ELTON JOHN
ALL THE SONGS
THE STORY BEHIND EVERY TRACK

ELTON JOHN
ALL THE SONGS
THE STORY BEHIND EVERY TRACK

ROMUALD OLLIVIER
AND
OLIVIER ROUBIN

BLACK DOG
& LEVENTHAL
PUBLISHERS
NEW YORK

CONTENTS

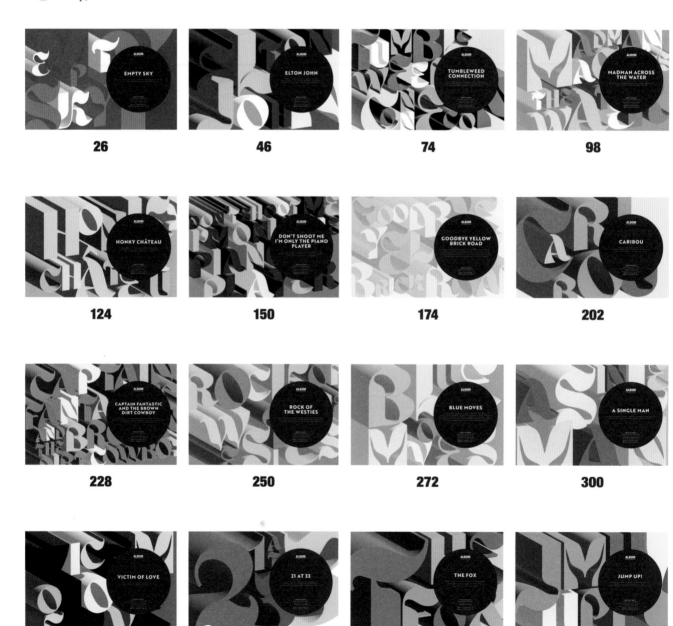

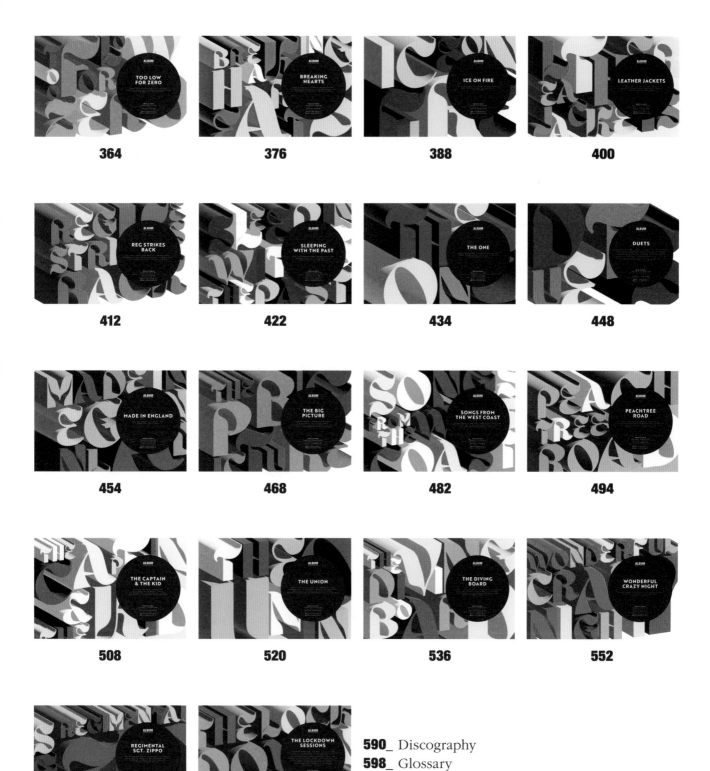

Elton John's father, Stanley Dwight, shown in 1976 with his second wife, Edna. (above)

Reg Dwight, the future Elton John, posing for his first publicity photo campaign in a park in Hampstead at the end of 1967. (right)

A NOT-SO-ABSENT FATHER

In 1947, Reginald's father, Stanley, was posted to the Royal Air Force maintenance unit No. 4 in Ruislip, England, which was not far from Pinner. Although he was there for his son's birth, Elton has always said that his father was barely present during his early years. However, biographer Philip Norman recently revealed that Stanley was home more often than was originally thought, thereby contradicting what Elton John claimed in 2019, when he said: "I was 2 when he came back home. My mother asked if he wanted to see me. He said: 'No, I'll wait until tomorrow morning.'"[4]

GLORY, WITHOUT HIS FATHER

Located twenty or so miles northwest of the British capital, Pinner lies somewhat outside the London field of attraction. Here, in an area still marked by the aftermath of the postwar era, life seemed to move more slowly than in the capital. It was here, in this peaceful mining town, where Reginald Kenneth Dwight, the future Elton Hercules John, was born on March 25, 1947.

Distant echoes of the major cultural upheaval happening in rock 'n' roll eventually reached young Reginald through his mother. Every Friday, Sheila Dwight received her weekly wages, and she would stop off at the electrical goods store on her way home from work. The store had a records department, and Sheila would select something new on 78 rpm. With a penchant for American music, and as an enthusiast for going out dancing, she lapped up the velvet melodies of crooners like Nat King Cole or Johnnie Ray. These early records introduced young Elton to the sounds of America. On one of these Friday evenings, Sheila brought home a record whose jacket bore the graceful features of Elvis Presley. Reginald had already spotted him in magazines he perused at the hairdresser the previous week, and the rocker awoke in him a certain unspoken fascination even before he had heard Elvis perform a single note. When the sounds of "Heartbreak Hotel" rang out, they came as a revelation. The physical energy exuded by the kid from Tupelo took hold of Reginald. The rocker, with his brilliantine pompadour and his cohort of imitators, became a fixture in Reginald's life and displaced his favorite musician up to that point: Winifred Atwell. Atwell was an exuberant ragtime pianist

who gave Reginald a taste for piano playing, and her records showed him an alternative to classical music and jazz, which were close to his father's heart. Her instrumental number "Poor People of Paris" (released in 1956) was the first piece that Reginald was able to play himself.

From the time of his discovery of rock 'n' roll, Reg, as he was called, dreamed of becoming Little Richard or Jerry Lee Lewis. He made the piano stool dance, playing the piano standing up in the tradition of his idols. "I heard Little Richard and Jerry Lee Lewis, and that was it,"[1] he declared to *Rolling Stone* magazine in 1973.

An Absent Father and an Explosive Mother

Reginald's personal and musical tastes were at odds with the rather more conservative rules and mores imposed on him by Stanley Dwight, a father frequently described as authoritarian and not given to emotional outpourings. On the rare occasion when Stanley would drop his guard, it usually happened while father and son were together at the local stadium supporting the Watford soccer team, or when Reg was playing the piano—in a more academic style, of course. Stanley had his own vested interest in music, having been encouraged by a friend to take up the trumpet in his youth, and eventually joining an orchestra called the Bob Miller Band. It was also during a gig at a hotel in North Harrow, while home on leave in 1942—he was a pilot in the Royal Air Force during the war—that he met a young milk delivery lady, Sheila Harris.

Trinidadian pianist Winifred Atwell served as an early source of inspiration for Elton John. (left)

Jerry Lee Lewis was one of the catalysts of Elton's passion for rock. The two musicians met for the first time in New Orleans in 2015. (above)

Whenever Reginald performed his piano exercises impeccably, he could expect to receive a compliment, albeit a measured one, but one that would fill his young heart with joy. Reginald was always eager for his father's affection, which was rarely expressed even in later years. According to Elton, Stan never expressed his pride, even when his son became one of the most popular pop stars in the world. "He was a tough and unemotional man. Hard. In the RAF. He was dismissive, disappointed and finally absent....I just wanted him to acknowledge what I'd done. But he never did."[2]

Unfortunately, Reginald could not seek emotional solace from his mother, either. Although she was a more modern and determined woman, Sheila also had a rather unsettling personality. She could be charming and good-natured but also explosive, and capable of "start[ing] an argument in an empty room,"[3] according to her brother. She frequently had monumental rages that could shake the walls, and she kept her family on a constant state of alert. Other players in young Reginald's life included a maternal grandmother, Ivy, whom he called "Nan," her second husband, Horace, and Uncle Reg.

None of these people had any illusions about the state of Sheila and Stanley's marriage. They came together precipitously in January 1945, and they were married at Pinner Parish Church when they were not even twenty. When Reginald was born two years later, the Dwights were living at 55 Pinner Hill Road, in a solidly built home with a red brick façade that they inherited from Sheila's parents. The house was tucked away at the top of a hill, beyond a belfry. Though it was modest in size, it was a household filled with life; there were always visitors stopping by, and the radio was always playing.

Stanley was eventually promoted to squadron leader and often called to serve overseas. His frequent absences meant that Reginald mostly avoided run-ins with this emotional brick wall of a man, and they also meant that his parents didn't have too much time to indulge in their favorite pastime: arguing. "They were both stubborn and short-tempered, two delightful characteristics that it's been my huge good fortune to inherit,"[3] Elton wrote humorously in his autobiography. In this context, it was difficult for young Reginald's personality to blossom. His insecurities concerning his slight stature, the space in his front teeth, and his weight made it difficult for him to feel comfortable in his own skin. His grandmother was a rare port in the storm during Elton's early years, and she was always quick to stand up for the little one. In particular, Elton's grandmother defended him when Sheila experimented with some very questionable upbringing techniques, which included hitting her son with a wire brush (sometimes drawing blood) in order to potty-train him as a child.[3]

Before needing glasses to correct his eyesight, Elton (on the right circa 1967) already wore them so that he would look like Buddy Holly (above). Elton subsequently developed a real passion for glasses as an accessory and he created his own line of designer glasses with Walmart and Sam's Club in 2021.

An Early Talent

Reginald played his first scales on his grandmother's piano. He showed signs of unusual abilities very early on, such as when he was able to reproduce "The Skaters' Waltz" by ear when he was only four. Apart from this talent, which was seen only by the family, Reginald blended into the background. He was a good student but never particularly excellent, and he was fine enough as an athlete, but never very remarkable. He was not overly popular, but he could count upon a band of loyal friends, even if they were indifferent to his mania for record collecting and his obsession with recording charts, which he studied with the care of a horse-racing expert.

At the age of six, he started to take piano lessons. At that time, rather presciently, he confided in a classmate: "When I grow up I'm going to be a concert pianist."[4] When he was eleven, his determination paid off: Reginald won a scholarship to study music at the Royal Academy of Music in London every Saturday from 9 a.m. to 2 p.m. He had to rein in his appetite for rock 'n' roll in order to fit into the academic mold, where only classical music was permitted. Always a smiling and respectful student, while he was there Reginald racked up hours of practice and lessons in musical theory that would be useful to him later in life. But he quickly became aware that his tastes lay outside of the classical canon, to which he much preferred Cliff Richard, Johnny and the Hurricanes, and Gene Vincent. His small fingers also meant that it was very unlikely he'd become a classical musician by trade. So, then, his decision was made: he would pursue rock 'n' roll. In the meantime, since he was unable to express himself as he'd have liked—his father would not tolerate seeing him dressed as a *teddy boy*—he wore glasses that he didn't really need to imitate Buddy Holly. All he achieved with this plan was diminished eyesight, but it was a small victory for a young artist trying to find himself.

Reg was fourteen when Stan and Sheila's divorce finally came through, in 1961. This separation led to a new companion for his mother, a painter-decorator named Fred Farebrother— or "Derf," as young Elton called him. Friendly, considerate, and a thousand times more personable than his father, Derf won the trust of Reg and became a stable presence in his family universe. Derf was the one who got Elton his first job as a pianist, at the Northwood Hills Hotel, which was actually a local pub. This was where the boy learned how to work with the public. Between playing the Ray Charles rhythm 'n' blues numbers that he started to master to perfection, and some compositions of his own that he was able to test under real conditions, Reginald also slid in some traditional pub songs to satisfy the regulars. Derf, who often accompanied him on his shifts, passed between the tables with an empty pint glass and collected some

At 18, Reg was the inconspicuous keyboard player with the group Bluesology (left to right): Stewart Brown, Terry Pattison, Rex Bishop, Reg Dwight, and Mick Inkpen.

In 1965, the young Reg Dwight worked as a packing agent with Mills Music, the music publishing house located in the heart of Denmark Street.

tips. Eventually, they saved enough money to enable the young prodigy to buy himself a Hohner Pianet electric piano. The denizens of the Northwood Hills Hotel were not always music enthusiasts, and Reginald sometimes struggled to make himself heard over the loud voices and brawls, the latter of which he would escape by crawling through a nearby window.

The Choice Is Music

During this time, Reginald had his first experience playing with a band when he joined the Corvettes, a group that straddled rock 'n' roll and blues. The Corvettes were founded by Stuart Brown, a guitarist, and Geoff Dyson, a bassist. The band's lineup was completed by Mick Inkpen on drums. Reginald was on piano, of course, and he sometimes sang on covers of Jerry Lee Lewis because he was the one member of the band who could project his voice the most easily. The group's life was soon cut short when Geoff Dyson decided to join the Mockingbirds, a rival group who managed to gain a slot as the opening band for the Yardbirds—birds of quite another feather.

In 1962, the Corvettes became Bluesology, named in homage to the album *Djangology* by the legendary jazz guitarist Django Reinhardt. The lineup consisted of Reginald, Stuart Brown, and Mick Inkpen. Rex Bishop was recruited on bass. The group set itself a rock 'n' roll emphasis, and they also worked up a set consisting of reimaginings of blues tracks by Jimmy Witherspoon and J. B. Lenoir. Bluesology played mostly in a bar called the Gate, which was owned by Mick's father and located near the ground-floor apartment where Reg's family now lived.

Among all these activities, the aspiring musician's academic performance was in free fall, and the prospect of going on to college was receding at an alarming rate. The young man decided to take some initiative, and he left school in March

1965 in favor of taking a job in the music business. Or, at least, in an area that was music-adjacent. Reginald was employed in the packing department of the Mills Music publishing house, located on Denmark Street in London's West End.

The act of abandoning his studies aroused the wrath of Stanley, who wrote a letter of protest to his ex-wife. With Stanley now living in Cheshire with his new family, his letter had the opposite of its intended effect, and it convinced Sheila that Elton's decision to leave school was the right one. "In a perverse way, my dad's attitude helped me, too. He never changed his mind about my career choice," Elton wrote in 2019. "He never said well done. Not long ago, his wife Edna wrote to me and told me that he was proud of me in his own way; it just wasn't in his makeup to express it. But the fact that he never expressed it instilled in me a desire to show him that I'd made the right decision."[3] Interestingly, the bleak picture that Elton John paints of his father, both in his autobiography and in the feature film *Rocketman* (2019), is a million miles away from the one painted by his half brother Geoff Dwight, who described Stanley as a loving and considerate father.

The Bluesology Adventure

Bluesology started to get its act together when the group found a manager in the person of Arnold Tendler, a Bond Street jeweler who worked with Mick Inkpen. He invested money in equipment and a van, and also paid for stage costumes in the form of roll neck sweaters, doubtless traumatized by the previous outfits worn by Reginald, who had yet to define his style. Tendler even financed the recording of a demo in a studio on May 13, 1965, which he then managed to have sent to Jack Baverstock, who was the artistic director of Fontana Records. Fontana, to the great surprise of Bluesology, agreed to release a single, and they

chose the only song written by Reginald. "Come Back Baby" was a syrupy, easy-listening-style track that the group had practiced at the Northwood Hills Hotel. Reginald sang lead vocals on the single, since Baverstock disliked the voice of the group's lead singer, Stuart Brown.[5] The single appeared on July 23, 1965, but it went totally unnoticed. The group's second attempt for Fontana Records, in November 1965, achieved the same disappointing outcome. "Mr. Frantic" was another number written by Reginald Dwight, and this time he was influenced by Motown soul, and by the B-side of B. B. King's "Every Day I Have the Blues." The group's second single made a timid appearance at the very bottom of the charts, and then disappeared.

The Long John Baldry Interlude

The group consoled itself by beginning a relationship with the agent Roy Tempest, a former boxer who made quite an impression on the young musicians with an aquarium filled with piranhas that he kept in his office. Roy obtained a number of contracts as a support band for Major Lance, Patti LaBelle and the Blue Belles, the Drifters, Doris Troy, the Ink Spots, the Isley Brothers, Lee Dorsey, and even Fontella Bass. The appearances made them a pittance, but even so Reginald decided to quit working at Mills Music to embrace the

life of the impoverished, hungry musician. This was a formative experience even though the pace, and performing conditions were grueling. Worn out by the expectations of their new agent, Bluesology threw in the towel at the beginning of 1966 and signed with Marquee Enterprises. This enabled them to perform at the Marquee Club, the focal point of the London rock scene at that time.

In March 1966, Bluesology took the path trodden by the Beatles six years earlier: they loaded their instruments onto a ferry and boarded a train for Hamburg, with a view to obtaining a residency at the Top Ten Club, not far from the Star-Club, which had hosted the Fab Four. Hamburg did not offer a particularly fancy existence (accommodation on the top floor of the club in spartan conditions and with five hours of gigs a day), but the musicians found consolation in performing as a group—at least, when they were not accompanying the Scottish vocalist Isabel Bond, who was quite a singer and who distorted the covers she sang by adding smutty words to the lyrics. For Reginald, who was just nineteen and had no knowledge of, and still less experience with, anything sexual, passing brothel windows filled with barely clothed prostitutes every day on his way to performing with this overtly sexual singer was quite a change of pace!

At the end of 1966, Bluesology became the backing band for a golden-haired singer who stood 6' 6" tall: Long John Baldry (left).

Bernie Taupin and Reginald Dwight shortly after their miraculous meeting, which was brought about by Ray Williams in 1967. (right)

This did not prevent him from becoming aware of the limitations of his group. Its repertoire had drifted from blues to soul so the group could stay fashionable, but soul was a genre in which Bluesology could not differentiate itself from the competition. While he was thinking of leaving the group, an opportunity presented itself to Reginald: Long John Baldry.

The bluesman with the golden hair, whose name was derived from his height—he stood at a little over six foot seven—Long John Baldry was a character as likeble as he was exuberant. He never hid his homosexuality, although he held back from announcing it publicly, since homosexuality was a criminal offense in Great Britain before 1967. A member of the Cyril Davies R&B All Stars, he headed up the group when Davies died in 1964, eventually renaming the group Long John Baldry and His Hoochie Coochie Men, and then changing the name again to Steampacket. For a while he shared the microphone with Rod Stewart, a rising star and future friend of Elton John. But the adventure was cut short, and the singer found himself without a group. In December 1966, Long John Baldry offered to hire the musicians of Bluesology, but only Stuart Brown (guitar), Fred Gandy (bass), and Reginald agreed to this proposal. Thus, a new incarnation of Bluesology emerged with Neil Hubbard on guitar, Elton Dean on saxophone, Pete Gavin on drums, Mark Charig on cornet, and Alan Walker and Marsha Hunt on vocals. Although excited about the magnetic presence of Long John Baldry and his strapping, charismatic personality, which coincided with a serious penchant for alcohol, Reginald nurtured bigger ambitions than simply playing music at the back of the stage. In 1967, Polydor Records released a new

single, "Since I Found You Baby." Sung by Stuart Brown, it was released under the name Stu Brown and Bluesology. Reginald's name was nowhere to be found, and this only increased his desire to take center stage.

The Envelope of Destiny

On June 15, 1967, while performing with Bluesology in Newcastle, England, Reginald chanced upon an advert published by Liberty Records in the landmark music publication *New Musical Express*: "Liberty is looking for talents. Artists-composers, singers-musicians. Call or write to Ray Williams." Once he was back in London, Reginald presented himself at this new record company in the hopes of securing a contract, and there he met the charming Ray Williams, whose youthfulness— he was twenty—belied his experience. At that point, Williams had worked in public relations for the Kinks, the Hollies, and Sonny & Cher. Reginald had no idea that Liberty Records was seeking to surf the psychedelic wave, which was very much in vogue at the time, and he so chose to play Ray Charles and Jim Reeves during his audition, and unsurprisingly he fell short of the mark! However, a stroke of luck transformed the audition into a turning point for Reginald's career. Just as Reginald was leaving the office, Ray Williams handed him an envelope that had been left behind by another candidate who called himself a poet. "He seemed to pull the envelope out at random. [...] I can't remember if he'd even opened it or not before he gave it to me. And yet that envelope had my future in it: everything that's happened to me since happened because of what it contained."[3] The envelope contained lyrics written by the young

Bernie Taupin, aged just seventeen. Taupin would become Reginald's musical partner for the next half century, as well as his soul mate and the author of all his greatest successes.

In the subway train that carried him away from Liberty Records, Reginald opened the envelope Williams had given him and found some strange titles ("Coffee Colored Lady," "Year of the Teddy Bear," and "Did Lightning Strike a Man," among others), but the lyrics seemed powerful to him. A meeting did not take place immediately. Before contacting Bernie, Reginald added melodies to the words inspired in him, and a kind of magic happened. Their musicality, their patterns and rhythm, and their depth could not have worked. Reginald composed twenty or so songs based on these lyrics before finally meeting the mysterious stranger face-to-face.

Meanwhile, Reggie took another piece of advice that Williams offered him on the fateful day of his Liberty Records audition, and he started working with Nicky James and Kirk Duncan at Niraki. The fledgling company took its title from the first few letters of its founders' names, and it worked with Gralto Publishing, the company founded by members of the Hollies. Gralto itself was a division of Dick James Music, the musical publisher who published the Beatles via Northern Songs. During the summer of 1967, Nicky, Kirk, and Reggie worked quite naturally in the studios that Stephen James—son

of Dick—had had installed at the DJM premises in New Oxford Street. Tony Murray, the future bassist with the Troggs, and Dave Hinds, a drummer, completed the team that had been hired by DJM to compose songs for other artists.

When Reggie Met Bernie

Bernie and Reggie met at the end of the summer in 1967, in the DJM studio and on the initiative of Ray Williams. When he arrived, the songwriter was asked to wait in the control room. Only seventeen years old at the time, the young man was very unsure of himself. This world was totally unknown to him, and until very recently he had been working on a poultry farm. The house sound engineer, Caleb Quaye, was known for being mischievous and he often playfully teased Reginald. Quaye jokingly asked Bernie if he was really supposed to be there. Bernie blurted out that he had a meeting with Reggie, who was busy finishing off a piano recording on the other side of the glass. The pianist eventually joined them and asked if Bernie was "the songwriter" before inviting him for coffee. They got on with each other immediately. "As far as the meeting, it was sort of uneventful, really. I mean, [Elton] was very pleasant. We just went and had a cup of coffee in a place called the Lancaster Grill on Tottenham Court Road just around the corner from Dick James Studios, which is where we actually met. [...]

This photograph of the young Reginald Dwight was used to illustrate the sleeve of his first single, "I've Been Loving You" in 1968.

We just talked. [...] I know we just agreed to keep in contact and try to write some songs."[6]

Their collaboration started almost instantly. Initially Bernie made return trips between his parents' farm and Putney, where his uncle put him up during his visits to London. "We used to communicate via post, which is kind of similar to the way it goes now. In fact, these songs have been found in someone's attic in London, and some of these songs are unbelievable: 'Mr. Lightning Strikerman,' 'Scarecrow' and 'The Witch's House' [...], and 'Regimental Sergeant Zippo.' We had a whole library of songs before we even started recording *Empty Sky*."[5] Bernie finally left the farm and moved into the family home in Frome Court. The duo that would go on to become one of the most famous pairs of collaborators in the world initially shared Reginald's room, which was dominated by posters of Dusty Springfield. They slept in bunk beds like a pair of brothers, which was what they felt like they had always been, and they talked into the small hours of the morning, dissecting their compositions and imagining their future fame. Despite their very close friendship, the two men were only just out of adolescence and they opted to work separately: Bernie isolated himself with the typewriter inside their shared bedroom, or with sheets of paper while perched in a tree. He would then submit the fruits of his labors to Reggie, depositing a packet of paper on his piano before slipping off again and getting back to work. Bernie was not constantly by Reginald's side, and Reginald gave him the space and the privacy he needed to do his work.

Elton Emerges

One evening, when everyone had left the DJM studios, the two men were working on their own projects. Totally committed to the musical world of Reginald and Bernie, Caleb Quaye had dropped his teasing and now took them seriously; he knew what kind of talents he saw before him. Quaye was willing to invest time in the two young upstarts, and he generally waited until the other staff left for the day in order to devote his nights to them, and to trying out new arrangements. He also called on his musician friends to fill out the sound on the new songs. This scenario lasted until the studio manager,

Ronnie Brohn, happened to drop by the premises late in the day and discovered what they were doing. He reported them to Dick James the very next day. As a desperate move before he lost his job, Caleb decided to ask the boss to listen to the fruit of their nocturnal labors. The music he played was so convincing that Dick James forgave Bernie and Reginald for using the studio outside of authorized hours. Dick also decided to offer them an author and composer contract under the aegis of DJM. The two men signed this agreement on November 7, 1967. As with Niraki, they were once again given the task of writing hits for other artists. The duo undertook a fairly schizophrenic approach to their work, compartmentalizing different final destinations for their songs: their music was either good enough to be incorporated into their personal repertoire, or they would offer the songs to other artists. Most often the mournful ballads they wrote took this second route, eventually being offered to other artists in the (vain) hope of convincing a Cilla Black or an Engelbert Humperdinck to sing them. Reggie and Bernie only managed to place songs with singers of a lesser caliber, such as Edward Woodward. However, Dick James's right-hand man—his son Stephen, who was in his twenties—was unstinting in his efforts to make Reggie and Bernie known as a top-notch creative duo. During a conversation with Johnny Franz, artistic director with the Philips Records label, Franz mentioned to Stephen that Elton might have a sufficiently interesting voice to perform his songs himself. Stephen shared this thought with his father, who agreed. On January 10, 1968, Dick James offered Reginald a recording contract for five years, combined with a requirement that he complete two albums a year.

The singer was over the moon. He was now recognized as an artist in his own right, and this new contract also allowed him to depart Bluesology. Having been deeply disappointed by the way in which the group's collaboration with Long John Baldry was turning out, Reggie no longer felt motivated to stay with Bluesology. He gave his last concert with the group in February 1968 in Glasgow. While riding in the bus that was taking the Bluesology musicians from Heathrow to London after their concert in Glasgow, Reginald was musing about the next stage in his career and thinking about a stage name for

his future solo career. He could not reasonably expect to bowl over crowds of people with a name as mundane and unglamorous as Reginald Dwight. Even his friends' names sounded a lot better than his: Elton Dean, for example, his saxophonist…That name had a nice ring to it. Without any sense of shame, Reg went up to the sax player and asked if he could use his name. "That's a bit much, Reg," Dean complained. The pianist considered combinations with the names of the other members of the band and stopped at Long John Baldry. He came back to Elton Dean: "And Elton John, would that do?" No objection, and it was adopted.[4]

Something else had also changed during the launch of his solo career, and Elton John started to take more liberties with his style of dress. He no longer held back in giving free expression to the eccentricity that had been building up inside of him. His initial attempts at expressing himself through fashion lacked cohesion: he grew a mustache and adopted a hippie style that mixed in deliberately childlike elements, such as a Noddy print shirt made by one his mother's friends. The seeds of his stylistic evolution had been planted, but there was still more work to be done.

The First Singles

Now in possession of a new name and a new look, Elton was ready to make the big leap and release his first single, "I've Been Loving You." Stephen James obtained a contract with Philips that allowed for the distribution of two singles via This Record Co., a subsidiary of DJM Records. Released on March 1, 1968, the single failed to make much headway with the public. This was only partly surprising for Elton, who would never have bet on its success, but Dick James, who was known for his penchant for sugary-sweet numbers, had insisted that this was the one to be chosen. This failure did not diminish Elton's thirst for change. Especially since his personal life was undergoing a major upheaval. Things were crystalizing with Linda Woodrow, Elton's ongoing girlfriend, and marriage looked to be on the horizon, with a date set for June 22, 1968. But the prospect of wedded bliss enchanted the young Reg less and less, as the pressure from his future spouse increased. Linda wanted to adopt a more conventional lifestyle, which Elton's more artistic temperament just wouldn't allow. Sensing a mounting panic inside of himself, as well as a feeling of unease concerning his sexual orientation, Elton's emotions eventually grew so fraught that he made a half-hearted suicide attempt in 1968.

These were hard times for Elton. Despite his contract with DJM, his career wasn't taking off in the way he'd hoped, and the probability of making it under his own name was also slipping away. In fact, outside of a few sessions done with the Hollies and Tom Jones, Bernie and Elton had the distinct impression that they were piling up songs that lacked originality and were not appealing to the working artists of the day. The duo seemed under threat of eviction when a new producer named Steve Brown arrived at Dick James Music in the autumn of 1968. When Brown called them into his office soon after arriving, Bernie and Elton were full of dread, and they were expecting to be shown the door.

BERNIE TAUPIN: THE KEY TO THE SONGS

When considering their respective backgrounds, Bernie and Elton could not be more different. The two men were united in their shared musical tastes—the Beatles, Bob Dylan, and so on—and by a fraternal affection, but they had diametrically opposite childhoods. For one, childhood meant a morose suburban life spent living in fear of his mother's mood swings, and the pain of seeing his affection for his father rejected; for the other, childhood meant cleaning out the stables on a quiet farm and enjoying a strong relationship with his loving parents. "We were complete opposites—town mouse and country mouse. But the one thing we had in common was being mad about pop music. And both being desperate to write songs,"[7] said Bernie in 2006.

The School of Life, in the Fields

Sleaford, a small town in Lincolnshire, England, had a population of barely more than seven thousand when Bernie Taupin was a young man. The town is located in the middle of the countryside, and far from many modern amenities offered by larger cities. Bernie was born on May 22, 1950, to Daphne (née Cort) and Robert Taupin. Their family name indicates French origins from his grandparents, who moved from Burgundy to live in London. His parents' history also seems to link the family to France, as Robert studied in Dijon, and Daphne studied French in Switzerland. The two young people met in London in 1947, but health worries kept Robert from taking on a career in law and obliged him to accept employment as a livestock breeder on a large farm near Market Rasen. Although verdant, the land in Lincolnshire was not easy to work, known as it is for its extreme winds.

It was here, on a farm surrounded by fields of kale and potatoes, that Bernie spent the first years of his life. There was no electricity, and his evenings were spent in candlelight. While their father was in the field and their mother was busy with household tasks, Bernie and his older brother, Tony, enjoyed the vastness of their playground, roaming around the farm on their tricycles. In the mornings and evenings, they took the run-down school bus to the nearby St. Joseph's Catholic school. A religious education appealed little to young Bernie, who had

to follow his family to Mass every Sunday. The two brothers remained at St. Joseph's despite a move that took them to live in a manor house. The contrast with the farm life of their first two years was striking. When they arrived in the elegant driveway that led to the imposing building where they would soon live, Bernie thought he was dreaming; he imagined that his father had maybe been involved in a robbery or that he had inherited the house from a rich ancestor. None of these daydreams were the case: his father's employer had simply had to sell his old farm and had relocated his family into one of his many other properties.

While Bernie learned about nature from the surrounding fields and countryside, he also spent a great deal of time listening to stories and lessons about life from his maternal grandfather, John Leonard Patchett Cort, nicknamed "Poppy." Even though Poppy died when Bernie was only nine, his influence on Bernie's life and his interest in writing was such that the songwriter later said that he owed his career to him. "Distinguished, kind and wise, his intelligence shone like a diamond in the rough. He instilled in me new passions, a caring for the quality of words and the stimulation of verse. Both as a botanist and naturalist, his enthusiasm for flora and fauna was unbridled. The study at his home in Baslow was a veritable goldmine of information on both subjects."[8] Clever, intellectually curious, freedom loving, and also reluctant to accept authority, Bernie revealed himself to be much more receptive to this type of nontraditional approach to education.

The Discovery of America

The life of relative luxury that they enjoyed in their new manor house did not entirely satisfy Robert and Daphne, who were ready to sacrifice their comfort in order to seek their independence. So it was that, in spite of the protests of young Bernie, the family moved once more. They didn't go too far, only to Maltkiln farm, in Bramby-by-Huddle, a minuscule village that does not even appear on many maps of Lincolnshire. The contrast with their previous residence was striking: two fairly dilapidated houses, located on a wasteland that looked like a real quagmire. Bernie's older brother adapted well to

After a rural upbringing, Bernie Taupin found himself caught up in the whirlwind of London musical life after his meeting with Elton.

this new life and made new friends due to his interest in soccer. Naturally a more solitary character, Bernie invented imaginary friends for himself, who filled his moments of contemplation in the fields, which were much warmer for him than time spent in the grim building that served as his family home, and which horrified him. He referred to his scruffy porch as the "Alamo," as though a long siege had reduced it to nothing more than a ruin. As though inspired by the pioneer spirit, his father decided to build a new house on the land. In the space of five months, and simply by the sweat of his brow and the modest sum of £1,000, Bernie's father managed to build a charming three-bedroom bungalow. Now that the Alamo had disappeared, Bernie started to create new fantasies for himself, and he began to write his own stories that were connected with the myths of America. These stories and myths would later infiltrate his songwriting. Bernie's

admiration for the New World is also evidenced by his uncle, who lived in London, and who helped him to discover another aspect of the United States: its music. Woody Guthrie and Leadbelly became heroes for Bernie, just as important to him as Wyatt Earp and Davy Crockett. When his uncle was not there to nourish him with new music, Bernie tuned into Radio Luxembourg, which broadcast country music and rock 'n' roll. Like his future accomplice, Reginald, Bernie swooned over the sounds of Little Richard, Jerry Lee Lewis, and Bob Dylan. In the latter, he discovered the power of words: "This voice was like broken glass. The words were like arrows being shot straight into the heart of the Establishment. That was what made me realize what the words of a song could do."TK With parents who were more permissive than Reggie's, Bernie was inspired by what he identified in Dylan as a form of rebellion, and he decided to follow his own creative path.

Since their earliest days of collaboration, the work of Bernie and Elton has been frequently celebrated, as it was in this image from the British Phonographic Industry in 2002.

Soon after meeting, Bernie and Elton quickly began to set records. Shown here celebrating four gold discs on April 26, 1973, together they racked up one diamond disc, 40 platinum discs, and 23 gold discs.

The Hand of God

Around the age of fifteen, Bernie started to live a marginal existence that included overindulging in alcohol. He tried to rein himself in and sought to exploit his passion for writing by becoming a journalist, but when he contacted the *Lincolnshire Standard*, all he was offered was an apprenticeship in the rotary press room.

Looking for other ways to kill time, Bernie hung out with the local pariahs for a while before finally managing to land a job as a handyman on a farm, where, among other chores, he had to take the bodies of chickens that had been decimated by avian flu to be incinerated. In the evening, in the privacy of his room, and without any real ambition, Bernie filled pages and pages of notebooks. He dreamed alternately of becoming a writer, a journalist, or a poet. It was under the last category that he described himself to Ray Williams when he responded to the advertisement that Liberty Records placed in the *New Musical Express*. The emergent record company was looking for "talents." Stuck in between an article on Judith Durham and the top albums and singles of the week, the quarter-page ad featured an image of the Statue of Liberty, which aroused Bernie's curiosity and helped him believe in the ascendancy of his own star. However, he never sent his response to the ad, the famous letter that would seal his future fate and that of Reginald Dwight. He did draft it and put it into an envelope but did not dare to post it. At the last moment, he told himself it would be a waste of time. Who

would want the services of a Lincolnshire farmer who thought he was a poet and lived with the calves, cows, and pigs? "I was so far away from the center of everything. I had no idea how record companies or song writers worked."[4] It was his mother who, having noticed the envelope hidden on the mantelpiece, sent off the letter on Bernie's behalf, unaware that she was setting the wheels of fate in motion, and turning her son into a future millionaire. "It [this letter] said, basically, 'I'm a poet and I think my words might be suitable as lyrics if set to music,'"[9] recalled Ray Williams, the letter's recipient, who was only just a little older than Bernie at the time, at the ripe old age of twenty. "There were dozens of people sending in lyrics. Most of them were 'moon in June' and that sort of stuff. But there was some sort of imagination attached to Bernie's. They weren't just the norm, even though we couldn't understand all of them. Now, it's fair to say I wasn't a great expert on lyrics, but there was definitely something that caught the imagination. I think that it was this that made me think that I should put him in touch with Elton...that he was the one."[9] Despite his aversion for Mass when he was young, Bernie saw it as a divine intervention in the chain of events that led to him becoming the lyricist for one of the greatest stars of pop music: "I believe God has a hand in everything. We had a one-time shot at meeting, and we got it. You can call it fate, kismet or, as they say, God's right hand. What made Paul McCartney turn up at the Woolton [Parish Church] garden fete and meet John Lennon? What made Keith Richards run into

Mick Jagger on the [train] station platform in Dartford? Like I say, God's right hand."[10]

The Ultimate Duo

Bernie met Reggie at the end of summer in 1967 at DJM Studios. The creative alchemy between the two men blossomed instantly. But success did not come overnight. It took nearly three years of lean times, disappointments, thankless tasks, and meager wages before their talent ripened and the sales figures became a little more impressive. Their initial attempts were not very assured, conceived as though they originated from a whiff of some acid trip (which Bernie had never tried at that point, but which he envisioned as some kind of surreal Technicolor dream): "The Chocolate Lakes of Your Mind," "The Year of the Teddy Bear," "Swan Queen of the Laughing Lake." Even the very first piece they wrote together, a song called "Scarecrow," was overly influenced by *Summer of Love* and did not give any inkling that three years later the pair would end up writing "Your Song," an accomplished model of the best that songwriting has to offer. This period of trial and error did, however, have the merit of sealing their friendship for decades to come. During this time of doubt and creative foment, their bond of collaboration rendered them invulnerable to the slings and arrows of fate and fortune. In fact, Reg was there when Bernie arrived in London, knowing nothing and no one, and needing a place to stay. Bernie was there when the forthcoming union of Reg

and Linda Woodrow would haunt the singer to the point of forcing him to stage his own suicide. Reg was there to give Bernie his first author's credit when the first single selected for release, "I've Been Loving You," was actually one of the rare songs written by Reg himself. The only time when they were not there for each other was in the actual creation of their art: "From 1967 they developed this incredible remote working relationship where they would never sit in the same room and write together. They only really ever [worked side by side] once or twice. So, it's not like a Lennon and McCartney where they are sitting knee to knee in the early days of the Beatles. Elton and Bernie were always writing separately. And there is something about that process that gave them a critical distance."[11]

If Lennon and McCartney managed to blossom artistically as individual entities, John and Taupin did not achieve this same feat. There was the gap between 1977 and 1979, when Bernie worked for other composers, such as Alice Cooper, while Elton, by default, hired the services of other writers such as Gary Osborne or Tom Robinson, but the results were never as good. The two partners determined that they were never better than when they worked together. For this reason, when it was time to create the monumental account of Elton's career in the biopic *Rocketman*, Elton once again put on his sequined costume, Bernie put on his work jacket, and they gave birth to a new song, in 2019: "(I'm Gonna) Love Me Again."

COVERS

One of the best rankings achieved by "Lady Samantha" was for the cover by the New Zealander Shane Hales, who released it as a single at the end of 1969. It rose to third place in his native country!

SIDE A

LADY SAMANTHA

Elton John, Bernie Taupin / 3:03

Single: *Lady Samantha / All Across the Havens* **UK Release:** January 17, 1969, on Philips (ref. BF 1739) **US Release:** January 17, 1969, on DJM Records (ref. 70,008) **Musicians:** Elton John: vocals, piano, organ / **Caleb Quaye:** electric guitar / **David Glover:** bass / **Roger Pope:** drums **Recorded:** Dick James Music Studios, London: October 18, 1968 **Technical Team:** Producer: Steve Brown / **Sound Engineer:** Frank Owen / **Assistant Sound Engineer:** Clive Franks **2nd Single Release:** *Lady Samantha / It's Me That You Need* **US Release:** January 1970 on Congress (ref. C 6017)

Genesis and Lyrics

Recorded before the start of the *Empty Sky* sessions, on October 18, 1968, "Lady Samantha" was issued as a New Year bonus on January 17, 1969. It came out in single format five months before the release of the official album, on which it was included. As the second Elton song intended for the public, this single is most notable as the first official offering by the John–Taupin duo, since the lyrics for "I've Been Loving You," Elton's first single, were written solely by Elton (though credit was given to Bernie as well).

With all of his seventeen years, the lyricist described the sepulchral silhouette of a woman who is both mysterious and disconcerting in equal measure; she was a woman straight out of a fireside story told at dusk. Although a troubling entity, the narrator cannot resist showing the most profound sympathy for this creature who seems to be overwhelmed by suffering. Are the mystical undertones of this early track responsible for its tepid reception by the public? Though impossible to say for sure, this first attempt by the duo resulted in a pretty resounding flop. The song was no more successful than the previous single Elton released in terms of chart placement or sales. This setback was not enough to dent Elton John's determination, however, and he was probably heartened by a more favorable critical reception, and by the very many airings the song received from famous English DJs of the time, such as Tony Blackburn and John Peel.

Production

In the autumn of 1969, Steve Brown was won over by the demo for "Lady Samantha" and suggested releasing it as a single on Philips. Elton asked guitarist Caleb Quaye to record it with him and to recruit a bass player and a drummer. He chose David Glover and Roger Pope, two DJM session musicians with whom he was accustomed to working. With this song, Steve took his first steps as a producer.

The piece contained all the hallmarks of a potential hit. It had an intro dominated by an assertive guitar that gave the song an enticing opening. This was followed by a sophisticated verse arrangement, led by an organ with a sinuous melody, and that welcomed the deliberately affected voice of Elton John. John's voice helped to reinforce the Baroque aspects of the story. In contrast to each other, the swaying rhythm section on the refrain and the change of key that accompanied Elton John's singing are very effective, while the guitar notes on the refrain fill out the arrangement considerably.

This track was Elton's last single under the Philips label in the United Kingdom, and it was also his first American single on the DJM label, though the record received a very lukewarm reception in the United States. In 1969, the rock group Three Dog Night covered this song on their album *Suitable for Framing*, and it gave the single another boost. The song was reissued on the Congress label, this time with the number "It's Me That You Need" on the B-side.

"Lady Samantha" had big potential, and it could have been the star piece on Elton's first LP, but DJM's choice of releasing it as a single sealed its fate. It had to wait for its "platinum success" when it was included as a bonus track on the rerelease of *Empty Sky* in 1995.

Tony Blackburn, the famous BBC DJ, regularly played "Lady Samantha" on his show, and helped make Elton John a household name in the UK.

ALL ACROSS THE HAVENS

Elton John, Bernie Taupin / 3:50

Single: *Lady Samantha / All Across the Havens* **UK Release:** January 17, 1969, on Philips (ref. BF 1739) **US Release:** January 17, 1969, on DJM Records (ref. DJM 70,008) **Musicians:** Elton John: vocals, piano, organ / Caleb Quaye: electric guitar / David Glover: bass / Roger Pope: drums **Recorded:** Dick James Music Studios, London: October 18, 1968 **Technical Team:** Producer: Steve Brown / Sound Engineer: Frank Owen / Assistant Sound Engineer: Clive Franks

Genesis and Lyrics

Included on the B-side of the single "Lady Samantha," "All Across the Havens" cannot compete with its partner's melodic immediacy. It is distinctive in its style and does have something interesting in its esoteric lyrics: "The sister of sunlight / Comes to my lonely life / Bearing the crosses I hung / I hung on my lonely wife." Here Taupin sets out the markers of a theme that will run through a number of the songs on *Empty Sky*, namely incarceration. This opens up the way for a religious interpretation of the subjects of torment and redemption: "I prayed by the river," "Then the mother of mercy / Showed me her stable," "I must stumble, locked in chains."

Production

Recorded at DJM on the same day as "Lady Samantha," "All Across the Havens" feels more like a stylistic exercise than a complete song. At the time, the musicians were looking at the United States, and they were very absorbed in the album *Music from Big Pink* by the Band, which they discovered at Musicland, their favorite record shop in Soho. They established this classically constructed ballad in a sort of comfortable Americana torpor in the vein of the Band.

This song was unexpectedly successful in Japan in 1971, reaching thirteenth place in Oricon sales rankings. It was Elton's biggest commercial success there until the double single "Something About the Way You Look Tonight" and "Candle in the Wind 1997" went to number one in 1997.

SIDE A

IT'S ME THAT YOU NEED

Elton John, Bernie Taupin / 4:04

Single: *It's Me That You Need / Just Like Strange Rain*
UK Release: May 16, 1969, on DJM Records (ref. DJS 205)
Musicians: Elton John: vocals, piano, Hohner electric Pianet / **Caleb Quaye:** electric guitar / **Clive Franks:** bass / **Roger Pope:** drums / **Strings arrangement:** Cy Payne **Recorded:** Olympic Studios, London, April 10, 1969 **Technical Team: Producer:** Steve Brown

London's Olympic Studios, where Elton John recorded his third single, "It's Me That You Need."

Genesis and Lyrics

"It's Me That You Need" is Elton John's third single but the first to be published by Dick James Music. Philips, with whom Elton had had an agreement since January 1968, covered the distribution of his singles before finally handing over his contract to DJM. Four months after "Lady Samantha," this new single could pass as just a love song but in fact has sophisticated lyrics, especially in comparison to the pop standards of the time. The story's narrator tries to convince the woman he loves that he is her ideal companion. The final verse suggests that this is a girlfriend who has left him: "You can fly home again / But don't, no don't forget yesterday / Pride is an ugly word girl / And you still know my name." Despite wide radio play and positive reviews, "It's Me That You Need" sold even fewer copies than Elton's two previous singles, and it was also not ranked on sales charts in the United States and the United Kingdom.

Production

On April 10, 1969, Elton recorded the A-side of his third single at Olympic Studios. Steve Brown was on production, Caleb Quaye was on electric guitar, and Roger Pope was on drums, but this time Clive Franks was on bass. The sound engineer moved to the other side of the glass for this song in order to provide Elton with his expertise as a musician—expertise that

had been forged in his group, the Claggers. Other members of the technical staff at DJM also played in the Claggers, including Stuart Epps (assistant producer for Brown), Kaplan Kaye (sound engineer), and Jeff Titmus (sound engineer).

The song opens with lots of tension in a strings section brilliantly arranged and directed by Cy Payne. Elton introduces the initial piano chords, and Caleb Quaye's electric guitar in turn makes a notable entry, with a finely measured wah-wah pedal. Quaye never seeks to establish himself in a psychedelic atmosphere, but rather to use a slightly crunchy sound in the higher frequencies to add some bite. The rhythm section, without being too flashy or busy, provides a fundamental basis to the arrangement. The strings, soaring and majestic, bring out the melody while Elton provides an assured vocal. In the final fifteen seconds, he rounds off this effective ballad on the piano alone.

Pleased with the recording of this track, Elton noted in his log book: "April 10. Recording at Olympic—"It's Me That You Need." Session was great. I also helped out at Musicland [his favorite record shop] today."

Rather unfairly shunned upon its release, "It's Me That You Need" was rediscovered when it was included on the reissue of *Empty Sky* in 1995.

Elton wore his memorable Noddy shirt during the promotional photo session for the single "Just Like Strange Rain."

JUST LIKE STRANGE RAIN

Elton John, Bernie Taupin / 3:44

Single: *It's Me That You Need / Just Like Strange Rain*
UK Release: May 16, 1969, on DJM Records (ref. DJS 205)
Musicians: Elton John: vocals, Hammond organ, piano / **Caleb Quaye:**
electric guitar, acoustic guitar / **Tony Murray:** bass / **Roger Pope:** drums
Recorded: Dick James Music Studios: November 1968–January
1969 **Technical Team: Producer:** Steve Brown / **Sound Engineer:**
Frank Owen / **Assistant Sound Engineer:** Clive Franks

Genesis and Lyrics

From his earliest days, Bernie Taupin had a rare capacity to take the listener on a journey from the intimacy of an ordinary place—most often the room in which he was writing—to somewhere else that was more appealing. "Just Like Strange Rain" is the perfect example of this talent at work: here Bernie describes in minute detail the most prosaic elements of his daily existence—the "rusty nail" that holds the calendar, his "comic book"—in order to provide a better contrast between their prosaic banality and the sumptuousness of the changing colors of the sky outside. The frontier between these two worlds is literalized by the "window pane." The patterns of stress and intonation in this song, from which emanates a constant musicality, do wonders with "Yellow, blue, green and gray / Settled on the window pane" and in the alliteration of "It made the rain that came seem strange / Just like a strange rain."

"Promoted" to the status of B-side on "It's Me That You Need," this track was revealed three weeks before the release of *Empty Sky*, on which it was not included. Like other early Elton singles, this song found its way onto the 1995 rerelease of *Empty Sky*.

Production

The song begins with a painterly intro, featuring Caleb Quaye cutting through the air with his saturated guitar bends and giving the piece a kinship with the song "With a Little Help from My Friends." But the group quickly performs a sidestep and reverts to a tangy pop melody with almost psychedelic accents. This song is interesting in its organization, which is centered around three distinct movements: verses and pre-refrains share the key of *Bb*, with refrains based in *F*. The piano and guitar lead an inspiring, coordinated dance.

Stephen (left) and Dick James (far right) were the father-and-son team who helped Elton John's career take off by providing him with the resources he needed.

THE *DICK JAMES DEMOS*

In 1992, the Yellow Dog Records label managed to exhume the famous *Dick James Demos*, which they combined into two volumes and released under the references YD 023 and YD 024. The volumes included all of the song demos created by Elton and Bernie for Dick James Music before Elton recorded *Empty Sky*. Amongst the famous tracks were "A Dandelion Dies in the Wind," "Tartan Coloured Lady," and "Regimental Sgt. Zippo," which were used again in 2020 for the *Jewel Box* set.

DICK JAMES:
THE ROCKETMAN PYROTECHNICIAN

Dick James, whose full name was Richard Leon Isaac Vapnick, was born to a family of Jewish immigrants living in the East End of London, in December 1920. He made his way into the music world as a singer, starting out in the Henry Hall jazz band before joining the army in 1942. After the war, he resumed his musical interests with Geraldo and the Stargazers, a popular vocal group in the early 1950s. Outside of his renditions of signature tunes for British television series such as *The Adventures of Robin Hood* and *The Buccaneers*, he did not achieve the success he had hoped for and ultimately changed his plans.

The Foundations of the DJM Empire

In 1958, James definitively left behind his career as a crooner and found a job with the publishing house Sidney Bron Music. Two years later, he decided to set out on his own and created his own music publishing company, Dick James Music (DJM), in offices that he rented at the intersection of Charing Cross Road and Denmark Street in London. His catalog stagnated until his providential encounter with Brian Epstein. Epstein, who was managing a new group called the Beatles, suggested jointly founding Northern Songs with James, the aim being to publish songs written by John Lennon and Paul McCartney. Although Brian Epstein would be the majority holder, with 51 percent of the shares, James agreed to his proposal. He activated his network of music industry contacts and managed to get the Beatles on television in *Thank Your Lucky Stars*…and the rest, as they say, is history. For DJM, this was the jackpot! The dividends earned in 1964 enabled James to relocate to a vast, four-floor building on New Oxford Street, and he devoted three floors of his new space to offices, leaving one entire floor to be used for recording studios. Stephen James, Dick's son, was behind the idea to create the record production company eventually known

as This Records Co., which was renamed as DJM Records in 1969. Dick James's expertise soon meant that they were working with numerous artists, including Gerry and the Pacemakers, Billy J. Kramer and the Dakotas, Herman's Hermits, and the Troggs, and he was a veritable "emperor" of the record world.

The Man Who Discovered Elton John

Although celebrated for his role in the Beatles' ascension, Dick James is also considered to be the man who discovered Elton John. Operating on the advice of his son, Stephen, in November 1967 James recruited Elton and Bernie Taupin to come work for him on a writer-composer basis. He gave them the task of writing hits for other artists like Lulu, Rod Stewart, and Edward Woodward. The duo performed this task while continuing to work on building their own repertoire. The men hoped to convince Dick to produce their first album, but when they submitted various songs to him, including "Regimental Sgt. Zippo" and "Watching the Planes Go By," he did not seem particularly enthused. It took all the determined efforts of Stephen James and Steve Brown, who was brought on to head up DJM Studios in the autumn of 1968, to persuade Dick to invest in the duo. Bernie and Elton then wrote a slew of numbers without any commercial pressure, such as "Lady Samantha," "Empty Sky," and "Skyline Pigeon." At the end of 1968, to their great surprise, Dick James finally agreed to finance an initial LP that would be called *Empty Sky*, and even founded the label DJM Records (which was the successor to This Record Co.) to provide the LP with the promotion it deserved. Elton became Dick's new protégé, and he eventually signed a five-year contract. Despite the clunky start of *Empty Sky*, which, unfortunately, moved only about four thousand copies, Dick James decided to offer Elton an advance of £6,000 for the production of a second opus. He

made this decision based on word of the potential of Elton's future songs, including "Your Song," "Sixty Years On," and "Take Me to the Pilot."

Elton John really owed his initial launch to stardom to Dick's flair. Dick declined Jeff Beck's offer to send Elton on tour with his group by retorting that "in six months' time, Elton John will be earning twice what Jeff Beck does,"[3] and he persuaded the singer to make America a priority. In 1970, shortly after the release of Elton's second album, *Elton John*, Dick found Elton a transatlantic distributor (the Uni Records label) and arranged for two tours in the United States (from August 25 to September 12, and again from October 29 to December 11, both in 1970). Although Elton dragged his feet somewhat on these early tour dates, they would propel him into the ranks of world stardom. When Elton John returned to England in December 1970, he had his first major hit, "Your Song," and he was well on his way to becoming an icon in his home country.

The End of a Collaboration

When John Reid became Elton's manager in 1973, the change put stress on the relationship between Elton and Dick. Elton felt that the terms of his contract were unfavorable, especially in regard to the royalties he earned. As a result, in 1973 Elton founded his own record label, which he called the Rocket Record Company. In spite of this development, his records were pressed on the DJM label until 1976. Elton's complaint against Dick James went on for years, working its way through the courts until 1986, when a court found in favor of the singer, who claimed back payment for the author's rights on 144 songs that were published during Elton's original five-year contract. A week after the verdict was announced, Dick James had a heart attack at the age of sixty-five. In the film *Rocketman*, which was produced by Elton John and released in 2019, the portrait of Dick James is unflattering. According to Dick's son, Stephen, he was reduced to the stereotype of the awful record executive "with a big, fat cigar, swearing every other word." In fact, again according to Stephen, Dick had served as a substitute father figure to Elton and had only ever done his best to give Elton the best career possible. The debate may never be resolved, but one thing is certain: James played a major role in launching Elton John's career and creating some of the most lasting and popular music of the twentieth century.

ALBUM

EMPTY SKY

Empty Sky . Val-Hala . Western Ford Gateway . Hymn 2000 . Lady What's Tomorrow .
Sails . The Scaffold . Skyline Pigeon . Gulliver / Hay Chewed / Reprise

RELEASE DATES
UK Release: June 6, 1969
Reference: DJM Records—DJLPS 403
Best UK Chart Ranking: Did Not Chart
US Release: January 13, 1975
Reference: MCA Records—MCA-2130
Best US Chart Ranking: 6 (1975)

Taking advantage of the opportunity he was given to record an album, Elton John tackled *Empty Sky* with all his might, working hard to ensure that his first album wouldn't be his last.

FOR ELTON ADDICTS

"Regimental Sgt. Zippo," a song composed and recorded at DJM Studios in May 1968, was supposed to be used as the title for Elton John's first album, which never saw the light of day! The song was eventually exhumed for the release of the *Jewel Box* box set in November 2020. The abandoned album was finally issued on June 12, 2021, for Record Store Day.

A PROMISING "FALSE START"

"You need to stop this rubbish. You're not very good at all."[3] This was the news that Steve Brown hit Elton John and Bernie Taupin with when he called them into his office on a rainy October morning in 1968, leaving them dumbfounded. What they didn't know yet was that Brown, who had been appointed director of DJM Studios the month before, was referring to their inability to write pieces for other artists, which they had done more or less happily since the signature of their author-composer contract on November 7, 1967. This contract was supposed to provide the publisher, Dick James, with resounding commercial success, but so far it was proving to be a failure.

A Duo with Plenty of Potential

In reality, Brown had noticed in the young duo the early stages of a rare symbiosis, and he encouraged them to assert themselves more forcefully in their work. "You need to do what you want to do, not what you think will sell. I'm going to talk to Dick and see if we can make an album."[3]

Elton and Bernie were transfixed. They had a distribution contract with Philips that was signed in January 1968, but this related only to singles, and soon it would no longer be in effect. In fact, having had its fingers burned from the lack of success of the duo's initial single, called "I've Been Loving You" (with "Here's to the Next Time" on the B-side), the company jumped at the opportunity to break its contract after the failure of the duo's second single "Lady Samantha (with "All Across the Havens" on the B-side). Steve Brown, however, had loved "Lady Samantha" from the time he heard its early demos, and finally managed to convince Dick James to take a chance on these two young upstarts.

He was not the only one pushing the producer in this direction. Dick's son, Stephen James, had sensed the potential of the two young musicians for a long time. He obtained the Philips distribution contract for them in January 1968 and had them sign an initial 45 rpm contract with This Record Co. at the same time. Caleb Quaye also appreciated their work so much that he secretly supported them during their nocturnal work sessions at DJM Studios, eventually sharing their recordings with his boss.

"So really, becoming Elton John happened as an accident," the singer confessed in 2020. "If Bernie and I had been any better at writing songs for other people, we would have carried on in that vein. But it was thanks to Steve Brown [DJM plugger, later to produce *Empty Sky*] who said to Dick [James, music publisher], 'Listen, these kids can't write pop songs for other people. But what they can do is write their own songs.' We played them the demos. That's when we got our contract. But we never felt any pressure to write hits for ourselves."[12]

Dick James was conscious that a lack of promotion had detracted from Elton and Bernie's singles sales, and so he decided not only to sign them both to work on albums but also to create a new record label, which would allow him to retain control of the recording process as well as the subsequent promotion. DJM Records was a new incarnation of This Record Co., and it was officially launched at the Revolution Club in London in early 1969. Steve Brown was appointed to run operations, assisted by Stuart Epps. Their mission was to succeed, whatever the cost!

A Multifaceted Album

Elton and Bernie, who had been working together for over a year, already had quite a few songs under their belts. In

Given the involvement of drummer Roger Pope and guitarist Caleb Quaye, the *Empty Sky* album was influenced by the band Hookfoot. The whole group is shown here in 1971. From left to right: Roger Pope, Dave Glover, Caleb Quaye, and Ian Duck.

A meeting with Nigel Olsson, the drummer with Plastic Penny (second from left) marked the beginning of a collaboration that would last for more than half a century.

addition to their previously released singles, they also completed a large number of new tracks in the spring of 1968. They felt that many of these songs could be made into a first LP called *Regimental Sgt. Zippo*, but Dick James was unconvinced, and so they went to work.

As had been their custom since their earliest collaboration, the two men operated independently of each other. Bernie wrote the lyrics on his own before handing them off to Reggie, who added the music that Bernie's lyrics inspired in him.

As far as the lyrics were concerned, Bernie made significant efforts to liberate himself from the stylized songs that Dick James had asked them to write up until that point. He delved into his own life for inspiration, drawing upon his rural roots, his personal experiences, his passions, and even certain societal issues. He addressed a varied range of subjects, many of which were rarely touched upon in the songs of the period: the Lincolnshire of his childhood inspired "Lady What's Tomorrow," incest was the theme of "Hymn 2000," America (which fascinated him even though he had yet to visit) took center stage in "Western Ford Gateway," and his (deceased) dog inspired "Gulliver." Two intimately linked subjects stand out in this first album, whose title, *Empty Sky*, is indicative of the themes discussed: confinement and freedom, and their inevitable corollary: escape—the need to break out from any form of constraint and oppression. We encounter these subjects in the songs "Empty Sky" and "Skyline Pigeon," among others.

From a musical perspective, Elton had a harder time channeling his influences. Elton, whose musical appetite was always increasing, wanted to try everything: psychedelic effects, harpsichord, inverted guitar solos, flutes, bongos, stereo panoramics, improvised jazz interludes, false endings where songs restarted... "If you listened carefully, you could hear the kitchen sink being dragged into the studio,"[3] Elton said with amused nostalgia many years later. In reality, the young composer was thinking that this first album was also, in many ways, his last chance. He knew he had to seize the moment, especially in light of the relative failure of his earlier singles. For this reason, the orchestrations show an astonishing ambition and melodic richness. Steve Brown, who was fairly green himself, sometimes struggled to keep up with the production.

An "All-Terrain" Team Led by Caleb Quaye

The *Empty Sky* sessions began in November 1968 and ended in late January 1969. They took place on the first floor of DJM Studios, located at 71–75 New Oxford Street, in a majestic building set in the heart of London's Soho neighborhood. The studio was equipped with an eight-track recorder, which allowed for multiple arrangements and overdubs. In order to conserve DJM's finances, the sessions were usually scheduled for later in the day, during off-peak hours, and it was not unusual for work to be completed in the middle of the night. Work on the album cost just over £2,000 in total, a very modest sum at the time.

Despite his lack of experience, Steve Brown, who was recently promoted to the role of director at DJM Records, was entrusted with production of the album. He managed the sessions with the support of his sound engineer, Frank Owen,

and his assistant, Clive Franks. There was a good atmosphere in the studio. Elton surrounded himself with his friends, notably Caleb Quaye and Roger Pope, who were the guitarist and the drummer with Hookfoot—Caleb Quaye's group—and who played on most of the songs. The latter described the huge potential felt in the sessions, even in spite of the limited range of equipment that was available. Other than a wah-wah pedal that was used sparingly, the guitarist emphasized the warmth and power of the combination of his 1964 Fender Stratocaster and a Marshall 50W amp. This was, after all, a classical combination. Tony Murray, a bass player who had escaped from the Troggs, was there too, while Nigel Olsson, the drummer with Plastic Penny and the Spencer Davis Group, made an appearance on one of the tracks, which marked the beginning of fruitful collaboration with the two men. Don Fay provided his bright flute sound on many of the numbers, and Graham Vickery performed on his harmonica. They were all DJM session musicians who were used to playing together on demos. "We would get out onto Oxford Street at four in the morning and we'd be so excited we couldn't sleep, so we'd just sit in the Wimpy Bar and talk about the album,"[1] recalls Elton. When sessions ended so late that Bernie and Elton missed their train for Pinner, Steve Brown put them up at his place, where they would sleep on the floor.

Little by little the songs took shape, and all of them were fortified with a blind confidence and unshakable faith in what the group was doing. "We were all playing live together in the studio—a lot of looking at one another and head-nods and everything. There was no glass window to the control room; the producer could see us via a [black-and-white] TV monitor hooked up to a camera in the studio, but we couldn't see into the control room. We wouldn't know to stop playing [if there was an issue],"[13] explained Caleb Quaye. Tony Murray remembers that recording with Reg and Bernie was straightforward,

and enjoyable. "Basically Reg would turn up with some lyrics that Bernie had written. He had some idea of what the melody should sound like and he just started playing it on the piano. I simply watched his left hand and started playing bass to his piano. It was as simple as that. Much of the playing was impromptu stuff. It really was like watching a song being written right in front of you."[20] In 2019, Elton recalled the astonishment he experienced as the work progressed: "It's difficult to explain the amazement we felt as the album began to take shape, but I remember when we finished work on the title track…it just floored me. I thought it was the best thing I'd ever heard in my life."[13]

Brown, who was conscious of the fact that he needed to create a big event for the launch of this first album, contacted the photographer and graphic designer David Larkham, who worked at the *Evening Standard* daily paper. Larkham remembers that Steve called him to ask him about doing the advertising, and to commission the cover art. David attended a photo shoot at DJM, where he met the team. The chemistry between David, Steve, Bernie, and Reggie was immediate, and they became fast friends. For the *Empty Sky* cover art, David selected a photo of Elton at the piano, which he reworked using cool tones. This marked the beginning of a long collaboration, which continued until the images for the singer's farewell tour that were used in 2018. Two influential DJs of the period were invited to draft a little note for the reverse side of the album jacket: David Symonds, of BBC Radio 1, and Tony Brandon, who loved "Lady Samantha" and broadcast it regularly.

A Mixed Reception

After its release on June 6, 1969, *Empty Sky* barely had an impact on audiences. Elton was nonetheless proud of it: he had finally managed to make things happen, and while the reviews might not have been ecstatic, they weren't bad, either. At least,

Elton John's famous acrobatic leaps
began very early in his career and helped
establish the young singer's reputation
for putting on stellar live performances.

BONUS TRACKS

Empty Sky was rereleased in CD format by Mercury Records in 1995 (ref. 528 157-2) and by the Rocket label in 1996, with four bonus tracks added. The new tracks were: "Lady Samantha" and "All Across the Havens," both originally released on January 17, 1969, and "It's Me That You Need" and "Just Like Strange Rain," which were both released on May 16, 1969.

Due to its relative lack of success in the United Kingdom, *Empty Sky* was not released on the other side of the Atlantic until 1975, after Elton John's success had been established in the United States. It had a different cover, created by the Belgian artist Jean-Michel Folon, which replaced the original artwork by David Larkham. It was massively successful, reaching sixth place on the *Billboard* charts.

they were not indifferent. In England, the *Disc & Music Echo* referred to a "youthful pretension" and a lack of "maturity,"[12] while in the United States, Eric Van Lustbader, a journalist with *Cashbox*, which, quite miraculously, had heard of *Empty Sky*, regretted that there was no planned American release.[14]

Elton had to face the facts: *Empty Sky* didn't seem destined to conquer the charts, and so he continued working on other projects, such as attempting to rework a song called "I Can't Go On Living Without You" in the hopes of taking it to the Eurovision song contest. Unfortunately, that plan didn't work out, either, and the song, which was entirely Elton's work (although Taupin was given a credit) came in last in the selection rankings. But "it's what kept you going," stressed Elton, "the hope that one day someone will have a hit with one of your songs."[15] The singer was also working in the studio, making his playing skills available to groups such as the Hollies, the Family Dogg, the Barron Knights, the Scaffold, and Argosy, which was Roger Hodgson's first group. Elton even contributed background vocals for two numbers by the Welsh singer Tom Jones, singing on "Delilah" and "Daughter of Darkness." He also continued to have fun creating budget compilations for the Woolworths brand; these were albums for which he and other studio musicians created covers of contemporary hit songs.

Learning About Stage Performance

Empty Sky did not achieve the level of success that its creators hoped for, but the album did make Elton aware that it was time to meet his public. With this first LP under his belt, he now had a repertoire, and next he needed to form a group. Elton first called upon Caleb Quaye and his group Hookfoot, but he soon opted for a trio formation. In the end, he went with Nigel Olsson on drums and Dee Murray on bass, both of whom were members of the Spencer Davis Group.

After some tentative early sessions, Elton and his group hit their stride. They still had a major obstacle to overcome: reproducing the ambitious studio arrangements onstage. The talent for improvisation that these excellent musicians possessed was very soon brought into play. For his part, Elton knew that he could not move around behind his piano like Mick Jagger behind his microphone! He needed to become a leader and to create a style. So he looked into the past for inspiration, analyzing how to handle the stage by following the example of his early models, Jerry Lee Lewis and Little Richard, as well as the charismatic Winifred Atwell. Studying them helped Elton learn to combine mastery of his instrument with an ability to capture the public's attention during a performance. *Record Collector* journalist Pete Paphides had the following question: "So the difference between Reg Dwight the songwriter and Elton John the performer is really…it's an apprenticeship of watching all these American soul singers at close quarters?" Elton had this to say in response: "Well, you learn. I've been learning ever since I saw Little Richard back in 1962—that was the night Elton John was conceived. You learn from everyone."[12] Elton, with his short arms, soon realized that playing the piano standing up was quite difficult. Opting to take deliberately extreme, and aggressive approach, he struggled to master his piano stool and learned how to send it off toward the back of the stage with a casual, gentle kick. Elton took his new moves and went out to meet his public, who were increasingly keen to attend his explosive concerts.

Bernie also started to open up to new ideas, and he wrote a huge number of new lyrics with an almost disconcerting level of ease and facility; these new numbers immediately inspired his co-collaborator on songs they worked on for future albums.

Empty Sky's initial release was only four thousand copies. Considered by many as a "false start" because of its financial failure, the album was actually Elton John's farewell to the sixties. The new decade of the 1970s would be the most successful of his career. After Dick James heard the new demos, he remained confident in the John–Taupin duo. This time, he put £6,000 on the table in order to record Elton once more.

EMPTY SKY

Elton John, Bernie Taupin / 8:30

Musicians
Elton John: vocals, piano, organ, Pianet
Caleb Quaye: electric guitar, congas
Tony Murray: bass
Roger Pope: drums, percussion
Don Fay: flute
Graham Vickery: harmonica

Recorded
Dick James Music Studios, London: January 14, 1969

Technical Team
Producer: Steve Brown
Sound Engineer: Frank Owen
Assistant Sound Engineer: Clive Franks

With two feet firmly planted in psychedelia, Elton John seems to be attempting to create his very own version of the Rolling Stones classic "Sympathy for the Devil," with the introductory conga drums calling back to Keith Richards's guitar, and with an abrasive vocal that takes inspiration from Mick Jagger. Elton himself admitted as much: "It sounded like a Stones song. I thought, 'I can do this.'"[15]

FOR ELTON ADDICTS
Elton John began to include the title song "Empty Sky" in his stage tour only in 1975. He played it nine times that year, most notably at the Dodger Stadium in Los Angeles on October 25 and 26.

Genesis and Lyrics
Whether it expresses a long-stifled sense of malaise that Elton John felt when faced with the prospect of his marriage to Linda Woodrow, or whether it portrays the singer's imminent artistic evolution when he'd become liberated from the constraints imposed by his role as a bespoke composer, "Empty Sky" evokes a man who has been locked up and who dreams of flying free. Bernie Taupin wrote the lyrics on January 7, 1969, in Frome Court, Elton's childhood home, where he lived as a joint tenant with the singer. He was firmly convinced that the best was yet to come: "Every day, the swallows play in the clouds of love / Make me wish that I had wings, take me high above." While confinement is portrayed with a chilling tone, Taupin somehow manages to hold on to a small sense of optimism.

Production
The imperative desire for escape is expressed as much in the text as it is through the music, via the intrusion of conga drums provided by Caleb Quaye, the pastoral flute of Don Fay in the bridge passage at 1:35, and the blues harmonica played with an American accent by Graham Vickery starting at 5:09. An ideal introduction to a first opus, "Empty Sky" affirms the artist's rejection of constraints, even if its duration (running at nearly 8:30) was quite a gamble for an album's opening track. Leaning into its sense of eccentricity, this piece is a theater of experimentation, including the sounds of a voice and guitar captured in a stairwell, and an instrument played backward beginning at three o'clock. This backward playing was managed in the same way as in "I'm Only Sleeping" by the Beatles, segueing into a false fade-out that leads to an end the harmonica does not manage to resolve. Like a slightly mad dog, Elton almost whispers "I want you to shhh…" before changing his mind and bringing everyone back in for a spirited finale to this devilish opening track.

The judicious mix of spontaneity and creative euphoria that characterizes "Empty Sky" does contain a certain contradiction: while seeking to circumvent stereotypical musical formulas, the song actually conforms to many of the tropes of psychedelic pop music from the era.

VAL-HALA

Elton John, Bernie Taupin / 4:12

Musicians
Elton John: vocals, piano, organ, harpsichord
Caleb Quaye: acoustic guitar
Tony Murray: bass
Roger Pope: drums
Recorded
Dick James Music Studios, London: January 28, 1969
Technical Team
Producer: Steve Brown
Sound Engineer: Frank Owen
Assistant Sound Engineer: Clive Franks

John Peel confirmed his reputation as a star maker by inviting Elton to take part in his *Night Ride* broadcast on the BBC in 1968.

Genesis and Lyrics

Elton played "Val-Hala" for the first time on November 27, 1968, on *Night Ride*, John Peel's program broadcast on the BBC. It was prereleased with two other songs whose recording was also planned for the coming two weeks, "Lady What's Tomorrow" and "The Scaffold." "Val-Hala" owes its title and lyrics to Bernie Taupin's personal inspiration. He is referring to Valhalla, the heavenly place of rest in Nordic mythology, where brave warriors are taken who die in combat. It is difficult to square this version of Bernie Taupin, with his passion for seals, sirens, and Thor, the god of thunder, with the man who would write some of the finest love songs in all of pop music history in just a few years' time.

Production

A huge lightness emanates from "Val-Hala," although it is far from being one of Elton and Bernie's favorite numbers. Elton has often explained that he composed this piece with a view to approaching the work of Leonard Cohen, whose songs he listened to a great deal in 1968. Elton introduces a perky and rather busy-sounding harpsichord, which he had hired for the recording session. The instrument is coupled with the warm notes of an organ and with some more solemn piano notes. All these sounds were doubled by Elton in the overdubs. Little by little, a long reverb is applied over his voice, thereby reinforcing the mystical nature of the song's lyrics. Set somewhat into the background of the song's final mix, Tony Murray's bass provides a fundamental structure for the piece along with a disciplined drum section that is slightly more business as usual than the rest of the song. The ornamentations provided by Caleb Quaye on acoustic guitar (in this case a 1964 Gibson J-45) are very refined: "My acoustic guitar was very easy to record; engineers loved it. It was microphone-friendly, with that old wood. It had a great low and mid—very warm but crisp in the highs. It just would sit very well in a track"[13] At the end of the song, Steve Brown opts to fade out the rest of the group, leaving the harpsichord on its own.

WESTERN FORD GATEWAY

Elton John, Bernie Taupin / 3:15

Musicians
Elton John: vocals, piano, organ
Caleb Quaye: acoustic guitar, electric guitar
Tony Murray: bass
Roger Pope: drums
Recorded
Dick James Music Studios, London: January 28, 1969
Technical Team
Producer: Steve Brown
Sound Engineer: Frank Owen
Assistant Sound Engineer: Clive Franks

Having fiercely defended Elton's potential to Dick James, Steve Brown became the producer of Elton's first LP, *Empty Sky*.

Genesis and Lyrics

"Western Ford Gateway" reflects Bernie Taupin's obsession with America, where he had never set foot at the time when he wrote the song. His imagination delivers an incalculable number of images while simultaneously musing on the ephemeral nature of life. He moves in turn from the present to the past and uses short but striking lyrics. The song is about a cold place where "the gas lamps grow" and the "garbage blows," where a baby cries, and lives are extinguished violently by alcohol. Placing himself among these lyrics as a passive observer, Bernie does not linger over the characters, thereby depriving the listener of all empathy for them. But one can sense the attention to detail that is present in many of Taupin's later works. The interest in this song is focused not on the narrator but on the location itself, which is both disconcerting and mysterious.

Production

Although Elton himself never spoke in very tender terms about *Empty Sky*, several sequences from the album attest to his immense talent as a melody writer, notably in "Western Ford Gateway," which offers one of the most indisputably intense songs on the entire album. Elton's work on the piano is explosive, while on organ he's more discreet and even velvety. During the recording session on January 28, 1969, Elton, who "would have the song laid out on the piano and he'd play it down with just a chord sequence for the intro," became aware that the piece was lacking a hook. Caleb Quaye explained what happened in an interview from 2019. "And [Elton and Steve] would say, 'Could you come up with some guitar thing for the intro?' So I'd come up with it. Necessity is the mother of invention, as they say. And on 'Western Ford Gateway,' I put down one guitar lick for the intro; everybody loved it and Steve said, 'Oh! Do you think you could put a harmony line on that?' [laughing] 'Okay, sure…no problem!'"[13]

As for Elton's voice, it's given added depth by a slight reverb, and it sounds slightly raw, a feeling that's reinforced by the warmth of the analog recording. Special mention is also due to drummer Roger Pope, who provides powerful boosts on the toms, and tracks his playing on cymbals very neatly alongside Caleb Quaye's guitar riff.

HYMN 2000

Elton John, Bernie Taupin / 4:30

Musicians

Elton John: vocals, piano, organ
Caleb Quaye: acoustic guitar
Tony Murray: bass
Roger Pope: tambourine
Don Fay: flute
Clive Franks: whistling

Recorded

Dick James Music Studios, London: January 22, 1969

Technical Team

Producer: Steve Brown
Sound Engineer: Frank Owen
Assistant Sound Engineer: Clive Franks

Elton John takes a break at the mixing console at the Dick
James Music Studios in 1969.

Genesis and Lyrics

This song is often used as evidence by detractors of *Empty Sky* when they accuse Elton John and Bernie Taupin of following the psychedelic pop trend of their contemporaries. In point of fact, "Hymn 2000" was never defended by Elton John, who even vilified it, describing the text as "psychedelic rubbish" and the music as a "painful Dylan-type thing."[16] Bernie Taupin's lyrics ("Collecting submarine numbers / On the main street of the sea") could have been right out of the Beatles' "Octopus's Garden," though that song was actually released three months later. Nevertheless, Taupin's surrealistic lyrics are meandering and obtuse. The author gives himself free rein to explore a baffling sense of cosmic humor: "And the comfort of mother / Was just an appeal for protection / For the cat from next door / Was found later at four / In surgical dissection." Philip Norman, author of *Sir Elton*, sees a "fable of maternal incest, church and chocolate"[17] in the song, apparently because it involves lines like "bed with her mother," a "chocolate center," and mention of a "vicar," but we're never certain what might be linking these diverse elements!

Production

Attempting to adopt some Dylan-esque nuances, Elton John seems to be debating with himself over the treatment of the lyrics in this song, choosing to linger on some syllables while accelerating through others. The result is neither fluid nor natural. In addition, the inclusion of a hippieish arrangement on the flute, the organ, and the tambourine aren't doing the song any favors. In the introduction, Elton John plants the chords inflexibly while Caleb Quaye adds in some dissonant guitar notes. The verse is destabilized through its frequent changes of tonality. Under these conditions, the refrains feel like bursts of oxygen because of their relatively normal harmonic nature. The cherry on top of this indigestible cake came when the assistant sound engineer, Clive Franks, was called upon to provide a whistled rendition of the piano's melody, thus finishing off a work that was destined to take its place as the most obvious misstep on Elton John's freshman album.

LADY WHAT'S TOMORROW

Elton John, Bernie Taupin / 3:09

Musicians: Elton John: vocals, piano, organ / Caleb Quaye: acoustic guitar / Tony Murray: bass / Nigel Olsson: drums **Recorded:** Dick James Music Studios, London: November 19, 1968 **Technical Team:** Producer: Steve Brown / Sound Engineer: Frank Owen / Assistant Sound Engineer: Clive Franks

Genesis and Lyrics

As one of the first tracks to be recorded in November 1968, "Lady What's Tomorrow" is probably one of the weakest songs on the album. Bernie's words have a touchingly naïve quality. He had grown up on a farm, and the listener can sense a mission statement of sorts in the words "lament for rural beauty in the voice of a child evacuee,"[17] as the author Philip Norman describes it in his book, *Sir Elton John*. Perhaps he is suggesting that he was exiled from the rural environment of his upbringing? Inspired by growing concerns about society's clash with nature, Taupin describes an older brother warning his younger brother of society's inevitable encroachment into nature. Although mentioned in the song's title, the "Lady" in question remains mysterious. She may be seen as a Mother Nature–like figure, or, conversely, as the source of all pain and suffering, as with the character Mame in "Put the Blame on Mame," a song sung by Rita Hayworth in the classic 1946 film *Gilda*.

Production

A conventional midtempo pop song of no particular interest, "Lady What's Tomorrow" remains important in the Elton John story because it marks his first collaboration with the drummer Nigel Olsson (Plastic Penny, the Spencer Davis Group, Uriah Heep), who remained with him until the 1975 album *Captain Fantastic and the Brown Dirt Cowboy*. Elton called upon Olsson again in the 1980s to work on the albums *21 at 33*, *The Fox*, *Too Low for Zero*, and *Breaking Hearts*. In this case, the drumming on the track sounds rather clumsy, and the organ is very discreet but oppressive, while Elton, who begins alone on the piano, lacks confidence in the first bars and seems to struggle to hold a straightforward tune.

SAILS

Elton John, Bernie Taupin / 3:45

Musicians: Elton John: vocals, organ / Caleb Quaye: electric guitar / Tony Murray: bass / Roger Pope: drums **Recorded:** Dick James Music Studios, London: January 1969 **Technical Team:** Producer: Steve Brown / Sound Engineer: Frank Owen / Assistant Sound Engineer: Clive Franks **Single Release:** *Levon / Sails* **New Zealand/Australia release:** 1971 on DJM Records (ref. DJK-4541)

Genesis and Lyrics

In "Sails," a midtempo blues-rock song, the narrator is sailing in the company of a certain Lucy; they're together on a merchant ship that's searching for "the spices of China." We do not know who Lucy is, or her age, but her behavior, particularly when she "walked gently / Between the damp barrels," and then "shut out my eyes / With the width of her fingers," leads the listener to suppose that she is the narrator's daughter. Bernie Taupin, the captain on Elton's long artistic voyage, had not yet experienced the joys of fatherhood when he worked on this song. His first daughter, Charley Indiana, was not born until 2005.

Production

"Sails" is a demonstration of the power of rhythm 'n' blues, and it attests to the group's growing sense of cohesion. Roger Pope demonstrates his versatility with a quite nervy, slamming play on the snare drum before adding a subtle caress to the ripple (at 1:15) just before placing a drumroll. During the refrains of this rhetorical fantasy, Elton shows that he is in charge, offering a Lennon-like intonation that's supported by precision playing from the studio musicians.

Caleb Quaye is given license to play a long and inspired solo beginning at 1:23, although the fuzzy sounds of his guitar leaves the listener wishing for a crisper sound. The instrument was recorded live and without any overdub. But it's Elton who reserves the star position in the finale for himself, featuring a vocal high point that includes a descending scale, while Caleb Quaye creates a violin effect with his volume pedal. "It's a track that I think is ahead of its time," Caleb said. "Compositionally, it's Steely Dan before there was a Steely Dan; listen to the chord changes. It absolutely stands the test of time."[13]

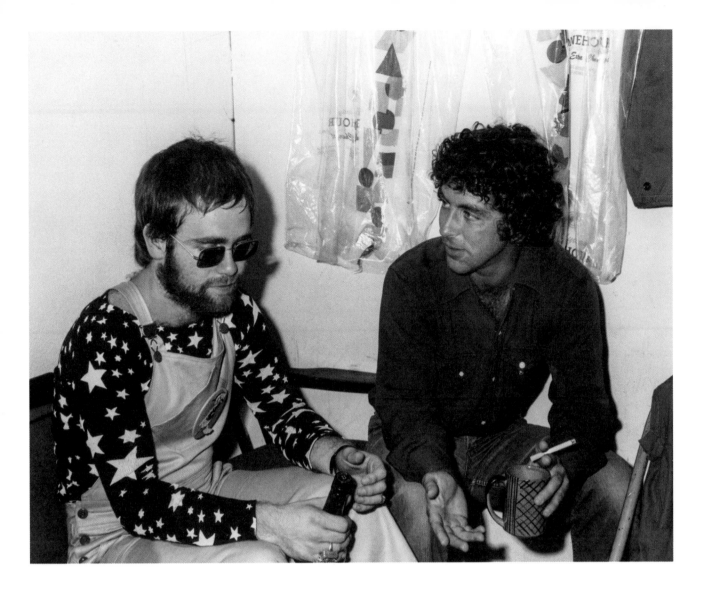

THE SCAFFOLD

Elton John, Bernie Taupin / 3:18

Musicians: Elton John: vocals, Pianet, organ / **Caleb Quaye:** acoustic guitar, electric guitar / **Tony Murray:** bass / **Roger Pope:** drums **Recorded:** Dick James Music Studios, London: January 1969 **Technical Team:** Producer: Steve Brown / **Sound Engineer:** Frank Owen / **Assistant Sound Engineer:** Clive Franks

Genesis and Lyrics

Bernie Taupin was clearly referring to the song "Long Black Veil" (released by the Band on their 1968 album *Music from Big Pink*) when he created "The Scaffold." It was in this venerated piece, both for the lyricist and for Elton, that they found verses to inspire their own number: "The scaffold was high and eternity neared!" Other than this obvious source of inspiration, the meaning of the words in this song remain somewhat impenetrable. There are strong images, such as "The Minotaur with bloody hands / [...] enraged by the sun / Caged he by the

corpses," as well as the desire to take the listener on a journey to the far corners of the world.

Production

"The Scaffold" is a light ballad, even glib, and it was conceived by Elton as an homage to the folk artists that he and Bernie were constantly listening to during this period. These artists included Bob Dylan, Leonard Cohen, and also David Ackles, who played in Elton's first American performances a year and a half later, and whose album *American Gothic* (1972) would be produced by...Bernie Taupin. The piano sequences in this song are very gentle and very well underpinned by the delicate arpeggios of Caleb Quaye, while the rhythm section is deliberately restrained. Elton, who ends the song on a low note, demonstrates his excellent vocal technique, and he is also responsible for the very successful backing vocals.

Elton focused a considerable amount of his efforts on "Skyline Pigeon," which proved to be the most successful song from *Empty Sky* and also the only song from the album that he continued to perform later in his career.

SKYLINE PIGEON

Elton John, Bernie Taupin / 3:38

Musicians
Elton John: vocals, harpsichord, organ
Recorded
Dick James Music Studios, London: January 1969
Technical Team
Producer: Steve Brown
Sound Engineer: Frank Owen
Assistant Sound Engineer: Clive Franks
Single Release
Daniel / Skyline Pigeon
UK Release: January 20, 1973, on DJM Records (ref. DJS 275)
Best UK Chart Ranking: 4
US Release: March 26, 1973, on MCA Records (ref. MCA-40046)
Best US Chart Ranking: 2

Another version of this song, recorded in London in 1974, was used as the opener of the live LP *Here and There*, which was originally released in 1976 and reissued on CD in 1995.

Paul Buckmaster, who reworked all of the arrangements for the 1972 version of the song, once confessed that he cried every time he heard "Skyline Pigeon"![20]

Genesis and Lyrics

The eighth and penultimate track on the album, "Skyline Pigeon" seems noticeably more accomplished than the previous pieces, showing a hitherto unseen maturity in the compositions of Elton and Bernie. This song is, in a way, the founding song of the duo (along with "Lady Samantha"), who often cite its fundamental role in the course of their career: "'Skyline Pigeon' was the first good song that Bernie and I wrote," Elton affirmed definitively in 2015. Five years later, the lyricist explained: "I think that happened when we found our own voice, when we weren't mimicking what was currently in vogue. I think the song that Elton and I always go back to is 'Skyline Pigeon.' [...] Bear in mind, this is before Elton was a performing artist, before we even realized that he was going to become the artist that was going to perform our songs."[18]

In fact, "Skyline Pigeon" is one of many songs written by the two musicians in 1968. It was not a novelty, strictly speaking, because it had already been released as a single in August 1968 on the Pye label (sung by Guy Darrell) and, almost simultaneously, by Roger James Cooke on Columbia Records. It was mainly after hearing this number that Steve Brown was convinced of the potential of the John–Taupin duo and decided to persuade Dick James to continue to invest in their future.

Cherished Freedom

"Skyline Pigeon" revisits once more the dominant theme of the album: freedom and the need to escape from all forms of constraint and oppression. The words, which are clearly metaphorical, describe a pigeon flying high into the sky after having been set free. One phrase in particular catches the listener's attention: "But most of all please free me from / This aching metal ring," possibly describing a man who wants to be free of a broken marriage so he can pursue his dreams and ambitions.

Some have seen in these lyrics an allusion to Elton John's personal situation, since his marriage to Linda Woodrow (whom he'd met in December 1967) was planned for June 1968. Caught in the crosshairs of his engagement, Elton realized that a wedding was not going to make him happy. Linda, on the other hand, seemed to be waiting for the moment when the aspiring singer would toe the line and finally become a good family man. What also did not help was the fact that they had never

been physically close. With little experience of her own, Linda did not initially find the situation abnormal, but, as time went by, she started to wonder. Long John Baldry also had his concerns about their relationship. He was the one who assumed responsibility for ending the romance when he, Elton, and Bernie met at the Bag O'Nails, a bar in Soho. Without pulling any punches, Baldry implored Elton to acknowledge the evidence of his homosexuality, and to admit that he could not marry a woman: "You're gay. You love Bernie more than you love her."[3] Elton did not dare to accept the truth of his own nature. Bernie was his best friend, but as far as Elton was concerned, their relationship was one of professional artistry and nothing else. All of these emotions were warring inside Elton when he broke

off his engagement with Linda later that night and moved back to live with Bernie in Frome Court.

Another, more prosaic interpretation has been provided for this song: that of a carrier pigeon used during wartime to transport urgent messages. The scope for interpretation is vast, which led Bernie to comment, in an October 4, 1997, interview in *Billboard* magazine, that he preferred to let people draw their own conclusions rather than to solve the mystery for them.

Production

"Skyline Pigeon" is the only track on the album in which Elton is alone at the harpsichord, which makes for a sort of procession that is moving in its minimalism as well as in its

Elton with Ryan White, who became a symbol in the fight against AIDS. Two years after the young man's death, the singer created the Elton John AIDS Foundation.

instrumental and vocal virtuosity. His voice seems fragile on the last notes of the piece, which helps this song retain all of its freshness and spontaneity, and it also emphasizes an extremely sophisticated melody. Elton often talked about the unconventional technique used to record his voice on this particular track. To create the slightly metallic echo that Steve Brown was looking for, the singer was positioned in the studio's emergency exit stairwell, thereby achieving the desired effect as well as a vocal depth that, combined with the music, proved to be quite striking. The harpsichord part delves into Elton's classical inspirations…and perhaps a little into the George Martin arrangement for "In My Life" by the Beatles, which appeared on the album *Rubber Soul* in 1965. To complete the arrangement and give the song an even more solemn tone, Elton added several organ tracks in the second verse.

A Late Single

Against all expectations, "Skyline Pigeon" became the most popular song from the early days of Elton John's musical career, even though it was not sold as a single straightaway. Fans had to wait until 1972 for Elton to rerecord the song alongside "Crocodile Rock," "Elderberry Wine," and "Daniel" during

the recording sessions for *Don't Shoot Me I'm Only the Piano Player* at the Château d'Hérouville. Elton recorded the track at the request of Sheila Dudgeon, Gus's partner. In this second version of the song, Elton retains the same tonality. The key is *Bb*, but he trades the harpsichord for the piano, and he does not play alone. Instead, he is accompanied by strings and an oboe under the direction of Paul Buckmaster, and supported by Davey Johnstone, Dee Murray, and Nigel Olsson. This new version, recorded in only two takes and with no overdubs save for the acoustic guitar, was not included in the track listing of the album, but it was used as a B-side for the single "Daniel" that was released in January 1973. It then appeared on the *Lady Samantha* compilation, which came out on cassette in 1974, then on vinyl in 1980, and finally on CD in 1988. Then, the song resurfaced again on *Rare Masters* in 1992, as a bonus on the reissue of *Don't Shoot Me I'm Only the Piano Player* in 1995, and, finally, on the third CD of the box set *Diamonds*, which came out in 2017.

With this majestic and inspiring piece, which liberated itself from all the musical categories of the time, Elton and Bernie set themselves on a path that would take them to the height of success in the following decade.

Steve Brown, looking very corporate as he proudly wears a shirt emblazoned with the Rocket Record Company image.

STEVE BROWN: GENTLEMAN PRODUCER

Steve Brown spent the first years of his life in Zimbabwe, where he was born in 1946. His father, Fred, was a pilot in the Royal Air Force, and his mother, Muriel, was an administrative manager. Eventually, the two of them decided to return to England with their four children, and they moved to Croydon, a large town in South London. After attending the local Heath Clark secondary school, the young Steve obtained his first job in music, working as a sales assistant in a shop called Potters, whose manager taught him how to play the baritone saxophone. Finding himself drawn to the lights of the stage, he joined a band called Emile Ford and the Checkmates, although only for a short while.

A Decisive Role in Elton's Career

Following his brief experience as a band member (Steve Brown is also rarely mentioned in the various biographies of the group), he entered the world of music production when he joined EMI in 1966, at the age of twenty. Two years later, in September 1968, he joined Dick James's stable, and James gave him the reins of his recording studio. Convinced of Elton's and Bernie's potential after hearing their early recordings, he managed to persuade the music publisher to take a chance as their producer. Steve was at the forefront of the subsequent creation of the DJM Records label; he produced its first album, Elton's very own *Empty Sky*, which came out in June 1969.

Given the paltry success of *Empty Sky*, Steve considered only his own limitations, rather than doubting Elton's talent. With good grace and style, he made way for Gus Dudgeon to take the reins on Elton John's self-titled second album, which turned the singer into a worldwide star. Steve Brown was one of Elton's earliest and most ardent supporters, and the singer never forgot the debt he owed to Brown. Brown and John were very good friends, and he remained Elton's mentor and his "musical coordinator" until 1976. In that time, he also worked with numerous other artists, including Kiki Dee and Ralph McTell.

From Stage to Farm...and Back Again

In 1976, Steve made a bold move that upended the course of his life. He left the music world and took his family to the countryside. With his wife, Gill Hook, whom he had married in 1968, he acquired a small farm in Kent. He discovered a fascination with sheep breeding and milk production. He also designed clocks, which Gill sold at market to supplement the farm revenues. In 1986, Steve, whose accounts were in the red, began to miss the good old days of music, and so he decided to backpedal: He sold the farm and returned to London, where he joined the team at John Reid Enterprises, working as the manager of the comedian Billy Connolly.

Following his divorce from Gill in 1998, Steve Brown married Sam Stell, his former assistant at John Reid. The two started a new life together in Malta in 2002, then returned to live in East Sussex in 2016.

When he died in 2018, at the age of seventy-two, Steve Brown left behind five children from his first marriage and four from his second. He also left behind the memory of a man who wanted to live life in his own way. He knew how to listen to his staff, and how to delegate tasks to people who knew what they were doing. Caleb Quaye, to whom Brown had ceded the management of DJM Studios after his departure, gave an interview in 2020 in which he said: "Steve was a great champion of us writing and pursuing the music that we felt. [...] Not only were we a [music] team, we were friends. We were mates. We all hung out together."[21]

Caleb Quaye was an exceptional guitarist, and he was one of Elton's earliest supporters.

CALEB QUAYE: "THE GREATEST GUITARIST IN THE WORLD"

"The greatest guitarist in the world": this is how Eric Clapton once described Caleb Quaye in an interview with David Letterman. Quaye was less well-known to the general public, but he was celebrated by other guitar heroes of his era. Not content to illuminate Elton's first compositions with his feverish playing, thereby enabling Elton to enter the pantheon of rock superstars, Caleb also played a key role in bringing Elton and Bernie Taupin to the attention of Dick James and his son, Stephen.

Caleb was born into a family of musicians, in London in 1948. His father, Cab Kaye, was a famous jazzman, and he introduced Caleb to the piano at the age of four, and to the drums at the age of seven. He also gave Caleb an old guitar, which had been purchased for £10 from a pawnshop, for his twelfth birthday. Three years later, after his father left home, Caleb left school and managed to find a job in England's equivalent of Tin Pan Alley, a wholesale music distribution outlet called Paxton's. "My job was to go around to the various music publishers on Denmark Street, and pick up their orders for sheet music. One of the places was called Mills Music and that's where I met Reg Dwight. He was their coffee boy kind of guy. We hit it off and became friends. That's where we first met, I was 15 and he was 16 going on 17."[78]

Having been raised on the jazz of Dizzy Gillespie and Ella Fitzgerald, Caleb had an exceptional ear for music. In 1965 he was recruited by DJM Studios, which was owned by Dick James Music, to work as an assistant, and this coincided with the creation of the recording studios that were being run by Stephen James. Caleb made himself useful by playing guitar during sessions, and in 1967, at age nineteen, he was promoted to studio engineer when Stephen James became more influential. It was at this time that Reginald Dwight took up his post there as a bespoke composer at the company. The two young lads often met in the studios, and they were also briefly in the groups Bluesology (at the end of 1967) and the Bread and Beer Band (1969).

Caleb liked Elton's compositions and even took the (not inconsiderable) risk of letting Reginald record his demos after hours, thereby putting his own job on the line. Eventually, Caleb's deception was uncovered by Dick James. But instead of falling on his sword, Caleb justified his actions by pointing to Elton's talent, and he urged his boss to listen to the young singer's demos. Quaye's nerve, combined with Stephen's lobbying, ultimately convinced Dick that signing Reginald was a good idea.

The Hookfoot Sound

In addition to his other responsibilities at work, Caleb also worked as a studio musician with DJM Studios. Quite naturally, he was the one to whom Elton turned in 1968 when he had to put together his first stage band. At that time Caleb was associated with Boots Slade on bass and Malcolm Tomlinson on drums, and then he formed a professional relationship with the indispensable David Glover and Roger Pope in the following year. Eventually, Glover, Pope, and Quaye combined forces with Ian Duck (singer, guitarist, and harmonica player) to form a band called Hookfoot, which lasted from 1969 to 1974. Active as an accompanying group for Elton both onstage and in the studio, Hookfoot was also a band in its own right, and the group released six studio albums with DJM Records in the span of five years. Following his separation from Hookfoot in 1974, Caleb Quaye went to the United States and worked as a studio musician. Elton called him back to the UK in 1975, and he worked in the studio and onstage with Elton until 1978.

A Voice That's Louder Than Rock 'n' Roll

On October 9, 1978, Caleb was celebrating his thirtieth birthday when he was struck by a mystical revelation. "I suddenly heard a voice speak to me and call me by my name to tell me: 'Caleb, from this point on everything in your life is going to be different and nothing is going to be the same for you ever again.'"[83]

From then on, he chose to embrace religion and he became an evangelist musician. Caleb went on to serve as a minister at the Foursquare Church in Pasadena until 1995, before being given the position of National Worship director for the denomination. In 2008 and 2009, he showed that the flame of music had not left him when he released two jazz rock albums: *One Night in San Dimas* and *Out of the Blue*.

GULLIVER / HAY CHEWED / REPRISE

Elton John, Bernie Taupin / 6:58

Musicians
Elton John: vocals, piano, organ
Caleb Quaye: acoustic guitar, electric guitar
Tony Murray: bass
Roger Pope: drums, percussion
Don Fay: tenor saxophone

Recorded
Dick James Music Studios, London: January 1969

Technical Team
Producer: Steve Brown
Sound Engineer: Frank Owen
Assistant Sound Engineer: Clive Franks

Caleb Quaye's instinctive guitar playing made its mark on the songs of *Empty Sky*, especially "Hay Chewed."

In 1995, "Hay Chewed" was reissued by the Rocket Record Company in the UK and by Island Records in the US. It was mistakenly titled "It's Hay Chewed."

Genesis and Lyrics

"Gulliver's gone but his memory lies there." The companion that Bernie created in the poignant ballad "Gulliver" is named after one of the dogs on the farm where he grew up. The death of the animal was a terrible blow for Bernie when he was a little boy. In this disarming song, he recalls the particular bond that united them. Careful to ensure that the text was respected by the other performers, the group fine-tuned the musical tension at the end of the piece in order to express the child's sense of anger and loss. "Gulliver" is a starting point for many future ballads written by the John–Taupin duo, which always managed to avoid subsiding into maudlin sadness, at least until "Sorry Seems to Be the Hardest Word" in 1976.

Production

Nearly seven minutes were set aside for this unusual song, though in actuality, "Gulliver" clocks in at just over three minutes. The last few minutes of the song become an extended jam session that turns the track into a massive achievement. Its structure remains relatively conventional: It begins with Elton's piano along with some guitar notes that are engorged with reverb. "That echo at the beginning was a board effect that the engineer would give back to me in my headphones while I was playing," confided Caleb Quaye. "In the verses, that's me just applying some of my Hendrix licks to what Elton was doing. That's 'The Wind Cries Mary.'"[13]

The rhythm section drives the song forward little by little, and Caleb raises the tension until Elton's final cry, which is drowned out by delay and reverb. He is the one who creates the transition into an unexpected, blues-jazz jam episode, called "Hay Chewed." This jam section demonstrates the group's musical tendency toward strengths. Although dominated by Caleb Quaye's guitar (slightly shrill on the solo) and the unbridled tenor sax of Don Fay, the sequence also shows off the refined playing of drummer Roger Pope: "Roger was a very versatile drummer," explained Caleb. "His dad was a jazz drummer and he grew up listening to that. So, we used to play jazzy stuff and bluesy stuff."[13] To conclude the piece, Steve Brown chose to place brief extracts from each of the album's songs into a sequence collectively called "Reprise." It ends in a "hard cut" similar to what was done on "I Want You (She's So Heavy)" from the Beatles' *Abbey Road*, an album that was released a few months later.

ALBUM

ELTON JOHN

Your Song . I Need You to Turn To . Take Me to the Pilot .
No Shoe Strings on Louise . First Episode at Hienton . Sixty Years On .
Border Song . The Greatest Discovery . The Cage . The King Must Die

RELEASE DATES
UK Release: April 10, 1970
Reference: DJM Records—DJLPS 406
Best UK Chart Ranking: 5
US Release: July 22, 1970
Reference: Uni Records—73090
Best US Chart Ranking: 4

Despite the relative lack of interest generated by *Empty Sky*, Elton was given the chance to record a second album with the Dick James Music team.

A VERY PRODUCTIVE DUO

Amazingly, when the recording sessions began on the second LP, the songs for Elton's next record, *Tumbleweed Connection*, had almost all been written.

A SKILLFULLY ORCHESTRATED METAMORPHOSIS

One has to face facts: *Empty Sky*, which was released in June 1969, barely appealed to the listening public. If Elton John did not want to see his career end before it had even really started, then it was essential for him to begin a new chapter. So, as soon as his first LP was released, he focused on the composition of his next album, with a view to doing something radically different. With this eponymous album, the singer would not only take the first steps on a new musical path, but he would also begin his transformation into a world-renowned rock superstar.

The Search for a Cohesive Sound

At the end of the summer, Steve Brown, who had produced Elton's first album, was listening to some of the new songs that John and Taupin had been working on, including "Take Me to the Pilot," "The Cage," and "Border Song." The question immediately arose of how to produce their future album so that the public answered the call. The quality of the songs was not in question; everyone in the DJM circle agreed that the new demos confirmed the potential they had first noticed when listening to early tracks from *Empty Sky*. Dick James himself seemed excited by the duo's new songs, even though their last album had performed well below expectations. James also knew that Elton and Bernie were spending lots of time with a bassist, Muff Winwood (the Spencer Davis Group, Traffic), who worked at Island Records. Probably concerned that his young protégé might be snapped up—and with good reason, since a deal between Elton and this other label was already being discussed—Dick James gave the green light to begin production of a new album, and he put £6,000 on the table to cover expenses, a considerable amount for the time, and much more than Elton and Bernie could've reasonably hoped for.

Although the duo already had a backlog of several numbers they hadn't included on *Empty Sky*, they showed no signs of slowing down in their creative process, and they continued to compose at full tilt. "There was so much output of music," recalled the guitarist Caleb Quaye. "[Elton and Bernie] loved writing the songs. They couldn't wait to get in the studio to do the demos!"[21] In his autobiography, Elton explains that all the songs from this period were composed in the pair's shared room at Frome Court, where they listened albums by the Band and Delaney & Bonnie on repeat. Those songs "felt like someone switching a torch on and showing us a new path to follow, a way we could do what we wanted to do. 'Chest Fever,' 'Tears of Rage,' 'The Weight,' this was what we craved to write. Bernie went crazy for the lyrics. Ever since he was a kid, he'd loved gritty stories about old America, and that was what the Band told."[3]

The problem lay not in the substance but in the form. In August 1969, Steve Brown called a meeting with Elton, guitarist Caleb Quaye, and drummer Roger Pope at Olympic Studios in London. The four men had worked on the previous album together, and Brown thought it was important for them to reflect on the sound identity they wanted to achieve on the new record. One of the major problems that Elton was aware of was giving cohesion to songs that were as heterogeneous in their form as in their inspiration: "Something like 'Border Song' or 'Take Me to the Pilot' had a sort of funk and soulfulness that I'd picked up backing Patti LaBelle and Major Lance, but they also had a classical influence that seeped in from all those Saturday mornings where I'd been forced to study Chopin and Bartók."[3]

The duo felt they needed to bring on a supportive manager, and they asked Ray Williams, the man who was behind their original meeting, to come on board.

The Song That Changed Everything

In the fall of 1969, Elton was still working on the demos of his songs at DJM Studios and focusing his energy on "The King Must Die," "No Shoe Strings on Louise," and "I Need You to Turn To." "Even I could tell that our new material was in a different league to anything we'd produced before. They were

1970

A collaboration with Gus Dudgeon (shown here in 1974), the brilliant producer of David Bowie's "Space Oddity," proved to be a decisive moment for Elton John.

A SMALL MISUNDERSTANDING!
The first time Gus Dudgeon met Elton John, he did not recognize him: "Actually, for the first half-hour of the meeting, I thought Bernie was Elton because Steve never introduces anybody to anybody; he just walks in and expects people to know who the hell they are. Bernie was kind of younger, thinner and didn't wear glasses and had longer hair. I thought [laughing], 'He must be the artist!' Mind you, Elton was dressed like a traffic light, which I guess should have been a bit of a clue."[25]

easy songs to write,"[3] he wrote in his autobiography. By October 27, a song appeared that would change everything for Elton: "Your Song." Reggie tried out the new song, which Bernie had written in five minutes flat during breakfast at Frome Court. Ray Williams was totally impressed by "Your Song," and he wondered how someone as young as Bernie could have written such lyrics. Steve Brown shared Ray's enthusiasm and started looking for an arranger who could maintain the impressive stature as the lyrics. He knew that the definitive launching of Elton's career could be a matter of releasing this particular song as a single. George Martin, the legendary Pygmalion behind the Beatles, was approached, but he wanted to manage both the production and the arrangements, and so Steve Brown did not pursue this option. Elton and Steve then thought of Paul Buckmaster, the bold arranger on David Bowie's "Space Oddity," which reached fifth place on the British charts at the beginning of November. Steve and Elton decided to meet Buckmaster at a Miles Davis concert given at Ronnie Scott's in London. Shortly after this meeting, Paul received the demo of "Your Song." "It only took the first hearing for me to call Steve and express my enthusiasm," recalled Buckmaster in a 2020 interview. "I heard the potential of what I was going to write. I had

already begun to hear what I was going to write on 'Your Song,' for a start. It was the sort of thing that I was dying to have a go at."[22] Steve had Paul listen to the other demos, with a view to selecting one to go on the B-side of "Your Song," but the arranger was so impressed with each new track that finally he confessed to Steve that he wanted to do the arrangements for the entire album. "We could afford strings and an arranger, Paul Buckmaster,"[3] confided Elton. "[...] Paul arrived looking like D'Artagnan—he had long center-parted hair, a goatee beard and a big hat. He seemed a bit eccentric, which, as it turned out, was a false first impression. Paul wasn't a *bit* eccentric. He was so eccentric as to suggest he might be genuinely nuts. He would stand in front of the orchestra and make noises with his mouth to indicate what he wanted them to do: 'I don't know how to describe what I want, but I want you to make a sound like this.' They got it exactly right. He was a genius."[3]

Carte Blanche for Gus Dudgeon

A dozen potential numbers came into view very quickly. At the end of winter, when all the pieces selected for the album had been locked into place, the team knew that they could record "an incredible, orchestral album," as Elton later explained to the

BBC in 1973: "The sort that had never been planned before. A really pop album with a lot of heavy orchestra in it but with a beat as well. You know, really sort of funky stuff."[23]

After careful consideration, Steve Brown then made the difficult decision to withdraw as producer. "I just realized that I hadn't got the experience and the expertise to produce an album that was going to involve a 50-piece orchestra and 16-track recording," he explained. "All that I had ever done before was with three or four musicians on a four-track studio."[24] *Empty Sky* had been a fascinating project for everyone involved, but Steve was the first to admit that Elton needed to call upon greater forces if he wanted to make a splash with his follow-up record. The two men asked Paul Buckmaster to suggest someone to produce the album. He immediately suggested Gus Dudgeon, who had produced David Bowie's landmark "Space Oddity."

A meeting was arranged, during which the demos were played for Gus. Steve and Elton had the impression that Gus didn't really seem interested: "Maybe I did it on purpose," Gus explained later. "I was trying to look cool or something. But [inside] I was leaping up and down thinking, 'Wow!'"[25] Later, Gus called up Steve and asked him for an advance of £2,500. Steve nearly choked. He explained that Dick had never paid money like that for an album before and added: "You might be lucky if you get a thousand." But Gus insisted, at the risk of losing the contract. In response to the question: "What sort of budget have you got in mind?" he responded without blinking, "Well…carte blanche?" Exasperated, Steve explained to Gus that he would have to give way on certain points. But Gus stuck to his guns, arguing that at this stage in the production process he could not predict the exact number of musicians he would need, or how long he might need them. He then went to see Dick James himself in order to find out if he would be given the money he needed. "No problem," Dick replied. "And finally," Gus later explained, "I never actually had to go back for more money; I had what I needed when I needed it. He just paid every bill and there was no further discussion. It cost £6,000 to make [about three times the budget for an established artist's album at the time], including the sleeve, which is absolutely peanuts. I mean, some people can't make a single nowadays for £6,000, myself included."[25]

Exquisite Work from the Best Musicians

Trident Studios, located at 17 St. Anne's Court in Soho, was selected as the recording site. This was the same studio where *Space Oddity* was recorded the previous year. It contained a legendary Bechstein piano that was one hundred years old, and it was not far from the Ship pub and the Marquee club. There were many attractions that drew people to Trident, and the artists had already found a fantastic Indian restaurant that delivered them all kinds of dishes during their recording breaks.

While waiting for the sessions to begin, Gus and Paul worked on the order of the songs. As they had done for Bowie, they decided to plan each detail of the recording process before any musicians had set foot in the studio. They were in Paul's office five days a week, running through the songs and writing down each note and rhythmic indication, scrutinizing the slightest lyric and determining where, exactly, they should incorporate the strings, drums, and other instruments. "Say it was a song where the piano started, for example, 'Your Song.' We would say, 'Okay, we will start with strings in the first verse. We won't bring the drums in until the second verse,'"[22] explained Paul in 1993.

When this work was completed, Paul took home the notes and gave free rein to his imagination. What the two men wanted to avoid at all costs was each musician coming to them with some preconceived idea for an intro or a solo that they wanted to record. The key was to conceive of a strict framework, but without being impervious to any brilliant studio "accidents" that might occur and could enhance the work. Elton decided to place his full trust in the duo and not to involve himself in the creative decisions taken on by Gus and Paul: "He was wonderful," recalled Paul. "It's not often that you have an artist do that. He had so much trust that he allowed us to do what we felt was right for each song. Each song was its own mini-film that had its own cast."[22]

The recruitment of musicians for the orchestra was the next step in the process; they needed twenty or so in total, which was the number of a small chamber orchestra. Logically, the best studio professionals were sought: "People like Terry Cox, who's with Pentangle," Elton told Terry Towne for *Jazz and Pop* magazine in 1971. "And Barry Morgan, the other drummer, is with an English group called Blue Mink [the British band also included bassist Herbie Flowers, who recorded on this album, and future Elton percussionist Ray Cooper]. All the other people are really sort of the top session guys, the backup singers are all the best backup singers."[26]

At the heart of this orchestra was a harpist named Skaila Kanga, who Elton had discovered for the first time when they were studying at the Royal Academy of Music. When she

Outside of Bernie Taupin, Elton's closest partner in his early days was this 1910 A-Day Birdcage Upright Piano, on which he composed many of the songs from his first five albums.

entered the studio, Skaila recognized not only Elton but also Paul Buckmaster, who had also been at the Royal Academy of Music after Elton had been there. As with the other musicians, she would follow the maestro almost blindly, reading the handwritten scores on sight and putting her faith in the process.

A Well-Planned Live Recording

On Monday morning, January 19, 1970, everything was finally ready. Engineers Robin Geoffrey Cable and David Hentschel were on the starting blocks and ready to go. There were just a few errant details that everyone had to wrap their minds around: first, while Trident Studios was among the first in the United Kingdom to offer sixteen-track recording, there were not enough headphones for sixteen musicians, so some had to make do with using tiny speakers in the floor during sessions. Second, in order to keep control of the budget, some of the recordings were made using only eight tracks instead of the full sixteen. This was the case with one of the first tracks to be put to bed, "No Shoe Strings on Louise."

The recording of the album, which was completed in just four days (from January 19 to 22, 1970), was divided into two 3-hour sessions per day: from 3 p.m. to 8 p.m., followed by a pause for dinner, and then again from 9 p.m. to 11 p.m. This was the norm, according to Musicians' Union rules; if a session lasted even a minute longer, every musician would be paid double. It was only at the end of each day that Elton could find the time to record his vocal parts along with the backing vocals. This meant that orchestral additions, if required, had to wait until the end of the week to be laid down. The piano was the first instrument to be recorded along with the rhythm section, if there was one. Gus Dudgeon became accustomed to locking away the drummer in a separate booth in order to put Elton's piano right in the middle of the studio.

"We did all the tracks live, with strings...," explained Elton in 1976. "I was very, very frightened in the recording studio being confronted with a 40-piece string section and having to do it live. So that was quite nerve-wracking but it was good experience. When we all finished it, we were knocked out."[24]

In his autobiography, which was published nearly forty years later, Elton retained an emotional memory of this period and details his experience thusly: "Everything about the sessions was weirdly magical. Me, Gus, Steve and Paul had planned everything out in advance—the songs, the sound, the arrangements—and it all just fell into place. I had barely touched a harpsichord before we hired one for 'I Need You To Turn To' [although he had played it on many of the *Empty Sky* pieces]; it was a really hard instrument to play, but I did it. I was petrified about playing live with an orchestra, but I psyched myself up, telling myself that this was it, something was finally coming to fruition. [...] It was all leading up to this. And it worked. The whole album was done in four days."[3] It was the same for Gus Dudgeon, who did not disguise his pride in the final result: "If I could go through that week again, I would just love it to death."[25]

As with the first album, the production of the second album's cover art was entrusted to David Larkham. "Because the music was dark, and very melodramatic," he explained, "I immediately thought of Rembrandt paintings and in particular those that were lit with a lantern from one side with a dark background and that was my vision of Elton for the cover of the album. The back cover was two shots joined together which was easy because of the black background."[20] Some were critical of the jacket's darkness, even suggesting that it had a negative impact on the album's sales.

America Opens Its Doors

Released by DJM Records on April 10, 1970, *Elton John* and its hit single "Your Song" turned the singer into a star. In England, the album received very good reviews and, thanks to the DJ John Peel, who broadcast it massively, it moved slowly but surely to the top of the charts, ultimately reaching fifth place.

In the United States, where it was issued on the Uni Records label a bit later in the year, many people thought this was Elton's first album, since *Empty Sky* crossed the Atlantic only in 1975. Even though it was still early days in the US, the best American reviewers were already analyzing the Elton John phenomenon: "In this age during which most everyone seems content to sing unison with moronic little guitar riffs, he writes attractive melodies,"[27] commented John Mendelsohn in *Rolling Stone*. However, he found the arrangements by Paul Buckmaster "pompous" and potentially undermining to the fine melodies created by Elton's imagination. He also felt that the album was overproduced in general. "Those acquainted with producer Gus Dudgeon's brilliant work with the Bonzos have ample reason to be mightily disillusioned with the good fellow for the excesses he allowed to run rampant here."[27] The reviewer had no such reservations for Elton John himself, writing: "But don't be scared away, for so immense a talent is Elton's that he'll delight you senseless despite it all."[27] He had no idea just how true that was.

YOUR SONG

Elton John, Bernie Taupin / 4:04

Musicians
Elton John: vocals, piano
Frank Clark: acoustic guitar
Colin Green: acoustic guitar
Clive Hicks: twelve-string guitar
Dave Richmond: bass
Barry Morgan: drums
Herbie Flowers (?): double bass (uncredited)
Skaila Kanga: harp (uncredited)
Unidentified musicians: uncredited
Paul Buckmaster: arrangements, direction

Recorded
Trident Studios, London: January 22, 1970

Technical Team
Producer: Gus Dudgeon
Production Coordinator: Steve Brown
Sound Engineer: Robin Geoffrey Cable
Tape Operator: David Hentschel
Mastering: Darrell Johnson
Editing: Gus Skinas

Single Releases
Take Me to the Pilot / Your Song
  US Release: October 26, 1970, on Uni Records (ref. 55265)
  Best US Chart Ranking: 8
Your Song / Into the Old Man's Shoes
  UK Release: January 8, 1971, on DJM Records (ref. DJS.233)
  Best UK Chart Ranking: 4

The importance of "Your Song" in the story of Elton John and Bernie Taupin is so great that they wrote a song about writing it! "We All Fall in Love Sometimes" appeared in 1975 on the autobiographical album *Captain Fantastic and the Brown Dirt Cowboy.*

Genesis and Lyrics

"Your Song" is the track that marked Elton John's ascent to musical stardom. It is the song through which the entire world was introduced to his talent. The legend of its origins, retold in the film *Rocketman*, emphasizes the importance of the partnership binding Elton and Bernie. In an iconic scene, the two men are eating at Elton's mother's house when Bernie hands the new song lyrics to his collaborator, who, incredulous, tells him: "There's some tea on it." While Bernie goes to the bathroom, Elton sits at his piano and starts looking for a melody, slowly begging to hum the outlines of "Your Song." Then, as though touched by grace, he gives birth to the song almost in its definitive format. When he is called, Bernie goes back down into the sitting room and smiles, as do Elton's mother and grandmother, both of whom are also charmed by the melody. Although romanticized, the celluloid evocation of this seminal moment in the duo's career is not so far removed from the truth, and it perfectly summarizes their way of working, which served them so well for more than fifty years.

Two Years . . . Twenty Minutes

Although Bernie took approximately two years to finalize the words of "Your Song," it took Elton just twenty short minutes to compose its melody. Bernie Taupin was only seventeen when he first put the idea for this song to paper. He was sharing an apartment with Elton in Pinner at the time, and he deplored the apparent paucity of his love life: "I've always written what's in my heart and on my mind and the thing about 'Your Song' is that it was born of absolute naivety. I was only 17 at the time . . . I'd experienced nothing and never been in any kind of substantial physical relationship. You can't fake that kind of naivety and it's what makes it work. These days the person who wrote 'Your Song' no longer exists, and I have no relationship with it whatsoever. All I'd say is: nice song."[28]

Bernie never changed his opinion on "Your Song," and he always felt that its greatest qualities were its freshness and its authenticity: "The great thing about that song is that the naiveté of it is truly honest. It's real. It's not somebody pretending to write a song that is simple and naive. It is a simple, naive song. And it still stands up."[29]

The lyrics remained in outline form until the morning of Monday, October 27, 1969. While he was reworking the lyrics

on paper normally used for math class exercises, Bernie was having breakfast and accidently stained what would turn out to be the final lyrics to one of Elton John's finest masterpieces. Elton, having just gotten out of the bath, joined Bernie in the dining room, where his friend promptly handed over his lyrics before disappearing. The rest is history.

"What can I say, it's a perfect song," explained Elton. "It gets better every time I sing it. I remember [...] sitting down at the piano [...] and going, 'Oh, my God, this is such a great lyric, I can't fuck this one up.' It came out in about 20 minutes, and when I was done, I called him in and we both knew. I was 22, and he was 19, and it gave us so much confidence. 'Empty Sky' was lovely, but it was very naive. We went on to do more esoteric stuff like 'Take Me to the Pilot,' of course, but musically, this ['Your Song'] was a big step forward. And the older I get, the more I sing these lyrics, and the more they resonate with me."[35]

For "Your Song," Elton only had to open up the floodgates of his creativity, though he was helped along by the famous opening words of the song: "It's a little bit funny." As he explained to Penny Valentine at *Sound* magazine in 1971: "When Bernie brings me the lyrics, I read them and then I get the first line of the song and deal with that first. I never work to the chorus or the hook. I start at the top and gradually work down, I can't do it any other way..."[30] Later, he added a nuance, recognizing that "'Your Song' is quite a complicated song as far as the chord changes are concerned" and explaining that "it was my first addiction to writing in the key of *E* flat."[31]

The authenticity of the song is reinforced by its interpretation, in which Elton enjoys hesitating and asking himself questions ("If I was a sculptor, but then again, no"), thereby giving the listener the feeling of being involved in a conversation.

Elton declared on many occasions that he felt unable to compose a song that could top "Your Song." In fact, it wonderfully combines his training as a classical musician and his unfailing musical instinct for creating disarming melodies that people love. "I knew I'd written something that was really good. And that happens very rarely...You can't pick those songs out. They just happen."[31]

Equally, it is impossible to know exactly who the song is about. For a long time Elton declared that Bernie wrote the song for a girl he was seeing at the time, but this has always been denied by the author, sometimes virulently, as in the famous interview granted by the two men to a *Rolling Stone* journalist in 1973: "I remember the girl you were going out with, the girl you wrote it about." And Bernie's categorical response: "I didn't write it about anybody, really."[1]

Production

"Your Song" was recorded at Trident Studios on the afternoon of January 22, 1970 (between 3 and 6 p.m.) with musicians

Elton John performed a very moving interpretation of "Your Song" when he appeared on the *Top of the Pops* broadcast on January 14, 1971.

1970

handpicked by Gus Dudgeon and Stuart Epps: as well as a thirty-six-piece orchestra of brass and strings. There was also a rhythm section consisting of bassist Dave Richmond and drummer Barry Morgan, guitarists Frank Clark, Colin Green, and Clive Hicks, as well as Herbie Flowers and Skaila Kanga on contrabass and harp, respectively (although neither were credited). "'Your Song' was recorded totally live," Gus Dudgeon recalled in 1975, "with the exception of the vocal. When he [Elton] walked in and saw an orchestra waiting to play his song I think he lost five pounds on the spot."[43]

They needed only three takes to wrap up this future hit. If the team was able to do the recording live, despite the large number of musicians present, it was only because Paul Buckmaster had planned everything in advance, writing out each orchestra member's part by hand and judiciously measuring out each individual's contribution. He left nothing to chance and was just as demanding of the orchestra as he was with the rhythm section. Although he was aware of Barry Morgan's frustration (Morgan only came in at the 1:50 mark, and he would have liked an earlier entry in the song or some extra drum strokes), Paul kept things as he had originally set them out so that the drums did not upset the overall equilibrium of the piece. The song was also deliberately mixed quite low. As for the bass, the trick here involved supporting the instrument with a discreet double bass, which added a sense of overall depth. The effect was so discreet that Herbie Flowers, who played bass on the album, was not credited on the jacket. Over these supportive foundations came a luminous Nylon guitar that was played by Clive Hicks and that Gus Dudgeon thought was a total marvel. Several times during the mixing, Dudgeon pushed up the volume a little more on the guitar track to give it more prominence. "Your Song" stands out as a model example of orchestral pop. At the end of the session, all those taking part were buzzing over what they had just accomplished.

"We couldn't stop smiling when we left the studio for the day," said Gus. He added, "It didn't sound like anything else that had ever happened before. It was completely unique. Basically, the way that Paul arranged the orchestra together with the rhythm section was so extraordinary that it just seemed to be completely fresh. I really wondered how people would take it."[43]

The booklet and original manuscript of "Your Song," written in Bernie Taupin's handwriting, sold at auction on November 19, 2018, for the sum of $11,250.

Conquering America

"Your Song" became a global hit almost by accident. In fact, although Elton's professional entourage was certain that this was an exceptional song, it was not the track they selected for the A-side of Elton's next single. Instead, they chose "Take Me to the Pilot" whose commercial potential was thought to be more promising. In addition to releasing a new single in America, Dick James had also decided to promote his protégé on the other side of the Atlantic, and he insisted on sending Elton out on tour. Elton was not convinced. He thought it was more prudent for him to consolidate the modest success he'd had with the album in the UK so that he could dominate that market definitively rather than setting out to conquer North America. But Dick held fast, and Elton took off for Los Angeles in August 1970 after performing a few concerts in Great Britain, one in Sweden (on June 19, 1970, in Östergötland), and one in Belgium (July 11, 1970, in Knokke). This first American tour ran from August 25 to September 12, 1970. Elton traveled from Los Angeles to Philadelphia, and in the process, he became a world-class rock star.

Driven by Elton's American label (Uni Records), which did not skimp on their advertising to promote his impending arrival, and by an inaugural series of six incendiary performances given at the Troubadour in Los Angeles, Elton drew in huge crowds and played to sold-out houses for six weeks straight.

"Your Song" became one of a trio of songs that opened Elton's concerts (alongside "Border Song" and "Take Me to the Pilot"), and it started to have its place in the sun. A lot of the song's success was due to support from radio DJs, who preferred to play "Your Song" rather than "Take Me to the Pilot." It should be said that "Your Song" was out of place in a musical landscape dominated by electric guitars, psychedelia, and concept albums. Surfing this unexpected success, Uni Records decided to release the song as a single in the United States—this time on the A-side!—to accompany the singer's second American tour, which was planned to run from October 29 to December 6, 1970. The sales of "Your Song" took off, and as Elton crossed the country, he became a phenomenon. The American press was ecstatic: "A 23-year old Englishman [...] extraordinarily original [...] magnificent in all respects [...]

defying all classification,"[50] were just some of the things written in local papers of the day. "The best thing Great Britain did since Churchill!"[50] proclaimed others, with some DJs going so far as to describe him as the "Messiah"![50]

When Elton returned to London in mid-December 1970, "Your Song" was in the top 40 in the United States and on its way to hitting eighth place in January 1971. Stephen James, who was still hesitating over its release as a single due to the song's stark contrast to the general exuberance of the British rock scene at the time, eventually gave in and sent the song to various DJs at the BBC. Tony Blackburn, a presenter during the influential Radio 1 breakfast time broadcasting slot, responded instantly, promising that if DJM released "Your Song" as a single, he would make it his disk of the week. The task of convincing Elton to move forward with the single in the UK was not easy, given his spate of failed British singles in the past. Dick James finally made the decision, and "Your Song" was released in Great Britain on January 8, 1971, with "Into the Old Man's Shoes" on the B-side. Tony Blackburn kept his word. On January 23—a year and a day after the song's recording—the single entered the British top 50. By the beginning of February, it was sitting at number seven. Elton was mightily relieved, as he later admitted: "Thank God we did happen in Britain as well. It would've been horrible to happen in America and not happen in Britain, because obviously that's where you were born and that's where you live. But it all fell into place."[11]

A Revolutionary "Classic"

Over time, "Your Song" has been cemented as a classic, alongside other songs from the era, including "Yesterday" by the Beatles. There have been some three hundred covers done by everyone from Andy Williams, the New Seekers, Cilla Black, Lena Horne, Jack Jones, Roger Whittaker, and Buddy Greco to Three Dog Night, Billy Paul, Ellie Goulding, Lady Gaga, Rod Stewart, Al Jarreau, and Roy Orbison. Even the actor Ewan McGregor took a turn in the film *Moulin Rouge*.

Not only did "Your Song" become a classic, but it also became a bridge between the deafening rock of the 1960s and the dawn of the *songwriters* era that began in the early 1970s. By demonstrating that the general public was amenable to simple melodies that were arranged with finesse, and that expressed the vulnerability of the author, "Your Song" marked a new direction in music, and a new musical age seemed to be taking shape within its verses. The typical thundering guitars of the era had been replaced by a discreet piano,

cliché-ridden refrains by poetic lyrics that reflected the singer's innermost, intimate thoughts. The sound of piano keys and a calm voice in an empty room were to become recurrent features on the British and American charts in the proceeding years. At the end of 1971, John Lennon released his own soliloquy for piano, "Imagine." The songwriter-composer Carole King came out of anonymity with her *Tapestry* album, and Gilbert O'Sullivan delivered a dark ballad called "Nothing Rhymed," not to mention new work from Cat Stevens, James Taylor, and Don McLean.

"Your Song" also gave Bernie Taupin his first major public recognition as a songwriter. In fact, the musical press of the time was astonished to discover that the hits did not come directly from Elton's head. Instead, they came from the mind of a writer with a name almost as improbable as that of Reginald Dwight. Up to this point, the pop geniuses of the era had always set their own words to music. Bernie can legitimately claim to be the first lyricist to achieve celebrity status since the age of Lorenz Hart and Ira Gershwin. According to Elizabeth Rosenthal, "'Your Song' was the first hit for Elton and Bernie and the first to be universally accepted as evidence of their songwriting talent."[32]

Writing the song, seeing it become a success, and savoring its development and maturation over time was like being present at the birth of a child for the two men, and then watching that child flourish.

Meanwhile, Bernie had set off in a new personal and artistic direction. He left behind the apartment he shared with Elton in Frome Court and got engaged to Maxine Feibelman. Next, he began planning their marriage with all the exhilarating urgency of his twenty years. The train of life had left the station, and the insouciance of "Your Song" was gone with it. Of course, Bernie was a writer and would always remain so, but things would be different going forward. Many years later, he confided: "Now I could never write that song again or emulate it because the songs I write now that talk about love coming from people my age usually deal with broken marriages and where the children go. You have to write from where you are at a particular point in time, and 'Your Song' is exactly where I was coming from back then.

[...] I think 'Your Song' is a gem. Our classic, I'm not sure. I'll let others decide that. But it's like an old friend, it means so many things on equally as many levels. It's certainly proved its worth, and I've heard it sung a million times. It's like a good dog, it's always there."[33]

John Lennon was a fan of "Your Song" from the first time he heard it. In 1975, he confided in *Rolling Stone* magazine that what he thought upon hearing the song for the first time, saying, "Great, that's the first new thing that's happened since we [the Beatles] happened." Following this declaration, the two artists became friends. John Lennon and Yoko Ono also made Elton their son Sean's godfather.

FOR ELTON ADDICTS

Elton John's diary entry for Monday, October 27, 1969 reads simply: "I didn't do anything, in the end. I wrote 'Your Song.'"

PORTRAIT

GUS DUDGEON:
THE AUTODIDACT'S INSTINCT

Gus Dudgeon and his wife, Sheila, were both killed in a car accident in 2002. Among the mountain of floral tributes that were sent to honor the couple, there was one bouquet of white lilies with the following handwritten note: "Thank you for the glorious times. May you be in Heaven together forever. Love, Elton."[40]

Elton never forgot the central role that his producer and friend played in his career.

From Coffee Boy to Producer

Angus Boyd Dudgeon was born on September 30, 1942, in Woking, which is located in the Surrey area of England. An undisciplined pupil, he was suspended from school several times before taking on a series of small jobs (eleven in four years) without any conviction. In 1961, he was offered a job in a recording studio somewhat by accident. "I had no idea what career I was going to have," he explained in an interview in 2002, "but I had always bought a lot of records. Records and clothes were my 'Achilles' Heel."[37]

"[...] By the time I'd walked up through the control room to meet the boss I was hooked. Anyhow, I somehow got that job and told myself, 'Gus, this is it. This is what you have to do. Don't lose this gig.' The other jobs I couldn't have cared less. I just used to get bored and f**k off, and sometimes they didn't even realize I'd gone! They must have thought, 'Hang on, we haven't seen him for a month, he must have left!'"[37]

Gus became the "tape op-tea-boy," which literally meant that he was the assistant tapes operator who was also responsible for bringing everyone their coffee—or tea, as was often the case in England. "You should know that at the beginning of the '60s, the remote control was an unknown concept. The sound engineer did not move from their console and it was the assistant, seated near the tape recorder, who had to do the recording drop-ins / drop-outs to ensure there were no 'dongs' on the tape. Quite an art in itself!"[38]

He remained in that post for several years before joining Olympic Studios in Baker Street, and then moving to Decca Records' studios around 1964.

Gus rose up the ladder and worked with the likes of John Mayall, the Small Faces, the Bluesbreakers, and Eric Clapton.

Without any formal musical training, and with no knowledge of electronics, Gus worked on instinct. He did not know how a microphone worked, but he knew how to differentiate between quality sound and rubbish sound. Above all, he knew how to make what he recorded sound good. "I had never considered myself as a great engineer. [...] I had my moments. [...] I'm not really interested in the mechanics of recording. I don't care why

a desk works, as long as you can push a fader up and hear something. I was always interested in the music itself."[37]

Nevertheless, Gus acquired considerable expertise during his years working with Decca. By the end of 1968, two major producers of the time, Andrew Lloyd Webber and Denny Cordell ("A Whiter Shade of Pale") encouraged him to become an independent producer. He left Decca and became one of the leading freelance producers in England alongside Joe Meek, Glyn Johns, and Tony Visconti.

In 1969, fortune came knocking when Tony Visconti, who had agreed to produce David Bowie's next album, *Space Oddity*, announced that he did not want to produce the album's lead song. Instead, he suggested that the duties be given to Gus. *Space Oddity* boosted Dudgeon's career[39] considerably and put him on the path to meeting Elton John. Paul Buckmaster recommended Gus to Steve Brown and Elton when they were looking for a producer to take on the singer's second album. Dudgeon took the job and fulfilled his task with panache. Released in April 1970, *Elton John* marked Elton's explosion onto the musical scene of the day, and it also marked the beginning of a long and fruitful collaboration between the two men.

A Magic Sound

Together, over the following years, they would write some of the finest chapters in Elton's discography: *Madman Across the Water, Honky Château, Goodbye Yellow Brick Road, Captain Fantastic and the Brown Dirt Cowboy*, and *Don't Shoot Me I'm Only the Piano Player*. Bernie provided the lyrics, Elton handled the piano and the vocals, and Gus contributed the magic of the sound. Things were not always idyllic between Gus and Elton, however, and Gus did not hold back in his criticism of *Caribou* (1974), even though he had produced the album. Their paths separated after *Blue Moves* in 1976.

Dudgeon launched his own recording studio, the Mill, which was run out of an old mill in Berkshire, to the west of London, and which he had purchased two years previously. Dudgeon produced many albums there and worked with artists like Solution, Shooting Star, Audience, Chris Rea, Ralph McTell, and Gilbert O'Sullivan. The Mill came to an abrupt close at the end of the 1980s thanks to the machinations of a shady accountant. However, Gus never gave up production.

He went back to Elton in 1985 and they worked together on *Ice on Fire* (1985) and *Leather Jackets* (1986), and then again on the famous *Live in Australia* (1987). They also worked together on a number of compilations and special projects, including *Two Rooms* (1991), on which Gus produced two tracks.

I NEED YOU TO TURN TO

Elton John, Bernie Taupin / 2:33

Musicians
Elton John: vocals, harpsichord
Roland Harker: guitar
Skaila Kanga: harp
Unidentified musicians: orchestra
Paul Buckmaster: arrangements, direction

Recorded
Trident Studios, London: January 21, 1970

Technical Team
Producer: Gus Dudgeon
Production Coordinator: Steve Brown
Sound Engineer: Robin Geoffrey Cable
Tape Operator: David Hentschel
Mastering: Darrell Johnson
Editing: Gus Skinas

After becoming a producer seemingly by chance, the instinctive Gus Dudgeon was fully in control when he took charge of the *Elton John* album.

Genesis and Lyrics
Elton John and Bernie Taupin have often joked about the fact that fans (and detractors!) always manage to find hidden meanings in their songs where none was intended. The anecdote with "I Need You to Turn To" is well-known: One day, a man accosted them and expressed his surprise that they had evoked the crucifixion of Christ in their song via the lyric "You are nailed to my love in many lonely nights." Stunned by this preposterous interpretation, the two friends and writing partners, who had composed this desperate love song in which the narrator has lost all control over his relationship, could only respond to the man with silence.

Production
As with many of the numbers on this second album, "I Need You to Turn To" was finalized very quickly, in the calm of a nighttime session that ran from 9 to 11 p.m. Initially recorded with just voice and piano for the demo, the song took a completely different turn once everyone got into the studio. Elton sat behind his harpsichord, which he had scarcely played, as he explained in his autobiography (leaving out the fact that a few months earlier he had written a very fine part for this instrument on "Skyline Pigeon"). Although he appreciated the sound it made, he found it difficult to master the instrument, with its slight lag separating the key touch and the production of sound. Following a short solo introduction, a Nylon string guitar played with delicacy by Roland Harker discreetly announces an arrangement of near-millimeter precision, which is embellished by the bewitching harp playing of Skaila Kanga and the sounds of the violins, all of which were directed live by Paul Buckmaster. Elton's vocals, both somber and luminous, provide a counterpoint to the ambient grandeur: In order to portray the narrator's distress, he avoids going to hard with the vocals and opts instead to remain very precise in his vocal intonation. The same mixing technique that was used for "Skyline Pigeon" is used again here. According to Gus Dudgeon, this was not entirely a coincidence: The harpsichord was mainly captured in the left stereo channel, while the vocals were captured in the right.

TAKE ME TO THE PILOT

Elton John, Bernie Taupin / 3:47

Musicians

Elton John: vocals, piano
Caleb Quaye: electric guitar
Alan Parker: acoustic rhythm guitar
Alan Weighall: bass, cello
Barry Morgan: drums
Dennis Lopez: percussion, congas
Madeline Bell, Tony Burrows, Roger Cook, Lesley Duncan, Kay Garner, Tony Hazzard: backing vocals
Unidentified musicians: orchestra
Paul Buckmaster: arrangements, direction

Recorded

Trident Studios, London: January 22, 1970

Technical Team

Producer: Gus Dudgeon
Production Coordinator: Steve Brown
Sound Engineer: Robin Geoffrey Cable
Tape Operator: David Hentschel
Mastering: Darrell Johnson
Editing: Gus Skinas

Single Release

Your Song / Take Me to the Pilot
US Release: October 26, 1970, on Uni Records (ref. 55265)
Best US Chart Ranking: 8

Genesis and Lyrics

Released first as a single in October 1970 in the United States, "Take Me to the Pilot" was soon surpassed by the commercial success of "Your Song," which definitively launched Elton's career. Bernie and Elton were constantly amused by the interpretations put forward for the lyrics of "Take Me to the Pilot," even though they often admitted that its cryptic reputation was not totally unfounded. "It's great that so many people have covered that and sort of put their all into it and that song [...] doesn't mean anything," explained Bernie in 1973. Elton, almost incredulous, added: "It's probably the most unlikely song of all time to be covered, because of the words. [...] It's had so many covers, Ben E. King..."[1] At least it does have a particular merit, according to Bernie: "It's the song that gives you most confidence [in yourself], because it proves to you what you can do, even if the words don't mean anything..."[1] Bernie confirmed on many occasions that he jotted down phrases on paper until he found something that pleased him, somewhat in the working style of the surrealist poets. A variety of subjects are addressed in the lyrics, such as betrayal, the illusion of danger, and also confidence and boldness. According to Elton, Bernie, who was reading lots of science fiction novels at the time, might have been inspired by their wild plots when he was writing "Take Me to the Pilot."

Production

Nasal like James Taylor's, rasping like Van Morrison's, Elton's voice takes center stage in the arrangement for this track, which was conceived by Paul Buckmaster. Elton's voice is the catalyst that propels the song's rock 'n' roll energy. *Rolling Stone* journalist John Mendelsohn described Buckmaster's work on *Elton John* as "pompous,"[27] but for the most highly produced numbers on the album, of which was "Take Me to the Pilot" was the most notable, history bears out the value of his work. The brilliantly surging strings, the gospel-inspired backing vocals, Elton's aggressive piano, and Caleb Quaye's mordant guitar light up the song and give it verve. The guitar player, equipped with his faithful 1964 Fender Stratocaster, also delivers his only solo of the album, doubling the strings based on an idea that came from Paul Buckmaster. Close listening reveals that two piano scores compete with each other in the middle of the song. In

fact, the respective scores are played simultaneously, but they're very complementary: On the left stereo channel is a part that plays throughout the song, and on the right is a small overdub for a sequence between the verses, which Gus Dudgeon explains quite simply: "He had trouble playing that little lick. Keeping it in time. So, we dropped [a piano overdub] in, with the drummer keeping time [off-mic]. And he comes back in on the left-side speaker with that big chord [to go to the next part in the song]."[25]

COVERS

"Take Me to the Pilot" is one of the Elton John songs that is covered most often. Over the years, numerous versions have been recorded. Among the most famous of these are versions by José Feliciano, folk-blues guitarist Buzzy Linhart, the rhythm 'n' blues singer Ben E. King, the blues icon Odetta, and also the keyboard player from Yes, Rick Wakeman, who covered the song on his first solo album, 1971's *Piano Vibrations*.

NO SHOE STRINGS ON LOUISE

Elton John, Bernie Taupin / 3:31

Musicians

Elton John: vocals, piano
Caleb Quaye: electric guitar
Clive Hicks: acoustic rhythm guitar
Alan Weighall: bass
Barry Morgan: drums
Dennis Lopez: percussion, congas
Madeline Bell, Tony Burrows, Roger Cook, Lesley Duncan, Kay Garner, Tony Hazzard: backing vocals

Recorded

Trident Studios, London: January 19, 1970

Technical Team

Producer: Gus Dudgeon
Production Coordinator: Steve Brown
Sound Engineer: Robin Geoffrey Cable
Tape Operator: David Hentschel
Mastering: Darrell Johnson
Editing: Gus Skinas

1970

The drummer Barry Morgan (shown here in 1982) was called back to play on *Tumbleweed Connection* and *Madman Across the Water.*

Genesis and Lyrics

Elton John and Bernie Taupin have always proudly declared their musical influences, which notably include the Band and Gram Parsons. These influences are directly discernable in "No Shoe Strings on Louise." If, as Bernie said, it seems out of context on this disk, which is resolutely pop, this country-rock roots waltz already telegraphs the color of the following album, *Tumbleweed Connection*. In his lyrics he uses clichés that illustrate his underlying vision of the American heartland. The song's narrator, who married at the age of fourteen, lays out general concepts like "All those city women want to make us poor men." According to the narrator, these city women are out to extract fortunes from the men they seduce.

Production

"No Shoe Strings on Louise" was one of the first songs on the album to be completed, with work finishing on January 19, 1970. It is one of the few tracks recorded on eight tracks (rather than sixteen), with a view to keeping costs down. Even though this is the work of British artists, the song is very credible in its homage to the American West; from the lap steel guitar to the precision of the backing vocals and the catchy refrain, it all works together to create a cohesive whole. Elton John delivers a mannered vocal performance on the track that's very close to Mick Jagger, which even led some to say that his was "an overly chewy impersonation."[11] However, Dudgeon was unflinching in his affection for the song: "I always sing along with this track. Without fail. When he goes 'There ain't NO...' I'm In!" he explains, before stating: "You can hear the Jagger influence in the vocal...[especially when he says] 'Caddilayak'!"[25] As for the production, Gus Dudgeon opted for a simple but formidably effective formula and that was already tried and tested by the American cousins: "The piano is on the left, simply providing more of a rhythm part and giving space for the big, chunky acoustic guitar on the right."[25] The drums part highlights an exceptional musician: Barry Morgan. "Great drummer on this (and most of the album), Barry Morgan," commented Dudgeon. "I remember him coming up to me and thanking me. Shaking my hand, I mean, really pumping my hand and saying, 'I'm just so pleased you asked me to come and do this album. I just love this guy's stuff.'"[25]

FIRST EPISODE AT HIENTON

Elton John, Bernie Taupin / 4:48

Musicians

Elton John: vocals, piano
Caleb Quaye: acoustic guitar
Skaila Kanga: harp
Diana Lewis: Moog
Unidentified musicians: orchestra
Paul Buckmaster: arrangements, direction

Recorded

Trident Studios, London: January 21, 1970

Technical Team

Producer: Gus Dudgeon
Production Coordinator: Steve Brown
Sound Engineer: Robin Geoffrey Cable
Tape Operator: David Hentschel
Mastering: Darrell Johnson
Editing: Gus Skinas

A member of the BBC Concert Orchestra, harpist Skaila Kanga also had a taste for pop that led her to collaborate with Elton John.

Genesis and Lyrics

Hot on the heels of the melodic clarity and musical immediacy of "No Shoe Strings on Louise" comes the complex structure and sophistical melody of "First Episode at Hienton." This track is probably one of the most underestimated of the timeless ballads that were included on Elton John's first albums. Unlike "Your Song," whose autobiographical inspiration Bernie always denied, "First Episode at Hienton" is expressly taken from his own discovery of love. The song evokes a person named Valerie who was close to the heart of the adolescent Bernie and is tenderly missed by the adult Bernie, who finds himself wallowing in melancholic nostalgia for the carefree days of his youth.

Production

The influence of classical music can be felt from the very first bars, via Elton's piano introduction. His voice is precise, warm, and intimate, although he intentionally molds it to the delicate curves created by the melody. The arrangement, marked by the absence of rhythmic elements, is governed by the strings and by the meticulous use of other instruments: The fairy-like harp of Skaila Kanga reinforces the nostalgic sentiment that's present throughout the song. Caleb Quaye's electric guitar is framed by an elegant chorus and doubled by a gentle tremolo. His acoustic guitar, a 1964 Gibson J-45, produces crystalline arpeggios mimicking the harp's motifs. "I tracked that live in the studio with Elton," he explained. "That was part of our musical chemistry since we first started playing together. It wasn't like 'work.' It was fun. I'd sit down and watch him play and figure out where he was going."[25] A few soaring notes from the Moog synthesizer were subsequently added by Diana Lewis, based on an idea from Paul Buckmaster, her future husband. "That wasn't an instrument that we knew very much about," confessed Gus Dudgeon. The Moog Modular was rented from George Martin's AIR Studios. "It consisted of four boxes about the size of medium suitcases and a 61-note keyboard. Only one note at a time could be played. The keyboard had a ribbon across the top, which Diana played with her left hand, to create those wonderful glissandi and the natural vibrato. Diana helped lift this beautiful song to heights none of us imagined. The excellent (totally analogue) reverb was applied, live, right there during Diana's one take, by engineer Robin Cable."[25]

PAUL BUCKMASTER: A "REVOLUTIONARY" ARRANGER

When Paul Buckmaster died on November 7, 2017, at the age of seventy-one, Elton John was one of the first to pay homage to him on Facebook, where we wrote: "Farewell Paul Buckmaster. So heartbroken. He helped make me the artist I am today. A revolutionary arranger who took my songs and made them soar. Irreplaceable."[41]

Classical Training in the Service of Pop

Paul Buckmaster was born in London on June 13, 1946, to an Italian mother and English father. He started playing the cello at the age of four, and he was imbued with a love for music by his mother, a concert pianist who taught him piano and music theory. Having noticed his aptitude for music, she introduced him to the maestro Willy La Volpe at the age of twelve. La Volpe became Buckmaster's cello teacher for the next four years, and they worked together for eight months a year. During this time, Paul broadened his love of music to include all of classical music, especially the works of Johann Sebastian Bach, and he also discovered a love for jazz. At the age of seventeen, he won a scholarship to the Royal Academy of Music in London, from which he graduated at twenty-one before going on to work as an accomplished cello soloist.

Having unsuccessfully auditioned with a French chamber orchestra, he started looking for work and played in baroque ensembles and also in small orchestras accompanying rock and pop groups like Bee Gees and Paul Jones. The turning point in his early career came in 1969, when one of his friends introduced him to the producer Gus Dudgeon and to an arranger named Tony Visconti. With these new connections secured, he started to work on arrangements in various London studios, especially at Abbey Road. In July 1969, Dudgeon introduced Buckmaster to a young David Bowie, with whom he was working on the single "Space Oddity" / "Wild Eyed Boy from Freecloud." Dudgeon asked him to write the arrangements for the two songs. The young musician, for whom this was not his primary training, acquitted himself with flying colors. From that point on, everything changed. Thanks to his influential manager, Tony Hall, Paul met Miles Davis backstage at his concert at the Hammersmith Odeon on November 1, 1969. They

got on well, and a solid friendship formed between the two men, eventually leading to a collaboration later on. The trumpet player invited Paul to come and hear him again the next day at Ronnie Scott's Jazz Club. This is where Buckmaster met Steve Brown and Elton John, who had come to ask him to work on the strings arrangements for their very promising song "Your Song." Paul was enthusiastic about the project, and he ended up working on the entire *Elton John* album. He also vigorously recommended Gus Dudgeon coming on as the producer. Paul eventually arranged no fewer than fifty-five songs for Elton John and worked on eight studio albums (*Elton John, Tumbleweed Connection, Madman Across the Water, Don't Shoot Me I'm Only the Piano Player, Blue Moves, A Single Man, Made in England*, and *Songs from the West Coast*), as well working on the original soundtrack for the film *Friends*. Many of the songs that Buckmaster worked on are among the singer's greatest commercial successes, most notably "Your Song" and "Tiny Dancer." Elton went as far as to describe some of Paul's contributions as "revolutionary."

Boundless Energy and Interest

Buckmaster's career was not limited to his work with Elton. He made his talents available in the world of pop music, of course, but he also dabbled in rock, country, jazz, and even variety music. He arranged a host of successful songs and albums for a variety of artists, including Leonard Cohen (on 1971's *Songs of Love and Hate*) and Carly Simon's famous "You're So Vain" off of 1972's *No Secrets*. He also collaborated with the Rolling Stones, the Grateful Dead, Stevie Nicks, and Miles Davis, whom he worked with in *On the Corner* (1972) and *Big Fun* (1974). After taking a break in the 1980s, which was a period focused on synthetic pop, he returned in the 1990s and collaborated with a wide variety of artists, including Céline Dion, Julio Iglesias, Faith Hill, Taylor Swift, Tim McGraw, Counting Crows, the Darkness, Bon Jovi, Guns N' Roses, and Ben Folds. In 2002, he won a Grammy for his arrangement of the song "Drops of Jupiter" by Train. He also left his name on the credits of numerous films, including *Son of Dracula, The Man Who Fell to Earth*, and *12 Monkeys*.

SIXTY YEARS ON

Elton John, Bernie Taupin / 4:35

Musicians

Elton John: vocals
Colin Green: classical guitar
Skaila Kanga: harp (uncredited)
Brian Dee: organ
Unidentified musicians: orchestra
Paul Buckmaster: arrangements, direction

Recorded

Trident Studios, London: January 22, 1970

Technical Team

Producer: Gus Dudgeon
Production Coordinator: Steve Brown
Sound Engineer: Robin Geoffrey Cable
Tape Operator: David Hentschel
Mastering: Darrell Johnson
Editing: Gus Skinas

An eminent figure on the London jazz scene, pianist and organist Brian Dee (shown here in 1985) contributed to "Sixty Years On" and "Border Song."

Genesis and Lyrics

Elton John was not the first person to have sung this song. Like "Country Comfort" and "Ballad of a Well-Known Gun," "Sixty Years On" was first performed by a rock group called Silver Metre, and it appeared on their self-titled album in 1969. A few months later, Elton reclaimed this humble, solemn, and poignant homage. It was written by Bernie to his grandfather, and in it he thanks the older man for giving a future to the lyricist by nurturing his interest in literature. This evocation is expressed with a magnificent Nylon string guitar of Spanish inspiration, and it's accompanied by a majestic orchestra. While Elton sometimes managed to sublimate Bernie's poetic texts within a minimalist arrangement, he also knew how to take hold and lean in to solemn texts that had a certain air of grandeur, as was the case in "Sixty Years On."

Production

Paul Buckmaster has received much praise over the years for the arrangement of the intro to "Sixty Years On," which was heavily influenced by the work of the Hungarian composer György Ligeti, and also possibly by Stravinsky. The intro's evocation of the buzzing of a swarm of wasps arose from the mind of Gus Dudgeon, since the sequences it contains were recorded independently of any song. "There was some downtime in the studio during a string session," Paul recounted. "So, just for fun, I dictated a set of notes to the string section, which they wrote down. Very simple—maybe one or two notes to each group of three or four players. We had 21 strings on that date. I proceeded to conduct them after having told Robin Cable to start recording. This was off the top of my head; there was nothing planned about this."[25] No one could have imagined that Gus Dudgeon would take this recording snippet and create the introduction to a song on the album. Paul also had the idea of introducing the harp just after the introduction. "In the case of the song 'Sixty Years On,' we had been given carte blanche by Elton and his personal manager Steve Brown to do whatever we wanted," explained Buckmaster in 2016. "The only thing we couldn't interfere with was his piano part. As we went on with the song I said, 'Look, we've got a little too much piano here. Let me transcribe that for harp' so that what you hear on the record is the piano part transcribed for harp with some modifications which were from my own taste. Essentially it was note for note."[45]

BORDER SONG

Elton John, Bernie Taupin / 3:22

Musicians

Elton John: vocals, piano
Clive Hicks: acoustic guitar
Colin Green: acoustic guitar
Dave Richmond: bass
Barry Morgan: drums
Brian Dee: organ
Barbara Moore Singers: backing vocals
Madeline Bell, Tony Burrows, Roger Cook, Lesley Duncan, Kay Garner, Tony Hazzard: additional backing vocals
Unidentified musicians: orchestra
Paul Buckmaster: arrangements, direction

Recorded

Trident Studios, London: January 22, 1970

Technical Team

Producer: Gus Dudgeon
Production Coordinator: Steve Brown
Sound Engineer: Robin Geoffrey Cable
Tape Operator: David Hentschel
Mastering: Darrell Johnson
Editing: Gus Skinas

Single Release

Border Song / Bad Side of the Moon
UK Release: March 20, 1970, on DJM Records (ref. DJS.217)
Best UK Chart Ranking: Did Not Chart
US Release: July 1970, on Uni Records (ref. 55246)
Best US Chart Ranking: 92

Genesis and Lyrics

When Bernie and Elton created "Border Song," they once again spent many hours in their room at Frome Court raving about the musical productions of the Band and Delaney & Bonnie. This latter rock-soul duo, who were accompanied by one of Elton's great idols, Leon Russell, managed to synthesize all the influences that Elton and Bernie dreamed of including in their music: rock 'n' roll, blues, gospel, and country. "They were white musicians making soul music without covering 'In the Midnight Hour,' or doing something that was just a pale imitation of what black artists did. It was a revelation,"[3] recounted Elton in his autobiography, before citing other sources of their inspiration at the time. About "Border Song," he had this to say: "Something like 'Border Song' or 'Take Me to the Pilot' had a sort of funk and soulfulness that I'd picked up backing Patti LaBelle and Major Lance, but they also had a classical influence that seeped in from all those Saturday mornings where I'd been forced to study Chopin and Bartók."[3] In the end, the gospel inspiration dominates this short and spiritual ballad. Interestingly, the song was chosen as the A-side of the first single released from the album.

One sufficiently unusual detail that's worth emphasizing is that this is one of the rare songs in which Elton intervened in the writing of the lyrics. In 1975, the singer confessed to Paul Gambaccini that he had added a third verse to Bernie's text: "It's never been disclosed, but lyrically I wrote the last verse of 'Border Song,' because it was only two verses long and we thought it really needed another verse. That's why the last verse is very mundane."[36] Bernie specified from his perspective that for him the song did not have much meaning until Elton involved himself in it: "The sentiments in that song, in fact, didn't mean anything. The great thing about Elton's last verse was he tried to put it all into perspective. That song is probably two totally separate songs."[36] The typed original manuscript that was sold in the fall of 2019 by Bernie does, in fact, show the additions and deletions made in Elton's hand. At this early stage, the song was called "The Border Song"; the offending *the* was subsequently deleted.

What did Bernie mean when he was talking about perspective and two songs in one? In 2001, Elton provided a key to understanding during a conversation with Elizabeth Rosenthal.[32] According to Elton, Bernie had expressed in the first two verses

Dusty Springfield was accompanied by her brother, Tom, during a performance on *Top of the Pops* in April 1970, where she spoke of her admiration for Elton.

One of Bernie's and Elton's idols, Aretha Franklin, really liked "Border Song" and decided to cover it on her seminal 1972 album *Young, Gifted and Black*. Unfortunately, the song was not a success for her. Franklin achieved multiple number one hits in the United States, but she reached only thirty-seventh place with "Border Song." In 1992, Elton and Aretha performed this number together onstage in a special televised appearance.

of the song the malaise he felt on his arrival in London, where he had not immediately found his place.

On the other hand, it's also possible that when Bernie refers to two songs in one, he is simply referring to the final verse: "There's a man over there / What's his color I don't care"; this verse resounds like a prayer for racial tolerance and harmony.

Production

"Border Song" was recorded on January 22, during an evening session. Elton begins alone on the piano, delivering an assured vocal performance that's soon supported by a gospel choir directed by Barbara Moore. The strings arrangement, discreet but impressively effective, was crafted by Paul Buckmaster, while the slightly laid-back drums were the work of Barry Morgan. At 1:50, the instrumental break arrives and Elton's moving piano playing is joined by the choirs, as though they are inviting him on an introspective journey into faith. It is unquestionably one of the most exciting and energetic moments on the album, especially as it introduces the famous final verse, written by Elton and calling for the reconciliation of mankind.

A Fan Called Dusty

The single was released in the UK a few weeks before the album (on March 20, 1970), and it got off to a slow start. It did not immediately enter the charts, but it generated sufficient interest to earn Elton John an invitation to appear on the April 2, 1970, broadcast of *Top of the Pops*. "Our appearance didn't do

much to help its sales as a single, but Dusty Springfield introduced herself to us in the dressing room and offered to mime backing vocals during our performance. My mouth just hung open. I'd traveled to Harrow to see her live with the Springfields when I was still at school, and hung around outside the stage door afterward, just to get another glimpse of her: She walked past in a lilac top and mauve skirt, looking incredibly chic. I'd joined her fan club in the early sixties and stuck posters of her on my bedroom wall."[3] Dusty's enthusiasm for "Border Song" "made my year,"[17] the star would later say. The show was broadcast a few days later. Elton watched the performance on the color television in Dick James's office, perspiring anxiously throughout. It was real: he was on television![11] However, the single still did not take off in Great Britain or in Europe, except for the Netherlands, where the song hit the charts in January 1971 and reached a fairly inexplicable twenty-ninth place.

In America, however, things were shaping up very differently. The simultaneous release of the song in the US and Canada at the end of April 1970 prudently allowed for the song's passing before the release of "Your Song," which came out as a single in October, and helped drive the lagging single release of "Border Song" into ninety-second place on the national charts. In Canada, "Border Song" was actually Elton's very first appearance on the charts, and the song went all the way to thirty-fourth place. Over the years, Elton grew humorously weary of playing this particular track, saying, "We've played that so much, now we call it the 'Boredom Song.'"[11]

THE GREATEST DISCOVERY

Elton John, Bernie Taupin / 4:12

Musicians: Elton John: vocals, piano / **Clive Hicks:** acoustic guitar / **Dave Richmond:** bass / **Terry Cox:** drums / **Skaila Kanga:** harp / **Paul Buckmaster:** cello, arrangements, direction / **Unidentified musicians:** orchestra **Recorded:** Trident Studios, London: January 20, 1970 **Technical Team: Producer:** Gus Dudgeon / **Production Coordinator:** Steve Brown / **Sound Engineer:** Robin Geoffrey Cable / **Tape Operator:** David Hentschel / **Mastering:** Darrell Johnson / **Editing:** Gus Skinas

With "The Greatest Discovery," Bernie Taupin created a family snapshot, portraying in an idealized way the moment when a young boy learns of the arrival of a little brother. Having arrived in the maternity ward after what one imagines might have been a short train journey, the protagonist discovers a new partner in life ("They have made for you a friend"), who emits "strange" sounds, hitherto unheard of. He is in wonderment of his "little feet" and his "small heart" beating and looks on with excited enthusiasm at the "Large hands [that] lift him through the air." The gentleness of the looks and smiles of the family reassure the little boy, eager to extend these "happy seconds" with this "brand new brother." A gentle ballad, the declaration "This is your brand-new brother" concludes the song.

A veritable bubble of placidity, the arrangement conceived by Paul Buckmaster manages to complement Elton's elegant melody and the tenderness expressed by Bernie's words. An introduction with trumpets, horns, and three tracks of strings was recorded during the session but didn't appear on any release until the Portuguese version of the album came out. But the warm brass sounds are indeed present later on in the song, even though they appear discreetly and are overshadowed by the majestic strings, which include Paul Buckmaster's graceful cello solo. Elton's delicate piano score is magnificently supported by the bewitching harp of Skaila Kanga, while the rhythm section completes the meticulous orchestration. The finale once again demonstrates Elton's wide vocal range, emphasizing his technical mastery, especially for a vibrato that's tinged with luminous spontaneity.

THE CAGE

Elton John, Bernie Taupin / 3:28

Musicians: Elton John: vocals, piano / **Caleb Quaye:** electric guitar / **Clive Hicks:** acoustic guitar / **Alan Weighall:** bass / **Barry Morgan:** drums / **Diana Lewis:** Moog / **Tex Navarra:** percussion, congas, shaker / **Madeline Bell, Tony Burrows, Roger Cook, Lesley Duncan, Kay Garner, Tony Hazzard:** backing vocals / **Unidentified musicians:** orchestra / **Paul Buckmaster:** arrangements, direction **Recorded:** Trident Studios, London: January 20 or 21, 1970 **Technical Team: Producer:** Gus Dudgeon / **Production Coordinator:** Steve Brown / **Sound Engineer:** Robin Geoffrey Cable / **Tape Operator:** David Hentschel / **Mastering:** Darrell Johnson / **Editing:** Gus Skinas

"Have you ever lived in a cage / Where you live to be whipped and be tamed?" This is the terrifying and uncharacteristically somber vision that begins "The Cage." This track is definitely the most feral piece on Elton's second album. It is a song of questionable morals and kisses offered to an "old daddy," but also dissipated and perpetuated by "bad whisky." The narrator has no hope of escaping his daily reality, but does he really want to? The question might be asked, since, having described his imprisonment, which is both psychological and physical, he explains that he does not know what they say about him ("Well I walk while they talk about virtue") and yet suffers because of it ("But I'm damned when I really care there").

"The Cage" generates an irresistible groove with brass that nestles in every corner of the song. It's glitzy, of course, and at the same time evocative of the Beatles' "Savoy Truffle" and heralding "You're So Static," which appeared on *Caribou* in 1974. Paul Buckmaster's arrangement was conceived—just this once—for the brass, and not for the strings, which are notably absent in this piece. The arranger even provided for a brass solo, which ended up being performed by Diana Lewis on the Moog keyboard. Unfortunately, the inclusion of the modular synthesizer pulls the carpet out from under this piece to a certain extent. Thus, despite a catchy melody and an uplifting refrain, "The Cage" is overshadowed by the other ballads on the album. Interestingly, some fans see this song as a necessary moment for exultation on an otherwise sensitive and sometimes melancholic album; others see it as an inexcusable mood killer!

1970

THE KING MUST DIE

Elton John, Bernie Taupin / 5:21

Musicians

Elton John: vocals, piano
Clive Hicks: acoustic guitar
Frank Clark: acoustic bass
Terry Cox: drums
Les Hurdle: bass
Dennis Lopez: percussion
Unidentified musicians: orchestra
Paul Buckmaster: arrangements, direction

Recorded

Trident Studios, London: January 20, 1970

Technical Team

Producer: Gus Dudgeon
Production Coordinator: Steve Brown
Sound Engineer: Robin Geoffrey Cable
Tape Operator: David Hentschel
Mastering: Darrell Johnson
Editing: Gus Skinas

Terry Cox played the drums on "The Greatest Discovery" and "The King Must Die."

Genesis and Lyrics

While generally reluctant to comment on the meaning of his lyrics, Bernie Taupin was obliged to shed light on his words in the case of "The King Must Die." The press suggested that the song was inspired by the death of the Rev. Martin Luther King Jr., who was assassinated on April 4, 1968, but Bernie explained that his lyrics were an evocation of the book of the same name, *The King Must Die*, which was written by Mary Renault in 1958, and focused on a very different kind of death. The book retraces the epic story of Theseus, who famously defeated the Minotaur. "It's a very famous book in England," he explained. "I just thought the title was nice. People say that (the song) is not about anything, but it's about something. It's about assassination. That's it. That's all."[31]

Production

Relegated to the last spot on the album, "The King Must Die" nonetheless had every attention lavished upon it, and therefore took on monumental proportions. The song begins with a piano playing in *D* minor, and it establishes its gravity through an alternation of notes and chords placed graciously but emphatically. Then the instrument becomes less loquacious as the emphasis is transferred to Elton's vocals. The chord change introduces the piece's dynamic, which leads to an orchestral interpretation with brass and strings, both rising with the same momentum from 1:26. They are joined in their ascension at 1:45 by the down-to-earth drumming of Terry Cox, who pounds out heavy rolls on the toms. The orchestral contribution provided by Paul Buckmaster proved crucial in the creation of this song. While Elton John and Caleb Quaye took great care to find the perfect combination with guitar and piano, the chief arranger illuminated the piece with his vision: "Instead of taking a paint brush, and putting a bank of strings here and there after the fact," Caleb Quaye recalled, "Paul really paid diligent attention to what the songs were about, the dynamics of the songs. [...] So, a song like 'The King Must Die'—it's just brilliant string writing."[31]

ROCK AND ROLL MADONNA

Elton John, Bernie Taupin / 4:18

Single: *Rock and Roll Madonna / Grey Seal* **UK Release:** June 19, 1970, on DJM Records (ref. DJS.222) **Best UK Chart Ranking:** Did Not Chart **Musicians:** Elton John: vocals, piano / Caleb Quaye: electric guitar / David Glover: bass / Roger Pope: drums / Unidentified musicians: orchestra / Paul Buckmaster: arrangements, direction **Recorded:** Trident Studios, London: January 21, 1970 **Technical Team:** Producer: Gus Dudgeon / Production Coordinator: Steve Brown / Sound Engineer: Robin Geoffrey Cable / Tape Operator: David Hentschel / Mastering: Darrell Johnson / Editing: Gus Skinas

Genesis and Lyrics

While Bernie Taupin's lyrics were increasingly inspired by his own experience, the author still maintained a veil of concealment when it came to the subjects of his songs. The attraction aroused in him by the elusive "Rock and Roll Madonna" ("Everybody wants her / But no one ever gets her") is clear, but her true identity is never made known. Defined by her association with the road ("a lady of the road"), she is a source of vices ("Breaking all the laws of the land") and dangers ("it's going to be the death of me").

Production

Obsessed with the idea of transcending the role of pianist in order to become a fully fledged onstage entertainer, Elton John looked to the source of his passion: rock 'n' roll. Like his models, Little Richard and Jerry Lee Lewis, he includes his inspiration overtly in the title of this song, developing a theme around a classical range of the genre, and giving full scope to his playing dexterity in a jubilant solo in the middle of the piece, which he performs in the style of his two musical heroes. In order to achieve this stylistic exercise in rock 'n' roll nirvana, which was scarcely original but still quite joyful, Elton John asked for the sound of a cheering audience to be added to the song in postproduction; the choice was made to use an extract from a concert given by the Jimi Hendrix Experience at the Royal Albert Hall, in London, on February 24, 1969. "Rock and Roll Madonna" was recorded during an evening session that took place January 21, 1970 (between 9 and 11 p.m.). This song was not included as part of the official album release, but it was chosen as the A-side of a single that was released two months after the album.

The rock 'n' roll fever that so often gripped Elton John onstage can also be found in certain tracks like "Rock and Roll Madonna" and "Bad Side of the Moon."

BAD SIDE OF THE MOON

Elton John, Bernie Taupin / 3:16

Single: *Border Song / Bad Side of the Moon* **UK Release:** March 20, 1970, on DJM Records (ref. DJS.217) **Best UK Chart Ranking:** Did Not Chart **US Release:** July 1970, on Uni Records (ref. 55246) **Best US Chart Ranking:** 92 **Musicians:** Elton John: vocals / Caleb Quaye: electric guitar / Alan Weighall: bass / Barry Morgan: drums / Dennis Lopez or Tex Navarra: congas / Madeline Bell, Tony Burrows, Roger Cook, Lesley Duncan, Kay Garner, Tony Hazzard: backing vocals / Unidentified musicians: orchestra / Paul Buckmaster: arrangements, direction **Recorded:** Trident Studios, London: January 21, 1970 **Technical Team:** Producer: Gus Dudgeon / Sound Engineer: Robin Geoffrey Cable / Tape Operator: David Hentschel / Mastering: Darrell Johnson / Editing: Gus Skinas

Genesis and Lyrics

A year after the release of "Bad Moon Rising" by Creedence Clearwater Revival, and three years before *The Dark Side of the Moon* by Pink Floyd, the future Rocketman put his platform boots on the "bad side of the moon" with the thunderous force of rock 'n' roll. Although just one small anecdotal step for mankind, it was a giant leap for Bernie Taupin, who revealed his true nature in his words, describing his position as a lyricist, and likening it to that of a man in the shadows "where the light has never shone" while also evoking his rural origins with references to a "rustic spoon."

Production

Barry Morgan engages with the song's hostilities via a militarily inspired drum sequence. After the drumroll on the toms, Elton John enters the stage, singing the melody at full tilt even before the orchestra enters. The orchestra takes its cue from the clear signal given by the snare drum, making its solemn entry before matching the guitar and bass groove, which in turn lead the number toward a machine-tight, roiling rhythm 'n' blues sound. The rounded, fluid playing of Alan Weighall on bass has a marvelous effect, dominating the proceedings and launching the signal for the refrain at 0:57 and again at 1:11. Conceived to be like a jam song without any real ending, the piece concludes with a very gradual fade-out, which commences at around two minutes in and runs all the way until the end. Recorded on the second day of the *Elton John* sessions, "Bad Side of the Moon" was not included on the album's definitive track list, but it was selected as the B-side for "Border Song" and released on March 20, 1970.

ALBUM

TUMBLEWEED CONNECTION

Ballad of a Well-Known Gun . Come Down in Time . Country Comfort .
Son of Your Father . My Father's Gun . Where to Now St. Peter? . Love Song.
Amoreena . Talking Old Soldiers . Burn Down the Mission

RELEASE DATES
UK Release: October 30, 1970
Reference: DJM Records—DJLPS 410
Best UK Chart Ranking: 2
US Release: January 4, 1971
Reference: Uni Records—73096
Best US Chart Ranking: 5

This advertisement promoted the *Tumbleweed Connection* album.

PASSING THE BATON

On April 10, 1970, while things were in full swing between the recording sessions for *Tumbleweed Connection* and preparation for the future concerts, Elton learned that the Beatles had officially split up. The news was announced on a small radio that was playing in the Indian restaurant where he was dining with his two bandmates. "The baton's been passed," the pianist teased.

A CONCEPT ALBUM THAT PAYS HOMAGE TO THE AMERICAN WEST

On March 20, 1970, the very day of the United Kingdom release of the single "Border Song," off of his second album (whose recording sessions had only just ended), Elton was back at Trident Studios to begin preparatory work on his third album, *Tumbleweed Connection*. An essential moment in his career, since the musician had accumulated so many songs. Indeed, all the songs making up this third opus were composed at the same time as the songs that appeared on his eponymous second album, *Elton John*. It was just a matter of making a selection.

Heading Way Out West

The choice of songs would prove easier than expected when Steve Brown had the idea of creating an Americana concept album. In their lyrics and musical tonality, many of the songs on this album evoke the United States, the conquest of the West, cowboys, and other classic images. In short, the world that had nourished Bernie Taupin's imagination during his childhood, a time that was spent reading comic books like *The Lone Ranger*, *Rawhide Kid*, and *The Authentic Life of Billy the Kid*. The songs are full of countless references to the West, including Pinkertons, Stage Coach Times, and Deacon Lee. "*Tumbleweed Connection* was something that I'd always wanted to do," confessed Bernie, "for I have always been most interested in the history of the Old West. In a way, I suppose you could say that they are just cowboy songs."[48] Paul Buckmaster

confirmed this vision in 1996: "The sound of the album is sepia-tinted, like the cover art. When I think of those songs, that is what I see visually. You think of old western steam trains and you think of clanking wheels on the rails. Hard-bitten creased faces of cowboys with squinty eyes looking off in the distance. You can almost smell the old leather. That's the feel of the album. It's very authentic. It's a tribute to the old American West."[22]

From a musical point of view, the ten songs on this record draw on new sounds originating from two opposite ends of the United States: California, where Delaney & Bonnie were located, and New York, where members of the Band were based. Both groups released albums that Bernie and Elton played on their turntables until they were practically worn out. Although most of the members of the Band were Canadian—Levon Helm was the only original member from the United States—the two British lads took this as a sign that images of the American West were up for grabs, and they felt they would be able to bring to life a fantasized past, far removed from the vicissitudes of the Cold War and the various political turmoils that shook America at the end of the 1960s.

Elton deliberately chose to focus on the West and to distance himself from what was starting to become his musical identity: mainly, well-packaged pop songs that exuded a very British form of preciousness in their outdated orchestration. "I was determined not to follow up *Elton John* with another orchestra

Tumbleweed Connection has a multitude of influences that coalesce into an immersive sound, rather than creating some kind of mish-mash musical soup.

album, because if I had done that in England, that would be me for life and I wouldn't get in that bag."[42] In another interview, the singer added that *"Elton* was a complicated album, really, whereas *Tumbleweed's* songs are much simpler, less orchestrated and easier for people to relate to."[56] The overall country, blues, and Americana colors, combined with an American accent deliberately adopted by the singer, helped with this immersion into nineteenth-century America. Quite a feat, given that neither Elton nor Bernie had yet set foot in the United States when they wrote these songs!

A Well-Rounded Track List

Elton had plenty of opportunities for rehearsing the pieces that formed this album during the demos he recorded with his friends from Hookfoot, the DJM house blues-rock group that consisted of Roger Pope and Caleb Quaye. "What would happen was, Elton would ask if he could come and sit with Hookfoot, to help flesh out his new songs," recalled Caleb. "[…] So by the time we went into the studio we had them down, because we'd already done them a million times on the road. Our rhythm section was hot. We knew those songs inside and out."[31]

Circumstances led Elton to consider making this disk under conditions that were as close to live as possible in order to take advantage of the live playing experience of his musicians. This approach manifested itself in the first bars of "Ballad of a Well-Known Gun," a dusty, decadent blues-rock number that opens the album. The musicians had already mastered this song a long time ago because they had been fiddling with the number since the period that followed the recording of *Empty Sky*, with a view toward constructing a song with the ideal formula in terms

of tempo and musical coloration. They approached the piece as a recreational jam session from which emanated a feeling of communion. The musicians and the backing vocalists turned up to record feeling mobilized and involved, while Elton seemed to set himself free from a certain self-imposed pressure by giving much more space to his musical colleagues. Starting from this declaration of intention, the songs flowed naturally.

A Piecemeal Recording Process

All the songs were written by Elton John and Bernie Taupin (apart from one). They were produced by Gus Dudgeon and recorded on sixteen tracks—except for "Love Song"—at Trident Studios in London. Paradoxically, while *Elton John* took only a week of recording despite its rich orchestrations, the *Tumbleweed* sessions stretched out over nearly four and a half months (March 20 to August 6), before Elton's American tour in the summer of 1970.

While some of the songs were more complex than others and required greater attention, such as "Burn Down the Mission," this extended recording period is more easily explained by the difficulty that the main protagonists had in freeing up time in their schedules. The worst offenders were Gus Dudgeon, who was booked on numerous projects, and Elton himself, who was lining up dates for concerts in Europe during this period (he played thirty dates in the United Kingdom and in Europe between March 20 and August 14, 1970). Paul Buckmaster recalls the sessions having a different vibe: "It was not recorded all at once. We weren't always available at the same time. […] Maybe studios weren't available."[22] Thus, when "Country Comfort" was being worked on, Elton was absent,

Like Bernie and Elton, Caleb Quaye (shown here in 1973) also immersed himself in American music and he often covered folk songs with his group Hookfoot.

BONUS TRACKS +

Tumbleweed Connection was given a rerelease in CD format in 1995 by Mercury Records in the United Kingdom (ref. 528 155-2) and by the Rocket Record Company / Island in the United States (ref. 314-528 155-2). The CD included two bonus tracks: "Into the Old Man's Shoes" and the first version of "Madman Across the Water," which featured Mick Ronson on guitar.

committed to being in the Netherlands to fulfill his promotional obligations. On the other hand, when the team members did meet, things proceeded very quickly. Six of the ten songs were recorded live, requiring only a few residual overdubs, most often in the form of a third guitar provided by Caleb. There was a good atmosphere in the studio as well. All the musicians taking part in these sessions were in agreement: It was a real pleasure to be directed by Dudgeon, who shared with Elton a constant need for involvement. The two men felt very free to share comic impressions, or to put on accents to give their colleagues a laugh between takes.

Two additional songs were recorded before being tossed aside because they did not fit with the theme of the album: "Into the Old Man's Shoes," a plaintive piano ballad that investigated a father-son relationship, and "Madman Across the Water," a song that would eventually be used on the following album. If Gus Dudgeon had been given the choice, he would have discarded this eight-minute number directly into the trash bin, although it was animated by the hallucinatory guitar of Mick Ronson, the famous colleague and confidant of David Bowie.

Paul Buckmaster found himself less in view on this "rustic" album than on the previous one. A certain disappointment can be sensed in the arranger's memoir, even though he understood the decision to go in a new direction for this latest album. "Come Down in Time" and "Burn Down the Mission" are the only two arrangements he completed for *Tumbleweed*.

A Sepia-Toned Album Cove

Sepia-toned photographs have a way of immediately evoking the American frontier, calling to mind vast open spaces haunted by the wandering souls of bounty hunters, pistoleros, and outlaws. The building on the cover of *Tumbleweed Connection* appears to be the ideal point of entry for this journey through space and time. Except that this "typical" Old West building was actually located in Horsted Keynes, a little village situated about thirty miles south of London. Once again, David Larkham was responsible for creating the album's cover art. Influenced by Bernie's vision of Americana, Larkham very quickly imagined illustrating the album jacket with a photo of a dilapidated waystation somewhere out west, which he eventually managed to find...in Sussex, on the Bluebell Railway. He also had an elaborate scheme in mind for the album's packaging: a double sleeve tucked inside of a special box that had the effect of a grainy, old sepia photo. The album would also contain a booklet with all the songs' lyrics. This was an expensive plan! "And remember, all this, the songs, the recording, the sleeve and all the associated artwork, was all done before the *Elton John* album was even released, and before the Troubadour trip that would establish Reg as a fully fledged rock star, so it was a pretty big deal to get DJM to agree to it,"[20] Larkham explained later.

The Search for an American Label

During the recording of Elton John's third opus, Lennie Hodes, DJM's representative in New York, was actively looking for an American distributor for the singer's burgeoning discography. He met with five consecutive rejections from different distributors, but he managed to secure the interest of Russ Regan, the boss of Uni Records, a subsidiary of MCA. Won over after listening to *Empty Sky*, Regan initially made his contact wait for an

The legendary rhythm section of the first Elton John Band consisted of Dee Murray (center) and Nigel Olsson (right), and they came together for the first time in the studio on "Amoreena."

answer, but once he had received a copy of *Elton John*, Regan realized he could delay no further. Normally a self-contained individual, he even became ecstatic in the intimacy of his office: "I looked up to the sky, and said, 'Thank you, God.'"[47] He then called thirty or so of his staff members into his office for a collective listening session. They also shared his enthusiasm straightaway. This divine surprise did not arrive on its own. Regan had already expressed his interest in another DJM project: a group called Argosy. This psychedelic pop project, led by Roger Hodgson, the future leader of Supertramp, was set to music that featured Caleb Quaye on guitar, Nigel Olsson on drums, and…Elton John on keyboards. Dick James drew up a $10,000 deal for Argosy, which included the United States licensing rights for Elton John's albums! Free of charge!

A New Group Takes the Stage: The Elton John Band

After securing an American label, Dick James seriously thought about having Elton do a tour of the United States, but not as a member of Hookfoot. Elton would have to choose new musicians for his rhythm section who were especially good at stage performance. During a little concert at the Roundhouse in London, which DJM had wanted him to take part in, Elton hired his future stage partners. Together, the three men would form the winning trio known as the "Holy

Trinity," which included bassist Dee Murray and drummer Nigel Olsson. They got on really well. Elton was delighted. "We did a couple of college dates. We went to Leeds and York (England). And every time we went on stage it was amazing,"[55] remembered the drummer. Nigel and Dee were recruited for Elton's upcoming US tour. The Elton John Band was born. As stage companions, they also increasingly dominated inside the studio, where they offered their services in the rhythm section, and also as backing singers.

Elton and his new group, accompanied by Bernie Taupin, Steve Brown, David Larkham, and roadie Bob Stacey, landed in L.A. on August 21, 1970, for an eleven-gig tour that would end on September 12, 1970. This tour set America alight due to the incredible promotion put in place by Uni Records, and by Elton's incendiary performances, most notably at the Troubadour. The US tour propelled the singer into rock star status.

The Conquest of England

Heartened by his series of triumphant gigs in the United States, Elton John approached his return to England with infinite confidence in himself, and in the Holy Trinity that he formed onstage alongside Dee Murray and Nigel Olson. The Royal Albert Hall, where he was set to perform on October 2, 1970, as the opener to the folk-rock group Fotheringay, was large enough in scale to help him get his hooks into the English

Herbie Flowers is shown here with his famous Fender Jazz Bass with its Lake Placid blue finish.

public. He hoped that this concert, which was scheduled to take place just a month before the release of *Tumbleweed Connection*, would be the springboard for his ascension to the top of the charts in Britain.

Elton, who had secretly hoped for a royal welcome upon his homecoming, complete with banners reading "Welcome Back!," had to face up to a harsh reality: People in the UK were just not that interested! An hour before the October 2 concert, no one paid the slightest attention to the singer as he waited for his mother and Derf on the steps outside the Royal Albert Hall. This was a major moment of disillusionment for the young artist. "When Reg got back from America that first time, he couldn't believe the reception he'd gotten [there]," Caleb Quaye said. "When he told us about their American gigs, his eyes just lit up. He couldn't believe how sudden it all was. From total anonymity to being mobbed on the street. No one could believe it, really. But back in England, it hadn't happened yet."[31]

This disappointment would reinforce the singer's determination. That evening, he appeared in majesty, dressed in a gold lamé tailcoat that was a gift from the impresario Bill Graham, and he got the crowd to their feet with an explosive show, which he concluded by flinging himself to his knees during a cover of "My Baby Left Me"—a song by Arthur Crudup that was popularized by Elvis Presley in 1956. The enthusiasm of the audience was in stark contrast with the disconsolate emotions

being experienced by the musicians of Fotheringay, who stood in the wings and watched in astonishment. They bitterly regretted giving Elton his chance, because he had made a mockery of their group even before they set foot on the stage. Sandy Denny, the group's singer, was panicked. How could they perform after a tornado like that? Elton, through no fault of his own, precipitated the end of the group. Having been effectively demobilized, Fotheringay disbanded a mere three months later! On the very next day, the rapturous British press began to widely report on the phenomenon that was Elton John.

Tumbleweed Connection came out on October 30, 1970, a month after the memorable night at the Royal Albert Hall, and two days after Elton's departure for his second American tour, which was scheduled to run from October 29 to December 6, 1970. To the singer's very great satisfaction, the reviews were as positive as they were numerous. The general public also reacted warmly, despite the absence of a massive hit like "Your Song." The gamble of the concept album, which seemed suicidal at this early stage in his career, proved to be a total success. *Tumbleweed Connection* reached second place in the UK charts, and it stayed there for an impressive twenty weeks, starting on January 16, 1971. The United States, who were the main protagonists in this album, was also besotted, and the album rose to fifth place on the *Billboard* charts, where it stayed for a remarkable thirty-seven weeks.

THE CONCERT AT THE TROUBADOUR ON AUGUST 25, 1970

Birth of a Star

Encouraged by Dick James, who was convinced that the future of his young protégé would take shape on the other side of the Atlantic, Elton reluctantly set off for Los Angeles on August 21, 1970. The singer did not feel ready to make the trip, and he would have preferred to stay home and work on conquering the British charts before branching out to new terrain. It took all of Bernie Taupin's powers of persuasion to convince Elton of the soundness of the enterprise. The songwriter, who had always dreamed about going to America, tempted Elton with the idea of vacations paid for at DJM's expense, during which they would visit Disneyland and "places [they] had only seen on TV or in films,"[3] not to mention the record shops they would go to, and the limousine that was bound to pick them up at the airport, courtesy of their Americana label. "Maybe a Cadillac. A Cadillac!"[3]

For his first American tour (August 25–September 12, 1970), Elton was accompanied by Bernie and his two new stage musicians, drummer Nigel Olsson and bassist Dee Murray. Also along for the ride were Steve Brown, Ray Williams, David Larkham, roadie Bob Stacey, and, later, songwriter Roger Greenaway. It was a real "gang," as Bernie put it.

As soon as they disembarked in Los Angeles, the gang faced their first disappointment: an imperial red bus displaying a large banner that "Elton John has arrived" that awaited them outside the Los Angeles International Airport. The Cadillac they had all fantasized about was nowhere to be seen. Norman Winter and the Uni Records team were highly motivated, and in spite of this inauspicious start, they had done everything they could to ensure that Elton's visit, and his series of concerts at the Troubadour, which was *the* club in L.A., were shaping up to be a true event. A bevy of stars were invited to the first concert, which was planned for the following evening, and stacks of his single were laid out in local record shops. A plethora of interviews were scheduled, and his name appeared in massive font size on concert posters. Neil Diamond had even been convinced by the staff of Uni Records to come and present the new British rising star onstage. Elton, who was very stressed, expressed his nervousness on the telephone to Dick James, who managed to calm down his protégé and reassure him about his performance. In the middle of the day on August 25, 1970, the trio's instruments were finally set up on the stage. Not one rehearsal had taken place since their departure from England. Elton took

his place at the piano, and, with Nigel and Dee behind him, he rattled through the songs that he was going to play later that evening. The label's personnel that were present could not believe their ears: these three men made such a powerful sound that it sounded like they had a full orchestral backing! "We just made a lot of noise," Murray told *Rolling Stone* in 1987. "It was new. Elton was experimenting. Plus we had to make up for the orchestra."[46] Despite how things sounded, there were just three of them onstage performing Elton's luxuriant and orchestral music, which was filled with guitars, backing vocals, and strings.

An Incendiary Set

The evening finally came, and when Elton made his entry onto the Troubadour stage, a low murmur emanated from the crowd, who applauded the musician. The audience was greeted by a little chap with an eccentric look, whose boisterous outfit was straight out of Mr. Freedom, a boutique in London. He looked worlds removed from the mysterious image that was offered on the cover of his second album. Neil Diamond grabbed the microphone and presented Elton to the handpicked audience of three hundred. Elton opened the set with "Your Song," which he played alone on the piano before being joined by his musicians, Nigel and Dee. The impact on the audience was immediate, and the group continued with "Bad Side of the Moon." Then the songs just flowed one after another: "Sixty Years On," "I Need You to Turn To," "Border Song," "Country Comfort," "Take Me to the Pilot," and also "Honky Tonk Woman" (a reinterpretation of the Rolling Stones hit) and "Burn Down the Mission," which contained a medley of "My Baby Left Me" (by Arthur Crudup) and "Get Back" (by the Beatles), which was easily longer than ten minutes in length. Of all the songs that were played that night, only five were officially on sale in the US on the *Elton John* album. *Empty Sky* wasn't released in the United States until 1975, and "Country Comfort" and "Burn Down the Mission" wouldn't appear for several more months, when *Tumbleweed Connection* was released in October 1970.

Elton was terrified by the presence of his idol Leon Russell, who was there in the third row, and he decided to improvise something: "I leapt up and sent my piano stool flying with a kick" he narrates in his autobiography. "I stood there, knees bent, pounding at the keys like Little Richard. I dropped to the floor, balancing on one hand and playing with the other, my head under the piano. Then I stood up, threw myself forward

and did a handstand on the keyboard."[3] Even though the songs were not yet familiar to the listeners, there was no mistaking the impact they had. The audience knew they had just witnessed the arrival of an immense new star. Even Neil Diamond, who, the evening before, welcomed Elton John at his house to get to know him, was blown away: "He sat in my living room holding his cap in his lap. He was super quiet and shy. I thought to myself, 'This kid's never gonna make it.' After introducing him from the stage that night, I joined our label president (we shared the same tiny record company, Uni Records), Russ Regan, in the audience. When Elton kicked back the piano bench and started playing and singing à la Jerry Lee Lewis, I knew I was wrong. I started cheering so loudly, I spilled my drink."[47]

The same Russ Regan was stunned by the successful gamble he had made, later confiding that: "It was magical, that night. August 25, 1970, is considered one of the ten greatest nights in Rock and Roll history."[7]

Even Doug Weston, the owner of the Troubadour, had never seen anything like it. "It was totally engulfing," he told *Rolling Stone* in 1987. "You were spellbound. Nobody had ever seen anybody playing a piano with their feet up in the air like that. He literally flew at the end. There were times when his hands were on the keyboard—and that was the only part of him that was in contact with the ground."[46]

Launched into Orbit

Elton had set the Troubadour audience alight, but it remained to be seen if he could continue his initial success during his subsequent concerts, which he did—brilliantly—over the next five days. Every evening was different, with a varying order of songs, but each night was a triumph. An ecstatic review by Robert Hilburn, who described the singer's performance as "magnificent," was displayed on the front page of the *Los Angeles Times* on August 27, 1970, which had a daily circulation of 900,000 copies: "Rejoice. Rock music [...] has a new star. He's Elton John."[50] Elton, who had played in front of the Hollywood elite, including his idol Leon Russell, T-Bone Burnett, Linda Ronstadt, Randy Newman, and the future Eagles Glenn Frey and Don Henley (the alleged presence of Janis Joplin has never been verified), had just seen his career sent into orbit: The American dream was in action. Following many other concerts, notably in San Francisco, New York, and Philadelphia, Elton returned to the London gloom on September 13, leaving behind a groggy America that was rooting to hear "Your Song" on the airwaves. Less than a month later, the song was relaunched as an official single in the US, and this marked the start of a new transatlantic tour: one that would cement Elton John's status as a rock legend.

Always ready to inject a rock 'n' roll momentum into Elton's sound, Dee Murray also had a highly developed sense of melody that complemented Elton's vocals.

DEE MURRAY: THE GUITARIST WITH GOLDEN FINGERS

Davie "Dee" Murray Oates, was born in Gillingham, Kent, in 1946, to a very conservative family that had very little time for distractions outside of piano lessons, which did not really appeal to the young boy. Music only really entered his life in 1962, when he was sixteen. A work colleague at the garage where he had started a job, after leaving school, suggested that he join his band, the Thunderbolts, as a bass player. With engagements playing events like weddings and bar mitzvahs, the young group earned itself quite a reputation with its enthusiastic covers of Shadows songs. Soon, Dee was poached by another band called the Mirage, which led to him being dismissed from the garage and kicked out of his house! Despite playing some gigs in Europe, and releasing a handful of singles, including "Mystery Lady," Murray quickly realized that the Mirage would not be able to take him far enough, and so he joined the Spencer Davis Group in 1969. During the same year, the group was joined by a new drummer named Nigel Olsson, whom they came across at Dick James Music Studios, where the musicians often visited. And so it was that the future Elton John rhythm section met for the first time, though it wasn't until later that Murray and Olsson would join Elton and form the so-called Holy Trinity.

Loyal and Faithful

Elton had just wrapped up production on his second album, and while he had hitherto been able to count on the musicians of Hookfoot to provide his backing band, he was now looking to form a team specifically focused on performing for the stage. Nigel and Dee were hired during a little concert given at the Roundhouse on April 21, 1970. Dee knew that he had at last found the musical partner who would enable

him to blossom fully. Initially confined to the stage, the two musicians would increasingly make themselves indispensable in the studio as well; they played a huge part in the design of the trilogy of albums recorded at the Château d'Hérouville, and they operated not only as drummer and bassist but also as backing vocalists.

In 1975, shortly after the recording of *Captain Fantastic and the Brown Dirt Cowboy*, Dee Murray and Nigel Olsson were offloaded by Elton, who wanted to try a new sound direction. According to Philip Norman's 2000 biography of Elton, Dee received a phone call that hit him like an earthquake: "It was Elton. [...] He said, 'I've decided to change the band. I think you, Nigel and I have gone as far as we can together.'"[17] But Olsson offered a different version of events in a 2011 interview,[54] stating that it was a DJM "lackey" who phoned to tell them the news and not Elton himself. Whatever the situation, the trauma and lack of understanding were quite intense. In 1977, Dee made a brief comeback working for Procol Harum during the promotional tour for *Something Magic*. But as far as he was concerned, the magic wasn't there. When Elton called him again in 1980, Dee made himself available for the following four years. Unfortunately, the discovery of skin cancer in 1984 forced him to work more intermittently so he could undergo treatment. He moved to Nashville, Tennessee, where he played during recording sessions for artists such as John Prine and Lewis Storey. He once again answered Elton's call to record some backings for the *Reg Strikes Back* album in 1988. Sadly, on January 15, 1992, at the age of forty-five, Dee Murray succumbed to a cerebrovascular accident. Elton John gave two concerts in Dee's memory to help support the late bassist's family.

Nigel Olsson and Dee Murray formed a key duo that became the bedrock of some of Elton's greatest hits between 1970 and 1975.

NIGEL OLSSON: MASTER OF TIME

As testimony to the important role that this legendary drummer played in the construction of the "Elton John sound," here are a few figures that show his commitment throughout his career: Nigel played and/or provided backing vocals on 186 songs recorded in the studio, and 59 songs that were recorded live. He has appeared on 18 of Elton John's studio albums and on 3 albums recorded onstage. Though he had a ways to go before tying his colleague Davey Johnstone's record of 3,000 concerts played with Elton, Nigel does have a very respectable total of 2,358 shows to his name.

A Perfect Understanding

Born on the tenth of February 1949, in Wallasey, Nigel Olsson started out in music as a guitarist playing with amateur groups. It was pure coincidence—the absence of the drummer at a concert given by a group called the Fireflies—that led him to taking his place behind the drums. In 1967, he auditioned for the group, Plastic Penny, who were managed by Dick James, and he got the job as their drummer. He went to London, where he contributed to two albums. Scarcely did he have time to enjoy the success of the single "Everything I Am," which was released by Page One Records and reached sixth place on the British charts, before he left the band and joined the Spencer Davis Group. This group now consisted of Davis, Olsson, bassist Dee Murray, and guitarist Ray Fenwick, and together they embarked on an eight-week American tour that began in the autumn of 1969. But, at the end of this series of concerts, Spencer Davis called the whole adventure to a close.

Nigel then met Elton and Bernie at DJM Studios. Elton, who was working on his demos, asked him to contribute some drums parts. "Within the first eight bars of the first song that we played together, I knew that this was the music that I wanted

to be playing. It had so much feeling and was so original."[53] Elton appreciated Olsson's playing, which was both economical and powerful. Olsson also knew how to be discreet when it was needed, and he allowed the songs to breathe, even though he liked to be able to add a decent fill here and there: "But knowing how to do more with less, that's what I've always found challenging. A simple, well-placed pattern stands out and announces itself."[54] Their first official recording together was for the group Argosy, formed around Roger Hodgson, and Nigel struck his first notes in for Elton on "Lady What's Tomorrow" (*Empty Sky*), in 1969. Little by little, he created a place for himself on subsequent albums before being invited to take part fully in the recording sessions for the three works created at the famous Château d'Hérouville recording studios.

The Rupture

As a member of Elton's inner circle, the drummer remained with him until 1975, when the singer decided to part company with his rhythm section and replace it with the duo of Roger Pope and Kenny Passarelli. Between 1975 and 1978, Nigel went on to record four solo albums. His discography was further extended in 2001 with *Move the Universe*, which included a song written by Bernie Taupin and Elton John called "Building a Bird." His return to form with Elton John took place in 1980, but it was short-lived and eventually ended in 1984. During this second stint, he was involved in *21 at 33*, *The Fox*, *Too Low for Zero*, and *Breaking Hearts*. Nigel Olsson also provided backing vocals on *Reg Strikes Back* in 1988, before devoting himself to the Warpipes project, which he ran with his friend Dee Murray. The sudden death of Dee, in 1992, led Nigel to step back somewhat from the music business. It was not until 2000 that Nigel officially returned to the business, rejoining Elton John's group, this time for good.

BALLAD OF A WELL-KNOWN GUN

Elton John, Bernie Taupin / 5:01

Musicians

Elton John: vocals, piano
Caleb Quaye: acoustic guitar, electric guitar
Roger Pope: drums
David Glover: bass
Dusty Springfield: cowbell, backing vocals
Madeline Bell, Tony Burrows, Lesley Duncan, Kay Garner, Tony Hazzard: backing vocals

Recorded

Trident Studios, London: March 20, 1970; April 4, 1970 (backing vocals)

Technical Team

Producer: Gus Dudgeon
Sound Engineer: Robin Geoffrey Cable
Editing: Gus Skinas

The influence of The Band's *Music from Big Pink* shines through on *Tumbleweed Connection*.

1970

Genesis and Lyrics

The song "Ballad of a Well-Known Gun" was not included on the track list of the previous album, and so it found its place as the lead-off song on *Tumbleweed Connection*. Not only does it open Elton's third opus, but it also sets the tone for the entire album, mostly due to the image-heavy lyrics written by Bernie, which tell the story of a fugitive ("a well-known gun"), in the American West during the nineteenth century. The fugitive is caught by the Pinkertons, private detectives working for a security agency created by Allan Pinkerton in 1850, who hunted down outlaws. The narrator decides, at long last, to stop running. In a few phrases, Bernie manages to create a feeling worthy of any classic Hollywood Western, which inspired an arrangement style that could have been straight out a saloon.

Production

"Ballad of a Well-Known Gun" was the fruit of a long period of gestation. Elton and the members of Hookfoot recorded an initial version of the song, produced by Steve Brown at Olympic Studios, in August and September 1969. Apparently unsatisfied with the result, they produced a second attempt during a session at the Dick James Music Studios the following autumn, where they laid down a more rhythmic and countrified version, which was also put to the side. The third version, recorded in four takes on March 20, 1970, at Trident Studios, appeared on this new album. Having finally found the desired tempo and musical color, the musicians approached the piece as a recreational jam session, from which there emanates a strong sense of communion. The musicians and their backing vocalists—which included some prestigious guest artists, Dusty Springfield and Lesley Duncan—seemed very involved, while Elton seemed to enjoy receding into the background slightly and letting his backing artists take on more of the spotlight.

The very first notes that are played on this new album do not come from Elton John's piano but from the edgy, chicken-picking guitar of Caleb Quaye. This stylistic contrast with *Elton John* is immediately obvious, although the singer's world remains intact, if slightly altered. "Ballad of a Well-Known Gun" is not a pop gem in the vein of "Your Song," but its depth still beguiles the listener, notably through a little trick that draws the listener in from the opening notes.

FOR ELTON ADDICTS

Other versions of this song appear on *Elton 60—Live at Madison Square Garden* (2007), *Tumbleweed Connection Deluxe Edition* (2008), and *Come Down in Time* (Jazz Version) (2020).

DYLAN LIKES "BALLAD OF A WELL-KNOWN GUN"

During a concert on Elton's American tour in 1970, Bob Dylan came to see the show, and he told Bernie Taupin how much he liked his work as a writer, singling out "Ballad of a Well-Known Gun" for special praise.

On first listening, the rhythm sounds slightly shaky, and the drummer, Roger Pope, seems to be out. This is far from the case. Pope is exactly in time, but the rhythm of the melody, written in 4/8 time, actually starts out in 4 time. All that is required to create a cohesive sound was a new guitar track that could help the intro flow more seamlessly into the piano and drums. This was not a straightforward proposition for Caleb Quaye, as the group had been playing the song for months in a particular way. In the end, Caleb did not have to look far. He simply changed the tuning of his guitar to *D*. The effect was immediate, and it managed to provide the missing ingredient that brought all the other pieces of the song together. After months of playing together, the musicians had developed an unconscious expertise that made their working relationship so irresistible and commercially effective. This new guitar sound was basically pulled out of a hat at the last second, and it provides a through line that enables all the other instruments to interweave naturally. It took some time…but the song was finally completed!

It is impossible not to hear the influence of the American rock masterpiece *Music from Big Pink* in this song. The Band released their classic album in 1968, and Elton and Bernie were both absolutely crazy for it. The exemplary interaction between the musicians on *Tumbleweed Connection*, and, in particular, the incredibly well-balanced rhythm section where drummer Roger Pope and bassist David Glover stand out, offered the best example of so-called swamp rock coming from a country other than the United States. The cherry on top? Dusty Springfield, Elton's idol, contributed fantastic backing vocals during an additional recording session on April 4, and she even added some cowbell!

COME DOWN IN TIME

Elton John, Bernie Taupin / 3:26

In 2020, Elton John decided to publish the demo version of this track, with its jazz inflection, as it was originally recorded on March 20, 1970. This was done to celebrate the fifty-year anniversary of *Tumbleweed Connection*. The number was released in a ten-inch version, which was a common format at the time of the recording.

Musicians

Elton John: vocals
Les Thatcher: acoustic guitar
Chris Laurence: acoustic bass
Herbie Flowers: bass
Barry Morgan: drums
Skaila Kanga: harp
Karl Jenkins: oboe
Unidentified musicians: orchestra
Paul Buckmaster: orchestration, arrangements

Recorded

Trident Studios, London: June 11, 1970

Technical Team

Producer: Gus Dudgeon
Sound Engineer: Robin Geoffrey Cable
Editing: Gus Skinas

1970

Karl Jenkins (bottom left) played the oboe on "Come Down in Time" and was also a member of Soft Machine.

Genesis and Lyrics

In 1991, while working on a song for the album *Two Rooms*, which was conceived as a celebration of the songs by Elton John and Bernie Taupin, Sting explained why he chose to cover "Come Down in Time" saying: "I love Bernie's lyrics (on that song), it's one of those songs you wished you'd written...It creates some very evocative images."[58] It involves a message left by a woman for the narrator, asking for a nocturnal rendezvous that she will never keep. The author skillfully conveys the sense of incredible joy turning into deep despair, and John and Taupin further twist the knife in as we realize that the narrator is telling his story from the perspective of many years later, and that his sadness is still as strong as it was on the day he was stood up.

Production

With the second song in the album, the new musical orientation chosen by Elton made an abrupt change in direction. As though experiencing a resurgence from his previous opus, "Come Down in Time" saw the reemergence of Paul Buckmaster's orchestration, and it broke with the country staging established in "Ballad of a Well-Known Gun." This was not the original intention, as the first instrumental takes of this track did include a rhythm section. But Gus Dudgeon was not satisfied with the resulting recordings. Paul Buckmaster, who had lost his central position in the recording process for this album, gained a new musical authority and used this opportunity to become much more involved in the decision-making process. He suggested finishing off the preliminary stage on his own before the voice tracks were added. Buckmaster endeavored to weave in some lighter elements, including the aerial harp of Skaila Kanga, which melds with the natural harmonies of the guitar and the languor of the oboe provided by Welshman Karl Jenkins. Gus Dudgeon rounded off the song by using the finale from a previous take. The result, with its baroque sound, is sumptuous and offers a vivid form of melancholy. It won over Elton, who was able to give full expression to his vocals and permitted himself the use of a little vibrato. "I love the melancholic," he confides, "and I love the sadness. I love writing sad songs. Not that I'm sad as a person—because I'm not—but they get to me. [...] I love 'Come Down in Time.' It was only our third album, and it's kind of something that a jazz singer would record. Chordwise, it was like nothing I'd ever written before."[35]

COUNTRY COMFORT

Elton John, Bernie Taupin / 5:07

Musicians
Elton John: vocals, piano
Caleb Quaye: acoustic guitar
Les Thatcher: acoustic 12-string guitar
Gordon Huntley: lap steel guitar
Herbie Flowers: bass
Barry Morgan: drums
Ian Duck: harmonica
Johnny Van Derek: violin
Dee Murray, Nigel Olsson: backing vocals

Recorded
Trident Studios, London: June 11, 1970

Technical Team
Producer: Gus Dudgeon
Engineer: Robin Geoffrey Cable
Editing: Gus Skinas

Rod Stewart has been a friend and collaborator of Elton John's since the early 1970s and he performed on "Country Comfort."

Genesis and Lyrics

"Country Comfort" might be thought of as a naïve interpretation of American living by British people who had never been to the other side of the Atlantic, had it not been legitimized by the rural experiences of Bernie Taupin. The lyricist transposes the everyday life of his country childhood to the heart of the United States. He immerses the listener in the daily routine of farmers, compiling a veritable gallery of characters whose names and activities help them feel familiar: Deacon Lee, who prepares his sermon; Grandma and the stature of her eighty-four years; the foreman and his new machine that presages the intensification of agriculture; old Clay and his aversion to modernity; the shepherd crossing the valley. With a restrained and precise pen, Bernie evokes the pittoresque in this well-beloved countryside, leaving out none of the senses in order to enhance the listener's sense of total immersion.

Production

More than any other song on the album, "Country Comfort" crystalizes the larger intentions of *Tumbleweed Connection*. Bernie Taupin willingly acknowledged as much when he said: "We put everything you'd find on a dozen country records on it. Steel guitars and fiddles. You name it."[31] Elton had such confidence in his musicians that, on the day they recorded this song, he himself was absent. He'd been previously committed to appear in the Netherlands in order to fulfill some promotional obligations for the *Elton John* album. The session pianist Pete Robinson replaced him on the day, but the feeling was not there. Elton John rerecorded his part during overdubbing, though he wasn't entirely satisfied with his version, either. He made up whatever failings he thought he might have with his strong vocal performance; he took great trouble to create a country singing voice that bordered on caricature. The intention is very obvious in phrases such as "it cuts man-power [pronounced *powa*) by fifteen," which he terminates with a nasal sound that's typical of the style (at 1:47). Contrived though it may seem, with its clichéd ingredients, "Country Comfort" is a testimony to an admirable devotion to musicality and craftsmanship. The rhythm section, in particular, warrants the listener's admiration: the laid-back playing of Barry Morgan on drums emphasizes the feeling of relaxation described by the lyrics, while the bass demonstrates a pop subtlety in the manner of McCartney.

SON OF YOUR FATHER

Elton John, Bernie Taupin / 3:49

Musicians

Elton John: vocals, piano
Caleb Quaye: electric guitar
David Glover: bass
Roger Pope: drums
Ian Duck: harmonica
Madeline Bell, Lesley Duncan, Kay Garner, Sue Glover, Tammi Hunt, Sunny Leslie: backing vocals
Unidentified musicians: orchestra
Paul Buckmaster: arrangements, direction

Recorded

Trident Studios, London: March 23, 1970

Technical Team

Producer: Gus Dudgeon
Sound Engineer: Robin Geoffrey Cable
Editing: Gus Skinas

Far removed from the nervy and exhilarating final version, the demo of "Son of Your Father" was recorded at the end of 1969 and it shows a glimpse of a very different musical path that Elton John might have taken. Performed as a piano and voice number, it is much slower, and it takes the form of a ballad with gospel overtones. This demo was revealed when *Tumbleweed Connection* was reissued in a deluxe format in 2008.

Genesis and Lyrics

The associations between "Son of Your Father" and "My Father's Gun," which both evoke a paternal figure, are noteworthy when one realizes the importance that the absence of a father had in Elton's life. The symmetry of the two numbers, the opposition of "your" and "my," and finally, the reconstitution of the expression "son of a gun" if the word "father" is removed from each of them, point to obvious links between these two songs, which also follow each other in the track list. This is a running order that is not coincidental, because "Son of Your Father" was originally intended to appear in the second slot, but it was dropped to the fourth position at the last minute. The song evokes a confrontation over money between Joseph and Van Bushell, though it's not stated if they are father and son. They end up shooting at each other in spite of a repeated supplication that exhorts them to draw upon their shared humanity, which nourishes the love that is often shared between a father and his son: "You're the son of your father / Try a little bit harder / Do for me as he would do for you / With blood and water, bricks and mortar / He built for you a home / You're the son of your father / So treat me as your own."

Production

Following the emotional rift and the stylistic side step of "Come Down in Time," it took the honky-tonk fantasy of *Son of Your Father* to compensate for this surfeit of emotions and to bring the team back into the welcoming embrace of country rock. Performed in the style of the Rolling Stones and driven by a bragging vocal line à la Mick Jagger, this number also incorporates the loquacious harmonica of Ian Duck. This member of Hookfoot was paid £30 for his contribution to the track. "I was sent an acetate of the song and I rehearsed the harmonica part at home first, and then went to the studio."[20] He played the entirety of his line through twice before the producer signaled to him that it was a wrap. This spontaneity guides the whole piece, which highlights the spirit of the group of musicians. As proof of its integration into the collective creation, Elton's piano is barely audible despite his feverish introduction. It is Caleb Quaye's instinctive guitar, to which he applies a wah-wah with great skill, that leads the playing and imprints a sustained rhythm between the numerous breaks and restarts.

MY FATHER'S GUN

Elton John, Bernie Taupin / 6:21

Musicians

Elton John: vocals, piano
Caleb Quaye: electric and acoustic guitars
David Glover: bass
Roger Pope: drums
Ian Duck: harmonica
Madeline Bell, Tony Burrows, Lesley Duncan, Kay Garner, Tony Hazzard, Dusty Springfield: backing vocals
Unidentified musicians: orchestra
Paul Buckmaster: arrangements, direction

Recorded

Trident Studios, London: March 23, 1970; April 4, 1970 (backing vocals)

Technical Team

Producer: Gus Dudgeon
Sound Engineer: Robin Geoffrey Cable
Editing: Gus Skinas

Elton John and Dusty Springfield were united by mutual admiration, and Dusty contributed backing vocals on the album.

Genesis and Lyrics

The last song to be composed for these sessions, "My Father's Gun" takes its title from a song written by Joe English during the American Civil War and sung by the soldiers of the Union who originally came from Ireland. Bernie Taupin adopts the perspective of a Confederate soldier who has sworn to avenge his fallen father. The warrior lyrics did not have much resonance with Elton, who was on cloud nine because his idol, Dusty Springfield, had come for a visit to the studio. Elton had managed to convince her of his talent two days earlier, on April 2, 1970, when he performed "Border Song" on Britain's popular TV show *Top of the Pops*. But the biggest surprise for Elton was not so much that she would accept his invitation to visit the studio, or that she eventually contributed some backing vocals; it was that Dusty seemed to be nervous about meeting him! She was even slightly panicking, and she felt concerned that she might spoil the song. Tony Hazzard, one of the other backing vocalists, recalled: "So it was crazy, me reassuring Dusty Springfield with her great voice, because she was worried about getting it wrong, which she didn't."[31]

Production

With the exception of the backing vocals and orchestral elements, the number was recorded live in order to retain its sense of freshness. During the first forty seconds, the group establishes a blues instrumental with nocturnal intimations. Elton's powerful voice rises up and Gus Dudgeon gives him a significant dose of reverb, which might have lost some of the DIY, "let's all gather around the campfire" spirit that the group seems to be going for. But the producer's generally good spirit meant that he could introduce ideas without causing ripples in the group. His best strategy lay in his use of humor. With Elton's participation, he could make everyone laugh and keep everyone feeling calm between takes, either by doing imitations or by putting on improbable accents. Paul Buckmaster was in a slightly awkward position during the recording of this album, since he was participating in a much more limited capacity than he had on the previous record. Still, he was totally engaged, and he provided precise directions to each of the musicians in his orchestra, which they followed with professional discipline and pride, even when they had only three notes to play.

WHERE TO NOW ST. PETER?

Elton John, Bernie Taupin / 4:11

Musicians
Elton John: vocals, piano
Caleb Quaye: electric and acoustic guitars (Leslie cabinet)
David Glover: bass
Roger Pope: drums
Dee Murray, Nigel Olsson: backing vocals
Recorded
Trident Studios, London: August 6, 1970
Technical Team
Producer: Gus Dudgeon
Sound Engineer: Robin Geoffrey Cable
Editing: Gus Skinas

Elton took a gamble when he changed direction after his first two albums and created a much more American-tinged sound on *Tumbleweed Connection*.

Genesis and Lyrics

Rolling Stone magazine ran a feature on *Tumbleweed Connection* on February 18, 1971, and the piece's silence on the subject of "Where to Now St. Peter?" speaks volumes. In the piece, the *Rolling Stone* writer, Jon Landau, praises the fundamental role played by Bernie in Elton's career, affirming that "*Tumbleweed Connection* centers around and is structured by Bernie Taupin's lyrics."[59] It is true that, despite a fine production quality, "Where to Now St. Peter?" is not given a particularly unforgettable melody, even while Bernie's lyrics are no less well put together than on any other track. It is easy to imagine, initially, that this is the same character that appears in "My Father's Gun," although now he's trying to resist madness by asking St. Peter for help despite his lack of religious faith. But a different interpretation is also possible: Could this be a dying soldier facing the apostle and wondering about his final destination…heaven or hell?

Production

Recorded at the beginning of August 1970, shortly before the group left for California, this piece with its sustained tempo shows Elton in good form: His falsetto voice and piano playing establish themselves at the heart of a very organic arrangement, which Paul Buckmaster initially hoped to handle himself. The drumming by Roger Pope is perfect, as is David Glover's bass, which is rounded and thrumming. As for Caleb Quaye, he lights up the song by using a Leslie pedal to augment his guitar, whose notes seem to flamboyantly conjure the flames of hell. This effect, which requires great precision, was generally used with Hammond organs. Its use with a guitar, by Jimi Hendrix three years earlier on his hit "Little Wing" (1967), ended up being influential for many guitarists and producers, including Gus Dudgeon. "Where to Now St. Peter?" reconnects with the simplicity of earlier songs from *Empty Sky*, including "Lady What's Tomorrow" and "Sails," and it was briefly considered as a possible single for the album. Although not chosen in the end, this track provided the album with a welcome contrast to some of its darker ballads.

1970

LOVE SONG

Lesley Duncan / 3:39

Lesley Duncan played her piece with Elton at the Royal Festival Hall in London on May 18, 1974. This moment was recorded, and it is immortalized on the live album *Here and There*. Elton continued to sing this number on his tours in 1976 and 1986 (on guitar in '86!). He also chose this piece for a charity concert given in California in 1992, where he was accompanied by Neil Young, James Taylor, and Shawn Colvin.

Musicians
Elton John: lead and backing vocals
Lesley Duncan: acoustic guitar, backing vocals

Recorded
Trident Studios, London: May 11, 1970

Technical Team
Producer: Gus Dudgeon
Sound Engineer: Robin Geoffrey Cable
Editing: Gus Skinas

Lesley Duncan shot to fame via a duet with Elton on "Love Song."

Genesis and Lyrics

"Love Song" is the first departure from the dominant Bernie–Elton compositional duo! This love song that Elton decided to feature at the heart of *Tumbleweed Connection* shows up like a bubble of melancholy, and it's disconnected from the rest of the album—which makes sense, since it's written by Lesley Duncan. Elton was a fan of Duncan, who was considered to be one of the best writer-composer-performers working in Great Britain. Although she never experienced great commercial success, many of her songs, including "Everything Changes" and "Sing Children Sing," enjoyed the support of the BBC, who broadcast them extensively. Adapting well to her relative anonymity, she offered her backing vocals to Dusty Springfield, who was one of Elton's idols. She also provided backings for some of the sessions on the singer's previous album, *Elton John*. It was during one of these sessions that Elton asked her for permission to sing "Love Song." Lesley did more than simply agree; she recorded this folk song with him. Its restrained and effective lyrics suggest that the idea of love itself cannot be contained by simple romance. Lesley Duncan had not even recorded the song herself when Elton took it up, though it would appear on her album *Sing Children Sing* in 1971.

Production

A somewhat beguiling interlude, "Love Song" was recorded as a direct take on only eight tracks with Elton and Lesley Duncan seated next to each other. Elton's foot beat the rhythm, and Lesley gently strummed chords on her acoustic guitar. The song is based on an arrangement that is as minimal as possible. It begins with a fade-in, over which the crystalline guitar arpeggios, played by Lesley Duncan, immediately establish an esoteric atmosphere. Elton's voice, separated from his piano, allows itself to be carried by sympathetic backing vocals, which he sculpted himself in overdubs with the assistance of Lesley Duncan. The sound of waves in the background, and of children playing on the beach, were added later to reinforce the melancholic aspect of the song. To achieve this effect, Gus Dudgeon searched through the BBC sound archives. Gus also kept in the sound of Elton tapping his shoe to preserve the spontaneity of the take. Apart from these unique details, the Elton John version of this song ended up being very similar to the one delivered by Lesley Duncan herself just a few months later.

AMOREENA

Elton John, Bernie Taupin / 5:03

Musicians
Elton John: vocals, piano, Hammond organ
Caleb Quaye: electric guitars (Leslie cabinet)
Dee Murray: bass
Nigel Olsson: drums

Recorded
Trident Studios, London: August 6, 1970

Technical Team
Producer: Gus Dudgeon
Sound Engineer: Robin Geoffrey Cable
Editing: Gus Skinas

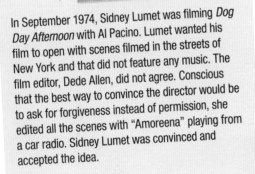

In September 1974, Sidney Lumet was filming *Dog Day Afternoon* with Al Pacino. Lumet wanted his film to open with scenes filmed in the streets of New York and that did not feature any music. The film editor, Dede Allen, did not agree. Conscious that the best way to convince the director would be to ask for forgiveness instead of permission, she edited all the scenes with "Amoreena" playing from a car radio. Sidney Lumet was convinced and accepted the idea.

1970

Genesis and Lyrics

"Amoreena" bears the same name as the daughter of Ray Williams, future godchild of Elton, who was born in 1970. But this song was not recorded in dedication to her. "Bernie came up to me and he said, 'We've got this idea for a song and it's called "Amoreena,"'" Williams recalls, still sounding amused. "And we wondered, if you have a little girl—this was before Amoreena was born, of course [...] would you call her Amoreena?' And I said 'Sure!'"[60] In light of these tail-wagging-the-dog circumstances, Bernie's narrative perspective seems surprising; outside of the pastoral landscape in which "Amoreena" takes place, the author offers an imprecise description of his character. He describes her in turn as a "lady" for whom he languishes, then as a "lusty flower" "rolling through the hay like a puppy child." In particular, he instills confusion with the suggestive verse: "The fruit juice flowing slowly [...] down the bronze of your body." The writer confirmed this sensual interpretation when called it a "bawdy love song."[16]

Production

The musicians tackled this piece for the second time on August 6, 1970, after an initial attempt with piano and voice on June 11. "Amoreena" was finally recorded in the studio with a reduced band consisting of Nigel Olsson and Dee Murray, who had been performing live onstage with Elton John for a while. The pianist knew that he had found the ideal duo to perform his richly orchestrated songs with the flesh and muscle necessary to make them work onstage, but he wanted to see how they would do in the studio. All three men knew this song by heart, having already performed it live. The results exceeded Elton's expectations, who said that he took the greatest pleasure in this track during the album sessions, even though it was eventually moved back from fourth to eighth place in the track listing. He made some noise about this with Gus Dudgeon, who was opposed to Elton's decision to record the song with his stage musicians. Whether or not it worked, Gus opted to play with the balance of the recording by bringing out the voice and piano during the mixing process. The cohesion between the musicians is nonetheless still vital to this song, with its New Orleans influence. The influence of Van Morrison is also very present in Elton's vocal inflections, especially in the lower register.

TALKING OLD SOLDIERS

Elton John, Bernie Taupin / 4:04

Musician
Elton John: vocals, piano
Recorded
Trident Studios, London: May 11, 1970
Technical Team
Producer: Gus Dudgeon
Sound Engineer: Robin Geoffrey Cable
Editing: Gus Skinas

The unique style of the songwriter David Ackles inspired Elton John in his interpretation of "Talking Old Soldiers."

Genesis and Lyrics

Contrary to a widespread opinion, numbers played only with the piano and voice are in the minority in Elton John's repertoire. "Talking Old Soldiers," a moving ballad that deals with friendship and despair, is the first of these songs to appear in his discography. In this number Bernie depicts a conversation between a young man and a veteran, all of whose comrades have died in combat and who, evening after evening, drowns his sadness in alcohol. He most likely regrets that he didn't die by their sides, and he explains to his interlocutor that he knows "how it feels to grow old." He knows that others just see him as this "old man Joe," having seen him gazing impassively at the walls and the lights in the bar. He does not deny a form of madness, as he is clearly suffering from posttraumatic stress disorder, and he knows he is condemned to live in the memories of his friends, with whom he used to raise a glass or two in the very same bar. "Do they know what it's like / To have a graveyard as a friend / 'Cos that's where they are," he says before disappearing like a ghost.

Production

An initial take of "Talking Old Soldiers" was attempted in the studio on April 15, 1970. The musicians, who were already focusing on the concert they would have to perform six days later (as the opening act for T. Rex at the Roundhouse in London), wanted to take things easy; this song was therefore the only one scheduled for the day. But it was not very convincing, and the first version was eventually trashed. A month later, on May 11, 1970, Elton tried his luck again, on the same day that he recorded "Love Song" with Lesley Duncan. Inspired by the intimate mood in the studio, he sat at his piano, and this time comfortably played the simple but effective chords of "Talking Old Soldiers." Above all, and through his mannered interpretation, he was totally at one with the dark lyrics written by Bernie. Both in his vocal mannerisms and in his playing on the piano, Elton gains in power as he evokes feelings of despair and anger, while also remaining in touch with the gentleness needed to emphasize the melancholic wanderings of the song's narrator. By taking a solemn approach, Elton allows himself to display all his vocal prowess in his phrase endings, particularly through the use of a perfectly controlled vibrato. This recording session wrapped after a single take.

BURN DOWN THE MISSION

Elton John, Bernie Taupin / 6:23

Musicians
Elton John: lead and backing vocals, piano
Les Thatcher: acoustic guitar
Mike Egan: acoustic guitar
Chris Laurence: acoustic bass
Herbie Flowers: bass
Barry Morgan: drums
Robin Jones: congas, tambourine
Brian Dee: organ
Unidentified musicians: orchestra
Paul Buckmaster: arrangements, direction

Recorded
Trident Studios, London: June 2, 1970

Technical Team
Producer: Gus Dudgeon
Sound Engineer: Robin Geoffrey Cable
Editing: Gus Skinas

Athough he plays acoustic bass on "Burn Down the Mission," Chris Laurence is best known for playing the double bass.

Genesis and Lyrics

The final track on *Tumbleweed Connection*, "Burn Down the Mission" emerges as one of the most complex numbers ever composed by Elton John. Even though Bernie Taupin's lyrics had systematically preceded the music since the beginning of their collaboration, de facto dictating the temperament of the songs, Elton never stuck as closely to Bernie's lyrics, and to the intensity of the action, as he does in this story of class struggle. The song tells of the descent of an oppressed individual, which eventually leads to revolt because he has no other motivation except to survive. Refuting any political motivation, Bernie did not seek to intellectualize this narrative, which came into his mind when he was walking in the street, and which seemed to him to be more interesting from an emotional, rather than a political, point of view.

Production

A gospel introduction with piano and voice sets the scene for the character's presentation: an impoverished father who is held down by his social and economic status. His transition to action—setting fire to a rich man's house—is described in the second verse, at 0:50, with the sharp intrusion of an acoustic guitar, and by the organ, which was played by Brian Dee. The organ gives the piece a certain solemnity, and it accentuates Elton's vocals. At 1:25, a long transition in suspension is marked by the rolling of the drums, played by Barry Morgan, who takes advantage of the change in tonality to adopt a very well judged jazzy style. At 2:09, Elton adds a new change in tonality when the brass section makes a powerful entry. After a rush of chords directed by Paul Buckmaster, the wave of instruments withdraws, leaving Elton on his own at the keyboard and linking back to the song's main character. The machine stirs up again at around 5:00 for a virtuosic finale. Elton later acknowledged that he was significantly inspired by the singer Laura Nyro in breaking out of the rules of composition and mastering this melodic odyssey. "She was the first person, songwriting-wise, that there were no rules. There were tempo changes, there wasn't a verse/chorus/verse/chorus/middle eight. She didn't write in that kind of way. And that put in my mind that you didn't have to write in that old template that everybody else did."[61]

With a cowboy hat set firmly on his head, Bernie Taupin dreamed of the arid Arizona landscape while writing the lyrics of "Into the Old Man's Shoes."

INTO THE OLD MAN'S SHOES

Elton John, Bernie Taupin / 4:17

Single: *Your Song / Into the Old Man's Shoes* **UK Release:** January 8, 1971, on DJM Records (ref. DJS.233) **Best UK Chart Ranking:** 4 **Musicians:** Elton John: vocals, piano / Caleb Quaye: acoustic and electric guitars / David Glover: bass / Roger Pope: drum / Unidentified musicians: orchestra / Paul Buckmaster: arrangement, direction **Recorded:** Trident Studios, London: March 23, 1970 **Technical Team: Producer:** Gus Dudgeon / **Sound Engineer:** Robin Geoffrey Cable / **Editing:** Gus Skinas

Genesis and Lyrics

The second song to emerge from the first recording sessions done in March 1970, "Into the Old Man's Shoes" failed to make it onto the definitive track list. It did, however, find favor with Elton, and it carries within it all the definitive markers of this album. In fact, it combines the personal and the historical sphere via the arid landscape of Tombstone, Arizona, which is famous for having been the location of the gunfight known as the showdown at the OK Corral. The showdown happened in 1881, and it involved Wyatt Earp, the hero that Bernie had worshiped since his childhood.

Production

The song presents two very melodious verses in the form of quatrains that are linked by transitions in which Elton John places his chords vigorously. In the middle of the piece, Caleb Quaye is provided with ample space to make his mark, and he drops in a crystalline blues-rock guitar solo that's punctuated by perfect, masterly shreds. The end of the track focuses on the refrain, which is played three times, allowing room for chords to develop with emphasis.

ALBUM

MADMAN ACROSS THE WATER

Tiny Dancer . Levon . Razor Face . Madman Across the Water . Indian Sunset .
Holiday Inn . Rotten Peaches . All the Nasties . Goodbye

RELEASE DATES
UK Release: November 5, 1971
Reference: DJM Records—DJLPH.420
Best UK Chart Ranking: 41
US Release: November 5, 1971
Reference: Uni Records—93120
Best US Chart Ranking: 8

EXTRAVAGANT RUNNING TIMES

Nineteen seventy-one was a pivotal year for Elton. The new "messiah of pop music" had won over the American and British public, the reviewers, and his peers. Everything reflected his newfound potential; he now just had to convert all of this into a successful new album. Elton, a man who was always working, released not just one album in 1971, but four, not counting the concerts he held, and the third tour! *Tumbleweed Connection* came out in the Unites States on January 4, 1971, the soundtrack to *Friends* came out on March 5, the live album *11-17-70* was released on April 1, and *Madman Across the Water* hit shelves on November 5. Four days of recording were sufficient to put the fourth studio album to bed. Filled with lengthy pop ballads featuring ambitious arrangements, the new album was very far from *Tumbleweed Connection*, which saw the arrival of the musician Davey Johnstone and marked the beginning of a new cycle in Elton's career. The first colleague to suffer the consequences of this new phase in Elton's career was Paul Buckmaster, and *Madman Across the Water* was the last recording in which he was so completely involved.

A Triumphant End to the Year

The end of 1970 was devoted to a second American tour (October 29 to December 12), which ended in triumph. For six weeks, Elton, Bernie, Nigel, and Dee toured the biggest cities in the country: Boston, Los Angeles, New York, Detroit, Chicago…Even though he was introduced as Elton "Jones" at his first stop, the singer very quickly made a name for himself. Each evening, he delivered a Dante-esque spectacle, transforming himself into an indefatigable rock star, even going as far as destroying a piano onstage just like Pete Townshend did with his guitar. Each evening, the atmosphere became more wild and enthusiastic. The group was living a real fairy tale. On November 6, at the Electric Factory in Philadelphia, the musicians met the members of the Band in the wings; they expressed their admiration of Bernie, who was thrilled to receive praise from his idols. But there were plenty more surprises still in store: At the end of the month, Bernie found himself face-to-face with Bob Dylan, who once again offered praise to Bernie for his work as a writer, adding that he particularly loved "Ballad of a

Well-Known Gun." His breath totally taken away, Bernie could not utter a word. "I wasn't ready for it. What can I say? I mean it was like 'Oh God' or 'You're god' or 'my god.'"[31] The next day, *Melody Maker* reported on this meeting with the headline: "Dylan Digs Elton!"[57] The "royal tour" stopped off once more in New York, on December 4, as the opening act for Derek and the Dominos, the group run by Elton and Bernie's other "god": Eric Clapton. Clapton also realized Elton's potential: "I was slightly threatened by all this. This guy had a hit album, he was really fashionable and everyone loved it."[58]

Back in England later that month, Elton took some time to search for a new home. He focused on finding a luxurious apartment in the center of London, finally settling on a place in Tottenham Court Road. It was filled with eccentric décor, and it had an elevator that directly connected the parking lot and the sitting room, both of which (the décor and the elevator) greatly appealed to Elton. It was in this new home where Elton experienced the excitement of a new relationship with John Reid, director of the British division of Tamla Motown, whom he had met at Christmastime festivities arranged by the record company. The affection that Elton felt for John was so deep that he could no longer have any doubts about his homosexuality. He decided to come out only to selected people, and when he told his mother she greeted the news with an amused composure.

At the same time, Elton's relationship with his manager, Ray Williams, had deteriorated since his first American tour and the fateful night at the Troubadour. In addition, Dick James was angry with Ray after learning that Ray had gone off to party in Palm Springs on the night of Elton's first concert at the Troubadour, leaving the young artist alone on what was perhaps the most important night of his career. In October 1970, Dick called Williams to his office for a "ticking off." Ray did not flinch, and he offered no argument. He knew he was on borrowed time. He was aware that, despite the road traveled so far, a road on which he had contributed a lot, he was not necessarily in a position to accompany Elton into the next phase of his professional life. This new phase would take him to the summit of the pop world. In fact, the top of the mountain was already well

within view: The *Elton John* album was released in the United States on July 22, 1970, and it reached fourth place on the charts on February 6, 1971. This was in large part thanks to the success of the single "Your Song," which was released in October 1970 and went to number eight on the charts on January 23, 1971. *Tumbleweed Connection* completed the hat trick: released in America on January 4, 1971, it had climbed to fifth place by February 13. The choice to not release a single from *Tumbleweed Connection* so that *Elton John* and "Your Song" could enjoy their moment in the sun had paid off.

New Sessions Lead to New Music

Elton was on cloud nine when he went back into Trident Studios on February 27, 1971, to record new tracks for his fourth album: *Madman Across the Water*.

Despite his confidence in Nigel Olsson and Dee Murray, the two men were, once again, not much required on this album. Gus Dudgeon preferred to call upon other studio musicians. He was known to be strict in his choice of personnel, but the producer was still open to suggestion in other areas. Only two songs were recorded on February 27: "Levon" and "Goodbye." This first session was restricted to one day, since the group was performing in Bradford later that evening, and they had other gigs coming up before hopping a flight to the United States for a third tour, which was planned between April 2 and June 18.

Just before this series of concerts, on March 27, the whole team met in Lincolnshire to celebrate Bernie's marriage to Maxine Feibelman.

During this time, two Elton albums were released: the original film score for *Friends*, on March 5, 1971, and a live album, *11-17-70*, on April 1, which was recorded at A&R Recording Studios in November 1970, for the New York radio station WABC. The live album rose through the charts and reached eleventh place in the United States and twentieth place in the United Kingdom. Elton had now become a bankable artist, and Dick James Music was in a position of strength at the beginning of 1971 when it came time to negotiate a distribution contract with MCA Records. The company guaranteed Elton a $2 million advance, subject to a commitment for seven albums, which were to be delivered over the coming seven years.

The first album that was contracted to be released in the US would therefore be *Madman Across the Water*, whose February sessions had to be interrupted for scheduling reasons. They resumed as a matter of urgency on August 9, 1971, once again at Trident Studios. The conditions were not ideal. Eighteen hours before starting, Elton and his musicians were still onstage at Vilar de Mouros in Portugal. They were completely exhausted. The final album consisted of nine songs, each of which (apart from the last track) ran to more than four minutes,

1971

Elton John at work with Paul Buckmaster on *Madman Across the Water* in a photograph taken by Mike Ross. (opposite)

Guitarist Davey Johnstone made his first appearance on *Madman Across the Water*. (left)

FOR ELTON ADDICTS

The cassette version of *Madman Across the Water* was reissued in 1980 with a slightly altered track list. "Razor Face" appeared as the seventh track while "Rotten Peaches" moved into third position.

sometimes even closer to five or six minutes. As for the lyrics, Bernie was back to focusing on romance, writing songs that were in some ways related to aspects of life he experienced during the first American tour. Often written in the first person, these lyrics forced Elton to assume a very wide range of voices and characters in order to live up to the promise of this rather ambitious album.

New Blood

The August sessions saw the arrival of a new musician in the group: Davey Johnstone, who had been a member of a group called Magna Carta, for whom Gus Dudgeon produced two albums, *Seasons* and *Songs from Wasties Orchard*. The producer, who had seen Johnstone's talents as a multi-instrumentalist (guitar, sitar, dulcimer, mandolin) firsthand, insisted that he should be given a chance. The newcomer not only showed his capacity for new ideas, but he would also play a peacekeeping role among a team that was experiencing some internal tensions. Johnstone turned up to the recording sessions filled with youthful enthusiasm, but without much of an idea of what he was getting himself into. He discovered an Elton John who was not particularly welcoming. Very reserved, and sometimes just silent, Elton often seemed too focused to engage in conversation. But Davey's good humor and useful suggestions gradually helped Elton relax.

Despite the urgency of the recording sessions and the relative lack of preparation, along with some tensions surrounding Paul Buckmaster, the recording progressed quickly and wrapped up in just three days, on August 9, 11, and 14, 1971 (or four days, if we include the earlier session on February 27).

"We recorded *Madman* in four days. It was supposed to be five, but we lost a day because of Paul Buckmaster. He stayed up the night before the sessions began to finish the arrangements—I suspect with a certain amount of chemical assistance—then managed to knock a bottle of ink all over the only score, ruining it. I was furious. It was an expensive mistake to make, and we stopped working together for decades afterward. [In reality, Buckmaster was back on *Don't Shoot Me* in 1973, but in a considerably reduced role.] But I was also quietly impressed when he wrote the whole score again, in twenty-four hours. Even when Paul screwed up, he screwed up in a way that reminded you he was a genius."[3]

Madman Across the Water was wrapped up twelve days before Elton and his band headed back to the United States for a new series of concerts. This was a grueling pace for the band to uphold, but it was the price that had to be paid in order to establish Elton John's supremacy as the reigning king of pop.

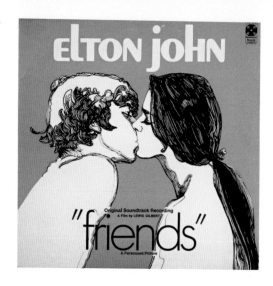

Elton was unhappy about *Friends* being promoted as his album since he composed only four complete numbers for the soundtrack.

THE *FRIENDS* ALBUM:
A DEMANDING EXERCISE

Friends (2:20)
Honey Roll (3:00)
Variations on "Friends" Theme (The First Kiss) (1:45)
Seasons (3:52)
Variations on Michelle's Song (A Day in the Country) (2:44)
Can I Put You On (5:52)
Michelle's Song (4:16)
I Meant to Do My Work Today (A Day in the Country) (1:33)
Four Moods (10:56)
Seasons Reprise (1:33)

ALBUM

Release Dates
United Kingdom: April 1971
Reference: Paramount Records—SPFL269
United States: March 5, 1971
Reference: Paramount Records—PAS-6004
Best UK Chart Ranking: Did Not Chart
Best US Chart Ranking: 36

Musicians
Elton John: vocals, piano
Caleb Quaye: guitar
Dee Murray: bass
Nigel Olsson: drums
Rex Morris: tenor saxophone
Madeline Bell, Lesley Duncan, Liza Strike: backing vocals
Paul Buckmaster: arrangements, direction

Recorded
Trident Studios, London

Technical Team
Producer: Gus Dudgeon
Engineer: Robin Geoffrey Cable
Executive Producer: John Gilbert

Single Release
Friends / Honey Roll
   UK Release: April 23, 1971, on DJM Records (ref. DJS.244)
   Best UK Chart Ranking: Did Not Chart
   US Release: March 5, 1971, on UNI Records (ref. 55277)
   Best US Chart Ranking: 34

Ray Williams was responsible for Elton John's involvement in the *Friends* album. When his young discovery's second album, *Elton John*, was released in April 1970, Williams sent a copy of the album to John Gilbert, son of the film director Lewis Gilbert (*Alfie* [1966] and *You Only Live Twice* [1967]). Ray had known John since the famous advert posted by Liberty Records in 1967; Gilbert was instantly won over by Elton's musical world, and he set about converting his father. Therefore, in September 1970, Elton was called upon to compose the music for Lewis's next film, *The Intimate Game*. The film relates the romance between two adolescents, Michelle and Paul, who leave Paris and become parents at a very young age. Bernie and Elton were hesitant about the film's title, and they suggested changing the name to *Friends*. The duo had not imagined just how much of their time would be required, or the time constraints that would be involved in the composition of a film soundtrack. Bernie, through sheer laziness, did not even bother to read the script, and he wrote his lyrics based on a verbal summary given to him by Lewis Gilbert!

Recording began in September at Olympic Studios. But the task proved more complicated than expected, and the process stretched out over five weeks. Elton and the musicians were placed in front of a giant screen and had to play live as the scene unfolded in front of their eyes. They were required to produce twenty- to thirty-second segments of music, which had to match the scenes precisely. The performance was timed, "sliced up," and constantly interrupted by the comments and recommendations of various film technicians. Elton, who liked things to be over and done with quickly, really hated the experience. He suggested to production that the complete pieces should be rerecorded in his natural environment at Trident Studios. As well as being comfortable, Trident Studios was equipped with separate booths for the drums, which helped avoid feedback on the microphones. The recordings done at Trident are of much better quality, and while the production team retained the takes from Olympic Studios and used them in the film, the Trident sessions were used for the release of the film soundtrack on March 5, 1971.

Elton recorded four numbers ("Friends," "Michelle's Song," "Seasons," and a short reprise of the main theme). Paul

(Left to right) Stephen James, Bernie Taupin, Elton John, and Dick James celebrated the success of the *Elton John* album in 1971.

Buckmaster supplied orchestral variations for the other tracks. However, embarrassed by the frugality of his offerings, Elton added two other numbers that had been meant for his next album, "Can I Put You On" and "Honey Roll"; both were pop songs with a lively groove.

Despite their initial reticence, Elton and Bernie managed to give form to this album while still being respectful of the film itself. There are a number of high points, including "Michelle's Song," which melds nicely with the juvenile optimism of the two main characters, while Bernie enriched the lyrics with idyllic images of the French countryside, and the danceable "Honey Roll," which was conceived as an homage to Fats Domino.

When the *Friends* soundtrack was released in the United States on March 5, 1971, it became the second Elton John album to appear in America since the beginning of the year, following *Tumbleweed Connection*. Apparently unsatisfied with his rate of output, Elton would also release a live album (*11-17-70*) and another full-length album (*Madman Across the Water*) in the same year.

FOR ELTON ADDICTS
Friends was certified a gold disk in April 1971 by the RIAA (Recording Industry Association of America). This was the third time in three months that Elton received this honor, following the consecrations of *Elton John* and *Tumbleweed Connection*.

AN ALMOST EMBARRASSING RECOGNITION
The original film score for *Friends* was nominated for a Grammy Award in the category "Best Original Film Soundtrack" in 1971. Elton John was flattered but he felt that, at most, the album deserved a rerelease with its reprises and variations removed.

11-17-70:
AN IMPROMPTU ALBUM RELEASE

Take Me to the Pilot (6:43)
Honky Tonk Women (4:09)
Sixty Years On (8:05)
Can I Put You On (6:38)
Bad Side of the Moon (4:30)
Burn Down the Mission (18:20)

ALBUM

Release Dates
UK Release: April 9, 1971, on DJM Records (ref. DJLPS 414)
Best UK Chart Ranking: 20
US Release: May 10, 1971, on Uni Records (ref. 93105)
Best US Chart Ranking: 11

Musicians
Elton John: vocals, piano
Dee Murray: bass, backing vocals
Nigel Olsson: drums, backing vocals

Recorded
A&R Recording Studios, New York: November 17, 1970

Technical Team
Producer: Gus Dudgeon
Sound Engineer: Phil Ramone
Production Coordinator: Steve Brown

FOR ELTON ADDICTS
Due to the different styles of date notation in England and the United States, this live concert album, which was recorded on November 17, 1970, was given the title *17-11-70* in the UK and *11-17-70* in the US.

The release of this live album was never actually meant to happen, but the record company had to provide a commercial response to the bootleg that was circulating on a very significant scale following the eighty-minute concert Elton gave on November 17, 1970, in the A&R Recording Studios in New York. The "concert" was broadcast by the New York radio station WABC, and it was decided that, as a matter of urgency, a live album should be released. Out of the thirteen songs played that evening, only six were kept, and the album had a total run time of forty-eight minutes. The remaining songs ("Indian Sunset," "Your Song," "Country Comfort," "I Need You to Turn To," "Border Song," and "My Father's Gun") would not be released until 2017 as part of a double LP created in support of Record Store Day. The album came out on April 9, 1971, in Great Britain, and a month later in the United States, and it was named for the date on which the concert was given.

A High-Frequency Live Concert

After a concert given in Santa Monica Civic Auditorium in Los Angeles, on November 15, 1970, Elton John and his band crossed the United States in the direction of the East Coast and went to A&R Recording Studios. This independent recording studio was run by the legendary producer Phil Ramone, who specialized in jazz and who was Burt Bacharach's and Louis Armstrong's preferred partner. He also worked with Paul Simon and Billy Joel during the second part of his career. Elton John, Dee Murray, and Nigel Olsson turned up at Studio 1A on November 17, situated on the top floor of a building located at 799 Seventh Avenue in New York City. They arrived just forty minutes (give or take) before delivering a set that was broadcast live. There was only enough time for a rehearsal of two or three numbers before they went live. The three musicians waited in silence for their cue to go on. Elton was staring into the distance, concentrating to the maximum, while Nigel and Dee shared a joint. Just over a hundred people were in the audience, including Mary Travers, of the group Peter, Paul and Mary. Buoyed by his proximity to

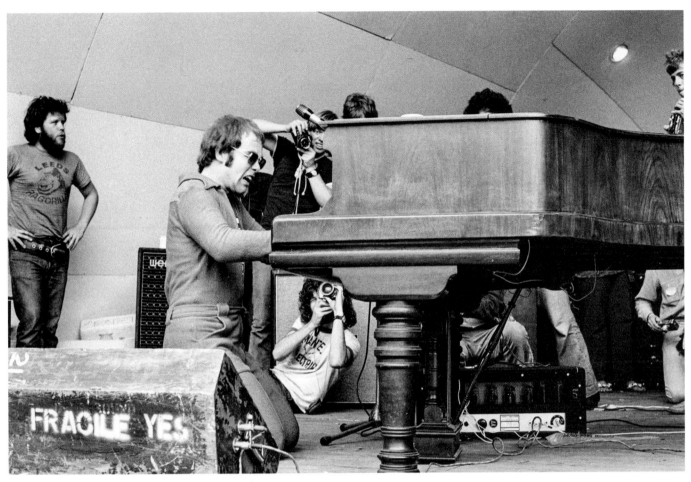

Beginning in 1970, Elton performed a series of concerts on both sides of the Atlantic, including an appearance at the Crystal Palace Garden Party II in London on July 31, 1971.

the audience, which reminded him of his early days playing small clubs, Elton decided to approach this performance as if it was a real concert. The musician, who very much preferred expressing himself onstage rather than in the studio, ended up giving what he felt was his best live performance, notably helped by the studio's optimal playing conditions. With Nigel Olsson and Dee Murray by his side, he was confident of proving that his atypical power trio—there was no guitar—was more than capable of playing rock 'n' roll. Following a short introduction provided by the station's DJ, Dave Herman, the group launched headfirst into a feverish version of "Bad Side of the Moon," followed by an animated rendition of "Amoreena" with very expressive vocals, and very technically astute drumrolls from Nigel Olsson. Following a fairly wild version of "Take Me to the Pilot"—Elton almost lost his voice by pushing the envelope in his top register—the singer then brought the tension down with "Sixty Years On," in a strikingly emotional performance that's even more impressive considering the absence of an orchestra. The song's power is also due to the

fabulous playing by Olsson, which concluded with crashing cymbals in the manner of Nick Mason from Pink Floyd. Elton's voice, enhanced by a reverb and echo judged to perfection, soars with a startling purity. But it is above all the devilish precision of his left hand playing, constantly in motion, that captured the attention of Phil Ramone, whose eyes were riveted on the musician from his perch at the console.

Elton felt very much at home, and he contributed lots of jokes during the session, such as when he warned to audience to take a bathroom break before "Indian Sunset," which had an epic seven-minute run time. The trio embellished their performance with covers that delighted the audience, including "Honky Tonk Women," borrowed from the Rolling Stones and subtly introduced a cappella, and in close harmony, with a slight rise at the end of the lyric that triggered some knowing laughter from the audience. References to two of Elton's other role models were also on the program: Arthur Crudup's "My Baby Left Me," which was popularized by Elvis Presley, and "Get Back" by the Beatles.

ROGER POPE: ANIMAL INSTINCT

While Nigel Olsson is identified as the drummer in the Elton John Band (he remained in the role from 1970 until the 2022 farewell tour), the absences that marked his career with Elton were filled with verve by Roger Pope. This drummer, with his precise and powerful playing, was affectionately nicknamed "Popey" by his entourage, and he was praised for his self-effacing qualities and his kindness, which he hid behind a slightly rough-cut manner. Unfortunately, he was not destined to become one of Elton's go-to collaborators. Only to the extent of illuminating with his subtle playing hits of the dimensions of "Tiny Dancer" or "Don't Go Breaking My Heart." Passionate in nature and brilliant in his adaptability, he was equally capable of great control, mastering complex jazz patterns such as the shuffle by Art Blakey, one of the masters of bebop. With a skill that convinced Caleb Quaye of his talent, Pope, who was destined to become a studio musician, eventually found himself working with the likes of Harry Nilsson, Kevin Ayers, and Cliff Richard. He was also a friend of Keith Moon and Ginger Baker, two of the greatest drumming legends of all time. Some suggest that Animal, the wild drummer in the Muppets, was inspired by a combination of these three men!

The Right Drummer at the Right Time

As a native of Whitstable, in the Kent region of England, Roger Pope discovered the drums in his early adolescence, when his family moved to Southampton. Aged fifteen, he joined the Soul Agents, a rhythm 'n' blues group led by keyboard player Don Shinn. In this group he met guitarist and harmonica player Ian Duck, and bassist David Glover, with whom he would later form the formidable rhythm section in the band Hookfoot. Specializing in covers, the Soul Agents played for a time as the backing group for Rod Stewart near the end of 1965. Two years later, Pope made the acquaintance of Elton John at the Dick James Music Studios, where he worked as a studio musician. The pianist-composer, who was still called Reginald Dwight at that time, regularly called upon his services to play on the compositions he wrote for other

artists. They created a short-lived group together in 1969: the Bread and Beer Band. Naturally, Elton called upon him for his first singles ("I've Been Loving You," "Lady Samantha," and "It's Me That You Need"), and then for his first album, *Empty Sky*. In addition to the studio sessions, Roger formed a group with other DJM musicians: Caleb Quaye, Ian Duck, and Dave Glover. They called the group Hookfoot, after a technique that Pope perfected to stop his high hat stand from falling over when he played.

A Missed Opportunity

Since he was busy working on construction sites to make ends meet, Pope missed being credited on "Your Song," an honor that would go to Barry Morgan. Pope eventually caught up with the album that would reveal Elton to the general public, *Tumbleweed Connection*, and above all with *Madman Across the Water*, during the production of which he made his mark on the future classic: "Tiny Dancer." But Elton, who had put together one team for stage gigs and another team for studio work, wanted to give his group a definitive form, and so he hired Nigel Olsson both for studio and concert work. It was not until 1975, with *Rock of the Westies*, that Pope found his place with Elton once more, sitting behind his famous walnut-caramel-colored Ludwig kit. On this occasion he delivered one of his best performances on "Billy Bones and the White Bird." Having joined the Kiki Dee Band around the same time, Pope remained available for Elton on the *Blue Moves* album in 1976. He formed a short-lived group with Davey Johnstone in 1977 called China, which disappeared after the recording of an eponymous album. Then he followed Caleb Quaye and joined the backing group for Hall & Oates in 1978. We find the two men together again in the Troops at the beginning of the 1980s, but a serious alcoholism problem kept Pope off the stage during the following decades, with the exception of a brief revival of Hookfoot in 1999. The drummer died of cancer on September 17, 2013, aged sixty-six. A few hours before his passing, he was officially married to his partner, Sue Tressider.

DAVID GLOVER: A BASSIST AND A MASTER OF MELODY

David ("Dave") Glover (not to be confused with Roger David Glover, of Deep Purple), together with Roger Pope, formed the rhythm section that accompanied Elton John's first steps on the road to rock megastardom. Theirs was a well-balanced association, with Glover providing a very rich and melodic playing style, contrasting with the vigorous playing of the drummer. The two men knew each other very well, having evolved together from their time in a youthful band called Soul Agents.

Glover was seventeen when he left his previous group, Men Friday, to join the Soul Agents, in December 1965. Their leader, Don Shinn, had just joined the group at the time when Rod Stewart jumped ship. In May 1966, Dave took part in his first recording for the group on their fourth and final single, consisting of "A-Minor Explosion" and "Pits of Darkness," two instrumental numbers. On June 6, sandwiched between a David Bowie concert and a Manfred Mann concert, the Soul Agents delivered one of their best performances at the Marquee Club, where they became regulars. Keith Emerson, who was an unknown at the time, was in the room and delighted in the nerve of the group, who executed a daring arrangement of Edvard Grieg's piano concerto in A minor. Unfortunately, the group split up in October 1966.

The Hookfoot Adventure

Dave Glover, Ian Duck, and Roger Pope decided to launch a new group: the Loot. The bassist composed some pieces, which the group recorded, including "I've Just Gotta Love You," "Whenever You're Ready," and "Don't Turn Around." With the arrival of guitarist Caleb Quaye, from Bluesology, the Loot turned into a new group that called themselves Hookfoot. This band brought to life Elton John's first demos, while at the same time building up their own repertoire: *A Piece of Pye* (1969), *Turn the Radio On* (1970), *Hookfoot* (1972), *Good*

Times a' Comin' (1972), *Communication* (1973), and *Roaring* (1973). They were fine musicians, very well matched, and Hookfoot enabled Elton John to give form to his compositions and try them out onstage. For this reason, when recording his first album, Elton decided to call upon these musicians, who knew his songs inside out. However, Dave Glover held back, and committed himself only to four songs on the *Tumbleweed Connection* in 1970 ("Ballad of a Well-Known Gun," "Son of Your Father," "My Father's Gun," and "Where to Now St. Peter?"). These were the songs on which his taste and aptitude for country music were fully expressed, with rich, fluid lines and round, deep sonorities that were primarily melodic rather than rhythmic, almost like solos, as on "My Father's Gun." The British bassist was also present on the fourth album, *Madman Across the Water*, in 1971, contributing on "Tiny Dancer," "Razor Face," and "Holiday Inn," pieces in which he presented another facet of his playing, which was more economical and provided a more melodic foundation than what's found in other tracks on the album. His gentle, discreet, and vital playing contributes to the beauty and timelessness of these songs.

From Bassists to Sound Engineer

Dave Glover's subsequent career, other than involvement on the albums *It Ain't Easy* by John Baldry in 1971 and *Dark and Devil Waters* by Mick Audsley in 1973, took an unexpected turn when he opted to put his instrument aside and place himself in the service of other musicians as an assistant sound engineer. He worked on *Different Light* by the Bangles in 1985, which contained the famous hit "Walk Like an Egyptian," and alongside producer Andy Johns on the album *Night Songs* by the glam metal group Cinderella in 1986. He also worked on *Big Generator* by Yes in 1987, and also on *Till I Loved You* by Barbra Streisand and Don Johnson in 1988.

TINY DANCER

Elton John, Bernie Taupin / 6:17

1971

Musicians
Elton John: vocals, piano
Caleb Quaye: electric guitar
B. J. Cole: lap steel guitar
Davey Johnstone: acoustic guitar
David Glover: bass
Roger Pope: drums
Tony Burrows, Roger Cook, Lesley Duncan, Dee Murray, Nigel Olsson, Barry St. John, Terry Steele, Liza Strike, Sue Glover, and Sunny Leslie: backing vocals
Paul Buckmaster: arrangements, direction

Recorded
Trident Studios, London: August 9, 1971

Technical Team
Producer: Gus Dudgeon
Engineer: Robin Geoffrey Cable
Mixing: Ken Scott
Production Coordinator: Steve Brown

Single Release
Tiny Dancer / Razor Face
US Release: February 7, 1972, on Uni Records (ref. 55318)
Best US Chart Ranking: 41

"THE CUT"
In 2017, as part of a celebration of his fifty-year partnership with Bernie, Elton launched a project called "The Cut," in association with YouTube. The idea was to offer clips in groups of three, from his classics released in the early 1970s, before the arrival of music videos. Among these was "Tiny Dancer," which was revisited by Max Weiland. In a few minutes, the producer painted a touching picture of California, with an unexpected actor appearing on screen: the gothic rock singer Marilyn Manson.

Genesis and Lyrics

The subject of the lyrics in "Tiny Dancer" has never been in doubt. From the outset, Bernie stated clearly that this piece was dedicated to Maxine, "with love," which one can see in the album credits printed on the sleeve. Two years later, Bernie also confirmed, in an interview given jointly with Elton to Paul Gambaccini for *Rolling Stone*, that the song is not just a piece dedicated to Maxine but also that it is a song about Maxine.[1]

The first song on the fourth album is therefore a declaration of love to Maxine Phyllis Feibelman, Bernie's first wife, whom he had met during the group's first tour of the United States, a year earlier. This was a meeting that occurred due to a twist of fate: Nigel Olsson, Elton's drummer, was stuck in the hotel and needed a hair dryer, and when a friend set out to look for one, he turned up back at the hotel with Maxine in tow. Bernie was immediately entranced by her charm. He was also struck by the contrast between American women, who he thought were very extroverted, and the women he had known in Great Britain, who he found to be rather straight-laced: "They were just so different from what I'd been used to in England," Taupin explained to Gambaccini. "They had this thing about embroidering your clothes. They wanted to sew patches on your jeans. They mothered you and slept with you. It was the perfect Oedipal complex."[36]

Little by little, Maxine and Bernie got to know each other, and she settled in with the group's entourage, devoting herself to maintaining their costumes. Every evening, Bernie watched her humming, her eyes riveted to the stage as she gently swayed to the music. She took him on a tour of Los Angeles, where he was soon to set up a home. Then the couple headed for Lincolnshire, and on March 27, 1971, Maxine walked up to the altar on the arm of her father, Lieutenant Colonel Max Feibelman, who had retired from the American Air Force. All of this happened under the benevolent gaze of Elton John.

A Snapshot of California

When Bernie wrote his lyrics, the young woman in the song crystallized his American dream. During a very busy year that flashed by at the rate of a galloping Thoroughbred, not only did he discover the America of his dreams, but he also found love in the person of Maxine. All of this is what he sought to summarize in "Tiny Dancer," a sort of snapshot of California,

Elton sporting a heavily patched denim jacket that was customized by Maxine, Bernie Taupin's partner.

which was the first state in which Bernie ever set foot: "We came to California in the fall of 1970 and it seemed like sunshine just radiated from the populace," recalled Taupin in 1973 concerning the writing of "Tiny Dancer." "I guess I was trying to capture the spirit of that time, encapsulated by the women we met, especially at the clothes stores and restaurants and bars all up and down the Sunset Strip. They were these free spirits, sexy, all hip-huggers and lacy blouses, very ethereal the way they moved."[36]

Through the course of the song, Bernie follows his "ballerina," re-creating along the way the atmosphere of the Golden State with its legendary open-mindedness, where one sees "Jesus freaks," probably converts handing out leaflets about faith on street corners. In the middle of all this, Maxine is indeed a "Blue jean baby, L.A. lady / Seamstress for the band / Pretty-eyed, pirate smile," whose future he pretends to predict, whereas he already knew the end of the story: "You'll marry a music man." "I knew it was about me," Maxine told the *New York Post* in 2019. "I had been into ballet as a little girl and sewed patches on Elton's jackets and jeans"[62] (two details cited in the lyrics). Furthermore, she remembers having goose bumps when hearing "Tiny Dancer" for the first time at Trident Studios, in London, in 1971:

"Elton was on one side of me and Bernie was on the other. That song was like having your really good friends give you the best gift you could ever receive."[62] Unfortunately, the couple divorced in 1976, apparently without acrimony. "Tiny Dancer" will forever remain the symbol of their heartfelt but ultimately ephemeral passion.

The Recording

"Tiny Dancer" was recorded on August 9, 1971, at the end of a day in which Elton also put to bed two other songs, "Razor Face" and "Holiday Inn." During discussions prior to recording "Tiny Dancer," the option of including a steel guitar was raised. It was 4 p.m., and Steve Brown lost no time in contacting B. J. Cole, a specialist in the instrument and a regular at Dick James Music Studios, having played there often with his group, Cochise. B. J. Cole appeared at 11 p.m., when the team was just starting to organize the number. He was included in the discussions straightaway, on equal footing with the other musicians. The guitarist appreciated this privilege, as he was aware that his instrument was usually added at the overdubs stage and relegated to a minor role. Amongst the musicians were David Glover, the bassist, and Roger Pope, the drummer, who was wearing work clothes that were covered with cement from his

Bernie Taupin, age 20, and Maxine Feibelman, age 19, were married on Saturday March 27, 1971, in Market Rasen, Lincolnshire. Elton served as best man and he wore a suit designed by Nudie Cohn, Elvis Presley's tailor.

day job working in construction. In fact, Glover and Pope were both working on a building site when they were called up at the last minute to come in for the recording. They did not hesitate. Having been on-site since seven o'clock in the morning, they left work at six thirty and went straight to the studio without changing or having a shower. Their hair was full of cement dust, which had been hardened by sweat, and they had the sensation of their heads weighing a ton as they played. Despite these less than ideal conditions, they still had time to record their parts in "Razor Face" and "Holiday Inn" before B. J. Cole arrived. As for the implementation of "Tiny Dancer," this took longer because the song had a complex structure that was fairly unusual for a pop song.

In order to deploy the gentle melody that had been conceived by Elton and that was meant to run for more than six minutes (unheard-of for a single!), "Tiny Dancer" made use of a subtle musical progression, which stayed with Elton on the piano and solo vocals, leading to the very inspired strings arrangement by Paul Buckmaster, which carries the song through to its end. Elton builds his voice progressively: Initially reserved, it grows steadily before it explodes, finally, in the refrain. Many years later, Elton did not beat about the bush when Bob Dylan asked him how he had conceived of the admirable crescendo of the refrain: "This is a very good question. 'Tiny Dancer' has a really long lyric. […] Writing a song like

that's a bit like having a wank, really. You want the climax to be good, but you don't want it to be over too quickly—you want to work your way up to it. Bernie's lyric took such a long time to get to the chorus, I thought, 'Fuck, the chorus had better be something special when it finally arrives.' And it's 'here I come,' literally."[63]

A total tour de force, the song immediately sets the tone of the rest of the album. The piano chords that open it, which are fairly close to the introductory harmonic sequence of "Country Comfort" from *Tumbleweed Connection*, offer an amplitude and depth that is immediately enthralling. The goal was not to create an intimate sound but to construct a multilayered musical effect, using a cohort of session musicians, much in the same way that things had been done on the *Elton John* album.

It was also on "Tiny Dancer" that the Scottish guitarist Davey Johnstone appeared for the first time, and he would shortly leave his own group, Magna Carta, to fill out the sound in Elton's band. His warm acoustic guitar, supported by Caleb Quaye's versatile electric guitar, establishes a solid sound that's illuminated by B. J. Cole's steel guitar pedal. The rhythm section is discreet but formidably well placed. The foundations are perfectly laid when Elton's piano becomes more expressive and Paul Buckmaster's arrangements, with full strings, help the song take off with the support of the soaring backing vocals. In

In between recording sessions for *Madman Across the Water*, Elton completed a whirlwind spring tour in the United States. Here he's shown at the San Francisco Civic Center on May 9, 1971. (above)

Elton John is in top form onstage at Tivoli Gardens in Copenhagen, Denmark, on July 9, 1971. (next page)

the backing vocals were the sisters Sue Glover and Sunny Leslie, and Lesley Duncan, who had given Elton her "Love Song" for *Tumbleweed Connection*. At around three in the morning, recording finally finished and all the musicians congratulated one another. They knew that they had just perfected a great song. Pope and Glover savored the moment with an added sense of irony. The next day would be a tough one for them. They would be going straight back to work at the construction site without getting any sleep.

Recognition That's Late in Coming

"Tiny Dancer" had two difficult missions to accomplish: opening the album *Madman Across the Water*, and helping the album mimic the success Elton had found with his previous album, *Tumbleweed Connection*. The track was selected for release as a single, with "Razor Face" on the B-side, and offered to the public in February 1972. But recognition was a long time in coming. In fact, the song did not make any headway in the United States. The six-minute running time was hindering the song's success. In fact, the radio stations did not hesitate to shorten the song, even cutting it after the first refrain because they found the verses repetitive, which also made things tough. Others simply censored it, considering the phrase "Jesus freaks out in the street" to be too transgressive for their airwaves. Given the song's seeming failure in

America, the record company decided not to release the track as a single in Great Britain, thereby depriving it of any chance of making its way up the charts. Elton regarded this as quite a blow. Disappointed and still giddy from the crazy year he had just experienced, he briefly entertained the idea of making a radical decision: "I thought of quitting. I really thought I'd gone as far as I was going to."[17]

Fortunately, in 1973 MCA released a different version of the song in AOR (Album-Oriented Rock) format, which was much better suited to radio broadcast. This helped "Tiny Dancer" find moderate success in Canada (nineteenth place) and in Australia (thirteenth). But Elton would have to wait until 2000 for the song to really to pass into the pantheon of classic singles and become one of the most emblematic standards of his entire repertoire. This all happened thanks to the Cameron Crowe–directed film, *Almost Famous*, which was a veritable love letter to *seventies* rock and heavily featured "Tiny Dancer" in its most iconic scene. "In fact, that scene turned 'Tiny Dancer' into one of my biggest songs overnight," wrote Elton in his autobiography. "People forget that when it came out as a single in 1971, it flopped. It didn't make the Top Forty in America, and the record label in Britain wouldn't release it at all. When it turned up on the soundtrack of *Almost Famous*, I think a lot of people had no idea what it was, or who it was by."[3]

LEVON

Elton John, Bernie Taupin / 5:37

Musicians
Elton John: piano, chant
Caleb Quaye: electric guitar
Les Thatcher: acoustic guitar
Brian Odgers: bass
Barry Morgan: drums
Rick Wakeman: piano
Brian Dee: harmonium
Tony Burrows: backing vocals (uncredited)
Unidentified musicians: orchestra
Paul Buckmaster: arrangements, direction

Recorded
Trident Studios, London: February 27, 1971

Technical Team
Producer: Gus Dudgeon
Engineer: Robin Geoffrey Cable
Mixing: Ken Scott
Production Coordinator: Steve Brown

Single Release
Levon / Goodbye
US Release: November 29, 1971, on Uni Records (ref. 55314)
Best US Chart Ranking: 24

1971

FOR ELTON ADDICTS
The headline "God Is Dead" appearing on the cover of the *New York Times* did not come from Bernie's imagination. The venerable newspaper had, in fact, printed this exact phrase on March 24, 1968, but as part of a longer headline that read in full: "'God Is Dead' Doctrine Loses Ground to 'Theology of Hope.'"

Genesis and Lyrics

"[This] song is about a little boy who gets fed up with what he's doing. And he just wishes he could get away from it, but he really can't. It's called 'Levon.'"[66] With these few words, Elton John presented the song during the live recording at the BBC studios for the TV series *Sounds for Saturday*, on November 11, 1971. The album had been released six days earlier. Elton confirmed this analysis to Susan Black in 1995: "It's just somebody who gets bored with blowing up balloons and he just wants to get away from it but he can't because it's the family ritual."[64]

In this song, Bernie evokes an older man who was born poor but made his fortune selling balloons after fighting in an unnamed war. His son, whose first name is Jesus, does not want to have anything to do with him, and refuses to blow up the balloons. He prefers to watch them fly away and dreams of "going up" to Venus and "leaving Levon far behind." When, in 2013, *Rolling Stone* asked Bernie Taupin about this song, he stressed that he had no idea about the meaning he wanted to give it: "Quite honestly, [the song] was written so long [ago] that I really don't know what was in my head at the time. It was a free-form writing. It's not David Bowie throwing words into a hat and picking them out. It's a totally different way. I think that Bob Dylan did that, too. It was just lines that came out that were interesting."[67]

Whatever he might say, the lyrics are derived from an intergenerational conflict that arose in the 1970s between the Greatest Generation (those born between 1905 and 1925) and the following one, which was attracted to the values of counterculture. The choice made by the character's son Jesus is also not without significance, as it was a question of rewriting his biblical destiny and turning him into a modern, rebellious figure, in the manner of *Jesus Christ Superstar* in the rock opera by Andrew Lloyd Webber and Tim Rice, which had debuted on Broadway a month earlier. The line "the *New York Times* said God is dead" would appear to confirm this interpretation.

Many people saw in the title of this song a nod by Bernie in the direction of his idol, Levon Helm, the singer in the Band, whom he had the opportunity to meet at an Elton concert in Philadelphia, on November 6, 1970. But, in an interview given to Andy Greene for *Rolling Stone* on September 26, 2013,[67] Bernie denied that this was the case, and said he simply picked the name because he liked it.

Elton gives an inspired performance on *Sounds for Saturday,* a BBC broadcast circa December 8, 1971.

Production

"Levon" was the first song in the album to be worked on and recorded on February 27, 1971, at Trident Studios, along with "Goodbye." Run through with an elan that is close to gospel, the number is performed with a Hammond organ played by Rick Wakeman, whose playing in harpsichord and on Mellotron on *Space Oddity* by David Bowie (released in November 1969) had pleased Elton John. Having been contacted by David Katz, who managed the session musicians, the keyboard player—who was about to join the group Yes—did not hesitate for second, seduced by Elton's technique and style. These qualities are given full expression in the introduction, with Elton John playing on the nuances in a pure, melancholic melody, instantly conferring a classical dimension upon this piece. Without it being possible to tell exactly at which moment, Wakeman's keyboard layers are inserted prior to the ascension of the refrain, before the cellos specifically requested by Gus Dudgeon enter the scene. Dudgeon also wanted to give the number a symphonic dimension, which Paul Buckmaster made to measure for him: "'Levon,' I think, is one of Paul's best arrangements of all time. That orchestra riff on the outro is fantastic."[68] In this orchestral

context, Barry Morgan, the drummer, found his place perfectly. He makes a thundering entry at 1:28, marking the peak of the emotional crescendo. As though touched by grace, he misread his score during the final prerefrain and inserted an impromptu roll on the toms when Elton was intoning, "He was born a pauper to a pawn on a Christmas Day." When the take was finished, the drummer rushed into the control cabin, his head held low, and apologized profusely to Gus Dudgeon: "I screwed up." The producer, though, was happily reassuring him: "Barry, that was a fucking brilliant drum fill. What on earth made you put it there? [...] It was a moment of genius."[68] The musician insisted on doing a retake, but Gus was firmly opposed to it and had the support of Robin Geoffrey Cable, his engineer. A sign from God like that does not happen twice!

"Levon," the first American single from *Madman Across the Water,* has a run time of 4:59 and still managed to hit number twenty-four on the *Billboard* chart, despite its length. Also it was slightly cut down for radio airplay; Elton refused to record a shorter version just to satisfy the disk jockeys! An honorable stance for a singer who was still not so well-known at the time.

RAZOR FACE

Elton John, Bernie Taupin / 4:42

Musicians

Elton John: vocals, piano
Caleb Quaye: electric guitar
David Glover: bass
Roger Pope: drums
Rick Wakeman: Hammond organ
Jack Emblow: accordion

Recorded

Trident Studios, London: August 9, 1971

Technical Team

Producer: Gus Dudgeon
Engineer: Robin Geoffrey Cable
Mixing: Ken Scott
Production Coordinator: Steve Brown

Single Release

Tiny Dancer / Razor Face
US Release: February 7, 1972, on Uni Records (ref. 55318)
Best US Chart Ranking: 41

Two days before beginning the recording of *Fragile* with the band Yes, Rick Wakeman laid down his Hammond organ for "Razor Face."

Genesis and Lyrics

The lyrics in *Madman*, often written in the first person by a Bernie who was always subject to autobiographical inspiration, obliged Elton to assume a very wide range of voices and characters. In "Razor Face," he seems to adopt the role of a young man seeking an older, reassuring figure or divine grace that "protects [...] like a glove." Is he scorning his destiny as a has-been, which he finds pathetic? Or, more likely, is he trying to show himself as being empathetic toward a paternal figure? In any case, he fully assumes his affection for the Razor Face of the title, his "old friend." All kinds of hypotheses have circulated concerning the real meaning of these words, from a disoriented Vietnam War veteran trying to find a place for himself upon returning home, to an older homosexual looking for a younger companion, to cocaine users chasing lines with a razor blade. But, as Bernie says through the voice of his character, "I'll never learn the reason why / I love your razor face." As such, the lyrics remain a mystery.

Production

"Tiny Dancer" and "Razor Face," the A- and B-sides, respectively, of the album's second single, were recorded during the same session on August 9, 1971. "Razor Face" is a very organic song, without superfluous arrangements, or big backing vocals. It has a very live sound, due partly to Caleb Quaye's electric guitar, which makes a remarkable entry in the piece at 1:17, as well as to the rock-solid rhythm section provided by Roger Pope and David Glover, and due also to a very clean production. One notes that Elton's vocals are regularly outside the frame, as though he was performing in a concert, placing the occasional little intervention between verses, especially in the finale, which introduces an accordion into the Elton John world for the first time. It is played by the veteran Jack Emblow, who delivers an astonishing solo, in a very effective question-and-answer section with Caleb Quaye's funky guitar. The piece ends with a fade-out, leaving the impression that, as with a musicians' jam session, the song really had no definite ending. The Super Audio CD version of the album, which was released in 2004, offers an extended version with nearly two extra minutes of track. The fact that this extended version clocks in at 6:39 would seem to support this theory.[TK]

MADMAN ACROSS THE WATER

Elton John, Bernie Taupin / 5:57

Musicians

Elton John: vocals, piano
Rick Wakeman: organ
Davey Johnstone: acoustic guitar
Chris Spedding: electric guitar
Herbie Flowers: bass
Terry Cox: drums
Diana Lewis: ARP synthesizer
Ray Cooper: percussion
Unidentified musicians: orchestra
Paul Buckmaster: arrangements, direction

Recorded

Trident Studios, London: August 14, 1971

Technical Team

Producer: Gus Dudgeon
Sound Engineer: Robin Geoffrey Cable
Mixing: Ken Scott
Production Coordinator: Steve Brown

Paul Buckmaster earned a serious reprimand from Elton for delaying the recording of the arrangements for "Madman Across the Water."

Genesis and Lyrics

First recorded at the end of the *Tumbleweed Connection* sessions, on May 8, 1970, "Madman Across the Water" was taken out of the final track listing due to an issue with its length (eight minutes). But it was also the victim of a harsh judgment by Gus Dudgeon, who would have happily trashed the piece. "It came out sounding like Led Zeppelin playing Elton John. A bit schizophrenic and boring,"[36] he wrote laconically on the label of the final recording of the first version! The faults he found in it were mostly related to the composer's attachment to giving form to the narrator's madness. One theory about the lyrics to "Madman Across the Water" has been resolutely denied by Bernie: that the song was a critique aimed the American president Richard Nixon. The link seems very tenuous, especially the idea that reference to water could make one think of Watergate, and the fact that the Watergate scandal didn't happen until 1972 only further confirms that this theory is a nonstarter.

Production

The album's title song was recorded on August 14, 1971. This time, multi-instrumentalist guitarist Davey Johnstone, a member of Magna Carta, was involved. He contributes a more solid structure that was missing from the earlier attempt. Its warmth—clearly audible on the strumming of the strings—contrasts with the gliding riff laid down by Mick Ronson. The creative madness of the guitarists infects the rest of the players, who seek to make the song as strange as possible. Gus Dudgeon even goes along with this; he applies a fade-out/fade-in on Elton's voice when he lets out the heart-rending cry at 2:00, giving the impression of the singer falling into the abyss, then rising back up again. The only dark shadow in the picture of this session: Elton John's anger with Paul Buckmaster. The arranger arrived at the studio without the scores, and there were nearly sixty musicians present who had been booked and were ready to play.

INDIAN SUNSET

Elton John, Bernie Taupin / 6:47

Musicians: Elton John: vocals, piano / Herbie Flowers: electric bass / Chris Laurence: acoustic bass / Terry Cox: drums / Cantores in Ecclesia (directed by Robert Kirby): backing vocals / Unidentified musicians: orchestra / Paul Buckmaster: arrangements, direction **Recorded:** Trident Studios, London: August 14, 1971 **Technical Team:** Producer: Gus Dudgeon / Sound Engineer: Robin Geoffrey Cable / Mixing: Ken Scott / Production Coordinator: Steve Brown

Genesis and Lyrics

In the lyrics of "Indian Sunset," Bernie Taupin puts himself in the shoes of an Amerindian warrior. Overcome by melancholy, he imagines the time when his destiny will change and probably end in defeat by the white men. Having been affected by a visit to an Native American reservation, the lyricist did not necessarily have a protest song in mind, as was the case with many artists at the end of the 1960s or early 1970s, but instead wanted to tell a story with cinematographic contours. This explains certain small inaccuracies, notably concerning the death of Geronimo, who is riddled with bullets in the song. In fact, the Apache chief surrendered to General Nelson Miles in 1886 and died of pneumonia in 1909, aged seventy-nine years.

Production

As an epic musical adventure lasting nearly seven minutes, "Indian Sunset" was constructed around an a cappella introduction by Elton, giving the impression that he is praying, invoking Native American ancestors. Little by little, discreet but solemn brass enters, opening up the way for Elton's piano. This is then supported by powerful drumrolls on the toms. While his voice seems to grow in anger, the rhythm section really gets started, as a bed for the majestic strings. This impressive movement is suddenly interrupted at 2:20 to give way to a more gentle, melancholic passage. This in turn leads into the instrumental storm from around 4:30, with a double sequence that repeats until the song's finale. Elton always preferred to perform this song in concert, as he stated in 2011: "Nobody knows that song at all, it's an obscure track from *Madman Across the Water*, and it gets a standing ovation every night. It's a six-minute movie in a song."[69]

HOLIDAY INN

Elton John, Bernie Taupin / 4:17

Musicians: Elton John: vocals, piano / David Glover: bass / Caleb Quaye: acoustic guitar / Roger Pope: drums / Davey Johnstone: mandolin and sitar / Tony Burrows, Roger Cook, Lesley Duncan, Dee Murray, Nigel Olsson, Sue Glover, Sunny Leslie, Barry St. John, Liza Strike, Terry Steele: backing vocals / Paul Buckmaster: arrangements, direction **Recorded:** Trident Studios, London: August 9, 1971 **Technical Team:** Producer: Gus Dudgeon / Sound Engineer: Robin Geoffrey Cable / Mixing: Ken Scott / Production Coordinator: Steve Brown **Single Release:** *Rocket Man (I Think It's Going to Be a Long, Long Time) / Holiday Inn; Goodbye* **UK Release:** April 7, 1972, on DJM Records (ref. DJX 501) **Best UK Chart Ranking:** 2

Genesis and Lyrics

During the first half of 1971, which was largely spent on the road, Bernie had plenty of opportunity to record life on tour in his notebooks. For him, having no occasion to enjoy the pleasures of stage performance, this daily reality was rather dull and repetitive. It was this unglamorous routine that he characterizes in "Holiday Inn," in the evocation of the hotel chains of the same name. But the song, seeming like a direct criticism of the brand, was the subject of some discussion within the team, who were concerned about a possible lawsuit. It was decided, therefore, to make some changes to the text to mitigate this. In the second verse, as a counter to the vitriol, the following was added: "Oh I don't even know if it's Cleveland or Maine / With the buildings as big and rooms just the same / And the TV don't work and the French fries are cold / And the room service closed about an hour ago." And one word, one single word but loaded with meaning, was introduced into refrain: "baby" was substituted for "prison," thereby completely altering Bernie's original intentions and transforming the song into a veritable advertising slogan in praise of the hotel chain—"And you ain't seen nothing till you've been / In a motel, baby, like the Holiday Inn." This change was also the source of the removal of the third verse, whose lack of coherence with the refrain would otherwise have been too flagrant.

Production

The instrumentation of this number, inherited from the *Tumbleweed Connection* period, was led by a mandolin, which gives it a folk-rock spirit similar to the Band. Davey Johnstone, who

The original version of "Holiday Inn," with the missing verse and the unmodified refrain, can be heard in a demo for piano dating from 1971 on the *Jewel Box* set, released in 2020.

played this part, had strongly advocated that it should replace the banjo that had been initially envisaged. The newcomer had plenty of ideas, and he even dared to suggest that Elton John abandon his usual melodic introduction on piano in favor of a very abrupt opening, with the voice starting at the same time as the mandolin. Elton, who appreciated the musician's enthusiasm, and the relevance of his suggestions, went with the idea and retained this version. The piano is only heard therefore at 1:37, accompanied by the orchestra, in a surprising twist involving the interleaving of violins with Indian sonorities, and a sitar, also played by Davey Johnstone, who was familiar with the instrument.

ROTTEN PEACHES

Elton John, Bernie Taupin / 4:58

Musicians: Elton John: vocals, piano / Chris Spedding: slide guitar / Davey Johnstone: acoustic guitar / Herbie Flowers: bass / Terry Cox: drums / Ray Cooper: percussion / Rick Wakeman: organ / Diana Lewis: modular ARP synthesizer / Tony Burrows, Roger Cook, Lesley Duncan, Dee Murray, Nigel Olsson, Barry St. John, Terry Steele, Liza Strike, Sue Glover, Sunny Leslie: backing vocals **Recorded:** Trident Studios, London: August 14, 1971 **Technical Team:** Producer: Gus Dudgeon / Sound Engineer: Robin Geoffrey Cable / Mixing: Ken Scott / Production Coordinator: Steve Brown

Genesis and Lyrics

"Rotten Peaches" tells the first-person story of a beleaguered chain-gang member. Condemned to forced labor, they spend their entire day breaking rocks along the railroads under construction. The unfortunate laments his condition and the monotony of the tasks that make his days so long and so predictable. But, above all, he acknowledges his wrongdoings, calling himself a "criminal" and an inveterate liar, who has had his "fill of cocaine and pills." He fears that he will never see the green grass, as there is none in the American prisons, and still less will he see his home, thousands of miles away from his place of detention. His only obsession becomes these fruits that rot every day in the sun, in front of his eyes—an appropriate metaphor for the fate of prisoners, which Bernie's perceptive imagination does not fail to identify.

Production

The first song recorded at the session on August 14, 1971, "Rotten Peaches" combines country, rock, blues, and gospel influences. It also highlights the playing of Terry Cox, drummer in the group Pentangle, who had come along to take part in the sessions. Other notable craftsmen on this number were Chris Spedding, on slide guitar—who stood out some years later by producing the first demos for the Sex Pistols—and Herbie Flowers and his floating thumb bass, also found the following year on the Lou Reed hit "Walk on the Wild Side," from his iconic *Transformer* album. No less important, Diana Lewis discreetly weaves a sound fabric in the background on her modular synthesizer.

ALL THE NASTIES

Elton John, Bernie Taupin / 5:09

Musicians: Elton John: vocals, piano / Dee Murray: bass / Nigel Olsson: drums / Ray Cooper: tambourine / Cantores in Ecclesia (directed by Robert Kirby): backing vocals / Paul Buckmaster: arrangements, direction **Recorded:** Trident Studios, London: August 11, 1971 **Technical Team:** Producer: Gus Dudgeon / Sound Engineer: Robin Geoffrey Cable / Mixing: Ken Scott / Production Coordinator: Steve Brown

Genesis and Lyrics

The rave reviews that blossomed in the American press in the wake of the singer's August 1970 concert tour were in very stark contrast to the severity of the British press. Elton interpreted this as a real snub against him, which led him to suggest to Bernie writing a song on this subject—an initiative he would never have allowed for himself. So it was that "All the Nasties" was born. This scathing text was crafted with sufficient skill as to offer a second level of interpretation…and sufficiently subtle for no one to see the second level immediately. Elton recalls: "'All the Nasties' was about me, wondering aloud what would happen if I came out publicly: 'If it came to pass that they should ask—what would I tell them? Would they criticize behind my back? Maybe I should let them.' Not a single person seemed to notice what I was singing about."[3]

Production

While one would have expected a muscular rock sound or a wild rhythm 'n' blues to be used for this vengeful diatribe, instead the composer-singer offers a delicious contrast, with a gospel sound that is informed by the vocal group Cantores in Ecclesia, directed by Robert Kirby. Sufficiently unusual to be noteworthy, Dee Murray and Nigel Olsson, the two musicians at the center of Elton John's stage team, were involved in the recording of "All the Nasties." In fact, Gus Dudgeon, who generally controlled what happened in the sessions, distinguished between the two activities, and usually preferred the professionalism of the studio musicians to the enthusiasm of Elton's two concert partners. The bassist and drummer make their entry only at 1:40. But when they come in, their smooth and precise playing gives the song a new direction—especially around 3:00, when the bass chimes out its notes, before imposing its full phrase, and the drumming of Nigel Olsson assumes a spatial dimension due to the echo applied to them by Gus Dudgeon. "The amount of reverbs we had available to us were very slim. I think there were a couple of EMT 240 Gold Foil verbs and maybe two or three EMT 140 Sheets, and that would have been it. You didn't have much control over them. About the most you could do was EQ the sound on the way into the Sheets and re-EQ it on the way back and set the delay."[68] The effect achieved by the combination of these processors, equipped with a metal plate re-creating the natural reflection of sound of a room with their vibrations, is impressive.

Phil Collins Before HE Was Phil Collins
The processing of the drum sound by Gus Dudgeon via reverb processors prefigures the sound processing applied to Phil Collins's drums a few years later. The latter perfected this due to a studio "accident" that happened during the recording of the song "Intruder" by Peter Gabriel in 1979: A microphone linked to the drums was mistakenly given a reverberation as well as a noise gate.

GOODBYE

Elton John, Bernie Taupin / 1:49

Musicians: Elton John: vocals, piano / Unidentified musicians: orchestra / Paul Buckmaster: arrangements, direction **Recorded:** Trident Studios, London: February 27, 1971 **Technical Team:** Producer: Gus Dudgeon / Sound Engineer: Robin Geoffrey Cable / Mixing: Ken Scott / Production Coordinator: Steve Brown **Single Release:** *Levon / Goodbye* **US Release:** November 29, 1971, on Uni Records (ref. 55314) **Best US Chart Ranking:** 24 *Rocket Man (I Think It's Going to Be a Long, Long Time) / Holiday Inn / Goodbye* **UK Release:** April 7, 1972, on DJM Records (ref. DJX 501) **Best UK Chart Ranking:** 2

Genesis and Lyrics

Elton plays with extremes on this album, where most of the numbers run close to five or six minutes each, and which ends with the shortest song in his repertoire to date: "Goodbye," coming in at just under one and a half minutes. The singer had experimented with it once before on the stage of *The Andy Williams Show* on December 11, 1970, in Los Angeles, a variety broadcast on which the Englishman was invited to appear alongside Ray Charles and Cass Elliot. But this number was not selected for the set, and only "Your Song" was performed.

Production

Along with "Levon," this final album track was completed on February 27, 1971. For this profound song of deep introspection, which is played in a minor key, sobriety is of the essence, and the piano and voice combo is a natural choice, highlighting the exceptionally expressive power of Elton's voice.

1971

ALBUM

HONKY CHÂTEAU

Honky Cat . Mellow . I Think I'm Going to Kill Myself . Susie (Dramas) .
Rocket Man (I Think It's Going to Be a Long, Long Time) . Salvation .
Slave . Amy . Mona Lisas and Mad Hatters . Hercules

RELEASE DATES
UK Release: May 19, 1972
Reference: DJM Records—DJLPH 423
Best UK Chart Ranking: 2
US Release: May 26, 1972
Reference: Uni Records—93135
Best US Chart Ranking: 1

Elton rewore his suit from Bernie's wedding in this photoshoot for 1972's seminal single "Rocket Man."

FOR ELTON ADDICTS

Honky Château was the last official album Elton John did with Uni Records in the United States and in Canada. In fact, MCA decided to combine all of their labels, including Uni Records, under the MCA banner. Future Elton recordings were done with MCA Records in the United States.

The cover art for Elton's fifth LP was entrusted to the American photographer Ed Caraeff and not to Elton's longtime collaborator, David Larkham.

AN ALBUM OF FIRSTS

Elton John worked at a frenetic pace in 1971, with release of four disks: two studio albums, (*Tumbleweed Connection* and *Madman Across the Water*), one live album (*11-17-70*), and the film score for *Friends*. But coming up for air was not really an option for the singer, who was bound by his contract (two albums a year) and was caught up in a promising upward spiral, which he wanted to perpetuate with his fifth studio album. He got started on it in January 1972. *Honky Château* took its name in reference to the location where it was created, the Château d'Hérouville in France, and it was completed in under three weeks.

A Year of Change

Taking one's time was not on the menu at this point in Elton's career. Just in time to enjoy his status as a rock icon, the singer changed his given name (Reginald Kenneth Dwight) to Elton Hercules John on January 7, 1972, honoring not the famous hero of Greek myth but, rather, the workhorse in the popular British 1960s sitcom *Steptoe and Son*! Psychologically, the switch was immediate: "It was like slipping into a Superman costume," he said. "I'd grown fed up with people saying, 'This is Elton John, but his real name is Reginald Kenneth Dwight.' Reg is the unhappy part of my life. I can't bear people calling me Reg. If people send me letters as Reginald Dwight, I don't even open them."[31] In his autobiography, Elton gave a more light-hearted version as the main reason for this change of name: "Basically,

I had got sick of the fuss in shops when the cashier recognized me but not the name on my checkbook."[3]

From a musical perspective, Elton also decided to change his method: He wanted to record this new opus with his stage group (Dee and Nigel) and not his usual studio musicians, and he also wanted to expand the group with the addition of guitarist Davey Johnstone, who had played acoustic guitar, mandolin, and sitar on *Madman Across the Water*. The coolness of Gus Dudgeon's reaction surprised him somewhat: "Davey was a wonderful guitarist, but he only played acoustic: as far as Gus knew, he'd never even played an electric guitar. He was in a band called Magna Carta, who specialized in bucolic folk, and there wasn't a lot of that in the Elton John repertoire."[3] Regardless of Gus's opinion, Elton opted to trust his own intuition once more, and offered the job to Davey. *Honky Château* would thus be an album of firsts: "It was the first time I'd tried to record an album with my touring band rather than crack session musicians; the first time that Davey had picked up an electric guitar; the first time we'd had the money to record abroad, in a residential studio."[3]

Exiled to Hérouville

The decision was made: In January 1972, Elton and his troupe set off for France. It is true that *11-17-70* had been recorded live in New York, but *Honky Château* was the first studio album

Left to right: Elton John, Gus Dudgeon, and Ken Scott sitting behind the console at the Hérouville studios.

that Elton recorded outside of Great Britain. Like the Rolling Stones, who set themselves up in the majestic villa Nellcôte in Villefranche-sur-Mer to record *Exile on Main St.* (and so they could circumvent the British tax authorities), Elton exiled himself to Hérouville for the time it took to wrap up his fifth LP. When his tax adviser recommended that he should record outside the country for financial reasons, Elton had no qualms about agreeing to this, but only as long as "we could find someplace peaceful [to record] without any interruptions."[1] It should be said that, while he had become a serious heavyweight in the music industry in the United States, it took a while before he was taken seriously in Great Britain, and this had an impact on his affection for his home country. But unlike the Stones, who recorded their double album over a long period of time and with a mobile studio, Elton wanted to move quickly and use a traditional studio, on the advice of Gus Dudgeon.

It was specifically Gus Dudgeon who had mentioned the unusual studio located not far from Paris in an eighteenth-century manor house that was famous for having been a location in the love affair between Frédéric Chopin and George Sand. Dudgeon had already visited it and had fallen under its spell: "When I entered the studio for the first time," he recalled, "a group called Zoo was doing their levels balancing, and I heard the drummer's cymbal, magnificent and crisp, which was making a sound like: 'Ting, ting, ting.' Then I went into the control room, and I heard exactly the same sound from the speakers, it was amazing, I had still never experimented with that level of fidelity in another studio."[127]

The Château d'Hérouville soon proved to be a viable option: The whole team could sleep there, working day and night if necessary, and they could take advantage of the luxurious facilities (including a private pool, game room, tennis

court, etc.) for relaxation. Furthermore, the home had its own vineyard, and the catering met with unanimous praise.

Elton was seduced by the place: "I loved the idea of working at the Château, even though it came with a reputation attached. It was supposed to be haunted, and the locals had apparently become wary of the studio's clientele after the Grateful Dead had stayed there, offered to play a free concert for the villagers, then taken it upon themselves to expand the minds of rural France by spiking their audience's drinks with LSD."[3] In the beginning of January, the team (along with their equipment and baggage) took over the premises for several weeks.

An Album Composed on Location

Elton had his work cut out for him when he arrived at the château with basically no melodies under his belt. He found the idea of writing the pieces in situ rather stimulating: "I'm not a musician who walks around with melodies in his head all the time," he explained in his autobiography. "I don't rush to the piano in the middle of the night when inspiration strikes. I don't even think about songwriting when I'm not actually doing it."[3] Furthermore, he was very much counting on breathing new life into his work by way of this new adventure. He wanted to get away from his typical symphonic arrangements and to sound like a group, in an organic way. For this reason, the team was cut down to a bare minimum upon arrival at the château: Elton, on vocals and keyboards, Dee Murray on bass, Nigel Olsson on drums, Davey Johnstone, the newbie, on guitars, mandolin, and banjo. Other musicians contributed from time to time, notably the French jazz violinist Jean-Luc Ponty, and the brass players Ivan Jullien (trumpet), Jacques Bolognesi (trombone), and Jean-Louis Chautemps and Alain Hatot (saxophones). The keyboards were played by either David

Elton, Dee, and Davey on a break between takes during recording sessions for *Honky Château*.

Hentschel or the jovial Larry Smith (alias "Legs," the drummer with the eccentric Bonzo Dog Doo-Dah-Band), who appeared unexpectedly on "I Think I'm Going to Kill Myself." Ray Cooper was along once again to play the conga drums. For the technical aspect, Gus Dudgeon was present with his wife, Sheila, and his assistant, Ken Scott. And of course, Maxine and Bernie came along, with the latter toting his trusty typewriter along in his luggage.

During the first two days, recording was put on standby because Gus and Nigel were involved with setting up and adjusting the drums in the studio, while Elton composed, Dee chilled, and Davey read *The Lord of the Rings*. This was a key phase for the producer, as he explained, "Within the drum kit you have every frequency you're ever going to have, from the highest high to the lowest low. Once you've got the drum sound together, someone can come in and say, 'What do you think of this bass sound?'—with it in solo. But you don't know how good it is until you've put it up against the drum kit, because it may be a great bass sound in its own right, but does it work with the bass drum?"[31] Everything eventually worked like a dream. Elton's vision was on point: The close-knit group was so used to playing together that the songs emerged with a disconcerting ease and steadily took shape in the luxurious comfort of the Château d'Hérouville. "We didn't have to pack everything away at the end of a session, and so we could work at night and sleep by day," Elton explained. "It is the only way to work. You come down to a place like this and you forget about all the troubles of the outside world. Nothing matters except getting your head straight and putting the music down."[31]

The inclusion of Davey Johnstone was a real success. However, neither Nigel nor Dee were aware of Elton's intentions for him before they saw him arrive at the airport. Only the possibility of inviting singer Mick Grabham—who later joined Procol Harum—had been floated before their departure for France. In an interview given the following year to *New Musical Express*, Elton affirmed: "I decided to use the band more prominently and add Davey. We didn't rehearse with him or anything, we just invited him to France with us."[73] Not only was his folk background a real asset for Elton's compositions, but his ideas would prove to be fundamental to the spontaneous approach that characterized this fifth opus.

To crown everything, Bernie was in very good form and feeling very inspired by life at the château, which helped to streamline the work even more. When he finished a song's lyrics, he put them on Elton's piano, a Steinway—his favorite, which regally dominated the dining room under a gigantic eighteenth-century chandelier. Other instruments were laid out just outside the studio to facilitate everyone seizing the moment of inspiration whenever it presented itself. From the third day, a routine had established itself: Elton got up before everyone else, went to the dining room, and had a look at Bernie's verbal creations while eating his breakfast. As though by magic, the melodies seemed to flow from his fingers, quite painlessly: "The first morning we were there, I had three done by the time the band drifted downstairs looking for something to eat: 'Mona Lisas and Mad Hatters,' 'Amy' and 'Rocket Man.'"[3]

Breakfast was eaten, not always very early in the day, but the method proved very effective: Elton sat alone at the piano with his croissant, joined by his lyricist and musicians who were in need of a black coffee, and the happy band could then go straight into collaboratively finalizing what they were preparing to record: "It was a pretty sensible way of doing things. It was very, very casual and very quick. It was such a creative hive of industry."[11]

Communal dinners at the end of the day quickly became a habit that reinforced the team's cohesion.

A Haunted Album?

All the group needed was a few ghosts to come along and disturb studious January spent at the Château d'Hérouville. One night, Gus Dudgeon's sleep was disturbed by the apparition of a silhouette floating at the foot of his bed. He woke up his wife, Sheila, who was petrified by this vision. The next day, at breakfast, the couple were gently mocked by the rest of the team, but the teasing stopped over the coming evenings, when the others also witnessed the same troubling apparitions. The château is reputedly haunted by the spirits of George Sand and Frédéric Chopin. "It had a very strange vibe about it," Bernie said of the château. "It was beautiful and tranquil, but at the same time there were definitely some sort of ethereal things in the air around there." "It was haunted," believes Davey Johnstone. "Almost every day somebody would be tapped on the shoulder when they were walking down the giant staircase."[11] Naturally, the consumption of marijuana by the members of the group probably heightened their capacity to connect with the strange vibrations given out by the place, but Elton was relatively sober at that time. He only shared his colleagues' interest in the local viticulture: "The band were doing drugs…puffing," he said. "And we'd have a glass of wine. But we couldn't afford not to be reasonably clean-living. We were doing too much work,"[11] he explained.

Elton nonetheless pursued his daily routine, beguiled by the magic of the location. The configuration was decidedly idyllic: In the studio, he played his Steinway. He sometimes looked out of the huge windows, soothed by the bucolic charm of the Val-d'Oise countryside. These windows could remain open during listening sessions, noisily reproducing the group's energy without disturbing any neighbors. As the recording progressed, Elton felt increasingly relieved: The songs were so powerful that they would not need much symphonic input. This time, the album was taking a concerted turn in the direction of rock.

"There's times in my life when music has been an escape, the only thing that worked when everything else seemed broken, but at that moment I had nothing to escape from. I was twenty-four, successful, settled and in love [with John Reid]. What's more, tomorrow we had a day off and I was going to Paris, with every intention of absolutely *looting* the Yves Saint-Laurent store."[3]

At the end of their stay, delighted by the direction in which things had gone, Elton called his musicians together in the château dining room. During this final dinner, he made an announcement to them that was unheard of at the time: The singer was so pleased that he decided to offer them royalties on the future sales of *Honky Château*. This was the least he could offer them, he thought, as they had exceeded all of his expectations, and assimilated so well into the cohesive group that he'd wanted to put in place upon Davey Johnstone's arrival.

The English Patient

On his return to the United Kingdom, Elton had to stand by, powerless, as the "Tiny Dancer" single from the *Madman Across the Water* failed to launch, not managing to rise higher than forty-first place in the United States, and not even released in England. This did not dent his morale, however, as he was so invigorated by the idyllic month he'd just spent at Hérouville. At this point it was Gus's turn to act. He took the masters from the château sessions with him to Trident Studios to start the mixing; he recorded some overdubs, including some from David Hentschel and his memorable synthesizer on "Rocket Man," as well as an inspired team of backing vocalists on "Salvation"; Ray Cooper added some bongo touches on "Amy." Then there was another mammoth task, lasting several weeks: Polishing a definitive mix for what was to become a key work in Elton John's career. The weight of responsibility on Gus's

In April 1971, Elton played "Rocket Man" on *Top of the Pops*. Unfortunately, the video from this performance was destroyed and only a brief extract remains. Note the rare appearance of John Reid on acoustic guitar.

shoulders was enormous. But he was determined to produce a perfect result.

During this time, Elton rehearsed with Paul Buckmaster and a philharmonic orchestra ahead of a long-scheduled concert he was to give at the Royal Festival Hall in February. But the rehearsals, and the resulting concert, were not the best; the fault lay, according to Elton, with the patronizing orchestra. When the press was harshly critical of his performance and wondered why a pop artist would feel the need to invite the classical world to his table, Elton was furious that the orchestra did not really take the concert seriously, and he internally confirmed for himself that the more organic artistic choices he had made for *Honky Château* were the right direction for him to take.

Upon its release, *Honky Château* found immediate support. Reviews were unanimously in line with the summary of the disk that appeared in *Rolling Stone*'s August 17, 1972, issue: "Musically more varied, emotionally less contrived, lyrically more lucid than *Tumbleweed Connection*, *Château* rivals *Elton John* as his best work to date and evidences growth at every possible level."[74]

The public also agreed: *Honky Château* became Elton's first album to reach the number one spot on the charts in the United States, where it remained (in one spot or another) for over a year. In the United Kingdom, the album

stalled just before the summit and never went higher than the number two spot on the chart. But this was just a temporary delay. *Honky Château* set out a template and methodology that would be applied to Elton's next spate of albums, and it opened up a clear artistic path for the singer to follow. Boosted by the success of its single, "Rocket Man (I Think It's Gonna Be a Long, Long Time)," *Honky Château* was the first of seven consecutive albums by Elton to hit the top of the American charts. The rocket had definitely taken off, and the 1970s would have to hold on tight.

FOR ELTON ADDICTS

In 2003, *Honky Château* was ranked as the 357th best album of all time by *Rolling Stone*, as part of a list of the top 500 albums. In 2012, its position went down two spots to 359th. In 2020 the album jumped up considerably in the rankings, to 251st place.

Michel Magne (in the suit) equipped the production cabin with a Diffona radio console customized by Gérard Delassus (left).

HÉROUVILLE: A PLACE FILLED WITH MAGIC

Not far from Auvers-sur-Oise, a town located just over fifteen miles from Paris, lies the Château d'Hérouville, an imposing residence with fifty-seven rooms distributed over three wings, and known as the location of the love affair that took place between the poet George Sand and the composer Frédéric Chopin. The solemnity of the location and its Romanesque grandeur immediately captivated composer Michel Magne when he discovered the building in 1962. The composer, who achieved fame thanks to popular film scores he created for films like *A Monkey in Winter*, *The Great Spy Chase*, and *Crooks in Clover*, decided to invest some of his wealth in creating an exceptional recording studio for use by other musicians. In 1969 a terrible fire ravaged the left wing of the château and destroyed most of Magne's archives, but the composer, then aged thirty-nine, chose not to be discouraged and took his plans for the house even further. Over the years he had only restored the swimming pool, a tennis court, and a music room, but now he decided to face up to this twist of fate and to double down on his dream of making the house something truly special.

The Birth of a Myth

Major developments were undertaken in the right wing of the château, and soon a very advanced residential studio would attract the biggest names in international pop and rock. Elton John recorded three albums there, *Honky Château*, *Don't Shoot Me I'm Only the Piano Player*, and *Goodbye Yellow Brick Road*. Pink Floyd recharged its batteries there during the creation of *The Dark Side of the Moon*, and in the space of two weeks they recorded *Obscured by Clouds* there. Many others famous acts passed through, including David Bowie, the Bee Gees, T. Rex, Iggy Pop, Michel Polnareff, Jacques Higelin, Canned Heat, and

Marvin Gaye. The band Uriah Heep, in particular, caused the walls of this noble home to tremble. It was a seductive concept, because the genius of Michel Magne's idea was not confined to creating the best recording studios possible; it was also to offer them a real place of relaxation, freedom, and comfort, which could then lead to renewed creativity for the artists who stayed there.

At Hérouville all the food was provided by a chef, and the musicians slept in the same place where they ate and recorded. Michel Magne was ahead of his time, and over the next decade or so, residential studios became the norm. In his book, *Love of Life*, published in 1980, he was full of proud bravado when he recalled this period: "In Paris, they told me that no one would travel thirty kilometers to record in the middle of the countryside. Then people saw that American groups were crossing the Atlantic to come here."[51]

Furthermore, the immense George Sand studio that Magne erected had a magnificent acoustic quality. The young sound engineer that Magne brought on, a man named Blanc-Francard, learned the ropes there with diligence and talent. Although French artists were hardly queuing up to go there in the early days, English and American artists were the first to request bookings at the château, which also boasted a restful five acres of wooded parkland complete with a lake.

Canned Heat was among the first groups to go there, along with Buddy Guy and Memphis Slim. As visitors from the other side of the Atlantic, they became formidable ambassadors for the château. In 1971, it was the Grateful Dead's turn to provide some unexpected publicity for Michel Magne's property. Their performance at the Auvers-sur-Oise festival, not far away from the home, was canceled due to bad weather, and Jerry Garcia

Michel Magne poses in the large recording hall of the legendary Georges Sand Studio in 1970.

and his companions decided to give a private concert at the château for an audience of several hundred privileged guests. A few months later, the Stones' bassist, Bill Wyman, spent some of the summer there. In January 1972, when Elton John was looking for some peace and quiet, he chose to set himself up in Hérouville, which resulted in the appropriately titled *Honky Château*.

Problems Arise

Unfortunately, Michel Magne ended up falling victim to his own generosity. With a staff of fifteen or so, the fixed costs of running the home literally exploded within the space of a few years. It was always out of the question to scrimp on the level of service offered to the clients, and the food served to the guests was growing ever more impressive, while sumptuous celebrations became more frequent and the leisure facilities more numerous (a game room with a foosball table, a swimming pool, tennis courts, etc.), and there was only one solution left to the owner: to optimize the use of the property by constructing a second studio. Despite the financial investments made, the acoustics of the brand-new space, called the Chopin, were not on the same level as the George Sand. As such, it was often used by French artists while the Sand studio was reserved for English and American big fish. But Michel Magne mistakenly took his eye off of the accounting ball. In 1973, the revenue authorities demanded astronomical sums that were owed to them, while the bills began mounting at an alarming rate. Magne tried to find someone he could trust who might enable him to step back a little and devote himself once more to his chosen profession as a composer. The Davout studios manager, Yves Chamberland, ran the studios for a while, while Magne remained the owner of the property. To stem the hemorrhaging

of money, the new manager cut back in all areas. But the level of debt was much higher than it had seemed at first, and Chamberland withdrew along with all of his equipment. Hérouville was left abandoned in the winter of 1973. In June 1974, Laurent Thibault, cofounder of the group Magma and a former château client, took up the mantle and took charge of the studios. In the space of three months, the impossible became possible once more. The clients returned, with Bowie leading the charge when he came to record *Low* in 1977 with Tony Visconti at the controls. Visconti described his experiences at Hérouville in an interview with the French-language magazine *Rock First*. He called them some of the "strangest" of his career: "The château was haunted by George Sand and Chopin. Finally, in any case, we were persuaded," he explained in the 2011 interview. "We were recording Bowie's album, *Low*, and Brian Eno was woken up every night by someone tapping him on the shoulder. But when he opened his eyes, there was no one there...The master bedroom was very dark and cold. Suddenly, Bowie decided he didn't like it, so I was the one who inherited it. I never felt at ease there. I always had the impression that I was been watched by someone, or something."[77] That year, 1977, the Bee Gees went to the château where they recorded six tracks for the legendary *Saturday Night Fever* soundtrack. Despite this resumption of activity, the château was once again on the edge of financial ruin. Eventually, the château was sold in the summer of 1979 to a property developer for 1.4 million francs—a modest sum, given the nature and history of the property. Laurent Thibault, who continued to run the studios for a while, finally threw in the towel in 1985.

Michel Magne never really recovered from the loss of his pride and joy. He died of a drug overdose in 1984.

HONKY CAT

Elton John, Bernie Taupin / 5:13

Musicians

Elton John: vocals, Fender Rhodes, piano
Dee Murray: bass
Nigel Olsson: drums
Davey Johnstone: banjo
Jacques Bolognesi: trombone
Jean-Louis Chautemps: saxophone
Alain Hatot: saxophone
Ivan Jullien: trumpet
Gus Dudgeon: arrangements, direction

Recorded

Château d'Hérouville, Hérouville, France: January 1972

Technical Team

Producer: Gus Dudgeon
Sound Engineer: Ken Scott
Production Coordinator: Steve Brown

Single Release

Honky Cat / Slave
 US Release: July 31, 1972, on Uni Records (ref. 55343)
 Best US Chart Ranking: 8
Honky Cat / Lady Samantha / It's Me That You Need
 UK Release: August 25, 1972, on DJM Records (ref. DJS.269)
 Best UK Chart Ranking: 31

"Honky Cat" is a play on words that will be obvious to any native French speaker. In French the English word *cat* is spelled "chat," which calls back to the album's title.

Genesis and Lyrics

In the first song of this new opus, Bernie returns once more with a great leap into the unknown, discussing how he felt when he left his native countryside for the magnetism of London. The writer's lyrics, which are much more direct than on previous albums, resonate with his own trajectory: "fishing in a stream / Looking for an answer, trying to find a sign / Until I saw your city lights, honey, I was blind." He is this "Honky Cat," this "redneck"—or "bumpkin"—struggling to find his way in the city, and who strangers encourage to return to his backwater hometown in the extensive refrain. But he will do nothing of the sort!

Production

On the fourth day of the recording sessions, having completed "Susie (Dramas)," "Salvation," and "Amy," the group relaxed with "Honky Cat," a number with a syncopated rhythm that's full of spontaneity and very much inspired by the musical scene of New Orleans (which is also referenced in the second verse). For this number, the services of a quartet of French musicians were called upon: the trombonist Jacques Bolognesi; trumpeter Ivan Jullien, a member of the Paris Jazz All Stars who accompanied Johnny Hallyday when he worked with Joey and the Showmen in 1964; and saxophonists Alain Hatot and Jean-Louis Chautemps, who played with Sidney Bechet and Django Reinhardt. With contributors of such an illustrious pedigree on board and given the usual band members' collective experience with stage performance, Gus Dudgeon felt that the best way to take advantage of the forces present was to have them play live. But while he knew he had the right formula, recording under these conditions was a real gamble. In fact, the studio's configuration did not enable each instrument to be isolated, and, fatally, the microphones arranged around the piano picked up the sounds of the other instruments. Gus could not therefore process the individual sounds of each instrument because they were being drowned out by surrounding sounds. So he resorted to drastic remedies: The team called on the services of a carpenter, who created a wooden casing around the shape of the piano with holes on each side to accommodate microphones. In this way, once the piano was placed in the middle of the rhythm section, the microphones picked up only the lower spectrum of the bass

and the kick drum, which made Gus Dudgeon's work much easier. All that remained left to do was to carry out the recording of the vocals, which Elton John performed with the sound on his headphones dialed up as loud as possible. Despite this sonar magma in his ears, which was almost deafening so that it could better simulate the aura of a live recording, the singer delivered a track that was perfect in every respect…and he did it in one take.

Davey Johnstone (shown here in 1976), has played alongside Elton John for over fifty years.

THE MULTITALENTED DAVEY JOHNSTONE

On October 1, 2019, during a stay in Saskatoon, Saskatchewan, in Canada, a stop on the "Farewell Yellow Brick Road Tour," Davey Johnstone celebrated playing his three thousandth concert alongside Elton John. The two men knew what they owed to Gus Dudgeon, who had introduced them to each other and who insisted on the singer allowing Davey to take part in the recording of *Madman Across the Water*.

Davey Johnstone was born on May 6, 1951, in Edinburgh, Scotland. After playing the violin from the ages of seven to eleven, he discovered the guitar—a present from his sister—which then became his preferred instrument. At the end of the 1960s, he joined the folk group Magna Carta, with whom he recorded two albums: *Seasons* (1970) and *Songs from Wasties Orchard* (1971). It was while recording the second of these albums that he got to know Gus Dudgeon, who was working in the control room at the studio. Thanks to Dudgeon's efforts, Johnstone became a member of Elton's inner circle, and also added some guitar chords to *Taupin*, Bernie's poetry album. As part of Gus's talent pool of session musicians, Johnstone had the opportunity to work on *Madman Across the Water* in 1971. Initially, he was considered to be a member of the rock 'n' roll section of the band. But his versatility, inventiveness, and irreproachable technique did their work, and the musician soon established himself as an essential cog in Elton John's system.

In 1972, Elton unilaterally decided to include him in his group. He took him to France for the recording of *Honky Château* in January. On February 5, 1972, Davey performed for the first time in public alongside Elton and his group at the Royal Festival Hall in London. "The first concert we did was at the Royal Festival Hall. Half [of] it was with an orchestra conducted by the late, great, amazing Paul Buckmaster. I played on both halves of the shows. Playing with the orchestra was a lot of fun and just insane. [...] I remember thinking, 'God, what am I doing up here? I'm not any kind of rock star. I'm a folk guitar player, basically, who plugged in and came up with some guitar parts.'"[75]

A Brother in Arms

Initially reticent, Dee Murray and Nigel Olsson quickly realized that Davey's presence in the group was a privilege. Despite the premature loss of Dee Murray, the trio that Davey and Nigel formed with Elton became a historical triangle that was the bedrock for Elton's greatest works. An enhanced musical cohesion was reinforced by an understanding that went beyond friendship, particularly with the bassist. "Dee and I were 'brothers' and that's never changed, even though he's long gone [Dee died in 1992]. I miss him every day,"[76] Johnstone said in 2019. As time went on, he established himself as Elton's right hand. Loyal above all others, he was never absent when Elton needed him, except during periods of inactivity when he took time out to perform onstage with Stevie Nicks, or to grapple with the hard rock of Meat Loaf and Alice Cooper. His fate must seem strange when one thinks that Gus Dudgeon had initially questioned the wisdom of hiring him. He doubted Davey could hack it due to his almost exclusively acoustic background. With sporadic studio engagements for artists like Olivia Newton-John (*The Rumour* in 1988), Rod Stewart (*A Spanner in the Works* in 1995), and Rick Astley (*Portrait* in 2005), he allowed himself only limited time for personal projects, which were limited to a solo album in 1973, *Smiling Face*. The album was released on Elton's label, the Rocket Record Company. He also worked on side projects with groups that never came to anything, such as China (with Roger Pope), and Warpipes (with Nigel Olsson). These were mostly meant as leisure activities, never taking priority over his relationship with Elton.

MELLOW

Elton John, Bernie Taupin / 5:33

Musicians

Elton John: vocals, Hammond organ, piano
Davey Johnstone: electric guitar
Dee Murray: bass
Nigel Olsson: drums, tambourine
Jean-Luc Ponty: violin

Recorded

Château d'Hérouville, Hérouville, France: January 1972

Technical Team

Producer: Gus Dudgeon
Sound Engineer: Ken Scott
Production Coordinator: Steve Brown

When he happened upon an album by Jean-Luc Ponty, Elton (shown here in 1972) called and asked him to collaborate.

Genesis and Lyrics

The amorous passion between Bernie Taupin and Maxine Feibelman, who had been married for less than a year, had not yet eroded (they separated in 1976), and their romantic life quite logically permeated the writer's lyrics, whose penchant for gravity and esoterism seemed to fade as more albums were produced. Having previously plunged into his deepest torments, and manipulated concepts by enveloping them in mysticism, he could now become ecstatic in front of the drawing of a nose, the curve of a toe, evoking the pleasure of diving back under the sheets when the rain is beating down outside, and even going to the shops…The writer finds new life in the evocation of ordinary things, and delights in introducing trivial elements into his poetry. The flow of the phrases itself also radically changed: shorter, more impactful, they seem more musical, particularly with this alternation of one rhyme with the other between the rounded vowels in "mellow" or "toes" and front vowels, as in "fine" or "time."

Production

To open up his mind to other musical territories and to stimulate his inspiration, the musician who usually arrived at the studio without a tune in his pocket (Elton) packed a huge pile of vinyls in his luggage. Among the offerings was the audacious album *King Kong* by the French violinist Jean-Luc Ponty, which was produced in 1970 by Frank Zappa and consisted of reworkings of songs by Frank Zappa. When he learned that the Frenchman was staying near Hérouville, he invited him to contribute on "Amy" and "Mellow." The latter, a smooth, midtempo ballad, has a simple and easily-to-follow structure, with piano and voice sections that are inspired by gospel sounds, and in which an almost funk bass note gradually crystallizes. But the song needed a catalyst to give it some bounce, and Jean-Luc Ponty's violon fit the bill perfectly. "It was a beautiful song, very inspiring to play on," recalled the violinist. "I forget who suggested I plug my violin into the Hammond organ, but I agreed and it worked great. I had tried this before with Eddy Louiss, who was a great organ player, and he knew how the organ should sound. I think I handled it really well by using a few violinistic expressions such as sliding notes that cannot be played on an organ, mixed with a more typical organ phrasing."[70]

I THINK I'M GOING TO KILL MYSELF

Elton John, Bernie Taupin / 3:35

Musicians
Elton John: vocals, piano
Davey Johnstone: acoustic guitar, backing vocals
Dee Murray: bass, backing vocals
Nigel Olsson: drums, backing vocals
Larry Smith: taps

Recorded
Château d'Hérouville, Hérouville, France: January 1972

Technical Team
Producer: Gus Dudgeon
Sound Engineer: Ken Scott
Production Coordinator: Steve Brown

Genesis and Lyrics

Composed straight after the transcendent and interplanetary classic "Rocket Man," "I Think I'm Going to Kill Myself" is that song's exact opposite, and it's both tragic and comical. In it, Bernie makes fun of an adolescent who complains about not being able to use the family car, having to be home by ten o'clock, being bored all the time, and asking himself, in passing, about how much space the newspapers would allocate to covering a depressed adolescent's suicide. The young narrator can only think of one thing that could possibly dissuade him from following through on his fatal plan: nightly visits from Brigitte Bardot!

Production

A saloon ambiance takes center stage on "I Think I'm Going to Kill Myself," mainly thanks to Elton's honky-tonk piano and his singing, which is done with a cheerful and communicative spirit even though the song is about such a dark topic. In this way, Elton cleverly holds on to the tragicomical message delivered by Bernie. After all, this is a song about a crabby adolescent who hardly seems credible in his intentions, except perhaps for a furtive touch of melancholy that shines through in the bride. Dee Murray's rounded, springing bass is one of the great attractions of the piece, with the taps provided by Larry "Legs" Smith, the drummer with the Bonzo Dog Doo-Dah Band, who experienced a moment of glory at the end of the 1960s when he played the number "Death Cab for Cutie" at the end of the Beatles film *Magical Mystery Tour*. Smith was so pleased to have been called upon by Gus Dudgeon to appear on the album (albeit not to play drums), that he brought his own piece of wood to use for the recording of his tap dancing part. "He danced his ass off. It went down a storm,"[31] Gus commented later.

Drummer Larry Smith and the Bonzo Dog Doo-Dah Band were a comedy rock group put together by art school students.

SUSIE (DRAMAS)

Elton John, Bernie Taupin / 3:25

Musicians
Elton John: vocals, piano
Davey Johnstone: electric guitar
Dee Murray: bass
Nigel Olsson: drums, tambourine
Recorded
Château d'Hérouville, Hérouville, France: January 1972
Technical Team
Producer: Gus Dudgeon
Sound Engineer: Ken Scott
Production Coordinator: Steve Brown

Davey Johnstone specialized in acoustic guitar and he recorded an electric-guitar solo for the first time on "Susie (Dramas)."

Genesis and Lyrics

As with "I Think I'm Going to Kill Myself," Bernie's lyrics center around the life of an adolescent. Blissful in admiration before the beautiful Susie, who "[lives] with her funky family," he is not fooled by her; he is aware that she "sure knows how to use me" and that she plays "hooky with my heart all the time." But he contents himself with enjoying every moment he can spend in her company, as he considers that he is not good enough for her. His greatest happiness is when he can strut by the side of "pretty little black-eyed Suzie" or go down by the river, where the two adolescents can "share a little loving in the moonshine." In simple language, he even considers that he is "the hit of the county fair." It would be tempting to think that the song alludes to the one by Guy Mitchell, "Pretty Little Black-Eyed Susie," but this is probably a coincidence. As there is also reference to a Susie in "Crocodile Rock," it is possible she might have been one of the first of the discreet Bernie Taupin's girlfriends.

Production

Naturally, there is an enjoyable honky-tonk piano played by Elton, who is also very expressive in his singing throughout the track. The very solid and funky rhythm section provided by the Dee Murray–Nigel Olsson duo also stands out, sticking like glue to the singer's slightest breath intake. But the real star of "Susie" is Davey Johnstone's psychedelic guitar, given a slight tremolo, which seems to owe as much to Frank Zappa as it does to Johnny Winter. For him, this was his first attempt at an electric guitar solo, as Gus Dudgeon explains with amusement: "When he hit the first note and this sound leapt out of his amplifier, he nearly fell over. It's a very structured solo because he just didn't know how to do a free solo…Davey was an acoustic guitarist, not an electric guitarist, and this was the first solo he had ever had to play."[31]

A slight diplomatic incident did, however, pull the group up short at the end of the recording. To congratulate Elton, Gus called out to him: "Really superb tune, Reg."

"Elton's face darkened," David John DeCouto recounted in 2018. "He bit his lip, pushed his glasses up his nose, and left the room without a word. Everyone looked at each other, mystified. A few minutes later, John Reid came into the control room and sat Gus and the rest of the band down. 'Listen guys, can you just call him Elton from now on? No more Reg. Just Elton, okay?'"[31]

ROCKET MAN (I THINK IT'S GOING TO BE A LONG, LONG TIME)

Elton John, Bernie Taupin / 4:42

Musicians
Elton John: vocals, piano
Davey Johnstone: electric and acoustic guitars, backing vocals
Dee Murray: bass, backing vocals
Nigel Olsson: drums, backing vocals
David Hentschel: ARP synthesizer

Recorded
Château d'Hérouville, Hérouville (France): January 1972

Technical Team
Producer: Gus Dudgeon
Sound Engineer: Ken Scott
Production Coordinator: Steve Brown

Single Release
Rocket Man / Holiday Inn; Goodbye
UK Release: April 17, 1972, on DJM Records (ref. DJX 501)
Best UK Chart Ranking: 2
Rocket Man / Susie (Dramas) [spelled Suzie on the single]
US Release: April 17, 1972, on Uni Records (ref. 55328)
Best US Chart Ranking: 6

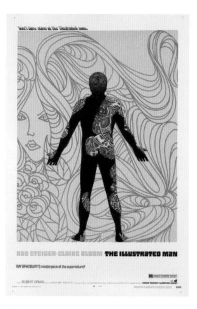

The Illustrated Man, a collection of science-fiction stories by Ray Bradbury, inspired Bernie to write "Rocket Man."

Genesis and Lyrics

After two days devoted to balancing the sound system, which required the expertise of Gus Dudgeon and Nigel Olsson and therefore give the other musicians plenty of free time for reading or visiting the grounds of Hérouville, the desire to begin their creative work was at its peak. On the third day, after a breakfast ingested in haste, Elton John sat at his piano and perused the lyrics of "Rocket Man," which Bernie had started to write a week earlier while still in England, but which he had finalized and typed up on his typewriter the previous evening. It was Maxine's job to place the lyrics on the piano in the small hours of the morning, while her writer husband was sleeping off a long night's work. Elton lingered over the text of "Rocket Man," which describes a spaceman setting off for Mars, who is gripped by the anguish of being separated from his loved ones, and the great solitude awaiting him during this "long, long" voyage.

Despite being similar in subject matter with David Bowie's classic "Space Oddity," which had a huge influence on Elton, Bernie's inspiration for "Rocket Man" came from the psychedelic folk group Pearls Before Swine, and a song they released on their 1970 album, *The Use of Ashes.* Its composer, Tom Rapp, was himself inspired by a Ray Bradbury novel, *The Illustrated Man,* that first appeared in 1951. The fascination with space had occupied Rapp's imagination since he was very young, when he lived close to the Kennedy Space Center in Cape Canaveral. As a child, he was very excited whenever a rocket was launched into the sky. His "Rocket Man" was written on the same day that Neil Armstrong stepped onto the moon, on July 21, 1969. However, the difference between Rapp's song, which takes the viewpoint of a mother and her child who don't know what has happened to their missing husband and father, Bernie takes the perspective of the man who goes to space. Moreso than the intoxication of going into orbit, it is the crushing feeling of isolation that takes hold of the narrator even as the rousing music seems to suggest a state of euphoria.

While Bernie very willingly acknowledges the inspiration he took from the Pearls Before Swine version of "Rocket Man," he explained that the idea had taken shape in his mind upon seeing a shooting star crossing the sky when he was returning from a dinner with his parents. The first phrases describing

According to Bernie, "Rocket Man" was written on July 21, 1969, the same day that Neil Armstrong stepped onto the moon.

a spaceman heading out on scientific mission also came to him straightaway: "She packed my bags last night pre-flight / Zero hour nine a.m."—but he had nothing with him that he could use to write them down. As soon as he got out of the car, he rushed in the house and asked that no one speak to him before he had got his ideas down on paper, conscious that what he had was a brilliant subject worth exploring further—mainly, the story of a man who's lost, alone, and cut off from the world; a "rocket man," for sure, but also Elton John.

A Monumental Recording

He had scarcely begun to peruse Bernie's lyrics when Elton already had his hands on the keyboard, rotating between a sequence of chords: Gm9, and then C9. It took him no more than ten minutes to complete the melody of what would become one of the great songs in his repertoire. While the other musicians finished eating, Elton John finalized two more songs, "Mona Lisas and Mad Hatters" and "Amy," to the great astonishment of newcomer Davey Johnstone. Unlike his colleagues, Davey was not yet used to the singer's explosive creativity and work ethic. As Elton would later testify in his autobiography: "Once Davey had been convinced that this

wasn't an elaborate prank at the expense of the new boy, that I really had written three songs while he was having a lie-in, he picked up his guitar and asked me to play 'Rocket Man' again. He didn't add a solo or do anything that a regular lead guitar player might do. He used a slide and played odd, lonely notes that drifted around and away from the melody. It was great."[3]

While the tune set out by Elton in the piano-voice combination already exudes a gentle perfume of timelessness, combining majesty and melancholy, Dee Murray's intervention on bass lays down the foundations for its grandeur with a very melodic play for this rhythm instrument. The drums come in with subtle contributions on the cymbal, before taking control of the refrain itself, giving the signal for take-off with a crash cymbal strike. This solar refrain exudes a rapture equivalent to the one that runs through "Tiny Dancer," opening up a luxurious soundscape with the four acoustic guitars, with their open tuning chords added by Davey in the overdubs. This dimension also owes a great deal to the backing vocals, which give the piece an incredible breadth. It was Gus Dudgeon, already familiar with this kind of thing on "Space Oddity," who suggested that the three musicians—Nigel, Dee, and Davey—should take charge of the vocal harmonies. Initially

In 2017, the Iranian refugee and filmmaker Majid Adin revisited *Rocket Man* on the occasion of a competition called The Cut, which was organized by YouTube and Elton John. The idea was to provide video clips for three of his biggest successes released at the beginning of the 1970s: "Tiny Dancer," "Rocket Man," and "Bennie and the Jets." Regarding "Rocket Man," which evokes the great solitude of an astronaut on a "long, long" voyage in space, the winner transposed the journey of an Iranian refugee separated from his family onto the song, discovering a different world (in England) rather than in outer space.

On October 30, 1972, Elton John performed several numbers from *Honky Château* at the London Palladium.

he placed the three men around a single microphone. But he quickly realized that he would get nowhere with this configuration. "It's like trying to take a trombone, a triangle and a bloody string bass and...get a balance. [...] The three of them had totally different types of singing voices. Nigel's voice is really high, he can hit those top notes really great but he doesn't have a lot of middle or bottom energy in his voice. Davey...has quite a husky voice and doesn't have a lot

of energy. Dee has just pure energy, and no top and no bottom."[31] After a couple of hours lost trying to get them to sing with the same voice level around a single microphone, Gus chose to give them a microphone each, which enabled him to process each voice separately. For Dee, he positioned a microphone behind him, as the bassist had to lean forward, almost singing between his legs to hit the highest notes. In order to achieve the futuristic and space aspect of the number, an

ARP synthesizer was added at around 2:20, during the mixing phase, at Trident Studios. As he was not so comfortable using synthesizers, Elton left this part to the studio engineer.

The result exceeded their expectations. Elton, first of all, could not contain his enthusiasm and attachment for this song: "The first huge single that I had. 'Your Song' was a hit; 'Rocket Man' was a big hit. It had an acoustic guitar on it, it was a different song for me—it was a simpler sound."[5]

The whole team was then conscious of having created a song with an exceptional destiny. Having reached the top of the charts, reaching second place in the United Kingdom by April 22, 1972, and sixth place on the American *Billboard* chart dated July 15, "Rocket Man" established itself in the pantheon of pop for decades to come. As a mark of great songs, it even gave Elton his nickname, as was the case later with "Material Girl" by Madonna.

SALVATION

Elton John, Bernie Taupin / 3:59

Musicians
Elton John: vocals, piano
Davey Johnstone: electric guitar and backing vocals
Dee Murray: bass and backing vocals
Nigel Olsson: drums and backing vocals
Madeline Bell, Larry Steel, Liza Strike, Tony Hazzard: backing vocals

Recorded
Château d'Hérouville, Hérouville, France: January 1972

Technical Team
Producer: Gus Dudgeon
Sound Engineer: Ken Scott
Production Coordinator: Steve Brown

Madeline Bell is an American singer who did backing vocals for Elton John and who also had a number 3 hit in the UK with the pop group Blue Mink.

Genesis and Lyrics

Following Elton John's slight vexation about the use of his former baptismal name, which chilled the atmosphere somewhat at the end of the recording of "Susie (Dramas)," the good mood was back once more, and the dark cloud dispersed as quickly as it had arrived. The team turned its attention to "Salvation," on which they had based all their hopes. Following the first attempts, everyone agreed that it had the makings of a single—even more so than "Rocket Man." All the ingredients were there, starting with the spirit of fraternity in the lyrics, launched by an ecumenical "I have to say my friends / This road goes a long, long way." Elton launches into what seems like a sermon on life and the need for us to help one another, delivered with an ardor suitable for gospel. Bernie thus seems to be calling up distant memories of childhood sermons heard with a distracted ear during interminable Sunday morning Masses. Its words, beyond the aspects of personal memory, touch the universality of those of the Beatles, as in "With a Little Help from My Friends."

Production

Starting with an *E-B-A-E* sequence, the piano settles into a sugary torpor, from which it is uprooted by the bass at 0:18, when it arrives in a high register, once again demonstrating the very melodic playing of Dee Murray. In a rather academic but effective way, Nigel Olsson follows Elton's rise toward the refrain. Davey Johnstone, by means of a gimmick landing on a *G#*, which guides the ensemble toward a change of key, infuses a scent of the unexpected in this very effective but linear construction. The backing vocals, although electrifying, rapidly descend into a gospel caricature, overly emphasizing the text: "Salvation spreads the gospel 'round." The doubled guitars played with bottleneck illuminate the end of the refrain before the backwash of the second verse. Then while the sound space is saturated, the horizon opens up, when Elton John is once more on his own, giving the second verse a charm of which the first was deprived. Despite its obvious qualities, the piece left the group feeling it was missing something. They rightly preferred "Rocket Man" as the lead-off single from the album.

SLAVE

Elton John, Bernie Taupin / 4:20

Musicians
Elton John: vocals
Davey Johnstone: acoustic guitar, pedal steel guitar, mandolin, banjo
Dee Murray: bass
Nigel Olsson: congas, drums
Recorded
Château d'Hérouville, Hérouville, France: January 1972
Technical Team
Producer: Gus Dudgeon
Sound Engineer: Ken Scott
Production Coordinator: Steve Brown

FOR ELTON ADDICTS

In 1995, Gus Dudgeon remastered *Honky Château* for rerelease in CD format. He added a bonus track: the up-tempo, rock 'n' roll version of "Slave" that had been put aside in favor of the LP version. This alternative version was originally going to be released as the B-side on the unreleased single "Hercules."

Genesis and Lyrics

Carried along by the piano bar–like atmosphere of "Honky Cat," the group was in a euphoric mood when they launched into a mind-blowing and helter-skelter version of "Slave." Elton John brings out the Mick Jagger that previously lay dormant within him, and Johnstone, Murray, and Olsson finish the song in a deluge of sound. Once the euphoria had passed, the musicians listened again to the recording and opted to do a second take. Clearly this rock frenzy did not fit with the concept of the song as imagined by Bernie Taupin. It was about a Black slave living just before the Civil War, in 1860. "Driven by a man with a bull-whip in his hand," the man chooses to rise up against his masters and calls upon the other slaves to rise up with him: "Oh we've got to free our brothers from their shackles if we can." While the violence is expressed bluntly in the lyrics—"I swear one day I'm gonna burn that whore house to the ground"—the musicians agreed that the music should be more controlled, so that the message would get across with even more force. Thus, their rollicking first take was shelved.

Production

Elton suggested that Davey take the song in hand and imbue it with his precise and evocative musicianship. Unusually, Elton decided to forgo his piano and to focus on the vocals, which still had elements of the Stones, as well as specs of the dusty and wild country music sound produced during the *Exile on Main St.* sessions. In fact, Davey brought out all his country music equipment for the occasion: mandolin, banjo, and steel guitar, and he proceeded to create the deepest-South, swampiest sound possible, following Elton's instructions. This version, which would not have been out of place on *Tumbleweed Connection*, met with universal approval.

AMY

Elton John, Bernie Taupin / 4:03

Musicians
Elton John: vocals, piano
Davey Johnstone: electric guitar, backing vocals
Dee Murray: bass, backing vocals
Nigel Olsson: drums, backing vocals
Ray Cooper: congas
Jean-Luc Ponty: violin

Recorded
Château d'Hérouville, Hérouville, France: January 1972

Technical Team
Producer: Gus Dudgeon
Sound Engineer: Ken Scott
Production Coordinator: Steve Brown

1972

Jean-Luc Ponty makes his electric violin sing on "Amy."

Genesis and Lyrics

With his characteristic efficiency, on the very first morning of work, Elton John polished off three new compositions with very different profiles: "Rocket Man," "Mona Lisas and Mad Hatters" and "Amy." Against the majesty of the first two songs, he contrasted the obvious blues effect combined with the affected airs of "Ballad of a Well-Known Gun." And with the solitude of a spaceman and neo–New Yorker, he contrasted the emotional dependency of a young man on a dominating woman. In doing this, Taupin dissociates himself from the sexist discourse that was common in the rock scene of his contemporaries, where the woman, the object of desire, is dominated by the man. The Amy in the song is a woman admired by all, and the narrator, who is young and inexperienced, assesses the distance that separates them: "You're far out, you're fab and insane / A woman of the world, it's quite plain." Ready to subject himself to all manner of torture ("Tread on my face if you like little lady"), the narrator ignores the advice of his friends.

According to Claude Bernardin, co-author of *Rocket Man: Elton John from A–Z*, the sadomasochistic love reading of the text is not correct: "According to Producer and former personal assistant Stuart Epps, this song lyrically is a joke to Elton and Gus Dudgeon's wife Sheila. It was her nickname. And apparently, she was not always keen on 'Elton' thus the teasing lines 'so if you don't want me around…and to you I'm an infection…' After the album's release Gus bought her a sports car with that name on the license plate."[72]

Production

When entering the walls of Château d'Hérouville, Jean-Luc Ponty knew very little about his host for the day. While Elton John had called upon his services, Ponty knew of him only by reputation. He quickly realized onstage that the singer's reputation was fully justified. He had the same effect on Elton, who confessed a boundless admiration for the violinist's empirical approach. Jean-Luc Ponty, enthused, agreed to take on the solos in "Amy," appearing at 1:40 and at 3:30. This enabled Elton to avoid a stock electric guitar solo. On top of this, the violinist's fiery and plaintive playing, particularly with the double-stopping in the finale, provided a marvelous illustration of the sense of frustration expressed in the lyrics.

MONA LISAS AND MAD HATTERS

Elton John, Bernie Taupin / 5:01

Musicians
Elton John: vocals, piano
Davey Johnstone: acoustic guitar, mandolin
Dee Murray: bass

Recorded
Château d'Hérouville, Hérouville, France: January 1972

Technical Team
Producer: Gus Dudgeon
Sound Engineer: Ken Scott
Production Coordinator: Steve Brown

FOR ELTON ADDICTS

Like "Tiny Dancer," "Mona Lisas and Mad Hatters" was also featured in the movie *Almost Famous*. It was used to illustrate the solitude of the groupie played by Kate Hudson, who takes an overdose at a hotel in New York City.

Elton has often said that "Mona Lisas and Mad Hatters" is one of his favorite songs out of his whole repertoire and probably one of the most underrated. It is probably for this reason that a sequel with the understated title "Mona Lisas and Mad Hatters (Part Two)" was released sixteen years later, on the album *Reg Strikes Back*. With a faster tempo and more complex arrangement, once again it makes New York the arena of Bernie's disillusionment.

Genesis and Lyrics

The poignant ballad "Mona Lisas and Mad Hatters" was written by Bernie after his first visit to New York in 1970. During this visit, a particular event had a striking impact on him: a shot was fired near the window of his hotel. A common scene for the inhabitants of New York, but one that made a sufficient impression on the young British lyricist for him to seek by means of his pen to release himself from this traumatizing memory. He was in part inspired by "Spanish Harlem," a piece written by Jerry Leiber and Phil Spector in 1960, in which it is suggested metaphorically that a rose grew in the notoriously violent district of Harlem. Ben E. King recorded it and had his first post-Drifters success with it. Accounting for his own mixed experience of the Big Apple, Bernie directly referenced the song by writing, "And now I know / Spanish Harlem are not just pretty words to say / I thought I knew / But now I know that rose trees never grow in New York City."

Production

In order to stay true to the melancholy heart of Bernie's lyrics, a minimalist arrangement was given precedence: With a full, warm acoustic guitar and a very beautiful line played by the mandolin, Davey Johnstone was in his usual folk garden, illuminating the melody crafted by Elton John the same morning as "Rocket Man" and "Amy." The piano was tracked by the versatile Dee Murray, who graciously contented himself with playing the basic bass line. Elton's vocal performance is remarkable on several counts: Throughout the song he is animated by this "soft power" that enables him to pick out high notes without ever giving the impression of forcing. There is a slight rising vibrato, which, without telegraphing the ends of certain phrases, adds a little more emotion to the interpretation, as in the final note descending into the lower register with a disconcerting ease and precision. Unlike the other pieces in the album where the backing singers are credited, the liner notes for "Mona Lisas and Mad Hatters" do not mention anyone. However, there is a second voice that supports Elton in the refrain, and it is...also Elton's! His own voice was used as a backing vocal.

HERCULES

Elton John, Bernie Taupin / 5:21

Musicians

Elton John: vocals, piano
Davey Johnstone: acoustic guitar, electric guitar, backing vocals
Dee Murray: bass, backing vocals
Nigel Olsson: drums, backing vocals
Gus Dudgeon: rhinoceros noises
David Hentschel: ARP synthesizer
Gus Dudgeon, Tony Hazzard: backing vocals

Recorded

Château d'Hérouville, Hérouville, France: January 1972

Technical Team

Producer: Gus Dudgeon
Sound Engineer: Ken Scott
Production Coordinator: Steve Brown

Hercules, the horse featured in the British series *Steptoe and Son* (1962), inspired the singer's new middle name.

Genesis and Lyrics

"Hercules" is probably the closest thing to a rock song on *Honky Château*. Like "Salvation," it was once considered as a single for the album. Various interpretations of the lyrics have been cited over time: Was this once again a song of adolescent obsession for an inaccessible woman and an impossible relationship? Was it a nod in the direction of the singer's residence in Virginia Water, Surrey, on the front door of which was inscribed the word *Hercule* (without an *s*)? Or does the song refer, quite simply, to Reg's change in name, since he had recently, and officially, become Elton Hercules John on January 7, 1972. Most people tend to think that the third hypothesis is the strongest. In 1974, during a BBC television broadcast of *Russell Harty Plus Pop*, Elton confided that he had a thing about the horse Hercules in the sitcom *Steptoe and Son*, to such an extent that he adopted the horse's name for himself. Ten years later, he confirmed at a concert given in Australia that "Hercules" did indeed refer to his change of name. Confusingly, the notes in the 1995 edition of *Honky Château* suggest that the song was about a rhinoceros...hence the rhinoceros noises added to the song by Gus Dudgeon.

Production

"Hercules" principally owes its propulsive energy to Dee's springing bass. Effectively, this is what instills the rock 'n' roll spirit in the piece, ably followed up by Nigel's disciplined drums. Davey's acoustic guitars are doubled in the stereo spectrum, thereby giving the song greater depth but also relegating Elton's piano to second fiddle. The function of the piano is basically rhythmic and nothing more, until his fiery solo at the end of the piece. The guitar solo played by Davey also has a central role in "Hercules" while responding to Gus Dudgeon, who indulges himself by adding rhinoceros noises using a whistle. Another strong point in the song: the backing vocals, which were initially provided by the Johnstone-Murray-Olsson trio. Their "doo-wop" and sixties pop intonation, which is not unlike the Beach Boys, was preserved while Gus Dudgeon and Tony Hazzard also contributed their own backing to reinforce the collegial aspect of "Hercules," ending the album on a friendly note.

ALBUM

DON'T SHOOT ME I'M ONLY THE PIANO PLAYER

Daniel . Teacher I Need You . Elderberry Wine . Blues for My Baby and Me .
Midnight Creeper . Have Mercy on the Criminal . I'm Going to Be a Teenage Idol .
Texan Love Song . Crocodile Rock . High Flying Bird

RELEASE DATES
UK Release: January 26, 1973
Reference: DJM Records—DJLPH 427
Best UK Chart Ranking: 1
US Release: January 22, 1973
Reference: MCA Records—MCT0 2100
Best US Chart Ranking: 1

Elton John, Marc Bolan, and Ringo Starr appeared at a promotional event for the film *Born to Boogie* in 1972.

HEAD IN THE STARS

On April 27, 1972, Elton and his group were in Houston preparing for a performance when the capsule that was bringing the Apollo 16 team back to Earth was scheduled to land. NASA invited the musicians to be present for the landing at the space center. They even had the privilege of dining with Al Worden, the pilot of NASA's previous space mission, Apollo 15; and they were also allowed to try out a space flight simulator.

1973

THE CREATIVE FLAME

From life at the Château d'Hérouville, to the princely existence at his own villa, Hercule, in Surrey, Elton John adapted marvelously well to his newly comfortable existence. Following the *Honky Château* recording sessions, the hope of British pop, who had worked doggedly on his first five albums, took advantage of the comfort of his new home, which he shared with John Reid, his partner and future manager. A large swimming pool, and a mini soccer pitch were the main attractions of this delightful haven of peace. As a perfect embodiment of the nouveau riche, Elton curated an eclectic collection of electronic devices in his home, including pinball machines and more, which stood alongside priceless works of art by Andy Warhol and Rembrandt. He also had some very luxurious and glitzy cars lined up in the driveway, including a Ferrari, a Rolls-Royce, an Aston Martin, and a Bentley. Clearly comfortable with extravagance, the singer was no less generous to those who were close to him. To his cousin Ray Dwight, who wanted to open a clothing shop, he gave £12,000. To his mother he gave an MG (Morris Garages) sports car and a three-bedroom house near Ickenham, in the suburbs of London—his own new house was also located just outside of London. He also gave his mother a magnificent wedding present when she married the likable Derf in May 1972, thereby adopting the name of Farebrother and finally dropping the name of Dwight, which was loaded down with unhappy memories. Sheila's name change happened just a few months after Elton had officially become Elton Hercules John for the purposes of the civil register. It was a point of honor for Elton to sign his mother's marriage certificate as a witness using his newly legal name.

New Friendships

The singer also took care of his circle of friends, which expanded proportionally with his fame. He added numerous stars of the music world to his sphere, who came to enjoy the hedonism of the wild parties that were thrown at villa Hercule, including people like Donovan, Ringo Starr, Keith Moon, Rod Stewart, and Marc Bolan. Hollywood stars were also known to drop by now that Elton had access to celebrities through his friend Bryan Forbes. The singer and Forbes met when he visited Forbes's secondhand bookshop, but the man himself, in addition to being a bookseller, was also an actor, a scriptwriter, and a producer. Once a bond had been established between the two men, Forbes regularly invited stars of the silver screen to Dionysian banquets arranged by Elton. Iconic stars like Mae West and Katharine Hepburn were among the guests who turned up. Fascinated by this world that he scarcely knew, Elton had the opportunity to take his first steps in front of the camera thanks to Marc Bolan, who invited him to the set of the film *Born to Boogie*, which was a documentary that Ringo Starr was making on T. Rex. Naturally, the three friends soon found themselves having a jam session, which was immortalized on film. They performed a frenzied version of "Tutti Frutti" by Little Richard. Elton also helped out on "Children of the Revolution," by T. Rex, for a version that the pianist later considered to be better than the one released as a single. Bernie also hung out with Starr and Bolan and lost himself in a haze of endless, sleepless nights, often concluding his partying sprees without having the slightest recollection of what had happened.

The tempo was in keeping with the speed of execution that was maintained during the recording sessions for *Don't Shoot Me I'm Only the Piano Player*. The songs gained several beats per minute based on the suggestion of the sound engineer, Ken Scott, who wanted to slightly increase the speed of Elton's piano to emphasize the rock 'n' roll dimensions of the tracks.

1973

Grains of Sand in the Machinery

While Bernie was dipping his pen more into alcohol more frequently than ink, Elton went back on the road with Dee, Nigel…and Davey, who officially joined the group for a United Kingdom tour that ended in March, then went on to join the American tour, which ran from April to June of 1972. The four colleagues found themselves relieved of the need to fill the soundscape with just their instruments, and they started playing less with a view to filling out the sound and in a way that was more nuanced, with the guitarist performing all the stylistic ornamentation.

Behind the façade of contentment that was on display to the outside world, Nigel and Dee were, in fact, not so happy. They were left feeling upset when they weren't consulted on creative decisions, and they saw that the foundations of their "magic trio" with Elton were starting to crack, especially with the arrival of Johnstone. It would take all the guitarist's talent and good humor to convince Nigel and Dee that he was, in fact, the right man for the job.

Elton was also preoccupied by a particular irritation: the sound systems in many of the concert halls where he performed, with all their ambient noise and audio feedback. The musician despaired, and when Elton despaired he became difficult to live with. He could no longer face having to deal with yet another sound engineer who seemed uninterested in his input, so Elton turned to Clive Franks, a sound engineer at Dick James Music. "I'd never done a live show in my life, but it was just fun to get out of the studio routine."[79] After only four numbers, a huge wall of audio feedback assaulted the audience's eardrums. Elton John stopped in his tracks and demonstrated his anger by kicking his piano stool. Clive was extremely concerned. At the end of the concert, he was close to tears and took himself away, feeling very stressed about his errors. John Reid recommended that he should have a talk with Elton. Transfixed by fear and shame, Clive went up to the singer, who greeted him with a huge smile. "I did the show but thought the sound was a disaster. But Elton said it was the best show they'd done! He asked me to join the team! I was overjoyed. He said we were going to America in a month! But I was also concerned because I was now studio manager and chief engineer […] and had a secure job earning a steady wage. You couldn't be sure that a singer or musician's career would last beyond one hit. But now I'm obviously glad I said yes."[79] The engineer

did not know it at the time, but he was effectively signing on for forty years in the service of one artist.

On February 24, 1972, there was a different kind of incident; it was much more annoying than a small sound issue and it put a wrench in the planning of the upcoming tour. That evening, Elton and his group were performing in Watford. Forty-eight hours earlier, members of the IRA exploded a bomb at the Aldershot military base, located a little farther to the south of England, and killing seven people. This attack was launched in response to the killings in Derry, in Northern Ireland, which took place on January 30, 1972, and which are referred to in the famous U2 song "Bloody Sunday." On the fateful Sunday in question, the British army targeted peaceful demonstrators. The mood on the night of Elton's show was dark, and the public was quick to realize what was going on when, in the middle of the show, one of the concert organizers rushed toward Elton and told him that the concert had to be stopped: The IRA had just warned that a bomb had been planted somewhere in the building. A police inspector took Elton's microphone and ordered the public to evacuate immediately. It turned out to be a false alarm.

Back to the Château

In spite of the occasional hiccup, things could not have been going better for Elton when it came to his music and its sales performance. "Rocket Man" was released as a single on April 17, 1972, the day after the Apollo 16 moon mission took off. Because of this finely orchestrated bit of marketing synergy, the song's "take-off" was also a foregone conclusion, and it stayed on the charts in America for fifteen weeks, climbing as high as sixth place. The United Kingdom loved the single so much they took it all the way to the number two spot. With his head in the stars, it was not yet time for Elton to descend from these heights, and on May 19, 1972, it was *Honky Château*'s turn to lift off, heading for number two in the British charts and number one in the United States.

Elton did not have too much time to savor his success, and he quickly had to get back to the studio to complete his next album. New recording sessions were scheduled to take place in June at the Château d'Hérouville. But Elton was not thrilled by the idea of going there. Suffering from a bout of mononucleosis and exhausted by the relentless pace of his touring and recording schedule, he felt very run-down. He asked for a postponement of the sessions until September, but then went back on his

decision when he realized that he was supposed to go on vacation in July. He felt it would be a good thing to have the new album already in the bag before he took a break; that way he could go away with complete peace of mind.

Maybe it was the euphoria generated by his ongoing fever, kind of like how Neil Young composed some of the songs on *Harvest* while suffering from horrific back pain. Elton was overflowing with creativity, as ever, and he composed twelve songs in two days! Seven on day one, and five on day two. He modestly attributes this mind-boggling level of productivity to the rich musical offerings of the day: "It was just the most exciting area. You could buy at least ten to fifteen great albums a week and be inspired. We were listening to bass sounds, drum sounds, piano sounds. Things that were happening technically

on records. And [we were] just filled with wonder."[31] Technically, Gus Dudgeon contributed to the continued success of his musicians by ensuring optimal recording conditions for them. He worked on creating the most refined premix possible so that the musicians had a precise idea of the soundscape for each song and knew what nuances to apply and when to push it or hold back in relation to the rest of the instrumentation. In other words, with such meticulous preparatory work already handled, the producer was killing two birds with one stone: The musicians were able to play in ideal conditions, and he was getting out ahead of the mixing process that happened once the musicians finished their work.

The speed of execution on *Honky Château* was pushed to the max on *Don't Shoot Me I'm Only the Piano Player*. Scarcely

While recording at the château, Elton and the rest of his team often relaxed by watching soccer.

had Elton composed a number, based on Bernie's lyrics, before the group took hold of it and rehearsed it with diabolical efficiency. "Day by day, we developed a way of working where nobody had to say anything to each other," explained guitarist Davey Johnstone, "Elton never said, 'Well, how about you play this?' or 'What about playing that?' He'd never tell me to play a part."[128] Davey Johnstone attributed this speed as much to Elton's talent as to his impatience, a notable trait in the musician: "Elton has a very short attention span. He always did, always will. When he sits down to write, if something doesn't come to him in 15 minutes, he's on to something else. He writes very spontaneously, and there's no fat on anything he does."[128] Everything went quickly: "Daniel" was recorded in just two takes, "I'm Going to Be a Teenage Idol" in only one. The recording process was so quick that the group had the time to fulfill a little request from Sheila Dudgeon, the producer's partner. They recorded a new version of "Skyline Pigeon," which was her favorite track. This reworking, which was better produced than the original, featured a piano in place of a harpsichord and lost some of the original's beautiful delicacy. In any case, it had the merit of providing a very different vision and showed the very quick maturation of Elton in the space of just three years. It was chosen as the B-side of the single "Daniel," which was released on January 20, 1973, in the United Kingdom. Elton also permitted himself the luxury of recording some new numbers around the same time, which he held in reserve, including "Screw You (Young Man's Blues)," "Jack Rabbit," "Whenever You're Ready (We'll Go Steady Again)," and "Tell Me What the Doctor Said." All but the last of these songs were released in 1995 when the album was put out in the relatively novel (for the time) CD format. The CD was released by Mercury (ref. 528 154-2).

An ambivalent atmosphere permeated the sessions: The group was tired from the to-and-fro travel between studio and stage performances, and they were also conscious that their sound was never as good as when it was played urgently, so they did not want to drag things out. This sense of urgency seemed to infuse itself in the songs, which retain the urgency of the tracks in *Honky Château* but are less weighed down by melodic detours, prioritizing rock 'n' roll immediacy over the baroque pop temptation that infuses songs like "Rocket Man." One consequence of the automatic reflexes that were adopted during this time of urgent creativity: Elton, Dee, Nigel, and Dave started to function as a real group. To be convinced of this, all one has to do is look at the number of contributors on Elton's first few albums and compare them to the number of people who were present for the last two recorded at the Château d'Hérouville. The (relative) simplicity of the new songs enabled Elton to focus more on his vocals, and it also let him experiment. This meant that he could achieve the huge range between the falsetto of "Crocodile Rock" and the plaintive, blue-eyed soul of "Blues for My Baby and Me."

Following the slick completion of the recording sessions, the team set aside an evening of relaxation, coming together in the large dining room at the château to discuss things like the progress being made on Davey Johnstone's first studio album, *Smiling Face*, in which Gus, Elton, Dee, and Nigel had all been involved. The guitarist was not sure he would be able to find a label to release it. This was something that his colleagues could not countenance, as they were convinced of the album's merit. Animated by the alcohol that was being consumed, one of them floated the idea of setting up their label to release the record, and the idea was met with general approval. The next day, still slightly foggy from the night before, the musicians wondered if this was really a good idea, or if the alcohol had made it seem that way. They quickly came to the conclusion that starting their own label was, in fact, a good idea. It took a few months more for the undertaking to take shape, but the seed had been sown.

At the end of the recording sessions, Elton lost no time before going to Paris, heading straight for the Champs-Élysées and a shopping session at all the best stores, just as he had done after wrapping *Honky Château*. He left the keys with Gus Dudgeon, trusting him to supervise the backing vocals recording, as well

Eltonmania was in full swing when *Don't Shoot Me…* was released. In this picture from January 1973, Elton is shown in the middle of a signing session at a record shop on King's Road, Chelsea.

as the overdubs for the percussion, synthesizer, and orchestra. This was a choice that did not help Paul Buckmaster feel valued as a stakeholder in the project, as he did not even get to meet Elton during the production process. The mixing was carried out entirely at Trident Studios in London.

An Album Cover Rich in References

The rock 'n' roll underpinnings on this album, coupled with its nostalgic viewpoint and Elton's growing interest in cinema, all came together in the visuals that Michael Ross and David Larkham designed for the cover. The image they chose, showing the entrance to a movie theater, was reminiscent of Edward Hopper. Immortalized by photographer Ed Caraeff, it features a young couple dressed in popular American fashions of the 1950s—jeans and a Perfecto jacket for the boy, and a long, full pleated skirt for the girl. The rear end of a Cadillac appears on the left-hand side of the image. Hidden behind the vehicle during the photo shoot, Larkham held a smoke machine while his assistant played the part of the ticket seller. For the first time, Elton was not physically represented on the sleeve of one of his albums. Instead, he shows up on one of the movie posters that's hanging outside the theater's entrance. "Elton was unavailable for a photo shoot, and he also hated having his picture taken,"[20] explained David Larkham.

The cover image also features a poster from the Marx Brothers film *Go West*. This was done as a gesture of thanks to Groucho Marx for the role he involuntarily played in helping Elton come up with the album's title. In fact, Elton and Groucho did meet once at a dinner in Los Angeles, thanks to Bryan Forbes. Despite his eighty-one years, the actor had lost none of his predatory humor, and he continuously teased Elton John throughout the evening. As soon as he arrived, Groucho feigned being in a bad mood, and, instead of greeting people, said: "When are we gonna eat? It's too cold in here!" before laughing loudly. Upon leaving, Groucho autographed a poster for Elton: "To John Elton, from Marx Groucho." "Because your name is backward," he commented, underlining his humor with a gesture mimicking a gunshot. Elton, greatly amused by this, put his hands up and replied: "Don't shoot me, I'm only the piano player!" with reference both to a version of a quote made famous by Oscar Wilde, "Don't shoot the pianist, he's doing his best," and to the classic François Truffaut film, *Shoot the Piano Player*. This was not the only time that someone got Elton's newly legal name backward. In 1995, the singer was appointed as a Commander of the Order of the British Empire, and when he was announced in front of the Queen, he was introduced as: "Sir John Elton!"

After a span of seven months between recording and release, the disk finally hit shelves in January 1973, at which point Elton had already moved on to his next smash record, *Goodbye Yellow Brick Road. Don't Shoot Me I'm Only the Piano Player* was met with enthusiasm from the public and went to the top of the charts in the United Kingdom, Canada, Australia, Norway, Spain, and the United States, where it was certified triple platinum.

DANIEL

Elton John, Bernie Taupin / 3:55

Musicians
Elton John: vocals, electric piano, Mellotron
Davey Johnstone: acoustic guitar, banjo
Dee Murray: bass
Nigel Olsson: drums, maracas
Ken Scott: ARP synthesizer

Recorded
Château d'Hérouville, Hérouville, France: June 1972

Technical Team
Producer: Gus Dudgeon
Sound Engineer: Ken Scott
Production Coordinator: Steve Brown

Single Release
Daniel / Skyline Pigeon
UK Release: January 20, 1973, on DJM Records (ref. DJS 275)
Best UK Chart Ranking: 4
US Release: March 26, 1973, on MCA Records (ref. MCA-40046)
Best US Chart Ranking: 2

ELTON VS. STEVIE
Recorded in June 1972, "Daniel" appeared as a single only in January of the following year. The release came too late for it to be eligible for the 1972 Grammy Awards, and it didn't earn the singer a nomination until 1973. The Grammy Awards were finally presented on March 14, 1974, two years after the song's creation, and Elton John was beat by Stevie Wonder and his hit "You Are the Sunshine of My Life."

Genesis and Lyrics

The recording sessions began with a choice piece: "Daniel," a calypso ballad set in *C* major. Behind its impulsive (synth) flute and caressing vocals, it portrays a sober destiny: that of a Vietnam War veteran, who, following the horror of war, did not expect that he would have to face a new battle in his search to find psychological peace. Unlike the many veterans who return home traumatized and alone, Daniel is feted upon his return, but all he seeks is some kind of normality after the atrocities he experienced. He decides to exile himself, and to leave his native Texas for Spain. This interpretation was not immediately clear to the audience, since at the time Bernie wrote the song, his text was cut drastically.

The problem lay in the way in which Bernie and Elton worked. Bernie, while he tried to inject a dose of musicality into his text with the incorporation of rhymes, the scansion, or repeated verses, did not get bogged down in all the musical contingences in terms of the length of the verses and refrains. Elton, when he picked up the texts, from that point was entirely free to do as he pleased, to change the order of sentences or paragraphs, and to remove parts of the text. Bernie's lyrics were often too long, intentionally so, in order to allow Elton the option of selecting a more musical phrase with a better rhythm to it. This was done with a view to effect and concision, and because "Daniel" was an obvious candidate for a single for the new album, given its melodic character. As a result, the song was somewhat mutilated, not unlike the hero who had lost his sight in combat, thereby also losing the verse in which the soldier's past of the protagonist was set out. All that remained was him fleeing to Spain. This was also a fortuitous choice of country, since Bernie was looking for a rhyme with *plane*, so the choice of *Spain* was a logical one. "'Daniel' had been the most misinterpreted song that we'd ever written," acknowledged Bernie in 2005, before explaining that the idea for this song had come to him while he was reading *Newsweek*. "[...] There was a piece about the vets coming home from Vietnam. The story was about a guy that went back to a small town in Texas. He'd been crippled in the Tet Offensive. They'd lauded him when he came home and treated him like a hero. They wouldn't leave him alone, they insisted that he be a hero, but he just wanted to go home, go back to the farm, and try to get back to the life that he'd led before. I

In a rare moment, Elton leaves his post behind the keyboards and takes center stage as the front man.

just embellished that and like everything I write, I probably ended up being very esoteric, but it is a song that is important to me, because it was the one thing I said about the Vietnam War. I wanted to write something that was sympathetic to the people that came home."[58]

It was the identity of the narrator that would give rise to the interpretation that was furthest off from the subject: Bernie adopts the perspective of Daniel's younger brother, rather than that of the war hero himself. For some, this "brother" is actually a euphemism for lover. For Bernie and Elton, this was a far-fetched interpretation, and they were surprised that the song was subject to such speculations, given that previously other songs had addressed the subject in a much more obvious way without anyone doubting that the subject had been Elton's homosexuality. "That whole 'Daniel' thing, that's just part of the myth," commented Bernie. "It's just one of those things that people just pick up on. There are a lot of other songs where there was probably something chopped off—'Candle in the Wind.' There was probably a verse chopped off in 'Bennie and the Jets.' The only reason it became such an issue with 'Daniel' was because some people thought the last verse totally changed what the

song was about. I don't remember what the last verse was, so I don't know whether it did or not, but I doubt it. I seriously doubt it."[6] Since the last verse was cut, no one will ever know whether the mysterious text could've shed any light. Davey Johnstone—unlike his colleagues, who have no recollection of it—suggested that it was a surrealist verse: "Elton had written this song which immediately we all loved. And he called me over and said, 'Look at this last verse, I think Taupin's on drugs. He must be taking acid or something.' And we looked at this verse, and I can vaguely remember something about a ship's dog named Paul. And I'm like 'What the fuck is he talking about?' Suddenly out of nowhere he starts talking about this dog. So Elton just kind of took the page and ripped that bottom part off very slowly and very definitely and said, 'Well, that's the end of that.' And that's why that verse was lost."[81]

Production

Having only just been composed and rehearsed, the instrumentation of "Daniel" was recorded in only two takes to retain the song's natural drive. The piece has an accomplished gentleness embellished with Davey Johnstone's acoustic guitar

On October 6, 1973, Elton John performed at Ohio State University's St. John Arena in Columbus, Ohio.

and banjo, which are subtly announced between two vocal parts (as at 0:57, in his rhythmic, fluid playing, and the pleasing harmonies of his guitar). It is also adorned with a flute solo, played by Elton John himself...on the Mellotron. The illusion is perfect, and it gives the song a light, illuminated character, which is supported by Nigel Olsson's congas. In order to counterbalance the sweetness of this melody and to give some relief to the interpretation, there was a lack of a certain bite and patina to this ensemble. But this initially made the music seem too smooth and distant from the gravity of Bernie Taupin's subject. This is where Gus Dudgeon's experience in managing the team came in. As an inventive producer, he always knew how to use the forces present to the best advantage. He was aware that the number's magic was derived not from the studio but from the artists' interpretation. For this reason, he decided to get Elton John unceremoniously out of bed early one morning and put him in front of the microphone, before he even had time to clean himself up or have something to eat. As an early riser, but not one to take kindly to being hustled, Elton still went with the flow, as he rapidly understood what the producer had in mind. The magic

worked straightaway: Elton's voice, still fairly gravelly and rasping, did not have its usual clarity, but it instantly injected a dose of drama into the interpretation, without him having to overplay it.

Meanwhile, as far as the recording was concerned, Gus Dudgeon was not entirely satisfied with the song. Davey's guitar solo did not quite sit right with him: Somehow it lacked punch. Ken Scott, therefore, doubled the part on an ARP 2600 synthesizer.

The whole team were charmed by "Daniel," which Elton John wanted to release as an initial single. But Dick James was vigorously opposed to this, and he was supported by MCA. They were convinced that this ballad would have catastrophic consequences if they took a chance with it. So "Crocodile Rock" was selected as the first single from *Don't Shoot Me I'm Only the Piano Player*. Since he did not have the final word on this decision, Elton John still managed to have "Daniel" released as a second single, and he agreed to assume personal responsibility for the promotional costs if the song was a flop. Fortunately for him, it rose to fourth place in the United Kingdom and to second place in the United States.

TEACHER I NEED YOU

Elton John, Bernie Taupin / 4:10

Musicians

Elton John: vocals, piano, Mellotron
Davey Johnstone: acoustic guitar, backing vocals
Dee Murray: bass, backing vocals
Nigel Olsson: drums, backing vocals

Recorded

Château d'Hérouville, Hérouville, France: June 1972

Technical Team

Producer: Gus Dudgeon
Sound Engineer: Ken Scott
Production Coordinator: Steve Brown

The lively character and catchy tune of "Teacher I Need You" made it a potential candidate for single status, but its path was blocked by "Daniel" and "Crocodile Rock." This song got its chance only in Norway, where, astonishingly, it was predicted to have a better future than elsewhere. However, the 45 rpm, which offered "High Flying Bird" on the B-side, did find favor in the charts in the land of the midnight sun.

Genesis and Lyrics

After "Daniel," which is a gentle calypso ballad, comes a swirling number halfway between rock 'n' roll and pop, and more in line with the album's general atmosphere. This musical evocation of the end of the 1950s accompanies lyrics that are infused with nostalgia for childhood. Bernie Taupin, who was at elementary school during this idealized era, remembers the feelings he had for his teacher. "She was long and she was lean / [...] a middle-aged dream." An amorous inclination very common in children, but which in this case plays very much on ambiguity, as the level of innocence in his lyrics veers between an almost maternal affection ("I need you like a little child") and a more carnal desire ("some further education / In connection with the birdies and the bees").

Production

In a departure from his usual practices, Elton John moves over to his Mellotron for this song, even though he prefers the sobriety of the piano. But he makes subtle use of this fascinating instrument, a sort of precursor of the sampler that was designed in 1963; its keys activate tapes that play sounds close to those of strings. Accompanying the series of introductory triplets on the piano that constitute one of Elton John's sound signatures, the instrument creates a moment for breath, replacing an intro on the cymbals that would have seemed rather conventional. Nigel Olsson perfectly matches the extension of this motif, making his entry at 0:13. While he had no problem following Elton John's syncopated rhythm, Dee Murray had more difficulty. As on "Crocodile Rock," he struggled to find an impactful approach for the bass. The trigger happened in the intro, on which he played just a few intriguing deep notes. In the end, he realized that the song did not necessarily require a complex line and that the main thing was to manage the attack on the notes and to establish his groove. For the voice takes, which started off the third day, Elton, as he specified himself, assumed the character of Bobby Vee,[80] his pop idol from the 1960s, well-known for his interpretation of Adam Faith's "What Do You Want." But the British singer has a wider tessitura than his American counterpart, which enabled him to go for the deeper register and also provided him with more rebound for hitting the high notes. To finish off, Gus Dudgeon draped his voice with a big reverb that could lead one to imagine that this was a live take.

ELDERBERRY WINE

Elton John, Bernie Taupin / 3:34

Musicians

Elton John: vocals, piano
Davey Johnstone: electric guitar
Dee Murray: bass
Nigel Olsson: drums
Alain Hatot: saxophone
Jean-Louis Chautemps: saxophone
Jacques Bolognesi: trombone
Ivan Jullien: trumpet
Gus Dudgeon: brass arrangements

Recorded

Château d'Hérouville, Hérouville, France: June 1972

Technical Team

Producer: Gus Dudgeon
Sound Engineer: Ken Scott
Production Coordinator: Steve Brown

Single Release

Crocodile Rock / Elderberry Wine
UK Release: October 27, 1972, on DJM Records (ref. DJS.271)
Best UK Chart Ranking: 5
US Release: November 20, 1972, on MCA Records (ref. MCA 40000)
Best US Chart Ranking: 1

A WINE BY ANY OTHER NAME

Elderberry wine is a fairly common beverage found in the southern United States and the United Kingdom, and it's made by mixing mashed elderberries, cane sugar, and water.

Genesis and Lyrics

"Elderberry Wine" employs a framework that is repeated several times on the album: a deliberate divergence between a text that is plaintively emphatic, and a soaring, almost joyful melody. Using this approach, Elton John sought to make a clean break from his first, intentionally elegiac albums. While Bernie's writing was moving more toward a simple style, it still had a melancholic tendency. Rather than being constrained on this aspect, Elton opted to inject some light into the pieces to create a chiaroscuro effect. The listener is carried along by this vigorous rock music, while Bernie depicts a man destroyed by the absence of his wife, who had left him nearly a year ago. The lyricist shows skill in describing what he has left around him—a dog, a trunk, some letters—all the better to evoke the vacuum left by the woman who is no longer there, and the memory of their pleasant evenings together. Similarly, all his purposelessness is focused on the observation of ordinary things, such as the fly on the window, the bills piling up, which emphasize the pathos of the situation. The elegance of his writing reaches the heights when, instead of "my wife," he uses the expression "wife of mine," which, if contracted, leads in the direction of "wine." This diffuses the much less elegant rhyme "You aimed to please me / Cooked black-eyed peas me," albeit that it adds humor.

Production

Establishing a catchy and very effective rhythm, Elton sets off on a series of classical chords developed in the left hand, in rhythm 'n' blues style (*Eb, G, G#, A*), over which is laid Dee Murray's bass, this time assuming a lightness in his supple and rounded playing. The more discreet guitar rotates around an *Eb-Bb* sequence. During the short rehearsals preceding the recording, Elton encouraged the group to play more quickly, bringing the final tempo up to 127 beats per minute, which makes this one of the fastest pieces on the album. In order to perfect the effervescent refrain and to give it an orchestral impetus, the team decided to call on four French musicians, who had already accompanied them rather impressively on *Honky Château*: saxophonists Alain Hatot and Jean-Louis Chautemps, trombonist Jacques Bolognesi, and trumpeter Ivan Jullien. They were, however, given some latitude to express themselves, as Gus Dudgeon himself had written the special brass arrangement.

BLUES FOR MY BABY AND ME

Elton John, Bernie Taupin / 5:39

Musicians
Elton John: vocals, piano
Davey Johnstone: electric guitar, acoustic guitar, sitar
Dee Murray: bass
Nigel Olsson: drums
Paul Buckmaster: arrangements, direction

Recorded
Château d'Hérouville, Hérouville, France: June 1972

Technical Team
Producer: Gus Dudgeon
Sound Engineer: Ken Scott
Production Coordinator: Steve Brown

OVATION
Charles Kaman was an aeronautical engineer and a builder of helicopters, and he was fascinated by guitars. He was the inventor of the Ovation acoustic guitar, which first appeared in 1966. Its bold design was created using aeronautical technologies, including an acoustically efficient resonating chamber and the use of a revolutionary composite material, which optimized the guitar's sound and enhanced its strength.

Genesis and Lyrics

Among the last songs to be finalized during the album recording sessions, "Blues for My Baby and Me" might not have been included in the final track list had Davey Johnstone not taken things in hand, thereby lifting the track into another dimension. He had in mind the psychedelic dynamic of "Alone Again Or," by the American group Love, and he wanted to give an exotic color to this story narrating the flight to the West of a young couple confronted with the strict attitude of a father who warns his daughter against her boyfriend's bad influence. Davey saw in this the ideal opportunity for using his new sitar, an instrument that had become very fashionable since the initial experiments by George Harrison on the Beatles' *Revolver* in 1966. The musician found this model in a magazine, and it had taken nearly a year to reach him in England. When it arrived, Davey was very surprised by the size of the instrument, which was housed in an enormous box that looked like a coffin! Davey, who really did not know how to play his colossal instrument, told himself that no matter how he played it, it would create an atmosphere, and that was all he was looking for.

Production

Also eager to give this number some more amplitude, Paul Buckmaster composed an orchestral arrangement that was of exceptional elegance. However, the man who had just demonstrated his talent with his arrangement of "You're So Vain" by Carly Simon had a bitter taste in his mouth after these sessions because he had been called in only after the recording portion was completed.

Although the structure of the pieces is very simple, alternating verse-refrain-verse-refrain, the riff in five bars, on which the song is constructed, confers upon it a certain sophistication because of its length. The motif is introduced on the keyboard by Elton, who starts on his own, in piano-vocals format, singing in what was a very low register for him. He then picks up the melody again in a shortened version during a harmonious transition into the refrain, where he is joined by violins, flutes, and horns directed by Paul Buckmaster, as well as Davey Johnstone's guitar. Johnstone was more at ease on his instrument of choice, in this case an Ovation acoustic guitar, although he did manipulate its sound by passing it through a Leslie cabinet and added to it a Uni-Vibe pedal and a wah-wah pedal.

MIDNIGHT CREEPER

Elton John, Bernie Taupin / 3:52

1973

Musicians
Elton John: vocals, electric piano
Davey Johnstone: electric guitar
Dee Murray: bass
Nigel Olsson: drums
Gus Dudgeon: brass arrangements
Alain Hatot: saxophone
Jean-Louis Chautemps: saxophone
Jacques Bolognesi: trombone
Ivan Jullien: trumpet

Recorded
Château d'Hérouville, Hérouville, France: June 1972

Technical Team
Producer: Gus Dudgeon
Sound Engineer: Ken Scott
Production Coordinator: Steve Brown

FOR ELTON ADDICTS
The original manuscript of "Midnight Creeper" was sold at the auction on September 11, 2018, for the sum of $3,437.50. Dated April 1972, the document also includes the lyrics for a song that was never produced: "Calamity Jane."

Genesis and Lyrics

"Midnight Creeper" features fairly transgressive lyrics that are not often found in the works of Bernie Taupin. Bernie, who usually had an affection for sympathetic antiheroes oppressed by destiny, instead opts to highlight a detestable and sadistic character who locked women into his cellar in order to inflict the worst kind of outrages imaginable upon them. Initially, the protagonist makes it clear that he is fully aware of his nature ("I'm a true rat for the things I done"), but this lucidity is not accompanied by the slightest sense of remorse. This sociopath feels no empathy. Of the two characters described in "Have Mercy on the Criminal" and "Midnight Creeper," the second seems to be the more dangerous. Bernie also includes some reflections during the course of this song: Imprisonment does nothing to resolve evil, and goodness in man is not determined by his acts, but by his capacity for redemption.

Production

Elton John approached "Midnight Creeper" with Mick Jagger's performance style in mind. His aggressive and swaggering vocals are perfectly in keeping with Davey's nervy, bluesy guitar, which is peppered with tiny, deliberately introduced imperfections, little notes that hang on. Inspired by Keith Richards, the guitarist, who devised a crunchy sound to suit the context, wanted to emphasize the intention rather than create a perfect copy, as he was normally capable of doing. But the group shied away from any imitation deviating toward rhythm 'n' blues, with the intervention of the brass section, consisting of four French musicians: Alain Hatot, Jean-Louis Chautemps, Jacques Bolognesi, and Ivan Jullien. The quartet gives the piece real dynamite, in the manner of a James Brown or an Ike and Tina Turner number. Tina Turner's name is also quoted in the first verse of the song, in the midst of a series of phrases without head or tail. This name dropping seems to focus the group's attention, who must take their inspiration from it for the degree of intensity to be instilled in the piece. In the middle of this joyous, groovy fury, Davey added a banjo in the style of the group McGuinness Flint, at the request of Gus Dudgeon. But this was met with a firm and categorical veto from Elton—to the producer's great astonishment, because the pianist had always given him carte blanche. But in this case, Elton was not in favor of this banjo idea. The instrument was quickly put back into its case.

HAVE MERCY ON THE CRIMINAL

Elton John, Bernie Taupin / 5:58

Musicians
Elton John: vocals, piano
Davey Johnstone: electric guitar
Dee Murray: bass
Nigel Olsson: drums
Paul Buckmaster: arrangements

Recorded
Château d'Hérouville, Hérouville, France: June 1972

Technical Team
Producer: Gus Dudgeon
Sound Engineer: Ken Scott
Production Coordinator: Steve Brown

Jailhouse rock turns dark and dramatic in "Have Mercy on the Criminal."

Genesis and Lyrics

Fifteen years after the explosion of Elvis Presley's "Jailhouse Rock," Bernie Taupin took up the subject of the convict and gave it a striking literary depth. With this text, the lyricist asserts himself as an inimitable storyteller. From the first verse, Bernie plunges the listener into the heart of the action: a manhunt. Even before describing the circumstances of the escape and the psychological state of the fugitive, he invites himself into his head. Then he suggests, in small brushstrokes, the humanity of this prisoner, that society denies him: "Oh there must be shackles on his feet / And [a] mother in his eyes." Further on, he introduces this glacial metonymy: "Now have you ever seen the white teeth gleam / While you lie on a cold damp ground?" White teeth that could also symbolize the jaws of dogs, or the smug smile of the policemen who captured him. It is therefore the justice of men that has the last word on the fate of this repentant individual whose prayers have not been heard ("Lord you got to help me / I am never gonna sin again"). Bernie offers a terrible conclusion to the reflexes for freedom already referred to in *Empty Sky*, and a criminal's struggles in "Rotten Peaches" on *Madman Across the Water*. The morning when Elton discovered these lyrics, he was very moved. He read them to the other musicians without delay, and they also shared his enthusiasm.

Production

"'Have Mercy on the Criminal' [is] a very dramatic song and we wanted to keep it as wild as possible—we recorded the guitar solo live, which was unusual but fun,"[31] testified Davey Johnstone, who authored the solo, that pierces the darkness at 3:54. In order to fill this out even more, the musician doubles and then triples with two additional guitars that both play an octave lower. In so doing, he shuts down any questions concerning his ability to express himself in the electric register, having hitherto been pigeonholed as essentially a folk musician. This number also saw the return of Paul Buckmaster to his former strength, who was eager to make the most of the scant space for expression left to him. And his symphonic orchestration is masterly, providing the dramatic and epic drive that the song merits. The introduction to "Have Mercy on the Criminal" presents a disconcerting kinship with the one in "Layla" by Derek and the Dominos, released in March 1971.

I'M GOING TO BE A TEENAGE IDOL

Elton John, Bernie Taupin / 3:56

Musicians

Elton John: vocals, piano
Davey Johnstone: electric guitar, acoustic guitar, backing vocals
Dee Murray: bass, backing vocals
Nigel Olsson: drums, backing vocals
Gus Dudgeon: brass arrangements
Alain Hatot: saxophone
Jean-Louis Chautemps: saxophone
Jacques Bolognesi: trombone
Ivan Jullien: trumpet

Recorded

Château d'Hérouville, Hérouville, France: June 1972

Technical Team

Producer: Gus Dudgeon
Sound Engineer: Ken Scott
Production Coordinator: Steve Brown

The embodiment of the glam-rock superstar, Marc Bolan was the leader of T. Rex, and he was immortalized on Elton's "I'm Going to Be a Teenage Idol."

Genesis and Lyrics

"He [Marc Bolan] had attitude, he had performing skills, he looked fabulous, he dressed the part. At a time when I was still becoming Elton John, he was a great role model,"[82] recalled Elton in 2020, explaining the extent to which he was captivated, in the early 1970s, as much by Bolan's exuberance and hyper-sexualization as by his capacity to create songs that were both hymnal and classy. Bolan, in turn, was intrigued by the image reflected back to him by Elton John, whose talent he also held in high esteem, and of whom he was also slightly jealous. The T. Rex leader called upon Elton in 1972 to take part in the documentary about him, *Born to Boogie*. The bond between the two men burst out in their wild cover of "Children of the Revolution," driven by Ringo Starr's battering rhythm on the drums. Afterward, with a view to returning the compliment, Elton wrote a song in honor of Bolan—or rather, he asked Bernie to write it. Bernie rolled out the stereotypical image of the glam-rock star, and in it he described his all-consuming ambition: "Put me on the ladder," "I'm gonna grab myself a place in history." This character trait always guided Bolan's artistic approach right up to his premature death in 1977, which tragically set his aura in stone for eternity. "We wrote that song about him because that's what he wanted to be [an idol], and he was living his part to the full and enjoying it, and meant no harm to anybody,"[32] said Elton in 1980.

Production

The seasoned professional musicians—trombonist Jacques Bolognesi, trumpeter Ivan Jullien, and saxophonists Alain Hatot and Jean-Louis Chautemps—were once again mobilized and tasked with giving this homage to the glam icon its groove, even though they were not particularly familiar with Bolan's sound. With formidable efficiency, the members of the group and the session musicians dispatched the number in a single take. The brass interventions are not numerous, but they are rhythmically demanding, and varied. The piano is not left out, distributing little ornamentations here and there or duplicating itself, as in the short sequence at 2:15 in which Elton John covers the entire keyboard.

"I'm Going to Be a Teenage Idol" is a celebratory song, unifying within itself many different musical influences, ranging from funk to sugary glam pop.

TEXAN LOVE SONG

Elton John, Bernie Taupin / 3:33

Musicians

Elton John: vocals, harmonium
Davey Johnstone: acoustic guitar, mandolin
Dee Murray: bass
Nigel Olsson: drums

Recorded

Château d'Hérouville, Hérouville, France: June 1972

Technical Team

Producer: Gus Dudgeon
Sound Engineer: Ken Scott
Production Coordinator: Steve Brown

Dee Murray and Davey Johnstone keep pace behind Elton during a performance on *Top of the Pops.*

Genesis and Lyrics

Like some kind of escapee from *Tumbleweed Connection,* "Texan Love Song" sees Bernie once again assuming the persona of a Texan while Elton returns to the Deep South accent that he'd mastered so well. However, Taupin has no intention of subsiding into blissful admiration, and even provides a vitriolic satire of a coarse redneck, which bears some comparison to "Lonesome Cowboy Burt" by Frank Zappa, released the previous year. Like Burt, he is comfortable in his own skin: "We're tough and we're Texan with necks good and red." Although it is no longer a matter of cowboys and outlaws, the Western style of confrontation is never far off: The narrator watches the arrival of hordes of hippies with a side glance and a knife between his teeth ("You long hairs are sure gonna die"). For him, the hippies are invaders, with their counterculture ("with your drug-crazy songs") and their leftist ideas ("With your communistic politics"). The narrator even adds in the specter of racism, making reference to "them Negro blues." Against the values of the "intruders," Bernie depicts those that are important to the song's narrator, mainly: work ethic, respect for the fatherland, and honoring the president (Richard Nixon, at the time the song was written). The caricature is taken so far as to leave no doubt about Bernie's and Elton's views. They are most definitely on the side of the "long hairs."

Production

Davey Johnstone was already chomping at the bit when he discovered the lyrics. The guitarist was on home territory in this respect: "Like most musicians, I was hugely impacted by blues—the blues scene in America and the folk scene, as well."[54] This was too good an opportunity to miss for getting his mandolin out of its case and sprinkling some delicacy over the refrains, which were performed on harmonium by Elton. But the main part of the song, halfway between Fairport Convention and Randy Newman, is provided on acoustic guitar, with Davey developing a subtle arpeggio melody while tapping his foot to keep the rhythm on the verses. Operating in the same way as in "Love Song" on *Tumbleweed Connection* (the link between the two songs is not coincidental), Gus Dudgeon placed a mic close to Davey's foot. Producing a pleasant muted sound, this "stomp" also contributes to the impression of proximity and intimacy with the four members of the group.

CROCODILE ROCK

Elton John, Bernie Taupin / 3:55

1973

Musicians

Elton John: vocals, piano, Farfisa organ
Davey Johnstone: electric guitar
Dee Murray: bass
Nigel Olsson: drums

Recorded

Château d'Hérouville, Hérouville, France: June 1972
Mixing: Trident Studios, London

Technical Team

Producer: Gus Dudgeon
Sound Engineer: Ken Scott
Production Coordinator: Steve Brown

Single Release

Crocodile Rock / Elderberry Wine
UK Release: October 27, 1972, on DJM Records (ref. DJS.271)
Best UK Chart Ranking: 5
US Release: November 20, 1972, on MCA Records (ref. MCA 40000)
Best US Chart Ranking: 1

FOR ELTON ADDICTS

In February 1978, Elton John was a special guest star on *The Muppet Show*. Always a good sport, he performed "Crocodile Rock" in the middle of the "jungle," while surrounded by the Electric Mayhem (the Muppets group) and with backing vocals provided by crocodiles who eventually tip Elton (dressed as a multicolored peacock for the occasion) into the water and eat him.

Genesis and Lyrics

In 1971, Australia pulsated to the rhythm of "Eagle Rock," the first single from the hippie blues-rock group Daddy Cool. The band was flying under the radar in Europe but they were omnipresent on the radio waves in Australia, where their song was ranked number one. Eventually, the song managed to reach Elton's and Bernie's ears during their trip to Australia at the end of October 1971. As proof of his attachment to the group, the lyricist proudly had a *Daddy Who?* badge (taken from the name of the band's first album), included in the promotional photos for *Don't Shoot Me I'm Only the Piano Player*. Although Bernie does not deny the earlier song's influence on "Crocodile Rock," they were inspired more by the spirit of the Daddy Cool song than by the name of the animal, and their song is really quite different from the earlier track. It was just a short step from an eagle to a crocodile. Bernie imagines a fictitious musical style, "crocodile rock," which the narrator says he remembers and claims to have had a passion for at a time when all anyone is listening to is "Rock Around the Clock" by Bill Haley. Taupin also invents an imagined past for this song, describing it as a classic—which, of course, it actually became in real life. The inspiration is also deliberately muddled with references to Bill Haley's song along with nods to "See You Later Alligator," by the leader of the Comets.

Drawing on nostalgia for a bygone era from the introductory "I remember," Taupin provides a rose-tinted image of the 1950s and its cohort of stereotypes: the Chevrolets and the Friday nights out dancing. It's a vision of the past that did not in any way belong to his own generation, because Bernie was only four when "Rock Around the Clock" was released. But the impact of this first wave of rock 'n' roll did leave its mark on Elton and Bernie, when they both purchased their first vinyls of Little Richard, Elvis Presley, and Jerry Lee Lewis. Like "American Pie" by Don McLean, which preceded this song by a few months, "Crocodile Rock" struck a nostalgic note with its audience. Interestingly, both songs made similar word choices, such as saying "Chevy" instead of "Chevrolet."

"Crocodile Rock" reveals a stark change in Bernie's writing. Here, there are none of the cryptic phrases, no unidentified characters appearing in the story out of nowhere...And

Elton John dressed as a peacock for an appearance on *The Muppet Show* in October 1977, where he performed "Crocodile Rock" for Kermit and his pals.

while diving into the past is a common currency in his narratives, this time he calls upon recent collective memories that can speak to a greater number of people. The author did not, however, seem to have particularly enjoyed this exercise. In a January 2012 article for *Esquire*, he commented that for him the writing of this song was "a strange dichotomy because I don't mind having created it, but it's not something I would listen to."[85]

Production

Following the same logic, Elton John set the table for a regressive rock 'n' roll fest. The pianist was in his own special corner, with the scales he had played an incalculable number of times sitting neatly under his fingertips. The number is full of inspiration taken straight from the likes of Eddie Cochran, Jerry Lee Lewis, and Johnny and the Hurricanes, whose characteristic Farisa organ is included in the number. Elton John fully embraces the distinctive sound of this instrument in the introduction, using it as a cohesive stylistic choice in order to achieve the desired retro vibe. Exercising a marvelous control over this exercise in pastiche, the former studio musician, capable of playing in any style, has a field day, particularly in the vocals, which borrow as much from Bobby Vee as they do from Del Shannon. Not to mention the obvious derivation from Pat Boone and his "Speedy Gonzales," to which the quasi infantile falsetto passage owes a great deal, and which is irritating and exhilarating in equal measure. While Elton was lapping it all up, Dee Murray was not so happy. Having grown used to more complex numbers, he was not sure how to take "Crocodile Rock." He seemed to have forgotten his basics and was at pains to create elaborate plans, although they did not naturally fit into the ensemble. "Every time I'd say, 'Why don't you play it like John Fred and His Playboy Band's 'Judy in Disguise'?" said Gus Dudgeon. "You know, just the basic root stuff that works in rock 'n' roll. And he'd pull a cheesed-off face, but he knew what I meant."[31]

HIGH FLYING BIRD

Elton John, Bernie Taupin / 4:12

Musicians
Elton John: vocals, piano
Davey Johnstone: electric guitar (Leslie cabinet), acoustic guitar, backing vocals
Dee Murray: bass, backing vocals
Nigel Olsson: drums, backing vocals

Recorded
Château d'Hérouville, Hérouville, France: June 1972

Technical Team
Producer: Gus Dudgeon
Sound Engineer: Ken Scott
Production Coordinator: Steve Brown

Nigel Olsson's playing contributed a great deal to the success of "High Flying Bird."

Genesis and Lyrics

Don't Shoot Me I'm Only the Piano Player closes with the poignant complaint of a man in tears over the loss of his partner. Despite Bernie's delicate phrasing, we understand that the young woman he loves suffered from serious psychological problems ("I thought myself her keeper / She thought I meant her harm") and probably ended her own life ("My high-flying bird has flown from out my arms," "The white walls of your dressing room are stained in scarlet red"). Recorded at the beginning of the sessions, this song was chosen to close the album because of the lightness of its tonality (contrasting with the oppressive atmosphere of the lyrics), a perfect, gentle conclusion for the album, and, above all, offering a last opportunity to take a breath after "Crocodile Rock." In the liner notes on the reissue of the album in 1995, Elton admits that he had tried to come close to Van Morrison in his interpretation, and to mimic the Van Morrison mode of vocal storytelling. Using a low vocal register, he takes the time to position his voice and to play on the modulations while allowing the silences to settle, even between two linked verses. At the beginnings of phrases, he adds some "mmm" sounds that are characteristic of his admired colleague, and he also applies sudden surges, or inserts that descend, while the backing vocals are rising. This variety creates a fascinating and particular flavor for this moving number.

Production

To accompany Elton's restrained piano playing, Johnstone opted for an Ovation acoustic guitar, which he passed through a speaker called a Leslie cabinet. "I really like the Leslie [speaker] sound and want to work it out a little more. It gives such a full sound,"[31] as he described it in *Guitar Player*'s January 1972 issue, published a few months before the recording. More than the sound, his very full gestures on the exchanges fill the space and convey this feeling of grandeur. Nigel Olsson also contributes significantly, with his very light and laid-back playing and his snare drum fills, almost groggy, that seem to mimic the narrator's dejection. But the credit for the real added value on this number has to go to the backing vocals, provided by Dee, Nigel, and Davey, whose harmony has rarely been so perfect. Ideally enhanced by a delightful reverb, they envelop the refrains in gentleness.

1973

Elton John and
Bernie Taupin pose
for Ed Caraeff at his
Coldwater Canyon
studio in the early
1970s.

JACK RABBIT

Elton John, Bernie Taupin / 1:50

Single: *Saturday Night's Alright (For Fighting) / Jack Rabbit; Whenever You're Ready (We'll Go Steady Again)* **UK Release:** June 29, 1973, on DJM Records (ref. DJX 502) **Best UK Chart Ranking:** 7 **US Release:** July 16, 1973, on MCA Records (ref. MCA-40105) **Best US Chart Ranking:** 12 **Musicians:** Elton John: vocals / Davey Johnstone: electric guitar, acoustic guitar, slide guitar, mandolin / Dee Murray: bass / Nigel Olsson: drums **Recorded:** Château d'Hérouville, Hérouville, France: May 1973 **Technical Team:** Producer: Gus Dudgeon / Sound Engineer: David Hentschel / Production Coordinator: Steve Brown

At the end of the recording sessions for *Don't Shoot Me I'm Only the Piano Player*, Elton, Davey, Dee, and Nigel decided to allow themselves some fun with "Jack Rabbit," a little country confection of just one minute and fifty seconds. Without depth or ambition, it is played simply for the pleasure of a jam session together in the manner of a hillbilly group, in the great tradition of the Farmer Boys, R. D. Hendon, or Carl Tanner and Ineva Buckins. Dee contributes a very traditional country feature by playing the basic notes and moving inexorably from one string to another. Davey pulls out all the stops, weaving a skipping air on the banjo, skillfully executed, trying out some fingerpicking on the acoustic guitar, then making his guitar sing with the bottleneck. Conceived almost like a children's nursery rhyme by Bernie Taupin, "Jack Rabbit" follows the tribulations of a rabbit who gives some farmers the runaround who want to turn him into stew. Obviously rejected at the time of selection, this perky little song was rerecorded in May 1973 and was used as a B-side for "Saturday Night's Alright (For Fighting)" the following month, where it was attached to another escapee from the *Don't Shoot Me…* sessions, "Whenever You're Ready (We'll Go Steady Again)." Both resumed their place on the album on a rerelease from Mercury in 1995.

WHENEVER YOU'RE READY (WE'LL GO STEADY AGAIN)

Elton John, Bernie Taupin / 2:51

Single: *Jack Rabbit; Whenever You're Ready (We'll Go Steady Again)* **Musicians:** Elton John: vocals, piano / Davey Johnstone: slide guitar / Dee Murray: bass / Nigel Olsson: drums **Recorded:** Château d'Hérouville, Hérouville, France: May 1973 **Technical Team:** Producer: Gus Dudgeon / Sound Engineer: Ken Scott / Production Coordinator: Steve Brown

Starting on the key of *C*, like the refrain in "Jack Rabbit," "Whenever You're Ready (We'll Go Steady Again)" follows on perfectly in its wake, which warranted these two numbers forming the shared B-side of the single "Saturday Night's Alright (For Fighting)" in 1973. This song, whose narrator mourns the absence of a woman who had clearly written him off, also has the advantage of having a musical relationship with the A-side song, with its rock 'n' roll edginess, which seems to flow right out the heart of some piano bar. The shadow of Jerry Lee Lewis floats over this rock number with its shuffle rhythm, in the way in which Elton hammers the keys, as from 1:43, where his speed of execution rivals Davey Johnstone's. In his enthusiasm, Johnstone makes his guitar sparkle, played as a slide, with a slight vibrato. In an interview for the official Elton John website in 2014, Johnstone revealed that Rod Stewart had considered recording his own version of this piece.

SELF-CENSORSHIP

In order to avoid upsetting the American public, who were sensitive on matters of propriety, the title "Screw You" was replaced by the very decorous "Young Man's Blues" on the artwork for the single. The lyrics, on the other hand, remained unchanged.

SCREW YOU (YOUNG MAN'S BLUES)

Elton John, Bernie Taupin / 4:43

A TROUBLING RESEMBLANCE

In 1976, a band called Boston had an ideal career launch with the single "More Than a Feeling," which jumped to fifth place on Billboard in the United States. Elton's fans were astonished by the strong resemblance the song's opening had with the intro to "Screw You (Young Man's Blues)."

Single: *Goodbye Yellow Brick Road / Screw You (Young Man's Blues)* **UK Release:** September 7, 1973, on DJM Records (ref. DJS.285) **Best UK Chart Ranking:** 6 **US Release:** October 15, 1973, on MCA Records (ref. MCA-40148) **Best US Chart Ranking:** 2 **Musicians:** Elton John: vocals, piano / Davey Johnstone: electric guitar / Dee Murray: bass / Nigel Olsson: drums / Leroy Gomez: saxophone **Recorded:** Château d'Hérouville, Hérouville, France: May 1973 **Technical Team:** Producer: Gus Dudgeon / Sound Engineer: Ken Scott / Production Coordinator: Steve Brown

This song portrays the struggles of an unfortunate man who sees himself as having been rejected systematically by everyone with a scathing "screw you." Its multiple rhythmic and stylistic breaks owe much to the Beatles, particularly in the middle section, at around 1:43, with its angelic choirs. The piece ends with a stirring saxophone solo provide by Leroy Gomez. He recalled with some emotion the welcome he was given on this occasion:

"Normally after a recording, the protocol was that I would pack up my sax, be paid, say thank you and leave. And for me that was always fine. But not with Elton and his mates, there was a different ambiance. It was like they let us in to sit at the round table as they discussed and contemplated the strategies of getting the music recorded just right. We were allowed to stay and watch as the Knights of the Round Table worked on one of Sir Elton's greatest works."[87]

ALBUM

GOODBYE YELLOW BRICK ROAD

Funeral for a Friend [Love Lies Bleeding] . Candle in the Wind . Bennie and the Jets .
Goodbye Yellow Brick Road . This Song Has No Title . Grey Seal . Jamaica Jerk-Off .
I've Seen That Movie Too . Sweet Painted Lady . The Ballad of Danny Bailey (1909–1934) .
Dirty Little Girl . All the Girls Love Alice . Your Sister Can't Twist (But She Can Rock 'n' Roll) .
Saturday Night's Alright for Fighting . Roy Rogers . Social Disease . Harmony

RELEASE DATES
UK Release: October 5, 1973
Reference: DJM Records—DJLPD 1001
Best UK Chart Ranking: 1
US Release: October 5, 1973
Reference: MCA—MCA2-10003
Best US Chart Ranking: 1

Among the titles considered for this album, the group suggested *How Many Guitar Sounds Can Davey Johnstone Get on This?* which gently mocked Davey's insatiable appetite for guitar overdubs!

A DOUBLE ALBUM FILLED WITH POP SONGS

1973

After a summer devoted to recharging his batteries following the recording of *Don't Shoot Me I'm Only the Piano Player*, September 1972 marked the beginning of Elton John's most ambitious American tour to date. It ran from September 26 through November 26 and made stops at four-thousand-seat halls and stadiums with a capacity to seat twenty thousand. In just a few days the entire tour sold out. "We could have done it a year and a half ago," explained Elton, "but we wanted to build up slowly. Anyway, I don't think we could have played the big halls as a trio."[31]

The Whirlwind of Life on the Road

Elton made sure that his closet matched the grandeur of his shows: ever more extravagant, and increasingly wild. Bernie was also carried along in the whirlwind of the concerts. He was a full member of the group even though he did not go onstage. An army of roadies was on hand starting early in the afternoon on show days, wheeling around tons of equipment to turn an arena that would normally accommodate basketball games into a suitable concert venue: lights, microphones, amplifiers, feedbacks, drum kit, and Elton's piano—a Steinway that measured nearly three meters long—were all installed in the space of a few hours. Due to the efficiency of their road crew, Elton and the group were able to grab a few hours before the curtain rose so that Clive Franks could get on with the difficult task of mixing the group's sound before they took the stage. In the immense open space of large arenas, the musicians focused totally on balancing their sound, and it was not until the engineer raised both thumbs that they could finally disappear into the wings. After an intense show, which would often be punctuated by half a dozen encores, the group would come offstage drenched in sweat.

This was the routine for Elton John and his team while they toured America; although Elton and his team took a brief hiatus in order to perform at the *Royal Variety Performance*, a televised variety show broadcast each year in the United Kingdom to raise funds on behalf of the Royal Variety Charity, for which Queen Elizabeth II serves as patron. For that show, Elton played his latest hit "Crocodile Rock," which was a massive success in

his home country. After this, the group went back to the United States, where they continued their traveling odyssey until their final show, on November 26, 1972, at the Bayfront Center in St. Petersburg, Florida. Upon his return to the UK at the beginning of December, Elton went to Pinner to play for the students at his old school at the request of his former teachers. When he was there, he took stock of how far he'd come in his life. It was the end of 1972 and he was flourishing, especially since *Madman Across the Water* had just hit tenth place in the *Billboard* rankings of best-selling albums of the year. *Honky Château* was also on that list, but it occupied the third spot. Could he have hoped for anything better? Probably not, but then one doesn't become a rock superstar by having low expectations.

The Jamaica Fiasco

Nineteen seventy-three began with a celebration of the success of "Daniel," a single taken from *Don't Shoot Me I'm Only the Piano Player,* both of which were released at the end of January in the United Kingdom. By that time, Elton was already far from the London gloom: The singer had flown off to enjoy the sun in Jamaica with his entire team. The plan was to record the next album there in the hopes of not being interrupted by the outside world. The Rolling Stones' drummer, Charlie Watts, recommended to Gus Dudgeon that he should go to Dynamic Sounds Studio in Kingston. The Stones had just recorded *Goats Head Soup* at this location, treasured in Jamaican musical history, which was also where Bob Marley and the Wailers recorded *Catch a Fire*. "We basically packed up the caravans and rolled on out there. And it just basically descended into shit, man. It was just a joke,"[88] Bernie would remember later.

The musicians discovered an electric, threatening atmosphere in the town, where violence was omnipresent. Elton was visibly frightened by the situation, and he locked himself away securely in his hotel room, where he was forced to compose on an electric Fender Rhodes while trying to forget that the girlfriend of Bill Wyman, the Stones' bass player, had been assaulted in the same neighborhood just a few weeks ago. He clearly succeeded in compartmentalizing his fears, and he

Gus Dudgeon realized that by having the group sing in the same voice around a microphone, Davey, Dee, and Nigel could form a formidable vocal trio.

managed to write eighteen melodies in three days. The only problem: A strike had paralyzed the studio where the musicians were supposed to record. "There was barbed wire around the studio. Guys with machine guns," recalled Bernie. "People yell[ed] obscenities at us in the street. There wasn't one positive vibe in the place."[88] Very quickly Dynamic Studios started to show that its name was not entirely accurate. "The first sign we got that something might be a bit wrong," recalled Davey Johnstone, "was that when the guy who ran the studio, we heard him say, 'Carlton, get the microphone.' [...] Like, 'Get *the* microphone.' You know, we use like twenty mics on the drums, even in those days."[88] Whenever Gus asked for a new piece of equipment, he was always given the same answer: "Tomorrow." But nothing ever arrived, and soon he had to face the facts: It would be impossible to record Elton John's next album under these conditions. The decision was therefore made to leave the place early, and to find a new studio to accommodate the sessions for the next album. "So we decided to leave early. And that didn't go down too well. They impounded our equipment. They took away our rental cars. And then Bernie and I were being driven to the airport. I thought, 'Oh my God, they're going to take us, they're just going to kill us.'"[88]

Return to Hérouville

The musicians went back to the Château d'Hérouville, the studio where they'd had so much previous success. "You know, in retrospect," Bernie later explained, "I think [...] it was preordained for that to happen. Simply because maybe we were so

relieved to get out of there, it maybe gave us a new lease on life. And a new enthusiasm for writing, because when we went to France, we wrote all of those songs in about two weeks."[88]

During the four months preceding their arrival at the studio, in May 1973, Elton was savoring the commercial success of *Don't Shoot Me I'm Only the Piano Player*, while also working to complete a short tour of England that ran from February 24 to March 27. During this time he also managed to finally turn the idea of creating his own label into a reality. The Rocket Record Company was officially launched in February 1973, having been announced with a full-page ad in *Melody Maker*. Each of the five musketeers behind the idea would have their own role to play: John Reid was in charge of the legal and contractual side of things, Steve Brown managed the day-to-day office business, and Elton, Bernie, and Gus took care of the creative aspects, constantly scouting for new talent.

May 1973 marked another turning point in Elton's career. The contract that bound him and Bernie to DJM officially expired on May 10, at which point John Reid would become the exclusive manager of their interests. Reid had noticed that Elton and Bernie did not own the rights to their own songs, which were held by Dick James until after their death. The businessman planned to profit from his "Elton investment" for as long as possible, and he refused to return the rights to Elton and Bernie in spite of repeated requests from Reid. But Reid was determined to give Elton and Bernie full ownership of their work, even if it meant going to court. No matter how things panned out in court, there was absolutely no question of renewing any

Released a few months after Pink Floyd's *The Dark Side of the Moon*, which had close associations with *The Wizard of Oz*, *Goodbye Yellow Brick Road* also made specific reference to the movie classic.

contracts with Dick James. What better place to go to clear one's head of ongoing legal battles than the beautiful, haunted old manor house in Hérouville?

Productive Sessions

The next round of recording sessions began on May 7, 1973. Comfortably installed in their familiar bubble, the musicians went with the flow. "Everybody seemed to be getting on very well," confided Bernie. "Again, I think after the whole debacle of Jamaica, I think anything would have worked. We were so relieved, and it just became this very conducive kind of atmosphere, to working. You know, we'd write in the morning, and sort of just walk around the grounds, and go and record whenever we felt like it."[88] And Davey added, "It was definitely right place, right time for us. [...] It was almost like we couldn't put a foot wrong. You know, everything we did was just the right thing, you know. Every part we put on was right."[88] They had indeed been on a long road. Nearly four months after their catastrophic sessions in Kingston, not much was left of the songs that were supposed to make up the new album. "I think we had nothing when we arrived, other than a few pieces written in Jamaica. It could really be said that it was a Bohemian undertaking,"[88] confessed Bernie.

Gus Dudgeon managed the sessions with a light touch, supported by his loyal lieutenant, David Hentschel. "I was basically in charge of setting up the instruments in the studio—putting them in the right areas. Choosing which microphones to use and placing them in the studio, plugging them into the console, getting the sounds…"[89] Dudgeon, who knew the exact sound he wanted to achieve, made some decisive choices that would affect the overall tone of the album. First: the piano. Gus quickly noticed that recording the piano with the lid down produced a terrible output and that there were "holes" in the sound, even after using two microphones. So he decided to create an "inverted" piano by mounting an "empty" piano on top of the normal piano (now sans lid), and placing microphones at a distance from the piano's strings. "The idea was to keep the sound from the drums from spilling on to the piano mics,"[89] explained David Hentschel.

Next: the backing vocals, which were often of vital importance on *Goodbye Yellow Brick Road*. Gus Dudgeon set out rules about the vocals that were not to be broken. Starting from the guiding principle that Nigel, Dee, and Davey owed their effectiveness as backing vocalists to the uniqueness of each of their voices—the guitarist's was rather throaty, the bass player's was high-pitched and penetrating, and the drummer's was very low—Gus refused to let them sing into the same microphone. Instead he insisted on recording them separately before mixing them together.

"Without that it we could never have obtained the sound required. It was like having a trombone, a triangle, and a double bass in front of the same microphone: it's not feasible," he confirmed. "So everyone had their own microphone. And this way they kept the same position and I had control. I controlled them individually in order to obtain a good mixture. Once we had this mixture, we kept it like that. So we tried to do the backing vocals over three or four days in a row, to avoid having to redo the installation and start again."[88]

Gus Dudgeon and David Hentschel worked hard to exploit the potential of each individual member of the group, while avoiding calling upon Elton unless they absolutely had to, so that they could refrain from wasting his creative energies. "He got bored very quickly. Sometimes, we did only backing vocals for three days, and he then came to listen to them," recalled Gus. "From the beginning the result pleased him. He said: 'That's fantastic, guys!' He always operated that way when I reworked his disks; he was only there for the final result."[88]

The sessions for recording as a group went off without a hitch. The key word from these days was *spontaneity*. "We probably did about four songs a day. Writing them and recording them. Plus overdubbing, plus vocals. It sounds insane. But that's the way it happened,"[88] insisted Elton. Three takes, four at the most, were necessary to wrap up each track. "But there was a lot of eye contact to make sure everyone [was] together. It was like a stage performance in some ways," added David Hentschel. "Generally, Elton would do the master vocals afterward. He'd do them really quickly: he'd just stand in the studio and sing two or three times. And once it was done it was done.

FOR ELTON ADDICTS

In 1987, after the release of "Candle in the Wind" on the album *Live in Australia*, *Goodbye Yellow Brick Road* had an unexpected return into the American top two hundred and it stayed there for another twelve weeks.

He's the consummate professional. He has wonderful concentration, and that is what it's all about in the studio…getting yourself in that 'zone' that sportsmen talk about. [...] Everyone was so focused. That is one thing that working in a residential studio gives you, if you can manage to be in the same room the entire time with the same people. It's like someone coming to stay at your house! But it does give you that wonderful focus, and I think that's why it happened so easily."[89]

Elton Sees Double

Working in this efficient manner, the group managed to outline the main album within a very short span of time—about three weeks in total. Very quickly it became obvious that they had enough material for a double album, although the competition was very stiff in this ambitious field: *The White Album* (1968) by the Beatles, *Electric Ladyland* (1968) by Jimi Hendrix, and *Exile on Main St.* (1972) by the Rolling Stones had all paved the way for this relatively new concept, but their success was a double-edged sword. It made the creation of a double album possible, but it also meant the risk of failure would be all the more humiliating. But Elton was confident. He knew that his melodies would hold up, and that Bernie's lyrics, as usual, complemented them perfectly, and vice versa. "The album is, in many respects, rather dark," the lyricist later explained. "Its songs evoke sadness and disappointment, there are alcoholics, prostitutes, and assassins, and also a lesbian who died in the underground."[88] It should be said that, based on the success of *Don't Shoot Me I'm Only the Piano Player*, with its universally appealing pop sound, Bernie felt the need to add a little bite to his lyrics: "I wanted to instill some anguish into what we were doing. I didn't want us to be considered just as a pop machine." In the end, "each song had its own specific identity,"[36] according to journalist Paul Gambaccini. "It wasn't just a love song. 'I miss you, I love you.' And then the next one is 'I love you, I miss you.' You had 'Saturday Night's Alright (For Fighting),' 'Candle in the Wind,' 'Bennie and the Jets,' I mean, completely different."[88]

After the sessions at the château, Gus and David went to Trident Studios in London to add the final touches and mix the album. Percussionist Ray Cooper notably played tambourine on "All the Girls Love Alice." Although he remained a fan of the strings arrangements previously written by Paul Buckmaster, this time Elton called upon another accomplished arranger to polish his new tracks: Del Newman had already worked with Elton on some demo sessions in 1968, and he had made a name for himself working alongside Cat Stevens on the album *Tea for the Tillerman* as well as with Paul Simon on the classic "American Tune." His melancholic approach to the orchestrations helped this next album to take a real step forward.

It all went fairly quickly: "We just spent maybe another week overdubbing and then two weeks mixing, probably. For a double album, that is very fast,"[89] David Hentschel recalled.

Through the Looking Glass

Shortly after the beginning of their recording sessions, Elton and Bernie started to throw around ideas for the title of their new opus: *Vodka and Tonics* and *Silent Movies Talking Pictures* were both considered as possibilities. In the end, *Goodbye Yellow Brick Road* was chosen in deference to the *The Wizard of Oz*, a film that was meaningful to both Elton and Bernie. As with most double albums, this one is experimental and can sometimes feel like a rough draft as it oscillates between songs with shades of light and dark, but it presents the listener with an impressive selection of musical styles.

This album was, without a doubt, the greatest creation Elton and Bernie had made by this point in their career. That meant it required an album cover to match is elevated stature. While working on the design, David Larkham reimagined an advertising image that he noticed in the portfolio of an illustrator named Ian Beck, which showed a man looking nostalgically at a poster on a wall. While developing this idea, he opted to show Elton wearing a jacket and satin pants along with a pair of platform boots in the same color as Judy Garland's famous ruby red slippers. Outfitted thusly, Larkham showed Elton in the process of crossing into—or backing out of?—a poster of the famous yellow brick road that winds its way through the so-called land of Oz. By depicting Elton passing, as if by magic, from a drab, urban, and industrial environment into a rural, sunny, and brilliant world, Larkham sums up the last four years of Elton's life in one symbolic image.

Goodbye Yellow Brick Road was released on October 5, 1973, on MCA Records in the United States and Canada. It was distributed by DJM Records in the rest of the world. Fifteen days after its release, it entered the *Billboard* charts in seventeenth place. In less than a month it was at number one, a position it maintained for eight weeks. After that, it stayed in the top ten for nine months and, it stayed in the top two hundred for two years!

FUNERAL FOR A FRIEND / LOVE LIES BLEEDING

Elton John, Bernie Taupin / 11:07

Musicians
Elton John: vocals, piano
Davey Johnstone: electric guitar, backing vocals
Dee Murray: bass, backing vocals
Nigel Olsson: drums, backing vocals
David Hentschel: ARP synthesizer

Recorded
Château d'Hérouville, Hérouville, France: May 7, 1973

Technical Team
Producer: Gus Dudgeon
Sound Engineer: David Hentschel
Assistant Sound Engineers: Andy Scott (Hérouville), Peter Kelsey (London)
Production Coordinator: Steve Brown

FOR ELTON ADDICTS
Axl Rose, the Guns N' Roses singer, acknowledged the influence of "Funeral for a Friend / Love Lies Bleeding" on his band's classic song "November Rain," which was released in 1991 on the album *Use Your Illusion I*. With its 8:57 running time, "November Rain" became the longest song ever to reach the top ten in the Billboard Hot 100.

Genesis and Lyrics

Before becoming part of an epic, eleven-minute piece that skillfully combines two numbers, "Funeral for a Friend" was just a sad piano ballad. That was one of Elton's favorite exercises when he was feeling a bit down: "I got very down one day. I'm hung up on things like that. I like tearful, plodding music," Elton once confessed to Tom Doyle.[11] In the first part, he imagines the type of music he would like to hear at his own funeral. But, having given it due consideration, he did not really see the album opening with a funeral march…Chance took care of the rest, as he explained in 2001: "Things are sometimes down to chance. This was the case with 'Funeral for a Friend,' a simple instrumental piece at the beginning, which became a cornerstone of my show. It shouldn't have been incorporated into 'Love Lies Bleeding.' I said to myself that it needed something after an instrumental part. It was a double album: The order of the songs mattered. We had 'Love Lies Bleeding,' a song in *A*, and 'Funeral for a Friend,' which finished in *A*. We then decided to assemble the two pieces and this worked, quite simply."[88]

For his part, as far as the piece was concerned, Bernie emphasized the performance of the musicians over his own: "For me this is what makes the distinctiveness of this number. The instrumental prowess is enormous. One is forced to sit down and listen. In other words: 'Take your seat, the journey is commencing.'"[88]

Production

It was with this Wagnerian piece that the team started the recording sessions at the Château d'Hérouville, on May 7, 1973. Ironically, it was also on this piece that that last notes of the album would be added during the mixing. In fact, although the piece stands out with the nuanced playing of Davey Johnstone, between the harmonics reminiscent of the sound of a flute—due to the judicious use of a volume pedal—and an incandescent solo, it also shines with a panting and enormous rhythm section on the second part, with an appropriate doubling of the cymbals, and also the magnificent backing vocals—"We nicked that from the Stones,"[88] said Gus later. But not initially planned was the famous introduction on ARP synthesizer by David Hentschel, which he recorded at Trident Studios during the mixing of the album. At this time, the

Platform boots, sparkling trousers, and a top hat: Elton sometimes appropriated the dress codes of glam rock onstage, as he did here in 1973.

plan was still to call Elton's seventh opus *Silent Movies and Talking Pictures*, and Gus Dudgeon envisaged opening it up with the famous 20th Century Fox jingle. The problem was, he could not obtain the rights. So he asked David Hentschel as a matter of urgency to write an arrangement, as he had done for "Hercules" and "Rocket Man" on previous albums. "I think I had three or four days to do it and write it down, and then when I got to the studio we did it all in about seven or eight hours,"[89] remembers Hentschel. He tackled this challenge like a mathematical exercise, looking in the album for things that worked easily together, from the point of view of the harmony, to create a melody. "I know I used some lines from 'Danny Bailey,' 'I've Seen That Movie Too,' 'Candle in the Wind,' and one or two others,"[89] he remembered in 2013. So his introduction was "stitched" onto the recording that had been made in Hérouville. This was only discovered by Elton's musicians right at the end of mixing.

At one time thought of as a possible single, "Funeral for a Friend / Love Lies Bleeding" was rejected on account of its length. This did not prevent some of the FM radio stations, especially those with prog-rock inclinations, from giving it significant airtime. This epic piece therefore gradually earned its stripes as an Elton classic and is always acclaimed in his concerts.

CANDLE IN THE WIND

Elton John, Bernie Taupin / 3:49

Musicians
Elton John: vocals, piano
Davey Johnstone: electric guitar, backing vocals
Dee Murray: bass, backing vocals
Nigel Olsson: drums, backing vocals

Recorded
Château d'Hérouville, Hérouville, France: May 7, 1973

Technical Team
Producer: Gus Dudgeon
Sound Engineer: David Hentschel
Assistant Sound Engineers: Andy Scott (Hérouville), Peter Kelsey (London)
Production Coordinator: Steve Brown

Single Release
Candle in the Wind / Bennie and the Jets
UK Release: February 22, 1974, on DJM Records (ref. DJS 10297)
Best UK Chart Ranking: 11

Marilyn Monroe was the original inspiration for "Candle in the Wind."

Genesis and Lyrics

Of all the classic songs featured on this album, "Candle in the Wind" was destined to become as legendary and eternal as the tragic subject that inspired it. Bernie, like millions of other people throughout the world, had been captivated by the glamour and fragility of Marilyn Monroe. In May 1971, for his twenty-first birthday, Elton had even given him one of the icon's dresses, carefully laid out in a glass-fronted case. The evocative title of the song is inspired by a comment from the record producer Clive Davis, who described Janis Joplin as a "candle in the wind." "I just, for some reason, kept hearing this term," explained Bernie in 2001. "I thought, what a great, great way of describing somebody's life. [...] To be quite honest, I was not that enamored with Marilyn Monroe. What I was enamored with was the idea of fame, or youth, or somebody being cut short in the prime of their life. I mean, basically, the song could have been about James Dean. It could have been about Montgomery Clift. It could have been about Jim Morrison. Anyone whose life is cut short at the prime point of their career. And how we glamourize death. How we immortalize people. And that's really what that song is about."[88]

Starting from that point of view, Bernie provides a beautiful homage to Norma Jeane Mortenson (Marilyn's real name), putting himself into the shoes of the "young man in the twenty-second row" who not only sees the cinema star on the screen but "sees you as something more than sexual / More than just our Marilyn Monroe." By calling her Norma Jeane, he rehabilitates her image as a human being, making us all fully aware that the young woman who became Marilyn Monroe had been commodified and relentlessly exploited by the film industry. As for Elton, he had no difficulty finding himself in the song, since he was a devout fan of Marilyn: "I was a huge Marilyn Monroe fan, as well as Elvis Presley. When you saw them, they looked like they came from another planet. In the fifties when I had my hair cut and I first saw a picture of Elvis Presley in *Life* magazine, I thought, 'My God, who is this guy?' And with Marilyn Monroe, it's like, 'That's the most glamourous woman that's ever been.'"[90]

Production

Recorded on May 7, at the very beginning of the sessions at Hérouville, "Candle in the Wind" caused a rare disagreement between Elton and Davey Johnstone. "When we first recorded

Elton delivered a faultless performance of the new version of "Candle in the Wind" during the worldwide broadcast of Princess Diana's funeral at Westminster Abbey.

At Diana's funeral, Elton was worried that he might not be able to remember the new words that Bernie had written for the occasion: "I'd performed 'Candle in the Wind' hundreds of times. It really wasn't beyond the realms of possibility that I might lose myself in the performance, forget about the teleprompter altogether and start singing the original lyrics.

it," the guitarist said, "I did it with electric guitar. Elton's feeling was, 'I want this to have a bit of a tougher feel.' In fact, he also had the idea for that guitar lick when he sings, 'candle in the wind...' When he sang the part to me, I went, 'That's so cheesy. You're not serious. I'm not going to play that.' It's one of the few times we've had an argument like that in the studio. And he said, 'Will you at least try it?' And I went, 'OK.'"[31] As an "Elton-compatible" guitarist, Davey did as he was asked, and, evidently, the singer's instinct was correct. "Since in the end it sounded good, we doubled it. So, right at the end of the piece, we added a nice harmony, but which appears only once. We could have added another one, but for what?"[88] The poignant quality of "Candle in the Wind" is derived above all from its soaring backing vocals, provided as usual by Nigel, Dee, and Davey. As was their custom, they preferred to wait until the recording was finished and Elton was occupied elsewhere before they recorded their voices.

A Delayed Success: Diana's Song

"Candle in the Wind" was only moderately successful when it was issued as a single in 1974 in the United Kingdom, where it leveled off at eleventh place in the charts. It had to wait until 1987, and a live version with the Melbourne Symphony Orchestra taken from *Live in Australia*, for the song to become a big hit in the United States, where it eventually went to number six. In 1997, the track was consecrated as "Diana's song," going to number one throughout the world, this time under the new title: "Candle in the Wind 1997."

The accidental death of Princess Diana on August 31, 1997, had a profound effect on Elton John, who was her friend.

After a period of despondency, he finally decided to pay homage to her by dedicating a song in her honor. He and Bernie decided to rewrite "Candle in the Wind." Elton agreed to sing this new version—which began with these now famous words: "Goodbye England's rose / May you ever grow in our hearts"—at Diana's funeral inside Westminster Abbey, on September 6, 1997. It was the only time he would sing it in public. Just after the ceremony, he went to Townhouse Studios, in Shepherd's Bush, where the legendary producer George Martin was waiting to record it. The author's and composer's royalties were entirely donated to the charitable foundation created in memory of the Princess of Wales. "I sang it twice, live at the piano, and went home, leaving George Martin to overdub a string quartet on it. [Later, watching TV, I saw] people were throwing flowers at Diana's hearse from the bridges over the motorway. That was when I finally broke down. I hadn't felt able to show emotion all day,"[3] Elton confided in his biography. The single, which sold more than 35 million copies, became the biggest selling single of all time, though some claim "White Christmas" by Bing Crosby still holds the top spot.

In the rockumentary *Elton John: Goodbye Yellow Brick Road*, produced in 2001, Bernie said: "The quality of the melody has such a powerful character that it almost becomes a hymn. Never mind the words that go with it. People let themselves be carried by it, carried along by this sumptuous melody. Really, you could be singing anything. This song is so rooted in the spirit of the public that the words don't matter anymore: it's 'Candle in the Wind.'"[88] Elton continues to consider the song magnificent.

BENNIE AND THE JETS

Elton John, Bernie Taupin / 5:23

Musicians

Elton John: vocals, piano, Farfisa organ
Davey Johnstone: electric guitar, acoustic guitar, backing vocals
Dee Murray: bass, backing vocals
Nigel Olsson: drums, backing vocals

Recorded

Château d'Hérouville, Hérouville, France: May 1973

Technical Team

Producer: Gus Dudgeon
Sound Engineer: David Hentschel
Assistant Sound Engineers: Andy Scott (Hérouville), Peter Kelsey (London)
Production Coordinator: Steve Brown

Single Release

Candle in the Wind / Bennie and the Jets
UK Release: February 22, 1974, on DJM Records (ref. DJS 297)
Best UK Chart Ranking: 37

Bennie and the Jets / Harmony
US Release: February 4, 1974, on MCA Records (ref. MCA-40198)
Best US Chart Ranking: 1

"Bennie and the Jets" is Elton John's third song, along with "Rocket Man" and "Tiny Dancer," to be turned into a music video as part of a 2017 YouTube competition called The Cut. Laura Brownhill and Jack Whiteley, two of the winners, created a very graphical, all black-and-white staging of the song.

Genesis and Lyrics

In this gently ironic satire of the 1970s music industry, Bernie relates the story of a fictitious glam-rock group, led by a scandalous singer with "electric boots" and "a mohair suit," and the fans. He explained his concept in *Esquire* magazine in 2012: "Because the whole idea of 'Bennie and the Jets' was almost Orwellian, you know—it was supposed to be futuristic. They were supposed to be a prototypical female rock 'n' roll band out of science fiction. Automatons."[85] Whether or not this was pure coincidence, Elton emphasizes the robot aspect with a very hypnotic and stuttering "B-B-B-Bennie…" combined with a falsetto voice, in the manner of Frankie Valli, whom Elton had seen in concert and really loved. "I don't remember what I wanted 'Bennie and the Jets' to be. For me, it was a real throwaway lyric. That was very much Elton's creation,"[6] explained Bernie modestly. He admitted that he drew his inspiration as much from comics as from the work of German fashion photographer Helmut Newton. Of course, not counting the musical fashion of the time, illustrated by the success of glam-rock stars David Bowie and Marc Bolan. "The 'Buh-buh-buh' was pure Elton," the lyricist said in admiration. "I didn't write it that way. But it was a great interpretation."[85] According to Gus Dudgeon, Bernie liked to communicate images: "It never mattered to him necessarily that the lyric told a story from front to back. What mattered to him was setting up […] little visual pictures in your mind. And if they didn't link together, well, so what? You know, the important thing is, does it sound good when it's sung?"[88] Some reviewers have subsequently interpreted Bennie as a reference to Benzedrine, and the Jets as representations of amphetamine, but this is far from the case. Elton has said at every opportunity that he was still very abstemious as far as drugs were concerned when *Goodbye Yellow Brick Road* was recorded.

Production

It is difficult to imagine that at the time of its recording, "Bennie and the Jets" was thought of as a future hit. However, Gus Dudgeon sensed that the hypnotic, staccato playing by Elton and his very particular diction, reinforced by the brilliant idea of the stuttering could assume a new dimension when the piece was played in concert. So he took the lead and worked on making it sound as live as possible when they were recording: "We

put on some sound effects, which are basically from an Elton concert at the Festival Hall, that he'd done about four or five years before. You've got Jimi Hendrix's applause [from his concert] on the Isle of Wight. [...] We threw a load of flat-back [guitar] on it to make it sound live. Dubbed on some whistles and hand claps doing the wrong beat because English audiences always do the wrong beat,"[88] he later confided. David Hentschel explains very clearly how this delay was handled: "That was one of the first uses of the Digital Delay Line, which was a digital method of producing (very short) delays. That was the main effect we used, on the hand claps. There were only three of us doing the hand claps, and we wanted to make it sound like a huge stadium audience clapping along to the song! So it was the three of us purposely trying to clap outside the time. We did it over and over again and for each pass that we did I could make it sound like nine people instead of the three, so it ended up sounding like about 40 people... and then with juggling reverbs and furthering the delays I made it sound like the real thing."[89] But despite all the efforts of Gus and David, Elton could not imagine releasing the song as a single: "The American record company kept pushing me to release 'Bennie and the Jets' as a single and I fought them tooth and nail: it's a really odd song, it doesn't sound like anything else I've done, it's five minutes long; why don't you just put out 'Candle in the Wind,' like we've done in Britain? Then they told me it was being played all over black radio stations in Detroit."[3]

In 1974, two Detroit radio stations, one of which historically had a Black following (WJLB), played the track in heavy rotation and received an incredible response. Pat Pipolo, who was working in promotion at MCA Records, urged Elton to acquiesce, and he finally allowed himself to be convinced: "I said, [...] 'I think you'll be an R&B artist as well as a pop artist.' So he called the main office, and he told them what we should do with 'Bennie and the Jets.' [...] We released it. And sure enough, it went to number one pop as well as number one R&B, which amazed the world, I think. It certainly amazed Elton."[88]

"Bennie and the Jets" was released as a single in the United States on February 4, 1974, and reached first place in the Billboard Hot 100 shortly afterward. At the same time, the song rose to fifteenth place in *Billboard*'s Hot Soul Singles rankings. In the light of this second stat, Elton was invited to appear on *Soul Train* in May 1975. "[It was] an unreal thing, seeing my name in among the singles by Eddie Kendricks and Gladys Knight and Barry White. I may not have been the first white artist to do that, but I can say with some certainty I was the first artist from Pinner,"[3] he wrote with amazement in his autobiography.

The meaning behind the title of the song is a subject of heated debate. A group called Bennie and the Jets was playing in the Detroit area long before Elton's song ever became a success. Could it have inspired the song's title? Or it could have been Frank Zappa's *Cruising with Ruben & the Jets*? Released in 1968, it depicted a fictional group from the 1950s called the Jets and a man named Ruben who owned three dogs: Baby, Martha, and Benny...! Further adding confusion, when Elton's song was released as a single in 1974, the "Bennie" in the title was misspelled as "Benny" on the album jacket.

GOODBYE YELLOW BRICK ROAD

Elton John, Bernie Taupin / 3:13

1973

Musicians
Elton John: vocals, piano
Davey Johnstone: electric guitar (Leslie cabinet), backing vocals
Dee Murray: bass, backing vocals
Nigel Olsson: drums, backing vocals
Del Newman: arrangements, direction
Unidentified musicians: orchestra

Recorded
Château d'Hérouville, Hérouville, France: May 1973

Technical Team
Producer: Gus Dudgeon
Sound Engineer: David Hentschel
Assistant Sound Engineers: Andy Scott (Hérouville), Peter Kelsey (London)
Production Coordinator: Steve Brown

Single Release
Goodbye Yellow Brick Road / Screw You
UK Release: September 7, 1973, on DJM Records (ref. DJS.285)
Best UK Chart Ranking: 6

Goodbye Yellow Brick Road / Young Man's Blues
US Release: October 15, 1973, on MCA Records (ref. MCA-40148)
Best US Chart Ranking: 2

Genesis and Lyrics

This moving ballad, which is not unlike the songs produced by Lennon and McCartney, is a perfect summary of the story that Taupin had already explored in "Mona Lisas and Mad Hatters" and "Honky Cat." It relates to this gentle, innocent country dweller attracted by the bright city lights. Having become a plaything for a high-society figure, and nostalgic for the more carefree times, he tries to escape from his gilded cage, to return to the farm, where less appealing but more rewarding tasks await. For Bernie, this song goes back to his roots of his first experience of London life in 1967: "It was about me being the country kid coming to town and being a little out of my depth. It was a sort of Dick Whittington tale—going to the city, making it big, but knowing that reality lay back where he came from. It just ended up being a song that seemed to echo those feelings of homesickness that I experienced in my first few months down in London. I was torn between the potential glamour of the bright lights and my country roots."[11] One verse had long been a source of amusement for the fans: "Back to the howling old owl in the woods." With amusement, Bernie commented: "You could point out that owls don't howl, but I love the way the words sound together and that's as important as anything. The song is a thinly veiled reference to the simple life and going back to your roots."[28]

The title "Goodbye Yellow Brick Road" is a direct allusion to the yellow bricks of *The Wizard of Oz*. It's a metaphor for success, but it also offers a path back to a simple way of life. It's as though Bernie is trying to answer an age-old question: Does fame really offer everything we expect, or is it not just as pleasing to live a peaceful lifestye? This song also could be a reference to the road paved with famous yellow bricks from William the Conqueror's brother's castle, which was demolished in 1964 and which passed not far from Bernie and Maxine's cottage in Tealby.

Production

In playing out the sequence of five chords already heard in "Son of Your Father," on *Tumbleweed Connection*, Elton shows himself to have been particularly inspired in starting off this piece. "What I do when I write, is I usually get a chord sequence," he explained. "[For this piece] it was the intro that I got first. [...] And the melody is very wistful, as well. [...] I

Davey Johnstone and Dee Murray performed tracks from the new album, *Goodbye Yellow Brick Road,* at London's Hammersmith Odeon on December 21, 1973.

have to take it down a key note because it's so high. My voice has changed so much. When I listen to that album, I sound like some castrati singing."[88]

Dee Murray initially accompanies Elton with simple bass line notes, until Nigel Olsson's drum makes its entrance. The mate sound of his snare drum and a few rolls on the toms become the solid marker for the song's rhythm; Dee and Davey are slightly in the background, with the guitarist reeling out attractive arpeggios simply to create subtle embellishments. Beyond the majestic strings arrangement created by Del Newman, it is the backing vocals that give the refrain its dreamlike ambiance.

Vocally, Elton is at the summit of his powers, both in the control of his very high register during the refrain, and in the magnetic phrasing of his verses. "One of the secrets in his piano playing," explained Gus Dudgeon, "was his ability to think where the vocal was going to lay against the track, and then put in certain piano lines that [...] would link the lines together vocally. [...] And the vocal, I mean it's just weird. [...]

He just went out and sang in a sort of sped-up voice. And [...] a lot of people asked me if I'd sped the tape up. But in fact, it's not sped up. It's just the weird way he decided to do it. That's Elton."[88]

On the evening when Elton completed the recording of his voice for "Goodbye Yellow Brick Road," a little after midnight, a young musician named Leroy Gomez entered the studio at the precise moment when the song ended. He had heard that Elton was at Hérouville and that he was looking for a saxophonist. He was there when Elton's voice died out on what was to be one of his future hits (number one in Canada, number two in the United States, and number six in the United Kingdom). Timidly, he introduced himself. Elton, still floating on the cloud of "Goodbye Yellow Brick Road," welcomed the young saxophonist and asked Gus to change their plans for the night: They would be recording the saxophone. Leroy Gomez appeared on two tracks from the album: "Screw You" (the B-side of the "Goodbye Yellow Brick Road" single) and "Social Disease."

THIS SONG HAS NO TITLE

Elton John, Bernie Taupin / 2:23

Musician
Elton John: vocals, piano, Farfisa organ
Recorded
Château d'Hérouville, Hérouville, France: May 1973
Technical Team
Producer: Gus Dudgeon
Sound Engineer: David Hentschel
Assistant Sound Engineers: Andy Scott (Hérouville), Peter Kelsey (London)
Production Coordinator: Steve Brown

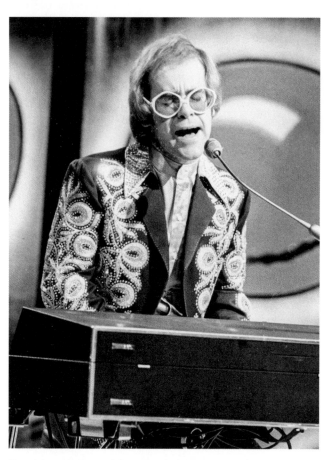

Elton John took charge of the various keyboards in "This Song Has No Title" while also handling lead and backing vocals.

Genesis and Lyrics

A novice with a curiosity for everything: this is the attire donned by Bernie this time, leaving Elton the job of applying a melody to his story. The desire to write and to experiment in his art is the raison d'être of this singular, appealing character. With his freshness and spontaneity, he has the rare, intangible power to turn each episode of learning into an authentic adventure. He wishes to be initiated into "the wild side of life," to visit the "alleys where the murders are done" and is happy to "learn just a little bit more" each day. In a hurry for everything, the narrator finally confesses: "If we're all going somewhere, let's get there soon." He does not even allow time to find a decent title for the song, concluding it with a simple but inventive: "Oh this song's got no title, just words and a tune." This does not mean that the lyrics are shallow. Bernie takes care to describe this thirst for knowledge as a true addiction: "If I was an artist who paints with his eyes / I'd study my subject and silently cry / Cry for the darkness to come down on me / For confusion to carry on turning the wheel."

Production

Elton John recorded this song on his own, including the backing vocals. In total harmony with himself, on the three vocal tracks that adorn the song, Elton overlays two tracks of Farfisa organ, three tracks of acoustic piano, one of electric piano, and one of the Mellotron. Light and airy, the arrangement leaves the biggest space for Elton's piano playing, which is expressive and powerful on the refrains, more detailed and nuanced on the verses, and well supported by the associated sonorities, in this case a flute, or strings, simulated by the Farfisa organ.

GREY SEAL

Elton John, Bernie Taupin / 4:00

Musicians
Elton John: vocals, piano, Mellotron, Fender Rhodes
Davey Johnstone: electric guitar
Dee Murray: bass
Nigel Olsson: drums, congas

Recorded
Château d'Hérouville, Hérouville, France: May 1973

Technical Team
Producer: Gus Dudgeon
Sound Engineer: David Hentschel
Assistant Sound Engineers: Andy Scott (Hérouville), Peter Kelsey (London)
Production Coordinator: Steve Brown

Considered to be too surreal for its own good, "Grey Seal" is one of the lesser-known songs in Bernie's repertoire.

Genesis and Lyrics

Just as "Skyline Pigeon" had been picked up and reused for *Don't Shoot Me I'm Only the Piano Player*, Elton was once again looking through his archives for an older number that could be given a new chance at life. This was the case with "Grey Seal," which was originally on the B-side of the 1970 single "Rock and Roll Madonna."

The singer has often described Bernie's lyrics as surrealistic in nature, while Bernie did not hesitate to confirm that they were quite simply lacking in meaning: "It's oblique," Bernie admitted. "I hadn't a clue what I was writing about. It was just images." "Bernie hates that lyric," Elton said. "But I like it, because of the mixture of music and lyrics which is kind of Procol Harum–ish absurd, like a Dali painting."[31] However, as with "This Song Has No Title," "Grey Seal" conveys the idea of a quest for knowledge.

As is always the case with Bernie's lyrics, this song and its predecessor have attracted their share of interpretations. For example, Neil Barrett, who runs the podcast *I Guess That's Why They Call It the Elton John Podcast*, believes that the song relates to Plato's allegory of the cave, in which Socrates describes a group of prisoners who are chained to the wall of a cave for their entire lives, and for whom the only experience of reality is that of the shadows they see projected on the opposite wall of the cave. It is only when one of the prisoners escapes that he realizes he was being held captive, and that life consists of so much more than shadows on a wall.

Production

"Grey Seal" is a constantly evolving song, and a symbol of the triumphant and clear-minded production values of Gus Dudgeon. Driven by Dee's syncopated and inventive bass, the song never wavers from the feeling of urgency expressed in its very first notes. As he had done previously on "Crocodile Rock," Davey Johnstone abstains from playing any notes on the guitar, except during the intro, refrain, and outro. "When the verse comes in, it's just bass and drums and piano," he explained. "And then the guitar comes in strong on the chorus. It would suddenly give the track a different dimension and highlight a part when it comes in...It's something I learned from George Harrison. I'm a huge Harrison fan, and if you listen to a lot of Beatles tracks, there will be songs where the guitar comes bombing in and then it will be out again."[31]

When "Jamaica Jerk-Off" was rescued from the canceled recording sessions in Kingston, Elton ventured into new recording terrain.

COVERS

"Jamaica Jerk-Off" was covered by the Pioneers in 1974 and by Judge Dread in 1977.

FOR ELTON ADDICTS

Elton and Bernie conferred together when it was time to confirm the song's title. It should be said that some sensitivities could have been offended by "Jamaica Jerk-Off." The more consensual "Jamaica Twist" was therefore also considered...briefly. Then again, you're either rock 'n' roll or you aren't!

JAMAICA JERK-OFF

Reggae Dwight, Toots Taupin / 3:38

Musicians: Elton John: vocals, organs / **Davey Johnstone:** electric guitar / **Dee Murray:** bass / **Nigel Olsson:** drums / **Prince Rhino:** "vocal interjections" **Recorded:** Château d'Hérouville, Hérouville, France: May 1973 **Technical Team:** Producer: Gus Dudgeon / **Sound Engineer:** David Hentschel / **Assistant Sound Engineers:** Andy Scott (Hérouville), Peter Kelsey (London) / **Production Coordinator:** Steve Brown

Genesis and Lyrics

Completely different from the rest of the album, the invigorating "Jamaica Jerk-Off" offers a nice slice of reggae-inflected pop, though it left no lasting impression on Bernie Taupin, who has said that he has no recollection of writing the lyrics for it. Those lyrics amount to a eulogy for Jamaica and its festive lifestyle. The whole team had beaten a hasty retreat from the country just a few months earlier, when they attempted to record the album in Kingston. The city was roiling with fear and violence, and the creative team was eventually forced to leave for fear of being attacked by angry strikers. They left in such a hurry that they didn't even stop to collect what little material they had created in the studio. Elton and Bernie had written only a handful of songs, including this one. The lyrics depict a rather idyllic experience, evoking a life of leisure and the good things of life on the island, "playing guitar all day" and where the people are "all happy."

Production

The album's liner notes credit the song to an unknown duo of writer-composers: "Reggae Dwight and Toots Taupin." The latter name is a reference to Toots Hibbert, a major reggae star, with his group the Maytals, in the early 1970s. In addition, some "vocal interjections" are credited on Elton's organ solo to Prince Rhino—actually Gus Dudgeon, whose enthusiastic efforts did indeed deserve recognition. The pseudonym is a nod to his well-known passion for rhinoceroses—which had already manifested itself in some curious trumpet passages in "Hercules" on the *Honky Château* album. In the rest of the piece, Dee and Nigel's swaying rhythm section does its job, relegating Davey's rhythm guitar to second string.

I'VE SEEN THAT MOVIE TOO

Elton John, Bernie Taupin / 5:58

Musicians: Elton John: vocals, piano / **Davey Johnstone:** acoustic guitar, electric guitar / **Dee Murray:** bass / **Nigel Olsson:** drums / **Del Newman:** arrangement, direction / **Unidentified musicians:** orchestra
Recorded: Château d'Hérouville, Hérouville, France: May 1973
Technical Team: Producer: Gus Dudgeon / **Sound Engineer:** David Hentschel / **Assistant Sound Engineers:** Andy Scott (Hérouville), Peter Kelsey (London) / **Production Coordinator:** Steve Brown

Genesis and Lyrics

Closing the first side of the double album with a harrowing ballad was a gamble, which would not necessarily encourage the listener to continue on to the next side. But Elton and Bernie understood their public, and, rather than finishing with the bouncing, positive weirdness of "Jamaica Jerk-Off," the choice was made in favor of the somber but effective "I've Seen That Movie Too." The piece shares some minor chords with "The Thrill Is Gone" by B. B. King. It has a very expressive blues tonality, but it's the powerful subject matter of lost love, to which Bernie adds the emotion of anger felt by the main protagonist. The films in question in "I've Seen That Movie Too" are like allegories of falsehood, in this game in which the narrator has become a victim, a game that, while smitten but also knowing he has been betrayed, he describes with philosophical resignation and realism. No one knows what happens to the two lovers at the end of the song, but misfortune and sadness prevail.

Production

The song begins with a cocooned feel to the introduction in minor key, immediately setting the scene between Nigel Olsson's bouncy and jazzy high-hat cymbals, and Elton's melancholic and bluesy piano. Quickly but discreetly, Davey Johnstone's acoustic guitar and Dee Murray's elegant bass join these two musicians, while Nigel's powerful side drum, embellished with some descents on the toms, loads up an atmosphere already heavy with meaning in this story told by Bernie's lyrics. The narrator's anger is magisterially assumed by Elton, who guides the vocals in the finale. This follows a psychedelic magical solo by Davey, which reflects the situation well: It's first played in inverted form (which could symbolize the individual who is lying), and is then joined by a second track, more decisive and assured (the narrator?). But their cohabitation is finally cut short by chords worthy of a classical composition. It was also to classical music that Guns N' Roses front man Axl Rose compared Elton John's composition when he inducted Elton into the Rock and Roll Hall of Fame in 1994. And in the Guns N' Roses hit "You Could Be Mine," he went so far as to directly quote "I've Seen That Movie Too," with the line "'Cause I think we've seen that movie too."

SWEET PAINTED LADY

Elton John, Bernie Taupin / 3:54

Musicians: Elton John: vocals, piano / **Davey Johnstone:** acoustic guitar / **Dee Murray:** bass / **Nigel Olsson:** drums, tambourine / **Del Newman:** arrangements, direction / **Unidentified musicians:** orchestra
Recorded: Château d'Hérouville, Hérouville, France: May 1973
Technical Team: Producer: Gus Dudgeon / **Sound Engineer:** David Hentschel / **Assistant Sound Engineers:** Andy Scott (Hérouville), Peter Kelsey (London) / **Production Coordinator:** Steve Brown

Genesis and Lyrics

"Getting paid for being laid": Bernie Taupin resumed work on "Sweet Painted Lady," an archetypical portrayal of the nameless girls ("the one with no name") who waited for sailors in various ports, to give them a bit of human warmth in exchange for a few bucks, after months spent at sea. This affectionate track takes a sour view toward the ingratitude of these men, who disappear as soon as their needs have been satisfied: "Just forget we ever slept in your rooms / And we'll leave the smell of the sea in your beds / Where love's just a job and nothing is said." A simple "name of the game," as Bernie later explained elsewhere: "We were just more interested in creating very visual pieces of work that went beyond what people imagined the pop song of that time to be. [...] Maybe in retrospect it subconsciously is a concept album because you're just presenting all these characters in a sort of cinematic framework, you know. You're bringing up Danny Bailey and sweet painted ladies and dirty little girls, and now they're all part of this big sort of complex movie."[88]

Production

Musically, "Sweet Painted Lady" suffers somewhat from its place in the track listing, following the splendid "I've Seen That Movie Too" and coming before the more cinematic "The Ballad of Danny Bailey." It is not without its qualities, however, with the "saloon" atmosphere of the port bars perfectly reproduced on Elton's versatile piano, and by his almost blasé voice. Especially as the arranger, Del Newman, had the good idea of requesting some discreet brass, and an accordion player to illustrate the second part of the piece, thereby adding a welcome dose of nostalgia. The song ends with the sound of seagulls and the tide, which, in a perpetual, routine movement recedes as quickly as it rose, just like the sailors in the life of these women.

THE BALLAD OF DANNY BAILEY (1909-1934)

Elton John, Bernie Taupin / 4:23

Musicians: Elton John: vocals, piano / Davey Johnstone: electric guitar, backing vocals / Dee Murray: bass, backing vocals / Nigel Olsson: drums, backing vocals / Del Newman: arrangements, direction / Unidentified musicians: orchestra **Recorded:** Château d'Hérouville, Hérouville, France: May 1973 **Technical Team:** Producer: Gus Dudgeon / Sound Engineer: David Hentschel / Assistant Sound Engineers: Andy Scott (Hérouville), Peter Kelsey (London) / Production Coordinator: Steve Brown

Genesis and Lyrics

Unlike "Goodbye Yellow Brick Road," most of which was brought back from Jamaica in various pieces of luggage, "The Ballad of Danny Bailey" is one of the very last songs written by Bernie for the album, and it was created after the team had set themselves up at the Château d'Hérouville and the recording sessions had really started. "Danny Bailey is John Dillinger, you know, or Pretty Boy Floyd, or Clyde Barrow. You know, again, he is my composite gangster. I just love creating characters,"[88] the lyricist explained. "A lot of the songs began when I came across a great first line," he also said. "The perfect example is 'The Ballad of Danny Bailey.' I don't know if I'd seen a movie or read a book, but I came up with the first line, 'Some punk with a shotgun killed Danny Bailey / In cold blood in the lobby of a downtown motel.' And that was it. It would have gone a number of different ways, but it ended up being a tune about a bootlegger"[90] from Kentucky, who was killed at the age of twenty-five.

Production

The short life of Danny Bailey makes for quite a musical journey. It starts with Elton's somber piano before a drum stroke on the snares breaks the ambient calm, although Nigel Olsson's playing is not the only thing responsible for startling the listener. For added realism, an authentic gunshot was fired at four o'clock in the morning out of one of the rooms in the château, and it was later superimposed into the track. "It really shows off Dee Murray's bass playing," Gus Dudgeon said, "which I think is superb. [...] He's an underrated and superb musician. His sense of melody and his sense of understanding the lyric, and the way that the whole thing has to feel was, as far as I'm concerned, faultless. I've never really come across a bass player quite as good as him."[88] But beyond the sliding bass, with its incredible versatility, were the arrangements by Del Newman, which give the piece its depth, particularly in the splendid intervention of the backing vocals (at 2:36), which precede the very intense, soaring strings. "The way that Del Newman has tied the orchestra to the backing vocals is really clever," said Gus Dudgeon. "[...] The secret of a good arrangement is not trying to be fancy and flow all kinds of stuff in. It's a question of trying to tie everything together. I mean, I love great arrangers. And Del is certainly in that league."[88] With this piece, Newman reaches the heights of the best orchestral arrangements of his predecessor, Paul Buckmaster.

DIRTY LITTLE GIRL

Elton John, Bernie Taupin / 5:00

Musicians: Elton John: vocals, Leslie piano, Mellotron / Davey Johnstone: electric guitar / Dee Murray: bass / Nigel Olsson: drums **Recorded:** Château d'Hérouville, Hérouville, France: May 1973 **Technical Team:** Producer: Gus Dudgeon / Sound Engineer: David Hentschel / Assistant Sound Engineers: Andy Scott (Hérouville); Peter Kelsey (London) / Production Coordinator: Steve Brown

Genesis and Lyrics

There is not much to be saved from the lyrics of the abject "Dirty Little Girl," without doubt the weakest link in *Goodbye Yellow Brick Road*. "I've seen a lot of women who haven't had much luck / I've seen you looking like you've been run down by a truck" is one of many questionable lines that Bernie includes in this song. The narrator, a brutish character, effectively states to the song's female protagonist that she might have been a fashion icon—or influencer, if we want to bring the concept up-to-date—but ultimately, all she is good for now is cleaning other people's stairwells. The showstopper: "I'm gonna tell the world, you're a dirty little girl / Someone grab that bitch by the ears [...] / I bet she hasn't had a bath in years [...] / So don't show up around here till your social worker's helped." There is a clear determination to sound like a "bad boy," but to what end? The song is without any redeeming features and is basely misogynistic. How did these lyrics manage to escape the trash heap?

Production

Despite its greasy, even glutinous groove, created with the help of Davey Johnstone's dirty guitar, the bounding bass of Dee Murray, and Nigel Olsson's solid drums, "Dirty Little Girl" remains a relatively conventional, even insipid rock number. But the musicians should be given credit for their capacity to mimic the Rolling Stones, a band they greatly admired. This song would not, in fact, have been out of place on the *Black and Blue* album (1976). Elton hams things up to the maximum, pushing his vocals to the extreme and accentuating the end of each phrase in an improbable way, while playing his piano heavily. Never released as a single, "Dirty Little Girl" was not a track that Elton was terribly fond of, and he never played it in concert; Bernie has never provided the slightest explanation for his lyrics. There are two prevailing theories as to why: fear of a defamation complaint in case the identity of the person who inspired this track ever becomes public, or simple embarrassment. The unanimous verdict: "Dirty Little Girl" is one of the duo's most forgettable numbers. If not for its presence on this classic album, it would undoubtedly have passed into history without further notice.

ALL THE GIRLS LOVE ALICE

Elton John, Bernie Taupin / 5:08

Musicians: Elton John: vocals, piano / Davey Johnstone: electric guitar / Dee Murray: bass / Nigel Olsson: drums / David Hentschel: ARP synthesizer / Ray Cooper: tambourine / Kiki Dee: backing vocals
Recorded: Château d'Hérouville, Hérouville, France: May 1973
Technical Team: Producer: Gus Dudgeon / **Sound Engineer:** David Hentschel / **Assistant Sound Engineers:** Andy Scott (Hérouville), Peter Kelsey (London) / **Production Coordinator:** Steve Brown

Genesis and Lyrics

The subject of the outsider in distress is a topic to which Bernie Taupin often returns, and it is a recurring theme throughout *Goodbye Yellow Brick Road*. This is the case in "All the Girls Love Alice," a song in which the main character, a sixteen-year-old lesbian, dies under mysterious circumstances and is later found in the London subway. While Elton sometimes left out the odd line from the song, even entire verses, he always remained very faithful to the dark story that Bernie tells here, of a desperate girl who can't find a way out of her problems: "Reality, it seems, was just a dream," "It's like acting in a movie when you got the wrong part," "And who could you call your friends down in Soho?"

Production

Rejecting Bernie's lyrics or completely setting aside a disturbing subject could have been considered an understandable choice. The only way to give life to this story was not to make it into a ballad, which would have rendered it even more maudlin. The path of least resistance was to veer into the domain of heavy rock, supported on this occasion by Ray Cooper's will-o'-the-wisp tambourine (recorded back in London), the slightly nonchalant backing vocals of Kiki Dee (who had just signed with the Rocket Record Company), and David Hentschel's ARP synthesizer. The battering ram guitar played by Davey Johnstone contributes to the hard-rock tonality of the piece, especially as it is passed through the wringer of an audacious Uni-Vibe pedal (phase shifter). Nigel Olsson's drums disappear discreetly from

the refrains before reappearing abruptly to give the finale its wild character. Davey Johnstone mixes his solo into this with several improvised bottleneck tracks, rapidly sliding a bottle over the neck of his guitar, while Nigel is recorded revving the motor of a Mini Cooper on the gravel drive outside the château. To emphasize this almost unhealthy atmosphere, a cacophonous ambient noise of street sirens is also added.

YOUR SISTER CAN'T TWIST (BUT SHE CAN ROCK'N'ROLL)

Elton John, Bernie Taupin / 2:42

Musicians: Elton John: vocals, piano, Farfisa organ / Davey Johnstone: electric guitar, slide guitar, backing vocals / Dee Murray: bass, backing vocals / Nigel Olsson: drums, backing vocals
Recorded: Château d'Hérouville, Hérouville, France: May 1973
Technical Team: Producer: Gus Dudgeon / **Sound Engineer:** David Hentschel / **Assistant Sound Engineers:** Andy Scott (Hérouville), Peter Kelsey (London) / **Production Coordinator:** Steve Brown

Genesis and Lyrics

Like "Dirty Little Girl" before it, "Your Sister Can't Twist" would probably not have been missed by anyone had it accidentally disappeared from the track listing of *Goodbye Yellow Brick Road*. In fact, the song fails in all the ways that "Crocodile Rock" succeeded in terms of creating an homage to the rock 'n' roll of the 1950s and 1960s. Try as Elton might in his frenetic flurries on his Farfisa organ, the magic does not work, and he struggles to create any interest in the story of this sixteen-year-old who does not know how to dance the twist.

Production

By his own admission, Elton wanted to drink from the same creative spring that inspired "Crocodile Rock." Without being unpleasant, because the piece is quite explosive, with fairly wacky keyboard lines and backing vocals impregnated clearly inspired by the famous harmonies of the Beach Boys, "Your Sister Can't Twist (But She Can Rock 'n' Roll)" remains middling. Just like "Crocodile Rock," the song does have the merit of definitively unlocking and removing Elton's complex about playing the organ, which he considered he was incapable of playing: "I can't play organ, I'm the worst," the pianist confessed. "I just love messing around with shitty organ sounds and things like that."[31] This does not prevent him from producing a fantastic solo, deliberately reminiscent of Freddy Cannon's hit "Palisades Park" released in 1962.

SATURDAY NIGHT'S ALRIGHT FOR FIGHTING

Elton John, Bernie Taupin / 4:55

1973

Musicians
Elton John: vocals, piano
Davey Johnstone: electric guitar, backing vocals
Dee Murray: bass, backing vocals
Nigel Olsson: drums, backing vocals

Recorded
Château d'Hérouville, Hérouville, France: May 1973

Technical Team
Producer: Gus Dudgeon
Sound Engineer: David Hentschel
Assistant Sound Engineers: Andy Scott (Hérouville), Peter Kelsey
(London)
Production Coordinator: Steve Brown

Single Release
*Saturday Night's Alright (For Fighting) / Jack Rabbit; Whenever
You're Ready (We'll Go Steady Again)*
UK Release: June 29, 1973, on DJM Records (ref. DJX 502)
Best UK Chart Ranking: 7
US Release: July 16, 1973, on MCA Records (ref. MCA-40105)
Best US Chart Ranking: 12

Genesis and Lyrics

The lyrics of "Saturday Night's Alright (For Fighting)" evoke an evening in town where the narrator plans to "get about as oiled as a diesel train." He knows that there will be plenty of provocations and that they will inevitably end up being settled in a physical way. "So much of my imagery at that time came from my childhood, you know," explained Bernie. "I mean, 'Saturday Night's Alright (For Fighting)' totally recalls [...] when I was, like, fourteen, fifteen, going to all these places in the north of England, like the Mecca Ballrooms and the Boston Gliderdromes. And that's what happened, you know. It was just too much beer. And [...] somebody would start a fight. [...] [It] was steeped in the days of the mods and the rockers, and all the sort of confrontations. It was just a straightforward 'Saturday night's all right for drinking, fighting, and getting screwed up.'"[88] The song came just at the right time for Elton, who thought that the public had too smooth an impression of him; he was determined to change this image of the nice musician churning out piano ballads on a production line, who was completely averse to controversy.

From a controversy point of view, Bernie and Elton were to be rewarded. Released as a single at the beginning of the summer of 1973 and used to promote an album that had not yet officially been named, "Saturday Night's Alright" caused controversy straightaway. The lyrics themselves offended some, but so did the record sleeve, which was fairly provocative. It was divided between an image of Elton drinking from a bottle and the title of the song, written in a tattoo typescript on a ribbon wrapped around a dagger. This was a bit much for some of the British radio stations, who opted to ban the number from their airwaves, considering it to be an incitement to violence. "I wouldn't want to be blamed for provoking anybody into a fight," said Bernie. "But at the same time it says a lot about the power of the song."[11]

Production

"Saturday Night's Alright (For Fighting)" was recorded for the first time in Kingston. But, despite days of hard work, the version they created there was unanimously considered to be catastrophic. The song only found its true identity with its finalization at the Château d'Hérouville. This process was not without difficulty, though, as Elton did not manage to

Davey Johnstone recorded even more guitar tracks on "Saturday Night's Alright (For Fighting)" and he was encouraged by Elton John, who wanted the song to have a fiery rock sound.

integrate his piano part with the ensemble. Following hours of attempts, he decided to record his track after the rest of the group was done, which was the only hitch in his process during the recording of the entire album. It was therefore behind the microphone, and not behind his piano, where Elton harangued his musicians, pushing them hard to make the machine throb wildly. The strength of the song comes from the edgy guitar chords, performed by Davey Johnstone on his 1962 Les Paul Gold Top. Excited by each

new dimension that the piece acquired every time a guitar track was added (now with a Fender Champ amp), Elton asked Davey to add more: No fewer than eight layers were superimposed to obtain the song's huge sound. They added some piano lines filled with glissandos before raving about the result, which lasted more than six and a half minutes. In order to adapt the piece to a more commercial format, its running time was brought down to 4:12 for the single, then extended to 4:55 for the album.

ROY ROGERS

Elton John, Bernie Taupin / 4:07

Musicians: Elton John: lead and backing vocals, piano / **Davey Johnstone:** acoustic guitar, steel guitar / **Dee Murray:** bass / **Nigel Olsson:** drums / **Del Newman:** arrangements, direction / **Unidentified musicians:** orchestra **Recorded:** Château d'Hérouville, Hérouville, France: May 1973 **Technical Team:** Producer: Gus Dudgeon / **Sound Engineer:** David Hentschel / **Assistant Sound Engineers:** Andy Scott (Hérouville), Peter Kelsey (London) / **Production Coordinator:** Steve Brown

With this song, inspired by the boundless admiration that Bernie had for the American actor and singer Roy Rogers, the lyricist departed from his usual creative process, evoking a character in his lyrics who actually existed. The cinematic character of Roy Rogers—his real name was Leonard Franklin Slye—was most famous from the 1930s to 1950s, during which time he acted in hundreds of films, mostly B-movie westerns that earned him the nickname "king of the cowboys." "Roy Rogers... really, really is so indigenous of my childhood," explained Bernie in 2001. "All I watched was westerns. It was either Champion the Wonder Horse or the Lone Ranger, you know. But I was watching Hopalong Cassidy and Roy Rogers [...] and my lunchbox mentality was overflowing. That was really a total homage. He was up there. He was my hero. He was my savior."[88]

In this melancholic ballad, Elton accompanies himself, providing the backing vocals, and he exaggeratedly emphasizes the name "Rogers" as Davey Johnstone backs him up with a thoroughly lachrymose steel guitar.

Once again, the song manages to find a perfect alliance between text and melody. Elton explained it as follows: "He was a genuine hero of Bernie and myself. [...] It's easy when you've got something that you know that you both connected with. [...] Sometimes I'm singing Bernie's lyrics and I'm singing what he wants to project. I don't mind that at all. But when you get a song with lyrics that, you know, that you both want to say, it's so much easier to write."[88]

SOCIAL DISEASE

Elton John, Bernie Taupin / 3:43

Musicians: Elton John: vocals, piano / **Davey Johnstone:** acoustic guitar, electric guitar, banjo / **Dee Murray:** bass / **Nigel Olsson:** drums / **Leroy Gomez:** saxophone **Recorded:** Château d'Hérouville, Hérouville, France: May 1973 **Technical Team:** Producer: Gus Dudgeon / **Sound Engineer:** David Hentschel / **Assistant Sound Engineers:** Andy Scott (Hérouville), Peter Kelsey (London) / **Production Coordinator:** Steve Brown

As amusing as they are pathos-ridden, the lyrics of "Social Disease" set the scene for the story of an alcoholic, who, in order to pay for his rent, has a relationship with his female landlord. When not complaining about his bulldog who barks in the courtyard, "enough to raise a dead man from his grave," he regrets that his days "get longer and longer" and that the night is of little use, as he is just getting "ugly and older." Purposeless, without hope, he decides to drown his sad life in tequila.

Recorded in a single take, the song quickly became one of the group's favorites, due to its swaying ambiance, conveying good humor, and the meticulous rhythmic work of the Olsson–Murray duo. Elton gave it his all on his honky-tonk piano, while Davey, having provided his acoustic guitar part, illuminates the piece with his banjo, and sprinkling throughout little catchy motifs played on electric guitar. But the real star of the piece was the surprise guest, Leroy Gomez, an American saxophonist living in Paris, who arrived at the end of the evening, unexpectedly, to offer his services spontaneously. Very skillfully, the musician managed to persuade Elton to change his plans, allowing him to contribute on "Social Disease," but he also provided a second intervention, on "Screw You." Once his part had been recorded, the singer, in very gentlemanly fashion, assured him that he would be paid at double the rate he'd originally requested.

HARMONY

Elton John, Bernie Taupin / 2:45

1973

Musicians

Elton John: vocals, piano
Davey Johnstone: acoustic guitar, backing vocals
Dee Murray: bass, backing vocals
Nigel Olsson: drums, backing vocals
Del Newman: arrangements, direction
Unidentified Musicians: orchestra

Recorded

Château d'Hérouville, Hérouville, France: May 1973

Technical Team

Producer: Gus Dudgeon
Sound Engineer: David Hentschel
Assistant Sound Engineers: Andy Scott (Hérouville), Peter Kelsey (London)
Production Coordinator: Steve Brown

Single Release

Bennie and the Jets / Harmony
  US Release: February 4, 1974, on MCA Records (ref. MCA-40198)
  Best US Chart Ranking: 1
Pinball Wizard / Harmony
  UK Release: March 12, 1976, on DJM Records (ref. DJS10652)
  Best UK Chart Ranking: 7

BIG MISTAKE!

Like Bernie, Gus Dudgeon regretted that "Harmony" was never used as a single: "4 or 5 years after the release of the album, one of the biggest American radio stations launched a survey with the public, asking its listeners to call in. It was a special Elton John week, and the question was: 'What is your favorite song on *Yellow Brick Road*?' Thousands chose "Harmony." Then we knew that it should have been on side A. It is very short, certainly, and we already had enough singles, but what a big mistake! It was on side B twice. I really regret our lack of finesse. This song is remarkable because of its backing vocals."[88]

Genesis and Lyrics

A love song, with luxuriant arrangements, "Harmony" seems above all to be dedicated to music. "If you take that song and read the lyrics to it," said Bernie, "it's really, really banal. But it's got a nice tune to it and the sentiments are quite nice."[31] It is true that, in order to celebrate the end of the album recording sessions, which had been idyllic in all respects, nothing seemed more appropriate than a positive song. This was a feeling generally shared by Bernie: "I don't necessarily think [*Goodbye Yellow Brick Road* is] our best album. But he [Elton] was on fire in the writing sense. And I guess I was in the lyrical sense." Elton concurred: "It was magic. [...] That creative period will never, ever come back again. You search for it, and you try and think, 'Oh, it would be great to do it.' But it will never happen like that again. It's a special time."[88]

Having been considered as a candidate for a single, "Harmony" was a victim of the singer's fiendishly impressive productivity: "We were asked to do a single of it. But I was working on *Caribou*. It was almost finished, when 'Bennie and the Jets' was released. We wanted to release a new single, but not to do it like Janet Jackson, releasing singles from the same album over a period of two years, that seems too mean. You can sell 25 million albums but then all you do is drip feed. We had 'The Bitch Is Back' and 'Don't Let the Sun Go Down on Me.' We could have used 'Harmony' or 'Roy Rogers,' but we preferred something new."[88] Too bad for "Harmony," then, which fell by the wayside much to Bernie's regret: "If it had been released as a single, it would have been very successful and it would have been better known now. But that's how it is. That's how things go. It's still a beautiful song and a good summary of the album. It has an ethereal aspect, quite cinematographic."[88]

Production

The alternation between minor key verses and major key refrains is undoubtedly the winning recipe behind the effectiveness of "Harmony." And even though it is a short song, its recording took a long time, especially due to the complexity of the vocal harmonies, which took two whole days to capture. "We went completely crazy with all these voices on the finale," said Dee Murray. "We also pinched some ideas."[31] "Especially from the Beach Boys," added Davey. "Such as, for example

Voice recording sessions on "Harmony" required an extensive amount of work from all involved to get the sound just right.

when following the bass line with our voices, this kind of thing. Everything was done track by track. In the end we were completely exhausted, but it was worth it."[88]

The mixing for the song proved to be complex, as the different vocal registers of the backing vocalists required a different equalization, therefore obliging David Hentschel to apply multiple adjustments: "Any sound that is a bit closed or warm, like 'Oono,' needs to be brought forward so that it can be more present in the mix, while when they are attacking the 'Aaahhh,' this is a very bright, open sound that is coming out of their

mouth, so the equalizer settings need to be turned down."[88] The responsibility of guiding the emotions conveyed during the song fell to the drums, which had a specific treatment applied by David and Gus; it was recorded on four tracks: one track was used for the bass drum, another for the snare drum, and the cymbals were recorded by a stereo pair. To ratchet back up the intensity, Gus worked mainly on the first two tracks. The vibrant strings added by Del Newman also added a lot to the song, just like the chord change on the word *harmony*, adding an even more melancholic touch to the finale.

CARIBOU

The Bitch Is Back . Pinky . Grimsby . Dixie Lily . Solar Prestige a Gammon .
You're So Static . I've Seen the Saucers . Stinker . Don't Let the Sun Go Down on Me . Ticking

RELEASE DATES
UK Release: June 28, 1974
Reference: DJM Records—DJLPH 439
Best UK Chart Ranking: 1
US Release: June 28, 1974
Reference: MCA Records—MCA 2116
Best US Chart Ranking: 1

RERELEASE WITH BONUS TRACKS

Caribou was rereleased in CD format in 1995, on Mercury Records in the United Kingdom (ref. 528 158-2) and from the Rocket Record Company / Island in the United States (ref. 314-528 158-2). The reissue included four bonus tracks: "Sick City," "Cold Highway," "Pinball Wizard," and "Step into Christmas."

A LASTING SUCCESS

While *Caribou* raced to the top of the American charts and stayed there for four weeks, the most notable aspect of this album's performance remains its longevity in the Billboard Top 200, where it stayed for more than a year.

A VALLEY BETWEEN TWO PEAKS

At the end of the summer of 1973, Elton set off once more for the United States on a new tour that would eventually include a storm of partying and excess. Onstage he took the trouble to wear different outrageous costumes for each concert, each more striking than the last. There was one exception to this bevy of variety: a cloak that measured nearly four meters (thirteen feet) long and a pair of luminous glasses displaying his name, made to measure by the company Optique Boutique. But the visual fireworks and good-natured atmosphere of the shows hid a much less glamourous atmosphere in the wings, where drugs and alcohol circulated in large quantities. Davey Johnstone admits as much: "Oh, we enjoyed ourselves, of course! [laughs] And believe me, there were many 'never again' nights. Many 'never again' three nights—72-hour stretches where you literally never went to sleep. And then, what did you do? You did it all over again, twice as hard! [laughs] Yeah, we did as many drugs as you can imagine, and drank as much alcohol as we could possibly pour down our throats. But because of the music we played, we were never linked to the drug culture like, say, the Rolling Stones. People didn't assume we could be decadent, even though we were. [laughs] We never got hassled, and we were twice as hardcore than so many other bands. There were some scary times, though, and periods that none of us are particularly proud of. In recent years, I've stopped everything, and I'm very grateful that I have my health. It's good to be able to show people that you don't have to be a raving maniac to be a rock 'n' roll star. We were very fortunate to have come through it alive."[54] Onstage, Elton and his crew did not allow any of their personal excesses to show, retaining perfect control over their art. Whatever issues they were dealing with offstage, when they were performing in front of an audience, those issues dropped away and they acquitted themselves as showmen of the highest order.

From the Haunted Castle to a Ghost Village

Having crisscrossed the South and the Midwest of the United States during the second half of August, Elton John stopped over in Denver, where he was scheduled to perform at the Coliseum on September 2, 1973. He wanted to visit a new studio with a view to recording his next album there. Elton was seduced by the picturesque setting of the Caribou Ranch recording studios, which was nestled at an altitude of eight thousand feet in the heart of the Colorado mountains, halfway between Boulder and Denver. The singer felt ready to break the spell that had bound him to the Château d'Hérouville. For an artist facing the crowds every night, a refuge like this offered him a place of complete escape and promised to be a propitious setting for creative inspiration. There would be no distractions to disturb the team, who would be able to focus on creating new compositions...or so he thought. The town closest to Caribou Ranch was literally a little ghost town! It had a population of three thousand at the height of its heyday as a center for silver mining in the nineteenth century, but it had been abandoned in the 1920s.

The studios, built entirely out of logs, evinced a rustic and authentically American atmosphere, which was rather exotic for

FOR ELTON ADDICTS

In 2015, the baby grand piano used by Elton John to record "Don't Let the Sun Go Down on Me" at the Caribou Ranch studios was sold at auction for $52,500. Frank Zappa and Michael Jackson had also made good use of the same instrument.

The rhythm section of the Elton John Band in 1974. From left to right: Nigel Olsson (standing), Davey Johnstone (seated), Dee Murray, and Ray Cooper.

a native of the London suburbs like Elton. He was very taken by the level of comfort on offer, and each musician was housed in their own individual log cabin. But above all else, the equipment provided was top tier, especially the three pianos: a Bösendorfer grand piano with ninety-seven keys (usually there are eighty-eight), a baby grand, and a 1910 mahogany Steinway that had previously belonged to CBS Records and had notably been used in the recording of "Bridge over Troubled Water" by Simon and Garfunkel. As the Bösendorfer was more of a concert instrument, most of the numbers were recorded using the Steinway, except for the more rock-inflected numbers, such as "The Bitch Is Back," which was played on the baby grand. Elton John had only two conditions in order to clinch the booking: that Tannoy speakers should be installed in the control room, and that the Olive brand recording console should be replaced by a Neve 8016. The Olive console was the latest model, but it emitted a continuous noise when it was operating that the technicians were unable to suppress. The studio owner, Jim Guercio, and the manager, John Carsello, met Elton's demands without batting an eyelash, even though they knew that a Neve 8016 mixing desk was not easy to obtain. After much careful research, they managed to locate one…at Abbey Road, thanks to machinations of the ex-Beatles producer, George Martin, who arranged to have one shipped over by plane.

Galvanized by the prospect of recording in this haven of peace, Elton continued with his American tour, which had begun on August 15 in Mobile, Alabama, and was due to end on October 21, in Gainesville, Florida. The highlight of the tour was to be an event played at the Hollywood Bowl on September 7, which turned out to be a triumph. After a few days of rest in Hawaii in mid-September, Elton performed at Madison Square Garden in New York on the twenty-third. At each appearance, Elton really stirred up the crowd. In Baltimore, on September 30, the concert turned into a riot after Elton dismissed the security staff, who had been too brusque for his taste. He was banned from Baltimore for the following seven years! In Memphis, on October 11, Elton delivered one of his best performances of the entire tour, hoping to impress Al Green, who was in attendance. His performance stirred up the public so much that hundreds of fans invaded the backstage area at the end of the concert, forcing the singer to barricade himself in his dressing room for two hours.

Significantly Scaled-Down Sessions

Given his performing conditions, recording his next album in the mountains sounded like a great plan. However, contrary to what Elton had imagined, these sessions of total immersion, which were supposed to offer the group a welcome creative interlude in the midst of a media tornado, did not turn out to be as relaxing as expected. In fact, the team found themselves wedged between a British tour, which ended on the evening of December 24, and upcoming tours in Japan and then in Oceania, which occupied the group from February 1 until March 18, 1974. This meant that Elton and his team could devote only nine days to the recording of the new disk. Not very relaxing!

Fortunately, by choice and by necessity, Elton saw this new album as a less ambitious work than *Goodbye Yellow Brick Road*. It would involve fewer arrangements, and it would be much more pared down. The arid environment of Caribou was in keeping with this kind of radical musical direction, which

was also influenced by Elton's proximity to Rod Stewart, his long-standing great friend, whose songs he admired for their simplicity and rough-and-ready qualities.

In the nine days of recording that were planned, the time for writing and composition was significantly scaled down because several days were taken up with the installation of equipment and the configuration of the studio. The technical team realized that, despite the quality of the equipment available, the acoustics of the studio were not ideal, and the sound was seriously lacking in comparison with Hérouville. Not only that, a suitable isolation booth had to be installed for the piano, like the system that had been designed at the château, so that the microphones (Neumann U87s) only picked up the sound of that specific instrument. During this phase, Elton was not really able to get ahead with the songwriting. This was because Bernie, who was applying the last finishing touches to his lyrics, had not yet arrived. Once everything was installed, there was very little time for the creative duo to conceive the entirety of the album, and then they had to turn around and record it with the group, who had to contend with the same time constraints they'd dealt with on previous albums.

Some New Blood

In November 1973, the group found a new member: percussionist Ray Cooper. Elton John, who was seeking to fill out the group's sound a bit more during their live performances, saw in Cooper the ideal candidate. His skills as a percussionist, his impressive CV (Carly Simon, Cass Elliot, Harry Nilsson), as well as his loyalty since the days of *Empty Sky*—these qualities all spoke highly in his favor. Ray Cooper was very surprised by

Elton's invitation, even slightly reticent, as he did not see himself in the context of Elton's rock 'n' roll exuberance and its effect on audiences. He agreed, somewhat cautiously. So when the other musicians asked his opinion, he responded modestly, saying that as someone who had not been historically part of the group, he should not necessarily have a vote in the matter. But his attitude onstage quickly evolved. Over time he loosened up more and more, sometimes almost to the extent of competing with Elton in his exuberance.

As the first album recorded on American soil, *Caribou* also marked Ray Cooper's first steps in the studio as a full member of the group. Also invited to the recording sessions was the brass section of the funk band Tower of Power, coming out of Oakland, California.

Tensions at Altitude

Although the team was larger, this did not mean they were more united. The first crack in the seams appeared in a debate over the choice of studio. Dee Murray and Davey Johnstone did not understand what suddenly attracted Elton to the Caribou Ranch studios, and they missed the comfort of the château and its more temperate climate. "When they [the musicians] showed up in January and the wind was blowing sixty miles an hour, it was shocking, especially [for] the bands that came here from England,"[93] recalled John Carsello, the studio manager. Not to mention the extreme altitude, which put a physiological strain on people's systems since many of them were already tired out by the grueling tours. Only Nigel could see a major advantage: "We found that on background vocals we could sing whole octaves higher. And we didn't realize that until we came down and tried

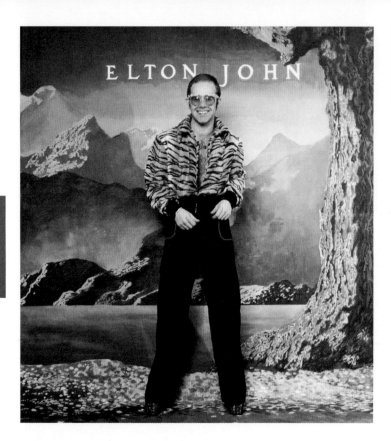

ELTON JOHN

Shot by Ed Caraeff, Elton posed in front of a fresco relief of the Colorado Mountains for the cover of his eighth studio album.

Another proposed title for *Caribou* was *Stinker*, which was taken from one of the songs on the album. However, the title seemed like too much of an unnecessary commercial risk. An alternative album image was also considered, featuring Elton doing his best Frank Sinatra, wearing a fedora, with a glass of scotch in his hand and a suit jacket nonchalantly draped over his shoulder.

to perform these songs onstage. And it was, 'Shit, I can't hit that note.'"[31] Elton John also experienced some difficulties with singing, due to the altitude. His voice tired quickly, and at one point things got so bad that he had a violent attack of nerves during the recording of "Don't Let the Sun Go Down on Me."

The cohesion of the team, already strained by the unfamiliar working conditions, also suffered from Elton's attitude, which was often moody and difficult to parse. On his good days, he seemed radiant, euphoric, and he took part in the informal soccer matches and the snow scooter outings that the rest of the group often had planned. But on a regular basis he would also sink into a profound silence or explode into a rage over trivial matters. The culprit was an increasing consumption of cocaine and alcohol—particularly whiskey. Fortunately, his musical abilities were unaffected by this, nor was his rate of output, which was still phenomenal. "Recording started in the afternoons and went on into the night. The next day, they listened to playbacks to see if they wanted to keep the songs, do a re-make or scrap them altogether,"[20] recalled David Larkham, the photographer responsible for the album cover art. Gus Dudgeon was far from happy with the result of the recordings. Once the recording sessions had been completed, he wanted just one thing: to forget this "crap" album—to use his expression. "The sound on it is the worst, the songs are nowhere, even the sleeve was wrong. [...] The lyrics weren't that good, the singing wasn't good, the production is just lousy,"[43] he complained in an interview in 1975.

This radical opinion did not prevent the album from reaching number one on both sides of the Atlantic when it was released on June 28, 1974. The public did not seem particularly taken by the album jacket created by David Larkham.

Naturally inspired by the unusual setting of *Caribou*, Larkham decided to use a photo of Elton with a vista of the mountains in the background, but he opted to paint the image in the manner of the artist Maxfield Parrish. Once the mountain backdrop had been completed, he sent Elton a Polaroid of himself posing in front of it, to give him an idea of what it would look like. On the day the snap was taken, the star, who did not like his picture being taken, arrived slightly the worse for wear. Consequently, the result was an image of Elton with an exaggerated smile, dressed in a panther jacket and wearing large pink glasses in front of a background of mountain peaks. The pinkness of the glasses stood out so much that Elton briefly considered calling the album *Ol' Pink Eyes Is Back*; in the end the more restrained title *Caribou* was selected. This was the second album, after *Honky Château*, to be given the name of the studio that had hosted it, which gave the locations an unexpected bid at posterity. This choice even became a habit, as four other works were named after the location, region, or country in which they had been recorded: *Rock of the Westies*, *Made in England*, *Songs from the West Coast*, and *Peachtree Road*.

Although the peaks of the majestic Rocky Mountains were the setting for the sessions, and were even featured on the album jacket visuals, *Caribou* would not be considered a high point in Elton's career. From the perspective of the reviewers, the album was saved by two incredibly effective singles, "The Bitch Is Back" and "Don't Let the Sun Go Down on Me." At best, *Caribou* can be thought of as a transitional album, a moment of respite between the career high points of *Goodbye Yellow Brick Road* and *Captain Fantastic and the Brown Dirt Cowboy*.

Elton, Bernie, and the whole touring team posing in front of their flying palace, the Starship, before setting off on their American tour in 1974.

STARSHIP:
ROCK 'N' ROLL ALTITUDE

After the outsized success of *Goodbye Yellow Brick Road*, Elton John was no longer able to envisage the rest of his career in reasonable, moderate proportions. Carried along by the star-making system in its extreme form in the 1970s, he played the game of excess that was expected from celebrities of the era, and he decided to hire a Boeing 720 for the first part of his North American tour, which ran from August to October 1973. This cost him a mere $2,500 a day! The 130-foot jet was given the glitzy name of *Starship*. The year of the tour was written on its fuselage in giant letters: "Elton John—1974 Tour."

The plane had already acquired a reputation as a flying brothel, having been used previously by members of Led Zeppelin. The hard rock group hired it just before Elton and used it between June and July of 1973. Bobby Sherman and Ward Sylvester were the two entrepreneur investors who owned the aircraft and sponsored its conversion into a luxury form of transportation for wealthy music stars.

The "starship" was equipped with a kitchen and a bar, as well as musical instruments (notably a Hammond organ for Elton). At the rear there was a cozy corner with a sofa and a large quantity of pillows that was nicknamed "the hippie room."

There was also a room with a king-sized waterbed covered in fake white fur.

On this flying behemoth, passengers scarcely had the sensation of regular workaday travel. Such a high degree of comfort enabled Elton to forget his motion sickness, as he was well-known for hating plane travel. The *Starship* hosted Alice Cooper, Bob Dylan, Deep Purple, the Allman Brothers Band, the Rolling Stones, and Peter Frampton in succession. But the artist who made most use of it was Elton: He leased it on four occasions all the way up to the "Louder Than Concorde Tour" in the summer of 1976. It enabled him to do a series of no fewer than 134 shows in total. In the intimacy of the aircraft, he did not deprive himself of any extravagance. Drugs and alcohol were consumed in abundance. Elton particularly remembers hosting a screening of the pornographic film *Deep Throat* while his mother and stepfather were on board and in the middle of eating their dinner. More than a means of transport, the plane became a VIP party venue where stars gathered before and after the concerts. Cher, Stevie Wonder, and John Lennon were all regularly listed on the flight manifest.

HOLLYWOOD BOWL, SEPTEMBER 7, 1973: THE CONCERT OF EXCESS

At the pinnacle of his fame and creativity, Elton John was also designing increasingly elaborate stage shows. The show he put on at the Hollywood Bowl in Los Angeles on September 7, 1973, was a high point at the nexus of rock and glam pop. In the streets of the city, extravagant billboards announced the arrival of the British star, who was photographed in top hat and tails, with a cane in his hand. But Elton would be wearing a much less restrained outfit while onstage at the Hollywood Bowl.

Rhinestones and Sequins

On one perfect California evening, the English singer made a majestic appearance before an audience of sixteen thousand people packed into the stands of the open-air arena. Although not ideally suited to a rock 'n' roll show, the Bowl did host the Beatles in August 1964 and 1965. The microphone crackled, and then the porn star Linda Lovelace stood up to welcome the audience before introducing Elton. "I'd like to welcome you to the Hollywood Bowl. On this spectacular night, we hope to revive some of the glamour that's all but disappeared from show business. We're very lucky in having this evening with us many distinguished guests from all parts of the world, none of whom would dare to miss this show tonight."[11] Elton John then appeared at the top of the staircase, as in a cabaret revue, dressed in an immaculate, white cowboy costume decorated with feathers. He descended the stairs, which were decorated in sequins of every color, to the sounds of the 20th Century Fox theme. At the bottom of the steps he was greeted by a dozen people disguised as celebrities or fictional characters: Groucho Marx, Batman and Robin, Frankenstein, the Beatles, and Queen Elizabeth II were all present. This tableau gave the impression that one was watching some animated version of the cover of *Sgt. Pepper's Lonely Hearts Club Band*. The star power onstage barely managed to rival the (real) stars in the audience, including Muhammad Ali, Carl and Brian Wilson, Carly Simon, Carole King, James Taylor, Steve McQueen, Peggy Lee, and Martha Reeves.

The disguised characters all stood before five fully painted pianos, each one wearing a different color of the rainbow. In synchronized movements, these pop culture representatives raised the lids of each piano, on which were written five letters spelling out the singer's name: "ELTON."

Doves and... Crocodiles

A hundred doves were supposed to spring forth from the opened pianos, but the birds had other ideas. A dozen or so did fly out, but the others decided that it was nicer to stay inside where it was warm. The technical team, accompanied by Bernie, had to rush around and encourage them to fly. Paying no attention to this, Elton removed his gigantic hat, took his place behind the piano, and frenetically hammered out the chords of "Elderberry Wine" over cheers from the public, who became ecstatic when he then launched into "Your Song." As though an indirect allusion to his failed bit of prop comedy, he then played "High Flying Bird." At this point there was one of those magical moments that happen so rarely in live performance: A stray dove suddenly appeared in the sky right above the stage of the Hollywood Bowl. One of the lighting crew had the presence of mind to track the bird in flight. The audience was captivated, convinced that this was an integral part of the staging of the show, which was certainly not the case.

By sheer happenstance, "Honky Cat" was the next song on the set list, which might have sounded like a threat of reprisal directed at the birds. "Goodbye Yellow Brick Road" was undoubtedly one of the highlights of the show. Even though Elton's voice seemed slightly frail when he was climbing into the higher register. When it came time to perform "Hercules," the singer changed into a new outfit, which would also be

etched into people's memories: a brown-sequined Lurex ensemble. Then came "Rocket Man" and "Daniel," which delighted the public.

For "Crocodile Rock," the roles were reversed, and this time a little surprise was reserved for Elton John. Joining in on the game of the burlesque staging, Clive Franks, who sometimes left his observation post as the sound engineer to play supporting keyboards, appeared behind the pianist disguised as a crocodile! His head, at least, was disguised. The rest of his costume was purchased secondhand and was so worn out that it couldn't be used. In the end, Clive wore a dark black cape from which an outsized crocodile head emerged. "I looked totally ridiculous. I didn't tell anybody in the band about the outfit."[31] Elton turned around and seemed to have difficulty focusing on

the singing, he was laughing so much. On "Saturday Night's Alright (For Fighting)," Elton seemed to go slightly wild. He left his keyboard while the group kept the main theme going. He positioned himself at the microphone, like a rock star, and harangued the crowd, who started to join in the refrain. In order to encourage them, he climbed onto his piano, and then nimbly got down again before performing some dance moves and returning to his instrument. The audience went wild. The group concluded the evening with a rendition of "Honky Tonk Women," a song borrowed from the Rolling Stones.

The next day, the press were unanimous in their rave reviews of the show. Elton's performance was called a crowning achievement in his career, and it further cemented his status as an amazing live performer.

THE BITCH IS BACK

Elton John, Bernie Taupin / 3:45

Musicians
Elton John: vocals, piano
Davey Johnstone: electric guitar
Dee Murray: bass
Nigel Olsson: drums
Ray Cooper: tambourine
Clydie King, Sherlie Matthews, Jessie Mae Smith, Dusty Springfield: backing vocals
Lenny Pickett: tenor saxophone
Tower of Power: brass

Recorded
Caribou Ranch, Nederland, Colorado: January 1974

Technical Team
Producer: Gus Dudgeon
Sound Engineer: Clive Franks
Assistant Sound Engineer: Peter Kelsey
Production Coordinator: Steve Brown

Single Release
The Bitch Is Back / Cold Highway
UK Release: August 30, 1974, on DJM Records (ref. DJS.322)
Best UK Chart Ranking: 15
US Release: September 3, 1974, on MCA Records (ref. MCA-40297)
Best US Chart Ranking: 4

SHOCKING!
The presence of the word *bitch* in a hit song of this caliber was a first. The Rolling Stones had included a song called "Bitch" on 1971's *Sticky Fingers*, but it was not selected as a single. Only Rod Stewart took the gamble in the charts when he released "Ain't Love a Bitch" in 1979.

Genesis and Lyrics

Elton never had any difficulty acknowledging that his irascible character was a major trait of his personality, fortunately counterbalanced by his capacity to wind down the pressure as quickly as it was raised. "The Bitch Is Back" is testimony to this, with a large dose of self-mockery, because "the bitch" is him! Two months previously, Maxine Taupin, Bernie's partner, exclaimed, on seeing Elton arrive with a look of thunder in his eyes, like he was ready to turn to stone the first unfortunate person to cross his path: "Oh God, the bitch is back." Bernie burst out laughing and logged the expression in some corner of his brain. Two months later, he took this expression out again for this fairly raw portrait of the singer. Far from being offended, Elton adored this hook, even to the extent of briefly considering it for the album's title. While it was not chosen in the end, the song itself was made prominent, as though to announce the artist's arrival. In this song it is a matter of his elevation to the rank of superstar and his descent into drug dependency: "I get high in the evening sniffing pots of glue." Even the way in which addicts deny the evidence is included in the lyrics: two lines of text later, the narrator claims to be "stone-cold sober." Elton takes on these words with an aplomb that is even more admirable, given that the words are not particularly favorable for him: "I can bitch, I can bitch 'cause I'm better than you / It's the way that I move, the things that I do."

Production

An absolute rager of a song, "The Bitch Is Back" owes its effectiveness to the mordant guitars of Davey Johnstone, who pulls out all the stops. It is no surprise that this is included among the musician's favorites songs; he managed to achieve a very individual sound by mixing two Gibson Flying Vs (these triangle-shaped guitars popularized by Jimi Hendrix and Billy Gibbons), with open strings in *G*, and equipped with humbuckers coupled with a single coil out-of-phase microphone. In fact, if the phase of one of the microphones is inverted, this inverts the sound curve: It rises on one microphone and descends on the other. This combination generates a very sophisticated sound, and was popularized by musicians such as Albert King and Peter Green. Completed by a precise and percussive attack, Johnstone's technique assumes its full dimension in the grandiloquent

Arrogance and self-mockery were the explosive cocktail at the center of "The Bitch Is Back," the hard-charging anthem of *Caribou*.

introduction of "The Bitch Is Back," which is not unlike the best moments of the Who.

Gripped by the same desire for experimentation, Dee Murray opts to double his bass and, for the second take, to pass it through a Pignose Hog 30 amp with low power, to produce a gentle, warm sound, perfect for precise articulation.

To complete this solid instrumentation, which asserts itself as a powerful single, there's a sugar-coated layer of incandescent, assured backing vocals, provided this time by a female team consisting of the loyal Dusty Springfield, Jessie Mae Smith, Clydie King, and Sherlie Matthews. The latter, who was very devout, at that time, raised an eyebrow when she discovered the lyrics and their "bitch" litany. Clydie, who had negotiated the contract for this session, was profusely apologetic, explaining that she did not know about the contents of the song. But Sherlie reassured her, and the two women burst out laughing. The four backing vocalists were very engaged and communicate their good humor, not hesitating to dance to the rhythm of

the music while recording their part. Elton, as a perfect gentleman, gave each of them an enormous bouquet of flowers at the end of the session, leaving them with the memory of a charming welcome...very far from the deplorable image of himself that Elton pretends to convey in this song.

The opening song on Elton's eighth album, "The Bitch Is Back" was also the track selected for the A-side of the album's first single, released on August 30 in the United Kingdom and on September 3 in the United States. When he selected the song to be the standard-bearer for his album, Elton was completely aware that he was exposing himself to the ax of censorship. Many DJs were horrified when they heard the single and refused to broadcast it. However, as it became increasingly successful with the public, the DJs were forced to put aside their moral sensitivities and add it to their playlists. Some tried to edit out the word "bitch" from the song, but the word appears forty times in less than four minutes, so they had their work cut out for them.

PINKY

Elton John, Bernie Taupin / 3:55

Musicians: Elton John: vocals, piano / Davey Johnstone: acoustic guitar, backing vocals / Dee Murray: bass, backing vocals / Nigel Olsson: drums, backing vocals / David Hentschel: ARP synthesizer / Ray Cooper: congas **Recorded:** Caribou Ranch, Nederland, Colorado: January 1974 **Technical Team:** Producer: Gus Dudgeon / Sound Engineer: Clive Franks / Assistant Sound Engineer: Peter Kelsey / Production Coordinator: Steve Brown

Genesis and Lyrics

Very much influenced by the harsh winter that Colorado was having during the album's recording session, which was even more aggressive at the altitude where Caribou Ranch was, the lyrics of "Pinky" are not brilliantly original. They are even borderline facile, with Bernie starting off the lyrics of his love song with a banal: "I don't want to wake you / But I'd like to tell you that I love you," effectively a rhyme of "you" with "you." Farther down, he used the breakfast menu to wind up his lyrics in haste; the listener purrs with pleasure at discovering the sense of hospitality at the studio, where one can have "toast and honey," having been served "breakfast in bed on a tray." Having ascertained that the outside temperature is not particularly inviting, Bernie suggests that the plans for the day should be shelved, doubtless to take advantage of the warmth of the duvet for a bit longer. This presumed idleness is, of course, not dissimilar to "Mellow" on *Honky Château*. However, Elton John later expressed his attachment to this song, which conjures up his own memories of this period.

Production

Although the lyrics are probably not destined to be remembered, the musical framework conceived of by Elton and his musicians does stand out as a model of soft rock. Davey's acoustic guitars are precise and inventive, while the rhythm section competently expedites the business in hand, leaving David Hentschel and his ARP synthesizer, and Ray Cooper with his skillful percussion, to add spice to this effective ballad. It is also surprising that "Pinky" was largely neglected upon its release and did not become a single or a staple in the huge repertoire of Elton ballads. However, its privileged position in the *Caribou* track list and the particular care taken over its production by Gus Dudgeon clearly show that a lot was invested in it. But one must not lose sight of the fact that the Elton "product" was over-represented at that time in the media and on the airwaves. "Pinky" might well have acted as a kind of unofficial single for *Caribou*, but this was clearly not enough to rescue it from the relative obscurity to which it has been unjustly relegated.

GRIMSBY

Elton John, Bernie Taupin / 3:47

Musicians: Elton John: vocals, piano / Davey Johnstone: electric guitars / Dee Murray: bass, backing vocals / Nigel Olsson: drums, backing vocals / Ray Cooper: tambourine **Recorded:** Caribou Ranch, Nederland, Colorado: January 1974 / **Technical Team:** Producer: Gus Dudgeon / Sound Engineer: Clive Franks / Assistant Sound Engineer: Peter Kelsey / Production Coordinator: Steve Brown

Genesis and Lyrics

Grimsby, a bustling town of approximately eighty-seven inhabitants, is located on the Humber estuary and is the principal town in North East Lincolnshire, in the East of England. It is known as a major fishing port. But other than the stock image promoted by the local tourist office, Grimsby is notable as being only fifty miles from the farm where Bernie grew up. Sufficient reason for Elton to suggest to his lyricist to make it the star of a song: "I once said to Bernie, 'Wouldn't it be nice to do a song about Grimsby?' It's such an absurd idea to write a song about Grimsby, it's one of the most putrid places. It's not romantic in the least. The song is up-tempo, I think it sounds like the Beach Boys. Anyway, Randy Newman did a song called 'Cleveland' [probably the song 'Burn On,' in which Cleveland is mentioned several times], so I thought we should do the English equivalent."[31] With a certain nonchalance, Bernie tried to create an ironically romanticized portrayal of this relatively uninteresting fishing port, with sarcastic reference to its unappetizing culinary delights.

Production

It would be an understatement to say that Gus Dudgeon was underwhelmed by "Grimsby" when Elton played the piece for him on the piano for the first time. But he held back from offending Elton's and Bernie's sensibilities, although he did have doubts about what he would be able to do with it; he then set to work with the group in the hope that one of the musicians would come up with some kind of inspiration to resolve the situation. Although it does not have the pretention of becoming an essential element in the singer's repertoire, "Grimsby" is still pleasant to listen to, particularly with Dee Murray's soft bass sound, and Davey Johnstone's flurrying guitars once again turning in a very catchy riff. Slightly in the background, the backing vocals are judiciously applied, while Ray Cooper's tambourine and Nigel Olsson's drums are categorically relegated to second place; they are very reliably performed and provide the assurance of the continuous energy of the song. As for Elton, neither his vocals nor his piano managed to enhance a fairly conventional melody.

Drummer Nigel Olsson performs at the King's Hall in Manchester, England, on November 29, 1973, shortly before the recording of *Caribou.*

DIXIE LILY

Elton John, Bernie Taupin / 2:55

Musicians: Elton John: lead and backing vocals, piano / **Davey Johnstone:** electric guitars, mandolin / **Dee Murray:** bass / **Nigel Olsson:** drums / **Ray Cooper:** tambourine, whistling / **Lenny Pickett:** soprano saxophone **Recorded:** Caribou Ranch, Nederland, Colorado: January 1974 **Technical Team:** Producer: Gus Dudgeon / Sound Engineer: Clive Franks / Assistant Sound Engineer: Peter Kelsey / Production Coordinator: Steve Brown

Genesis and Lyrics

While "Dixie Lily" stakes its claim from the outset to an affiliation with Dixieland, the jazz style that is the bedrock of New Orleans music, the song moves into a more country register. In fact, this pleasing ballad scrupulously ticks all the boxes of the genre in under three minutes. The lyrics, which are almost anecdotal, set out a picture-postcard Louisiana decor, with the evening crickets, the boats quietly plying the river, and the fishermen tirelessly catching the catfish. The lyricist focuses particularly on one of these boats, heading for Vicksburg, on the Mississippi.

Production

Elton's honky-tonk piano exudes good humor, while Davey Johnstone plays the lead role at the core of this rich instrumentation, first providing a guitar riff with a warm crunch, and then his cheerful mandolin, which chips away in the background. Bassist Dee Murray and drummer Nigel Olsson form a compact, minimalist rhythm section, while saxophonist Lenny Pickett delivers a limpid solo. Elton was rather unsatisfied with his voice on some of the songs on *Caribou* because the altitude tired out his vocal cords. He admitted that "Dixie Lily" was the only song on which he entirely rerecorded his part, after they left the ranch. But the result was worth it: Elton, who also provided the backing vocals, is skillful in his use of the Southern US accent, which he masters perfectly. The song was covered in 1974 by the American country singer Roy Drusky, who managed to get his version into the top 50 on the Billboard country charts. Lonnie Donegan, a Scottish skiffle singer, also produced a version that same year, with a frenetic bluegrass interpretation, on his album *Lonnie Donegan Meets Leinemann.*

Elton came to rely on solid support
from Davey Johnstone, which opened
up new possibilities for the singer,
including the operatic production of
"Solar Prestige a Gammon."

SOLAR PRESTIGE A GAMMON

Elton John, Bernie Taupin / 2:53

1974

Lenny Pickett, a member of Tower of Power
between 1973 and 1981, and subsequently of the
Saturday Night Live band beginning in 1985, also
created a solid reputation for himself as a session
musician.

Musicians

Elton John: vocals, piano
Davey Johnstone: acoustic guitars, backing vocals
Dee Murray: bass, backing vocals
Nigel Olsson: drums, backing vocals
Ray Cooper: vibraphone
Lenny Pickett: clarinet, soprano saxophone
David Hentschel: ARP synthesizer

Recorded

Caribou Ranch, Nederland, Colorado: January 1974

Technical Team

Producer: Gus Dudgeon
Sound Engineer: Clive Franks
Assistant Sound Engineer: Peter Kelsey
Production Coordinator: Steve Brown

Lenny Pickett (seen here in 1992) played saxophone and
trumpet on "Solar Prestige a Gammon."

Genesis and Lyrics

With celebrity, a veritable cult grew up around the works of
Elton and Bernie. Incredulous, the duo could only conclude
that some kind of intellectual hysteria had taken hold of the
most tenacious fans when each album was released; Bernie's
sometimes abstruse lyrics were intensely studied and dissected
as though they contained the Holy Scriptures. The wildest interpretations and most convoluted theories flowed from these
semantic analyzes. This was nothing new: As an admirer of the
Beatles, Elton had witnessed this phenomenon already. John
Lennon's response to it resulted in one of his most famous
pieces of bravado: "I Am the Walrus." The singer had conceived this concoction of images without head or tail in 1967,
after he received a letter from a student at his old school, who
confided in him that he had made a study of the Beatles' lyrics. Lennon was curious to know what they would manage to
extract from a surreal text worthy of the Oulipo, such as "I Am
the Walrus." He repeated this experience with "Sun King." As
an admirer of this kind of audacious display, Elton suggested
the same thing to his lyricist, and set him the challenge of producing an incomprehensible set of lyrics. "I love it, because I
always suggest things that Bernie Taupin's going to get knifed
in the back for. I thought it would be great to write a song with
English words that didn't mean a thing, but that sounded fantastic when put together."[32] For this occasion, Bernie did not
seek to disguise anything: Unlike Lennon, whose syntax at least
remained coherent, the lyricist totally fragmented his text, pul-
verizing it to ensure that no trace of meaning remained. Some
words remained such as "loto," "salmon," "solar," or "prestige"
alongside unknown terms and onomatopoeias that were alliterative ("kool kar kyrie kay salmon").

Production

Elton John devised an operatic feel to the score of this track,
which seemed to pave the way for "Bohemian Rhapsody" by
Queen the following year, 1975. With a very large dose of
self-mockery, encouraged by some ad hoc vibraphone from
Ray Cooper, Elton launches emphatically into a lyrical interpretation, rolling his *r* and exaggerating the accentuations, as
an Italian tenor might do. But Dee Murray's playful bass prepares a delightful twist, with a bouncing bridge passage that
Paul McCartney would not have been unhappy with. Dee's

debonair irregular line is reminiscent of McCartney's on "Maxwell's Silver Hammer" in particular. On the second refrain, Cooper's vibraphone croons its own individual music in the midst of the dance hall style orchestra, reprised by the unison duo of Lenny Pickett's clarinet—at the same time proving that he is not just a virtuoso saxophonist—and David Hentschel's ARP synthesizer. The combination makes this parody an appealing number, oscillating as it does between the fantastically absurd and the brilliant.

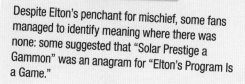

Despite Elton's penchant for mischief, some fans managed to identify meaning where there was none: some suggested that "Solar Prestige a Gammon" was an anagram for "Elton's Program Is a Game."

YOU'RE SO STATIC

Elton John, Bernie Taupin / 4:53

Musicians
Elton John: vocals, piano
Davey Johnstone: electric guitar (Leslie cabinet)
Dee Murray: bass
Nigel Olsson: drums
Ray Cooper: snare drum, castanets, tambourine
Clydie King: backing vocals
Tower of Power: brass

Recorded
Caribou Ranch, Nederland, Colorado: January 1974

Technical Team
Producer: Gus Dudgeon
Sound Engineer: Clive Franks
Assistant Sound Engineer: Peter Kelsey
Production Coordinator: Steve Brown

Behind Ray Cooper's impenetrable gaze, the percussionist's imagination was always capable of adding interesting new sounds on Elton's recordings.

Genesis and Lyrics

Frustrated by the delays caused by the equipment installation, the musicians lost no time in setting up the new songs as soon as they had the green light from the technical team. The first of these to take shape, "You're So Static," shows evidence of this impatience in an all-pervasive nerviness. The lyrics perfectly illustrate the oppression exerted by New York on a narrator on vacation, who seems very out of step with the lifestyle in this megalopolis. He shares his experience with the listener, accompanied by a warning: He was snared by a woman that he met in a bar. A flirtatious look was all it took for him to succumb to temptation. But a bad surprise awaited him when he woke up: The young woman wanted his watch instead of money. A second reading shows another meaning: This female character could also symbolize the city, inviting the newcomer into vice.

The song was composed before the recording sessions at Caribou Ranch, and an initial demo had been made of "You're So Static." But Gus Dudgeon felt that it was lacking in relief and variety, and that it needed additional arrangements. The producer thought once more about the brass sections that had been put in place on the Château trilogy; these had proved their worth. Why not do the same again? Gus ran the idea past Elton, who gave his approval straightaway. Dudgeon therefore recruited the brass section of Tower of Power, a funk group based in Oakland, who had managed to have two singles hit the American charts in 1972: "You're Still a Young Man" (twenty-ninth) and "Down to the Night Club" (sixty-sixth). "I met them and I talked to Greg Adams, the lead trumpeter and arranger," said the producer. "I said, 'I want you to bring the band up [to] the office and have them play the parts to me over a backing track.' So about a week later, these guys showed up. They get their horns out and I ran the track. I thought, 'Well, I'd better play it fairly loud,' because six of them stood there. I played the track really loud. I mean, the speakers were jumping off the bloody wall. And they hit the first thing and completely drowned the tape out. I'd never heard anybody play that loud or that tight (before). It was just unbelievable."[31]

Production

In something of a paradoxical situation, the team, working in the most extreme isolation of the Colorado mountains on a song evoking the bustle and hustle of New York, decided to

Elton had little involvement in the post-production phase of *Caribou*, and he heard the end result only after the album was complete.

start with a tango…! As well as the sensual overtones that this created, it worked very well with the presence of the castanets played by Ray Cooper. The new member was being given a central role right from the first song. This percussion instrument acted as a metronome for the entire group, starting out with a sustained rhythm, never neglecting the groove, provided particularly by the vibrant bass of Dee Murray, who lays into the pace with demonic energy. Davey Johnstone remains more in the background, not helped by the mix, which relegates him to a secondary level. He uses his guitar, passed through a Leslie cabinet, as though providing an ornamental element, floating in the background, that contributes an element of freedom in this orchestration that is otherwise somewhat rigid. It took all

the kick provided by Tower of Power, consisting of Emilio Castillo (tenor saxophone), Stephen Kupka (baritone saxophone), Lenny Pickett (tenor and soprano saxophone, and clarinet), Mic Gillette (trombone and trumpet), and Greg Adams (trumpet) to ignite the full R&B potential of the piece. When Elton, who never concerned himself with what happened after the recording (overdubs, additional arrangements, mixing, mastering, etc.), discovered what Gus had done with the song in the mixing, he was in awe, and he even declared that this was one the most accomplished songs on the album. So much so that he was tempted to choose it as a single, before finally giving precedence to "Don't Let the Sun Go Down on Me" and "The Bitch Is Back."

I'VE SEEN THE SAUCERS

Elton John, Bernie Taupin / 4:43

Musicians
Elton John: vocals, piano
Davey Johnstone: electric guitars, backing vocals
Dee Murray: bass, backing vocals
Nigel Olsson: drums, backing vocals
Ray Cooper: tambourine, congas, water gong, vibraphone
Gus Dudgeon: tambourine

Recorded
Caribou Ranch, Nederland, Colorado: January 1974

Technical Team
Producer: Gus Dudgeon
Sound Engineer: Clive Franks
Assistant Sound Engineer: Peter Kelsey
Production Coordinator: Steve Brown

Genesis and Lyrics

Even before the cinema focused on stories about space, beginning in the second half of the 1970s, with *Star Wars, Close Encounters of the Third Kind*, or later with *E.T. the Extra-Terrestrial* spawning a proliferation of creatures more or less hostile to human kind, UFO literature already had wind in its sails. The spectacular "I've Seen the Saucers," which evokes extraterrestrial abductions, therefore owes a great deal to Bernie's passion for science fiction, fed by the works of George Adamski, Erich von Däniken, J. Allen Hynek, and Bruce Cathie. The lyricist describes the irresistible power of attraction exercised over the narrator by these mysterious saucers, once the fear of the unknown has passed. As though he was trying to make a permanent escape from the banal reality of his day-to-day existence, he hopes to relive this experience and this all-powerful feeling over his fellow men. But he does not know whether he should keep the secret surrounding this encounter or reveal it to the whole world: "Maybe if I promise not to say a word / They can get me back before the morning light."

Production

An elegant track with impeccable production value, "I've Seen the Saucers" shines brightly with the solid drumming of Nigel Olsson, but also the versatile guitars of Davey Johnstone. In order to fill out the sense of mystery sustained in the text, Johnstone uses a phaser effect, which consists of copying the original signal and sending it through a series of all-pass filters that act like a phase shifter and produce a cyclical sweeping, or wave, effect. The guitarist's marked interest in experimentation, which almost anchors the piece in prog rock, is quickly counterbalanced by delicate, pragmatic congas—one might almost say down to earth—by Ray Cooper. Elton also provides one of his finest vocal performances on the album (especially from 1:38), magnificently supported by Dee, Nigel, and Davey on backing vocals.

In this song the artist delivers a sincere, poetic, and irony-free homage to a subject that would later be largely the object of derision: the extraterrestrial encounter. Sadly, somewhat neglected, including by Elton, who commented later that it was "not the greatest song in the world,"[11] "I've Seen the Saucers" certainly suffered in the context of previous "space" hits such as "Space Oddity" or "Rocket Man." However, it is undoubtedly one of the best numbers on *Caribou*.

STINKER

Elton John, Bernie Taupin / 5:20

Musicians
Elton John: vocals, piano
Davey Johnstone: electric guitars
Dee Murray: bass
Nigel Olsson: drums
Ray Cooper: tambourine
Chester Thompson: organ
Tower of Power: brass

Recorded
Caribou Ranch, Nederland, Colorado: January 1974

Technical Team
Producer: Gus Dudgeon
Sound Engineer: Clive Franks
Assistant Sound Engineer: Peter Kelsey
Production Coordinator: Steve Brown

The Oakland Tower of Power (shown here in 1974) added a new layer to "Stinker" with its brass ensemble.

It was with jubilation that Bernie Taupin abandoned all semblance of literary ambition with "Stinker" in favor of filling this text with the worst kind of inanities. Complying with Elton's wish to sprinkle some sulfur on any suspicion of his image becoming too comfortable, the lyricist focused, as he had done in "Saturday Night's Alright (For Fighting)," on constructing an unsavory character. He goes even further in rendering him detestable and disgusting, with the narrator shamelessly boasting of his deplorable hygiene: "I come crawling up out of my hole / Dirt in my toes, dirt up my nose / I'm a perfect curse to pest control"; and later, he refers to his "burning vermin stink." Getting into the spirit of this repugnant litany, Elton even went as far, at one point, as considering called the whole album *Stinker*, though that plan was eventually flushed.

Production
With such a portrait in relief, the instrumentation had to keep pace. Elton focuses on a rampant, unhealthy blues sound, delivered with vigor. This is not something that just comes out of the blue: the pianist picked the chords from a Beach Boys song that he is very fond of, "Sail On, Sailor," which appeared in 1973. Notwithstanding the prosody, Davey's shredding guitar solo, Dee's unstoppable bass, and the rhythm 'n' blues arrangements distance his version from the original. He later acknowledged the relationship between the two numbers, presenting "Stinker" as a homage to those who had gone before. At the heart of the mechanism, the Tower of Power brass section blasts through the piece with fervor, together with the group's keyboard player, Chester Thompson, who contributes some well-judged accentuations. Emilio Castillo, on tenor saxophone, remembers: "The opening horn riff totally stands out in the mix but does *not* get in the way of Elton and his band. That became a signature for ToP [Tower of Power] horns: The arrangements never got in the way. We had perfected the 'less is more' concept and that allowed the artists to mix us high up in the mix without taking over the song."[94] Although the recording of the instrumental part took place without a hitch—in a single take—Elton John had severe difficulties recording his own vocals, which was unusual. Gus Dudgeon, in the face of a possible meltdown on the part of the singer, decided to combine six different takes to create the main vocals.

DON'T LET THE SUN GO DOWN ON ME

Elton John, Bernie Taupin / 5:37

Musicians

Elton John: vocals, piano
Davey Johnstone: electric and acoustic guitars
Dee Murray: bass
Nigel Olsson: drums
Ray Cooper: tambourine, bells
David Hentschel: Mellotron
Del Newman: arrangements, direction
Tower of Power: brass
Carl Wilson, Bruce Johnston, Toni Tennille, Billy Hinsche: backing vocals
Carl Wilson: backing vocals arrangements, direction
Daryl Dragon: backing vocals arrangements, direction

Recorded

Caribou Ranch, Nederland, Colorado: January 1974

Technical Team

Producer: Gus Dudgeon
Sound Engineer: Clive Franks
Assistant Sound Engineer: Peter Kelsey
Production Coordinator: Steve Brown

Single Release

Don't Let the Sun Go Down on Me / Sick City
  UK Release: May 24, 1974, on DJM Records (ref. DJS.302)
  Best UK Chart Ranking: 16
  US Release: June 10, 1974, on MCA Records (ref. MCA-40259)
  Best US Chart Ranking: 2

In 1991, *Two Rooms: Celebrating the Songs of Elton John & Bernie Taupin* brought together a constellation of celebrities, including George Michael, the Who, Sting, Kate Bush, Tina Turner, Rod Stewart, and Phil Collins, to pay homage to the duo formed by Elton John and his historical lyricist, Bernie Taupin. The version of "Don't Let the Sun Go Down on Me" by jazz singer Oleta Adams had the honor of being selected as a single; it eventually reached 33 in the UK sales charts.

Genesis and Lyrics

So far, Elton had recorded numerous high-quality ballads that maintained a solemn tone of sobriety, such as "Candle in the Wind," or that were adorned with sinuous chord sequences and abstract lyrics, such as "Goodbye Yellow Brick Road." But he had not yet engaged completely with the "tearful ballad" genre, like the ones that had filled the airwaves since 1973. Paul McCartney and Wings and Barbra Streisand set the ball rolling with, respectively, "My Love," released in March 1973, and "The Way We Were," in November of the same year. Elton was therefore ripe to enter this world on an even footing and develop this new strain in the DNA of pop, which was to become one of his specialties over the coming decades. However, the creation of this piece was not destined to be an easy process. One morning, as usual, Bernie gave his text to Elton, who went straight to his Wm. Knabe & Co. baby grand—on which he also composed "Philadelphia Freedom." "It was early morning and I was upstairs in my room, half awake," recalled Nigel Olsson, "and I could hear Elton downstairs...sort of plunking out the first few verses [of 'Don't Let the Sun Go Down on Me']. He seemed to be struggling with the first line of the chorus, when all of a sudden he got it and the whole chorus started to come out." The drummer ran downstairs, stood beside Elton's piano, and told him that was going to be a number one hit.[16]

Bernie's lyrics depict a failed relationship that the narrator refuses to abandon in spite of everything, effectively showing himself to be disproportionately possessive: "I'd just allow a fragment of your life to wander free / But losing everything is like the sun going down on me." An even darker aspect emerges with this line: "Don't discard me just because you think I mean you harm." Would he be willing to intimidate the object of his love, so that she would distance herself from him for good?

Production

It presents a strange paradox for a singer to want to scrap a song that he has just composed. This is nonetheless what happened with Elton and "Don't Let the Sun Go Down on Me." "When Elton sang the vocal track, he was in a filthy mood," Gus Dudgeon remembers. "On some takes, he'd scream it, on others he'd mumble it. Or he'd just stand there, staring at the control room. Eventually, he flung off the cans [earphones]

COVER
In 1991, Elton did a cover of "Don't Let the Sun Go Down on Me" with George Michael, and it reached number one in the United Kingdom and United States (the original version only reached numbers sixteen and two, respectively). The two artists had already reworked this ballad at the legendary Live Aid concert in 1985, but only the ex-Wham! singer sang it during that event, accompanied by Elton on piano.

George Michael and Elton John initially collaborated on "Ice on Fire" in 1985. "Don't Let the Sun Go Down on Me" sealed their friendship six years later.

and said, 'Okay, let's hear what we got.'"[17] The singer, totally exasperated by the uncontrollable variations in his voice—doubtless due to the altitude—grew furious and stormed into the control room, his mind already made up, and leaving no doubt about it. "After announcing that I hated the song so much we were going to stop recording it immediately and send it to Engelbert Humperdinck—'and if he doesn't want it, tell him to send it to Lulu! She can put it on a B-side!'—I was coaxed back to the vocal booth and completed the take. Then I yelled at Gus Dudgeon that I hated it even more now it was finished and was going to kill him with my bare hands if he put it on the album."[3]

It goes without saying that Gus had an immense task on his hands with refining the arrangement while Elton flew off for a tour of Japan, convinced that his song would end up in the trash. But Gus was inspired: he recorded some sumptuous backing vocals provided by Beach Boys Carl Wilson and Bruce Johnston, supported by Toni Tennille and Billy Hinsche. From this point, the magic started working: The song assumed an almost mystical dimension, as though Elton were pleading for his happiness with some superior being.

Gus also called upon Del Newman to add a brass arrangement to the piece. The two men had a mutual respect for each other and, above all, trusted each other. Things went even better, since Del Newman was convinced that "Don't Let the Sun Go Down on Me" was one of the best songs Elton had composed to date. Thanks to the backing vocals and the brass, the song was saved, and even assumed grandiose dimension: David Hentschel's Mellotron, Nigel Olsson's epic drumming, Ray Cooper's tambourine, and Dee Murray's powerful bass each contributed to the structure. Having been later nominated for Grammy Awards for both Record of the Year and Best Male Pop Vocal Performance, "Don't Let the Sun Go Down on Me" proved all of Elton's early assessments to be completely wrong. Having been convinced to allow the piece to be included in *Caribou*, he still did not want it released as a single. Eventually, Elton had to admit that he had been way off in his assessment of this song and its quality.

TICKING

Elton John, Bernie Taupin / 7:34

Bernie never confirmed this, but the fictitious massacre could have been inspired by the Texas Tower shooting at the University of Texas, perpetrated in 1966 by Charles Whitman, a twenty-five-year-old ex-marine who killed eighteen people and shocked the nation. The "Ticking" in the title could be an allusion to the clock tower.

Musicians

Elton John: lead and backing vocals, piano
David Hentschel: ARP synthesizer

Recorded

Caribou Ranch, Nederland, Colorado: January 1974

Technical Team

Producer: Gus Dudgeon
Sound Engineer: Clive Franks
Assistant Sound Engineer: Peter Kelsey
Production Coordinator: Steve Brown

Sound Engineer Clive Franks established himself as an essential element in Elton's team.

Genesis and Lyrics

After the diplomatic crisis triggered by "Don't Let the Sun Go Down on Me," the group set off on a snowmobile excursion to see the Continental Divide, and to let off the pressure that had been building up. This return to calm was a lifesaver for Elton, who stayed at the studio with David Hentschel and the technical team, and it coincided with the recording session for "Ticking." This poignant ballad did not require the presence of the other musicians. Since, in order to set Bernie's rich lyrics to music, which was eminently cinematographic, Elton focused on the emotional power of a piano-and-voice formula. The song powerfully conveys a detailed description of the events of a massacre perpetrated in a bar in Queens by a disturbed young man. The text begins skillfully with a flashback ("'An extremely quiet child' they called you in your school report"), which makes the return of the action to the present even more shocking, in the midst of the blaring police sirens. With an interest in the study of human weaknesses and the mechanics of what turns people to crime, Bernie opts to address the criminal directly, approaching from a different perspective a subject that had already been addressed in "Have Mercy on the Criminal" on *Don't Shoot Me I'm Only the Piano Player*. Pinned down by the police, the young man is finally shot down.

Production

Elton breaks with his usual recording method, in this case trying to lay down the vocals and the instrumental at the same time. On one hand, he did this in order to preserve the dynamic emotion of his interpretation, but also because, strangely enough, he found it harder to play his syncopated piano part without the vocals, as these inevitably filled his head and interfered with the normal playing of the keyboard score. "Gus [Dudgeon] was always a stickler for separation, but I had to tell him, 'Look, the only way we're ever going to get this thing done is by doing the voice and piano together, and forget about the leakage.' It would only be the voice leaking anyway, so why care?"[95] Having won this point, Elton still had to resolve the issues caused by the imbalanced verse lengths in Bernie's lyrics. This meant that the singer had to fit eight words into one phrase and three into another, in the same melody. Elton finally managed to overcome these difficulties by playing on the silences and prolonging certain syllables.

SICK CITY

Elton John, Bernie Taupin / 5:24

Single: *Don't Let the Sun Go Down on Me / Sick City* **UK Release:** May 24, 1974, on DJM Records (ref. DJS.302) **Best UK Chart Ranking:** 16 **US Release:** June 10, 1974, on MCA Records (ref. MCA-40259) **Best US Chart Ranking:** 2 **Musicians:** Elton John: vocals, piano / **Davey Johnstone:** electric guitar, backing vocals / **Dee Murray:** bass, backing vocals / **Nigel Olsson:** drums, backing vocals / **Ray Cooper:** percussion / **Tower of Power:** brass **Recorded:** Caribou Ranch, Nederland, Colorado: January 1974 **Technical Team:** Producer: Gus Dudgeon / **Sound Engineer:** Clive Franks / **Assistant Sound Engineer:** Peter Kelsey / **Production Coordinator:** Steve Brown

After Elton recorded the very serious "Ticking," the other musicians rejoined him in better spirits than when they had left him, following the episode with "Don't Let the Sun Go Down on Me." They worked on finalizing the energetic number "Sick City," driven by the vigorous rhythm section of Tower of Power. This cynical number mercilessly highlights the groupies and freeloaders who gravitated around the group during their tours.

The piece led to a failed experiment. The team took it into their heads to record the backing vocals backward…In other words, Dee, Nigel, and Davey recorded their voices normally, repeating "Sick City" over and over again; then they played the tape back in reverse and listened carefully to the phrase produced when played in reverse, which amounted approximately to "Ahy-is-cus"; finally, the idea was to sing this word, which was in turn played backward to reproduce "Sick City." But the effect fell totally flat, and the three backing singers were unable to synchronize. Giving up on their strange idea, they agreed to record the backing vocals in the traditional way.

"Sick City" did not appear on the track list of the album but was selected for the B-side of the "Don't Let the Sun Go Down on Me" single, and it was released in the spring of 1974 on both sides of the Atlantic. It also appeared as a bonus track on the CD reissue of *Caribou* in 1995 (on both Mercury Records and Rocket).

COLD HIGHWAY

Elton John, Bernie Taupin / 3:25

Single: *The Bitch Is Back / Cold Highway* **UK Release:** August 30, 1974, on DJM Records (ref. DJS.322) **Best UK Chart Ranking:** 15 **US Release:** September 3, 1974, on MCA Records (ref. MCA-40297) **Best US Chart Ranking:** 4 **Musicians:** Elton John: vocals, piano, organ / **Davey Johnstone:** electric guitar, acoustic guitar, backing vocals / **Dee Murray:** bass, backing vocals / **Nigel Olsson:** drums, backing vocals **Recorded:** Caribou Ranch, Nederland, Colorado: January 1974 **Technical Team:** Producer: Gus Dudgeon / **Sound Engineer:** Clive Franks / **Assistant Sound Engineer:** Peter Kelsey / **Production Coordinator:** Steve Brown

No pun intended, but from the very first bars of "Cold Highway" Bernie and Elton take us down all kinds of strange routes. It was left off the album because of its complexity and its numerous contrasting stylistic strands. The song is challenging, due to the discrepancy between Bernie's chilling lyrics and Elton's rather pleasing and engaging music, with its sophisticated rhythm 'n' blues, punctuated by frequent key changes and rhythm breaks. The lyrics describe the death of a childhood friend in a car accident, on a notoriously dangerous stretch of road. The author confronts the harshest aspects of reality ("all they bought you was a hole in the ground") with delicate metaphors ("Your life stepped lightly out our hands"). The tragic irony is that, as children, they joked together about this deadly section of the road, the black spot.

This moving number was released on the B-side of the "The Bitch Is Back" single in 1974, and it was given new life as a bonus track on the 1995 reissue of the *Caribou* album.

SIDE A

STEP INTO CHRISTMAS

Elton John, Bernie Taupin / 4:32

Single: *Step into Christmas / Ho, Ho, Ho (Who'd Be a Turkey at Christmas?)* **UK Release:** November 26, 1973, on DJM Records (ref. DJS.290) **Best UK Chart Ranking:** 8 **US Release:** November 1973, on MCA Records (ref. MCA-65018) **Best US Chart Ranking:** 1 (US Billboard Christmas Singles) **Musicians:** Elton John: vocals, piano / **Davey Johnstone:** electric guitar, acoustic guitar, backing vocals / **Dee Murray:** bass, backing vocals / **Nigel Olsson:** drums, backing vocals / **Ray Cooper:** percussion / **David Hentschel:** ARP synthesizer / **Kiki Dee:** backing vocals (uncredited) / **Jo Partridge:** backing vocals (uncredited) / **Roger Pope:** tambourine (uncredited) **Recorded:** Morgan Studios, Willesden, London: November 11, 1973 **Technical Team:** Producer: Gus Dudgeon / Sound Engineer: David Hentschel

Genesis and Lyrics

Two months before arriving at the studio for the *Caribou* album, on November 11, 1973, Elton and his colleagues went to Morgan Studios, made available to them by the owner of the premises, Barry Morgan, the drummer who had worked on *Elton John*, *Tumbleweed Connection*, and *Madman Across the Water*. The idea was to finalize the two sides of a single that was to appear before the Christmas season. Without dipping into the stereotype of church bell–ridden arrangements, "Step into Christmas" perfectly encapsulates the spirit of Christmas with its perky melody and regressive, catchy refrain that lends itself to being sung at the top of one's voice. Envisaged as a light and inconsequential piece, even as a joke—in the spirit of the Christmas songs issued by the Beatles for members of their fan club—this would be something to be wrapped up in double-quick time. The B-side, "Ho, Ho, Ho (Who'd Be a Turkey at Christmas?)," with its chunky, cartoonish bass, and eccentric recording in which we hear loud background conversations, did indeed receive this treatment. But "Step into Christmas," on the other hand, was packaged in the most glitzy of arrangements.

Production

Elton asked Gus Dudgeon to assume the character of Phil Spector. Elton had met him the month before, at the sessions for the John Lennon album *Rock 'n' Roll* and had been able to get the measure of the producer's Napoleonic complexity, as well as his musical talent. Without launching into multiple arrangements to obtain the symphonic pop density of Spector's famous Wall of Sound, Gus Dudgeon focused on compression during the mixing and added a mammoth dose of echo to give depth to the ensemble.

Elton appeared as the Pinball Wizard in The Who's seminal film, *Tommy*.

A TUNE THAT RINGS A BELL
Elton leans into the length of his version by including a long outro that also contains a surprise: he includes the chords of "I Can't Explain."

SIDE A

PINBALL WIZARD

Pete Townshend / 5:09

Single: *Pinball Wizard / Harmony* **UK Release:** March 12, 1976, on DJM Records (ref. DJS 10652) **Best UK Chart Ranking:** 7 **Musicians:** Elton John: vocals, piano / **Davey Johnstone:** electric guitar, acoustic guitar, backing vocals / **Dee Murray:** bass, backing vocals / **Nigel Olsson:** drums, backing vocals / **Ray Cooper:** tambourine, congas **Recorded:** Ramport Studios, London: April 15, 1974 **Technical Team:** Producer: Gus Dudgeon

Following their tour through New Zealand and Australia, Elton and his musicians went to Ramport Studios in South London, where the Who had invited them to record a contribution to the film adaptation of the rock opera *Tommy*, which they were promoting, and in which Elton agreed to play a champion pinball player who would be matched against Tommy. All the musicians were ecstatic about this and very conscious that they had hit the jackpot with "Pinball Wizard," whose flamboyance would fit them like a glove. Elton managed to have it agreed that they would use his musicians, as well as Gus Dudgeon to finalize his reworking of the 1969 hit. Attired in the same way as on the album jacket of *Caribou*, with his leopard pattern jacket and big pink glasses, Elton took his place in the insulated booth containing the piano, on the left-hand side of the studio. The instrument in the structure replaces to great advantage the original acoustic guitar. Under the manic gaze of a Keith Moon slightly the worse for wear, and watched like a hawk by his fellow musicians, the group executed the number in only two takes. Elton, totally relaxed, gave the vocals everything he had in order to match the register of Roger Daltrey; he sipped mouthfuls of pure malt Laphroaig during his take, between phrases. He completed his (rather demanding) part in just ten minutes, while it took Dee, Nigel, and Davey an hour to finish their magnificent backing vocals. Then it was time for Dee to finalize his smoking solos. The whole thing was wrapped up in just four hours, to the total amazement of Pete Townshend, guitarist with the Who and the song's composer.

CAPTAIN FANTASTIC AND THE BROWN DIRT COWBOY

Captain Fantastic and the Brown Dirt Cowboy . Tower of Babel . Bitter Fingers .
Tell Me When the Whistle Blows . Someone Saved My Life Tonight . (Gotta Get a) Meal Ticket .
Better Off Dead . Writing . We All Fall in Love Sometimes . Curtains

RELEASE DATES
UK Release: May 23, 1975
Reference: DJM Records—DJLPX 1
Best UK Chart Ranking: 2
US Release: May 19, 1975
Reference: MCA Records—MCA-2142
Best US Chart Ranking: 1

A 1976 pinball machine combined images from *Tommy* and *Captain Fantastic*.

Elton John started working on the songs for his ninth album during a transatlantic boat trip.

Captain Fantastic was rereleased in CD format in 1995, with the original US CD release coming in 1987 on MCA. The new reissues included three bonus numbers: a cover of "Lucy in the Sky with Diamonds" by the Beatles (released as a single in 1974), a cover of "One Day at a Time" by John Lennon (released as the B-side on the 1974 "Lucy in the Sky with Diamonds"), and "Philadelphia Freedom" (released as a single in 1975).

THE PAST RECOMPOSED

As the doors of Caribou Ranch closed on a series of recording sessions that were as rapid as they were chaotic, Elton John and his team could hardly believe the news coming from the outside world. "Bennie and the Jets," a track Elton had never had much faith in, was becoming a bona fide hit on the radio. The song was so popular, in fact, that MCA Records worked hard to persuade Elton to release the song as a single in the United States instead of "Candle in the Wind," which had been the initial choice. "Bennie and the Jets" was released on February 4, 1974, and it easily sold over a million copies before settling at the top of the record sales charts.

While simultaneously conquering North America with his new track, Elton also began a Japanese tour with a concert in Tokyo on February 1, 1974. After Japan, Elton and the rest of his crew moved on to Australia and New Zealand. Fans in New Zealand gave him a royal welcome during his appearance at Western Spring Stadium on February 28, 1974, where he was met by an audience of thirty thousand people. Backstage at a press conference held at Auckland Park on the day before the concert, Elton's partner, John Reid, drew attention to himself when he lashed out physically at some of the journalists in attendance. This altercation was the culmination of Reid's ongoing struggles with drugs and alcohol. On the day of the concert, Reid was arrested by police and had to spend forty-eight hours in jail. Fortunately for Elton, the case did not register with the British press, but it was still a serious warning. John Reid might, at any time, endanger Elton's career and his physical well-being. In fact, the singer himself was sometimes a victim of his irascible companion: "It wasn't until John hit *me* that I came to my senses,"[3] Elton confessed in his autobiography.

A Nostalgic Opus Composed at Sea

Perched within the ivory tower that fame had afforded him, but under the unhealthy influences of drugs and an unfaithful and sometimes violent companion, Elton needed to get back to a simpler way of living. He wanted to spend time with so-called normal people who had authentic emotions. So he turned to his home soccer club: Watford. Knowing that the club was facing some difficulties, Elton helped them out by giving a concert at the town stadium on May 5, 1974, in front of a crowd of thirty-one thousand people who had all come to admire the local boy made good. For the occasion, Elton wore black and yellow, the colors of the club. That evening he played a cover of a Beatles song: "Lucy in the Sky with Diamonds." Surprised by the standing ovation that he received when he finished playing, he made a mental note that the song could well be a hit single for his own repertoire. This passing fancy came to fruition the following year when Elton recorded a version of the song with John Lennon appearing as a surprise guest. On May 18, 1975, Elton once again gave a charity concert, this time in support of disabled children. He gave an exceptional show, retracing his entire career from his earliest recordings all the way through *Caribou*. Some of the songs from this show were later immortalized on the first side of the live double album *Here and There*, which was released on April 30, 1976. This nostalgic retrospective provided an indication of where Elton intended to take his career.

After this concert, the singer decided to take a break from appearing onstage, and he also opted not to head back on out on tour. Frustrated by the latest sessions at Caribou Ranch, he was impatient to get back into the studio, but this time he wanted to avoid having to rush the recording process.

Elton's core team on *Captain Fantastic*: Davey Johnstone, Nigel Olsson, Dee Murray, and Ray Cooper.

THE LES PAUL CUSTOM SHOP ANNIVERSARY

In 2005, for the thirtieth anniversary of *Captain Fantastic*, the Custom Shop department of Gibson called upon the artist Pamelina H. to reproduce the *artwork* of the album on the body of a Gibson Les Paul specially made for Davey Johnstone.

Elton was thinking about his next album. He had a dream of creating a conceptual project in the same vein as *Tommy*, the celebrated album from the Who that was eventually turned into a movie in which Elton appeared. He discussed this with Bernie, who welcomed the idea of pursuing a conceptual album with enthusiasm. He also needed a new challenge. Between May and July 1974, the lyricist was involved in constructing an autobiographical narrative that covered the period of his early days with Elton, all the way through to the recording of *Empty Sky*. In these lyrics, he tells the story of their fateful first meeting and the formation of their friendship, which came together as naturally as if they had been two brothers separated at birth.

Bernie wrote the entirety of the album's autobiographical lyrics before returning to each individual song and working to fashion it into a gem. "With this, I took much more time. I would write something, then I'd go to something else, then go back and work some more on what I'd done previously. It was a new exercise, and I think it really paid off."[97] Bernie presented his finalized lyrics to Elton on July 20, the day after their boat departed for New York. At Elton's behest, the group opted to make a transatlantic voyage from Southampton, England, to New York onboard an ocean liner called, simply, *France*. The thinking was that they should separate the creative phase of the album from the recording phase. Elton thought that a six-day trip across the Atlantic would give him the time he needed to compose without interruption or pressure from the outside world.

Only Dee Murray out of the whole team was absent from the voyage, as he was on vacation in Barbados with his family.

Elton worked tirelessly in the boat's luxuriously gilded Debussy saloon, and he was often joined by Davey Johnstone, who had brought along an old acoustic Yamaha. Elton tackled the numbers one by one, following the chronological order originally conceived by Bernie. Working for two hours a day, he constructed the entire album in the exact order of the final track list. This process of working allowed Elton to take a bird's-eye view of how the entire album would operate as a cohesive whole, and it enabled him to plan for changes in mood as he saw fit. He managed to create five new songs while on board: "Captain Fantastic and the Brown Dirt Cowboy," "Tower of Babel," "Bitter Fingers," "Tell Me When the Whistle Blows," and "Someone Saved My Life Tonight." He also finalized "(Gotta Get a) Meal Ticket."

A Recording Done in Chronological Order

Upon their arrival in New York, the team was welcomed by John Lennon. On July 31, Elton went to the Record Plant studios to listen to the rough cut of *Walls and Bridges*. When the ex-Beatle suggested that Elton take on the piano part in "Whatever Gets You thru the Night," Elton managed to learn the part after listening to the song a single time. He showed his talent under the admiring eye of Lennon, who was in awe of his skill. Elton was enthusiastic about the song, and he was convinced that this would be a number one hit. Lennon had his doubts, so Elton offered him a bet. If Elton won, Lennon would have to come out of retirement from live performing and accompany him onstage.

Once the recording of *Walls and Bridges* had been completed—Elton also ended up playing the Hammond organ on "Surprise, Surprise (Sweet Bird of Paradox)"—the team then made their way back to Caribou Ranch, this time under much more welcoming conditions than they'd experienced during their previous recording sessions. Under the welcoming rays of the July sun, the mountains presented quite a different landscape from the desolate winter climate they'd encountered in January. This time, they booked the studio for a month.

Gus Dudgeon, who had experienced great difficulty in adapting to this remote location, was finally starting to acclimatize to his surroundings. In order to get over certain acoustic problems, he decided to record the takes without effects and with no

NUMBER-ONE RECORD
Upon its release in May 1975, *Captain Fantastic and the Brown Dirt Cowboy* became the first Elton John album to be ranked number one in the United States in its first week of release. This feat was repeated later in the same year by *Rock of the Westies*.

Elton sporting a
Captain Fantastic
T-shirt during his
promotional tour for
the album in 1975.

Elton joined John Lennon onstage at Madison Square Garden on November 28, 1974, which was the ex-Beatle's last major stage performance.

The Caribou Ranch studio was frequented by many artists over the years, including Chicago; Earth, Wind & Fire; Frank Zappa; Billy Joel; and Supertramp. Forty-five albums recorded at the studios are ranked in the top ten best sales of all time.

reverb, and to incorporate these later during the mixing stage. The songs were recorded one after the other, in accordance with the chronology of the story: "Captain Fantastic and the Brown Dirt Cowboy" lays out a comic scenario with the appearance of two characters symbolizing Elton and Bernie: Captain Fantastic (the superhero of the title) and the Brown Dirt Cowboy (a young British farmer who dreamed of being a cowboy and a poet, and who became a lyricist). Bonded together by their mutual passion for music, they apply their combined perseverance in an attempt to penetrate a very challenging location (the "Tower of Babel"). Ironically, the most original and ambitious song on the album in terms of its construction is "Bitter Fingers," which evokes the pressure Elton and Bernie felt early in their careers to create simple songs that would sell well for other artists. At the time of their initial partnership, Bernie had just arrived in London straight from the countryside, and he had difficulty adapting to city life. This struggle to find himself became the subject of "Tell Me When the Whistle Blows." Elton had barely managed the transition to adulthood himself, and he still felt a lack of clarity concerning his sexuality. This led to an attempted suicide that became the subject of "Someone Saved My Life Tonight." The failures and disappointments they experienced in the early days of their career would go on to fuel a sense of jealousy toward other artists that the duo covers on "(Gotta Get a) Meal Ticket." Lest we think their younger days were all a drag, Bernie and Elton also created "Better Off Dead," which portrays evenings spent drinking and eating burgers after days of long recording

sessions. The artistic partners also took an opportunity to reflect on their creative partnership in the song "Writing," and in the pleasures of sharing all the perks of fame with someone else, on the song "We All Fall in Love Sometimes." Bernie concludes the album by returning to his rural childhood with these words of summation from "Curtains": "And just like us / You must have had / A once upon a time."

Some Innovations

The recording of the album was managed by a smaller team than the crew who had handled *Caribou*. Other than David Hentschel, who was invited to provide the ARP synthesizer on the numbers "We All Fall in Love Sometimes" and "Curtains," and Gene Page, who was responsible for the orchestral arrangements on "Tell Me When the Whistle Blows," the Elton John Band was on its own. This was done against the advice of Gus Dudgeon, who advocated for luxurious soul-inspired arrangements for most of the tracks. Notwithstanding this slight artistic disagreement, the producer got his smile back and almost managed to forget the previous album, of which he was highly critical. He really liked the quality of the new compositions and the level of Elton's performances on vocals. The sessions went brilliantly, and the work was facilitated by the straightforward concept of the album; this was a product of the new chronological approach that the team adopted, which enabled them to gauge each new track against the one they had just worked on, and therefore led to an overall sense of cohesion.

The group's taste for innovation also applied at a technical level. The sound on "Bitter Fingers" was created in part by using a new effect produced by an Eventide Harmonizer, which had only recently arrived on the market. For a musician like Elton John, who was far less inclined toward innovation than some of his contemporaries (the Beatles, for example), this was a giant leap forward. In fact, the influence of the Beatles is very present on this album, and John Lennon actually visited the studio during recording at Elton's express invitation. In order to thank him for his recent contribution on *Walls and Bridges*, the ex-Beatle provided backing vocals and played guitar on a song that he knew rather well—"Lucy in the Sky with Diamonds," which Elton wanted to revisit.

Elton's and Bernie's *Garden of Earthly Delights*

The album's cover art shows the pianist wearing a top hat and Zorro mask while holding a cane and a rose and sitting astride a piano. Elton appears in the midst of repulsive creatures with half-human, half-animal forms. Designed by artists Harry Willcock and Alan Aldridge (the latter was known for his design for the album *A Quick One* by the Who, and for numerous psychedelic illustrations he created for the Beatles), it was strongly influenced by the painting *The Garden of Earthly Delights* by Hieronymus Bosch. This influence is corroborated by the presence of a globe enclosing Bernie Taupin on the back of the album. A globe can also be found on the back of *The Garden of Earthly Delights* when the triptych panels are closed. Bernie's

wife, Maxine, also appears inside the globe with the body of a dove. Situated all around them are other members of the group as well as Dick James. Already rich in symbolism, the 33 rpm was also sold with two booklets, one containing the lyrics to all the album's songs along with one that wasn't included: "Dogs in the Kitchen." The other booklet took the form of a scrapbook, and it was illustrated with numerous youthful photos, press articles, a comic strip covering Elton's early days, and various drawings and notes.

Captain Fantastic and the Brown Dirt Cowboy went straight to the top of the *Billboard* charts, which was a first for Elton and Bernie. It remained in the top spot for six weeks, and it stayed in the top 200 for nine months!

The back of the *Captain Fantastic* album cover features a grotesque character in the process of defecating. A subtle (or not-so-subtle) reference to the unofficial motto of the Dick James label, This Record Co.: "Turning shit into hits."

CAPTAIN FANTASTIC AND THE BROWN DIRT COWBOY

Elton John, Bernie Taupin / 5:45

Musicians
Elton John: lead and backing vocals, piano, Fender Rhodes electric piano
Davey Johnstone: acoustic guitar, electric guitar, mandolin
Dee Murray: bass
Nigel Olsson: drums
Ray Cooper: shaker, congas, quijada, gong, tambourine

Recorded
Caribou Ranch, Nederland, Colorado: August 1974

Technical Team
Producer: Gus Dudgeon
Sound Engineer: Jeff Guercio
Assistant Sound Engineer: Mark Guercio

Elton was never short of tricks when it came to amusing himself at the expense of his lifelong colleague.

Genesis and Lyrics

The recording sessions for Elton John's ninth studio album began with the title song "Captain Fantastic and the Brown Dirt Cowboy," which does a…fantastic job of presenting Elton and Bernie in the guise of two antiheroes who are "still green and growing." Between their overflowing ambition (characterized by their assumed superhero names) and their attachment to the comforts of childhood (suggested by foods such as "corn flakes," tea with sugar, and "chocolate biscuits"), the two young men have not yet moved fully into the world of adulthood. The autobiographical elements in this song are numerous and subtly integrated into the text. Take the inclusion of the word "regimented," which harkens back to the military-like education imposed by Elton's father, a flight lieutenant in the Royal Air Force. The word also calls back to Elton's given name, Reginald, and to the title considered for an early album title that never saw the light of day, *Regimental Sgt. Zippo.*

Production

Elton hewed closely to the general structure of the piece, but his introductory piano playing was not very full, and it was deemed insufficient on its own to sustain the introduction to the album. The pianist therefore called upon Davey Johnstone to add some drive and color to the song. From his point of view, this meant anchoring the song with a sense of the bucolic country-folk sound that called back to Bernie's childhood in Lincolnshire. Davey deployed a gentle melody on the acoustic guitar in the spirit of the community of Laurel Canyon beloved by artists like Joni Mitchell, Crosby, Stills & Nash, and Jackson Browne. "I came up with that riff, which was to be the first thing you hear on the record. Elton said to me, 'I need an intro,' and it was the first thing that I came up with as he was playing a G chord to an E-minor chord in kind of a lazy, country vibe."[31] Beyond the introduction, the whole track was structured around the sunny guitar sound, which Davey opted to supplement at the last minute with a mandolin. This further emphasizes the lightness of the piece, and it's an ideal preparation for the listener, setting them up for the harder driving final section of the song. In the last couple of minutes, the track abruptly changes tempo and turns up the groove. Nigel makes his Slingerland kit swing, and Ray Cooper backs him up on the conga drums.

TOWER OF BABEL

Elton John, Bernie Taupin / 4:28

Musicians
Elton John: vocals, piano
Davey Johnstone: electric guitar
Dee Murray: bass
Nigel Olsson: drums
Ray Cooper: tambourine

Recorded
Caribou Ranch, Nederland, Colorado: August 1974

Technical Team
Producer: Gus Dudgeon
Sound Engineer: Jeff Guercio
Assistant Sound Engineer: Mark Guercio

On June 21, 1975, Elton presented the *Captain Fantastic* album to the public in its entirety during a performance at London's Wembley Stadium.

Genesis and Lyrics

This delightful ballad with its highly polished production focuses an objective gaze on the decadent world of the London music industry at the end of the 1960s. The image that the song paints is uncompromisingly somber, despite a very pop feel: drugs, alcohol, prostitutes, dealers, adulation, and, finally, boredom and spiritual degradation all make an appearance. Everything has a price in this "Tower of Babel." Once they have become famous, the two men also plunge into a world that is numbed by excess. At first, they observe this stultifying world with a mix of innocence and skepticism. Some journalists have advanced the theory that the song was inspired by a specific event: the death of the Scottish drummer Robbie McIntosh, who was a founding member of the Average White Band. McIntosh died of a heroin overdose during a party at the Troubadour in Los Angeles, and Bernie had also been present. The only problem with this theory is that it's impossible! McIntosh died on September 23, 1974, and "Tower of Babel" had been written and recorded a month earlier.

Production

As a model of instrumental balance and continuity, "Tower of Babel" has the benefit of a clear production quality. Dee Murray's dominant bass bounds off in all directions, while Nigel Olsson's percussion sits on top of the mix with the power of the snare, ably highlighted by Ray Cooper's tambourine. Above all, the versatile guitars of Davey Johnstone illuminate the song, with little licks in A minor that expertly exploit the spaces leading up to the formidable solo, even if it's not the most inspired of the guitarist's repertoire. These valuable guitar moments were not planned; Elton intended to leave as much breathing space as possible in the song. But when Davey offered his inventive idea, his suggestion was enthusiastically received by the other musicians. Elton is also in top form with his vocals, which are commanding in their splendid isolation. There is clearly no need for additional backing to give body to a melody that's full of angst in the refrain. The singer adds a velvety electric piano sound, which blends admirably into the ensemble. Astonishing as it may seem, and despite its undeniable effectiveness, "Tower of Babel" was only ever played onstage once, during a concert at Wembley Stadium on June 21, 1975.

BITTER FINGERS

Elton John, Bernie Taupin / 4:32

Musicians
Elton John: vocals, piano
Davey Johnstone: electric guitar, backing vocals
Dee Murray: bass, backing vocals
Nigel Olsson: drums, backing vocals
Ray Cooper: tambourine, bells, bell tree, congas

Recorded
Caribou Ranch, Nederland, Colorado: August 1974

Technical Team
Producer: Gus Dudgeon
Sound Engineer: Jeff Guercio
Assistant Sound Engineer: Mark Guercio

With its catchy melody, "Bitter Fingers" could have been an excellent single, but the song was not promoted by Elton and his team. The singer performed it onstage a dozen times in 1975 before it disappeared from his stage repertoire for the following three decades. He played it again during his 2005 tour: in Boston, in New York, and then in Atlanta.

Genesis and Lyrics

After their early days of fascination with the music industry, the Taupin-John duo had to go through a thankless and rather unfulfilling phase spent writing pieces for other singers. One of them encounters these people and implores them in the first verse: "I'm going on the circuit, I'm doing all the clubs / And I really need a song, boys, to stir those workers up / And get their wives to sing it with me just like in the pubs."

"It's hard to write a song with bitter fingers," says the refrain. Impeded in their advancement by this side work, Elton and Bernie found this period of working as songwriting mercenaries to be a difficult one, which is evoked in "Bitter Fingers." "This is a song about having to write songs for people you don't really want to write songs for," explained Elton. "This song is about having to write with bitter fingers. What [Bernie and I] went through when we were writing all the shit we had to write before we eventually started making records that we wanted to make. I'm glad that happened, though, because without the struggle you don't appreciate anything."[99]

Production

Gus Dudgeon's intuition is once more in evidence from the opening moments of the song. It was his idea to double the triplets played on the piano by speeding up the tape to obtain a harmonized effect that sounds as though it's coming from some other world. But his really brilliant idea was passing the instrument through a Leslie cabinet and an Eventide Harmonizer, a completely new digital effects processor developed by the Eventide brand in 1974. Then Davey Johnstone made a remarkable entry, becoming an explorer of sound and experimenting with the microphone selector on his guitar, and on his tonality potentiometers until he obtained a sound close to that of a trumpet. Gus doubled the guitar to give it even more depth, and he also doubled Elton's voice in the refrain, using a technique known to help confer more presence and explosivity to the main vocals. The backing vocals provided by Dee, Davey, and Nigel intentionally lacked the same degree of clarity, and they were cleverly placed into the background to add color to the arrangement in the style of the Beatles.

TELL ME WHEN THE WHISTLE BLOWS

Elton John, Bernie Taupin / 4:20

Musicians
Elton John: vocals, electric piano, Clavinet
Davey Johnstone: electric guitar
Dee Murray: bass
Nigel Olsson: drums
Ray Cooper: tambourine, congas
Gene Page: arrangements, direction
Orchestra: uncredited

Recorded
Caribou Ranch, Nederland, Colorado: August 1974

Technical Team
Producer: Gus Dudgeon
Sound Engineer: Jeff Guercio
Assistant Sound Engineer: Mark Guercio

Famous arranger Gene Page directed the orchestra on "Tell Me When the Whistle Blows."

Genesis and Lyrics

One memorable lyric from "Tell Me When the Whistle Blows" sums up the song in just a few words: "Has this country kid still got his soul?" The kid, in this case, is clearly Bernie, and the verse in question says everything about the issues that were plaguing him as his career started to take flight. Growing up on a farm and then becoming a world-famous lyricist for an already revered rock artist was clearly no trivial matter. In the song, Bernie reminisces about the train he rode at the end of each week from London's King's Cross Station back to his family's home in rural Lincolnshire at the end of the 1960s. This weekly transition from hectic London life to the quiet countryside inexorably led him to notice the huge gulf that separated his two worlds. When he was still having difficulty making it as a professional songwriter, Bernie was often happy to go back to the comforting surroundings of his childhood home, but part of him was also ashamed that he had not yet managed to take control of his destiny: "You're just a black sheep going home / I want to feel your wheels of steel / Underneath my itching heels."

Production

Anchored by the sounds of rhythm 'n' blues and soul, "Tell Me When the Whistle Blows" owes a great deal to the work of the famous arranger Gene Page. While the strings are sometimes pompous in their sound, they remain very smooth throughout the piece, and they're complemented well by the funky brass that is so perfectly balanced by Gus Dudgeon. The recording process (before the overdubs were added) required only a single take. Everything fits together naturally, and the strings harmonize with Elton's sinuous Clavinet without difficulty. The instruments also meld nicely with Davey Johnstone's bluesy guitar, which recalls the sounds of groups such as Steely Dan. The rhythm section provides the essentials for the song without adding any embellishments, and Dee manages to mesh his plummeting bass impeccably with Nigel's slightly flat-sounding snare drum.

"Tell Me When the Whistle Blows" was performed a dozen times onstage between 1975 and 1976, but the song then disappeared from Elton John's set lists for thirty years. It wasn't until 2005 that this well-liked track was performed again onstage.

SOMEONE SAVED MY LIFE TONIGHT

Elton John, Bernie Taupin / 6:45

Musicians

Elton John: vocals, piano, Fender Rhodes electric piano, ARP String Ensemble synthesizer
Davey Johnstone: electric guitar (Leslie cabinet), acoustic guitar, backing vocals
Dee Murray: bass, backing vocals
Nigel Olsson: drums, backing vocals
Ray Cooper: tambourine, shaker, cymbals

Recorded

Caribou Ranch, Nederland, Colorado: August 1974

Technical Team

Producer: Gus Dudgeon
Sound Engineer: Jeff Guercio
Assistant Sound Engineer: Mark Guercio

Single Release

Someone Saved My Life Tonight / House of Cards
UK Release: June 20, 1975, on DJM Records (ref. DJS.385)
Best UK Chart Ranking: 22
US Release: June 23, 1975, on MCA Records (ref. MCA-40421)
Best US Chart Ranking: 4

Linda Woodrow (shown here in 1984) was Elton's onetime fiancée, and the focus of the psychodrama that served as the origin of "Someone Saved My Life Tonight."

Genesis and Lyrics

At the age of twenty, Elton John was still called Reg Dwight, and he was the pianist with Bluesology, a group led by Long John Baldry. At a concert at the Mojo in Sheffield, he met a tall blond woman named Linda Woodrow who was three years older than him. Eventually, Elton and Linda moved into an apartment together, and Bernie Taupin was invited to join them as a tenant. Bernie was not really a fan of Linda's. He thought that she was going to interfere with the close relationship he was forging with Elton, and that she would hold back their burgeoning lyricist-composer partnership, especially since Linda never held back with her opinion on their compositions. Soon enough, Elton and Linda were engaged and, although Elton himself did not seem entirely sure of their partnership, he could not find the courage to leave Linda. Apparently feeling trapped and unable to give voice to his concerns, Elton panicked and attempted suicide…albeit only after taking certain precautions: "I'd not only put a pillow in the bottom of the oven to rest my head on, I'd taken the precaution of turning the gas to low and opening all the windows in the kitchen…. There wasn't enough carbon monoxide in the room to kill a wasp."[3]

Although it was Bernie who came to the assistance of his friend on that fateful day, "Someone Saved My Life Tonight" does not refer to him. The "someone" in the song who really saved his life was Long John Baldry. As an openly gay man, Long John Baldry was the one who took things in hand, sensing that his friend did not have the courage to end his relationship with Linda. "You're gay," he told Elton. "You love Bernie more than you love her."[3] This discussion came as a shock to Elton, who was still uncertain about his own latent homosexuality. He was sure that his feelings toward Bernie were only friendly, but as for the larger question of his sexuality, he was suddenly plagued by doubts. Elton realized that he did not love Linda enough to make a commitment of marriage: "I did not know how to deal with this, so I got drunk and went home and told myself I was not going to get married."[3] Before the night was through, several arguments with Linda sealed the fate of their relationship. As a firsthand spectator to this difficult moment, Bernie Taupin later used his memories to create lyrics.

Long John Baldry provided a shock to the system that helped Elton realize his homosexuality.

In fact, the lyrics leave little doubt as to the lyricist's animosity toward Linda Woodrow, whom he portrayed as a "dominating queen," "sittin' like a princess perched in her electric chair."

Production

This song is without doubt one of the most intimate and autobiographical songs in Elton John's catalog, and it clearly stands out from the rest of *Captain Fantastic*. Due to its length (it comes in at 6:45), it is also the longest single in the singer's repertoire. From the first moments of the track, the piano is tense and unsettling while the drums mix discreetly with the cymbals. The bass begins modestly before gradually expanding with some very effective slide notes (0:36). Symbolically, it is on the "anymore" of the phrase "And it's one more beer, and I don't hear you anymore" where Elton John really lets his vocals go, taking flight alongside backup vocals just like the butterflies in the song's lyrics: "You're a butterfly, and butterflies are free to fly." The major influence of the Beach Boys is clearly perceptible in the song's harmonies. This is even more obvious when Elton deploys his falsetto range for the first time (1:43), in an apparent nod to Brian Wilson. Elton's vocal performance, which is intense and sensitive, left Gus Dudgeon completely cold at the time of the song's recording. He kept pushing the singer to do more takes until the guitarist, Davey Johnstone, leaned over to him and murmured: "He's talking about attempting suicide!"[100] Mortified by this revelation, the producer did not dare to say anything more.

The second sequence of the song is marked by the appearance of the matte-sounding snare drum at 2:20. Gus Dudgeon slightly overmixed this contribution in order to give the ballad more punch. For the producer, the drums were the cornerstone of this piece. During the recording, he noticed a peculiarity of Nigel's playing: When he switched from the high hat to the ride cymbal, he could not stop hitting the high hat with his foot pedal, whereas any other drummer would have stopped to create a softer effect. This idiosyncrasy became an integral part of his playing, and Gus decided to leave the sound as it was.

The backing vocals establish a charming question-and-answer exchange with the lead vocals. The lead vocal line expresses anger for the first time (at 2:35) in the highly symbolic and liberating lyric: "Listen to me good / I'm sleeping with myself tonight / Saved in time, thank God my music's still alive." The last line, introduced by an exaggeratedly loud snare drum, starts with an inventive bridge that leads into a richly orchestrated finale set within a dreamlike atmosphere. The song ends with a skillful fade on the phrase "Someone saved my life tonight." The words are hammered out like a mantra, or like an expression of Elton's eternal gratitude for his savior, Long John Baldry.

Naturally, Elton had already recorded ballads, like "Levon," "Rocket Man," and "Daniel," but never had his despair and anger been as palpable as they were in "Someone Saved My Life Tonight." This cry for help bowled over not just the fans, but also the famous rock critic Jon Landau, who had this to say when the single was released: "As long as Elton John can bring forth one performance per album on the order of 'Someone Saved My Life Tonight,' the chance remains that he will become something more than the great entertainer he already is and go on to make a lasting contribution to rock."[102]

(GOTTA GET A) MEAL TICKET

Elton John, Bernie Taupin / 4:00

Musicians

Elton John: vocals, piano, Clavinet
Davey Johnstone: electric guitars, acoustic guitars, backing vocals
Dee Murray: bass, backing vocals
Nigel Olsson: drums, backing vocals
Ray Cooper: tambourine

Recorded

Caribou Ranch, Nederland, Colorado: August 1974

Technical Team

Producer: Gus Dudgeon
Sound Engineer: Jeff Guercio
Assistant Sound Engineer: Mark Guercio

A veritable army of fans showed up to support the show at Madison Square Garden in August 1976.

Genesis and Lyrics

"That's a song about jealousy and envy and about seeing people being successful while you're not," acknowledged Elton John. "I was always desperate to become a success, and I was envious and very bitter and very narrow-minded about anybody who was successful. At the time [...] I'd put down anybody who was making it, just because we weren't. I think a lot of artists go through a stage like that."[101] Fully espousing this hardly noble attitude, which he shared with his colleague, Bernie adopts a posture that is both bitter and deliberately miserable: "The world's in front of me in black and white / I'm on the bottom line, I'm on the bottom line." Focusing on the despair of the situation in which the duo found themselves at this stage in their career, the "meal ticket"—or, by extension, the fee or contract after which the artist has to chase—is shown in contrast with a concert ticket. Similarly, the line for a meal, or to join a record company, is contrasted with the line for a concert.

Production

When Elton completed "(Gotta Get a) Meal Ticket" on July 22, the song had not yet revealed all its rock potential, which would be brought out by Davey Johnstone's electric guitar during the recording sessions. From his thundering riff, largely inspired by the flamboyant playing of Pete Townshend and by the Beatles' "Day Tripper," the group agreed to add an intro that would serve as a gimmick throughout the song. Nigel Olsson proposed beginning with a crash cymbal beat acting as a detonation, which grips the listener from the song's first second. This marks the starting point for Davey Johnstone's six-note motif, which anchors the piece into hard rock, at least until the arrival of the piano, which creates a change in tonality, and a switch toward rock 'n' roll. Elton's rough and bitter voice rises over an edgy, tight orchestration, with Nigel leading the assault on a sustained rhythm. Dee Murray's fully rounded bass, which sometimes merges with the groovy Clavinet notes, is given space to breathe. To round off this sonic offensive, which would not have been out of place next to "Midnight Creeper" or "Saturday Night's Alright (for Fighting)," Elton adds some voice takes with "Feel no pain, no pain / No regret, no regret" and interweaves them in response to his own singing, to accentuate the urgency of the words.

BETTER OFF DEAD

Elton John, Bernie Taupin / 2:35

Musicians: Elton John: vocals, piano / Davey Johnstone: acoustic guitar, backing vocals / Dee Murray: bass, backing vocals / Nigel Olsson: drums, backing vocals / Ray Cooper: triangle **Recorded:** Caribou Ranch, Nederland, Colorado: August 1974 **Technical Team:** Producer: Gus Dudgeon / Sound Engineer: Jeff Guercio / Assistant Sound Engineer: Mark Guercio

Genesis and Lyrics

At the bottom of the page on which he wrote the lyrics to "Better Off Dead," Bernie scribbled, as a note for the composer, the reference "John Prine." One supposes that this was done to indicate that a country-folk arrangement would be ideal for this song. It should be said that these lyrics evoked other, more rhythmic memories for the singer: Bernie drew his inspiration from the restless nights during which friends watched from behind the window of a bar as drunkards and prostitutes were picked up by the police. The song's message, addressed to all these unfortunate people who had been so battered by life, is clearly expressed by words that are repeated several times: "Then you're better off dead if you haven't yet died." The recollection of these heavy-handed arrests might have pushed Elton to distance himself from John Prine's poetic milieu, even in spite of Bernie's suggestion, choosing instead to concoct a musical setting that is as temperamental as the characters in the song.

Production

The sequence of chords created by Elton is absorbing right from the introduction, making "Better Off Dead" one of the most melodically catchy songs on the album. Dee's bass, the main vector of the urgency sensed by the listener, seems to provide a marvelous image of the arrival of the police, sirens blaring, to grab recalcitrant offenders trying to escape before the trap closes in on them. The galloping rhythm is sustained by Nigel in top form behind his drums, and by the acoustic guitar tracks of the Martin D-28 played by Davey. To obtain his distinctive drum sound, Gus passed Nigel's kit through an Eventide Harmonizer and created a slight delay—a technique also used by John Lennon on his solo track "Instant Karma! (We All Shine On)." Another of this song's strong points is the sophisticated arrangement of the backing vocals, which Gus Dudgeon placed in the center of the panoramic spectrum to make them more direct for the listener. Bernie, who heard the song only after it was finished, was somewhat taken aback by the result, which is light-years away from the warm folk sound he had originally imagined. "Better Off Dead" is clearly one of Elton's favorites, and he has since performed it more than four hundred times onstage.

WRITING

Elton John, Bernie Taupin / 3:38

Musicians: Elton John: vocals, electric piano / Davey Johnstone: piano, acoustic guitar, backing vocals / Dee Murray: bass, backing vocals / Nigel Olsson: drums, backing vocals / Ray Cooper: triangle, shaker, bongos **Recorded:** Caribou Ranch, Nederland, Colorado: August 1974 **Technical Team:** Producer: Gus Dudgeon / Sound Engineer: Jeff Guercio / Assistant Sound Engineer: Mark Guercio

Genesis and Lyrics

In the columns of the *Radio Times*, in 2002, Bernie Taupin answered the question left in suspense in the song "Writing," mainly: "Will the things we wrote today / Sound as good tomorrow?" Bernie's response was simple and straightforward. "I guess the answer is 'yes,' they do! Although this is from a mid-seventies concept album, it's about when we started out in the late sixties, surviving writing in that Tin Pan Alley of Denmark Street in London. I'm very happy that our songs have lasted and become part of modern culture—it's the biggest compliment you can get."[28] Writing a song about writing songs is always a gamble. Bernie fondly remembered the gamble when he and Elton, oscillating between lightheartedness and recklessness, learned to get to know each other and to write songs together.

Production

Given that this song is about how Elton's songs are written, it's ironic that Elton shared piano playing duties with Davey Johnstone on the track. Davey also distinguishes himself with the precision of his acoustic guitar playing, which delivers a very catchy gimmick and a lively solo from 2:27, heightened by a light reverb. On this rhythmic and sparking number, the bass and drums are deliberately held back in order to give prominence to the unexpected triangle played by Ray Cooper. The enthusiastic voice of Elton is supported by some unusual vocals, on the verses, that are provided by the impeccable Davey-Dee-Nigel trio. While "Writing" is not one of Elton's best songs, due to its predictable melody, it remains one of the most convivial moments on this album. The song has been completely disregarded by Elton, who only performed it once onstage in 1975.

WE ALL FALL IN LOVE SOMETIMES / CURTAINS

Elton John, Bernie Taupin / 4:13 and 6:35

Musicians
Elton John: vocals, piano, harpsichord, Mellotron
Davey Johnstone: electric guitar, acoustic guitar
Dee Murray: bass
Nigel Olsson: drums
Ray Cooper: tambourine, bells, congas
David Hentschel: ARP synthesizer

Recorded
Caribou Ranch, Nederland, Colorado: August 1974

Technical Team
Producer: Gus Dudgeon
Sound Engineer: Jeff Guercio
Assistant Sound Engineer: Mark Guercio

Pop singer Neil Sedaka (above, right) was present in the studio when the group was working on "We All Fall in Love Sometimes/Curtains."

Genesis and Lyrics

Captain Fantastic and the Brown Dirt Cowboy closes with a diptych of tracks that clocks in at nearly ten minutes in total. "We All Fall in Love Sometimes" and "Curtains" are presented as two distinct tracks on most versions of this album (see For Elton Addicts); however, these tracks form one distinct entity, especially when considering that they were also recorded in one go. Musically linked, the two songs are nonetheless distinguished by their respective subjects. "We All Fall in Love Sometimes" expresses an uncommon melancholy, but the mood evolves with the text: A timely change of key accompanies the light that pierces the lyrics, which describe the power of the relationship between the lyricist and the singer. "It made me well up because it was true. I wasn't in love with Bernie physically, but I loved him like a brother; he was the best friend I'd ever had,"[3] confided Elton in his autobiography. "Curtains" shows this close relationship even more clearly, with Bernie speaking directly to Elton and inviting his memories through the evocation of their first songs and of the conditions in which he wrote: "Beneath these branches / I once wrote / Such childish words for you." The piece, and the album itself, both end on the powerful "A once upon a time" in the final coda.

Production

Only two takes were needed to complete this bravura recording. Neil Sedaka, one of the house artists with the Rocket Record Company, was passing through the studio during these sessions. When the group began their second attempt, he popped into the cabin and asked Gus if he could sit down. Gus was inwardly delighted to have a spectator, whose reaction he could observe. The minutes went by. After approximately nine minutes, Neil Sedaka quietly leaned over to Gus and murmured: "My God, are they doing this all in one go, or are they dubbing on?" Pleased with his reaction, the producer whispered back: "No, it's all in one go."[31] The performer of "Oh! Carol" was impressed by the technical skill of the group and by their extreme consistency—none of the musicians had put a foot wrong for nearly ten minutes. "Jesus, they been going on for *hours*,"[31] he whispered.

The close relationship between the singer and his lyricist is at the heart of this track's lyrics.

"We All Fall in Love Sometimes" paved the way for "Sorry Seems to Be the Hardest Word," to which it is melodically very close. It distills its angst through Elton's emotional singing and the use of the Mellotron, which imitates the sound of a flute. Meanwhile, Davey provides a delicate guitar motif that's sprinkled with bends and is reminiscent of David Gilmour's refined playing. Continuing at the same tempo and in the same key, "Curtains" concludes the album with a brilliant crescendo. It stars Nigel Olsson, who delivers his fullest and most narrative score, with varied rolls and cymbal beats. It also made Olsson break out in a cold sweat; the drummer was conscious during the recording of the risk involved if he made the slightest mistake. This fabulous finale also owes a great deal to the angelic backing vocals that accompany Elton's singing with diabolical precision. Gus Dudgeon suggested that Davey, Dee, and Nigel should harmonize over Elton's voice, thereby supporting it and adding necessary emphasis.

FOR ELTON ADDICTS

On the CD version of the album these two numbers are listed as one track, reducing the album's track listing to nine songs in total. When MCA released its version the songs were listed as separate tracks.

SIDE A

LUCY IN THE SKY WITH DIAMONDS

John Lennon, Paul McCartney / 5:58

Single: *Lucy in the Sky with Diamonds / One Day at a Time* **UK Release:** November 15, 1974, on DJM Records (ref. DJS.340) **Best UK Chart Ranking:** 10 **US Release:** November 18, 1974, on MCA Records (ref. MCA-40344) **Best US Chart Ranking:** 1 **Musicians:** Elton John: lead and backing vocals, piano, Mellotron, harpsichord / John Lennon (credited as Dr. Winston O'Boogie): guitars, backing vocals / Davey Johnstone: electric guitar, sitar, backing vocals / Dee Murray: bass, backing vocals / Nigel Olsson: drums, backing vocals / Ray Cooper: tambourine, tubular bells, gong, maracas, congas, chimes **Recorded:** Caribou Ranch, Nederland, Colorado: August 1974 **Technical Team: Producer:** Gus Dudgeon / **Sound Engineer:** Jeff Guercio / **Assistant Sound Engineer:** Mark Guercio

Genesis and Lyrics

"I met John last year," Elton explained. "Then when I was in New York getting off the SS *France* I saw him again and he said, 'Come down to my sessions.' So I did, and ended up doing, 'Whatever Gets You thru the Night' and 'Surprise' from the album. And he was going to LA to do a song which he had written for Ringo and I said, 'On the way back why don't you come up to Caribou? Cos we're gonna do "Lucy in the Sky." And he said, 'Sure.'"[103] John Lennon kept his word and arrived with May Pang at the Caribou Ranch studios. The singer was good company and enjoyed spending time with Elton and his musicians, despite some breathing difficulties due to the altitude (during the vocal takes, he regularly asked to use the oxygen tank). The presence of the ex-Beatle resulted from Elton's boundless admiration for his colleague, and it was a sign of a conspicuous opening up on the part of the singer, who before this point had not been keen to let other artists into his world. But in 1974, Elton

John Lennon was invited to Caribou Studios for a reworking of "Lucy in the Sky with Diamonds."

had played and sung on "Let Me Be Your Car" on Rod Stewart's album *Smiler*, and he played piano on Ringo Starr's "Snookeroo," a song Bernie had written for *Goodnight Vienna*. Elton also provided backing vocals on "Bad Blood" by Neil Sedaka, who was signed to the Rocket Record Company.

Production

John Lennon immediately demonstrated a remarkable modesty during the creative process. He did not wish to interfere in the reworking of "Lucy," and he even suggested going so far as to just watch and not contribute during recording. Davey Johnstone insisted that he should play. Seemingly shocked by Lennon's reticence, Davey said simply: "Just play on it. You're fucking great. You're a fucking *Beatle*."[31] John initially gave the excuse that he did not have a guitar. Undeterred, Davey put his Gibson Les Paul over Lennon's shoulder. The ex-Beatle then confessed that he could not remember how the guitar part of the song went. Davey happily reminded him of the chords of his own song. Once his memory had been jogged, Lennon agreed to take part, but without impinging on Elton's direction. In fact, Lennon was the one who pushed the musicians to take liberties with the original song, and he even suggested including a surprising ska-inflected sound at the end. Elton's version, therefore, offers a very different vision of this classic track; it's less psychedelic, despite the "subaquatic" treatment of the sound and the sitar played by Davey. Instead, Ray Cooper's percussion and chimes contribute a refreshing and new sound to the song. Dee Murray's highly melodic bass playing also received John Lennon's warmest compliments, and Lennon was delighted with the entire experience.

ONE DAY AT A TIME

John Lennon / 3:49

Single: *Lucy in the Sky with Diamonds / One Day at a Time* **UK Release:** November 15, 1974, on DJM Records (ref. DJS.340) **Best UK Chart Ranking:** 10 **US Release:** November 18, 1974, on MCA Records (ref. MCA-40344) **Best US Chart Ranking:** 1 **Musicians:** Elton John: vocals, piano, keyboards / Davey Johnstone: acoustic guitar, backing vocals / Dee Murray: bass, backing vocals / Nigel Olsson: drums, backing vocals **Recorded:** Caribou Ranch, Nederland, Colorado: August 1974 **Technical Team:** Producer: Gus Dudgeon / Sound Engineer: Jeff Guercio / Assistant Sound Engineer: Mark Guercio

Genesis and Lyrics

The day after he finished recording "Lucy in the Sky with Diamonds" with Elton, John Lennon left Caribou Ranch with May Pang. Still on cloud nine after Lennon's departure, Elton launched into the cover of another John Lennon song: "One Day at a Time." The ex-Beatle had recorded this number for his solo album *Mind Games*, released in 1973. More intimate, introspective, and abstract, *Mind Games* was completed shortly before Lennon's separation from Yoko Ono and the start of his relationship with May Pang. "One Day at a Time," with its lyrics about intense and unconditional love, therefore seemed slightly out of step with Lennon's new life. After all, this was a man who had written about himself and Yoko: "I'm a fish and you're the sea," "I'm the apple and you're the tree," and "I'm the door and you're the key."

Production

In the original version of the song, John Lennon's gentle voice is overlaid with aerial backing vocals, and the drums are very discreet. Elton remained true to the spirit of the song, while offering his musicians a leading role, both in the backing vocals and in their musical contribution. Unlike the original version, the backing vocals do not "answer" the lead voice but accompany it throughout the song. As for the instruments, the rhythm section provides a well-balanced beat, while Davey's guitar is once again in the foreground, this time at the suggestion of Gus Dudgeon. The producer proposed that the guitar be systematically doubled; by doing this he was looking for a sound close to that of a saxophone. As for Elton, he provides a fine piano score and fills the overall sound of the verses with layers of keyboards before entering into a delicate solo, which Davey doubles in the background. A slight vocal approximation (perhaps deliberate?) on the part of Elton in the final refrain—when singing the "for" in "is good for you"—seems slightly forced and lacking in accuracy.

COVER
"House of Cards" was covered by British singer and actress Linda Kendrick in 1975, the same year in which the single was released. Kendrick was famous for her role as Jeanie in the musical *Hair* (1968).

HOUSE OF CARDS

Elton John, Bernie Taupin / 3:09

Single: *Someone Saved My Life Tonight / House of Cards* **UK Release:** June 20, 1975, on DJM Records (ref. DJS 385) **Best UK Chart Ranking:** 22 **US Release:** June 23, 1975, on MCA Records (ref. MCA-40421) **Best US Chart Ranking:** 4 **Musicians:** Elton John: vocals, electric piano / Davey Johnstone: acoustic guitar, electric guitar, backing vocals / Dee Murray: bass, backing vocals / Nigel Olsson: drums, backing vocals / Ray Cooper: shaker **Recorded:** Caribou Ranch, Nederland, Colorado: August 1974 **Technical Team:** Producer: Gus Dudgeon / Sound Engineer: Jeff Guercio / Assistant Sound Engineer: Mark Guercio

Genesis and Lyrics

Released as the B-side of "Someone Saved My Life Tonight," "House of Cards" was not included on the original *Captain Fantastic and the Brown Dirt Cowboy* album. It was rehabilitated for the deluxe version of the album that was released in 2005, in celebration of the album's thirtieth anniversary. This edition included the three bonus tracks from the previous CD reissues, to which, finally, "House of Cards" was added. The "house of cards" described here by Bernie is one in which the rich and famous are confined, and which may collapse in the blink of an eye. The lyricist provides some paternalistic verses delivering a warning for those who would allow themselves to be deluded by the smoke and mirrors of success: "I hear tell some playboy has kidnapped your heart / With his plane and his plans for games after dark" [...] / "If there's sharks in the water, don't swim where it's deep." Bernie also issues a reminder that the taste for success may be both "bitter and sweet," and can also be very risky.

Production

In contrast to the song's argument that fame is not a game, Elton and his musicians created a country-pop sound with a playful and irresistible groove. The springing bass of Dee Murray is once again the invisible pillar in this solid musical structure, sticking close to Nigel's relaxed drums while adding an uninterrupted flood of notes with remarkable dexterity and musicality. Davey Johnstone is less present than on many other cuts from the album, even though his interwoven notes remain impressive. The backing vocals that shine through to the last bar of the song rigorously track Elton's lead. Here, Elton leaves off his piano for an electric piano that ably slides between the other instruments.

SIDE A

PHILADELPHIA FREEDOM

Elton John, Bernie Taupin / 5:38

Single: *Philadelphia Freedom / I Saw Her Standing There (live)* **UK Release:** February 28, 1975, on DJM Records (ref. DJS 354) **Best UK Chart Ranking:** 12 **US Release:** February 24, 1975, on MCA Records (ref. MCA-40364) **Best US Chart Ranking:** 1 **Musicians:** Elton John: vocals, electric piano / **Davey Johnstone:** acoustic guitar, electric guitar / **Dee Murray:** bass / **Nigel Olsson:** drums / **Ray Cooper:** tambourine, maracas, congas / **Gene Page:** arrangements, direction / **Orchestra:** uncredited **Recorded:** Caribou Ranch, Nederland, Colorado: August 1974 **Technical Team:** Producer: Gus Dudgeon / **Sound Engineer:** Jeff Guercio / **Assistant Sound Engineer:** Mark Guercio **2nd Single Release:** *Philadelphia Freedom / Lucy in the Sky with Diamonds* **UK Release:** September 1978, on DJM Records (ref. DJS 10911)

Genesis and Lyrics

Over the years, many singers have written tributes to great figures in the world of sport. From Teresa Brewer's ecstatic ode to the swing of baseball icon Mickey Mantle, to Lil' Wayne deifying Kobe Bryant on his track "Kobe Bryant," the exploits of athletes feed an artist's appetite for modern epics. So, it stands to reason that Elton John, who was famously a fan of soccer and served as the chairman of the Watford Hornets club from 1976 to 2002, dedicated one of his most famous songs to a female tennis player. While tennis came right after soccer in his personal hierarchy of favorite sports, above all Elton wanted this song to pay homage to an exceptional personality: Billie Jean King.

The pop star met the tennis star in 1973 at a society event organized by promoter Jerry Perenchio. In the midst of a room filled with wealthy patrons, Elton only had eyes for the world number one and a heroine of the feminist cause. At the time, Billie Jean was preparing to confront Bobby Riggs, a former number one himself and winner of four Grand Slam titles. Riggs was boasting to anyone who would listen that female tennis players belonged in the kitchen and not on the court. According to Riggs, female players were inferior to men, and he would have no difficulty, despite his fifty-five years, in beating Billie Jean King. Billie Jean accepted this challenge and decided to challenge Riggs to a match referred to by the press as "the battle of the sexes," on September 20, 1973, at the Astrodome in Houston, Texas. The match wasn't much of a contest, and Billie Jean ran rings around Bobby Riggs, winning in straight sets: 6-4/6-3/6-3.

A few months later, Elton and Billie met on a tennis court to exchange a few serves. Honored by this privilege, the singer became an assiduous supporter of the Philadelphia Freedoms, a tennis team managed by Billie Jean King.

There are various stories about how this song came into being. There are the words of the singer himself, who had this to say on the set of the *Tonight Show* on September 20, 1993: "I wanted to pay tribute to her because [...] Billie Jean is such a motivating and fantastic person. [...] If you're in a sick bed and you can't walk, she'll make you walk. [...] She's been there [during the] worst moments in my life."[104] Strangely, Elton would later cast doubt over the circumstances of the birth of this song, when he wrote in his autobiography: "Billie Jean King had asked me to write a theme song for her tennis team, the Philadelphia Freedoms. I couldn't refuse; I adored Billie Jean."[3]

Either way, he still had to convince Bernie Taupin to work on the subject. The lyricist was very reticent. He did not see himself writing about tennis, a subject that was unknown to him, and he also did not feel inspired by the title chosen by the singer: "Philadelphia Freedom." But he managed to put aside his reservations and write lyrics that were more universally accessible, celebrating independence and freedom with a tinge of nostalgia: "Oh, Philadelphia freedom, shine on me, I love you / Shine a light through the eyes of the ones left behind," Elton sings in the postrefrain. As a native of Pinner, that small town in the London suburbs, Elton went on to conquer the world, and Taupin uses the lyrics in this song to express the feelings of pride that Elton had in all the success he had achieved. Bernie wrote about their penniless years of apartment-sharing, and about how far they had both come: "Some people choose the city / Some others choose the good old family home / I like living easy without family ties."

Elton said that a song called "Philadelphia Freedom" would be a dream opportunity to pay homage not just to Billie Jean (with the plural -*s* dropped in the title) but also to *Philadelphia soul*, or *Philly soul*, a musical style that was very much in fashion at the beginning of the decade, and that he greatly appreciated. The British artist made no secret of his love for the musical style, and he wrote the following dedication on the back of the record sleeve "With love to B. J. K. and the music of Philadelphia." "We wrote 'Philadelphia Freedom' as a tribute to the music that sounded so Philadelphia, like Philadelphia. The O'Jays and the Three Degrees and MFSB, Harold Melvin and the Blue Notes. It was just such great stuff,"[105] he declared in a 2018 interview.

A lifelong friendship between Elton John and Billie Jean King began with "Philadelphia Freedom."

Production

Elton John wanted to add a galvanizing dimension to this track by making it a dancing and celebratory song. He knew from the time he composed the song on the Wm. Knabe & Co. baby grand that it would be released as a single and not on the album, and he wanted it to be a hit.

To sustain its fiery rhythm and to imitate the Philadelphia soul sound, he needed a full orchestra, complete with strings and brass sections, as well as flutes (on the postrefrains). The creation of these pyrotechnics was provided by Gene Page, who had earned praise for his orchestral work with Barry White, and with icons like Aretha Franklin, the Temptations, and the Four Tops. Exultant brass and plummeting strings launch the song, picking up on the famous overtures from classic songs like "Hold On, I'm Coming" by Sam & Dave and "Respect" by Aretha Franklin. Keeping in mind the luxurious sound structures of Kenny Gamble, Leon Huff, Thom Bell, or Bobby Martin, Elton John starts out with solid foundations by entrusting the implacable groove of this number in A# to the voluptuously rounded bass provided by Dee Murray. The musician's supple and elastic playing (which bursts out in the transition between the intro and verse) was much admired by producer Gus Dudgeon, who was very enthusiastic about the sound from his place in the control room. Though it is the center of attention in the verses, the bass lets the strings take a starring role in the refrains. Given free rein, they stand out from the main melody sung by Elton John. His voice, which is rather muscular in comparison to the usual gentleness of Philadelphia soul, adds an even more unique energy to his performance. This also means that he does not fall into the trap of allowing the piece to become a pastiche of the musical genre that inspired it.

Once recorded, and before it was mixed, Elton John took a portable tape recorder to the Philadelphia Freedoms in Denver and asked to meet with Billie Jean King. He joined her in the locker room, and after they exchanged affectionate greetings, he eagerly played her the tape in the hope that she would approve. She waited and listened carefully until the end of the piece, unable to hold back her smile. She reacted just as Elton hoped she would, delighted at the end of the five minutes of the song: "I don't like it, Elton, I love it, love it, love it!"[109] she exclaimed. The single, released in February 1975, is one of the longest ever issued by the artist—probably as a repudiation to the DJs of the era who were clamoring for him to record shorter numbers that would fit into radio standards. This slightly defiant stance did not in any way affect the success of the single, which, alongside "I Saw Her Standing There," a duet recorded live with John Lennon, went to the top of the American *Billboard* charts and achieved a platinum certification when it sold one million copies.

ALBUM

ROCK OF
THE WESTIES

Medley (Yell Help, Wednesday Night, Ugly) . Dan Dare (Pilot of the Future) . Island Girl .
Grow Some Funk of Your Own . I Feel Like a Bullet (in the Gun of Robert Ford) .
Street Kids . Hard Luck Story . Feed Me . Billy Bones and the White Bird

RELEASE DATES
UK Release: May 23, 1975
Reference: DJM Records—DJLPX 1
Best UK Chart Ranking: 2
US Release: May 19, 1975
Reference: MCA Records—MCA-2142
Best US Chart Ranking: 1

Elton John dressed in sequins for an appearance in front of a sold-out crowd at LA's Dodger Stadium in October 1975. This performance was one of the high points of his triumphant tour in the States.

ELTON TURNS THE TABLES

In the middle of the 1970s, Elton John could look back upon what he had achieved with some satisfaction. On November 9, 1974, midway through his triumphant tour of the United States, which ran from September 25 to December 3, 1974, with Kiki Dee as the opening act, he released his first "best of" album, called *Elton John's Greatest Hits*. On the album cover, Elton appears dressed in an elegant, immaculate suit, with a smile on his face. His expression, which one imagines to be cheerful, was concealed behind large white-framed glasses with tinted lenses. He is shown posing in his sitting room, in front of his piano, with a cane that matches his suit resting on the instrument. Despite the fairly simple composition of the photo, Elton was very persnickety about it and he had the image reworked an incalculable number of times by the designer, Hogie McMurtrie. By all reports, the designer was tearing out his hair in the face of these endless changes. Elton seemed almost more demanding in the supervision of his image than he was during the recording of his songs in the studio. The compilation consisted of ten hits: "Your Song," "Daniel," "Honky Cat," "Goodbye Yellow Brick Road," "Saturday Night's Alright (for Fighting)," "Rocket Man," "Candle in the Wind," "Don't Let the Sun Go Down on Me," "Border Song," and "Crocodile Rock." "Bennie and the Jets" was left off the British version, paying the price for its lackluster performance in his own country in February 1974 (thirty-seventh), while the American version included it instead of "Candle in the Wind." The compilation went to the top of the charts in both the United Kingdom and the United States, and its success had only just begun. The greatest hits album remained in the Billboard Top 200 for two years.

An Inexplicable Decision

Elton was delighted to perform at Madison Square Garden in the company of his idol, John Lennon, on November 28, 1974. This performance was given in part to honor Lennon's wager concerning the performances of "Whatever Gets You thru the Night," which became a number one hit in the United States, just as Elton had predicted. Nobody knew it at the time, but this show would be the ex-Beatle's last, as he subsequently devoted himself to his role as a father before being shot by Mark David Chapman six years later, on December 8, 1980. A few days after the New York concert, *Billboard* called *Goodbye Yellow Brick Road* the album of the year, and then Elton's cover of "Lucy in the Sky with Diamonds" went to number one in the United States charts in January 1975, before eventually giving "Philadelphia Freedom" the top spot in the following month. The singer took advantage of all the work he had done and allowed himself to savor this triumph.

But in the end, this moment of enjoyment was short-lived. After years of hard work, Elton became depressed, and lost no time identifying the origin of his malaise: He had a deep need for change. On April 19, 1975, he decided to change things up and he sacked some of his musicians. "I've always wanted to be part of a good, driving rock 'n' roll band. The old band never used to drive—we just used to rattle along," he confided to journalist Caroline Coon two months later. "Whenever we played anything live, it was always twice the tempo of the recording, and that was always a bit off-putting to me. I wanted to chug rather than race."[101] This was a harsh conclusion, and the culprits identified were Dee Murray and Nigel Olsson. They comprised the rhythm section of the Elton John Band, and they were supposed to ensure a reliable tempo. Their sentence was passed without the slightest warning. "I rang them myself. They took the news quite well—Dee was more upset than Nigel, but there wasn't a huge row or a feeling of bad blood from either of them. I feel worse about it now than I did at the time. It must have been devastating for them—they'd been integral for years and we were at the peak of our careers. Back then, I was always looking forward, and I felt in my gut that I needed to revamp our sound: make it funkier and harder-driving."[3] The version of events that Elton gives in his autobiography does not match the one given by Nigel Olsson in a 1999 interview, which affirmed that Elton had not taken the trouble to announce the news to them directly: "I got this call from Steve Brown saying 'Elton doesn't want you guys involved in gigs or recordings

A STAR AMONG THE STARS

Three days after the release of *Rock of the Westies*, Elton John received his star on the Hollywood Walk of Fame. He arrived at the ceremony in a customized golf cart, wearing glasses in the shape of giant stars.

anymore, what are you going to do?' all in one sentence. I was floored."[55] Later in the same interview he added: "I had wished Elton had made the call himself. It would have been much easier. [...] Dee went to his grave not knowing why. [...] One of the last things Dee said to me was: 'Nige, I wish we'd been told what the hell we did to be fired. We never got the right story.' That really saddens me, and there's really not a day that goes by I don't think about Dee. It was the best band Elton's had—ever."[55]

The New Team

When it happened, the star's entourage also did not understand his decision. Everyone, including John Lennon, Gus Dudgeon, and John Reid thought, that Elton had lost his senses. Davey Johnstone and Ray Cooper were miraculously spared. Paradoxically, as he was moving forward, Elton chose to bring back some old acquaintances: guitarist Caleb Quaye and drummer Roger Pope. Caleb was ready to roll with his Gibson Les Paul and his Fender Stratocaster, but he imposed a single condition: never to play "Crocodile Rock," which he loathed. Two American session musicians were also recruited. The first was Kenny Passarelli, a trained classical trumpet player who became a bass player, and who was accustomed to playing a fretless bass. Passarelli was asked at the same time to join Peter Frampton's group, but he gave precedence to Elton. The second musician, a twenty-four-year-old keyboard player named James Newton Howard, was recruited without ever having to play in front of Elton. He was hired based only on his CV, which was pretty respectable for someone his age (Melissa Manchester, Ringo Starr, Carly Simon). He subsequently went even further in his career, becoming one of the most famous film composers of his generation. Howard was nominated for nine Oscars, and he was famously involved in the soundtracks for *Batman*, *Hunger Games*, and *Fantastic Beasts and Where to Find Them*.

The newly constituted group went to Amsterdam in June to rehearse for two weeks before performing at Wembley in a much-anticipated concert in front of eighty thousand people, on June 21, 1975. The rehearsal sessions went really well. Elton was very pleased with his new group, which showed power and cohesion. As for the new recruits, Kenny and James, he was ecstatic, to the extent of claiming that he himself was now the worst musician in the group: "I've got to work hard to keep up with them, which is going to make me play harder and

better."[101] However, the first performance given by the new version of the Elton John Band at Wembley nearly ended in disaster: This mini festival, programmed by Elton himself, promised to have an American feel to it with Joe Walsh, the Eagles, the Beach Boys, and more. But Elton could think of no better idea than to round off the concert by playing the entirety of the *Captain Fantastic* album, which the audience scarcely knew since it had only been released a month earlier. Unsurprisingly, the welcome it received was not terribly warm.

The Guitars Take Power

This slight setback, which was unconnected with the quality of the group, did not dent Elton's confidence in what he was doing. At the end of June, the musicians went to Caribou to record the next record: *Rock of the Westies*. This tenth studio album—as well as many of the songs on *Blue Moves*—was composed and recorded at Caribou Ranch during July. Most of the recordings were completed in a single take, and very few overdubs were added. As Elton had hoped, and as its title indicated, *Rock of the Westies* fostered a rock 'n' roll attitude and put power guitars on center stage. The album included only one ballad, "I Feel Like a Bullet (in the Gun of Robert Ford)," which was also the only song to pose difficulties for the group during recording. The gentle "Sugar on the Floor" was not included in the track list.

At times quite raucous, the album did not escape the funk fashion of the time, which gave it flexibility and groove, both qualities that had hitherto been lacking from Elton's point of view. Although the opus is ambitious in its construction, starting with the surprising introductory medley, "Yell Help / Wednesday Night / Ugly," it is far less forward-thinking in its arrangements, of which there are not many. The variety of sounds on the record is mainly derived from the use of different keyboards by James Newton Howard, who alternates between ARP synthesizer, Mellotron, Hohner Clavinet, ELKA synthesizer, and harpsichord, and by the impressive panoply of percussions provided by Ray Cooper (bells, castanets, shakers, maracas, congas, timbales, etc.). The gang mobilized on *Rock of the Westies* was augmented by backing vocalists Patti LaBelle and Kiki Dee, who managed to make herself indispensable in Elton's eyes. Dee appears on all the tracks on the album, with the exception of the introductory medley and "I Feel Like a Bullet (in the Gun of Robert Ford)." Without exactly revolutionizing

Elton's musical formula, the new team did mark a difference, most notably in the way the tracks were tackled. This new team approached the creative process head-on, as testified by the throbbing bass and edgy snare drum beats on "Grow Some Funk of Your Own." In general, emphasis was placed on the homogeneity of the sound between the pieces (to the detriment of richness and variety, which had characterized Elton's previous recordings), which resulted from the bass being placed very much to the fore in the mixing. The bass sound alone almost defines the identity of this work, almost to the point of interfering with the listening experience. The homogeneity of the lyrics, however, seems nonexistent. There is a kind of thread that progressively emerges in the songs: Like Lou Reed, Bernie Taupin highlights marginal characters and social pariahs, whose alienation fascinated him, as he became increasingly isolated and increasingly reliant on alcohol to help him forget his separation from Maxine.

Very Bad Trips

True to his usual practice, from the first day, Elton was on duty from six thirty in the morning, well before the other musicians. This was done because of his preference for working early in the morning, but also to ensure that there was sufficient material to work on with them when they joined him after breakfast.

Gus Dudgeon arrived twenty-four hours after the others. Suffering from jet lag, he planned to have a rest when he arrived, but he was met by Elton full of smiles behind his Steinway, which was a huge piano that measured nearly ten feet long. Elton proudly announced that he had already composed six songs, all of them done in the style of rock 'n' roll. With almost child-like excitement, Elton could barely wait until Gus had put his bags down to have him listen to the most mordant piece in this new corpus: "Street Kids." He started to play the chords and he was soon joined by the whole group, with Caleb making his Epiphone roar on some tempestuous solos. The producer expressed his enthusiasm, filled with confidence about these sessions that seemed as though they were going to be exceptional. He was supported by Jeff Guercio and his brother Mark, who had been present on the previous album. Jeff had agreed to help Mark, who was still easing into his role as an assistant sound engineer during these recording sessions.

Despite this early sense of promise, as well as the convivial atmosphere and newfound serenity for Elton John, whose sense of guilt concerning his former partners did not exactly seem to have engulfed him, the sessions were rendered chaotic by the gargantuan consumption of cocaine and LSD by the musicians. Caleb Quaye, in particular, was so out of it sometimes that Elton had to explain the chord sequences to him while the

Elton John and Gus Dudgeon sit in front of the mixing table at Caribou Ranch in August 1975.

guitarist struggled to understand! Davey combined drugs with an immoderate consumption of alcohol, to the extent that he couldn't remember having been involved in the recording of "Grow Some Funk of Your Own"; blissfully oblivious, he redis-covered the number, as though for the first time, the follow-ing day. In spite of this, however, the guitarist had never been so productive. He was even involved in the writing process, gleaning some credits as a composer on this album. This was a novelty for Elton, for whom composition was normally his sole preserve.

Most of the team at these recording sessions were mak-ing risky choices, but during their month at Caribou, Elton was the one who came the closest to death. On July 20, hav-ing finalized "Feed Me," the pianist took off in a helicopter with Quaye, Pope, Passarelli, and Dudgeon to go to Hughes Stadium, in Fort Collins. They were on their way to perform with the Rolling Stones. As soon as he went onstage to per-form "Honky Tonk Women," Elton understood that he was not welcome. Were The Stones having a bad day? Had his suc-cess caused some jealousy? Was his euphoric behavior, fur-ther encouraged by the drugs he was taking, bothering them? He was getting lots of angry looks, and Mick Jagger added to the affront by introducing Elton to the crowd as "Reg, from Watford," which was clearly intended as a put-down. The ten-sion remained throughout the show. Back at Caribou, and

now feeling demoralized by this glacial reception, Elton went to his room without a word and swallowed some Valium tab-lets. Davey and Kenny found him in time to induce vomit-ing. A day later, Elton was up again and ready to continue working, acting as though nothing had happened. At the end of the session, a courtesy visit by Stevie Wonder changed his frame of mind. The soul prodigy had brought along tapes of *Songs in the Key of Life*, and the music left Elton and his team in awe.

Kenny's Technical Woes

This restored good humor lasted until the end of the record-ing sessions, with the exception of Kenny Passarelli. While the bassist was preparing to celebrate the album's completion, Gus took him to one side and explained that they had a big prob-lem with the bass takes: Gus was unable to process the sound of his fretless properly. The musician could hardly believe this news, but the fact remained—it would be necessary to redo all the bass parts as overdubs! This was heartbreaking for Kenny, who knew that all his live takes, which he considered to be very well done, would be lost. In the end it was possible for two of these live takes to be salvaged—"Feed Me" and "Street Kids"—and the difference is glaring in terms of fluidity and har-mony. For the other songs, Kenny had to search the studios to find a standard bass because he had only a fretless with him.

Elton has breakfast al fresco in the rural Caribou setting during the summer sessions of 1975.

He found several and did some tests with Dudgeon. But Gus had the same difficulties in using their sound. Only one of the instruments worked: a Höfner bass that had belonged to Paul McCartney. This was a model of choice for the ex-Beatle, the "violin bass" with its straight body was the diametric opposite of the Fender Jazz Bass. Paul had given it to Jim Guercio (owner of Caribou Ranch and big brother of Jeff and Mark) as a thank-you for his work on the mixing of the album *Ram*. Grumbling throughout the process of recording the overdubs, Kenny eventually fulfilled his task, but still with a sense of defeat. The new cuts were less fluid and organic, and they were not as good as the original takes. However, when he heard the final mix, Passarelli changed his opinion, and expressed his gratitude to Gus since, in his view, he had managed to enhance the sound of his bass. Not all of Elton's fans shared this opinion. Some were critical of Kenny's overly predictable and mechanical playing, especially in comparison to Dee's.

These bumps in the road could do nothing to prevent the popularity of the album, which came out on October 4, 1975, in England, and on October 20, 1975, in the United States. Not even the strange album cover, which featured a quick snap taken by photographer Terry O'Neill during an al fresco breakfast, could stop the album's ascent. Elton was shown with sunglasses on his nose and he was wearing a deerstalker hat, which was made famous for its associations with Sherlock Holmes. The group photo that illustrates the back of the album cover offered an opportunity for fans to make the acquaintance of the new members of the Elton John Band, who were humorously presented on the inside of the sleeve with some odd little texts; Elton describes himself as a "a boring little musician." Curiously, the disk is "dedicated" to Dee and Nigel. Whether it was crass irony or clumsy sincerity, either way the reference would have been no consolation for the two men who had been so unceremoniously given the boot.

As for the title of the album, *Rock of the Westies* was eventually chosen over *Bottled and Brained*, a phrase taken from "Street Kids," which was a song about adolescence. *Rock of the Westies* was a purposeful play on "West of the Rockies," and this was done in reference to the newcomers in Elton's group. Howard was a native of California, and Kenny hailed from Colorado. The album title is also an homage to the rock 'n' roll sound coming out of the West Coast, especially from bands like the Doobie Brothers, the Eagles, and Little Feat.

Despite various technical hitches and ongoing issues with drugs and alcohol, the "boring little musician" managed to place his new opus, with its rock contours and strong groove, at the top of the *Billboard* charts. Just as its predecessor, *Captain Fantastic and the Brown Dirt Cowboy*, had done, *Rock of the Westies* went to number one in its first week of release, thanks to more than one million preorders.

MEDLEY (YELL HELP, WEDNESDAY NIGHT, UGLY)

Elton John, Bernie Taupin, Davey Johnstone / 6:15

Elton John opted to be credited for the backing vocals on several of the numbers on the album under the name of Ann Orson, a pseudonym that he had already used when he provided backing vocals on Neil Sedaka's album *The Hungry Years.*

Musicians
Elton John: lead vocals, piano, backing vocals (credited as Ann Orson)
Davey Johnstone: electric guitar
Caleb Quaye: electric guitar
Kenny Passarelli: bass
Roger Pope: drums
James Newton Howard: harpsichord, ELKA Rhapsody String Synthesizer, ARP synthesizer, Hohner Clavinet
Ray Cooper: bell, tambourine, congas, quijada
Patti LaBelle, Nona Hendryx, Sarah Dash: backing vocals

Recorded
Caribou Ranch, Nederland, Colorado: July 1975

Technical Team
Producer: Gus Dudgeon
Sound Engineer: Jeff Guercio
Assistant Sound Engineer: Mark Guercio

Nona Hendryx, Sarah Dash, and Patti LaBelle of the R&B vocal trio Labelle, circa 1972.

Genesis and Lyrics

Despite their marked differences, the three songs in this medley were composed with a view to forming one single piece. This highly repetitive number was constructed with the help of Davey Johnstone, during a day of substance abuse of all kinds. Holding in mind the laid-back playing of J. J. Cale, Davey compiled the haunting riff that is the backbone of "Yell Help"—and as such earned the inclusion of his name in the song credits— before moving the song to the edge of boredom around the musical bridge, "Wednesday Night," which shares some subtle rhythmic and melodic elements with "Ugly." The rhythms were more subtle, in any case, than the verses in this third and final part, with their crass misogyny ("I'll even pay sometimes for a woman that's ugly"). These lyrics were picked out by chance from a pile of sheets of Bernie's manuscript, and without any consideration for textual cohesion.

Production

The drummer, Roger Pope, gave the initial pulse that the number needed. During the second take, he instinctively reversed the rhythmic motif, creating a pleasant surprise. Howard's playing constitutes the musical element that is most on display, with its multiple interventions and the variety of sounds used (Clavinet, synthesizers, harpsichord). At times almost cartoonish, they offer a soul–rhythm 'n' blues color, in the spirit of Stevie Wonder and to great effect. Ray Cooper closely follows the detail of Roger Pope's solid groove, with a bell, tambourine, congas, and even a quijada. Finally, Patti LaBelle, Nona Hendryx, and Sarah Dash take care of the backing vocals. Elton had previously provided vocals for Patti and her group, the Bluebelles, during a British tour in 1966, when he was a member of Bluesology. The recording of Patti, Nona, and Sarah proved to be complicated. Although perfectly synchronized when they performed in the control cabin, they lost their vocal line when they went into the studio. After numerous attempts, they managed to get back together again. During the mixing, Dudgeon was horrified to discover that part of their performance (on the final refrain that precedes the break at 5:08) had been accidentally erased…assuming it was ever recorded at all. Gus Dudgeon decided to salvage this by doing the "*do-do-dos*" himself: "So I made myself an enormous joint, walked into the studio and imitated LaBelle. Nobody's spotted it—not even Elton."[31]

DAN DARE
(PILOT OF THE FUTURE)

Elton John, Bernie Taupin / 3:29

Musicians
Elton John: lead vocals, piano, backing vocals (credited as Ann Orson)
Davey Johnstone: electric rhythm guitar, talk box, backing vocals
Caleb Quaye: electric guitar, backing vocals
Kenny Passarelli: bass, backing vocals
Roger Pope: drums
James Newton Howard: Clavinet Hohner
Kiki Dee: backing vocals

Recorded
Caribou Ranch, Nederland, Colorado: July 1975

Technical Team
Producer: Gus Dudgeon
Sound Engineer: Jeff Guercio
Assistant Sound Engineer: Mark Guercio

A copy of the *Eagle* comic book from 1964 featuring Dan Dare, the science fiction hero that was much loved by Bernie in his youth.

Genesis and Lyrics

"Dan Dare (Pilot of the Future)" celebrates the cartoon science fiction hero of the same name, created and drawn by the Englishman Frank Hampson for the *Eagle* weekly, and whose first issue was datedApril 14, 1950. Daniel MacGregor Dare, first terrestrial pilot of the Interplanetary Space Fleet, experiences numerous exploits due to his courage, his legendary good luck, his strength in hand-to-hand combat, and his virtuosity in piloting craft of all kinds: spacecraft, monorails, jetfoils, helicopters, and submarines. Bernie links this evocation of a fictitious hero from his childhood to growing up and being forced to abandon childhood dreams. The contrast is striking between the qualifying terms used for Dan ("pilot of the future," "champions of destiny," "Captain Dan") and the failures of the narrator ("I don't have the energy," "I fail to see," "I couldn't make his flight"). At the end of the song, he confesses a slight betrayal: His boundless admiration for his hero did not prevent him from also having a certain admiration for his sworn enemy, the Mekon, who is referred to in the coda of the piece.

Production

Davey Johnstone makes his mark on this funk number, which stands out in the midst of the other rock pieces on the album. He uses a talk box, an effect popularized by Peter Frampton on "Do You Feel Like We Do" in 1973. Davey makes the sound of his guitar come out through a plastic tube that he placed in his mouth. Then, by "vocalizing," he modulates the sound. This literally brings his guitar to life, which seems to talk with the voice of a robot. James Newton Howard and Elton John contribute a percussive and groovy element to the song via their keyboards. The rhythm section, led by the slightly laid-back drums of Roger Pope and the very measured bass of Kenny Passarelli, provides an impeccable base for Elton, whose vocals are particularly inspired. He is supported by the backing vocalists in a very well-thought-out balance between the female voice of Kiki Dee and the male voices of Davey, Caleb, Kenny, and Elton himself. This piece, which is somewhat reminiscent of "I've Seen the Saucers" on *Caribou*, is definitely one of the best songs on *Rock of the Westies*. Elton would have liked to release it as a single, but in the end "Island Girl" was selected.

ISLAND GIRL

Elton John, Bernie Taupin / 3:42

Musicians

Elton John: lead vocals, piano, backing vocals (credited as Ann Orson)
Davey Johnstone: electric guitar, acoustic guitar, slide guitar, banjo, backing vocals
Caleb Quaye: acoustic guitar, backing vocals
Kenny Passarelli: bass, backing vocals
Roger Pope: drums
James Newton Howard: ARP synthesizer, Mellotron
Ray Cooper: congas, tambourine, marimba
Kiki Dee: backing vocals

Recorded

Caribou Ranch, Nederland, Colorado: July 1975

Technical Team

Producer: Gus Dudgeon
Sound Engineer: Jeff Guercio
Assistant Sound Engineer: Mark Guercio

Single Release

Island Girl / Sugar on the Floor
UK Release: September 19, 1975, on DJM Records (ref. DJS.610)
Best UK Chart Ranking: 14
US Release: September 29, 1975, on MCA Records (ref. MCA-40461)
Best US Chart Ranking: 1

In addition to working with Elton John, James Newton Howard (shown here in 2009) has composed more than one hundred film soundtracks.

Genesis and Lyrics

"I knew I'd written a hit even before I heard the melody,"[31] Bernie Taupin once said with more than a trace of self-satisfaction. However, he must have also been a visionary, since, on paper, no one would have guessed that the story of a Jamaican prostitute who is lost on the sidewalks of New York (at the junction of Lexington Avenue and Forty-Seventh Street) would have fascinated the listening public. But perhaps it was the choice melody concocted by Elton that helped ensure the song's success. Bernie, who thought up this story when he was passing through the Caribbean, described the situation of the young girl lost in a "white man's world," under the control of her pimp. Her companion, who stayed on the island, wants her back; he wants to "save" her, but the fatalistic narrator lets it be known: "the cause is lost."

Production

The rhythm is so rapid and frenetic that the lyrics pass almost unnoticed, and they are hard to make out. Elton wanted a "tropical" arrangement for this song, but Davey Johnstone's snarling guitar slide is more evocative of Hawaii than Jamaica, the country of origin for Bernie's protagonist. Maybe a reggae overlay to the lyrics would have been too predictable? The guitarist is one of the main architects of the musical bedrock of "Island Girl," both in his slide playing, which highlights the power of the rhythm section on its repetitive gimmick, and with his acoustic playing on his Ovation guitar, which is quite unruly. The choice of percussion was key for this number: Ray Cooper chose a marimba, whose sounds are close to those of the steel drum, which is widely used in Jamaican music. Elton's piano is restrained, although still decisive in Gus Dudgeon's mix. Above all it is the Mellotron solo by James Newton Howard that contributes all the originality of "Island Girl." This single was released in September 1975, with "Sugar on the Floor" on the B-side. The single stayed at number one in the United States for three weeks.

GROW SOME FUNK OF YOUR OWN

Elton John, Bernie Taupin, Davey Johnstone / 4:48

Musicians

Elton John: vocals, piano
Caleb Quaye: electric guitar, backing vocals
Davey Johnstone: electric guitar, backing vocals
Kenny Passarelli: bass, backing vocals
Roger Pope: drums
Ray Cooper: castanets, tambourine, vibraphone, bell tree
Kiki Dee: backing vocals

Recorded

Caribou Ranch, Nederland, Colorado: July 1975

Technical Team

Producer: Gus Dudgeon
Sound Engineer: Jeff Guercio
Assistant Sound Engineer: Mark Guercio

Single Release

Grow Some Funk of Your Own / I Feel Like a Bullet (in the Gun of Robert Ford)
UK Release: January 9, 1976, on DJM Records (ref. DJS.629)
Best UK Chart Ranking: Did Not Chart
US Release: September 29, 1975, on MCA Records (ref. MCA-40505)
Best US Chart Ranking: 14

Genesis and Lyrics

This number first saw the light of day at the beginning of the group's stay at Caribou Ranch. Elton and Davey shared the same cabin. Davey was intoxicated and in need of a break, but Elton was working at the piano on the melody for "Grow Some Funk of Your Own." Unable to get any rest, the guitarist got out of bed and picked up a guitar. After a few minutes he had the opening riff, which was sharp and explosive. This riff gave substance to Bernie's lyrics, which are richly self-deprecating. They portray a man who has escaped from a bad dream. In it, he fell in love with a pretty woman in a frontier town, but the young woman's macho and rather unpleasant boyfriend interrupted the protagonist's attempted advances, firmly suggesting that he should turn around and go back home: "Take my advice, take the next flight / And grow your funk, grow your funk at home." The term *funk* might have been chosen because of its phonetic closeness to another, less socially acceptable four-letter word.

Production

During the recording, the group displayed some real muscle, staring with the energetic drums of Roger Pope and the springing bass of Kenny Passarelli. Even so, "Grow Some Funk of Your Own" struggled to go beyond the classicism of its rock melody, which was too predictable to shine on the record charts. Released as a double A-side single (a concept introduced by the Beatles, which allowed for no hierarchy between the A-side and the B-side) with "I Feel Like a Bullet (in the Gun of Robert Ford)," the song was a commercial flop and was not ranked, except in Canada (number eight) and in New Zealand (number thirty-nine). It owes this lack of success partly to the hesitations surrounding its release; "I Feel Like a Bullet" was initially presented as the potential hit, before "Grow Some Funk of Your Own" was offered in response to the cool reception from radio programmers. Davey Johnstone, author of the edgy riff on the intro, is credited as a joint composer of the piece, even though the guitarist admitted that he had no recollection of having written this riff: "I had zero recollection [of] writing that one," the guitarist admitted. "I'd been so drunk, the whole thing just escaped me till Elton played it for me the next day."[31] Another joy offered by this piece: the spectacular vibraphone solo performed by Ray Cooper from 3:30, which intervenes as a fairly unstructured jam session for the finale.

I FEEL LIKE A BULLET (IN THE GUN OF ROBERT FORD)

Elton John, Bernie Taupin / 5:27

Musicians
Elton John: vocals, piano
Davey Johnstone: electric guitar, acoustic guitar
Caleb Quaye: electric guitar, acoustic guitar
Kenny Passarelli: bass
Roger Pope: drums
James Newton Howard: electric piano, synthesizer
Ray Cooper: tambourine, vibraphone

Recorded
Caribou Ranch, Nederland, Colorado: July 1975

Technical Team
Producer: Gus Dudgeon
Sound Engineer: Jeff Guercio
Assistant Sound Engineer: Mark Guercio

Single Release
Grow Some Funk of Your Own / I Feel Like a Bullet (in the Gun of Robert Ford)
  UK Release: January 9, 1976, on DJM Records (ref. DJS.629)
  Best UK Chart Ranking: Did Not Chart
  US Release: January 12, 1976, on MCA Records (ref. MCA-40505)
  Best US Chart Ranking: 14

LIVE VERSION
The box set *To Be Continued...*, which appeared in 1990, contains a live version of this song, which was recorded in May 1977 and performed only by Elton John and Ray Cooper.

Genesis and Lyrics

From "Tiny Dancer" to "I Feel Like a Bullet," Bernie charts the course of his relationship with his wife, Maxine. Through a text in which each image seems to have been carefully judged, the lyricist focuses in prolific detail upon the failure of his marriage, for which he assumes most of the responsibility: "I threw the last punch too hard," "I had lost what should have been found," "I'm cold as a hired sword," "I'm damned if I'll ever get rid of this guilt that I feel." In the midst of this sad conclusion, a slight hope of reconciliation seems to emerge in the following line: "I'm so ashamed, can't we patch it up?" This was not the case, however, since the phrase was modified by Elton to help facilitate his diction: In fact, Bernie had originally written "We can't patch it up," but Elton sings "Can't we patch it up?"

The choice to draw an audacious parallel between the singer and the outlaw Robert Ford, who killed his friend Jesse James with a bullet in the back, speaks volumes about the sense of guilt that assailed Bernie. Interestingly, at the same time that Elton was giving form to this highly personal song, Maxine took refuge in the arms of Kenny Passarelli, the new bass player. This was a relationship that they tried to keep secret, before Caleb and his wife, Patricia, discovered what they were up to.

Production

A great responsibility weighed on Elton's shoulders, who had to provide these lyrics with a fine framework. A ballad-like approach seemed appropriate, and this would go on to be the only such song on the album. The musicians had to stay particularly focused while recording this song, which starts out in G major and moves to F minor in the refrain. This is a change of tonality of fantastic elegance, which is further enhanced by Elton's melancholic vocals. His voice is doubled, and it rises to a perfectly controlled falsetto, but the transition between the two parts of the song posed a problem for the musicians, who had to do several takes to achieve a natural-sounding result. Another delicate passage: the interaction established between the piano arpeggios and Ray Cooper's vibraphone, to which were added some fairylike harmonies that sometimes got mixed up with the piano. This was easily done, since, although the vibraphone is a percussion instrument (it is made from strips of metal mounted over resonators and has a keyboard element), it can sometimes have a keyboard-like sound.

STREET KIDS

Elton John, Bernie Taupin / 6:25

Musicians
Elton John: lead vocals, piano, backing vocals (credited as Ann Orson)
Davey Johnstone: electric guitar, slide guitar, backing vocals
Caleb Quaye: electric guitar, backing vocals
Kenny Passarelli: bass, backing vocals
Roger Pope: drums
Ray Cooper: tambourine, congas
Kiki Dee: backing vocals

Recorded
Caribou Ranch, Nederland, Colorado: July 1975

Technical Team
Producer: Gus Dudgeon
Sound Engineer: Jeff Guercio
Assistant Sound Engineer: Mark Guercio

Elton John and his guitarist Caleb Quaye in 1974.

Genesis and Lyrics

At the end of the album's recording sessions, shortly after Stevie Wonder's visit to the studios, Elton seemed to be in much better form. He came back up to his usual level of performance after the insult at the Stones concert at Fort Collins, and his episode with the Valium. He seemed in better shape than Bernie, who was drowning his sorrows in alcohol and spent a lot of time brooding in his room. Depressed about the end of his relationship with Maxine, the lyricist felt a certain anger, which he expressed in "Street Kids," in which he portrays himself as a member of an East End gang. Projecting himself into what his destiny might have been if he had not met Elton, Bernie piles on the provocations ("I'm a juvenile delinquent," "I run the toughest bunch this side of town," "I was born to sin").

Production

When recording "Street Kids," Elton was in a rather playful mood, especially with his keyboard colleague, James Newton Howard, who was four years his junior. A little rivalry was established between the two musicians and was largely promoted by Elton. Thus, by the time they started recording this piece, Elton, as though inspired by the bellicose spirit of "Street Kids," played a sixteen-note riff of triplets, moving from A to D, then to F, with a fairly blustering feel to them. The idea must have been to show Howard what he was capable of. Gus includes this very inventive descending phrase, which takes Elton through the entire keyboard and down into the low notes, within the sound wall constructed by the other musicians, especially by the guitars. One of these guitars, starting with feedback created by moving the microphones on the instrument toward the amp, develops a deliciously crunchy, unhealthy riff, whose first notes are slightly reminiscent of "Layla" by Derek and the Dominos. During this time the other guitar exhales stridently, playing plaintive sounds in the second layer. In the midst of this deluge of decibels and virility, the gentle voice of Kiki Dee struggles to make itself heard, as the sound delivered by the group seems so compact. Interestingly, this track was made in a direct recording, and without any overdubs, including Caleb Quaye's invigorating solo, which was executed instinctively. Wild, and intrinsically rock 'n' roll with its numerous bends, the solo can be heard at 3:48 before winding up in the high notes in the finale. This is the longest solo on any Elton song.

HARD LUCK STORY

Elton John, Bernie Taupin (credited as Ann Orson and Carte Blanche) / 5:16

Musicians

Elton John: vocals, piano
Davey Johnstone: electric guitar
Caleb Quaye: electric guitar, backing vocals
Kenny Passarelli: bass, backing vocals
James Newton Howard: electric piano
Roger Pope: drums
Ray Cooper: congas
Kiki Dee: backing vocals

Recorded

Caribou Ranch, Nederland, Colorado: July 1975

Technical Team

Producer: Gus Dudgeon
Sound Engineer: Jeff Guercio
Assistant Sound Engineer: Mark Guercio

Kiki Dee in 1973, shortly after signing a contract with Elton's label, Rocket Record Company.

Genesis and Lyrics

At this stage in their collaboration, Elton had yet to compose the song that would make Kiki Dee, his muse, famous—"Don't Go Breaking My Heart"—but he had created "Hard Luck Story," which was originally envisaged as a single before being reassigned to the album. Bernie and Elton wrote the song together, assuming the character of an exhausted man who's deeply unhappy because of his work, and who has nothing else to share with his wife in the evening except for boring stories. In order not to overshadow Kiki's version of the song, which was released separately, the two men credited themselves as Ann Orson and Carte Blanche, a play on "a horse and a cart."

Production

Kenny Passarelli, to some extent affirming the differences between himself and Dee Murray, opted to reduce his playing to the simplest possible form, playing fundamentals in a very pulsating way, and in very direct support of Roger Pope. Gus also ensured that the sounds of the two instruments functioned well together. "I have to start with the bass and drums. Within the drum kit you have every frequency you're ever going to have, from the highest high to the lowest low. Once you've got the drum sound together, someone can come in and say, 'What do you think of this bass sound?'"[127] Kenny's approach also highlighted Elton's piano playing, which was genuinely virtuosic. While Kiki's version of this song evolved with restraint, ending up somewhere between blues and pop, and with a steel lap guitar in the foreground, Elton's version takes a harder edge before the backing vocals come in. Before launching this sonic fury, Gus Dudgeon chose to keep the introduction of the song very gentle, bringing up the fade-in very slowly. The song reaches its full volume when Ray Cooper starts on the congas, which mark the beginning of this new, wild jam session that seems like it never wants to stop. Eventually, Gus opted to bring down the curtain with a long fade-out.

FEED ME

Elton John, Bernie Taupin / 4:01

Musicians

Elton John: lead vocals, backing vocals (credited as Ann Orson)
Davey Johnstone: electric guitar, backing vocals
Caleb Quaye: electric guitar, backing vocals
Kenny Passarelli: bass
Roger Pope: drums
James Newton Howard: electric piano
Ray Cooper: congas, shaker, vibraphone, wind chimes
Clive Franks, Kiki Dee: backing vocals

Recorded

Caribou Ranch, Nederland, Colorado: July 1975

Technical Team

Producer: Gus Dudgeon
Sound Engineer: Jeff Guercio
Assistant Sound Engineer: Mark Guercio

Bernie Taupin wrote some uncompromising lyrics for "Feed Me," which very bluntly lays out some of Elton's worst excesses.

Genesis and Lyrics

"No one forced me to do drugs and drink. In fact, more than a few people tried to warn me I was out of control,"[107] Elton John acknowledged in retrospect. His accomplice at the time, Bernie Taupin, was also indulging heavily during the time this album was recorded. He expressed his concern in the way he knew best: through writing. In powerful, uncharacteristically short lines, he shines a harsh light on the realities of the life of a junkie. The words are chosen carefully. He combines elements of the drug environment ("basement") equipment ("razor blade"), with dark thoughts ("shades," "darkness"), derangement ("madness," "They're all trying to kill me," "screaming," "mad shadows"), and dependency ("Feed my needs and then just leave me," "Let me go back where you found me").

Production

While the text of this song would logically call for shadowy instrumentation, Elton chose to take the number into the realms of jazz, and he starts with a decisive step by abandoning his piano and focusing solely on vocals. Elton also demonstrates his confidence in his new colleague, James Newton Howard, by handing him the piano reins in this piece. They work together beautifully in this instance, with one track for the voice and another for the Fender Rhodes. The gentle, ringing tone of the instrument contrasts with Elton's grainy, penetrating voice. This makes for a fine combination, needing only a single element to help bind them. This is provided by the guitar, with light saturation, which follows the same line as the electric piano before the addition of perfectly controlled harmonics, despite the difficulty the team experienced in making them sound out distinctly. Passarelli and Cooper overlay a serene groove that leads the number in the direction of easy listening, assisted by the whisper of slightly insipid backing vocals that suffer in comparison to what the Murray-Olsson duo were capable of creating.

Davey Johnstone and Elton
John perform at Dodger
Stadium in October 1975.

BILLY BONES AND THE WHITE BIRD

Elton John, Bernie Taupin / 4:40

Musicians
Elton John: lead vocals, backing vocals (credited as Ann Orson)
Davey Johnstone: electric guitar
Caleb Quaye: electric guitar
James Newton Howard: electric piano, synthesizer
Roger Pope: drums
Ray Cooper: timbales, maracas, tambourine, cowbell
Kiki Dee: backing vocals

Recorded
Caribou Ranch, Nederland, Colorado: July 1975

Technical Team
Producer: Gus Dudgeon
Sound Engineer: Jeff Guercio
Assistant Sound Engineer: Mark Guercio

Roger Pope asserts the exceptional power of his drumming on
"Billy Bones and the White Bird."

Genesis and Lyrics

One day, while the group was in the middle of a recording session, they were interrupted by the deafening sound of a helicopter that was preparing to land on the roof above the studio. As if they were living inside a parody of an action movie, impeccably besuited men with dark glasses and briefcases got out of the helicopter. These were lawyers who had come to have Elton sign the contracts for an American tour that was scheduled for the following autumn. For the old Hookfoot alumni and for the newcomer, James Newton Howard, this was a striking scene: Elton's fame had moved into another dimension, well beyond anything they could ever have expected. Following this surreal interruption, the group got back to work on the song "Billy Bones and the White Bird," whose lyrics focused on a much less urbane character than the men in suits who had just departed in their flying machine: the old sea dog Billy Bones, straight out of Robert Louis Stevenson's *Treasure Island*. The drunken, violent pirate, who kicks the bucket at the beginning of the adventure, leaving behind a treasure to be discovered, comes back to life under Bernie's pen, in an otherwise relatively forgettable song.

Production

The song carries a feeling of stress and urgency that comes from the guitars and their fuzzy sound, with Roger Pope's battering percussion doing its part to raise the dead on a very particular rhythm that originated in "Cadillac" by Bo Diddley. Gus does wonders with his handling of the snare drum, which rings out like thunder; it bangs like blows from metal bars, as imagined by Ivy Jo Hunter, Marvin Gaye, and Mickey Stevenson on "Dancing in the Street," which was eventually performed by Martha Reeves and the Vandellas. Elton's jerky piano playing, progressing toward the high notes before interrupting itself via a rather strange chord that sounds almost like a mistake, is sometimes drowned out by this sonic magma. This is readily understandable, since, on the piano's isolated track, it lacks body, and the voice passes back through the microphone. As a direct recording, this song exudes the spontaneity of a free-wheeling jam session, as suggested by the laid-back "Check it out" spoken by Elton from 2:45 and several times again before the end of the piece.

Kenny Passarelli (center) joined the Elton John Band between 1975 and 1976 and he worked on the albums *Rock of the Westies* and *Blue Moves*.

COVER

Having failed to find favor with Elton John, "Planes" did find its place with Colin Blunstone, the singer for the Zombies, who had been signed by the Rocket Record Company. In November 1976 he released "Planes" as a single, with "Dancing in the Dark" on the B-side (ref. Epic EPC4752).

PLANES

Elton John, Bernie Taupin / 4:32

Musicians: Elton John: vocals, piano / **Davey Johnstone:** acoustic guitar, mandolin, backing vocals / **Caleb Quaye:** acoustic guitar, backing vocals / **Kenny Passarelli:** bass, backing vocals / **Roger Pope:** drums / **Ray Cooper:** tambourine? / **James Newton Howard:** synthesizer? / **Kiki Dee:** backing vocals **Recorded:** Caribou Ranch, Nederland, Colorado: July 1975 **Technical Team:** Producer: Gus Dudgeon / **Sound Engineer:** Jeff Guercio / **Assistant Sound Engineer:** Mark Guercio

The ill-fated "Planes" was a song imagined by Bernie Taupin, who was dreaming of romantic destinations while watching the planes overhead as he was out walking his dog, Jessie. The song was originally sketched out during the recording sessions for *Captain Fantastic and the Brown Dirt Cowboy*, where it was initially sandwiched between the title song and "Tower of Babel" before finally being left out. More in step with the delicacy of Elton's first albums—with the American sound from *Tumbleweed Connection*, for example—this folk song with its discreet, bucolic charm was once again brought out for *Rock of the Westies*. However, the refinement of the piece did not align with the artistic direction of an album that was conceived to be instinctive, and that was intended to convey the image of a rock group recording on the fly and in the moment. "Planes" was finally added to the album in 1996, as part of its reissue on the Rocket Record Company label. The song was not lacking in justifications for inclusion, however, with its introductory backing vocals and its shrewd construction that features instruments giving way to the vocals-guitar duo on the verses, a gentle torpor lavished by the keyboards, and a mandolin that elegantly anchors itself into the arrangement.

Elton John borrowed *"Sugar on the Floor"* from his colleague Kiki Dee.

On the following pages: Elton John peforms in front of an audience of 50,000 at LA's Dodger Stadium in October 1975.

SUGAR ON THE FLOOR

Kiki Dee / 4:32

Single: *Island Girl / Sugar on the Floor* **UK Release:** September 19, 1975, on DJM Records (ref. DJS.610) **Best UK Chart Ranking:** 14 **US Release:** September 29, 1975, on MCA Records (ref. MCA-40461) **Best US Chart Ranking:** 1 **Musicians:** Elton John: vocals, piano / **Davey Johnstone:** electric guitar **Recorded:** Caribou Ranch, Nederland, Colorado: July 1975 **Technical Team:** **Producer:** Gus Dudgeon / **Sound Engineer:** Jeff Guercio / **Assistant Sound Engineer:** Mark Guercio

In the wake of "I Feel Like a Bullet," Elton John finalized "Sugar on the Floor," with a view to it being a B-side (to accompany the "Island Girl" single in its ascension to the top of the *Billboard* chart in September 1975). The singer knew this song well, having already played electric piano on it during recording sessions for Kiki Dee's album, *Loving & Free*. Elton played a big part in these

sessions, which took place between April and June 1973, along with Clive Franks, Dee Murray, Nigel Olsson, and Davey Johnstone. This piece, composed by Kiki Dee herself, already had the benefit of Davey's delicate touch, and he played his guitar with the bottleneck slide. Although Elton retained this sound for his own version, this was the only part of the original that remained. Seduced by the emotional power of this song's simple melody, which evokes the imminence of a separation and feelings of guilt for being the cause of it, Elton opted for a more austere sound: using piano and vocals, and nothing more. Even for his playing, Elton, who usually liked to add ornamentations, just plays a few slow chords, allowing the silence to give this song a feeling of solemnity. The only flourish he allows himself is this fabulous outpouring at 1:40, which clearly carries the vocal signature of one of his idols, Ray Charles.

ALBUM

BLUE MOVES

Your Starter For… . Tonight . One Horse Town . Chameleon . Boogie Pilgrim .
Cage the Songbird . Crazy Water . Shoulder Holster . Sorry Seems to Be the Hardest Word .
Out of the Blue . Between Seventeen and Twenty . The Wide-Eyed and Laughing . Someone's
Final Song . Where's the Shoorah? . If There's a God in Heaven (What's He Waiting For?) . Idol .
Theme from a Non-Existent TV Series . Bite Your Lip (Get Up and Dance!)

RELEASE DATES
UK Release: October 22, 1976
Reference: Rocket Record Company / EMI Records—ROSP 1
Best UK Chart Ranking: 3
US Release: October 28, 1976
Reference: Rocket Record Company / MCA Records—MCAT2-11004
Best US Chart Ranking: 3

THE END OF THE GOLDEN AGE

After delivering epic and flamboyant performances on October 25 and 26, 1975, at LA's Dodger Stadium, the likes of which the park had not seen since the Beatles nine years earlier, Elton ended the *Rock of the Westies* tour and gave himself some well-deserved time off in Barbados. At the end of his stay, he felt revitalized. He had not had a break for quite some time, and he enjoyed spending his days playing Scrabble with his guests, as well as the good climate, listening to Bob Marley and Pink Floyd, and occasionally just sitting and looking out at the ocean, a glass of something in his hand as he counted the waves and contemplated his future.

At the beginning of March 1976, the recording sessions for Elton's next studio album, *Blue Moves*, began to take shape. This would be the first Elton album that was produced by the Rocket Record Company, the label Elton created in 1973. The singer still contractually owed one disk to DJM Records, which he would honor on April 30, 1976, with *Here and There*, a hybrid live album consisting of two parts: *Here*, which was the recording of the concert at the Royal Festival Hall on May 18, 1974, and *There*, which was the recording of a concert at Madison Square Garden on November 28, 1974. Once he was officially liberated from his obligations to DJM, Elton could finally start to focus seriously on the next phase of his career.

Nothing Stays

Another new feature on this album were the studios. The Caribou Ranch studios in Colorado were officially in the rearview mirror; this time, the British singer chose to work out of Eastern Sound Studios in Toronto, the first studios in Canada with twenty-four-track technology. The musicians did not want to wind up rerecording some of their performances, as they had on *Rock of the Westies*. They made it known to Gus Dudgeon that they wanted a really live, direct recording, as had been the original intention for the previous opus.

Bernie, realizing that the sessions were fast approaching, shut himself away and wrote two dozen new songs. His lyrics were full of references that were triggered by the breakup of his marriage with Maxine and by her affair with Kenny Passarelli. He was in a deep depression, accentuated by the uncontrolled consumption of alcohol and cocaine. In addition, although not broken, the fraternal link between Elton and Bernie had started to unravel slightly. The pace of their working life was frenetic, and they never quite seemed to be in sync with each other. Bernie also struggled, despite many attempts, in finding a consistent role beyond his writing partnership with Elton. Even the book he published in 1976 carried allusions to the scars he'd gotten while working for the successful singer: *Bernie Taupin: The One Who Writes the Words for Elton John.* Bernie was not in a good place: He devoured cocaine, tried heroin, lived at night, slept by day, and woke up to only reach painfully for the bedside fridge, grabbing a beer, drinking half, and then filling the rest of his drink with vodka.

Unsurprisingly, the latest batch of lyrics Bernie came up with clearly reflected his overall despondency, which was fueled by chemical substances and suicidal ideation and was filled with melancholic narratives about broken hearts; his work had become dark and desperate.

The lyricist's desolation had reached such a level that Elton, although rarely critical of his colleague's work, was particularly disheartened; he was also going through a not particularly happy time himself, having just ended his toxic amorous relationship with John Reid, who had become his manager and whom he opted to keep on in this role after the end of their romantic partnership. "I never rejected one of his lyrics before," he said, "but some of the stuff he did for [the new sessions] … I said, 'Taupin, for Christ's sake, I *can't* sing that.' They were just plain hateful, three or four of them."[31] So, for the first time ever, Elton asked Bernie to revise his lyrics. Bernie, who was really not in the mood to take part in the Toronto sessions, remained in Barbados, trying to deal with the fallout from his divorce.

An Unpredictable Elton

As he had at Caribou, Gus Dudgeon called upon high-caliber studio musicians to augment Elton's group. The guest artists

The team from *Rock of the Westies* was reunited on *Blue Moves*. Left to right: Elton John, (front) Kenny Passarelli, Roger Pope, Caleb Quaye, (rear) Davey Johnstone, Ray Cooper, and James Newton Howard.

included, among others, the Brecker Brothers and saxophonist David Sanborn, while the backing vocals were provided by Toni Tennille, Beach Boy Bruce Johnston, and Curt Becher, founding member of the psychedelic group the Millennium. Even Paul Buckmaster, absent from the picture since 1972 and the *Don't Shoot Me I'm Only the Piano Player* album, was called back to create a number of arrangements.

The sessions were directed with surgical precision by Gus Dudgeon, despite Elton being on something of a short fuse, with his addictions causing him to swing rapidly between times of general euphoria and dark periods of taciturn sadness. One day, the group set off on a thunderous version of the funky rock number "Bite Your Lip (Get Up and Dance!)." At the end of the piece, Elton stood up and called out: "OK, that's going to be a hit!" Problem was, as Gus Dudgeon informed him, the last take had only been meant as a tryout to gauge the studio's sound levels. Furious, Elton refused to do any more recording that day!

In spite of all these ups and downs, thirty days after pushing open the doors of the studio, the group closed them with the satisfaction of a job well done: seventeen numbers had been recorded for the album, and also a duet with Kiki Dee called "Don't Go Breaking My Heart," which would hit

number one in the British charts when it was released as a single in June 1976. Even so, Elton had not quite finished with *Blue Moves* yet, and he recorded a final song for it on his return to England in March 1976: "Tonight" was almost eight minutes long, which in a way summed up the malaise Bernie faced after the failure of his marriage. The final track was recorded live at Abbey Road with the London Symphony Orchestra.

"I'll Be Back...Someday"

Exhausted, Elton had now finished *Blue Moves*, which would be his first double album since *Goodbye Yellow Brick Road* and, above all, the first album as part of his new and lucrative contract with MCA, negotiated by John Reid in the United States. In spite of these outward appearances, *Blue Moves* did not mark a new departure for Elton John; rather, it marked the end of a golden age. Reaching only third place on the charts in the United States, it was the close of a glorious string of six number one albums for Elton, which had begun with *Honky Château* in 1972. *Blue Moves* was also the last album produced by Gus Dudgeon for a decade, and above all the last one entirely written by Bernie Taupin until 1983's *Too Low for Zero*.

Elton John at Radio One studios in London, promoting *Blue Moves* in 1976.

Of course, Elton couldn't know any of this as he launched into his "Louder Than Concorde Tour" on April 29 in Leeds, which was supposed to promote his previous album, *Rock of the Westies*, in England and the United States. Even before *Blue Moves* was released, an overtired Elton John announced his intentions to take a break from stage performances after a series of performances at Madison Square Garden. On August 16, 1976, on the occasion of his penultimate concert in New York, he gathered his group together in his dressing room to tell them his decision, having first taken care to ensure his musicians had a year's salary in advance.

That night, in front of an audience of twenty thousand, he painfully picked up the microphone and told them: "You'll not be seeing me for a while, but I'll be back…someday." Elton was only twenty-nine, but he was at the end of his tether, and, although the stand-alone single "Don't Go Breaking My Heart" was a triumph in the charts, he had no idea how *Blue Moves* was going to be received. After agony of his relationship with John Reid, and after the demise of Bernie's marriage, which gave birth to one of his future greatest hits, "Sorry Seems to Be the Hardest Word," Elton had a profound sense that an era in his life and career had come to an end. In an October 1976 *Rolling Stone* article, Elton opened up on the subject of his

bisexuality. In the United States, the announcement caused a stir and threatened to derail the star's status as a rock 'n' roll icon. "A few radio stations were a bit upset," he said, "and people burnt my records. But you know what? It was a very small price to pay for the freedom that it gave me."[11] In the United Kingdom, however, the news passed almost unnoticed. When *Blue Moves* came out on both sides of the Atlantic in October, the whole world got its first glimpse of the new Elton John via a purposefully anticommercial album with a mysterious album cover that reproduced a painting by the Irish artist Patrick Procktor, called *The Guardian Readers*. This was a painting that Elton had purchased, and it depicted mostly bare-chested men with indistinct facial features, sunbathing in a park. The *Sun* newspaper, which was initially supposed to give away copies of the disk, refused to do so on the pretext that there were no women on the cover. The album itself was met with mixed reviews that often criticized the artist for overly long tracks, and for an excessively mournful sound overall. *Blue Moves* has always occupied an important place in Elton John's catalog, and the time and circumstances under which it was recorded represent a moment of extreme upheaval in his life. Despite the mixed reviews, Elton has always defended this album and ranked it as one of his favorites.

DON'T GO BREAKING MY HEART

Elton John, Bernie Taupin (credited as Ann Orson and Carte Blanche) / 4:35

Single: *Don't Go Breaking My Heart / Snow Queen* **UK Release:** June 21, 1976, on Rocket Record Company (ref. ROKN 512) **Best UK Chart Ranking:** 1 **US Release:** June 21, 1976, on Rocket Record Company (ref. PIG-40585) **Best US Chart Ranking:** 1 **Musicians:** **Elton John:** vocals, electric piano / **Kiki Dee:** vocals / **Davey Johnstone:** electric guitar / **Caleb Quaye:** electric guitar / **Kenny Passarelli:** bass / **Roger Pope:** drums / **James Newton Howard:** piano, arrangements, direction / **Ray Cooper:** tambourine, congas, bongos / **Orchestra:** uncredited / **Backing vocals:** Curt Becher, Cindy Bullens, Ken Gold, Jon Joyce (uncredited) **Recorded:** Eastern Sound Studio, Toronto: March 27, 1976 **Technical Team: Producer:** Gus Dudgeon / **Sound Engineer:** Jeff Guercio / **Assistant Sound Engineer:** Mark Guercio

Genesis and Lyrics

On March 27, 1976, at the end of a month spent recording at Eastern Sound Studio in Toronto, the musicians had almost finished the sessions for the double album *Blue Moves.* But this was not taking into account the hyperactivity of their leader, who, taking advantage of a pause imposed by technical issues, allowed his fingers to wander over his Wurlitzer electronic piano. Elton started to set in motion an agreeable chord sequence (F, C, Bb), while humming in a loop: "Don't Go Breaking My Heart." This song aroused Gus Dudgeon's curiosity; he could not remember having seen a text by Bernie containing this phrase. And, quite rightly so, since Elton had just invented it. For some time he had been thinking of doing a disco-soul duet with a female partner. He was particularly thinking of one song featuring Marvin Gaye and Tammi Terrell in April 1967: "Ain't No Mountain High Enough." Elton did not have his lyricist on hand in the studio because Bernie preferred the Barbados sun to the Canadian cold. Also, Bernie really did not wish to come into contact with Maxine, with whom he was in the middle of divorce proceedings; she was pursuing

a new relationship with Kenny Passarelli…who was participating in these recording sessions. Given the awkward situation, Elton still picked up the phone. "[I] said, 'Write a duet,' and Taupin nearly died 'cause he'd never done one,"[113] as Elton John recalled in the famous 1976 interview with *Rolling Stone*, in which he also revealed his bisexuality. Bernie complied and wrote the lyrics for the future hit that Elton would share with Kiki Dee. Pauline Matthews (Kiki Dee's real name) was not the singer's first choice, and Elton originally suggested Dusty Springfield, the heroine of his adolescence. But the performer of "Son of a Preacher Man" was unwell, so he decided to offer the song to his friend and protégée, Kiki Dee.

Production

The singer announced to his musicians, who thought that they had finished recording the album, that there was one more song for them to work on. Roger Pope, who always spoke his mind, expressed his discontentment, but Elton's response was just a black look, which extinguished any appetite for rebellion in the drummer. The singer's reaction had its effect on the musicians: As impatient as they were to wrap up the session, they were still as dedicated as ever, and they managed to immortalize the number in a single take. In a register that was rather alien to him, somewhere between funk and disco, the rocker Caleb Quaye accepted the challenge with a disconcerting facility, imprinting a lively groove with funk rhythm bump notes of impeccable precision, while Ray Cooper's congas and bongos provided the piece with a touch of originality.

Then it was Elton's turn. "He actually sang about three quarters of the song and gave Kiki about four lines," explained Gus Dudgeon. "I said 'Hang on a minute, is this supposed to be a duet or a guest appearance?' Elton replied, 'A duet.' Then you've got to give her at least 50 percent of the song."[114]

Although the promotional video created by Mike Mansfield shows the two singers in the studio, this was not how it was at

"Don't Go Breaking My Heart," a duet with Kiki Dee (shown here in 1977), brought Elton his first number one hit in the UK.

the time of the recording, which was done remotely because Kiki was in London. As a consequence, Elton recorded not only his own parts, but also those of his partner, performing at an exaggeratedly high pitch so that she would easily be able to identify the phrases. The tape was then sent to England.

To complete the track, Gus Dudgeon wanted to add an orchestral arrangement. Ray Cooper suggested entrusting this mission to James Newton Howard. The keyboard player, who did not flaunt his talents, was more than capable of directing

orchestral arrangements. He proved this brilliantly with the support of twelve violins, four violas, and four cellos. His orchestration, which was superlative, was totally in keeping with soul classics by the Temptations and the Supremes, which the musician studied in minute detail. Some backing vocals were added at the end, including the "woo-hoos," "don't go breaking my heart," and "nobody knows it."

Released on June 21, 1976, "Don't Go Breaking My Heart" enabled Elton to rectify a historical anomaly: He finally had a number one hit in his home country, the United Kingdom.

YOUR STARTER FOR...

Caleb Quaye / 1:23

Musicians
Elton John: piano
Davey Johnstone: mandolins
Caleb Quaye: acoustic guitars
Kenny Passarelli: bass
Roger Pope: drums
James Newton Howard: synthesizer
Ray Cooper: glockenspiel, marimba

Recorded
Eastern Sound Studio, Toronto: March 1976

Technical Team
Producer: Gus Dudgeon
Sound Engineer: John Stewart
Audio Editing: Arun Chakraverty

Guitarist Caleb Quaye wrote one of the rare numbers in Elton's discography on which the singer is not credited.

Genesis and Lyrics

This entirely instrumental sequence was recorded during a break in the Toronto recording sessions, which Elton used to visit some local radio stations and to attend a hockey game. The song was not based on any work of Bernie's, so Elton arbitrarily chose to give it the title "Your Starter For..." This strange title refers to a private joke between the musicians relating to a verbal gimmick by Bamber Gascoigne, host of the British TV quiz show *University Challenge*, who always began the starter questions with the phrase "Your starter for ten..."

Production

"It was something I've written actually when I was living in Chicago" in the early 1970s, explained guitarist Caleb Quaye, who wrote and was credited for one of the few songs in Elton John's repertoire that was not credited to the singer himself. "It was just a practice piece that I wrote. It was something that I used to play to warm up during the cold winter on my acoustic guitar [laughs]." Elton John was looking for an instrumental introduction for his double album and asked his musicians for ideas and suggestions. "[Gus asked,] 'Anybody got any ideas?' And so I just said, 'Well, you know, I've got this little piece.' [...] I played it to Elton, [and he said], 'Oh yeah, that's great.' Because, you know, he comes from a classical background, and it's a kind of a classical piece and he really liked it so everybody jumped on it."[110] The impulsive motif, which incorporated an interesting rhythmic change, and was supplemented by the cheerful notes of the marimba, is also accompanied by the glockenspiel, and both are played by Ray Cooper. The piece then develops with a light touch, embellished only with subtle changes. Less subtle was James Newton Howard's synthesizer, whose almost burlesque and rather dated sound incrementally detracted from this moment of melodic joyfulness, which ends prematurely at 1:23. Only two takes were needed to complete the recording of this song.

TONIGHT

Elton John, Bernie Taupin / 7:52

Musicians
Elton John: vocals, piano
London Symphony Orchestra: orchestra
James Newton Howard: arrangements, direction
Recorded
Abbey Road, London: March 1976
Technical Team
Producer: Gus Dudgeon
Sound Engineers: John Stewart, John Kurlander
Audio Editing: Arun Chakraverty

James Newton Howard assumed responsibility for directing the orchestra on "Tonight."

Genesis and Lyrics

After an instrumental introduction that lasts until 1:23, the listener might reasonably expect that "Tonight" would get down to the heart of the matter. But, in fact, the veil of the curtain is lifted only to reveal another veil, namely another instrumental part that lasts nearly three minutes, meaning there was a total absence of vocals for four and a half minutes. Gus Dudgeon was the first to express his astonishment: "He'd written the whole thing, top to bottom, [as] a complete piece. The first time I heard it, Elton kept going on and on, one movement after another, and I just sat there thinking, 'Well, okay, is he ever going to start singing?' But I shouldn't have worried. He knew what he was on about, he knew what he was doing."[31] Bernie's lyrics managed to provide an outpouring of resentment and remorse, and their darkness left Elton feeling uneasy. With "Tonight," Bernie captured a moment of heartbreak and fatigue, when two lovers opt to go to sleep rather than to start yet another argument: "Tonight / Do we have to fight again / Tonight? / I just want to go to sleep." "It [this phrase] was very difficult for me to listen to at one time, but my life has changed a lot and it doesn't have that torturous edge for me anymore."[111]

Production

In his own estimation, this turned out to be one of Elton's finest creations, even though it was recorded after the group had left Toronto. Back in London, Elton felt the need to immortalize this song that, until that point, had only existed in his head. He decided to book the Abbey Road studios for himself and James Newton Howard. Howard took care of directing the orchestra—the London Symphony Orchestra, which is one of the most highly regarded ensembles in the world—which agreed to perform the piece live along with Elton's piano and vocals. The majestic symphonic arrangement envelopes Elton's piano, and then his voice, which is submerged with emotion. In the actual take, which required the greatest concentration on the part of the pianist, Elton gently played the last chord of D, then delicately placed his forehead on the Steinway. Morally and physically exhausted, he had at last finished this demanding album.

ONE HORSE TOWN

Elton John, Bernie Taupin, James Newton Howard / 5:57

Musicians
Elton John: vocals, piano
Caleb Quaye: electric guitar
Davey Johnstone: electric guitar
Kenny Passarelli: bass
Roger Pope: drums
James Newton Howard: electric piano, synthesizer
Ray Cooper: gong, tambourine, vibraphone, tubular bells
Michael Hurwitz: cello
The Martyn Ford Orchestra: orchestra
Paul Buckmaster: arrangements, direction

Recorded
Eastern Sound Studio, Toronto / Abbey Road, London: March 1976

Technical Team
Producer: Gus Dudgeon
Sound Engineer: John Kurlander
Audio Editing: Arun Chakraverty

ON YOUR HEADPHONES
Just before Caleb Quaye's guitar solo, which lasts for more than thirty seconds, Elton calls out with an enigmatic *"Gonzales!"* Many thought that this was the name given by the pianist to his guitarist. This was far from the case: It was simply meant to encourage the musicians to continue with the same propulsive drive as the famous cartoon mouse Speedy Gonzales.

Genesis and Lyrics
When not chronicling his descent into relationship hell following his separation from Maxine, Bernie Taupin returned to his comfort zone: the evocation of a fantasized America as seen through the lens of his countryside childhood in Lincolnshire. Here, the lyricist constructed the décor of a little village in Alabama that has been left behind by progress, where there is no crime, because "there's nothing to steal." There is an element of boredom running through the description of the town, but when he evokes his impatience to grow up and leave home, a glimmer of hope appears and gives rise to a dynamic, galloping interpretation of song in Elton's music.

Production
More than with any other album, Elton John was eager to have his musicians involved in the creation of the tracks. In "One Horse Town," it was James Newton Howard's turn to step up to the plate, and he was credited for his electric piano introduction to the piece. Delicate and nuanced, his part is wonderfully complemented by the luminous notes of a vibraphone. Ray Cooper then comes in with the tubular bells, whose tones integrate perfectly with the continuity of James Newton Howard's electric piano in the introduction and help to maintain the gentleness previously established. He counterbalances the biting intervention of Caleb's and Davey's hard rock guitars, which then move toward modern jazz. Progressively, the tubular bells emerge alongside the orchestra's elegiac strings, which were directed by a revenant Paul Buckmaster, who had not been called upon since the *Don't Shoot Me* sessions in 1972. In an interview given in 2010, Buckmaster explained his approach to bringing in the instruments: "One general rule is to hold back as much as possible, to give the listener the chance to let the song grow and unfold, introducing new sonic elements, such as new instruments or sectional groupings. If you use everything from the beginning, you have nowhere to go."[112] With the same care for managing the surprise, and true to the objectives of the song, Buckmaster ensures that the orchestra grows in parallel with the group and sometimes reduces the intervention of the violinists to a melodic comma, as at 4:36, when coming out of Caleb's rapid solo.

CHAMELEON

Elton John, Bernie Taupin / 5:28

Musicians

Elton John: vocals, piano
Caleb Quaye: electric guitar, acoustic guitar
Kenny Passarelli: bass
Roger Pope: drums
Ray Cooper: vibraphone, shaker
Curt Becher, Cindy Bullens, Ron Hicklin, Bruce Johnston, Jon Joyce, Gene Morford, Toni Tennille: backing vocals
Bruce Johnston: backing vocals arrangements

Recorded

Eastern Sound Studio, Toronto / Brother Studios, Santa Monica: March 1976

Technical Team

Producer: Gus Dudgeon
Sound Engineer: Earle Mankey
Audio Editing: Arun Chakraverty

Single Release

Bite Your Lip (Get Up and Dance!) / *Chameleon*
US Release: January 31, 1977, on MCA Records / Rocket Record Company (ref. MCA-40677)
Best US Chart Ranking: 28
Crazy Water / Chameleon
UK Release: February 4, 1977, on Rocket Record Company (ref. ROKN 521)
Best UK Chart Ranking: 27

Toni Tennille and Daryl Dragon, who formed the pop duo Captain & Tennille.

Genesis and Lyrics

When he went onstage with his new group for Midsummer Music at Wembley Stadium, on June 21, 1975, Elton was still in the learning phase. The members of this new version of the Elton John Band, who had only two weeks' playing experience behind them, were still learning and getting to know one another. While calming his nerves by practicing on his instrument, Davey Johnstone created a ravishing melody on his acoustic guitar, under the admiring gaze of James Newton Howard, who was amazed by the playing of this tall, lanky, blondhaired bloke. Elton John shared the billing with the Beach Boys that day, and the pianist took advantage of the occasion to submit the now-famous composition "Chameleon" to the California group. The reaction was no more than polite interest, and the piece went back into Elton's box of ideas. It came out again eight months later during the *Blue Moves* sessions, on a prolific day in Toronto, which also saw the creation of "Shoulder Holster" and "Cage the Songbird."

Production

The indifference of the Beach Boys is even more surprising, given the rampant melancholy of this slow number, the content of the lyrics (love, summer, nostalgia for a carefree youth), and the splendor of the assertive backing vocals accompanying the rising vocals of Elton, which were all ingredients readily recognizable as being similar to the California group. The spirit of the Beach Boys does permeate this song with the contribution of Bruce Johnston, a member of the group from 1965 to 1972 (before rejoining in 1978), who was assigned the task of directing the backing vocals on this track. Also present was Toni Tennille, of Captain & Tennille, who played keyboards for the Beach Boys during their 1972 tour, and whose husband, Daryl Dragon, assisted the band as a session musician. Five other singers completed the team, which gently envelops Elton's lamentations with background vocals recorded during the overdub sessions at Santa Monica: Curt Becher, Cindy Bullens, Ron Hicklin, Jon Joyce, and Gene Morford.

BOOGIE PILGRIM

Elton John, Bernie Taupin, Davey Johnstone, Caleb Quaye / 6:06

Musicians

Elton John: vocals, piano
Davey Johnstone: slide guitar
Kenny Passarelli: bass
Roger Pope: drums
James Newton Howard: organ
Ray Cooper: tambourine
The Brecker Brothers (Randy Brecker, Michael Brecker), Barry Rogers, David Sanborn: brass
The Cornerstone Institutional Baptist and Southern California Community Choir: backing vocals
Rev. James Cleveland: backing vocals direction

Recorded

Eastern Sound Studio, Toronto / Sunset Sound Recorders, Los Angeles: March 1976

Technical Team

Producer: Gus Dudgeon
Sound Engineer: Mark Howlett
Audio Editing: Arun Chakraverty

The Brecker Brothers were highly sought after session musicians and they also had a successful career as a duo that released seven studio albums.

Genesis and Lyrics

If "Boogie Pilgrim," which ends with an ad lib punctuated with claps, sounds like a live recording, it's because it came out of a midnight jam session. "Elton said, 'Let's all perform as much as possible like a band. Let's take ideas into the studio and see what we come up with,'" Davey Johnstone recalled. "This was a great opportunity for everyone in the band to throw in their ideas and their tools and see what happened. And 'Boogie Pilgrim' was like that. It was a jam, and it came out great."[31] Bernie's lyrics were conceived as a prayer delivered by a "boogie pilgrim" who lived frugally and observed the vicissitudes of modern life.

Production

Placed on different sides of the album, "Boogie Pilgrim" and "Where's the Shoorah?" both communicate their themes with the same good humor. There is a reason for this: Both songs were recorded in the same session. They represent the two sides of gospel music that Elton John liked: a contemplative sound that appears in "Where's the Shoorah?" and a more festive tone like what appears on "Boogie Pilgrim." Infused with rhythm 'n' blues, the piece still retains the marks of gospel: the organ, the backing vocals, and an instinctive, warm singing style. Carried along by the enthusiasm of the moment, Elton delivers an astonishing vocal performance, moving directly from falsetto to singing the low notes in a deliberately stereotypical way. Nothing was calculated, and he performs the song instinctively, strictly respecting the guidelines he had laid down for this album: a minimum of takes and no overdubs, at least for the main musicians.

CAGE THE SONGBIRD

Elton John, Bernie Taupin, Davey Johnstone / 3:26

Musicians
Elton John: vocals
Davey Johnstone: acoustic guitar, dulcimer
Caleb Quaye: acoustic guitar
James Newton Howard: synthesizer, Mellotron
Ray Cooper: triangle, finger cymbals, bell tree, shaker
David Crosby and Graham Nash: backing vocals

Recorded
Eastern Sound Studio, Toronto / Brother Studios, Santa Monica: March 1976

Technical Team
Producer: Gus Dudgeon
Sound Engineer: Earle Mankey
Audio Editing: Arun Chakraverty

French singer Edith Piaf (shown here in 1955), was sometimes known as "The Sparrow," and she inspired Bernie to write "Cage the Songbird."

Genesis and Lyrics

From Dusty Springfield to Aretha Franklin, Elton John and Bernie Taupin had always had a reverential fascination for great female singers, but there was one singer whose tragic destiny and force of character struck them to such an extent that it inspired a song: Édith Piaf. Often referred to as "the Little Sparrow," she became the "songbird" of Elton and Bernie's song. The track was hatched during the recording sessions of *Rock of the Westies* at Caribou Ranch, in January 1974. It was six o'clock in the morning when the musicians felt the need for some fresh air. They marched outside, and Davey Johnstone, who had brought along his acoustic guitar, launched into a gentle melody inspired by "The Skaters' Waltz." This waltz by Émile Waldteufel stuck with Elton, who had played his scales along to this piece when he was a child. The singer enthusiastically returned to the ranch and came back with a sheet of paper in his hand, on which Bernie had written the lyrics of "Songbird." Everything fell into place as though by magic. In this requiem, Bernie evokes the death of an icon, the rumors that grew surrounding her demise, especially about her last thoughts and her solitude. The circumstances of her death are only touched upon, but the lyricist seems to be suggesting that she died of suicide. In reality, the famous French singer died, aged forty-seven, of an aortic aneurysm following liver failure. This dramatic rendition of the life of a famous but tragic woman places "Cage the Songbird" in the same ranks as the first version of "Candle in the Wind," which was written in homage to Marilyn Monroe.

Production

This song was left off the *Rock of the Westies* album, probably because of that album's folk ambitions. "Cage the Songbird" eventually joined the track list of *Blue Moves*, which had a more diverse range of sounds. Davey Johnstone used a dulcimer, and its sonorities brought an aspect of mystery to the recording. The musician added an acoustic guitar track, which he played using a finger-picking technique that created a gentler sound and greater melodic richness. Finally, to enhance the rustic vibe of the song, two exceptional singers were called upon to illuminate the backing vocals with their complementary timbres: David Crosby and Graham Nash, from the trio Crosby, Stills & Nash.

CRAZY WATER

Elton John, Bernie Taupin / 5:42

Musicians
Elton John: vocals, piano
Davey Johnstone: electric guitar
Caleb Quaye: electric guitar
Kenny Passarelli: bass
Roger Pope: drums
James Newton Howard: Clavinet
Ray Cooper: congas, tambourine
Cindy Bullens, Ron Hicklin, Bruce Johnston, Jon Joyce, Gene Morford, Toni Tennille: backing vocals
Daryl Dragon: backing vocals arrangement
The Martyn Ford Orchestra: orchestra
Paul Buckmaster: arrangements, direction

Recorded
Eastern Sound Studio, Toronto / Brother Studios, Santa Monica: March 1976

Technical Team
Producer: Gus Dudgeon
Sound Engineer: Earle Mankey
Audio Editing: Arun Chakraverty

Single Release
Crazy Water / Chameleon
UK Release: February 4, 1977, on Rocket Record Company (ref. ROKN 521)
Best UK Chart Ranking: 27

Genesis and Lyrics

Once the first single of the album, "Bite Your Lip (Get Up and Dance!)," was safely consigned to tape at the beginning of the sessions, the group could relax in the knowledge that *Blue Moves* had set off on the right track. "Crazy Water" shows the band having fun with a jazz-funk, up-tempo song that's boiling with energy. A new variation on the theme of separation, the lyrics explore its causes, pointing the finger at the dissolute lifestyle of the lyricist, who compares the obligations linked to the artistic life with those of a whale hunter reported missing at sea. The central metaphor of the song was inspired by a true story that happened in 1972, and that particularly affected Bernie Taupin: the loss of the ship *FV Gaul* and its crew, which disappeared without trace in the Barents Sea.

Production

The extravagant stylistic orientation of "Crazy Water" says a great deal about how Elton composes. He often chose a word in the text, in this case "crazy," and then oriented the music according to the way this word inspired him. Elizabeth J. Rosenthal refers to this way of working in her book *His Song: The Musical Journey of Elton John*,[32] explaining, for example, that the term "ballerina" in "Tiny Dancer" led the singer to create a single with a music box feel to it, and that the cowboy in "Captain Fantastic and the Brown Dirt Cowboy" took him in the direction of country folk. The "madness" of "Crazy Water" is expressed through the speed of execution on the funky Clavinet, Elton's flamboyant playing, and, above all, the astonishing backing vocals conceived by Daryl Dragon. This member of the Captain & Tennille duo, whose involvement was suggested by Bruce Johnston, offered some surprising and very brief vocals with a deliberately deep register. Gus Dudgeon was initially skeptical of how this would sound, but when he listened to the final result, he realized just how brilliant this unexpected idea was.

SHOULDER HOLSTER

Elton John, Bernie Taupin / 5:09

Musicians

Elton John: vocals, piano,
Kenny Passarelli: bass
Roger Pope: drums
Ray Cooper: tambourine
The Brecker Brothers (Randy Brecker, Michael Brecker), Barry Rogers, David Sanborn: brass

Recorded

Eastern Sound Studio, Toronto / Brother Studios, Santa Monica: March 1976

Technical Team

Producer: Gus Dudgeon
Sound Engineer: Mark Howlett
Audio Editing: Arun Chakraverty

Single Release

Sorry Seems to Be the Hardest Word / Shoulder Holster
UK Release: October 29, 1976, on Rocket Record Company (ref. ROKN 517)
Best UK Chart Ranking: 11
US Release: November 1, 1976, on MCA Records / Rocket Record Company (ref. MCA-40645)
Best US Chart Ranking: 6

A former member of the Butterfield Blues Band, David Sanborn became one of the most sought-after saxophonists of the 1970s.

Genesis and Lyrics

With a view toward intellectual honesty, and also toward writing a song in the vein of the traditional American storyteller-songwriter tradition, Bernie put his cards on the table from the first verse of this song, announcing that the story that follows is identical to the one told in the traditional American song "Frankie and Johnny." As with Frankie, Dolly Summers, this song's main character, is "a simple girl / From a Midwest family" who realizes that she has been betrayed and then executes the adulterous couple. "Frankie and Johnny" was first published in 1904, by Hughie Cannon, a New York Tin Pan Alley composer. By coincidence, the part of London where Elton and Bernie made their professional debuts, Denmark Street, is also nicknamed Tin Pan Alley, and it is considered to be the London equivalent of American music's nerve center during the early twentieth century.

The second verse of Bernie's song links the story to another traditional American song, "Stagger Lee," the most famous version of which is performed by Lloyd Price. The link is less obvious here as it involves the assassination of William "Billy" Lyons by his friend "Stagger" Lee Shelton, a St. Louis pimp. By nodding toward other famous songs, Bernie almost seems to be apologizing for the possible mediocrity of his own lyrics when he includes the following: "it seemed just like a movie / Or a night of bad TV."

Production

In the spirit of homage, Elton refrained from creating sinister-sounding music to illustrate this sordid story. On the contrary, he chose to create a catchy rhythm 'n' blues piece, with distant, sidelong glances in the direction of honky-tonk. The song positions itself quite rapidly due to its simple construction, with a heady brass motif played by the Brecker Brothers, Barry Rogers, and David Sanborn (which was added during additional sessions at the Sunset Sound Recorders studio). The listener's attention stays focused on the lyrics, and the piano is accompanied only by the rhythm section, which provides the song's main groove without adding additional ornamentation. Elton even made the radical decision not to include any guitar on this song. As such, the mandatory solo at the end of the song is therefore assigned to David Sanborn's alto saxophone.

SORRY SEEMS TO BE THE HARDEST WORD

Elton John, Bernie Taupin / 3:48

Musicians
Elton John: lead and backing vocals, piano
Kenny Passarelli: bass
James Newton Howard: electric piano, arrangements, direction
Ray Cooper: vibraphone
Carl Fortina: accordion
Orchestra: uncredited

Recorded
Eastern Sound Studio, Toronto / Brother Studios, Santa Monica: March 22, 1976

Technical Team
Producer: Gus Dudgeon
Sound Engineer: Mark Howlett
Audio Editing: Arun Chakraverty

Single Release
Sorry Seems to Be the Hardest Word / Shoulder Holster
UK Release: October 29, 1976, on Rocket Record Company (ref. ROKN 517)
Best UK Chart Ranking: 11
US Release: November 1, 1976, on MCA Records / Rocket Record Company (ref. MCA-40645)
Best US Chart Ranking: 6

"Sorry Seems to Be the Hardest Word" is one of the most poignant ballads in Elton John's repertoire.

Genesis and Lyrics

The biggest hit off the *Blue Moves* album, "Sorry Seems to Be the Hardest Word" required only modest resources for its recording. For some months, the melody had been going around in Elton's head. It haunted him, and he could hardly wait for a set of lyrics whose prosody matched the melody's rhyme in order to give the song life. So he decided to submit the tune to Bernie when he called in to see him one afternoon. "He was tinkling on the piano," recalled the lyricist, "and I just listened for a while. Finally, I thought of the title line and went home and completed the song."[111] Elton was very emotionally involved with this ballad, which was inspired by yet another amorous disappointment since his relationship with John Reid ended. Although it might have appeared that he tended to flit about, the singer was very emotionally whole-hearted, even excessively so, launching himself very quickly into serious relationships with people he just met, but his emotional commitments were not always reciprocated. This absence of reciprocity was frequently a source of disappointment...and sometimes also of inspiration: "What have I got to do to make you love me? / What have I got to do to make you care?" Elton asks like a jilted lover who's gripped by sadness, but who has no intention of giving up.

Production

On March 22, 1976, during the recording, Elton finally gave voice to his internal lament. He presented the composition to the musicians, playing it slowly before an initial bass was laid down. The bass was done in a direct recording with just Elton's piano and vocals and Kenny Passarelli's bass to serve as a rhythmic guide. As had been done at Caribou Ranch, Gus Dudgeon installed a wooden shell over the piano, isolating its sound and enabling Elton to sing while playing without the voice being too audible over the piano track. The strings, vibraphone, and famous plaintive accordion that all contributed to the song's identity were recorded in a second stage. With its piano arpeggios and descending chords, the song is emotionally captivating in its simplicity. "For me, it's one of the best ballads we've ever written," said Elton, "which is why it has stayed in the show for a long time."[111] It received a fairly cool reception when it went to eleventh place in the United Kingdom and sixth place in the United States. But as the years have passed, "Sorry Seems to Be the Hardest Word" lodged itself in the hearts of fans.

OUT OF THE BLUE

Elton John, Bernie Taupin / 6:15

Musicians

Elton John: piano
Davey Johnstone: electric guitar
Caleb Quaye: electric guitar
Kenny Passarelli: bass
Roger Pope: drums
James Newton Howard: synthesizer
Ray Cooper: vibraphone, congas

Recorded

Eastern Sound Studio, Toronto: March 1976

Technical Team

Producer: Gus Dudgeon
Audio Editing: Arun Chakraverty

Kenny Passarelli, Elton John, and Roger Pope during the Louder Than Concorde Tour in May 1976.

Genesis and Production

Recorded at the end of the *Blue Moves* sessions, the appropriately named "Out of the Blue" really did come out of nowhere to become the third instrumental piece on the album. Not that there was any lack of lyrical options from Bernie to supply this double album. The lyricist, on vacation on Barbados, had provided dozens of options, but Elton realized that the addition of lyrics might break the fine dynamic of this new composition. He started by presenting the introductory motif to the other members, which was quickly enhanced by Caleb Quaye's electric guitar with its fuzz sound. The picture grew bigger with Roger Pope's drums, triggering the forward movement of the song, and James Newton Howard's synthesizer, which added tension, acting like a guitar played very assertively. Howard managed to get hold of a polyphonic synthesizer, due to his friendship with the instrument's designer, Bob Moog. But the real stroke of genius was the trenchant guitar riff by Caleb, which was doubled by Ray Cooper on vibraphone. Following this sweet-and-sour riff, it was Kenny Passarelli's turn to step forward, with some bass phrases that are both melodic and rhythmic, including the use of the highest range on his four-string. These stand out even more, given that at the beginning of the piece he was relegated to playing the fundamentals, and sometimes just one single note. He had been particularly frustrated by the sessions for *Rock of the Westies* and now had the opportunity to take his rightful place on Elton John's team. His exceptional technical prowess fully justified the confidence that the pianist had placed in him. Developing between jazz and an almost garage-sounding rock, the piece concludes with a frenetic jam session on which Elton John and Ray Cooper take over the controls.

BETWEEN SEVENTEEN AND TWENTY

Elton John, Bernie Taupin, Davey Johnstone, Caleb Quaye / 5:18

Musicians
Elton John: vocals
Caleb Quaye: electric guitars
Davey Johnstone: mandolin
Kenny Passarelli: bass
Roger Pope: drums
James Newton Howard: organ
Ray Cooper: congas, tambourine, shaker
Curt Becher, Cindy Bullens, Joe Chemay, Bruce Johnston, Jon Joyce, Toni Tennille: backing vocals
Bruce Johnston, Curt Becher: backing vocals arrangement

Recorded
Eastern Sound Studio, Toronto / Brother Studios, Santa Monica: March 1976

Technical Team
Producer: Gus Dudgeon
Sound Engineer: John Stewart
Audio Editing: Arun Chakraverty

Bruce Johnston of the Beach Boys contributed his expertise in backing vocals arrangements on *Blue Moves*.

Genesis and Lyrics

Can one imagine a worse position to be in than the one occupied by Kenny Passarelli at the time of recording "Between Seventeen and Twenty"? The bass player, who still had to prove himself to some of the group members, was in the process of playing a piece that told the story of his relationship with Maxine, the former wife of Bernie Taupin. The song had lyrics like "I wonder who's sleeping in your sheets tonight [...] / Could it be a close friend I knew so well?" Kenny remembered how uncomfortable this felt: "When I was playing the bass line during that song, it was pretty heavy. I was around Bernie enough to see how upset [he was] about his marriage falling apart but he didn't know in the beginning that I was involved. It was difficult to watch what he was going through as his marriage was breaking up, me knowing that I was on the other side."[20] The lyrics leave no doubt as to Bernie Taupin's thoughts concerning the reasons for his separation. The song's title "Between Seventeen and Twenty" reflects their ages when he and Maxine became a couple. Their relative youth, mixed with Bernie's rock 'n' roll lifestyle, made for an untenable relationship.

Production

Despite the content of the lyrics, the piece has a certain serenity to it coupled with a Led Zeppelin–ish air on the the acoustic side. Credit is due to Davey Johnstone, whose mandolin adds some subtle ornamentations to the overall effect, while Caleb Quaye reserves for himself the finale to highlight his controlled playing, developing little by little on the electric guitar. But the added value on this piece resides in the backing vocals directed by Curt Becher and Bruce Johnston. The latter, an ex–Beach Boy, was back with Elton two years after working on "Don't Let the Sun Go Down on Me" from *Caribou*. More elaborate but less memorable in "Between Seventeen and Twenty," these backing vocals were created by Johnston at Brother Studios in Santa Monica, California. This was the local studio for the Beach Boys, and was founded in 1974. The background vocals carry the imprint of the California group, with a clear distinction between the basses, which are short and accentuated, and the high notes (the register used by Bruce), which were more sustained.

Graham Nash and David Crosby gave Elton the benefit of their vocal harmonies on "The Wide-Eyed and Laughing."

The CD version of *Blue Moves* was released in Europe in 1988. The album had three numbers excised from it so that it would fit onto a single disc without increasing its cost: "Shoulder Holster," "Out of the Blue," and "The Wide-Eyed and Laughing."

THE WIDE-EYED AND LAUGHING

Elton John, Bernie Taupin, James Newton Howard, Davey Johnstone, Caleb Quaye / 3:28

Musicians: Elton John: vocals / Caleb Quaye: six- and twelve-string acoustic guitars / Davey Johnstone: sitar / James Newton Howard: synthesizer / Ray Cooper: rototoms / David Crosby, Graham Nash: backing vocals **Recorded:** Eastern Sound Studio, Toronto / Brother Studios, Santa Monica: March 1976 **Technical Team:** Producer: Gus Dudgeon / **Sound Engineers:** Gus Dudgeon, Earle Mankey / **Audio Editing:** Arun Chakraverty

It was in Caleb Quaye's hotel bedroom, at the Park Hyatt hotel, that "The Wide-Eyed and Laughing" emerged during an improv jam session with Davey Johnstone and James Newton Howard. Davey jumped at the chance to get his sitar out of its box, which he had used for the first time in 1971, on "Holiday Inn" (*Madman Across the Water*). He was wary of misusing this instrument, which had been designed in Bombay by Chaitsingh Gurbaxsingh and ordered from a magazine, "because it's such a traditional sacred instrument."[115] Howard added the modulations on a Moog, which fitted perfectly with the ambiance of the track. The result of this jam session was presented to Elton, who was immediately enthusiastic and came up with the title of "The Wide-Eyed and Laughing," which tells the story of an amorous liaison between Bernie and Wendy Adler, daughter of harmonica player Larry Adler. From the first attempt, the words meshed perfectly with the music. To record the sitar, a microphone was positioned at the jivari (the bridge on the sound box), and another was set inside the tumba (the resonating chamber, which is near the head of the instrument). Only one take was needed for the group to complete this dreamlike interlude.

SOMEONE'S FINAL SONG

Elton John, Bernie Taupin / 4:11

Musicians: Elton John: vocals, piano / James Newton Howard: Fender Rhodes, synthesizer / Curt Becher, Clark Burroughs, Joe Chemay, Bruce Johnston, Toni Tennille: backing vocals / Bruce Johnston, Curt Becher: backing vocals arrangement **Recorded:** Eastern Sound Studio, Toronto / Brother Studios, Santa Monica: March 1976 **Technical Team:** Producer: Gus Dudgeon / **Sound Engineer:** Earle Mankey / **Audio Editing:** Arun Chakraverty

Bernie Taupin's depression reached the zenith of its expression in "Someone's Final Song," a song in which the lyricist clearly evokes his own suicide. This "someone" is not anonymous; it is Bernie himself who is described in this phrase: "He put a pen to paper for one final song." Elton fell into step with the grim mood of the lyrics with an angst-filled melody, which is exemplary in its chordal economy, the handling of silences, and the expressivity of his singing, especially at the end, with long, sustained notes. However, Elton might have found himself gasping for breath, since, just before the session, he had been obliged to sprint! In order to reconnect with real life, and to take in some of the ambiance of Toronto, the singer and his musicians had opted to go to the studio each day on foot rather than by car. To avoid being recognized in the street, Elton wore a hockey mask. But on the day of the recording of "Someone's Final Song," he was spotted by some young people, who started to chase him. So, the musicians arrived at the session out of breath…But, like Elton, the backing vocalists were not out of breath, and they overlaid their angelic vocals on this delicious melody under the supervision of Bruce Johnston and Curt Becher.

WHERE'S THE SHOORAH?

Elton John, Bernie Taupin / 4:10

Musicians: Elton John: vocals, piano, harmonium / Kenny Passarelli: bass / The Cornerstone Institutional Baptist and Southern California Community Choir: backing vocals / Rev. James Cleveland: backing vocals direction **Recorded:** Eastern Sound Studio, Toronto / Sunset Sound Recorders, Los Angeles: March 1976 **Technical Team:** Producer: Gus Dudgeon / Sound Engineer: Mark Howlett / Audio Editing: Arun Chakraverty

Genesis and Lyrics

While Elton wonders where "the Shoorah" is, the listener is probably wondering what the word actually means. This is very uncertain. While the phrase "Where's the Shoorah?" is sung by the narrator's mother, addressing the narrator and his companion, there have been numerous conjectures concerning the meaning of this. As it is sung, it could be a reference to a preexisting song. There are two possibilities, as suggested by Elizabeth J. Rosenthal in *His Song: The Musical Journey of Elton John*[32]: In the song "Shu Rah," released by Fats Domino in 1961, the word appears like an exclamation to celebrate the pleasures of life. Another song, "Shoorah! Shoorah!" was composed by Allen Toussaint—a colleague of Fats Domino—and recorded by Betty Wright in 1974. Stephen Spignesi and Michael Lewis, in their work *Elton John: Fifty Years On: The Complete Guide to the Musical Genius of Elton John and Bernie Taupin*,[116] suggest the idea of a Hebrew origin of the word that could refer to a verse of the Bible, or could mean "counsel." Both these hypotheses could concern the prospect of marriage of the two characters: The narrator's mother could be trying to find out what text will be read at the ceremony, or when the counsel will take place to authorize them to marry outside a given religion.

Production

Regardless of the lyrics' meaning, spirituality permeates this song, which was sketched out at Caribou Ranch and finalized after the "Out of the Blue" instrumental was recorded during the *Blue Moves* sessions. As though to emphasize the ceremonial aspect, Elton excludes the guitars and the rhythm section, and plays only piano and harmonium, whose sonority is similar to a church organ's. He is accompanied by the singers of the Cornerstone Institutional Baptist and Southern California Community Choir, directed by the Reverend James Cleveland. Rev. Cleveland was the first gospel musician to have his star on the Hollywood Walk of Fame, and by the time of this recording had won a Grammy Award; he would win three more between 1977 and 1990. The rounded and contemplative singing of the choir, assisted by a nice reverb, comes in at the start and then disappears for a long time, before returning in the refrain and leaving such a religious imprint on the piece that it ceases to be just a romantic ballad. Elton delivers vocals with soaring gospel accents alongside some electrifying passages, such as the superb rise at 3:06, and the falsetto at 3:51.

IF THERE'S A GOD IN HEAVEN (WHAT'S HE WAITING FOR?)

Elton John, Bernie Taupin, Davey Johnstone / 4:25

Musicians: Elton John: vocals, piano / Caleb Quaye: electric guitar / Davey Johnstone: electric guitar / Kenny Passarelli: bass / Roger Pope: drums / James Newton Howard: organ / Ray Cooper: congas, tambourine / The Martyn Ford Orchestra: orchestra / Paul Buckmaster: arrangements, direction **Recorded:** Eastern Sound Studio, Toronto / Abbey Road, London: March 1976 **Technical Team:** Producer: Gus Dudgeon / Sound Engineer: John Kurlander / Audio Editing: Arun Chakraverty

Genesis and Lyrics

While reviewing the lyrics that Bernie had given him, Elton came across "If There's a God in Heaven (What's He Waiting For?)," one of the rare songs, along with "Philadelphia Freedom," whose subject he had imposed on his co-writer. This time his justification was his admiration for the group the Chi-Lites. He wanted Bernie to write a song for him in the spirit of the Chicago vocal quartet's tune entitled "There Will Never Be Any Peace (Until God Is Seated at the Conference Table)." He liked their engaging, finely harmonized voices, and this pleasantly wrapped, sugary soul sound, with its elegant strings, but he gently mocked their pious lyrics, which, for his taste, were lacking in restraint. Bernie approached this pastiche in a very academic way, reproducing the form of the title, and then picking up on the subject of divine intervention hoped for by mankind. However, he takes things a little further: Whereas, in the song by the Chi-Lites, there was a certain benevolence on the side of mankind—doing their best to make the world a better place. Bernie, in his version, berates the rich who keep the poor hungry and, in passing, wonders about God's perspective on human injustices.

Production

Elton also sticks close to his model, with a caressing soul style in his vocals, reaching the high notes with ease. The strings of the Martyn Ford Orchestra bring personality to the piece, very skillfully reproducing the vocal line. Their leader, Richard Studt, placed himself under the responsibility of Paul Buckmaster, and he could not believe it was happening: Buckmaster was his absolute idol. He had been wonderstruck by Elton John's second album, and as a young arranger, he considered Buckmaster the embodiment of his musical ideal: creating orchestral arrangements for rock music.

IDOL

Elton John, Bernie Taupin / 4:09

Musicians
Elton John: vocals, piano
Kenny Passarelli: bass
Roger Pope: drums
The Brecker Brothers (Randy Brecker, Michael Brecker), Barry Rogers, David Sanborn: brass

Recorded
Eastern Sound Studio, Toronto / Sunset Sound Recorders, Los Angeles: March 1976

Technical Team
Producer: Gus Dudgeon
Sound Engineer: Mark Howlett
Audio Editing: Arun Chakraverty

In 1976, Elton met his idol, Elvis Presley, but the "king" was a shadow of his former self.

Genesis and Lyrics

In the third line of the bridge, between the phrases "He was a light star" and "But his face has changed, he's not the same no more," "Idol" chronicles the pathos of the end of career of a former music star. There can be no possible doubt as to his identity: "the lamé suits," "the fifties"...this is Elvis Presley. In 1976, the "King" was a shadow of his former self, his puffy face showing the outward signs of his ill health. By definition, for Elton, there was a second level of interpretation: the fear of seeing his own career taking the same turn over time. By chance, Elton had the opportunity to meet his idol, between the recording and the release of *Blue Moves*, on June 27, 1976, in the wings of a concert given by the rock star at the Capital Centre Arena, Landover, in Maryland, where Elton was to perform two days later. "When I [shook] his hand, my heart broke," the singer confessed in his autobiography. "There was something desperately, visibly wrong with him. He was overweight, gray and sweating."[3]

Production

This evocation took the form of a jazz ballad based on a chord sequence that Elton ran through while the technical team was fixing some issues in the control booth. In under a quarter of an hour, the song was set up, and it was recorded in just a couple of takes. For this occasion, Roger Pope, known to be a hard hitter, proved his adaptability by transforming into a jazz drummer, swapping his sticks for brushes. He provides the gentlest accompaniment to the slow brass laments exhaled by the Brecker Brothers, Barry Rogers, and David Sanborn. Kenny plays an Alembic bass, an instrument with an exceptional fidelity of sound and refined finishes, designed by the company founded in 1969 by Owsley Stanley, the Grateful Dead sound engineer and also a chemist. "My approach was as if I was playing an upright bass [...] in a jazz trio in some smoky club."[117]

THEME FROM A NON-EXISTENT TV SERIES

Elton John, Bernie Taupin / 1:19

Musicians
Elton John: electronic harpsichord
Caleb Quaye: acoustic guitars
Kenny Passarelli: bass
Roger Pope: drums
James Newton Howard: synthesizer, electric piano
Ray Cooper: glockenspiel, marimba

Recorded
Eastern Sound Studio, Toronto: March 1976

Technical Team
Producer: Gus Dudgeon
Sound Engineer: John Stewart
Audio Editing: Arun Chakraverty

On this album, Elton tried to free himself from expectations and he even offered a few instrumental numbers.

Genesis and Lyrics

Mobilizing the same instruments and the same musicians—with the exception of Davey Johnstone—that worked on "Your Starter For...," this track is the shortest piece on the album, with a running time of only 1:19. This completely instrumental piece—which might have closed the album, had Gus Dudgeon not opted to allocate this last slot to "Bite Your Lip (Get Up and Dance!)"—was credited to Elton John and Bernie Taupin in spite of the fact that the lyricist played no part in its creation. For its musical design, Caleb Quaye and Roger Pope remembered the reworking they had done in 1969 (as part of the Bread and Beer Band) of the "Dick Barton Theme (the Devil's Gallop)," a piece of light music by Charles Williams that was used as the theme for the radio series *Dick Barton: Special Agent*, broadcast by the BBC between 1946 and 1951. "Theme from a Non-existent TV Series" proved to be very musically similar to this cover. The title simultaneously references this historical milestone in their musical association and emphasizes its potential effectiveness as a TV series theme, due to its instrumental format and its easily recognizable tune.

Production

Retaining the same baroque spirit by mobilizing Elton John's rapid keyboard playing, this time the musicians provided an electronic ambiance via the electric piano and James Newton Howard's synthesizer, which follows the melody established by Elton's harpsichord, an octave higher. Initially he repeats the entire phrase before playing only the second parts, so that there is a question-and-answer between the two musicians. This is a minor piece, conceived as an interlude, but it did, however, receive unexpected recognition from the Ivors Academy, an independent professional association of music creators that since 1956 has been recognizing British songwriters and composers. In 1977, the institution nominated the song for an Ivor Novello Award for best instrumental work.

BITE YOUR LIP
(GET UP AND DANCE!)

Elton John, Bernie Taupin / 6:43

Musicians
Elton John: vocals, piano
Davey Johnstone: slide guitar, backing vocals
Caleb Quaye: electric guitar, backing vocals
Kenny Passarelli: bass
Roger Pope: drums
James Newton Howard: synthesizers
Ray Cooper: bongos, congas
Harry Bluestone: arrangements, strings direction
The Gene Page Strings: orchestra
The Cornerstone Institutional Baptist and Southern California Community Choir: backing vocals
Rev. James Cleveland: backing vocals direction

Recorded
Eastern Sound Studio, Toronto: March 1976

Technical Team
Producer: Gus Dudgeon
Sound Engineer: John Stewart
Audio Editing: Arun Chakraverty

Single Release
Bite Your Lip (Get Up and Dance!) / Chameleon
  US Release: January 31, 1977, on MCA Records / Rocket Record Company (ref. MCA-40677)
  Best US Chart Ranking: 28
  Split Single Release with Kiki Dee
Bite Your Lip (Get Up and Dance!) / Chicago
  UK Release: June 3, 1977, on Rocket Record Company (ref. ROKN 526)
  Best UK Chart Ranking: 28

Additional tweaks were made before the US release of "Bite Your Lip" on January 31, 1977. Tom Moulton, a disco specialist, was brought on board to give added shine to Johnstone's slide guitar and Elton's voice in the recording booth.

Genesis and Lyrics

While tears inundated the lyrics of Bernie Taupin, who had been inconsolable since his rupture with Maxine, the text of "Bite Your Lip (Get Up and Dance!)" is a ray of light in the midst of all this darkness. Elton John, who had been looking for a way of constructing an energetic number that would set the tone for his new opus, *Blue Moves*, seized on this. The lyrics, which were simple, short, and repetitive, fitted well with the trends of the time. Elton took the pulse of the music and put his own stamp of the vocabulary of the disco movement that was emerging in the charts in the mid-1970s, driven by Donna Summer and Gloria Gaynor. So we find various injunctions called out to the dancers of the kind frequently found in hits of this kind ("Get up and dance"), although Bernie introduces a heavy dose of cynicism ("Move that muscle and shake that fat"), while the disco atmosphere is heady in this song ("disco heat," "strobe light," "funky feet"). Whether critical or sincere, these lyrics are transcended by the hedonism of the music that Elton John puts in place, his own vision of disco—in fact a hybrid formula of rock, disco, pop, and funk.

Production

Elton was unable to play "Crocodile Rock" during his stage performances because Caleb Quaye refused to play it, so Elton conceived a similar type of anthem that would seem more acceptable to his guitarist and would offer his musicians the opportunity to play at their full power. He launches the assault with staccato playing, vigorously hammering at his keyboard, while Caleb, who was always at his best when delivering a strong rhythm, dominates with his muscular playing, in the vein of Keith Richards. Roger Pope and Ray Cooper launch into a frenetic race at a high rate of bpm, hitting the skins as though their lives depended on it. In contrast, Davey Johnstone's guitar seems to glide serenely over the mêlée, occasionally punctuated by huge downward-driving swoops with the slide. He is given two solos, and the piano is given three, evidence of the creative latitude provided by this piece, which, in consequence, runs for more than six minutes in the album version. At the end is a majestic finale in which the musicians, braced on their instruments, give it their all, and after the moment of release is sounded by Roger Pope's authoritative drum roll. After they finished recording it, Elton

"Bite Your Lips (Get Up and Dance!)" is a demonstration of strength by Roger Pope, who really gives his drums a beating.

frantically rushed into Gus Dudgeon's control booth. He was convinced that he had a hit with this number, and that the first version was so fabulous that the group would be unable to beat it. Gus tempered his excitement: Some residual technical issues had spoiled this first take despite the distance between the instruments that was made possible by the huge recording studio. The direction of the microphones needed to be corrected. Elton did not care about any of that. He insisted on the producer listening to the tape again; he thought that even if the group played it again a thousand times, they would be unable to do better than they had on their first take. The musician won the argument, but maybe not the war. As a reprisal, Dudgeon relegated the number to the last spot on the track list. In the meantime, he had to remove the imperfections in the sound. He was able to erase and hide imperfections during the overdubbing phase, especially with the additions of the orchestra and the gospel choir, whose vocal fervor reached the top of the human register in the finale.

Elton John onstage at
Madison Square
Garden in August
1976. Ray Cooper can
be seen on the drums
in the background.

ALBUM

A SINGLE MAN

Shine on Through . Return to Paradise . I Don't Care . Big Dipper . It Ain't Gonna Be Easy .
Part-Time Love . Georgia . Shooting Star . Madness . Reverie . Song for Guy

RELEASE DATES
UK Release: October 16, 1978
Reference: Rocket Record Company—TRAIN 1
Best UK Chart Ranking: 8
US Release: October 1978
Reference: MCA Records—MCA-3065
Best US Chart Ranking: 15

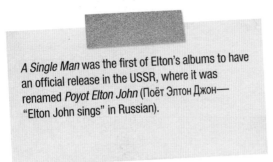

A Single Man was the first of Elton's albums to have an official release in the USSR, where it was renamed *Poyot Elton John* (Поёт Элтон Джон— "Elton John sings" in Russian).

OFF THE ROAD

As the title suggests, *A Single Man* describes a man alone and preparing for the most important turning point in his career. Elton, completely exhausted, gave his tour group a break from their duties in midsummer 1976, several months after the recording sessions for *Blue Moves*. At the annual meeting of his record label, which took place on October 22, 1976, Gus Dudgeon asked to speak. Strongly opposed to the management of the Rocket Record Company by the strongmen at the top, and in particular by John Reid, Bernie, and Elton himself, the producer banged the table and reeled off half a dozen problems that, in his view, needed to be remedied as a matter of urgency. When he finished, there was a long silence. "Well, quite honestly, Gus," John Reid said, "we don't agree with you." Then Gus answered, "So what you're saying is that you don't agree with anything I've proposed, and you understand that if these things aren't sorted out, I'm going to have to go?"[31] Combining actions with words, Gus left the room. He was expecting to be called back in, but this did not happen. Elton was of the view that after they had produced so many albums together, the time had possibly come for them to take a break, and he allowed the drama to play out without intervening.

This separation, and the disappointing results of *Blue Moves*, prompted Elton to reassess his partnership with Bernie as well. Did they still want the same things? Were they still on the same planet? The lyricist also had questions about their working relationship: "I didn't think we had any choice but to take a break," Bernie later confessed in an interview. "I had to run away from it, because I was frightened to keep going. I was frightened of failure. I'm sure drugs, alcohol, the geographical thing, it all contributed. But the base core of it was, I don't know if we knew what we wanted to do next. Or if we could do it. But we never argued about it."[31] In fact, the professional break was decided upon in common agreement between the two men, and it took place without acrimony. It did, however, bring to

an end a golden age of record making during which Elton had earned his stripes as a global star and joined the ranks of the richest recording artists in the world.

A World Waiting to Be Reinvented

Without Bernie and Gus, two of the biggest pillars in his world, Elton had to envisage what the rest of his musical journey was going to look like. But there was no hurry. He lived almost as a recluse in London. He only came out of his seclusion to give a handful of concerts with Ray Cooper at the Rainbow Theatre in Finsbury Park, north of London. He would also appear fleetingly onstage with China, a group signed to the Rocket Record Company that counted Davey Johnstone and Roger Pop as members. Even the death of Elvis, on August 16, 1977, did not bring Elton out of his torpor. He restricted himself to commenting, like everyone else, that Elvis was the King and that without him nothing would have happened for anyone in the world of rock. He was more shaken by the loss of his friend Marc Bolan, aged nearly thirty, one month later, on September 16, 1977. He attended Marc's funeral alongside other artists such as Rod Stewart, David Bowie, and Linda Lewis, before disappearing into the back of his Rolls-Royce.

Beyond this tragic event, neither the first spasms of the punk movement that might have left him obsolete, or the milestone of his thirtieth birthday, which he had just passed, seemed to reach him. He took advantage of his retreat as much as he could, trying out hair implants and taking part in *The Muppet Show* before becoming chairman of his beloved Watford soccer club.

In the autumn of 1977, Elton went to the United States to work on an album project with producer Thom Bell, one of the precursors of Philadelphia soul and a collaborator with R&B and soul groups like the Stylistics, the Delfonics, and the Spinners. But relations were strained, and the sessions were curtailed: Only a few numbers were produced, which would give

1978

rise to *The Thom Bell Sessions '77* EP two years later. Nineteen seventy-seven had been a decidedly strange year, and it produced only one compilation: *Elton John's Greatest Hits Volume II*, whose main merit was bringing a definite end to Elton's relationship with Dick James.

Life without Bernie

The biggest change in Elton's professional life was, of course, the absence of Bernie Taupin. Taking advantage of this break, Bernie spent time writing lyrics for the new album by his California companion in debauchery, Alice Cooper. That album, called *From the Inside*, was released on November 17, 1978. This did not prevent Elton and Bernie from meeting up from time to time, nipping in the bud any rumors of a falling-out, such as on the evening of March 1, 1977, at the Royal Albert Hall, where they watched transfixed as Frank Sinatra performed a cover of "Sorry Seems to Be the Hardest Word." The two men were even more shocked when "the Voice" asked the crowd to give them an ovation.

Elton considered picking things up with Bernie once more for the writing of his new album, which he planned to release in 1978, but eventually he turned to another lyricist. In May 1977, he called up Gary Osborne, now newly released from his recent work on Jeff Wayne's first album, which would come out on June 9, 1978. The two men had known each other for a long time (Osborne was the writer of the English-language lyrics for his friend Kiki Dee's French hit, "Amoureuse," in 1973) and they got on very well. They regularly took part in interminable

nocturnal poker or backgammon games, and TV viewing sessions washed down by good red wine. It was therefore natural that Elton would turn to Jeff for the first number, "Shine on Through," thereby opening up the way to an official collaboration on *A Single Man.*

A New Era

At the beginning of 1978, Elton was back at work. Finally, the siren call of showbiz had become too loud for him to ignore. He asked the sound engineer Clive Franks to support him as producer and bass player on the recording of a piece called "Ego," which was a song left over from his partnership with Bernie. Elton did consider working with Chris Squire, the bass player with Yes, but he was not available. The role therefore fell to poor Clive, who was thrown into the deep in more ways than one.

Elton chose to record his new opus in Gus Dudgeon's studio, the Mill, which was located in the Berkshire countryside. The producer had created the space three years earlier inside an old mill that straddled a backwater of the Thames. A waterwheel remained from the building's former use. It is represented on a stained-glass window on the control booth, a room of modest dimensions, with a low ceiling, and quite dark with its redbrick walls, dark beams, and rustic décor. The gigantic MCI 24 track console with its leather-bound edges and quadriphonic speakers filled the whole room. After Elton was there, the Mill also seduced Jimmy Page, and then Chris Rea, who each worked there in turn.

BONUS TRACK

The 1998 reissue of *A Single Man* offered
five bonus tracks: "Strangers," the single
"Ego" and its B-side, "Flinstone Boy," as well as
"I Cry at Night" and "Lovesick," which were the
B-sides of "Part-Time Love" and "Song for Guy,"
respectively. Some versions of the album *21 at
33* (1980) also included "Strangers" as a bonus.

Although Elton and Gus were not officially working together, there was no coldness between the two men. Drummer Steve Holley and guitarist Tim Renwick joined Elton and Clive for the "Ego" session, which came out as a single on March 21, 1978, with "Flinstone Boy" on the B-side. From that point on, the sessions for the album *A Single Man* began in earnest, and they were guided by a seemingly regenerated Elton. Three anchor points from his glorious past did stay on to work on the new album: Ray Cooper was present on the majority of the tracks, and Paul Buckmaster's talents as an arranger were required for six of the eleven pieces. Finally, the indefatigable guitarist, Davey Johnstone, was brought on to play on the song "Part-Time Love."

Slightly anxious about his comeback, Elton was leaving nothing to chance, and he extended the sessions from January to September 1978, even though the main part of the recording process was wrapped up by March. He knew that without Bernie and, to a lesser degree, without Gus, *A Single Man* would be scrutinized down to the smallest detail. By pure coincidence, and without expressing any resentment toward Bernie, the great majority of the lyrics in *A Single Man* took infidelity or separation as their subject.

For this new opus, Elton wanted to make a complete break from the past. The singer chose a very sober album cover, as though he was seeking to erase the flamboyance of his former persona. He is dressed with funereal sobriety, as though preparing to attend a Victorian burial, in a long overcoat, boots (with heels, not platforms!), and a top hat. He is shown standing with a cane in his hand in the majestic Long Walk that leads to Windsor Castle, which can be seen in the distance. His serious gaze is focused on photographer' Terry O'Neill's lens. The media, who were accustomed to focusing on the superficial aspects of Elton's persona, even to the extent of placing his musical value second, were quick to note that he appeared without glasses and thereby radically modified his image. The inside of the album cover shows him wearing a cap and a tweed jacket at the steering wheel of his vintage Jaguar. One thing was certain: Elton wanted to be freed from his glam rock past, which was now outdated, but he did not wish to jump onto the bandwagon of the punk or new wave movements. He was thus imposing a new persona as a member of an imaginary rock aristocracy.

Mixed Results

Musically, *A Single Man*, which came out on October 16, 1978, struggled to win the enthusiasm of the music press. Reviewers stigmatized its lack of homogeneity and the fact that some powerful ballads rubbed shoulders with some much more forgettable pieces. The journalist Stephen Holden, in the January 25, 1979, edition of *Rolling Stone*, did not beat around the bush: "If John and Taupin's final collaboration, *Blue Moves*, was a disastrous exercise in inflated pop rhetoric, *A Single Man* is an equally disastrous exercise in smug vapidity. The songs here are barely songs at all, but childish Neil Sedaka–style ditties with characterless little nursery rhymes for lyrics. [...] *A Single Man* demonstrates just how thin the line really is between disposable radio pop and elevator music and suggests that for all of Elton John's public whining about not being taken seriously, the only thing that's ever mattered to him is that the hits keep coming. May they not."[118] Against all odds, the album had a reasonably decent career, although it did not enable Elton to have another number one hit. It was, however, certified as a gold disc in the United States, where it reached fifteenth place on the *Billboard* charts.

As for the United Kingdom, it was "Song for Guy," which was written by Elton in homage to Guy Burchett, a young seventeen-year-old messenger with the Rocket Record Company who was killed in a motorbike accident, that attracted the public's attention on its way to fourth place in the British single charts. This tribute was much better than songs like "Georgia" and "Big Dipper," whose only particular feature of note was that it included backing vocals by the Watford soccer team as well as the mysteriously credited South Audley Street Girls' Choir, which consisted of the employees of the Rocket Record Company (whose head office was on South Audley Street). In the end, *A Single Man* went to number eight on the British charts.

Without making a huge fuss, Elton had just set out on the second part of his career.

THE THOM BELL SESSIONS

EP The Complete Thom Bell Sessions

Nice and Slow / 4:41

Country Love Song / 5:03

Shine on Through (Thom Bell Version) / 7:45

Mama Can't Buy You Love / 4:05

Are You Ready for Love / 8:16

Three Way Love Affair / 5:00

US Release: February 1989, on MCA Records (ref. MCA 39115)

Musicians

Elton John: vocals

Bobby Eli: guitar

Tony Bell: guitar, backing vocals

LeRoy M. Bell: guitar

Casey James: guitar, synthesizer, backing vocals

Bob Babbitt: bass

Charles Collins: drums

Larry Washington: percussion

MFSB: orchestra

Thom Bell: arrangements, direction, keyboards

Carla Benson, Evette Benton, Barbara Ingram, Bill Lamb, the Spinners: backing vocals

Recorded:

Kaye-Smith Studios, Seattle: October 1977

Overdubs: Sigma Sound Studios, Philadelphia

Technical Team

Producer: Thom Bell

Sound Engineer: Don Murray

Assistant Sound Engineers: Buzz Richmond, Jeff Stewart

Mixing: Thom Bell (1977); Clive Franks, Elton John (1979)

An Attempt at Soul

The *Thom Bell Sessions* took place at a particular moment for Elton. Virtually inactive musically since the recording of *Blue Moves* in March 1976, he had neither lyricist, musicians, nor producer with him. Gradually rediscovering a taste for creativity after a year and a half of silence, he felt ready to return to the studio to record a complete album. Having long reflected on who the ideal person would be to take charge of the control room, he approached Thom Bell, who had proven himself with groups that Elton liked, such as the Delfonics, the Stylistics, and the Spinners. Bell was one of the creators of the Philadelphia soul sound, the same one that had inspired "Philadelphia Freedom." It was precisely this musical direction that Elton intended to give to his new opus. But from the outset, he made something clear to Bell: Elton wanted to give him the keys to the van. In other words, he did not want to have any involvement in directing the project. For the first time, Elton wanted to allow himself to be guided and to release himself from all the pressure that weighed on him in each recording. Thom Bell was not sure he had really understood this, but Elton confirmed it to him: Thom would be the sole decision maker, including in choices of an artistic nature. Elton let him direct the sessions completely. The producer was amazed at having been handed such a carte blanche by an artist like Elton, who was known for his strong personality. He agreed with good grace, hoping that once through the studio door, the singer's natural instinct would click in again straightaway and that he would take back the reins that had been so easily handed over. This was not the case—quite the opposite, in fact. In October 1977, Thom Bell left Philadelphia for Seattle, where Kaye-Smith Studios were located. The studios, which had been chosen by Elton for the recording sessions, were the best equipped in the "Emerald City."

Elton Falls Back on Old Habits

Bernie was present for the recording sessions, but neither he nor Elton seemed to be in a mood to celebrate the reunion, as they were chilled in the presence of Thom Bell and seemed to be apprehensive about his reactions. Observing Elton's initial instructions to the letter, Bell behaved in a prescriptive way with the singer. He even gave him advice about how to sing, which none of his colleagues would have otherwise dared to do. Before Elton recorded his voice takes, the producer explained to him how to manage his breathing. He also told him that he often sang too high, and that he did not make sufficient use of his lower register, whereas his vocal range was more extensive than he had used hitherto. This came out particularly in "Are You Ready for Love," in which the voice has new depth and serenity, and on "Shine on Through," including

Elton John and Thom Bell at the recording sessions for the EP in Seattle in October 1977.

On *The Complete Thom Bell Sessions*, released in 1989, the original mixing by Thom Bell was chosen for "Are You Ready for Love," "Three Way Love Affair," and "Mama Can't Buy You Love," rather than the mixing done by Elton and Clive Franks for *The Thom Bell Sessions '77*, which was released in 1979.

the final sequence where the backing vocals come in, and where Elton adopts a more staccato rhythm 'n' blues singing style. In his autobiography, Elton explains: "I could experiment with music in ways I never had before. […] He [Thom] made me sing lower than I previously had and wrapped the songs in luxurious strings."[3] But at the time, his feelings were polarized: On the one hand, he was aware of his producer's legitimacy and the relevance of his advice; on the other hand, he really did not appreciate being treated like a beginner…even though he was the one who had facilitated this situation.

In a day and a half, Elton came to the end of his voice tracks on the six numbers recorded in these sessions. On the edge of disco, which was the rage in 1977, these pieces had the marks of Philadelphia soul: sugary, warm backing vocals, precise guitar playing, sparkling violin arrangements, and a comfortable groove. Apart from "Shine on Through," they were far removed from Elton's usual formula, and for a good reason: only the title song and "Nice and Slow" (constructed from unused lyrics from the *Rock of the Westies* period) were by him. "Country Love Song" was the work of Joseph B. Jefferson, who had worked with the Spinners and the O'Jays, while "Mama Can't Buy You Love," "Are You Ready for Love," and "Three Way Love Affair" were developed by Thom Bell's nephew LeRoy M. Bell, and by Casey James.

Although innovative, this recording session did not please Elton John: He found the result too soft and sorely lacking in energy. To make things worse, he realized that he was really not featured other than in a single verse in the song intended to be an A-side, "Are You Ready for Love," with the backing vocals completely eating up his performance on the rest of the piece. While a second session was to have been scheduled to make up a full album, Elton decided to sweep these recordings under the carpet and showed no interest in what became of them.

It would take nearly three years for these songs ("Are You Ready for Love," "Three Way Love Affair," and "Mama Can't Buy You Love") to be remixed by Elton John and Clive Franks, and distributed in 45 rpm maxi format in the United Kingdom with the title *The Thom Bell Sessions '77* and in the United States under the title *The Thom Bell Sessions*. They were also released in regular 45 rpm format: In the United Kingdom, "Are You Ready for Love" was split into two parts on one single, and another single featured "Mama Can't Buy You Love" with "Strangers" on the B-side. In the United States, "Mama Can't Buy You Love" was backed with "Three Way Love Affair." A decade later, all the 1977 tracks were released by MCA on the EP *The Complete Thom Bell Sessions* in February 1989.

SHINE ON THROUGH

Elton John, Gary Osborne / 3:45

Musicians
Elton John: lead and backing vocals, piano
Clive Franks: bass
Steve Holley: drums
Ray Cooper: tambourine
Paul Buckmaster: direction, arrangements
Orchestra: uncredited
Gary Osborne: backing vocals

Recorded
The Mill, Cookham, Berkshire, UK: January 1978

Technical Team
Producers: Clive Franks, Elton John
Sound Engineers: Phil Dunne, Stuart Epps, Clive Franks
Production Coordinators: David Croker, Alex Foster

Bernie Taupin and Alice Cooper. During his "exile" from Elton, Bernie wrote the Alice Cooper album *From the Inside* (1978).

Genesis and Lyrics

In the absence of Bernie Taupin, separated by the distance of an ocean, who had found a new drinking and musical partner in Alice Cooper, Elton came closer to Gary Osborne. There had been no question of a collaboration between the two friends before now (early June 1977). Elton, who was visiting the Osbornes, sat at the grand piano that belonged to Gary's father and started to play a sober, melancholic melody in *Eb*, in the vein of "Sorry Seems to Be the Hardest Word" or "Your Song." After Osborne showed enthusiasm for this composition, Elton suggested that he could write the lyrics for it. But Gary did not wish to interfere in the relationship between Elton and Bernie. Elton reassured him: He had already submitted this number to Bernie who, for now, had done nothing with it, as he was too busy with his new activities. Even though he guessed at a proposal motivated by jealousy, Gary was no less flattered, and lost no time getting out his book of words once Elton had left. He spent the next two days refining his lyrics, then submitted them to the singer the following weekend. He gave him a manuscript called "Smile That Smile." The singer was impressed. Following a few modifications suggested by Elton, the new lyrics were adopted, with the new title "Shine on Through." This was about a love that had withstood many tests. It began each paragraph with a different apostrophe: "oh my love," "oh my dear," then "oh my friend." This last word permits a different interpretation: a message to his friend, Bernie.

Production

Having been absent from recording studios for some time, Elton rediscovered his desire to return with "Shine on Through." It really was the catalyst in his new creative phase. With Thom Bell, Elton recorded an initial version of the song that emanates an almost religious serenity with a carefully applied reverb and finale somewhere between soul and gospel, which was in the spirit of Philly soul. The second version, the one included on *A Single Man*, was recorded on the first day of the new sessions in the wake of the single "Ego." It sounded much more "British," more precious—with its slightly higher key and refined strings created by Paul Buckmaster and his orchestra—and more "aristocratic."

RETURN TO PARADISE

Elton John, Gary Osborne / 4:16

Musicians: Elton John: lead and backing vocals, piano / **Tim Renwick:** acoustic guitar / **Clive Franks:** bass / **Steve Holley:** drums / **Ray Cooper:** marimba, shaker / **Henry Lowther:** trumpet / **Gary Osborne:** backing vocals / **Paul Buckmaster:** arrangements, direction / **Orchestra:** uncredited **Recorded:** The Mill, Cookham, Berkshire, UK: March 1978? **Technical Team: Producers:** Clive Franks, Elton John / **Sound Engineers:** Phil Dunne, Stuart Epps, Clive Franks / **Production Coordinators:** David Croker, Alex Foster

Genesis and Lyrics

The only piece on the album in which all the instrumentation is arranged by Paul Buckmaster, the swaying, sunny rhythm of "Return to Paradise" gives the impression that it is recycling "Island Girl," which appeared on *Rock of the Westies* in 1975. It could surely have been a hit if the punk wave had not contrived to make the previous generation of musicians, including Elton, seem obsolete. "Return to Paradise," a song about a vacation romance with its banal lyrics and fairly predictable melody, would also probably have made a young Reginald's hair stand up on end, given that he had balked against Long John Baldry's tendency toward mawkishness in 1967. Nobody was really convinced of its originality when it was being recorded. By way of proof, when Elton was preparing to record his vocals, Gary Osborne was seized by panic at the idea that the refrain would be too reminiscent of the Harry Belafonte 1957 hit, "Jamaica Farewell." Rapid adjustments were made. The recording was then supplemented by a bright solo by jazz trumpeter Henry Lowther, who had already worked with artists such as Bryan Ferry and Richard Thompson.

I DON'T CARE

Elton John, Gary Osborne / 4:24

Musicians: Elton John: vocals, piano, Clavinet / **Tim Renwick:** acoustic guitar / **Clive Franks:** bass / **Steve Holley:** drums / **Ray Cooper:** tambourine / **Vicky Brown, Stevie Lange, Gary Osborne, Joanne Stone, Chris Thompson:** backing vocals / **Paul Buckmaster:** arrangements, direction / **Orchestra:** uncredited **Recorded:** The Mill, Cookham, Berkshire, UK: March 26, 1978 **Technical Team: Producers:** Clive Franks, Elton John / **Sound Engineers:** Phil Dunne, Stuart Epps, Clive Franks / **Production Coordinators:** David Croker, Alex Foster

Genesis and Lyrics

Neither fundamentally disco nor soul, nor pop, nor really rock, "I Don't Care" is something of a mixture of all these genres but is above all marked by the return to Paul Buckmaster's tumbleweed strings and a vocal track from Elton that is lower than on his previous albums, a trend that was also followed on the rest

of *A Single Man.* The contrast between the urgency conveyed by the strings and the swaying guitars drowned in the flanger effect (which mixes two audio signals together but then delays one signal to often disorienting results) may be disconcerting. But the melodic effectiveness of the refrain is indisputable, and its hedonistic message unifying, by definition. The narrator is down on his luck: He has holes in his shoes, the bills are piling up, and his car refuses to start, but this does not demoralize him, as he seeks refuge in love. With these simple lyrics, Elton produces a jubilant piece of music in G major, in itself a joyful key par excellence, without getting bogged down in frills in order to develop it; two chords suffice, and a third (B minor) is added for the refrain. His piano playing is powerful, and the backing vocals inspired. Although it does not have the substance of a timeless hit, "I Don't Care" is by no means a disappointment.

BIG DIPPER

Elton John, Gary Osborne / 4:04

Musicians: Elton John: vocals, piano / **Tim Renwick:** electric guitar / **Clive Franks:** bass / **Steve Holley:** drums, percussion / **Ray Cooper:** tambourine / **John Crocker:** clarinet / **Jim Shepherd:** trombone / **Pat Halcox:** trumpet / **The South Audley Street Girls Choir, Watford Football Team:** backing vocals **Recorded:** The Mill, Cookham, Berkshire, UK: January 1978? **Technical Team: Producers:** Clive Franks, Elton John / **Sound Engineers:** Phil Dunne, Stuart Epps, Clive Franks / **Production Coordinators:** David Croker, Alex Foster

Genesis and Lyrics

A playful clarinet appears supported by roguish brass, a sliding bass, some electric guitar notes, and a very laid-back groove that mixes rock and blues, and it all works! A New Orleans ambiance takes hold in this audacious, thinly disguised story of a gay flirt, with the Watford soccer team (presided over by Elton) ironically turning up to overlay their masculine backing vocals. "It had to be slightly disguised," Gary Osborne said about the lyrics, which were carefully adapted from the 1928 standard "Makin' Whoopee," written by Gus Kahn and Walter Donaldson. "Because, firstly, it was 1978. And secondly, we wanted the Watford football team to sing on it and we couldn't have them singing words that were...too poofy. I was trying to put a bit of Elton's wicked sense of humor into his songs."[31] This relates to two men with "big dippers"—such a flagrant metaphor requires no further explanation. This was also probably what the Russian authorities thought, when, despite the very avant-garde treatment of the song, they simply removed it from the version of *A Single Man* issued in the USSR.

Elton John convinced his Watford football team (shown here in 1982) to take part in the backing vocals on "Georgia."

IT AIN'T GONNA BE EASY

Elton John, Gary Osborne / 8:28

Musicians: **Elton John:** vocals, piano / **Tim Renwick:** electric guitar / **Clive Franks:** bass / **Steve Holley:** drums / **Ray Cooper:** tambourine, vibraphone / **Paul Buckmaster:** arrangements, direction / **Orchestra:** uncredited **Recorded:** The Mill, Cookham, Berkshire, UK: March 1978 **Technical Team:** Producers: Clive Franks, Elton John / **Sound Engineers:** Phil Dunne, Stuart Epps, Clive Franks / **Production Coordinators:** David Croker, Alex Foster

Genesis and Lyrics

A haunting blues ballad, "It Ain't Gonna Be Easy," in its running time of more than eight minutes, deploys a warning from a man to his lover who has been unfaithful: acting as though nothing had happened and starting again with a peaceful relationship "ain't gonna be easy."

Gary Osborne's lyrics are not the most original, and the song in itself is long, some would say too long (it originally ran twelve minutes!), because this also emphasizes its weaknesses. Steve Holley's playing on the drums is sometimes clumsy; the guitar playing by Tim Renwick, former member of Junior's Eyes, who contributed to David Bowie's *Space Oddity*, does not mesh straightaway with the subject and struggles in comparison with the richness of Davey Johnstone's playing, while Elton's improvised singing from the sixth minute does not contribute much, such as with the disastrous scat singing around 7:25, or of the multiple "yeahs" that only weigh down the final sequence. When listening to "It Ain't Gonna Be Easy," it is impossible not

to think of the minor mode intro on "Sixty Years On," released on *Elton John* eight years earlier, or even the piano chords in this song (which were even more evident in the live version on the album *11-17-70* in 1971). The strings entry on the second bridge is also incredibly reminiscent of another piece on the *Elton John* album, "The King Must Die."

PART-TIME LOVE

Elton John, Gary Osborne / 3:16

Musicians: **Elton John:** vocals, piano / **Tim Renwick:** electric guitar / **Davey Johnstone:** electric guitar, backing vocals / **Clive Franks:** bass / **Steve Holley:** drums / **Ray Cooper:** tambourine, congas / **Vicky Brown, Stevie Lange, Gary Osborne, Joanne Stone, Chris Thompson:** backing vocals / **Paul Buckmaster:** arrangements, direction / **Orchestra:** uncredited **Recorded:** The Mill, Cookham, Berkshire, UK: March 1978 **Technical Team:** Producers: Clive Franks, Elton John / **Sound Engineers:** Phil Dunne, Stuart Epps, Clive Franks / **Production Coordinators:** David Croker, Alex Foster **Single Release:** *Part-Time Love / I Cry at Night* **UK Release:** October 4, 1978, on Rocket Record Company (ref. XPRES 1) **Best UK Chart Ranking:** 15 **US Release:** November 1979, on MCA Records (ref. MCA-40973) **Best US Chart Ranking:** 22

Genesis and Lyrics

With "Little Jeannie" in 1980 and "Blue Eyes" in 1982, "Part-Time Love" is probably one of the most popular and also one of the most effective tracks that Elton John and Gary Osborne

Guitarist Tim Renwick (right) and Gavin Sutherland, who helped make up the group Sutherland Brothers & Quiver.

managed to compose. It was also chosen to be the first single off the album (except in the United States, where it was released a year later), twelve days before the official release of the album itself. Providing a joyful treatment of adultery and full of spirit, the lyrics kept it from being included in the Russian version of *A Single Man*. This enthusiastic rocker, bathed in backing vocals with a gospel ambiance, also has the benefit of Davey Johnstone's only contribution to the album, a luminous and inspired guitar solo. Paul Buckmaster is on "autopilot" this time with the orchestral arrangements, especially with the predictable albeit still effective strings, while Clive Franks's bass stands out with a rounded, dancing groove. Although the following single, "Song for Guy," did better in the British charts, "Part-Time Love" remains one of the better numbers on the album.

GEORGIA

Elton John, Gary Osborne / 4:50

Musicians: Elton John: vocals, piano, harmonium, organ / **Tim Renwick**: electric guitar (Leslie cabinet), mandolin / **B. J. Cole**: pedal steel guitar / **Clive Franks**: bass / **Steve Holley**: drums / **Ray Cooper**: tambourine / **The South Audley Street Girls Choir, Watford Football Team**: backing vocals **Recorded:** The Mill, Cookham, Berkshire, UK: March 1978 **Technical Team: Producers:** Clive Franks, Elton John / **Sound Engineers:** Phil Dunne, Stuart Epps, Clive Franks / **Production Coordinators:** David Croker, Alex Foster **Single Release:** *Johnny B. Goode / Georgia* **US Release:** December 1979, on MCA Records (ref. MCA-41159) **Best US Chart Ranking:** Did Not Chart

Genesis and Lyrics

The second number to include the contribution of the Watford soccer team on backing vocals, "Georgia" stands out as the best song on the album, with its elegant introduction and Elton's multiple appearances on piano, harmonium, and organ. Very fortunately, the soccer players are not the key contributors to the backing vocals, who provide all the gospel dimension to the song. In fact, the South Audley Street Girls Choir took control and provided grace and lightness. As an ode to this particular Southern state, "Georgia" is based upon a personification of this territory, whose charm is set out in bas relief in its comparisons with other states, such as Maine or California. Gary Osborne instills a melancholy that is musically translated by the warm pedal steel guitar of B. J. Cole, a sonority that had not appeared in an Elton John recording since "Tiny Dancer" in 1971. Cole finds an Elton changed from having gone through the wringer of all the excesses of superstardom. But their musical understanding had remained intact, and it was translated into the excellent vibrations of the song.

Elton John, Rod Stewart, and Stewart's partner Alana, at Studio 54.

SHOOTING STAR

Elton John, Gary Osborne / 2:44

Musicians: Elton John: lead and backing vocals, Fender Rhodes / Herbie Flowers: acoustic bass / Steve Holley: drums / Ray Cooper: shaker / John Crocker: tenor saxophone **Recorded:** The Mill, Cookham, Berkshire, UK: March 1978 **Technical Team:** Producers: Clive Franks, Elton John / **Sound Engineers:** Phil Dunne, Stuart Epps, Clive Franks / **Production Coordinators:** David Croker, Alex Foster

Genesis and Lyrics

It was probably with this evanescent saxophone sprinkled ballad in mind particularly that the journalist Stephen Holden, in the January 25, 1979, issue of *Rolling Stone*, suggested that Elton's music was becoming more suitable for use as elevator music. Even so, this was one of the singer's favorite songs, and he wanted to use his suave and melancholic voice to transcribe a sort of emotional "descent." The jazz color added by the musicians is perfectly compatible with the drifting mood of Elton's Fender Rhodes, this instrument with its crystalline harmonics favored by the likes of Ray Charles, Ray Manzarek (the Doors), and Billy Preston. The delicate lines contributed by John Crocker's saxophone and the generous bass of Herbie Flowers, who had not appeared in Elton's world since *Madman Across the Water* in 1971, effectively seem to offer the singer a form of consolation. Derived from the same musical vein as pieces such as "Come Down in Time" on *Tumbleweed Connection* in 1970, or "Idol" on *Blue Moves* in 1976, "Shooting Star" might have seemed out of place on *A Single Man*. But the tragedy contained in the words of Gary Osborne (a narrator in love with a "shooting star"), as well as Elton's fine and audacious performance, prepare the way for one of his greatest ballads, "Blue Eyes," which came along in 1982.

1978

MADNESS

Elton John, Gary Osborne / 5:53

Musicians: Elton John: vocals, piano / Tim Renwick: electric guitar / Clive Franks: bass / Steve Holley: drums / Ray Cooper: tambourine, congas, timbales / Paul Buckmaster: orchestral arrangements / Orchestra: uncredited **Recorded:** The Mill, Cookham, Berkshire, UK: March 1978 **Technical Team:** Producers: Clive Franks, Elton John / Sound Engineer: Phil Dunne, Stuart Epps, Clive Franks / Production Coordinators: David Croker, Alex Foster.

Genesis and Lyrics

Rarely did an Elton John song incorporate so many contradictory sentiments: musically jubilatory, despite its minor key (D), Clive Franks's elastic bass, and Ray Cooper's frenetic congas, "Madness" induces a slight feeling of malaise when one listens to the lyrics. It addresses the problems of the world, and includes many terrifying refences to fires, catastrophes, poverty, war, and a "final countdown," "walls [that] collapse," a "child screams out in fear," or "the smell of death [that] hangs in the air." Without doubt, this "world gone mad" shows the darkest thoughts Elton John ever recorded. He has no difficulty in transcribing the ambient chaos depicted by Gary Osborne, who was visibly nostalgic for his work on the concept album *Jeff Wayne's Musical Version of the War of the Worlds*, completed shortly before his collaboration with Elton. At no point does the lyricist seek to sweeten his words, marking his complete difference from Bernie Taupin, who enjoyed abstract metaphors. Elton creates for this number the only rock oasis on the album with the discoid support of strings arranged by Paul Buckmaster. No happy endings for this number, because "nothing survives of all those lives."

REVERIE

Elton John / 0:54

Musicians: Elton John: piano / Paul Buckmaster: ARP synthesizer **Recorded:** The Mill, Cookham, Berkshire, UK: March 1978 **Technical Team:** Producers: Clive Franks, Elton John / Sound Engineers: Phil Dunne, Stuart Epps, Clive Franks / Production Coordinators: David Croker, Alex Foster

Genesis and Lyrics

Less than a minute was all the time needed by Elton to unleash all of his melancholy. It ably prepares the terrain, and even serves as a sort of introduction for "Song for Guy," which is surely the most moving number on the album. More melodically complex than it seems, this gentle and enchanting bagatelle, inspired by Elton's long hours of classical studies, particularly the repertoire of Chopin, is not lacking in charm. After its recording, Elton was unable to conceal a slight smile, indicating his satisfaction and also his emotion.

SONG FOR GUY

Elton John / 6:54

Musicians: Elton John: vocals, piano, Mellotron, synthesizers (Polymoog, Solina String Synthesizer) / Clive Franks: bass / Ray Cooper: chimes, shaker, rhythm box **Recorded:** The Mill, Cookham, Berkshire, UK: September 1978 **Technical Team:** Producers: Clive Franks, Elton John / Sound Engineer: Phil Dunne, Stuart Epps, Clive Franks / Production Coordinators: David Croker, Alex Foster **Single Release:** *Song for Guy / Lovesick* **UK Release:** November 28, 1978, on Rocket Record Company (ref. XPRES 5) **Best UK Chart Ranking:** 4 **US Release:** March 1979, on MCA Records (ref. MCA-40993) **Best US Chart Ranking:** 37

Genesis and Lyrics

One Sunday, in a bad mood, and with a face like thunder, Elton sat at his piano and started to play a few notes. A little phrase had been running around in his head for quite a while: "Life isn't everything." As though by magic, this fit like a glove with the melancholic melody he was imagining. When he learned the next day that Guy Burchett, a young seventeen-year-old courier employed by Rocket, had died in a motorbike accident at the very moment when he had been creating this piece—composed in the same key as "Let It Be"—Elton decided to dedicate the song to him. He called it "Song for Guy." The homage profoundly touched Ann Spano, the young man's mother.

Production

In the studio, Elton added several layers of synthesizer to add an aerial dimension to the melody. For this he used the Solina String Synthesizer by ARP Instruments, of which only a hundred or so were produced. This model, which is presented as a combination of the Solina String Ensemble and the ARP explorer, produced a singular polyphonic sound that enables it to emulate the sounds of trumpets, flutes, or clarinets. This synthesizer part is sublimated by the fairylike chimes of Ray Cooper, while a rhythm box discreetly marks the tempo of this essentially instrumental piece. It is only in the last moments that Elton's distant and ghostlike voice appears and proclaims the only phrase written for the occasion, like a mantra. Having been cut down by one minute, "Song for Guy" rose to fourth place in the British charts, but the American label released the single the following year, triggering Elton's obstinate wrath. Its 110th-place finish led him to reconsider his partnership with MCA. "My favorite track from *A Single Man* is 'Song for Guy'—it was different, it was an instrumental, it was just me doing everything. It meant so much to me, that track. It was a huge record in England and everywhere else in the world, but it was my first single that didn't make the Top 100 in the U.S. That was the reason I got bloody-minded and left MCA Records. I wanted to have an instrumental on the charts. They said, 'You can't.' So I said, 'Fuck you, I'm joining Geffen' [which he did with *The Fox* in 1981]. 'In retrospect, that was a big mistake.'"[35]

Elton was photographed by Terry O'Neill for the cover of the "Ego" single, which was released in March 1978.

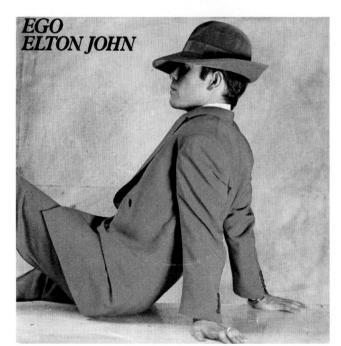

EGO
ELTON JOHN

SIDE A

EGO

Elton John, Bernie Taupin / 4:00

Single: *Ego / Flinstone Boy* **UK Release:** March 21, 1978, on Rocket Record Company (ref. ROKN 538) **Best UK Chart Ranking:** 34 **US Release:** March 1978, on MCA Records (ref. MCA-40892) **Best US Chart Ranking:** 34 **Musicians:** Elton John: vocals, piano, synthesizer, organ / **Tim Renwick:** guitar / **Clive Franks:** bass / **Steve Holley:** drums / **Ray Cooper:** tambourine, vibraphone, train whistle / **Paul Buckmaster:** direction, arrangements / **Orchestra:** uncredited **Recorded:** The Mill, Cookham, Berkshire, UK: January–March 1978 **Technical Team:** Producers: Clive Franks, Elton John / **Sound Engineers:** Phil Dunne, Stuart Epps, Clive Franks / **Production Coordinators:** David Croker, Alex Foster

Genesis and Lyrics

While he enjoyed the status of pop superstar and readily acknowledged his egomaniacal shortcomings, Elton undertakes to do the same for some of his contemporaries: "It's dedicated to the Jaggers and Bowies of this world," the pianist said, "and especially to Mr. McCartney."[11] He also acknowledges his part in the responsibility for the media circus perpetuated by rock stars and assumes the first person in singing these lyrics, written by Bernie Taupin during the *Blue Moves* period: "Inflate my ego gently / Tell them heaven sent me."

Production

The first song recorded during the *A Single Man* sessions, "Ego" marks the baptism of Clive Franks as producer. Far from having sought this role, the sound engineer did not understand that Elton wanted to make him the prime mover for this disc. But the singer had sufficient faith in his songs and people's capacity to exceed themselves when he presented them with a fait accompli. Clive was well placed to understand this, as he had himself been propelled to the position of sound engineer for the live performances…So, conscientiously, Clive set to his task, stuck small bits of tape to each of the faders on his mixing table

noting the names of the instruments, as he had done for the concerts, and undertook to treat each song with care but without flourish. When Elton joyfully presented this first song, he was met with enthusiasm from his new producer, who thought it sounded like music for a silent film. Elton liked this comparison and went back to his Steinway grand piano. Tim Renwick, the former member of the Sutherland Brothers & Quiver, and Steve Holley, a future member of Wings, were recruited for the new sessions. Alongside these musicians, experienced in the demands of studio work, Clive Franks felt somewhat unconfident. He recorded his bass parts for "Ego" live while seated in the control room, directly plugged into the console; this was a luxury he would not allow for the other musicians. Given the numerous key changes and tempo of this melodically rich song, changing from a straight 4/4 to a waltz rhythm, he sweated a lot, but came through in the end. However, the bass player–producer was not yet fully at one with his playing. He had a tendency to turn down his bass track on numerous occasions. But each time Elton came back to turn up the volume. At the end of the piece the singer was so pleased with this song that he decided to continue composing and recording, gripped by what he defined later as creative "diarrhea."

FOR ELTON ADDICTS

"Ego" did not appear in CD format until 1990, when the box set *To Be Continued…* was released. It was also included in the reissue of *A Single Man*, which came out from Mercury in 1998.

FLINSTONE BOY

Elton John / 4:13

Single: *Ego / Flinstone Boy* **UK Release:** March 21, 1978, on Rocket Record Company (ref. ROKN 538) **Best UK Chart Ranking:** 34 **US Release:** March 1978, on MCA Records (ref. MCA-40892) **Best US Chart Ranking:** 34 **Musicians:** Elton John: lead and backing vocals, piano, synthesizer, organ / **Tim Renwick:** guitar / **Clive Franks:** bass / **Steve Holley:** drums **Recorded:** The Mill, Cookham, Berkshire, UK: March 1978 **Technical Team:** Producers: Clive Franks, Elton John / **Sound Engineers:** Phil Dunne, Stuart Epps, Clive Franks / **Production Coordinators:** David Croker, Alex Foster

Recorded during the sessions for "Ego," for which it served as an inoffensive B-side, "Flinstone Boy" is of little interest. Elton, to whom we owe both words and music of this slightly lazy number, later admitted that before deciding to work with Gary Osborne as lyricist, he had written frenetically, as though in order to cope better with digesting the temporary dissolution of his partnership with Bernie Taupin. He was so pleased with the way "Flinstone Boy" had gone, which is a surreptitiously subversive piece about lost love, that he even very briefly considered writing the lyrics for an entire album, before returning to his senses: "[My lyrics] might come out very raw and very crude," he reasoned. "Also, I'm quite positive it would be extremely bitter. There have been periods in my life where, if I'd had the ability to write good lyrics and write them down, they would have been quite heavy statements for me to make, but I just couldn't do it so I didn't even bother to try. If I had, I would've probably ended up in jail with libel suits."[31] This piece, which was recorded quickly, has some endearing qualities: The backing vocals work well, as do the catchy acoustic guitar and the particularly stoical bass line. But the synthesizer overdubs are painful, and the melody is completely forgettable.

I CRY AT NIGHT

Elton John, Bernie Taupin / 3:16

Single: *Part-Time Love / I Cry at Night* **UK Release:** October 4, 1978, on Rocket Record Company (ref. XPRES 1) **Best UK Chart Ranking:** 15 **US Release:** November 1979, on MCA Records (ref. MCA-40973) **Best US Chart Ranking:** 22 **Musicians:** Elton John: lead and backing vocals, piano, electric piano **Recorded:** The Mill, Cookham, Berkshire, UK: March 1978 **Technical Team:** Producers: Clive Franks, Elton John / **Sound Engineers:** Phil Dunne, Stuart Epps, Clive Franks / **Production Coordinators:** David Croker, Alex Foster

On March 25, 1978, Elton celebrated his thirty-first birthday at the Vicarage Road stadium, and watched the victory of his club, the Watford Football Club. Having tasted a cake in the shape of the Rocket Record logo, made by the wife of coach Graham Taylor, the singer was on cloud nine. He went to the studio the following afternoon. Along with the numbers "Hello Campers" (which was quickly abandoned), "Dreamboat" (which can be found on the B-side of "Kiss the Bride," released in 1983) and "I Don't Care," Elton produced in the same session the heartbreaking "I Cry at Night," a piece whose lyrics had been written by Bernie Taupin during the *Blue Moves* sessions. The lyricist seems to be referring to his stricken marriage and uses numerous metaphors to explain that nothing has any meaning ("This house that I live in has no reason"). He assumes responsibility for his own mistakes and acknowledges having not been present often enough because he had been "ten years a slave to rock and roll." The musical transcription by Elton is extremely melancholic: alone at the piano, which he plays strongly with powerful chords, still keeping back the volume for the more delicate passages, he enriches his very assured vocal line with instinctive backing vocals, and then adds some electric piano notes to fill out the melody. Probably too somber to be included straight into the album, the song failed as the B-side to "Part-Time Love" and was rehabilitated as a bonus track on the reissue of *A Single Man* by Mercury in 1998.

LOVESICK

Elton John, Bernie Taupin / 3:59

Musicians: Elton John: vocals, piano / Tim Renwick: electric guitar / Clive Franks: bass / Steve Holley: drums / Ray Cooper: percussion / Paul Buckmaster: direction, arrangements / Orchestra: uncredited **Recorded:** The Mill, Cookham, Berkshire, UK: March 1978? **Technical Team:** Producers: Clive Franks, Elton John / Sound Engineers: Phil Dunne, Stuart Epps, Clive Franks / Production Coordinators: David Croker, Alex Foster **Single:** *Song for Guy / Lovesick* **UK Release:** November 28, 1978, on Rocket Record Company (ref. XPRES 5) **Best UK Chart Ranking:** 4 **US Release:** March 1979, on MCA Records (ref. MCA-40993) **Best US Chart Ranking:** 37

"Lovesick," as its name suggests, is one of the numbers written by Bernie Taupin at the time of his divorce from Maxine Feibelman, during the sessions for the album *Blue Moves*. The words naturally relate this profound conjugal crisis and the lyricist's state of mind, having become "lovesick" and tired of having "heard too many lies." Initially released as the B-side on the single "Song for Guy," "Lovesick" did not find a place on *A Single Man*, but it was included in the remastered version of the album in 1998. Musically, this is a rapid piece, with several variations in tempo, with its hybrid disco and soul ambiance. The percussion by Ray Cooper stands out in particular, as do the strings arranged by Paul Buckmaster. The strings, which start out timidly, become increasingly edgy, flighty, and thus also increasingly interesting as the piece develops. But the real moment of bravura, is of course the long electric guitar solo performed by Tim Renwick; it must be placed at the peak of his personal pantheon, on a level with his contribution to the Al Stewart hit "Year of the Cat," in 1976.

STRANGERS

Elton John, Bernie Taupin / 4:47

Single: *Victim of Love / Strangers* **UK Release:** September 14, 1979, on Rocket Record Company (ref. XPRES 21) **Best UK Chart Ranking:** Did Not Chart **US Release:** September 14, 1979, on MCA Records (ref. MCA 41126) **Best US Chart Ranking:** 31 **Musicians:** Elton John: lead and backing vocals, piano / Tim Renwick: electric guitar / Clive Franks: bass / Steve Holley: drums / Ray Cooper: vibraphone **Recorded:** The Mill, Cookham, Berkshire, UK: March 1978 **Technical Team:** Producer: Clive Franks, Elton John / Sound Engineer: Clive Franks, Phil Dunne, Stuart Epps / Production Coordinators: Alex Foster, David Croker / Mastering: Ian Cooper (Utopia Studios, London)

Recorded on the same day as "Georgia," "Strangers" is a new song in the story of a love that is coming apart. Although the metaphors used are evocative of Bernie Taupin's work, it was in fact Gary Osborne who wrote the lyrics. In it he describes two people drifting apart and meeting again as strangers to each other, even reaching the conclusion that they were "strangers from the start," although they had together completed "the long and the lonely climb." This very melancholic slow number, with its equally slow tempo, is mainly based on Elton's busy piano part and the edgy guitar of Tim Renwick. Despite an interesting contribution on vibraphone by Ray Cooper, the song quickly turns to marshmallow, and the melody is cruelly lacking in relief. This is undoubtedly why "Strangers" was not included on the track list of *A Single Man* and had to wait until September 14, 1979—after the success of "Mama Can't Buy You Love" (a single from *The Thom Bell Sessions*)—to be given a second chance as the B-side on the "Victim of Love" single release from the eponymous album.

ALBUM

VICTIM OF LOVE

Johnny B. Goode . Warm Love in a Cold World . Born Bad .
Thunder in the Night . Spotlight . Street Boogie . Victim of Love

RELEASE DATES
UK Release: October 13, 1979
Reference: Rocket Record Company—HISPD 125
Best UK Chart Ranking: 41
US Release: October 13, 1979
Reference: MCA Records—MCA-5104
Best US Chart Ranking: 35

In May 1979, Elton performed in
Leningrad and Moscow. He was one of
the first pop stars authorized to perform
on the other side of the iron curtain.

FOR ELTON ADDICTS

The original title for *Victim of Love* was *Thunder in the Night*, the title of another song in the track list.

THE DISCO FLOP

After a year of almost no concerts, sales that were stalling (*A Single Man* reached only fifteenth place in the United States), and a spell in the hospital following a panic attack that could probably be ascribed to his state of extreme exhaustion, Elton John was in a hurry to turn the page on 1978. Still quick to put himself at risk, he launched into a world tour from February 5 to May 28, 1979, with only Ray Cooper accompanying him. This was quite a gamble, which Elton took on in order to feel the adrenaline and excitement of stage performance that he felt he was starting to lose. The singer found this tour rather fulfilling because he was able to see his songs in a different light, and because the public enjoyed these more intimate performances. Elton also stopped in some countries, like France, Spain, Israel, and the then-named USSR for the first time. He obtained authorization to perform on the other side of the Iron Curtain after an emissary from the Soviet Ministry of Culture attended one of his concerts at England's Oxford Theatre on April 17, 1979. Then he confirmed his visit from May 21 to 24 in Leningrad, and May 25 to 28 in Moscow. This was a historic moment for a country that was relatively cut off from Western culture at the time. Elton John had to withstand certain complaints from the authorities the day after his initial concert—these remonstrances were mostly about kicking his piano stool around and playing "Back in the USSR" by the Beatles—but the series of shows was a real success, and that certainly did not escape the attention of the Western press. Elton's appearance in Moscow gave rise to another historical event when his final concert on May 28 was broadcast live by the BBC throughout Europe. It was the first satellite connection set up between the two blocs. This legendary recording, which had long been circulating in a pirated version, was officially released under the title *Live from Moscow* on January 24, 2020.

Elton John: The Performer

In the wake of the release of the 45 rpm maxi format of *The Thom Bell Sessions '77*, Elton John went to Grasse, in France's Côte d'Azur, to compose some new pieces. He returned with enough material to fill the forthcoming disk, *21 at 33*, as well as some of the following one, *The Fox*. However, another album would be created before these two were released: *Victim of Love*. This arose from a suggestion by producer Pete Bellotte, who had earned a reputation through his collaboration with Giorgio Moroder on several of Donna Summer's hits, including "Love to Love You Baby," "I Feel Love," and "Hot Stuff." Elton had known him for a long time; the two men had become friends in Hamburg in March 1966, when Reginald was performing there with Bluesology, and Pete was there as part of the Sinners. In April 1978, Bellotte asked the singer if he would be willing to record a disco album. Against all expectations, Elton said yes. Although he had never played disco, Elton was familiar with this musical genre, to which he would dance away the night at wild parties inside New York's famed Studio 54, the most eccentric and selective nightclub of the era, which was frequented by the likes of Liza Minnelli, Andy Warhol, Lou Reed, Mick Jagger, and Rod Stewart. Elton did impose some conditions upon Bellotte, which were curiously reminiscent of those he imposed two years earlier on Thom Bell: Bellotte was to take total charge of supervision of the disk, on which Elton would only be the performer. He would not play any instrument or compose. "I'd just sing whatever Pete and his staff writers came up with," Elton wrote in his autobiography. "I suspect the thinking behind this idea was influenced by the fact that I only owed my American label, Uni, a couple more albums. I was still furious about them refusing to release 'Song for Guy' and had decided that I wanted to get out of my contract as quickly as possible, with the minimum of effort."[3]

1979

Pete Bellotte (shown here on the left alongside singer Andrea and Giorgio Moroder in 1979) was at the helm during the *Victim of Love* shipwreck.

Elton had a very lucid awareness that he would be panned by reviewers for compromising himself in an opportunistic project, and for selling out to the sirens of disco, but he did not care. He decided that he was going to do what he wanted, regardless of the opinions of outsiders. If he had cared about such things, he would not have just done an intimate tour with Ray Cooper, and that had worked out relatively well.

An Impressive Commando Unit

In August 1979, Elton met Bellotte in Munich, at Musicland Studios, which was housed in the basement of the Arabella High-Rise Building. The studios were owned by Giorgio Moroder, and they had hosted the recordings of *It's Only Rock 'n Roll* by the Rolling Stones, *Stormbringer* by Deep Purple, and *Presence* by Led Zeppelin. Bellotte presented Elton with seven songs that would make up the future album—the shortest album in the star's discography at a scant thirty-six minutes. The producer called upon some fine professionals for the recording.

Keith Forsey, a drummer and percussionist from London, who had played for some years with German rock legends Udo Lindenberg and Amon Düül II, both pioneers of so-called krautrock. At the end of the 1970s, he climbed aboard the disco train and worked with La Bionda and Boney M. His links with the German scene and his affinity for this musical style led him to work with Giorgio Moroder and Pete Bellotte on some Donna Summer albums, including the famous *Bad Girls* in early 1979. He stands out for his precise, clinical drumming, and he had been actively involved in writing hits, notably "Hot Stuff." As a close colleague of Bellotte's, he naturally formed part of this adventure.

For the bass, Bellotte called upon a young player barely into his twenties, whose youth and stunning potential encouraged him to try out all kinds of experiences: this was Marcus Miller, future bass legend, who would shortly earn his colors alongside Miles Davis. Paulinho da Costa, the most famous percussionist of his generation, who would appear on hundreds of albums ranging from *Thriller* by Michael Jackson to *Dirty Dancing*, was also called in at the last minute. Other studio musicians completed the team: Roy Davies and Thor Baldursson were put on keyboards, Craig Snyder and Tim Cansfield were on lead guitar and rhythm guitar. Since most of the work had been done in advance, Elton spent only eight hours working on the album; this was enough time to record his vocals in a single session. Elton departed just as he had arrived, leaving Bellotte to handle the overdubs on his own. This took place in Los Angeles, at Rusk Sound Studios, and consisted mainly of the addition of female backing vocals with contributions from Stephanie Spruill, Julia Tillman Waters, and Maxine Willard Waters. Three pieces received particular attention during these sessions: "Johnny B. Goode," the main number that opens the album, was augmented by a vibrant saxophone solo by Lenny Pickett, who had performed with his colleagues from Tower of Power on *Caribou* in 1974. The Doobie Brothers' Patrick Simmons and Michael McDonald—whom Elton had joined onstage on June 29, 1975, to perform "Listen to the Music" at the Oakland Coliseum—contributed their gentle voices to the backing vocals of "Victim of Love." Last but not least: Steve Lukather joined the crew. At just twenty-two, he was a young guitarist leading the group Toto, which had just arrived in the United States with its first eponymous album (that went to number nine on the *Billboard* charts). Lukather would eventually sell 40 million albums and win five Grammy Awards, and he was also the pyrotechnician responsible for the famous guitar line on Michael Jackson's "Beat It." His playing, which is as melodic as it is flamboyant, made him a guest artist who was very much in demand.

Marcus Miller, the bass virtuoso, managed to swim to the surface in the midst of the syrupy sweetness of *Victim of Love*.

He shows his exceptional dexterity on "Warm Love in a Cold World" and "Born Bad."

Saturday Night Hypothermia

A black-and-white photo adorns the *Victim in Love* album sleeve. Only part of Elton's face is visible, and, once again, he's swallowed up by a pair of futuristic tinted glasses. The image, shot by David Bailey, perfectly symbolizes the album: an unrecognizable Elton looks bland, colorless, with seemingly avant-garde intentions that are terribly behind the times. Indeed, disco was already falling out of fashion by the time this album was released.

"Not everything on *Victim of Love* was terrible," Elton said by way of defending himself in his autobiography, "if the title track had come on at Studio 54, I'd have danced to it—but making an album in bad faith like that is never a good idea. No matter what you do, it somehow gets into the music:

you can just tell it's not coming from an honest place. Furthermore, it was released at the end of 1979, just as a huge backlash against disco started in the States, with particular venom reserved for rock artists who had dared to dabble in the genre."[3] *Victim of Love* eventually went to thirty-fifth in the charts in the United States, and to forty-first in the United Kingdom. Elton had not experienced such a level of indifference since *Madman Across the Water*, which achieved the same ranking in his homeland in 1971. Unsurprisingly, the reviews completely stalled the disc. Stephen Holden, of *Rolling Stone*, called it "empty of ideas."[119]

Recorded very quickly and released only two months later, *Victim of Love* received no promotion. Elton never performed any of the seven songs on the album, with the exception of his cover of "Johnny B. Goode," which he performed on the Australian television show *Countdown* on December 2, 1979.

Elton and Ray Cooper in front of the Peterhof Palace in Saint Petersburg during their tour of the Soviet Union in May 1979.

Ray Cooper has fun playing onstage at the Royal Albert Hall on September 20, 1983.

RAY COOPER:
PERCUSSION PhD

Ray Cooper entered Elton John's life when he was invited to join the 1971 recording sessions for *Madman Across the Water*. The percussionist was at the start of his career as a studio musician, which was subsequently enriched by a series of collaborations with some prestigious names, including Harry Nilsson, the Rolling Stones, Carly Simon, and America.

From the outset, Ray showed himself to be a consummate professional, although he was particularly invested in Elton's project, which he tackled like it was just any other session. It should be said that his contribution was initially restricted to adding some percussion on the title song, as well as some tambourine beats on "Rotten Peaches" and "All the Nasties." He was also underemployed on *Honky Château*, for which he was asked only to play the congas on "Amy." But his magnetism ended up convincing Elton to have him join his stage group. Elton initially saw in this the opportunity to (re-)distribute the responsibility for rhythm so that he could concentrate more on the melodic dimension. Then, progressively, the singer discovered in this musician, with his three-piece suit, and his strict, tax inspector–like demeanor, a real stage-performing animal. Ray, who had been classically trained in piano, percussion, woodwinds, and strings, managed to overcome his instinctive distaste for Elton's rock following by drawing on his theatrical training—his other passion—in order to construct an exuberant onstage personality. "I was given the credit (or discredit perhaps, from a classical point of view) for being one of the first people to bring classical percussion instruments into rock 'n' roll: timpani, tubular bells, vibraphone, all that stuff which looks spectacular in classical orchestra."[80] As a veritable will-o'-the-wisp, he flitted from one instrument to another, from the congas to the maracas, from the bongos to the marimbas, from the castanets

to the triangle. He put together this huge arsenal on a disc for the first time during the trilogy that was recorded at Caribou Ranch. "As a percussionist I have before me an incredible range of sound color to orchestrate or illuminate lyrics or certain nuances of music. I can, therefore, generally be more liberated than the kit drummer."[80]

The Pillar

Ray Cooper became an important pillar in the Elton formula. He also became the only man standing after the pianist implemented a cruel clear-out of his usual roster of musicians. After performing as a duo from May 2 to 7, 1977, at the Rainbow Theatre, Elton and Ray did a tour in 1979 that went to Paris and Moscow, among other stops. This was an intimacy they re-created several times between 1993 and 1995, and again between 2009 and 2010. Still present by Elton's side after half a century of collaboration, this native of Watford (born in 1947, like his colleague) also took part in the "Farewell Yellow Brick Road Tour." This loyalty did not prevent him from satisfying his musical curiosity with other artists, such as the Rolling Stones. After taking part in *It's Only Rock 'n' Roll* (1974), Ray helped out Bill Wyman on his eponymous third solo album (1982), and took part in Mick Jagger's first solo effort, *She's the Boss* (1985). He also had a strong friendship with George Harrison, which culminated in five albums as well as in film when Ray joined his friend's production company, HandMade Films. This led him to get to know another member of Harrison's artistic entourage, Terry Gilliam. Ray Cooper has appeared in several of the films made by this Monty Python alumnus, including *Brazil*, *The Adventures of Baron Munchausen*, and *The Imaginarium of Doctor Parnassus*, all works that are as fantastical and intriguing as Cooper himself.

Toto guitarist, Steve Lukather, was a budding prodigy at the age of 22 and he had a reputation as a paragon of efficiency in the studio.

JOHNNY B. GOODE

Chuck Berry / 8:06

Musicians: Elton John: lead and backing vocals / Craig Snyder: guitar / Tim Cansfield: guitar / Marcus Miller: bass / Keith Forsey: drums / Thor Baldursson: keyboards, arrangements / Roy Davies: keyboards / Paulinho da Costa: percussion / Lenny Pickett: saxophone / Stephanie Spruill, Julia Tillman Waters, Maxine Willard Waters: backing vocals **Recorded:** Musicland Studios, Munich / Rusk Sound Studios, Hollywood: August 1979 **Technical Team:** Producer: Pete Bellotte / Sound Engineer: Peter Luedmann /

Assistant Sound Engineers: Hans Menzel, Carolyn Tapp / **Technical Engineer:** Roman Olearczuk / **Album Coordinator:** Jerry Simpson
Single Release: *Johnny B. Goode / Thunder in the Night* **UK Release:** December 1979, on Rocket Record Company (ref. XPRES 24) **Best UK Chart Ranking:** Did Not Chart *Johnny B. Goode / Georgia* **US Release:** December 1979, on MCA Records (ref. MCA-41159) **Best US Chart Ranking:** Did Not Chart **12-Inch Single:** *Johnny B. Goode / Thunder in the Night* **UK Release:** December 1979, from the Rocket Record Company (ref. XPRES 2412) **Best UK Chart Ranking:** Did Not Chart

With little involvement in this album, Elton seemed ready to accept all the musical incongruities of this song as long it took a minimum amount of his precious time. So he did not balk when Pete Bellotte presented to him a hideous version of "Johnny B. Goode," the standard by Chuck Berry, a pioneer of rock 'n' roll and a benchmark in Elton's own personal pantheon. Everything that added spice to the original—the timeless riff, the organic dimension of the song, the speed of execution of the guitar layers—was entirely deconstructed and swept away. The tempo was slowed to an indecent degree, with a flaccid guitar riff, and turned it into a song without backbone. The excessively busy guitar launches into a verbiage of stereotypical rock 'n' roll guitar layers, while the Yamaha CP-70 electric piano struggles to exist, and the drums, synthetic and rigid to the maximum, all turn this into a totally irrelevant number. Elton sings at the top of his voice, but in vain, not helped by mixing that puts him into the background. Only the virtuosic bass of Marcus Miller manages to float on top of this mush, appearing bright and precise with its groove, especially when it is left on its own at 4:33. Lenny Pickett's saxophone also succeeds when he steps outside the usual scenarios and literally shouts out at around 2:40, almost approaching the sound of a human voice.

WARM LOVE IN A COLD WORLD

Pete Bellotte, Stefan Wisnet, Gunther Moll / 4:30

Musicians: Elton John: lead and backing vocals / Craig Snyder: guitar / Tim Cansfield: guitar / Steve Lukather: guitar / Marcus Miller: bass / Keith Forsey: drums / Thor Baldursson: keyboards, arrangements / Roy Davies: keyboards / Paulinho da Costa: percussion / Stephanie Spruill, Julia Tillman Waters, Maxine Willard Waters: backing vocals **Recorded:** Musicland Studios, Munich / Rusk Sound Studios, Hollywood: August 1979 **Technical Team:** Producer: Pete Bellotte / Sound Engineer: Peter Luedmann / Assistant Sound Engineers: Hans Menzel, Carolyn Tapp / Technical Engineer: Roman Olearczuk / Album Coordinator: Jerry Simpson

"Warm Love in a Cold World" fits perfectly in the wake of "Johnny B. Goode" in terms of tonality and tempo. It includes bass playing that is perfectly authentic disco with improvised slaps contributing a bounding, dancing dimension to the piece. Nothing very original enables it to be differentiated from other disco productions of the time, because it follows the code of the genre to the letter. And the romantic lyrics do not provide depth to this number either:

"I feel so good, yeah I feel so fine / I know I'm yours and I know you're mine." The only creative imagination allowed is found in Paulinho da Costa's cowbell, which provides some relief to a monolithic rhythm, despite an exemplary recording quality that highlights a very matte snare drum sound. This cowbell can be heard in particular at 2:30 before the

intervention of the young Steve Lukather, who avoids the pitfall of a sound that is worked too hard and prefers to focus on the melodic originality of his guitar layer, which presents an almost oriental color. "When I am in the studio, I avoid using too many effects," explained the Toto guitarist, in 2003. "I tried two methods. The problem was that in terms of mixing you end up with a plethora of effects and you get confused. You find yourself nitpicking details that make you lose sight of the overall picture, the main thing, in other words, the emotion. And then this denatures your sound. OK, it sounds good, you add the overdubs, you overlay guitar tracks, but these are just layers of varnish over the guitarist's talent."[121]

BORN BAD

Pete Bellotte, Geoff Bastow / 5:12

Musicians: Elton John: lead and backing vocals / Craig Snyder: guitar / Tim Cansfield: guitar / Steve Lukather: guitar / Marcus Miller: bass / Keith Forsey: drums / Thor Baldursson: keyboard, arrangements / Roy Davies: keyboard / Paulinho da Costa: percussion / Stephanie Spruill, Julia Tillman Waters, Maxine Willard Waters: backing vocals **Recorded:** Musicland Studios, Munich / Rusk Sound Studios, Hollywood: August 1979 **Technical Team:** Producer: Pete Bellotte / Sound Engineer: Peter Luedmann / Assistant Sound Engineers: Hans Menzel, Carolyn Tapp / Technical Engineer: Roman Olearczuk / Album Coordinator: Jerry Simpson

Here, too, the stylistic cohesion of the album remains a solid constant. "Born Bad" asserts itself as a more polished version of "Warm Love in a Cold World" thanks to a more effective melody and refrains, carried by the female voices of Stephanie Spruill and sisters Julia Tillman Waters and Maxine Willard Waters. But the lively, energetic tune, driven from time to time by congas and sometimes evoking Kool & the Gang, does not mesh with the seriousness of the lyrics. Here, a narrator addresses their partner, admitting to being "born bad" and saying that they cannot be sorry because they are "never gonna change." Unlike the previous song, the intervention of Steve Lukather on guitar seems rather conventional, with a solo (at 3:16) constructed on ordinary scales. Almost thirty seconds long, it is nonetheless of admirable clarity. An inspiration that came to the young musician on the spur of the moment, and all in one go. "I created my own solo parts on the spot. I sometimes had to play from written scores. But most of the time I was free to play what I wanted. For better or for worse [laughter]."[121] The vocal trio created for the album *Victim of Love* brought together Stephanie Spruill and sisters Julia Tillman Waters and Maxine Willard Waters. They were experienced in studio work, and together they had already taken part in dozens of sessions, notably for Larry Carlton (*Singing / Playing* in 1973) and Tina Turner (*Acid Queen* in 1975). They also sang on Yvonne Elliman's "If I Can't Have You" from the *Saturday Night Fever* soundtrack in 1977.

THUNDER IN THE NIGHT

Pete Bellotte, Michael Hofmann / 4:40

Musicians: Elton John: lead and backing vocals / **Craig Snyder:** guitar / **Tim Cansfield:** guitar / **Marcus Miller:** bass / **Keith Forsey:** drums / **Thor Baldursson:** keyboards, arrangements / **Roy Davies:** keyboards / **Paulinho da Costa:** percussion / **Stephanie Spruill, Julia Tillman Waters, Maxine Willard Waters:** backing vocals **Recorded:** Musicland Studios, Munich / Rusk Sound Studios, Hollywood: August 1979 **Technical Team:** Producer: Pete Bellotte / Sound Engineer: Peter Luedmann / Assistant Sound Engineers: Hans Menzel, Carolyn Tapp / Technical Engineer: Roman Olearczuk / Album Coordinator: Jerry Simpson **Single Release:** *Johnny B. Goode / Thunder in the Night* **UK Release:** December 1979, on Rocket Record Company (ref. XPRES 24) / **Best UK Chart Ranking:** Did Not Chart **12-Inch Single:** *Johnny B. Goode / Thunder in the Night* **UK Release:** December 1979, on Rocket Record Company (ref. XPRES 2412) **Best UK Chart Ranking:** Did Not Chart

The staggeringly vacuous lyrics of "Thunder in the Night" (whose title was almost used for the name of the album) make us regret the absence of Bernie Taupin. Based on lazy ("get her" / "begged her" / "loved her" / "lost her") or improbable rhymes ("tonight" / "fight" / "right"), they evoke a man jilted by his partner because he cheated on her. Now he sees the gathering of dark clouds over his head, announcing an imminent storm. Any originality is best sought in the instrumentation, which has a certain urgency, propagated by the rounded, bounding bass and the guitar with its syncopated attacks.

SPOTLIGHT

Pete Bellotte, Stefan Wisnet, Gunther Moll / 4:24

Musicians: Elton John: lead and backing vocals / **Craig Snyder:** guitar / **Tim Cansfield:** guitar / **Marcus Miller:** bass / **Keith Forsey:** drums / **Thor Baldursson:** keyboards, arrangements / **Roy Davies:** keyboards / **Paulinho da Costa:** percussion / **Stephanie Spruill, Julia Tillman Waters, Maxine Willard Waters:** backing vocals **Recorded:** Musicland Studios, Munich / Rusk Sound Studios, Hollywood: August 1979 **Technical Team:** Producer: Pete Bellotte / Sound Engineer: Peter Luedmann / Assistant Sound Engineers: Hans Menzel, Carolyn Tapp / Technical Engineer: Roman Olearczuk / Album Coordinator: Jerry Simpson

Though it is in keeping with the relative flimsiness of the rest of this album, the lyrics for "Spotlight" do, however, cast light on Elton John's motivation for making this album in the first place. He is trying to occupy a musical terrain that is in keeping with his youth, which had not given in to the siren call of punk and, instead, embraced the hedonism of the discotheques. He sings: "I know that these guys are cool / But I'll show this kid is more than ready / I sure got something to prove." His capabilities as a singer, however, are very real on this number, as he provides a more varied, nuanced, and, above all, more rhythmic performance, encouraged by the numerous claps and more lively playing of drummer Keith Forsey, who places some drum rolls coordinated with the guitar, and steps outside his role as a rhythm box.

STREET BOOGIE

Pete Bellotte, Stefan Wisnet, Gunther Moll / 3:57

Musicians: Elton John: lead and backing vocals / **Craig Snyder:** guitar / **Tim Cansfield:** guitar / **Marcus Miller:** bass / **Keith Forsey:** drums / **Thor Baldursson:** keyboards, arrangements / **Roy Davies:** keyboards / **Paulinho da Costa:** percussion / **Stephanie Spruill, Julia Tillman Waters, Maxine Willard Waters:** backing vocals **Recorded:** Musicland Studios, Munich / Rusk Sound Studios, Hollywood: August 1979 **Technical Team:** Producer: Pete Bellotte / Sound Engineer: Peter Luedmann / Assistant Sound Engineers: Hans Menzel, Carolyn Tapp / Technical Engineer: Roman Olearczuk / Album Coordinator: Jerry Simpson

Far from the dance floor, the action in "Street Boogie" takes place…in the street, as though to underline the fact that disco, like any popular musical movement, extended beyond the official boundaries of the nightclub. It is given a new language ("hot thing," "boogie," "city beat," "catch the sound") and is broadcast through the media of the time, in this case the radio ("yes, that's the radio") and word of mouth ("sharing, music, sure thing"). More cheerful, and more pop sounding than the other tracks on *Victim of Love*, "Street Boogie" offers a refrain that is perfectly calibrated for the radio waves, which is eminently effective, mostly due to the female backing vocals provided by the Waters sisters and Stephanie Spruill. The song could have been a single—it had no competition. Rhythmically impressive, with the profusion of effects by Marcus Miller, with slaps all over the place, nonetheless the number has not aged well, due to its dated keyboard sounds supervised by the Icelander Thor Baldursson.

THE MAN WHO CAME IN FROM THE COLD
Following the release of his solo album in 1970, Thor Baldursson became a keyboard player and arranger, and he offered his services to artists such as Giorgio Moroder and Donna Summer.

The Doobie Brothers (shown here in 1976) had an infectious joie de vivre. From bottom left: Jeff "Skunk" Baxter, John Hartman, Patrick Simmons, Keith Knudsen, Tiran Porter, and Michael McDonald (center).

VICTIM OF LOVE

Pete Bellotte, Sylvester Levay, Jerry Rix / 4:52

Musicians: Elton John: lead and backing vocals / Craig Snyder: guitar / Tim Cansfield: guitar / Marcus Miller: bass / Keith Forsey: drums / Thor Baldursson: keyboards, arrangements / Roy Davies: keyboards / Paulinho da Costa: percussion / Michael McDonald, Patrick Simmons, Stephanie Spruill, Julia Tillman Waters, Maxine Willard Waters: backing vocals **Recorded:** Musicland Studios, Munich / Rusk Sound Studios, Hollywood: August 1979 **Technical Team:** Producer: Pete Bellotte / Sound Engineer: Peter Luedmann / Assistant Sound Engineers: Hans Menzel, Carolyn Tapp / Technical Engineer: Roman Olearczuk / Album Coordinator: Jerry Simpson **Single Release:** *Victim of Love / Strangers* **UK Release:** September 14, 1979, on Rocket Record Company (ref. XPRES 21) **Best UK Chart Ranking:** Did Not Chart **US Release:** September 1979, on MCA Records (ref. MCA 41126) **Best US Chart Ranking:** 31

"Victim of Love" gave its name to the album, and rightly so, as this is certainly the song with the most successful melody on the disc. It was co-written by composer Sylvester Levay, who was already working on the international hit "Fly Robin Fly" for the German disco group Silver Convention. "Victim of Love" is thus the natural single from the album, and it is founded on the millimeter-precise vocal harmonies of Doobie Brothers Michael McDonald and Patrick Simmons. But it is really the Marcus Miller–Keith Forsey duo that holds the key to the effectiveness of this high-tempo (128 bpm) number that quickly begins to purr. Sticking very close together, they cannot really help overdoing this a little. The bassist provides his overelaborate and stodgy slap after three minutes, when the matt and hypnotic sound of the drummer's snare finally sends the listener to sleep. Try as Elton might in scrambling to deliver the vocals, he often gives the impression of being underpowered, and his lack of finesse only echoes the unctuous keyboards that are peppered throughout the piece. The last number on this clumsy album, "Victim of Love" puts an end to Elton's foray into disco.

ALBUM

21 AT 33

Chasing the Crown . Little Jeannie . Sartorial Eloquence
(Don't Ya Wanna Play This Game No More?) . Two Rooms at the End of the World .
White Lady White Powder . Dear God . Never Gonna Fall in Love Again .
Take Me Back . Give Me the Love

RELEASE DATES
UK Release: May 13, 1980
Reference: Rocket Record Company—HISPD 126
Best UK Chart Ranking: 12
US Release: May 13, 1980
Reference: MCA Records—MCA 5121
Best US Chart Ranking: 13

Elton John went to the South of France to work on his new album.

BACK IN THE REALM OF POP

After wrapping the USSR tour for *A Single Man*, Elton John headed for the south of France. He planned to take advantage of the warmer climate in June 1979 to relax and to get started on the composition for his next album, *21 at 33*. From the day he began to work, Elton found to his great relief that inspiration had not left him in spite of his hectic and exhausting schedule. He finalized six songs, including "Little Jeannie," which would be the future single for the album. He broke off work after a few days to join Pete Bellotte in Munich, and then returned to Grasse and picked up his creative thread.

The Return of Bernie

The panoply of writers for this album included Gary Osborne, who was back again as the main lyricist; Tom Robinson, a gay rights activist Elton had met the previous autumn, and whom he called upon for "Sartorial Eloquence" and "Never Gonna Fall in Love Again"; and Judie Tzuke, a British pop singer who was on the roster of the Rocket Record Company. But the presence of one name in the album credits of *21 at 33* monopolized the attention of the public, and that was Bernie Taupin. Everyone applauded the reconciliation between Elton and Bernie. For their part, the two parties were amused by this perspective, since there had never been any falling-out. Quite simply, the two men had incompatible schedules, some major emotional issues, and, for Bernie, an alcohol addiction that had to be sorted out. Even so, the two men had never doubted that they would be back together again. Bernie managed to break

out of his self-destructive spiral after going into total isolation in Acapulco and getting sober. Relieved to know that he had come out of his hibernation in good health, Elton invited Bernie's soul mate and new companion, Toni Lynn Russo—sister of the actress Rene Russo—to his rented house along with the lyricist to take part in creating the album. Bernie accepted with an enthusiasm that spilled over into his writing. Their first collaboration in three years, "Two Rooms at the End of the World" evokes in a transparent way the whispers that accompanied their separation ("Will they ever get together?" "There's a change in their thinking / And their habits seem uneven"). In the face of these rumors, Bernie announces their resounding success: "But together the two of them were mining gold."

The other tracks that were destined for *21 at 33*, such as "Chasing the Crown" and "White Lady White Powder," were also in the offing, and they were part of a major catharsis for the writer.

The recording sessions took place in August at Super Bear Studios, whose name refers to its location at Berre-les-Alpes, located in the Alpes-Maritimes region of France. The young Steve Lukather, whose musical prowess Elton had so appreciated on *Victim of Love*, barely had time to discover and explore the studio before work began. Elton welcomed him with open arms and thanked him for interrupting the recording sessions on *Hydra*, Toto's second album, to come and work with him. Along with Lukather, the album included an enlarged team of musicians. Times had changed since the days when Elton would

shut himself away with his quartet behind the walls of the Château d'Hérouville. Among those in attendance during recording were the rhythm section formed by Dee Murray and Nigel Olsson, keyboard player James Newton Howard, and backing vocalists Bruce Johnston, Curt Becher, and Toni Tennille.

A Good Hand

Most of the recording was wrapped up during the month of August, but it would be necessary to wait until March for the finishing touches to be completed during two overdub sessions. One of these sessions took place at Sunset Sound Studios in California, under the direction of Clive Franks, who was assisted by sound engineer Steve Desper. They put to bed the backing vocals on "Dear God," which were provided by Bruce Johnston, Curt Becher, Joe Chemay, Jon Joyce, Peter Noone, and Toni Tennille. The other overdub session took place at the Rumbo Recorders studio, which was a new recording complex, also in California, that Daryl Dragon had invested in. "It was

Elton John facing a sea of 400,000 people during a performance in New York City's Central Park on September 13, 1980.

always Daryl's dream to own a state-of-the-art recording studio. He wanted a place where he could record and maintain complete control of all of the equipment and staff."[122]

Although Elton was not yet thirty-three when he started the composition of this album, he was about to celebrate his birthday when work was completed. One day, he surprised himself by counting up the number of albums he had recorded: thirteen studio albums (including two double albums—*Goodbye Yellow Brick Road* and *Blue Moves*), two live albums (*11-17-70* and

Here and There), a film soundtrack (*Friends*), and three compilation albums (*Elton John's Greatest Hits, Elton John's Greatest Hits Volume II,* and *Lady Samantha*). By his own count, this next album would be his twenty-first, at the age of thirty-three, and thus the title was born: *21 at 33*.

The album's cover design was done by George Osaki, a Hawaiian graphic artist who had twice been nominated for Grammy Awards, and by Norman Moore, a Scotsman who lived in Los Angeles, and who became artistic director for MCA before founding his own company, DesignArt Inc. The cover for *21 at 33* tends toward abstraction, showing disembodied hands playing a game of cards.

As for Elton's hand, in this case it was a lucky one. When *21 at 33* was released in May 1980, the artist returned to sales levels that were more in keeping with his status. The record went to number twelve in the United Kingdom and to number thirteen in the United States. This success was sufficient enough to erase the blunder of *Victim of Love* from memory.

CHASING THE CROWN

Elton John, Bernie Taupin / 5:38

Musicians: Elton John: lead and backing vocals, piano / **Steve Lukather:** electric guitar / **Reggie McBride:** bass / **Alvin Taylor:** drums / **Victor Feldman:** tambourine / **Venette Gloud, Stephanie Spruill, Carmen Twillie:** backing vocals **Recorded:** Super Bear Studios, Berre-les-Alpes, France / Sunset Sound Recorders, Los Angeles / Rumbo Recorders, Los Angeles: August 1979–March 1980 **Technical Team: Producer:** Clive Franks, Elton John / **Sound Engineers:** Clive Franks, Patrick Jaunead / **Assistant Sound Engineers:** David Burgess, David Leonard, Peggy McCreary, Stephen McManus / **Mastering:** Bernie Grundman / **Album Coordinator:** Adrian Collee

Steve Lukather had worked on two numbers for *Victim of Love* without ever actually meeting Elton John. Nevertheless, Elton had appreciated his work, and so he was invited back to work on *21 at 33*. The young Toto guitarist sets this piece on fire with a sustained tempo. Elton is not left out with his impossible piano playing and mannered vocals, which are well supported by jubilatory backing vocals. The rhythm section is solid, and Reggie McBride's groovy bass appropriately inserts itself into the few available gaps in the song. Somewhere between the Rolling Stones and Roxy Music, "Chasing the Crown" marks a return to grace for Bernie Taupin, whose lyrics express the imaginary thoughts of a fictitious character who has traversed various moments in history in his quest for domination, from the construction of the Great Wall of China to the Boston Tea Party.

LITTLE JEANNIE

Elton John, Gary Osborne / 5:17

Musicians: Elton John: lead and backing vocals / **Richie Zito:** acoustic guitar / **Reggie McBride:** bass / **Nigel Olsson:** drums / Chuck Findley: trumpet, trombone / Jerry Hey: bugle / Jim Horn: direction, arrangements, piccolo, alto saxophone / **James Newton Howard:** Fender Rhodes, Yamaha CS-80 / Tambourine: uncredited / Bill Champlin, Max Gronenthal, **Dee Murray:** backing vocals **Recorded:** Super Bear Studios, Berre-les-Alpes, France: August 1979 **Technical Team: Producer:** Clive Franks, Elton John / **Sound Engineers:** Clive Franks, Patrick Jaunead / **Assistant Sound Engineers:** David Burgess, David Leonard, Peggy McCreary, Stephen McManus / **Mastering:** Bernie Grundman / **Album Coordinator:** Adrian Collee **Single Releases:** *Little Jeannie / Conquer the Sun* **UK Release:** April 28, 1980, on Rocket Record Company (ref. XPRES 32) **Best UK Chart Ranking: 33 US Release:** May 17, 1980, on MCA Records (ref. MCA-41236) **Best US Chart Ranking:** 3

Some muffled keyboard notes accompanied by a disciplined acoustic guitar open up this brilliant soft rock ballad, whose sole defect may be a horrendous (uncredited) tambourine that

bangs on in a sterile way in the background. The warm brass, on the other hand, is perfectly calibrated, as are the backing vocals, which include the voice of Dee Murray, a great artisan of vocal harmonies that so elegantly adorned Elton's productions from the beginning of the 1970s. Nigel Olsson also took his place at the drums for this track, delivering his inimitable signature matte-sounding snare rhythm. Elton limits himself to the main vocals and some backing vocals. The single rose to third place on the American charts, but only after it was cut in length by twenty or so seconds. This was the singer's best commercial performance since "Don't Go Breaking My Heart," which had appeared three years earlier.

SARTORIAL ELOQUENCE (DON'T YA WANNA PLAY THIS GAME NO MORE?)

Elton John, Tom Robinson / 4:42

Musicians: Elton John: lead and backing vocals, piano / **Steve Lukather:** electric guitar / **Reggie McBride:** bass / **Alvin Taylor:** drums / James Newton Howard: keyboards / **Victor Feldman:** tambourine / **Venette Gloud, Stephanie Spruill, Carmen Twillie:** backing vocals **Recorded:** Super Bear Studios, Berre-les-Alpes, France: August 1979 **Technical Team: Producer:** Clive Franks, Elton John / **Sound Engineers:** Clive Franks, Patrick Jaunead / **Assistant Sound Engineers:** David Burgess, David Leonard, Peggy McCreary, Stephen McManus / **Mastering:** Bernie Grundman / **Album Coordinator:** Adrian Collee **Single Releases:** *Sartorial Elegance / White Man Danger; Cartier* **UK Release:** August 1, 1980, on Rocket Record Company (ref. XPRES 41) **Best UK Chart Ranking: 44 US Release:** July 1980, on MCA Records (ref. MCA-41293) **Best US Chart Ranking:** 39

Elton begins this languorous ballad alone on the piano, singing lyrics by Tom Robinson, a gay rights activist. The musician then later plays a piano solo, deliberately underutilizing guitarist Steve Lukather in order to avoid needlessly distracting the listener and thereby undermining the song's catchy refrain. As well as its effective melody, above all this song has the benefit of a magisterial contribution from Venette Gloud, Stephanie Spruill, and Carmen Twillie on backing vocals. The discreet rhythm section is no less important in providing an impeccable foundation for the piece. The only negative here, which is not a trivial one, is the dated sound of the keyboards. Their syrupy tone simulates violins and a cello, and definitively anchors the piece in the 1980s.

Two Englishmen in Paris: Bernie and Elton enjoyed a break on the terrace of the famous literary café Aux Deux Magots.

TWO ROOMS AT THE END OF THE WORLD

Elton John, Bernie Taupin / 5:39

Musicians: Elton John: vocals, electric piano / **Steve Lukather:** electric guitar / **Reggie McBride:** bass / **Alvin Taylor:** drums / **Clive Franks:** tambourine, bell / **Chuck Findley:** trombone, trumpet / **Jerry Hey:** trumpet / **Jim Horn:** direction, arrangements, tenor saxophone / **Backing vocals:** uncredited **Recorded:** Super Bear Studios, Berre-les-Alpes, France / Sunset Sound Recorders, Los Angeles / Rumbo Recorders, Los Angeles: August 1979–March 1980 **Technical Team:** Producer: Clive Franks, Elton John / **Sound Engineers:** Clive Franks, Patrick Jaunead / **Assistant Sound Engineers:** David Burgess, David Leonard, Peggy McCreary, Stephen McManus / **Mastering:** Bernie Grundman / **Album Coordinator:** Adrian Collee

Throughout the lyrics of "Two Rooms at the End of the World," Bernie Taupin seeks to celebrate his unconventional partnership with Elton. In fact, despite the distance and different life journeys of the previous few years, Bernie was officially back at center stage on *21 at 33*. Without any doubt, "Two Rooms," which gave its name to a tribute album in 1991, is one of the best pieces on the record. With its flashy brass, its ideally compressed bouncing bass, its precise backing vocals (which are uncredited, but in which one can definitely recognize the voice of Elton himself), and the surgical accuracy of Steve Lukather's guitar, the song was curiously not chosen as a single to promote the album. As for Elton's vocals and Yamaha electric piano playing, they seem to exude happiness throughout the piece.

Musician Tom Robinson (shown here in 1986) worked as Elton John's lyricist for the *21 at 33* album.

WHITE LADY WHITE POWDER

Elton John, Bernie Taupin / 4:35

Musicians: Elton John: lead and backing vocals, piano / **Richie Zito:** electric guitar / **Dee Murray:** bass / **Nigel Olsson:** drums / **Lenny Castro:** congas / Glenn Frey, Don Henley, Timothy B. Schmit: backing vocals **Recorded:** Super Bear Studios, Berre-les-Alpes, France / Sunset Sound Recorders, Los Angeles / Rumbo Recorders, Los Angeles: August 1979–March 1980 **Technical Team:** Producers: Clive Franks, Elton John / **Sound Engineer:** Clive Franks / **Assistant Sound Engineers:** David Leonard, Peggy McCreary, Stephen McManus / **Mastering:** Bernie Grundman / **Album Coordinator:** Adrian Collee

A nebulous bass plays elusively as the drums beat on with deceptive simplicity: There can be no doubt that this is the rhythm section of Elton, Dee Murray, and Nigel Olsson at work. This piece sounds resolutely positive with its lively melody, but the theme of the lyrics written by Bernie is, to say the least, explicit and the expresses the opposite of this happy mood: "You didn't have to be a genius to work out what he was driving at when he sent me a song called 'White Lady White Powder,' a portrait of a hopeless cocaine addict,"[3] explained Elton. "I had the brass balls to sing it as if it was about someone else."[3] Davey Johnstone was missing from these recording sessions, so it was Richie Zito who delivered an inspired score on his six-string, while the Eagles' Glenn Frey, Don Henley, and Timothy B. Schmit provide sublime vocal harmonies.

"Dear God" was originally intended for release as a single with "Tactics" on the B-side. But it was also released as a double 45 rpm; the second disc consisted of "Steal Away Child" and "Love So Cold." The three B-side tracks were included on *Jewel Box* in 2020.

DEAR GOD

Elton John, Gary Osborne / 3:45

Musicians: Elton John: lead and backing vocals, piano / **Steve Lukather:** electric guitar / **Reggie McBride:** bass / **Alvin Taylor:** drums / **David Paich:** organ / **James Newton Howard:** Fender Rhodes / **Clive Franks:** tambourine / Curt Becher, Joe Chemay, Venette Gloud, Bruce Johnston, Jon Joyce, Peter Noone, Stephanie Spruill, Toni Tennille, Carmen Twillie: backing vocals / Bruce Johnston: backing vocals arrangements, direction **Recorded:** Super Bear Studios, Berre-les-Alpes, France: August 1979 / Rumbo Recorders, Los Angeles: January 1980 **Technical Team:** Producers: Clive Franks, Elton John / **Sound Engineers:** Clive Franks, Steve Desper / **Assistant Sound Engineers:** David Burgess, David Leonard, Peggy McCreary, Stephen McManus / **Mastering:** Bernie Grundman / **Album Coordinator:** Adrian Collee **Single Release:** *Dear God / Tactics* **UK Release:** November 21, 1980, on Rocket Record Company (ref. XPRES 45) **Best UK Chart Ranking:** Did Not Chart

"Dear God" is the shortest song on the album, and not necessarily the most inspired, both in terms of lyrics and the music. The lyrics, by Gary Osborne, take the form of a prayer to God, an appeal to his mercy, and cause Elton to take a step in the direction of Christian rock. The song is clearly peppered with gospel inspirations. An impressive choir was assembled to further emphasize this gospel coloration and was recorded afterward, at the beginning of 1980, at Rumbo Recorders in Los Angeles. Electric guitar arpeggios fairly limply accompany the rather lazy piano. Soporific to the maximum degree, especially in the wake of the energetic "White Lady White Powder," "Dear God" even managed to send the general public to sleep. The public effectively denied the single any presence in the charts, except in Australia, where it was ranked eighty-second.

NEVER GONNA FALL IN LOVE AGAIN

Elton John, Tom Robinson / 4:07

Musicians: Elton John: lead and backing vocals / **Steve Lukather:** electric guitar / **Richie Zito:** acoustic guitar / **Reggie McBride:** bass / **Alvin Taylor:** drums / **James Newton Howard:** Fender Rhodes, keyboards / **Richie Cannata:** alto saxophone **Recorded:** Super Bear Studios, Berre-les-Alpes, France / Sunset Sound Recorders, Los

Judie Tzuke, whose song "Stay with Me Till Dawn" was a hit in the UK and Australia, co-wrote "Give Me the Love" with Elton.

Angeles / Rumbo Recorders, Los Angeles: August 1979–March 1980 **Technical Team: Producers:** Clive Franks, Elton John / **Sound Engineers:** Clive Franks, Patrick Jaunead / **Assistant Sound Engineers:** David Burgess, David Leonard, Peggy McCreary, Stephen McManus / **Mastering:** Bernie Grundman / **Album Coordinator:** Adrian Collee

Elton John has never shown any regard for the ballad "Never Gonna Fall in Love Again." He also never played it in concert... And from the recording, his lack of motivation is palpable: He does not take the trouble to accompany himself on the piano, and his vocals sound rather characterless. The soft rock music is very predictable, with thick, indigestible layers of keyboards, and a saxophone solo worthy of elevator music. Three guitarists were lined up for this piece, without their parts being fundamentally distinct: The few acoustic arpeggios by Richie Zito, which are very precisely executed, would probably have sufficed, but the electric guitars contribute little to filling the void, which extends even to the particularly insipid lyrics.

TAKE ME BACK
Elton John, Gary Osborne / 3:52

Musicians: Elton John: lead and backing vocals, electric piano / **Richie Zito:** electric guitar / Steve Wrather: electric guitar / **Reggie McBride:** bass / Alvin Taylor: drums / Byron Berline: violin **Recorded:** Super Bear Studios, Berre-les-Alpes, France / Sunset Sound Recorders, Los Angeles / Rumbo Recorders, Los Angeles: August 1979–March

1980 **Technical Team: Producers:** Clive Franks, Elton John / **Sound Engineers:** Clive Franks, Patrick Jaunead / **Assistant Sound Engineers:** David Burgess, David Leonard, Peggy McCreary, Stephen McManus / **Mastering:** Bernie Grundman / **Album Coordinator:** Adrian Collee

With its rhythm guitar played on the backbeat, "Take Me Back" plays its cards close to its vest. Simple and cheerful, the melody is catchy, especially given that Elton's backing vocals are almost as effective as his main vocals, which are slightly nasal, sometimes giving the impression of the end of the refrain being a little forced. The Wurlitzer piano played by Elton provides a rich and varied score, while Reggie McBride's jovial bass bounds gracefully in all directions. Richie Zito enriches his guitar playing with delicious, precise arpeggios fitting closely with a finely adjusted chorus. As for Byron Berline's inspired violin, this switches the song into a very agreeable soft country register. A fine surprise for the end of the album, which fits musically very well with the hopes of the narrator, conspicuously evident in Gary Osborne's lyrics, that his lost love is giving him a second chance.

GIVE ME THE LOVE
Elton John, Judie Tzuke / 5:23

Musicians: Elton John: vocals / **Steve Lukather:** electric guitar / **Reggie McBride:** bass / **Alvin Taylor:** drums / **James Newton Howard:** piano / **Victor Feldman:** tambourine / **Lenny Castro:** congas / **Larry Williams:** tenor saxophone / **Bill Reichenbach Jr.:** trombone / **Larry Hall:** trumpet, bugle / **Jerry Hey:** bugle, trumpet, direction, brass arrangements / **David Foster:** direction, strings arrangements / **Bill Champlin, Venette Gloud, Stephanie Spruill, Carmen Twillie:** backing vocals **Recorded:** Super Bear Studios, Berre-les-Alpes, France / Sunset Sound Recorders, Los Angeles / Rumbo Recorders, Los Angeles: August 1979–March 1980 **Technical Team: Producers:** Clive Franks, Elton John / **Sound Engineers:** Clive Franks, Patrick Jaunead / **Assistant Sound Engineers:** David Burgess, David Leonard, Peggy McCreary, Stephen McManus / **Mastering:** Bernie Grundman / **Album Coordinator:** Adrian Collee

Elton brings out the heavy artillery for this piece, whose sensual lyrics, written by the British singer Judie Tzuke, are given a torrid treatment with an indulgent arrangement. Vibrant strings, a languorous rhythm section, warm brass, and impressive backing vocals make us forget Elton's half-shaded backing vocals, with him choosing to focus on his lead vocals. He leaves the keyboards to James Newton Howard, who turns in one of the finest sequences on the album, bringing finesse and lightness to the verses, and a groove that is decisive for the success of the piece in the refrains. Despite this, Elton has never played "Give Me the Love" onstage.

The collaboration with Judie Tzuke was implemented remotely: Elton sent the lyricist a demo in which the singer enunciated some phrases that he wanted to be retained. In return, Judie Tzuke sent him a very long list of verses adhering to the required meter, from which she invited him to make his selection.

Michel Berger and France Gall joined Elton John on two songs, "Les Aveux" and "Donner Pour Donner."

LES AVEUX

Elton John, France Gall, Michel Berger / 4:11

Musicians: Elton John: vocals / France Gall: vocals / Richie Zito: guitar / Tim Merrizk: guitar / Dee Murray: bass / Nigel Olsson: drums / James Newton Howard: keyboards / Paulinho Da Costa: percussion / Orchestra: uncredited / Marty Paich: direction, arrangements
Recorded: Sunset Sound Recorders, Los Angeles: August 15, 1980
Technical Team: Producers: Clive Franks, Elton John, Michel Berger / Sound Engineer: Clive Franks **Single Release:** *Les aveux / Donner pour donner* **France Release:** October 1980, on Atlantic (ref. 11635)
Best French Chart Ranking: 6

A phone call and a misunderstanding were at the origins of this pleasant encounter between the Michel Berger–France Gall duo and Elton John. In 1980 Elton was spending July in the Côte d'Azur. On the radio, he heard the latest hit: "Il jouait du piano debout" (He played the piano standing), written by Michel Berger. He decided straightaway to phone the French singer, who hung up on him, thinking it was some kind of bad joke. Finally, Elton managed to make contact, and he became friends with the couple, to the extent of recording two numbers with France Gall, "Donner pour donner" (Giving for giving's sake) and "Les aveux" (Confessions). The latter, an agreeable soft rock ballad, was created from "Reach Out to Me," a number that had remained at the demo stage, recorded with lyrics by Tom Robinson. The piece is worth it above all for Elton's delightful French accent, its indisputable compatibility with the voice of France Gall, and Dee Murray's skillfully woven bass line.

DONNER POUR DONNER

Bernie Taupin, Michel Berger / 4:28

Musicians: Elton John: vocals / France Gall: vocals / Richie Zito: guitar / Tim Merrizk: guitar / Dee Murray: bass / Nigel Olsson: drums / James Newton Howard: keyboards / Paulinho Da Costa: percussion / Lon Price: saxophone / Orchestra: uncredited / Marty Paich: direction, arrangements **Recorded:** Sunset Sound Recorders, Los Angeles: August 15, 1980 **Technical Team:** Producers: Clive Franks, Elton John, Michel Berger / Sound Engineer: Clive Franks **Single Release:** *Les aveux / Donner pour donner* **France Release:** October 1980, on Atlantic (ref. 11635) **Best Chart Ranking:** 6

Of the two numbers recorded by Elton John and France Gall, "Donner pour donner" (Giving for giving's sake) is probably the best known, although it appeared as the B-side of "Les aveux" (Confessions). The music is not by Elton, but by Michel Berger, who oddly shares the credits with Bernie Taupin. Elton sings first in English before joining France Gall in French on the refrain. The song is very catchy from the melodic point of view. Already successful in "Les aveux," the vocal marriage of the two artists is disconcertingly natural on "Donner pour donner," which offers some nice high points, such as Lon Price's saxophone solo, James Newton Howard's enveloping groovy keyboards, the very high register used by France Gall in some of the sequences, and above all Elton's incomparable composure on the phrase: "C'est la seule façon d'aimer" (It's the only way to love).

CONQUER THE SUN

Elton John, Gary Osborne / 4:16

Single: *Little Jeannie / Conquer the Sun* **UK Release:** April 28, 1980, on Rocket Record Company (ref. XPRES 32) **Best UK Chart Ranking:** 33 **US Release:** May 17, 1980, on MCA Records (ref. MCA-41236) **Best US Chart Ranking:** 3 **Musicians:** Elton John: vocals, piano / Other musicians: uncredited **Recorded:** Super Bear Studios, Berre-les-Alpes, France: August 1979 **Technical Team:** Uncredited

"Conquer the Sun" was recorded during the album sessions for *A Single Man*. This is one of the very first collaborations between Elton John and Gary Osborne, who produced a soft rock ballad that unfortunately suffers from a clumsy first half without any real relief. It was logically left out of the final track listing and used later as a B-side to "Little Jeannie." The song is played on the piano by Elton, supported by some rather monotonous strings, and its value lies above all in the different colors provided by the guitars, especially after 2:39—the acoustic arpeggios, tinged with slight reverb effect, give the response to an electric guitar, producing some floating notes with excellent effect, before giving way to a sequence drowned in wah-wah pedals.

WHITE MAN DANGER

Elton John, Gary Osborne /5:26

Single Side B: *Sartorial Eloquence / White Man Danger; Cartier* **UK Release:** August 1, 1980, on Rocket Record Company (ref. XPRES 41) **Best UK Chart Ranking:** 44 **US Release:** July 1980, on MCA Records (ref. MCA-41293) **Best US Chart Ranking:** 39 **Musicians:** Elton John: vocals / Other musicians: uncredited **Recorded:** Super Bear Studios, Berre-les-Alpes, France: August 1979 **Technical Team:** Uncredited

With a fine intro that includes a particularly venomous guitar, "White Man Danger" then moves into a lighter tone with the contribution of silky keyboards that stand in strange opposition to the song's lyrical indictment of conquest and colonialism. The electric guitar still has a sharpness to it, and although the piece bogs down in a certain monotony, due to its length, it is still a showcase for some fine musical performances. This is particularly true of the rhythm section—which is firmly in place and combines simplicity and effectiveness in the imperious keyboard solo between 2:43 and 3:13—and above all in the impressive female backing vocals, which supplant Elton's slightly timid voice in the refrains.

CARTIER

Elton John, Gary Osborne (credited as Dinah Card and Carte Blanche) / 0:54

Single Side B: *Sartorial Elegence / White Man Danger-Cartier* **UK Release:** August 1, 1980, on Rocket Record Company (ref. XPRES 41) **Best UK Chart Ranking:** 44 **US Release:** July 1980, on MCA Records (ref. MCA-41293) **Best US Chart Ranking:** 39 **Musicians:** Elton John: vocals, piano **Recorded:** Sunset Sound Recorders, Los Angeles: March 17, 1980 **Technical Team:** Uncredited

In the fifty-four seconds during which Elton is alone at his piano, he does all he can to ensure that this subtle, elegant, short, but also forgettable song resembles as much as possible an advertisement for the famous Cartier brand. In it he encourages the rich clientele to spend their cash with Cartier, without it being entirely clear whether this is really what he is doing, or if there is a certain cynicism at play. Although credited with the lyrics, Gary Osborne explained that Elton had mostly written and composed this cruise anthem on his own, and that he might have contributed "a line or two at most."[123] "Cartier" is one of the rare B-sides that Elton has sung many times onstage, and famously so in an a cappella version on September 17, 1980, on *The Tomorrow Show with Tom Snyder*.

Elton John poses with his personal vinyl collection at home in Windsor, England.

TACTICS
Elton John / 0:54

Single Side B: *Dear God / Tactics* **UK Release:** November 21, 1980, on Rocket Record Company (ref. XPRES45) **Best UK Chart Ranking:** Did Not Chart *In Neon / Tactics* **US Release:** November 1984, on Geffen Records (ref. 7-29111) **Best US Chart Ranking:** 38 **Recorded:** Super Bear Studios, Berre-les-Alpes, France: August 1979 **Musicians:** Elton John: vocals, piano, keyboards / **Other musicians:** uncredited

After a very attractive introduction of classical inspiration, "Tactics" starts to sink at 0:44. There ensues some appalling keyboard tones that are doing their very best to imitate brass and strings, while the listener is left to wonder if it is possible that the composer of "Your Song" and the composer of "Tactics" could really be the same person. This instrumental track was recorded during the *21 at 33* sessions, and it was initially called "Football Theme." Incredible as it may seem, "Tactics" was exhumed in 1984 and placed on the B-side of "In Neon" in the United States, although the American public had done nothing to deserve this.

STEAL AWAY CHILD
Elton John, Gary Osborne / 3:06

Musicians: Elton John: vocals, electric piano **Recorded:** Super Bear Studios, Berre-les-Alpes, France: August 1979 **Technical Team: Producers:** Clive Franks, Elton John / **Sound Engineer:** Clive Franks / **Assistant Sound Engineers:** David Burgess, David Leonard, Peggy McCreary, Stephen McManus **Mastering:** Bernie Grundman **Album Coordinator:** Adrian Collee? **Single Release:** *Dear God / Tactics / Steal Away Child / Love So Cold* **UK Release:** November 21, 1980, on Rocket Record Company (ref. ELTON 1) **Best UK Chart Ranking:** Did Not Chart

Surprised by the melody written by Elton John that was both elegiac and childlike, and that sounded almost like a lullaby, Gary

Osborne allowed himself to be submerged in a wave of sadness. Far from his family and his three-year-old son due to his booking with Elton, he committed his sorrow to paper: "Our love is too precious for distance to kill." And as he wrote the lyrics that he hoped would be soothing for his son (and Elton's godchild), and as he described for him "a place peaceful and calm / Where no one and nothing can harm you," the emotion affected him.

LOVE SO COLD
Elton John, Bernie Taupin / 5:08

Musicians: Elton John: vocals, piano / **Other musicians:** uncredited **Recorded:** Super Bear Studios, Berre-les-Alpes, France: August 1979 **Technical Team:** Uncredited **Single Release:** *Dear God / Tactics / Steal Away Child / Love So Cold* **UK Release:** November 21, 1980, on Rocket Record Company (ref. ELTON 1) **Best UK Chart Ranking:** Did Not Chart *I'm Still Standing / Love So Cold* **US Release:** April 1983, on Geffen Records (ref. 7-29639) **Best US Chart Ranking:** 12

"Love So Cold" assumes its humorous character and limited commercial ambition from the first moments when Elton launches into an imitation of Ricky Ricardo from *I Love Lucy*. The song itself is colored with a swaying rhythm and improvised castanets, but it takes a turn toward honky-tonk when a piano erupts at 3:11 and plunges the listener right into an old-time saloon.

ALBUM

THE FOX

Breaking Down Barriers. Heart in the Right Place . Just Like Belgium .
Nobody Wins . Fascist Faces . Carla/Etude . Fanfare . Chloe .
Heels of the Wind . Elton's Song . The Fox

RELEASE DATES

UK Release: May 20, 1981
Reference: Rocket Record Company—TRAIN 16
Best UK Chart Ranking: 12
US Release: May 1981
Reference: Geffen Records—GHS 2002
Best US Chart Ranking: 21

Struggling with addiction and other personal setbacks, Elton John poured his melancholy into *The Fox*.

A MOMENT OF MELANCHOLY

The genesis of *The Fox* can be traced back to *21 at 33*, as almost half of the album was composed in Grasse during the summer of 1979. Still, it would be wrong to think that *The Fox* consists merely of a collection of rejected songs and studio outtakes from earlier albums. Despite a long and intermittent gestation period, and a recording process that was spread over nearly eighteen months and five different studios, Elton was surprisingly able to give coherence to both sides of a disk that's imbued with an almost magical sense of creativity.

A Year and a Half in the Making

When he arrived in Grasse in the early summer of 1979 to compose the songs for *21 at 33*, Elton John allowed himself one month to create the equivalent of a double album. In August, he moved into Super Bear Studios, a former restaurant that had been transformed into a generously equipped studio where Pink Floyd recorded *The Wall*. Elton's team consisted of Clive Franks in production, Reggie McBride and Alvin Taylor in the rhythm section, Victor Feldman on percussion, and the ever-loyal James Newton Howard on synthesizer. It was an intense period of work, and by the end of this summer session, Elton abandoned the idea of a double album. *21 at 33* was released as one disc, which meant that many tracks were left unused. Only five of these unused songs appeared on his next LP, *The Fox*: "Heart in the Right Place," "Fanfare," "Chloe," "Elton's Song" and the ambitious symphonic medley "Carla/Etude." Even at the demo stage, this instrumental composition set the tone for the rest of the album, which was a melancholy affair that was brought on by a period of depression surrounding Elton's unrequited love affairs and ongoing drug use. It was not until a series of later recording sessions at Davlen Sound Studios in Los Angeles that Elton recorded the final pieces of the album. On December 31, 1979, the London Symphony Orchestra recorded James Newton Howard's orchestral parts at the fabled Abbey Road Studios.

Back in Los Angeles, recording sessions for the album continued through January 1980 at the Sunset Sound recording studio. A year later, Elton's new record company, Geffen Records, persuaded Elton to go back into the studio—this time without Clive Franks—to record six additional tracks. More rock 'n' roll in style, these new tracks were: "Breaking Down Barriers," "Just Like Belgium," "Nobody Wins," "Fascist Faces," "Heels of the Wind," and "The Fox." One possible silver lining to the prolonged recording process for *The Fox* was that it gave Elton's fans time to absorb his abundant creative output. In the space of just two years, Elton released *Victim of Love* and *21 at 33* along with the compilation albums *The Complete Picture—Milestones*, *Lady Samantha*, and *The Very Best of Elton John*.

A New Producer and Old Friends

Elton turned to one of his old friends from the Royal Academy of Music, Chris Thomas, to handle the production supervision on the second half of the recording sessions for *The Fox*. Hiring Thomas meant that Clive Franks was out, and Franks learned of his dismissal through a brief phone call made by an assistant to John Reid. There was nothing surprising about this move since Chris Thomas had an excellent track record: he worked as a personal assistant to George Martin on the Beatles' *Abbey Road* (1969), he produced three Procol Harum albums and also the Sex Pistols' *Never Mind the Bollocks* (1977). Guitarists Richie Zito and Steve Lukather also returned for the second round of recording sessions along with Elton's old friends Dee Murray and Nigel Olsson. These four musicians provided a new dynamism to the forthcoming tracks by adding a midtempo rock feel, which provided a striking contrast to the album's more intimate orchestral numbers.

Outside of the studio, a battle was raging between Geffen Records, the new label Elton had signed with on September 21, 1980, and MCA; the latter company argued that Elton had begun work on *The Fox* in 1979 and 1980 before the termination of his contract with their company. The case ended up in court and was eventually settled in favor of Geffen. Public and critical reception of *The Fox* were muted. Reviewers acknowledged the general quality of the disk but were not overly impressed. A similar lack of public enthusiasm resulted in a respectable but not noteworthy placing of the album at number twelve on the UK charts and number twenty-one in the United States.

BREAKING DOWN BARRIERS

Elton John, Gary Osborne / 4:41

Musicians: Elton John: lead and backing vocals, piano / **Richie Zito:** guitar / **Dee Murray:** bass / **Nigel Olsson:** drums / Stephanie Spruill: tambourine, backing vocals / **James Newton Howard:** synthesizer / Bill Champlin, Venette Gloud, Tamara Matoesian: backing vocals
Recorded: Sunset Sound Recorders, Los Angeles: January 1981
Technical Team: Producer: Chris Thomas / **Sound Engineer:** Bill Price / **Assistant Sound Engineers:** Peggy McCreary, Stephen McManus / **Mastering:** Tim Young

Full of earsplitting bravado, this rock song features dazzling piano-playing that takes center stage with fearless arpeggios executed at breathtaking speed. "Breaking Down Barriers" was not a recent creation; instead it had been improvised by Elton during an interview with Paul Gambaccini for the BBC in the summer of 1980. During the program, Elton had asserted that he could set any text to music in the span of just a few minutes. Gambaccini challenged him to compose a song using the words of John Donne's poem "No Man Is an Island." The version that appeared on the album was revived when Geffen asked Elton to produce some new songs with words written by Gary Osborne. Less than inspired, the lyrics describe the speaker feeling emotionally rescued when he opens his heart after years of denying himself love and affection.

The effectiveness of the song owes a lot to Dee Murray and Nigel Olsson's rhythm section, which is energetic enough to make you forget Richie Zito's rather conventional guitar playing. Zito's mock solo fades away as quickly as it appears, and Elton's voice is lower than usual, though it is supported by magnificent backing vocals from Stephanie Spruill, Venette Gloud, Tamara Matoesian, and Bill Champlin.

HEART IN THE RIGHT PLACE

Elton John, Gary Osborne / 5:15

Musicians: Elton John: lead and backing vocals, piano / **Reggie McBride:** bass / **Steve Lukather:** guitar (not credited) / **Alvin Taylor:** drums / **James Newton Howard:** synthesizer, vocoder **Recorded:** Super Bear Studios, Berre-les-Alpes, France: August 1979 / Sunset Sound Recorders, Los Angeles: January 1980 **Technical Team: Producers:** Clive Franks, Elton John / **Sound Engineer:** Clive Franks / **Assistant Sound Engineer (Super Bear):** Patrick Jauneaud / **Assistant Sound Engineers (Sunset Sound):** Peggy McCreary, Stephen McManus / **Mastering:** Tim Young

Arguably one of the best tracks on *The Fox*, the ominous-sounding "Heart in the Right Place" owes much of its torrid atmosphere to Steve Lukather's magnificent electric guitar. From the wah-wahs of the intro to the electrifying solos, the six-string guitar also acts as an essential link between Elton's restrained bluesy piano and the solid rhythm section, notable particularly for the brilliant bass playing done by Reggie McBride, with his striking use of pick technique. James Newton Howard's vocoder is effective even if the addition of a synthesizer feels overly obvious. It all works, though, and "Heart in the Right Place" is a genuine success and also the first properly blues-inflected song that Elton tackled since the rather tentative "Stinker" from 1974's *Caribou*. As for the lyrics, Gary Osborne steps up with the story of an unprincipled journalist who is prepared to do anything to attract readers, including slandering his subjects.

JUST LIKE BELGIUM

Elton John, Bernie Taupin / 4:10

Musicians: Elton John: vocals, piano / **Richie Zito:** guitar / **Dee Murray:** bass / **James Newton Howard:** synthesizer / **Jim Horn:** alto saxophone / Colette Bertrand: French vocals / **Nigel Olsson:** drums (not credited) **Recorded:** Sunset Sound Recorders, Los Angeles: January 1981 **Technical Team: Producer:** Chris Thomas / **Sound Engineer:** Bill Price / **Assistant Sound Engineers:** Peggy McCreary, Stephen McManus / **Mastering:** Tim Young Released as **Single:** *Just Like Belgium / Can't Get Over Getting Over Losing You* **UK Release:** July 3, 1981, on Rocket Record Company (ref. XPRES 59) **Best UK Chart Ranking:** Did Not Chart

"Just Like Belgium" was originally composed by Elton and Bernie for Rod Stewart, who turned it down because he felt the tune did not match the words. It is true that the cheerful tune accompanies a melancholy text about alcoholic homeless people looking back on the carefree and glamorous days of their youth in Belgium. Although Elton took note of Rod Stewart's comments, he was happy to include this piece when Geffen asked him to add more songs to *The Fox*. The upbeat rhythm section, together with the full sound of Dee Murray's lively bass playing and Nigel Olsson's accurate drumming, provides an ideal support for Elton's extended passages of luminous piano playing. These moments are interspersed with discreet interventions from James Newton Howard on the synthesizer, and a few whispered words in French that are intended to give the story a hint of local color. Elton's assured singing does little to express an appropriate nostalgia that fits with the hazy, alcohol-filled memories of the Belgian tramps at the center of the song, except perhaps in the final "oooh" that is dragged out as if to emphasize the evocation of a long-lost happiness.

NOBODY WINS

Jean-Paul Dréau, Gary Osborne / 3:39

Musicians: Elton John: lead and backing vocals / James Newton Howard: synthesizers / Roger Linn: rhythm box / Steve Porcaro: synthesizers (not credited) / **Jeff Porcaro:** rhythm box (not credited) **Recorded:** Sunset Sound Recorders, Los Angeles: January 1981 **Technical Team:** Producer: Chris Thomas / **Sound Engineer:** Bill Price / **Assistant Sound Engineers:** Peggy McCreary, Stephen McManus / **Mastering:** Tim Young Released as a **Single:** *Nobody Wins / Fools in Fashion* **UK Release:** May 8, 1981, on Rocket Record Company (ref. XPRES 54) **Best UK Chart Ranking:** 42 **US Release:** April 1981 by Geffen Records (ref. GEF49722) **Best US Chart Ranking:** 21

While staying on the French Mediterranean coast in the summer of 1980, Elton found himself stuck in a traffic jam on the outskirts of Saint-Tropez. His attention was suddenly caught by an unusual song coming from the car radio. It was "J'veux de la tendresse" (I want tenderness), sung by Janic Prevost with a linear and restless electronic backing. Elton was instantly hooked: He shared his discovery with Gary Osborne, who undertook to adapt the original text, written by Jean-Paul Dréau, into English. Unlike the French version, in which the singer cries out for her share of happiness, Osborne's version lacks the same emotional impact because here the singer becomes a neutral observer of a young couple whose relationship is falling apart. It's not until the latter verses that the singer himself takes center stage.

Elton's version does not attempt to mimic the original song. The tempo is much steadier, and it has a strong rhythmic power provided by one of the first rhythm boxes in use, a Linn LM-1 programmed jointly by Jeff Porcaro, the distinguished drummer from Toto, and Roger Linn, the creator of this little technological treasure. Based on just twelve drum samples, almost one hundred different patterns were available on the Linn LM-1. Although the result was a bit inflexible, the sound was amazing, and it closely resembled an acoustic drum kit. The synth-pop sound of the song was further achieved by the insistent layering of James Newton Howard's synthesizers, thereby placing the track squarely in the musical trends of the period. But this song is chiefly notable for Elton's visceral vocal performance, which gives it its dramatic impact.

Elton also recorded the song in French, this time using the words written by Jean-Paul Dréau and sung with a notably good French accent. This French version was released under the title "J'veux de la tendresse" for the French and Québécois releases of *The Fox*. It was also issued as a 45 rpm in France and Canada, with "Fools in Fashion" as Side B.

Putting on a smile in spite of his internal torment, Elton combined joyful melodies with Bernie's often grief-tinged lyrics.

FASCIST FACES

Elton John, Bernie Taupin / 5:11

Musicians: Elton John: lead and backing vocals, piano / Richie Zito: guitar / Dee Murray: bass / Nigel Olsson: drums / The Cornerstone Institutional Baptist Choir: vocals / **Rev. James Cleveland:** spoken voice, choir conductor / **Recorded:** Sunset Sound Recorders, Los Angeles: January 1981 **Technical Team:** Producer: Chris Thomas / **Sound Engineer:** Bill Price / **Assistant Sound Engineers:** Peggy McCreary, Stephen McManus / **Mastering:** Tim Young

The result of a new collaboration between Elton and Bernie, this title is filled with bitterness and anger. Rarely does Bernie choose such direct words in his songwriting, but here the title alone is enough to express the contempt that both men felt for the radicalization of right-wing thinking. The lyrics tell the story of a man who seeks to reveal information hidden by the so-called establishment and who resents accusations that he's a communist sympathizer.

Musically, Elton opts for a slow and somewhat heavy tempo that's created by his go-to rhythm section comprised of Dee Murray and Nigel Olsson. Murray confines himself to providing penetrating and fundamental notes, while Olsson seems like he's about to destroy his drums with his militaristic, rhythmic playing. Elton's piano, initially relegated to the background, emerges to become an essential part of the composition, particularly when he cleverly fleshes out the relatively simple bass line played by Dee Murray. Elton's singing is accompanied by a gospel choir, and it becomes progressively more aggressive as his indignation grows. Richie Zito's incisive guitar adds a certain flamboyance, symbolizing the confrontation between the opposing forces of justice and oppression.

CARLA/ETUDE/ FANFARE/CHLOE

*Elton John / Elton John, James Newton Howard /
Elton John, Gary Osborne 10:51*

CARLA/ETUDE
Elton John

Musicians: Elton John: piano / London Symphony Orchestra: orchestra / James Newton Howard: direction, arrangements **Recorded:** Piano: Davlen Sound Studios, Los Angeles: ? Orchestra: Abbey Road, London: December 31, 1979 / Synthesizers and percussion: Sunset Sound Recorders, Los Angeles: January 1980 **Technical Team:** Producers: Clive Franks, Elton John / Sound Engineer: Clive Franks / Assistant Sound Engineers: Patrick Jauneaud (Super Bear), John Kurlander (Abbey Road), Peggy McCreary, Stephen McManus (Sunset Sound Recorders) / **Mastering:** Tim Young

FANFARE
Elton John, James Newton Howard

Musicians: Elton John: piano / London Symphony Orchestra: orchestra / James Newton Howard: synthesizer, direction, arrangements / Victor Feldman: percussion **Recorded:** Piano: Davlen Sound Studios, Los Angeles: ? / Orchestra: Abbey Road, London: December 31, 1979 / Synthesizers and percussion: Sunset Sound Recorders, Los Angeles: January 1980 **Technical Team:** Producers: Clive Franks, Elton John / Sound Engineer: Clive Franks / Assistant Sound Engineer (Super Bear): Patrick Jauneaud / Assistant Sound Engineer (Abbey Road): John Kurlander / Assistant Sound Engineers (Sunset Sound Recorders): Peggy McCreary, Stephen McManus / **Mastering:** Tim Young

CHLOE
Elton John, Gary Osborne

Musicians: Elton John: vocals, piano / Steve Lukather: guitar (not credited) / Reggie McBride: bass / Alvin Taylor: drums / London Symphony Orchestra: orchestra / James Newton Howard: Fender Rhodes, direction, arrangements / Marty Paich: arrangements / Victor Feldman: percussion / Bill Champlin, Max Gronenthal, Dee Murray, Gary Osborne: backing vocals **Recorded:** Piano: Super Bear Studios, Berre-les-Alpes, France: August 1979 / Orchestra: Abbey Road, London: December 31, 1979 / Synthesizers and percussion: Sunset Sound Recorders, Los Angeles: January 1980 **Technical Team:** Producers: Clive Franks, Elton John / Sound Engineer: Clive Franks / Assistant Sound Engineer (Super Bear): Patrick Jauneaud / Assistant Sound Engineer (Abbey Road): John Kurlander / Assistant Sound Engineers (Sunset Sound Recorders): Peggy McCreary, Stephen McManus / **Mastering:** Tim Young

Genesis

A predominantly instrumental suite of songs: "Carla/Etude," "Fanfare," and "Chloe" occupy an important place at the heart of *The Fox*, not merely because they arrive midway through the track list but also because this group of songs were recorded at the start of this new album's sessions in August 1979 and thereby set its melancholy tone.

Following "Amoreena," "Alice," and "Amy," "Carla" can be added to the list of Elton's songs that use a woman's name as their titles. This one is named after the wife of Clive Franks, Elton's sound engineer. Even years later, Franks still found this hard to believe: "I asked him what it was called, and Elton said he was trying to title it in an anagram of our names. I said, 'You're kidding me,' and he said 'No, leave it with me for a while.' And Elton is very clever with words, even though he doesn't write lyrics. After 10 minutes he came back into the control room where me and my wife, Carla, were sitting and said: 'I can't get an anagram of your names, so sod you, I'm just calling it the Carla Suite!' or whatever it was."[65] When *The Fox* was reissued as a CD in 2003, "Carla/Etude," "Fanfare," and "Chloe" became a single piece and thereby reduced the track list from eleven to nine.

Production

"Carla/Etude" draws on the classical training acquired by Elton when he attended classes at the Royal Academy of Music in his teens. The slow, lamenting melody on the piano acquired an astonishing elegance when the orchestration was added later. This orchestration was performed by the prestigious London Symphony Orchestra in the no-less-legendary Abbey Road studios at the end of 1979. James Newton Howard conducted the orchestra, revealing that he had skills beyond those of a simple keyboard player. A graduate of the Music Academy of the West (located in Santa Barbara, California) and the University of Southern California, Newton Howard would eventually go on to compose music for many popular movies. With a delicacy no less subtle than that of his predecessor, Paul Buckmaster, James Newton Howard here composed beautiful passages for flutes and strings. This section comes to a quiet end with the chords fading out and just a hint of a flanging effect, as the synthesizer is introduced to provide a bridge into "Fanfare." The effect is to shift the whole sound toward the new age while distilling some melodic elements from "Chloe," which is the only section in this triptych where Elton sings. Further arrangements for strings are introduced, and they include work from Marty Paich, who was one of the best West Coast jazz arrangers and the father of David Paich, the previously mentioned keyboard player for Toto. These arrangements fit perfectly with Steve Lukather's subtle guitar and Elton's vocals. Elton's tone moves between light and dark, setting the mood of the piece and perfectly adapting to the lyrics, which express the narrator's feelings of guilt over the lies that he's told, as well as his gratitude to his partner for her unfailing affection.

Elton John at his Windsor property on June 4, 1981, during the filming of the documentary accompanying the release of *The Fox*.

HEELS OF THE WIND

Elton John, Bernie Taupin / 3:34

Musicians: Elton John: lead and backing vocals, piano / **Richie Zito:** guitar / **Dee Murray:** bass / **Nigel Olsson:** drums / **James Newton Howard:** synthesizer / **Stephanie Spruill:** tambourine, backing vocals / Bill Champlin, Venette Gloud, Tamara Matoesian: backing vocals
Recorded: Sunset Sound Recorders, Los Angeles: January 1981
Technical Team: Producer: Chris Thomas / **Sound Engineer:** Bill Price / **Assistant Sound Engineers:** Peggy McCreary, Stephen McManus / **Mastering:** Tim Young

Although he had managed to extricate himself from a self-destructive depressive spiral, Bernie Taupin was still affected by the failure of his marriage. His pain can be felt in "Heels of the Wind." The very first line provides the following comparison: "Just like a broken marriage, when two people just don't care / Like when the cupboard is empty or there's no food in the Frigidaire." The speaker seeks to made amends, admitting that

a relationship with him is not always a "cushy first-class flight," and that he hasn't always been "nice." As so often happens in similar cases, Elton John chooses to counterbalance the darkness of the lyrics with a musical composition that is relatively light in tone. Supported by gospel-like backing vocals, Elton's voice sounds cheerful as it stresses certain, important words like "hope," as a way of almost negating sad phrases like "no closer to my hope." James Newton Howard follows Elton's lead here and injects a few happier moments with the synthesizer. In the background, Richie Zito lends density and substance with his saturated electric guitar.

ELTON'S SONG

Elton John, Tom Robinson / 3:02

Musicians: Elton John: vocals, piano / James Newton Howard: synthesizer **Recorded:** Super Bear Studios, Berre-les-Alpes, France: August 1979 / Sunset Sound Recorders, Los Angeles: January 1980 **Technical Team:** Producers: Clive Franks, Elton John / Sound Engineer: Clive Franks / Assistant Sound Engineer (Super Bear): Patrick Jauneaud / Assistant Sound Engineers (Sunset Sound Recorders): Peggy McCreary, Stephen McManus / Mastering: Tim Young

"Elton's Song" is one of the five songs on *The Fox* that was composed in August 1979, but not used on *21 at 33*. Before it was recorded, this song had a baptism by fire during the American tour "Back in the USSA," which ran from September 19 to November 11, 1979. Elton John has said of this number: "'Elton's Song' is so beautiful, and Tom Robinson's lyric is so beautiful. It reminded me of the film *If...*, by Lindsay Anderson. It was very homoerotic. I could imagine the boy that I wanted to be, on the parallel bars, swinging with his tight little outfit on and his bare feet. It was the first gay song that I actually recorded as a homosexual song. Rather than 'All the Girls Love Alice,' it was the first boy-on-boy song I wrote—because Tom, of course, is a gay man, and we became great friends."[35] As far as Elton is concerned, the autobiographical element of the song must be fairly limited, since he did not discover the truth of his own sexual orientation until much later in life, and long after his adolescence. This is not to say that he did not identify with and feel sympathy for the young narrator who was ostracized by his classmates because of his sexuality.

Similar to the classical style of "Carla/Etude," the melancholy of "Elton's Song" is expressed by Elton's dreamy piano playing, which is featured almost entirely on its own in this intimate song, and which alternates between major and minor chords to create an unusual and off-kilter atmosphere. Preferring not to let the song become overarranged, Elton confined additions to James Newton Howard's gentle synthesizer layers, which resemble the sounds made by typical stringed instruments.

1981

THE FOX

Elton John, Bernie Taupin / 5:20

Musicians: Elton John: vocals, piano / Richie Zito: guitar / Dee Murray: bass / Nigel Olsson: drums / James Newton Howard: organ / Mickey Raphael: harmonica / Ronald Baker, Carl Carwell, Chuck Cissel, Clarence Ford, Roy Galloway, James Gilstrap, John Lehman, Oren Waters: backing vocals **Recorded:** Sunset Sound Recorders, Los Angeles: January 1981 **Technical Team:** Producer: Chris Thomas / Sound Engineer: Bill Price / Assistant Sound Engineers: Peggy McCreary, Stephen McManus / Mastering: Tim Young

When Geffen asked Elton to come up with a title for the album, he thought immediately of a fox, an animal whose cunning struck him as an appropriate symbol for the way in which he had led his own life. Added to that, it is an animal associated with the English aristocracy. He asked Bernie for lyrics about this clever beast and Bernie obliged. Elton had become the fox, "like it or not," identifying totally with the fox that, thanks to its many talents and shrewdness, has survived innumerable attacks, managing to reverse apparently desperate situations. He knows that the critics (the hunters) will never let up, that he will always be hunted, but he vows that: "I'm always gonna be there running over the rock" and "I'll keep moving through the night."

Elton's voice is backed by impeccable and beautiful gospel vocals. Nigel Olsson and Dee Murray prove reliable as always, and their groove on this track is both inventive and rigorous. Richie Zito fits into the arrangement perfectly with his subtle injections of electric guitar.

As the final track on the album, "The Fox" represents an emotional triumph for an artist who was determined not to accept feelings of depression that overcame him from time to time. His piano playing is both inspired and persuasive here, and it is enlivened by the sound of Mickey Raphael's harmonica.

FOOLS IN FASHION

Elton John, Bernie Taupin / 4:12

Single: *Nobody Wins / Fools in Fashion* **UK Release:** May 8, 1981, on Rocket Record Company (ref. XPRES 54) **Best UK Chart Ranking:** 42 **US Release:** April 1981 on Geffen Records (ref. GEF49722) **Best US Chart Ranking:** 21 **Musicians:** Elton John: vocals, Fender Rhodes / James Newton Howard: synthesizer / Mickey Raphael: harmonica / Victor Feldman: percussion / Unidentified musician: guitar / Unidentified musician: bass / Unidentified musician: drums / Unidentified singers: backing vocals **Recorded:** Sunset Sound Recorders, Los Angeles: January 1980 ? **Technical Team:** Producers: Clive Franks, Elton John / Sound Engineer: Clive Franks / Assistant Sound Engineers (Sunset Sound Recorders): Peggy McCreary, Stephen McManus / Mastering: Tim Young

Chosen for Side B of "Nobody Wins," "Fools in Fashion" is a well-made track, with its balanced mix of pop and rhythm 'n' blues. Originally intended to be included as a track on the album, the song was rejected by Geffen Records for reasoning that remains unclear. Listening to the nervy, groovy keyboard sounds on this track, one is immediately reminded of the work of Stevie Wonder. With its many changes of rhythm and short pauses, the track only intermittently features drums, preferring to entrust its groove to percussion. The drums eventually come in for the finale, joining the excitingly sensual duo of the deep, full bass and the deliciously retro-sounding Fender Rhodes.

CAN'T GET OVER GETTING OVER LOSING YOU

Elton John, Gary Osborne / 4:16

Single: *Just Like Belgium / Can't Get Over Getting Over Losing You* **UK Release:** 3 July 1981 by Rocket Record Company (ref. XPRES 59) **Best UK Chart Ranking:** Did Not Chart **Musicians:** Elton John:

lead singer, piano, vocals / Richie Zito: guitar / Reggie McBride: bass / Alvin Taylor: drums / Lenny Castro: percussion / Byron Berline: violin **Recorded:** Super Bear Studios, Berre-les-Alpes, France: August 1979 / Sunset Sound Recorders, Los Angeles: January–March 1980 **Technical Team:** Producers: Clive Franks, Elton John / Sound Engineer: Clive Franks / Assistant Sound Engineer (Super Bear): Patrick Jauneaud / Assistant Sound Engineers (Sunset Sound Recorders): Peggy McCreary, Stephen McManus / Mastering: Tim Young

Recorded during the sessions for *21 at 33*, "Can't Get Over Getting Over Losing You" was released as the B-side of the "Just Like Belgium" single in 1981, and it would later gain in popularity when it was included on *Jewel* in 2020. "Can't Get Over Getting Over Losing You" is a charming and unpretentious country ballad that features a saloon-like atmosphere created by the relaxed sound of a lap steel guitar. Elton's voice is just right for the style of the song and Richie Zito's electric guitar appears between verses to help provide transitions between the piano and the lap steel guitar.

TORTURED

Elton John, Bernie Taupin / 4:37

Singles: *Chloe / Tortured* **US Release:** July 1981 on Geffen Records (ref. GEF49788) **Best US Chart Ranking:** 34 • *Who Wears These Shoes? / Tortured* **UK Release:** October 15, 1984, on Rocket Record Company (ref. EJS 612) **Best UK Chart Ranking:** 50 **Musicians:** Elton John: vocals, piano / **Recorded:** Super Bear Studios, Berre-les-Alpes, France: August 1979 / Sunset Sound Recorders, Los Angeles: January–March 1980 **Technical Team:** Producers: Clive Franks, Elton John / Sound Engineer: Clive Franks / Assistant Sound Engineer (Super Bear): Patrick Jauneaud / Assistant Sound Engineers (Sunset Sound Recorders): Peggy McCreary, Stephen McManus / Mastering: Tim Young

A weepy soft-rock ballad, "Tortured" features a man who's in love with someone who seems to delight in sentimental torture. The song seems more than once to end (for example, at 1:35), only to start up again with renewed vigor. The arrangement is not particularly original with a restrained piano and rhythm section and a rather conventional guitar solo, but the melody of the chorus is catchy. Released in the United States in 1981 as the B side of "Chloe," the song went to number 34 on the charts. In 1984 it appeared as Side B of "Who Wears These Shoes?" and went to number 50 on the UK charts.

ALBUM

JUMP UP!

Dear John . Spiteful Child . Ball & Chain . Legal Boys . I Am Your Robot .
Blue Eyes . Empty Garden (Hey Hey Johnny) . Princess .
Where Have All the Good Times Gone? . All Quiet on the Western Front

RELEASE DATES
UK Release: April 9, 1982
Reference: Rocket Record Company—HISPD 127
Best UK Chart Ranking: 13
US Release: April 19, 1982
Reference: Geffen Records—GHS 2013
Best US Chart Ranking: 17

THE *JUMP UP!* TOUR

On March 6, 1982, in Auckland, New Zealand, Elton John began a vast world tour that finished more than a year later on October 15, 1983. The massive tour included 135 gigs throughout Australia, New Zealand, Europe, North America, and Africa. The tour also marked the return of Davey Johnstone after eight years away, and the re-forming of the historic quartet of the 1970s: Dee, Nigel, Davey, and Elton.

BLUES IN THE SOUL

The ink was barely dry on the contract binding Elton John to Geffen Records when the first tensions arose between the artist and his new partners. After *The Fox*, Elton was dying to record an instrumental album, but this whim did not mesh with the record company's plans. With the exception of "Song for Guy," "Mama Can't Buy You Love," and "Little Jeannie," Elton had not reached the top of the charts in the United States or the United Kingdom since 1977, and his new record company felt that an instrumental album was not going to get him back on top.

Elton Falls in Line

The artist, who was mostly unmoved by Geffen's fears, was determined to record his instrumental numbers. He set himself up in the Pathé-Marconi studios in France on June 21, 1981, which happened to be the day after a party he'd attended at which he met Lady Diana Spencer for the first time. Because Elton's plan was to use just piano and synthesizers to enrich this new crop of songs, only James Newton Howard was with him in the studio. But the experiment soon ground to a halt; or, at least, it began to take on a much more conventional tone. As he worked, Elton realized that the melody for a song he had just created was ideally suited for lyrics that had been sent to him by Tim Rice, the lyricist behind *Jesus Christ Superstar*. The song "Legal Boys" took shape, and Elton felt that it had huge potential. Elton then decided to perform a complete about-face. He put his instrumental compositions (including "The Man Who Never Died," an homage to John Lennon that remained unused until its appearance on Side B of "Nikita" in 1985) to the side and began a new creative phase, this time involving songs with lyrics. With the notable exception of "Empty Garden," the music for all of the songs created during this new phase came before the word, including tracks with lyrics written by Bernie Taupin. Whether or not this cart-before-the-horse style of writing music would become a regular way of working remained to be seen, but the fact remained that Elton was overflowing with new and exciting ideas.

The Possibility of an Island

All the songs on *Jump Up!* originated in Paris, but they were recorded at the George Martin–owned AIR Studios located in the British Lesser Antilles. Parisian studios were not suited to the acoustic requirements of Chris Thomas and Elton John. So it was on the idyllic paradise setting of Montserrat, a tiny volcanic island of barely twenty-five acres, that the album assumed its final form. In this setting, which offered calm and ensured an absence of distractions, Elton could focus on the input of his loyal band of trusted musicians. This time, there were no upheavals in personnel, no psychodramas to contend with: Richie Zito was back in the role of guitarist, Dee Murray was back on bass (this time without the fear of competition), and Jeff Porcaro was brought in on drums after providing some sporadic additions on *The Fox*. Once again, James Newton Howard retained his place on keyboards. As for Gary Osborne and Bernie Taupin: they shared the lyrical duties on an equitable basis, with Gary focusing on his favorite subject of love (and loss), and the Taupin taking care of a variety of different themes, including death ("Empty Garden"), war ("All Quiet on the Western Front") and nostalgia ("Where Have All The Good Times Gone"). The gravity of these subjects found a natural extension when Elton chose to produce his voice in a lower register, which can be heard on "Spiteful Child," "Blue Eyes," "Princess," and "Ball and Chain," although this weighty subject matter isn't apparent in the album's title, *Jump Up!*, which comes from a common festive expression used on the island of Montserrat.

This enthusiasm won over the general public, but Bernie Taupin was never really taken with this album and considered it be a relative disappointment in relation to some of his other work. Nevertheless, *Jump Up!* did reach seventeenth place in the United States, and thirteenth in the United Kingdom. With the exception of "Blue Eyes," which went to number eight in the United Kingdom, the singles released from this album did not enjoy the same level of success, and they have since disappeared from Elton's set lists.

DEAR JOHN

Elton John, Gary Osborne / 3:33

Musicians: Elton John: vocals, piano / Richie Zito: electric guitar / Dee Murray: bass / Jeff Porcaro: drums / James Newton Howard: synthesizer **Recorded:** AIR Studios, Montserrat (Caribbean): February 9, 1982 **Technical Team:** Producer: Chris Thomas / Sound Engineer: Bill Price / Assistant Sound Engineers: Nigel Barker, Mike Stavrou / Mastering: Greg Fulginiti

"Dear John, so long…" Contrary to what the first verses of this song may seem to suggest, this tense rock number is not an homage to Elton's friend, John Lennon, who was assassinated in 1980. Elton and Bernie dedicated the seventh track on this album, "Empty Garden (Hey Hey Johnny)" to Lennon, and this opening number has a more straightforward meaning. The words of "Dear John" were written by Gary Osborne and they refer to a mostly friendly breakup that is announced via letter. There's nothing particularly original about this concept, since the "Dear John letter"—which is a letter written by one person to inform their partner that their relationship is over—occupies a well-known space in the epistolary universe. The edgy guitar of Richie Zito is combined with Elton's swirling piano, and together they offer the only completely novel moment on this track, though they are weighed down somewhat by the presence of James Newton Howard's synthesizer. While the melody here is superficially effective upon first listening, it soon grates on the nerves and only adds further banality to an already fairly lackluster piece.

SPITEFUL CHILD

Elton John, Bernie Taupin / 4:16

Musicians: Elton John: vocals, piano / Richie Zito: electric guitar / Dee Murray: bass / Jeff Porcaro: drums / James Newton Howard: synthesizer **Recorded:** AIR Studios, Montserrat (Caribbean): February 9, 1982 **Technical Team:** Producer: Chris Thomas / Sound Engineer: Bill Price / Assistant Sound Engineers: Nigel Barker, Mike Stavrou / **Mastering:** Greg Fulginiti

"Spiteful Child" has some positive aspects, including an infectious groove provided by an impeccable rhythm section. Dee Murray's plunging bass and Jeff Porcaro's disciplined drums effectively maintain a breathless tempo for more than four minutes, and Richie Zito's guitar aligns itself with gusto. Elton's voice emerges deep and clear, and it's lifted up by the supportive backing vocals of a gospel choir. Elton's piano, which inserts a captivating gimmick into the piece's introduction, gradually cedes space for James Newton Howard's synthesizer, which has a merely anecdotal role in the track and accompanies the piano solo later in the track. Unfortunately, some of the effects in the arrangement are a little predictable, such as the

incessant clicking of fingers and the unnecessary chimes. Overall, this is a decent song with some nice lyrics from Bernie that focus on the possible vengeance of a narrator who has been badly treated by a "spiteful child."

BALL & CHAIN

Elton John, Gary Osborne / 3:29

Musicians: Elton John: vocals, piano / Richie Zito: electric guitar / Pete Townshend: acoustic guitar / Dee Murray: bass / Jeff Porcaro: drums / James Newton Howard: synthesizer / Steve Holley: tambourine **Recorded:** AIR Studios, Montserrat (Caribbean): February 9, 1982 **Technical Team:** Producer: Chris Thomas / Sound Engineer: Bill Price / Assistant Sound Engineers: Nigel Barker, Mike Stavrou / Mastering: Greg Fulginiti **Single Release:** *Ball & Chain* / *Where Have All the Good Times Gone?* (alternative version) **US Release:** November 1982 with Geffen Records (ref. 7-29846) **Best US Chart Ranking:** Did Not Chart

As a mix of pop and country, "Ball & Chain" suffers from Gary Osborne's rather two-dimensional lyrics, which are laced with clichés.

As he already did on "Dear John," Gary Osborne tries in vain to inject some nuance by adding a few lyrics in French, this time using a very clumsy "Oh oui." Fortunately for all involved, Pete Townshend of the Who contributes a punchy acoustic guitar that saves the song from anonymity and made it worthy of release as a single. Dee Murray's bass line remains the most interesting part of the arrangement while Richie Zito, Steve Holley, and James Newton Howard all turn in fairly ordinary performances that don't contribute any additional feeling to the song. This song's inoffensive melody proved to be too much of a hindrance when it was released as a single in the United States, and the track never hit the charts.

LEGAL BOYS

Elton John, Tim Rice / 3:08

Musicians: Elton John: vocals, piano / Richie Zito: electric guitar / Dee Murray: bass / Jeff Porcaro: drums / James Newton Howard: synthesizer, string arrangements / Unidentified musicians: strings **Recorded:** AIR Studios, Montserrat (Caribbean): February 9, 1982 **Technical Team:** Producer: Chris Thomas / Sound Engineer: Bill Price / **Assistant Sound Engineers:** Nigel Barker, Mike Stavrou / **Mastering:** Greg Fulginiti

Lyricist Tim Rice and composer Andrew Lloyd Webber were to musicals what Bernie and Elton were to pop. Together, they shocked the public with *Jesus Christ Superstar* and then followed up on their success with *Evita* and *Cats*. By working with Elton, Tim Rice was taking a first step toward the world

1982

Working at AIR Studios on the Caribbean island of Montserrat during the recording of *Jump Up!*

of pop, and in so doing gave Elton one of the most success-ful tracks on the album, even though it had previously been rejected by Lloyd Webber. "Legal Boys" is about a couple that's in the midst of an acrimonious divorce. The man in the song thinks of the accountants and lawyers involved who are par-ticipating in his divorce as gravediggers of his lost love. When faced with fighting for his material property, the narrator feels a mixture of anger and melancholy that serve as a projection of his painfully hurt feelings. Elton's voice is both powerful and assured, as is the rhythm section in which the multiskilled Dee Murray shines. Overall, the arrangements are perfectly managed and constructed, from Elton's nervy piano playing to the fleet-ing but always useful contributions of James Newton Howard's synthesizer, and of course Richie Zito's electric guitar. A special mention is owed to the soaring stings and gentle backing vocals that appear to great effect beginning at 2:28.

This early collaboration between Elton John and Tim Rice proved fruitful when, many years later, the two men worked together again on the soundtracks for *The Lion King* (1994) and *The Road to El Dorado* (2000), as well on the original score for a Broadway musical adaptation of *Aida* (1999).

I AM YOUR ROBOT

Elton John, Bernie Taupin / 4:45

Musicians: Elton John: lead and backing vocals, piano / Richie Zito: electric guitar / Dee Murray: bass, backing vocals / Jeff Porcaro: drums / James Newton Howard: synthesizer / Steve Holley: Syndrum / Gary Osborne: backing vocals **Recorded:** AIR Studios, Montserrat (Caribbean): February 9, 1982 **Technical Team:** Producer: Chris Thomas / Sound Engineer: Bill Price / Assistants Sound Engineers: Nigel Barker, Mike Stavrou / **Mastering:** Greg Fulginiti

Elton's piano playing on "I Am Your Robot" is dynamic and his voice is assured despite some rather random backing vocals, but the repetitive melody and the unpalatable keyboards quickly sink the whole endeavor. At the heart of a rhythm sec-tion, Dee's bass bounces around in multiple directions while Jeff Porcaro's metronomic playing provides the song with a foundation that's based in minimalism and efficiency. Richie Zito's very crunchy guitar soon joins the fray, but the use of a cartoonish synthesizer and a truly strange, synthetic bass means this song falls victim to some of the worst excesses of the era.

BLUE EYES

Elton John, Gary Osborne / 3:26

Musicians

Elton John: vocals, piano
Dee Murray: bass
Jeff Porcaro: drums
James Newton Howard: Fender Rhodes, synthesizers, direction, arrangements
Martyn Ford Orchestra (credited as "The Mountain Fjord Orchestra"): orchestra
Gavyn Wright (credited as "Gavin Wright"): orchestral direction

Recorded

AIR Studios, Montserrat (Caribbean): February 9, 1982

Technical Team

Producer: Chris Thomas. Sound Engineer: Bill Price. Assistant Sound Engineers: Nigel Barker, Mike Stavrou. Mastering: Greg Fulginiti

Single Release

Blue Eyes / Hey Papa Legba
UK Release: March 19, 1982, on Rocket Record Company (ref. XPRES 71)
Best UK Chart Ranking: 8
US Release: July 1982 on Geffen Records (ref. 7-29954)
Best US Chart Ranking: 12

"Blue Eyes" was presented as an homage to Elizabeth Taylor before Elton confessed that this song is about one of his lovers.

Genesis and Lyrics

A retro love song with a haunting tempo, "Blue Eyes" is far and away the best track on *Jump Up!* For a long time, the origins of the song were shrouded in mystery. Written by Gary Osborne, some suggested that the lyrics were an homage to Frank Sinatra, and others thought the song was about Elizabeth Taylor, or possibly addressed to a lover of Elton's named Gary Clarke. In his 2019 autobiography, Elton shed some light on this hit when he discussed the explosion of AIDS at the beginning of the 1980s: "My ex-boyfriend Tim Lowe had tested positive. So had another ex, Vance Buck, a sweet blond boy from Virginia, who loved Iggy Pop and whose photo was on the inside cover of my album *Jump Up!*, just below the lyrics to 'Blue Eyes,' the song Gary Osborne and I had written with him in mind."[3]

Production

As the last song recorded for the album, "Blue Eyes" was almost abandoned after six takes because Elton felt he hadn't been able to achieve the right tone with his vocals. From a harmonic point of view, "Blue Eyes" is very complex, and it features verses written in *Bb* alongside a refrain written in *D* minor. The string arrangements are one of the biggest successes of the piece, as are the nuances provided by James Newton Howard's gentle Fender Rhodes. The minimalist rhythm section provides full but discreet support to Elton's moving piano. Jeff Porcaro performs a very fine drum line that's played mainly with brushes, while Dee Murray adds great depth to the track by focusing on fundamentals. Even if only for the incredible emotion contained in Elton's wavering vibrato on the word "eyes" at the 0:29 mark and again at 1:30, "Blue Eyes" is very much worth a listen.

EMPTY GARDEN
(HEY HEY JOHNNY)

Elton John, Bernie Taupin / 5:08

Musicians
Elton John: lead and backing vocals, Yamaha CP-70 electric piano, harpsichord
Richie Zito: acoustic guitars
Dee Murray: bass, backing vocals
Jeff Porcaro: drums, LinnDrum
James Newton Howard: synthesizer
Gary Osborne: backing vocals
Unidentified musicians: castanets, maracas, tambourine

Recorded
AIR Studios, Montserrat (Caribbean): April 1982

Technical Team
Producer: Chris Thomas / **Sound Engineer:** Bill Price / **Assistant Sound Engineers:** Nigel Barker, Mike Stavrou / **Mastering:** Greg Fulginiti

Single Release
Empty Garden / Take Me Down to the Ocean
UK Release: May 28, 1982, on Rocket Record Company (ref. XPRES 77)
Best UK Chart Ranking: 51
US Release: March 1982 on Geffen Records (ref. GEF50049)
Best US Chart Ranking: 13

John Lennon's death two years earlier was still an open wound for Elton.

Genesis and Lyrics
On December 8, 1980, the day when John Lennon was assassinated in New York, Elton John was traveling from Melbourne, Australia, to Brisbane. When he got off the plane, John Reid told him the terrible news. Incredulous, Elton arranged a memorial service at the cathedral of St. Patrick in Melbourne, during which he performed Psalm 23. He then had an enormous chocolate cake with the message "Love from Elton" sent to his godson Sean Lennon. Bernie, who was in Los Angeles when this tragedy was announced, was in a similar state of despair. Incapable of watching television or reading any newspapers, he took up his pen and notebook and began to write the lyrics of "Empty Garden," evoking the last place where John Lennon played in public, New York's Madison Square Garden. Emotion abounds in "Empty Garden," and it is for precisely this reason that Elton only rarely performs this song onstage. However, he did notably perform the song in a series of concerts given at Madison Square Garden between August 4 and August 7, 1982, with Yoko Ono and Sean Lennon in attendance.

Production
Despite its personal significance to Elton and Bernie, "Empty Garden" did not achieve real chart success and eventually had to settle for thirteenth place in the United States while never reaching the top fifty in the United Kingdom. However, the arrangement on this track is a successful one, with a fine harpsichord part performed by Elton alongside the copiously sliding bass of Dee Murray and backing vocals whose emotional power is subtly alleviated by some high synthesizer notes. Jeff Porcaro slots in some intense breaks on the drums that enable Elton to relaunch into vocals that are loaded with anger and sadness. These fleeting moments prepare the way for a magnificent finale, during which the backing vocals completely take off and envelop the entire track.

PRINCESS

Elton John, Gary Osborne / 4:56

Musicians: Elton John: vocals, piano / Richie Zito: electric guitar / Dee Murray: bass / Jeff Porcaro: drums / James Newton Howard: synthesizer **Recorded:** AIR Studios, Montserrat (Caribbean): February 9, 1982 **Technical Team:** Producer: Chris Thomas / Sound Engineer: Bill Price / Assistant Sound Engineers: Nigel Barker, Mike Stavrou / Mastering: Greg Fulginiti **Single Release:** *Princess / The Retreat* **UK Release:** September 3, 1982, on Rocket Record Company (ref. XPRES 85) **Best UK Chart Ranking:** Did Not Chart

A "prisoner," "buried alive," is "suddenly [...] freed" by the love of his "princess": this is the theme developed by Gary Osborne in the lyrics of "Princess." Elton does not perform any miracles with this text, and melodically the verses verge on banality. Thankfully, Dee Murray once again demonstrates the full elasticity of his bass, which is complemented by Jeff Porcaro's drums to create a solid rock 'n' roll intonation. Richie Zito's surprising guitar provides very decent licks that highlight the finesse of Elton's voice, which is well supported by very attractive backing vocals. It is such a pity, then, that the end of the song is annihilated by a painful synthesizer solo from James Newton Howard. Unsurprisingly, the door to the charts remained closed to this third single released from the album.

WHERE HAVE ALL THE GOOD TIMES GONE?

Elton John, Bernie Taupin / 4:01

Musicians: Elton John: vocals, piano / Richie Zito: electric guitar / Dee Murray: bass / Jeff Porcaro: drums / James Newton Howard: synthesizer / Unidentified musicians: orchestra **Recorded:** AIR Studios, Montserrat (Caribbean): February 9, 1982 **Technical Team:** Producer: Chris Thomas / Sound Engineer: Bill Price / Assistant Sound Engineers: Nigel Barker, Mike Stavrou / Mastering: Greg Fulginiti **Single Releases:** *All Quiet on the Western Front / Where Have All the Good Times Gone?* (remix) **UK Release:** November 12, 1982, on Rocket Record Company (ref. XPRES 88) **Best UK Chart Ranking:** Did Not Chart • *Ball & Chain / Where Have All the Good Times Gone?* (alternative version) **US Release:** November 1982 on Geffen Records (ref. 7-29846) **Best US Chart Ranking:** Did Not Chart

Not to be confused with the song of the same name by the Kinks that was released in 1965, "Where Have All the Good Times Gone?" suffers from the same shortcomings as most of the other numbers on *Jump Up!*: It has a good refrain but extremely ordinary verses. The lyrics from Bernie Taupin express a rather forced nostalgia for a lost age. The lyricist indulges himself in the evocation of these "good times" when people were "captured by romantic things" in a succession of clichés that include "Crazy summers that would never end" and "Monday mornings that would come too soon"! To sugarcoat these platitudes, Elton provides a melody that owes a lot to the soul music of the 1970s, and which is supported in particular by soaring violins and Dee Murray's assured and penetrating bass. Elton's voice, although very much at ease in the lower register and ably assisted by the millimeter-like precision of the backing vocals, was not enough to appease the general public, who shunned the single when it was released.

ALL QUIET ON THE WESTERN FRONT

Elton John, Bernie Taupin / 6:07

Musicians: Elton John: vocals, piano / Richie Zito: electric guitar / Dee Murray: bass / Jeff Porcaro: drums / James Newton Howard: synthesizer **Recorded:** AIR Studios, Montserrat (Caribbean): February 9, 1982 **Technical Team:** Producer: Chris Thomas / Sound Engineer: Bill Price / Assistant Sound Engineers: Nigel Barker, Mike Stavrou / Mastering: Greg Fulginiti **Single Release:** *All Quiet on the Western Front / Where Have All the Good Times Gone?* (remix) **UK Release:** November 12, 1982, on Rocket Record Company (ref. XPRES 88) **Best UK Chart Ranking:** Did Not Chart

With "All Quiet on the Western Front," which evokes the First World War, Bernie intended to publish an antimilitaristic manifesto in the vein of the classic novel with the same title. In this famous book, which appeared in 1929 and was written by Erich Maria Remarque, the German writer describes the horror of the Great War through the eyes of a young German solder sent to the Western Front. Transferred to the screen the following year, the novel became a huge success and an enduring pacifist symbol. Elton's song was released as a single in 1982, but the public shunned the long track that clocked in at more than six minutes of running time (although a shorter version was marketed). As the final track on *Jump Up!* this song takes its time to establish a touching atmosphere and a powerful refrain that's magnified nicely by James Newton Howard's keyboards, Richie Zito's discreet guitar, and a few rolls on the toms provided by Jeff Porcaro. These reappear on the song's intense finale, which feels somewhat reminiscent of other songs from Elton's catalog, including "The King Must Die" and "Burn Down the Mission."

"All Quite on the Western Front" is one of the rare instances in which Elton made a change to one of Bernie's lyrics. The singer asked the songwriter to delete a line portraying soldiers as "thin white men in stinking tents." Curiously, Elton sang this exact phrase when he performed the song during his 1982 tour.

Posters for *Jump Up!* covered the streets of Paris to announce Elton's performance at the Palais des Sports on May 17, 1982.

TAKE ME DOWN TO THE OCEAN

Elton John, Gary Osborne / 4:06

Single: *Empty Garden / Take Me Down to the Ocean* **UK Release:** May 28, 1982, on Rocket Record Company (ref. XPRES 77) **Best UK Chart Ranking:** 51 **US Release:** March 1982 with Geffen Records (ref. GEF50049) **Best US Chart Ranking:** 13 **Musicians:** Elton John: vocals, piano / Richie Zito: electric guitar / Dee Murray: bass / Jeff Porcaro: drums / James Newton Howard: synthesizer / Daryl Dragon, Bruce Johnston, Peter Noone, Toni Tennille: backing vocals **Recorded:** Super Bear Studios, Berre-les-Alpes, France: August 1979 / Sunset Sound Recorders, Los Angeles: January to March 1980 / Brother Studios, Santa Monica: ? **Technical Team:** Producers: Clive Franks, Elton John / **Sound Engineer:** Clive Franks / **Assistant Sound Engineer (Super Bear):** Patrick Jauneaud / **Assistant Sound Engineers (Sunset Sound):** Peggy McCreary, Stephen McManus / **Mastering:** Tim Young

Having been recorded during multiple sessions, the production of "Take Me Down to the Ocean" was finalized by Gary Osborne supporting Clive Franks, instead of Elton, who was indisposed during the final sessions. Beach Boy Bruce Johnston supervised the backing vocals, and it shows. Daryl Dragon, Toni Tennille, and Peter Noone also contributed to the vocal harmonies, which are irreproachable, particularly on the bridge, which extends from 2:45 until the end of the piece. Musically, Richie Zito's guitar is at the forefront, as is Elton's well-judged piano playing. But once again it is Dee Murray's unchained bass that makes the strongest impression, even though it sometimes seems slightly out of sync with Elton's honky-tonk gimmick, mainly on the introduction. This sense of confusion very logically kept the song off the album.

HEY PAPA LEGBA

Elton John, Bernie Taupin / 5:11

Single: *Blue Eyes / Hey Papa Legba* **UK Release:** March 19, 1982, on Rocket Record Company (ref. XPRES 71) **Best UK Chart Ranking:** 8 **US Release:** July 1982 on Geffen Records (ref. 7-29954) **Best US Chart Ranking:** 12 **Musicians:** Elton John: vocals, piano / Richie Zito: electric guitar / Dee Murray: bass / Jeff Porcaro: drums / James Newton Howard: synthesizer / Unidentified musicians: brass **Recorded:** Super Bear Studios, Berre-les-Alpes, France: August 1979 **Technical Team:** Producers: Clive Franks, Elton John / **Sound Engineer:** Clive Franks / **Assistant Sound Engineer:** Patrick Jauneaud / **Mastering:** Tim Young

Papa Legba is a voodoo spirit who acts as a gatekeeper between the human world and the spirit world. Here, Bernie devotes his lyrics to Papa Legba in a song that appeared on the B side of "Blue Eyes" and is basically the polar opposite of its Side A companion, which is a fairly somber ballad. Elton imposes an imposing rock sound on the track complete with an intense tempo that centers around a haunting piano and Richie Zito's effusive guitar. The rhythm section revolves around Dee Murray, whose bass delivers an insatiable groove, and Jeff Porcaro with his edgy playing. Together, they reliably sustain Elton's powerful voice. The cherry on top: a glitzy brass section that provides an extra dose of spirit.

ALBUM

TOO LOW FOR ZERO

Cold as Christmas (In the Middle of the Year) . I'm Still Standing .
Too Low for Zero . Religion . I Guess That's Why They Call It the Blues . Crystal .
Kiss the Bride . Whipping Boy . Saint . One More Arrow

RELEASE DATES
UK Release: May 30, 1983
Reference: Rocket Record Company—HISPD 24, 811 052-1
Best UK Chart Ranking: 7
US Release: May 30, 1983
Reference: Geffen Records—GHS 4006
Best US Chart Ranking: 25

FOR ELTON ADDICTS

Although he was not the producer of *Too Low for Zero*, Gus Dudgeon took over the remastering of the album when it was reissued by Mercury as a CD in 1998.

1983

RETURN OF THE DREAM TEAM

Elton John's creative impulsivities meant that he often didn't make concrete plans from one album to the next, so it must have come as a pleasant surprise when the team from the golden years of the early '70s reunited. Dee Murray, Nigel Olsson, and Davey Johnstone all signed up to join Elton on the *Jump Up!* world tour (March 6, 1982, to October 15, 1983), and although Bernie was preoccupied with writing for other artists like Rod Stewart, the Motels, and Bruce Hornsby, he, too, was keen to work with Elton once again. Elton was equally enthusiastic at the prospect, and he was able to meet up with Bernie in California at the beginning of June 1982 before embarking on the North American stage of his tour (June 12 to August 7). The two men hoped to re-create the conditions that had been so favorable to the production of their earlier masterpieces. By shutting themselves up in the studio with a pared-down team, they planned to see where inspiration might take them. They agreed to get together at George Martin's AIR Studios in Montserrat in September 1982, during a break from the *Jump Up!* world tour. Elton allowed for two weeks of recording, which was an almost unheard-of amount of time for a team that was used to the high-speed sessions of the early '70s, when entire recording sessions were often completed in a single week. Elton John wrote in his autobiography that this was the first album since 1975's *Captain Fantastic* to properly reunite the old Elton John Band. "It was like a well-oiled machine coming back to life, but the results didn't sound like the albums we had made in the 1970s, they sounded really fresh."**³**

A New Direction in Sound

Elton, who had begun to find the sound of the acoustic piano somewhat limiting, felt the need to expand the range of sounds available to him on what would become his seventeenth album. Although previously reluctant to use them, Elton now turned to the electric keyboard, which would become a major factor in creating his new, more modern sound. The electric keyboard

meant he could play much faster than on a traditional piano, which was especially helpful on tracks with a more rock 'n' roll style to them. The fact that he now composed on an electric Yamaha CP-80 certainly helped Elton adapt to this type of instrument, after previously finding them too complicated. Presented with the knobs and controls of electronic keyboards, Elton would previously throw up his hands and abandon it. Now he began to add synthesizers—Fender Rhodes and Clavinet—to his lineup, performing the role usually filled by James Newton Howard. The latter was involved in only one number on the album, "One More Arrow," on which he provided the string arrangements. In his pursuit of something new, Elton adopted the going fashion for synth-pop. Not only did he make greater use of synthesizers (probably under the influence of Prince, who's music was massively popular at the time), but he also used a rhythm box for tracks like "Crystal" and the eponymous "Too Low for Zero."

The album's modern sound also owes a lot to Chris Thomas's fine production, which brings out the singer's voice in the mix thanks to the addition of a carefully calibrated reverb. Working alongside Chris Thomas were sound engineer Bill Price and assistant sound engineers Peggy McCreary and Renate Blauel. As work progressed, a strong rapport was established between Elton and Renate, a twenty-nine-year-old born in Berlin.

The evident pleasure the team felt in working together again infuses many of the tracks on this album with an infectious energy, particularly on the powerful "Whipping Boy" and "Kiss the Bride" and of course on the hit song, "I'm Still Standing." The Fab Four—Elton, Dee, Nigel, and Davey—were almost single-handedly responsible for the majority of the musical compositions on the album, with only occasional added assistance from Kiki Dee on vocals, Skaila Kanga on harp, Ray Cooper on percussion, and the amazing Stevie Wonder on harmonica for "I Guess That's Why They Call It the Blues."

Davey Johnstone, Elton John,
Nigel Olsson, and Dee Murray:
The outstanding team reunited
in the studio and onstage for
the *Jump Up!* Tour.

Confident in his team, and now endowed with a renewed taste for sound experimentation, Elton delivered vocal performances that are both more elaborate and more instinctive than some of his previous work. While *Jump Up!* marked a foray into a more serious register, here Elton returns to his former style of singing and revives his famous falsetto, much to the delight of fans, on tracks like "One More Arrow."

A Difficult Time

When recording was completed, *Too Low for Zero* was eventually settled on as the title of the album. It's an odd choice given that it seems to totally contradict the return to form that was so evident during the recording sessions, and the declaration of intent that comes on "I'm Still Standing." The artistic direction of the record cover was entrusted to Rod Dyer, with design work done by Clive Piercy; their task was to create a minimalist representation of the album's title. Shown several rough drafts, Elton selected a version with a spare and geometric design that used symbols and the numbers 2 for "Too" and 4 for "For."

Before assessing the public impact of the new album, the Elton John Band was back on the road in November with the *Jump Up!* tour. Great Britain was waiting for them and they were ready to conquer it. But now a series of mishaps occurred that would upset the good dynamics of the group. On the one hand, sales on the *Jump Up!* album were less than stellar. "Ball & Chain" and "All Quiet on the Western Front" (a title that turned out to be prophetic) failed to sell, and the Geffen Record Company was becoming impatient with Elton's seemingly chronic inability to place his new singles on the charts, with the sole exception of "Blue Eyes." The compilation album *Love Songs*, which was comprised of a selection of songs taken from recent Elton albums starting with 1976's *Blue Moves*, also proved to be a disappointment when it stalled out at number thirty-nine on the UK charts in November 1982. A later compilation album from Elton, also called *Love Songs*, did much better when it hit the fourth spot on the UK charts upon release in 1995.

Elton hoped to revive his fortunes with an ambitious residency planned for the Hammersmith Odeon in London between December 9 and December 24, 1982, but he was once again disappointed. He had gone all out for the occasion, spending nearly $13,000 on decorations to give the famous venue the appearance of a gift-wrapped Christmas present. In the first week of concerts problems began to arise when Nigel

Olsson fell ill but didn't tell anyone he was struggling. During one performance, the group was forced to go on as a trio. The three musicians stuck together and were able to compensate for the absence of their colleague, but Elton became increasingly angry as the evening progressed. As the trio performed "Better Off Dead," Elton shared his fury at the drummer's absence with the audience. When he introduced each musician, Elton looked hard at the drum kit where Nigel should have been sitting and gave a groan that made the audience laugh, but that also said a lot about his anger. The same evening came to a fairly disastrous conclusion when, during "Bennie and the Jets," Elton pushed his stool forcefully toward the edge of the stage, assuming that it would fall into the orchestra pit. Unfortunately, the pit was covered and the stool ended up falling into the audience and injuring a woman. Instead of asking if the young woman was all right, as the other musicians did, Elton awkwardly tried to justify himself. Later in the evening, the band was backstage and waiting to return for an encore. Elton spotted John Reid laughing and drinking champagne with guests even as he was experiencing the worst evening of his tour. He stormed out of the theater and got into his car. The road was jammed with traffic and the car couldn't move. This seemed to be a sign telling him that he had to go back onstage, apologize, and finish the show. Elton eventually made amends, inviting the injured audience member backstage and promising her a day of shopping at his expense.

On February 23, 1983, the 25th Grammy Awards took place, and Elton once again went home empty-handed. Then, two canceled projects further undermined Elton's morale. The first was an idea for a movie with Liza Minnelli and Rod Stewart, in which Elton and Rod were supposed to appear dressed as women a la *Some Like It Hot*. The other canceled project was a proposed world tour featuring Elton and Rod Stewart, which Rod declined.

It was in the midst of this inauspicious career moment when the singles from *Too Low for Zero* were released, in April 1983. "I Guess That's Why They Call It the Blues" started the ball rolling in the UK, and it marked Elton's artistic comeback by going to fifth place in the sales charts—a ranking that Elton had not achieved since "Song for Guy" in 1978. Meanwhile, "I'm Still Standing" was dominating the airwaves in the United States, eventually reaching twelfth place on the *Billboard* charts. The track did even better in the UK, where it reached number four on the singles charts in July 1983. "Kiss the Bride" also hit a very respectable twentieth position.

COLD AS CHRISTMAS (IN THE MIDDLE OF THE YEAR)

Elton John, Bernie Taupin / 4:22

Musicians: Elton John: vocals, piano, Fender Rhodes, synthesizer / Davey Johnstone: acoustic guitar, backing vocals / Dee Murray: bass, backing vocals / Nigel Olsson: drums, backing vocals / Ray Cooper: percussion / Skaila Kanga: harp / Kiki Dee: backing vocals
Recorded: AIR Studios, Montserrat (Caribbean): September 1982 / Sunset Sound Recorders, Los Angeles: January 1983 **Technical Team:** Producer: Chris Thomas / Sound Engineer: Bill Price / Assistant Sound Engineers: Renate Blauel, Peggy McCreary / Mastering: Chris Thomas (UK), Greg Fulginiti **US Single Release:** *Cold as Christmas (In the Middle of the Year)* / *Crystal* **UK Release:** November 1983 on Rocket Record Company (ref. ESJ 3, 814 862-7) **Best UK Chart Ranking:** 33

The contrast between the title and the surroundings evoked in the words of "Cold as Christmas" creates a striking thermal shock. Bernie paints a picture of a man of a certain age who, we gather, lives with his wife in some Caribbean-like idyllic tropical location. The shade from the palm trees does nothing to offset the burning July heat, but the temperature seems to have cooled considerably between this pair of one-time soulmates who now eat at different tables and no longer share the same bed. The man laments this "marriage minus heart," and a "love burned out by silence." He tells his children, "there's a winter look in your mother's eyes." This song, with a melody composed by Elton, is full of a morose sadness, and it provides a strangely low-key opening to the new album. The vocal line does not entirely suit Elton, who has to force his voice in the refrain, but the arrangement works well in part thanks to the gentle backing vocals from Kiki Dee. Dee Murray's flexible bass, and some particularly magical harp playing by Skaila Kanga, also help keep the song afloat. Although not the most memorable song created by the pair, "Cold as Christmas" effectively reasserted Elton's fruitful collaboration with his lyricist.

I'M STILL STANDING

Elton John, Bernie Taupin / 3:03

Musicians

Elton John: lead and backing vocals, piano, synthesizer
Davey Johnstone: electric guitar, backing vocals
Dee Murray: bass, backing vocals
Nigel Olsson: drums, backing vocals

Recorded

AIR Studios, Montserrat (Caribbean): September 1982

Technical Team

Producer: Chris Thomas
Sound Engineer: Bill Price
Assistant Sound Engineers: Renate Blauel, Peggy McCreary
Mastering: Chris Thomas (UK), Greg Fulginiti (USA)

Single Release

I'm Still Standing / Earn While You Learn
UK Release: July 3, 1983, on Rocket Record Company (ref. EJS 1, 812 776-7)
Best UK Chart Ranking: 4

• *I'm Still Standing / Love So Cold*
US Release: April 1983 on Geffen Records (ref. 7-29639)
Best US Chart Ranking: 12

Elton in Montserrat in Autumn 1982.

Genesis and Lyrics

"I'm Still Standing" is undoubtedly the biggest hit from *Too Low for Zero* and, in the way it mirrors his life, it's also one of the most symbolic songs in Elton John's entire catalog. Shaken by the seeming disenchantment of the public, who had ignored his singles for several years, Elton picked himself up with a song that celebrated his resilience like a mantra: he is "still standing." This was not, however, the original meaning of the lyrics; Bernie Taupin wrote the song as though he were speaking to an ex-lover and telling her that the end of their relationship has not brought him down, in the vein of Gloria Gaynor's classic, "I Will Survive." For Elton, the song took on a different meaning, symbolizing the rebirth of an artist and his musicians, who had now been reunited.

Together once more, the legendary group's magic does the trick. "'I'm Still Standing' sounded like the whole album's calling-card," Elton explained in his autobiography. "The lyric was about one of Bernie's exes, but I also thought it worked as a message to my new American record company [Geffen], who were, quite frankly, turning out to be a terrible pain in the arse."[3] In fact, the recently formed company had been forced to put up with the commercial failures of Elton's two previous albums, and they were beginning to doubt if he would ever return to his previous heights of popularity and commercial success; these were concerns that they did not hesitate to share with Elton. The company showed the same failures in its management of other artists such as John Lennon, Donna Summer, Joni Mitchell, and Neil Diamond. Looking back, Elton had this to say: "I didn't like the look of any of it, and thought 'I'm Still Standing' sounded like a warning shot across their bows. It was a big, swaggering, confident fuck-you of a song."[3]

Production

In the tropical heat of AIR Studios, energy flowed between the musicians, who were seemingly galvanized by the lyrics of the song. Elton's singing is astonishing, and the piano playing is incisive. Added to that was a background of the ever-present synthesizers, which Elton played himself. The acoustic piano and the synthesizer are each used in their own specific way: the piano hammers out a percussive rhythm while the electric sounds of the synthesizer back up the guitar. In this number,

Elton and Bernie were close as ever during recording sessions in Montserrat on October 11, 1982.

Davey Johnstone delivers one of the most memorable guitar solos in the whole of Elton's discography. Dee Murray's energetic bass and Nigel Olsson's aggressive drumming seem ready to steamroll over anything that might stand in their way. And who could resist the phenomenal backing vocals from Davey, Dee, and Nigel with their repeated interjections of "yeah, yeah, yeah"?

For the accompanying video, Elton dreamed up a totally over-the-top production and gave the reins over to Russell Mulcahy, who would go on to direct the feature film *Highlander* (1986). Filmed on the beachside promenade at La Croisette in Cannes, France, the video features overhead shots taken from a helicopter along with an army of dancers wearing multicolored bodysuits, and Elton's Bentley, which had been shipped over specially for the occasion. This time, Elton agreed to feature himself prominently in the video, something he had previously

refused to do. Elton proved to be a hopeless dancer and so the choreographer, Arlene Phillips, had to tactfully arrange things so that his appearance in the dance scenes was reduced to a minimum. Behind the scenes, Elton partied hard with members of Duran Duran and ended up smashing John Reid's face (and hotel room). He then returned to finish shooting the video, insisting on being filmed as he rolled around on the ground stark naked. "That's the thing about success. It gives you a license to misbehave, a license that doesn't get revoked until your success dries up completely, or you man up and decide to hand it in yourself. And, for the time being, there was no danger of either of those things happening to me."[3] Although the video contributed greatly to the popularity of "I'm Still Standing," the song's success also owed much to a very positive reception from the press, who were almost universally supportive of the single.

TOO LOW FOR ZERO

Elton John, Bernie Taupin / 5:46

Musicians: Elton John: vocals, piano, synthesizer / **Davey Johnstone:** electric guitar, backing vocals / **Dee Murray:** bass, backing vocals / **Nigel Olsson:** rhythm box programming, backing vocals / Unidentified musician: percussion **Recorded:** AIR Studios, Montserrat (Caribbean): September 1982 **Technical Team: Producer:** Chris Thomas / **Sound Engineer:** Bill Price / **Assistant Sound Engineers:** Renate Blauel, Peggy McCreary / **Mastering:** Chris Thomas (UK), Greg Fulginiti (USA)

Bernie offers a radical and disconcerting change of mood after the triumphant "I'm Still Standing." In this piece, from which the album takes its name, Bernie explores in a rather lackluster way the theme of the antihero, who is "too tired to work" but unable to sleep and reduced to "watching flies with my eyes till sunrise." But this "bad patch" that the narrator cannot shake off is not interpreted by Elton via a typically sad melody. Cheerful if hardly original, the song quickly veers into the irritating. The arrangement suffers from poorly integrated synthesizers, artificial handclaps, and crude percussion. That said, there are one or two lovely moments, including the reverse guitar effect used with restraint by Davey Johnstone, as well as Elton's vocals and a delightful piano solo.

RELIGION

Elton John, Bernie Taupin / 4:07

Musicians: Elton John: vocals, piano, synthesizer / **Davey Johnstone:** acoustic guitar, electric guitar, backing vocals / **Dee Murray:** bass, backing vocals / **Nigel Olsson:** drums, backing vocals **Recorded:** AIR Studios, Montserrat (Caribbean): September 1982 **Technical Team: Producer:** Chris Thomas / **Sound Engineer:** Bill Price / **Assistant Sound Engineers:** Renate Blauel, Peggy McCreary / **Mastering:** Chris Thomas (UK), Greg Fulginiti (USA)

"Religion" has a country feel to it, and the lyrics feature tales of a thief and a prostitute who are both touched by grace. Their sudden religious conversion does not, however, stop them from carrying on just as they had before acquiring their newfound faith. "Religion, well, you do the best you can / 'Cause we all make the same mistakes." The fatalistic implication here is clear enough: Religion is helpless in the face of human nature, which is always ready to sink into vice. The very effective arrangement of "Religion" owes a lot to Davey Johnstone's

ever-inventive guitar playing, here backed by an effective, if rather academic, rhythm section. The vocals are refined, and Elton delivers a convincing and jubilant performance. As for his uninhibited piano playing, he seems to have escaped from a honky-tonk saloon in an attempt to evoke the musical traditions of the Southern United States and the Bible Belt.

I GUESS THAT'S WHY THEY CALL IT THE BLUES

Elton John, Bernie Taupin, Davey Johnstone / 4:45

Musicians: Elton John: vocals, piano, synthesizers / **Davey Johnstone:** electric guitar, acoustic guitar, backing vocals / **Dee Murray:** bass, backing vocals / **Nigel Olsson:** drums, backing vocals / Stevie Wonder: harmonica **Recorded:** AIR Studios, Montserrat (Caribbean): September 1982 / Sunset Sound Recorders, Los Angeles: September 1982 **Technical Team: Producer:** Chris Thomas / **Sound Engineer:** Bill Price / **Assistant Sound Engineers:** Renate Blauel, Peggy McCreary / **Mastering:** Chris Thomas (UK), Greg Fulginiti (USA) **Single Release:** *I Guess That's Why They Call It the Blues / Choc Ice Goes Mental* **UK Release:** April 1983 on Rocket Record Company / Phonogram (ref. XPRES 91, 812 168-7) **Best UK Chart Ranking:** 5 • *I Guess That's Why They Call It the Blues / The Retreat* **US Release:** October 1983 by Geffen Records (ref. 7-29460) **Best US Chart Ranking:** 4

Bernie Taupin wrote "I Guess That's Why They Call It the Blues" as a love letter to his then wife, Toni Russo. Despite the idyllic surroundings on Montserrat, which was where the song was composed, Bernie was missing his wife. Looking back to songwriting style of Tin Pan Alley, and particularly to the songs of the 1940s and '50s written about wartime separations, he captures his feelings in simple words: "Just stare into space / Picture my face in your hands / Live for each second / Without hesitation / And never forget I'm your man." This sentiment becomes universal when Elton sings: "And while I'm away / Dust out the demons inside / And it won't be long / Before you and me run / To the place in our hearts / Where we hide."

Elton John has an unparalleled ability to employ a straightforward melody as a means of capturing universal moods and feelings, and this time he makes homesickness seem almost bearable. His piano playing draws randomly on influences from jazz to a warm, '50s-style version of rhythm and blues. The full sound of Dee Murray's bass speaks with depth and fine technique, while Davey Johnstone's electric guitar offers a wide variety of elements: powerfully marking the beats and then spilling out into limpid arpeggios that are finely shaped by a hint of refrain and a touch of reverb. The laidback atmosphere of the song is further underlined by Nigel Olsson's seemingly lazy drums. Stevie Wonder's harmonica comes in at 2:47 with an inspired solo set down in the spirit of the famous Belgian harmonica player, Toots Thielemans. Each note evokes the writer's loneliness, which is further underlined by Elton when he sings, "Wait on me, girl / Cry in the night if it helps" over a pre-refrain that magnificently illustrates the musicality of his singing.

'50S FAN

The video by Russell Mulcahy closely reflects the Tin Pan Alley inspiration for Taupin's lyrics. The action takes place in the 1950s: two lovers are forced to part because the man is being called up to the army. The video was filmed in the Rivoli Ballroom in Crofton Park, London, and at the Colchester Barracks in Essex, England.

CRYSTAL

Elton John, Bernie Taupin / 5:06

Musicians: Elton John: vocals, synthesizers / **Davey Johnstone:** electric guitar, acoustic guitar, backing vocals / **Dee Murray:** bass, backing vocals / **Nigel Olsson:** rhythm box programming, backing vocals **Recorded:** AIR Studios, Montserrat (Caribbean): September 1982 **Technical Team: Producer:** Chris Thomas / **Sound Engineer:** Bill Price / **Assistant Sound Engineers:** Renate Blauel, Peggy McCreary / **Mastering:** Chris Thomas (UK), Greg Fulginiti (USA) **Single Release:** Cold as Christmas (In the Middle of the Year) / Crystal **UK Release:** November 1983 on Rocket Record Company (ref. ESJ 3, 814 862-7) **Best UK Chart Ranking:** 33

The compelling ballad "I Guess That's Why They Call It the Blues" must've felt like a hard act to follow. The musicians' solution is to offer a complete contrast to that song in the form of "Crystal." Vocally, Elton sings with a slightly hoarse timbre to beautiful effect, and the song's arrangement is also quite different from the preceding track. The overlapping sounds of Elton's keyboards seem confused at first, especially in the dissonant bridge starting at 2:14, as does the rhythm section that suffers from the decision to use a rhythm box in place of Nigel Olsson.

Olsson tried a take with his drum kit but was met with Elton's categorical veto. The song's melody is very catchy despite the strictness of the rhythm. Dee Murray's bass comes vibrantly alive in the finale, which also features Elton's cracked voice and some excellent bluesy guitar playing from Davey Johnstone. Often forgotten about in favor of bigger hits, "Crystal" represents one of the nicest surprises on Too Low for Zero. Bernie's touching and sensitive words are carefully crafted, just like the crystal after which the girl in the song is named. Crystal is the focus of a love triangle that is composed of the singer, the singer's (male) friend, and Crystal herself. The narrator has come to the painful realization that he needs to step back, leaving Crystal and his friend to pursue their love affair. But he begs his friend not to hurt her, comparing her to a pearl and saying the world is her oyster.

KISS THE BRIDE

Elton John, Bernie Taupin / 4:22

Musicians: Elton John: vocals, synthesizers / **Davey Johnstone:** electric guitar, backing vocals / **Dee Murray:** bass, backing vocals / **Nigel Olsson:** drums, backing vocals **Recorded:** AIR Studios, Montserrat (Caribbean): September 1982 **Technical Team: Producer:** Chris Thomas / **Sound Engineer:** Bill Price / **Assistant Sound Engineers:** Renate Blauel, Peggy McCreary / **Mastering:** Chris Thomas (UK), Greg Fulginiti (USA) **Single Release:** Kiss the Bride / Dreamboat **UK Release:** October 1983 on Rocket Record Company (ref. EJS 2) **Best UK Chart Ranking:** 20 • Kiss the Bride / Choc Ice Goes Mental (Lord Choc Ice) **US Release:** July 1983 on Geffen Records (ref. 7-29568) **Best US Chart Ranking:** 25

Sometimes in life, fate has a way of intervening. "I want to kiss the bride," Elton sings emphatically on this song with words written by Bernie Taupin. A year and a half later, Elton would repeat these words in front of the woman he married, Renate Blauel. Elton and Renate met and fell in love when Renate worked as an assistant sound engineer on...Too Low for Zero. In "Kiss the Bride," Bernie imagines raising his hand at a wedding when the priest asks if anyone has any reason to oppose the marriage. His reason is a selfish one: "I want to kiss the bride yeah / Long before she met him / She was mine, mine, mine." But, out of respect for his ex, the narrator doesn't utter a word. Instead, he takes small comfort from a tiny detail: "Underneath her veil I could see / A tear."

Constructed over a solid but quite conventional guitar riff, the song remains effective thanks to a strong refrain and a robust rhythm section. Elton sings in a clear, powerful, and confident voice, supported by restrained but essential backing vocals. Unless you count the bridge beginning at 2:53, Davey Johnstone doesn't really get a guitar solo here, but he has plenty to do throughout the remainder of the piece. Elton's synthesizers are intelligently used in the rhythm section to help flesh out the song's rock bona fides. "Kiss the Bride" is another undeniable success for this album.

WHIPPING BOY

Elton John, Bernie Taupin / 3:44

Musicians: Elton John: vocals, piano / Davey Johnstone: electric guitar, backing vocals / Dee Murray: bass, backing vocals / Nigel Olsson: drums, tambourine, backing vocals **Recorded:** AIR Studios, Montserrat (Caribbean): September 1982 **Technical Team:** Producer: Chris Thomas / Sound Engineer: Bill Price / Assistant Sound Engineers: Renate Blauel, Peggy McCreary / Mastering: Chris Thomas (UK), Greg Fulginiti (USA) **Single Release:** Town of Plenty / Whipping Boy **UK Release:** August 1988 on Rocket Record Company / Phonogram (ref. ESJ 17, 870 618-7) **Best UK Chart Ranking:** 74

"Whipping Boy" literally copies the intro and tempo of the hit "I'm Still Standing," which may help explain why this song is so appealing. However, this is also probably the reason why the former track ruled the charts while "Whipping Boy" hardly registered. Bernie's daring words talk about an "illegal kind of lovin' / that keeps my motor runnin' / From the start to the finish line." The narrator is the song is having a relationship with a much younger partner, which makes him "feel like sixty-three." The edgy rock vibe of "Whipping Boy" also features a pretty unforgettable refrain. Elton's voice is assured, the backing vocals are perfectly placed, and the musical arrangement shows each musician working at his best. Davey Johnstone's incisive guitar punctuates each couplet or refrain with memorable electric interjections. In the rhythm section, we are reminded again of the cheeky synergy of the Dee Murray–Nigel Olsson duo. Backed up once again by his old team, Elton is at the top of his form with this appealingly straightforward number.

SAINT

Elton John, Bernie Taupin / 5:20

Musicians: Elton John: vocals, synthesizers, Clavinet / Davey Johnstone: electric guitar, acoustic guitar, backing vocals / Dee Murray: bass, backing vocals / Nigel Olsson: drums, backing vocals **Recorded:** AIR Studios, Montserrat (Caribbean): September 1982 **Technical Team:** Producer: Chris Thomas / Sound Engineer: Bill Price / Assistant Sound Engineers: Renate Blauel, Peggy McCreary / Mastering: Chris Thomas (UK), Greg Fulginiti (USA)

Elton and Bernie needed to find enough numbers to make up an album, so "Saint" was eventually included. It is one of the more dispensable tracks on *Too Low for Zero*. Drowning in the dreamy sound of Elton's Yamaha synthesizer, this long track clocks in at more than five minutes, and it gains momentum only from the layers of electric guitar that are piled on by Davey Johnstone. Dee Murray manages to slip in some expressive bass notes, but Nigel Olsson confines himself to accompanying Elton's vocals. The singer's voice feels heavy and awkward, and he also reveals its limitations in the higher register when he verges on falsetto at the 3:11 mark. The pounding melody of the refrain is like a sledgehammer on the listener's skull, and the only enjoyable section of the song is the delicate vocals that begin at 2:14. The meaning of Bernie's highly abstract lyrics is unclear. Although this is the kind of unwelcome tune that can somehow get stuck in a listener's head, "Saint" is one song from Elton John's repertoire that should be forgotten as quickly as possible.

ONE MORE ARROW

Elton John, Bernie Taupin / 3:48

Musicians: Elton John: vocals, piano / Davey Johnstone: electric guitar, backing vocals / Dee Murray: bass, backing vocals / Nigel Olsson: drums, backing vocals / Kiki Dee: backing vocals / James Newton Howard: direction, arrangements / Unidentified musicians: orchestra **Recorded:** AIR Studios, Montserrat (Caribbean): September 1982 **Technical Team:** Producer: Chris Thomas / Sound Engineer: Bill Price / Assistant Sound Engineers: Renate Blauel, Peggy McCreary / Mastering: Chris Thomas (UK), Greg Fulginiti (USA)

Bernie's touching lyrics seem to be addressed to an idealized father figure whose loss the speaker finds it hard to come to terms with. This man is "strictly from the old school," "quiet about his pain," and "could have been a boxer." At one point in the song, Bernie seems touched by the remorse the fictional father figure feels after an argument: "he knocked me down / And he cried when he thought / He'd hurt me." The speaker's admiration is expressed by a specific poetic metaphor, comparing this father to "one more arrow / Flying through the air" that, when it lands, "can always feel the sun." He will be "forever always young."

In setting these words to music, Elton returns to his piano instead of the synthesizers that he used on all the other tracks. The touching melody is further developed by the elegant string arrangement created by James Newton Howard, who joins the band for this track. Dee Murray does sterling work with the dark and serious notes of his bass, while Nigel Olsson executes some beautiful rolls on the drum kit. Davey Johnstone stays in the background, appearing only where needed. Elton gives us an accomplished vocal line that is one of the best of the entire album, and it's both powerful and refined. Elton's singing is perfectly supported by the well-coordinated backing vocals from his musicians with an assist by Kiki Dee.

EARN WHILE YOU LEARN

Lord Choc Ice (Elton John) / 6:47

Single: *I'm Still Standing / Earn While You Learn* **UK Release:** July 3, 1983, on Rocket Record Company (ref. EJS 1, 812 776-7) **Best UK Chart Ranking:** 4 **Musicians:** Elton John: piano, organ, Mellotron / Tim Renwick: electric guitar / Clive Franks: bass / Steve Holley: drums / Ray Cooper: tambourine **Recorded:** The Mill, Cookham, Berkshire, UK: 1978 **Technical Team:** Producers: Clive Franks, Elton John / Sound Engineers: Phil Dunne, Stuart Epps, Clive Franks / Coordinators: David Croker, Alex Foster

An instrumental track that resulted from the recording sessions for *A Single Man* in 1978, "Earn While You Learn" hinges on a slightly chaotic guitar riff performed by Tim Renwick (who also plays an inspired solo at the end of the piece) along with an unrestrained Elton improvising on piano and a selection of various keyboards. This exploration of new sounds establishes Elton's desire to take control of all, or almost all, of the keyboards that were available to him. This piece was saved from likely oblivion when it reemerged as Side B of the hit number "I'm Still Standing."

DREAMBOAT

Elton John, Tim Renwick, Gary Osborne (not credited) / 7:35

Single Release: *Kiss the Bride / Dreamboat* **UK Release:** October 1983 on Rocket Record Company (ref. EJS 2) **Best UK Chart Ranking:** 20 **Musicians:** Elton John: vocals, organ, Fender Rhodes / Tim Renwick: electric guitar / Clive Franks: bass / Steve Holley: drums / Ray Cooper: tambourine / Paul Buckmaster: direction, arrangements / Unidentified musicians: orchestra / Unidentified singers: backing vocals **Recorded:** The Mill, Cookham, Berkshire, UK: 1978 **Technical Team:** Producers: Clive Franks, Elton John / Sound Engineers: Phil Dunne, Stuart Epps, Clive Franks / Coordinators: David Croker, Alex Foster

As a contributor to the composition of "Dreamboat," guitarist Tim Renwick is credited on this disk along with Elton. The words are uncredited but were written by Gary Osborne. A pleasant surprise, this song was added to *Too Low for Zero* for the 1998 Mercury reissue. "Dreamboat" was another number that was originally recorded in 1978 during the *A Single Man* sessions, and it reappeared on Side B of "Kiss the Bride" when it was issued as a single in 1983. Light and cheerful, the song owes much to the sublime and airy string arrangement by Paul Buckmaster. Tim Renwick provides a catchy gimmick at the beginning of the piece, providing a support for the soft Fender Rhodes played by Elton, which intervenes here and there to great effect.

THE RETREAT

Elton John, Bernie Taupin / 4:46

Single Release: *Princess / The Retreat* **UK Release:** September 3, 1982, on Rocket Record Company (ref. XPRES 85) **Best UK Chart Ranking:** Did Not Chart • *I Guess That's Why They Call It the Blues / The Retreat* **US Release:** October 1983 by Geffen Records (ref. 7-29460) **Best US Chart Ranking:** 4 **Musicians:** Elton John: vocals, piano / Steve Lukather: electric guitar / Reggie McBride: bass / Alvin Taylor: drums / James Newton Howard: synthesizers / David Paich: Hammond organ **Recorded:** Super Bear Studios, Berre-les-Alpes, France: August 1979 / Sunset Sound Recorders, Los Angeles: January 1980 **Technical Team:** Producers: Clive Franks, Elton John / Sound Engineer: Clive Franks / Assistant Sound Engineers: Patrick Jauneaud (Super Bear), Peggy McCreary, Stephen McManus (Sunset Sound) / Mastering: Tim Young

Composed in 1979 during the recording sessions for *21 at 33* and *The Fox*, "The Retreat" was intended for the latter album but was vetoed by Geffen. It only appeared later, as Side B on "Princess" and then on "I Guess That's Why They Call It the Blues." This second B-side appearance resulted in the song being included as a bonus track on the CD reissue by Mercury in 1998. "The Retreat," like "My Father's Gun" and "Where to Now St. Peter?" before it, returns to the theme of the American Civil War. It describes an army withdrawing in response to a bugle call. Bernie's words convey the mixed feelings of the soldiers: the joy of returning home but the bitterness of leaving behind their fallen comrades. "God had saved the chosen few and the devil took the rest," Elton sings poignantly. The synthesizers and Hammond organ, played by James Newton Howard and David Paich respectively, make a magnificent contribution to the finale of this unjustly ignored piece, which was fortunately rediscovered on the *Jewel Box* set that was released in 2020.

ALBUM

BREAKING HEARTS

Restless . Slow Down Georgie (She's Poison) . Who Wears These Shoes? .
Breaking Hearts (Ain't What It Used to Be) . Li'l 'Frigerator . Passengers . In Neon .
Burning Buildings . Did He Shoot Her? . Sad Songs (Say So Much)

RELEASE DATES
UK Release: July 9, 1984
Reference: Rocket Record Company—HISPD 25, 822 088-1
Best UK Chart Ranking: 2
US Release: June 18, 1984
Reference: Geffen Records—GHS 24031
Best US Chart Ranking: 20

1984

A RETURN TO GRACE

In 1983, Elton John opted to spend his end-of-year vacation in the studio, although his musical comrades may well have preferred to spend the time with their families. Back at the AIR Studios in Montserrat, and in the company of the Elton John Band, Elton also brought Chris Thomas on to handle production, and Renate Blauel was appointed as sound engineer. As a sign of the increasing importance of Renate Blauel in Elton's eyes, her name was clearly visible on each of the covers of the four singles derived from *Breaking Hearts*, shortened to simply "Renate." With this new opus, Elton intended to make good on the experiment of *Too Low for Zero* and to win back his public.

Back to His Roots

As in the earliest days of their collaboration, Elton and Bernie Taupin renewed the creative process that had been their standard from the very beginning: after writing late into the evening, the lyricist would leave a pile of sheets for Elton to read when he woke up. Elton, who was an early riser, set to work at about eight thirty in the morning. Little had changed since the days at the Château d'Hérouville, with the exception of the equipment, which had developed significantly over the past decade. The Steinway piano had given way to a Yamaha synthesizer, to which was added a drum machine. The other musicians in the band made their appearance around midday, when the rehearsal sessions began on whatever new song had just been composed. The day ended at around ten in the evening. This familiar routine reassured Elton, who was feeling

the pressure after the success of *Too Low for Zero*. That album had provided the singer with a second chance after the lackluster sales of his previous offerings, and Elton didn't want to squander this new opportunity. He also knew that his resurgence in popularity would not last if he kept releasing the same kinds of music over and over again. Thus, following *Too Low for Zero* and its slick sounds, which were dominated by keyboards, Elton opted to give his guitarist, Davey Johnstone, a starring role in this next production.

All the conditions were set for Elton to make a return to rock, which started right from the first track, which is a Stones-like song called "Restless" that features a venomous guitar riff. The album then continues with "Slow Down Georgie (She's Poison)," in which Elton's keyboard features heavily; later, Elton offers the listener a very rock 'n' roll–tinged track called "Li'l 'Frigerator." Like the previous album, this album presents a dichotomy between style and substance. The virile rock sounds and characters sometimes flirt with misogyny on the first half of the record, but they are followed by more mixed ambiances and more recognizably human subject matter on the album's second half.

A common thread runs right through *Breaking Hearts*, which justifies the choice of its title: a certain sadness, born of an accumulation of disappointments and injustices. This common thread is translated in the final song of the track list, "Sad Songs (Say So Much)," which was the song that Elton and Geffen planned to release as a single. This piece, which was released as a 45 rpm in May 1984, did slightly less well

On February 14, 1984, Elton John and Renate Blauel were married during a quickly arranged ceremony at St. Mark's Church in Sydney, Australia.

in the UK (number seven) than "Passengers" (number five), which in turn was released as a single three months later. But "Sad Songs (Say So Much)" traveled rather well as an export, especially in the United States, where it hit fifth place in the rankings.

Although the album was marked by something of a return to Elton's roots, two elements shone out particularly because of their absence: Ray Cooper was largely absent, and there was a paucity of orchestral arrangements. In fact, every album since *Victim of Love* included at least one contribution from a strings or brass section, but *Breaking Hearts* broke the mold.

Three Tours and a Wedding

On February 10, 1984, when Elton John was still in Sydney, Australia, finalizing the overdubs for *Breaking Hearts* and rehearsing before the *Too Low for Zero* tour in Oceania (February 19–March 25), the singer made an explosive announcement that surprised even his close personal entourage. Shortly after midnight, Elton declared with a big smile that he was going to marry his sound engineer, Renate Blauel, on Valentine's Day. The close friends that made up the star's inner circle did not take him seriously. None of them had noticed the bond that had been formed between Elton and Renate over the past few months. The media was even more circumspect, given the numerous unequivocal declarations about his homosexuality that Elton had made during the year. To everyone's surprise, the two Valentines did indeed tie the knot, as announced, on February 14, 1984.

Two months later, with the *Too Low for Zero* tour barely completed, Elton began his European Express Tour (April 5–June 25, 1984), which was the European phase of his *Breaking Hearts* tour. He was then scheduled to tour North America from August 17 to November 18, 1984, to promote

his eighteenth album. The Elton John Band traversed Eastern Europe and performed behind the Iron Curtain with a series of concerts in Yugoslavia, Poland, Hungary, and Czechoslovakia. This new incursion into the Eastern Bloc, barely five years after their 1979 tour of the Soviet Union, fueled Elton's and Bernie's imaginations to the extent that it inspired their next album, *Ice on Fire*. After giving a concert at Wembley Stadium on June 30, 1984, Elton took a break at Saint-Tropez to relax before flying off to start his tour dates in North America. While staying at this famous haunt of the jet set, Elton met George Michael and Andrew Ridgeley from the popular group Wham!

The news from the United Kingdom was excellent: *Breaking Hearts* hit number two on the UK album sales charts. This performance delighted the singer, who had been hurt by his recent poor sales in the UK. This ranking confirmed his return to grace.

Despite his vacation in Saint-Tropez, Elton arrived on the other side of the Atlantic feeling completely wrung out. His fatigue, coupled with the absence of Renate and set alongside his various addictions and the bulimia that had started to plague his day-to-day life, all combined to weigh heavily on his morale. On several occasions, Elton talked openly of announcing his retirement from stage appearances. However, at the end of the tour it was Dee Murray and Nigel Olsson who headed for the exit, and not Elton. Once again, the artist very abruptly parted company with two of his closest musicians. There was no way Elton could have known that *Breaking Hearts* would be the last album to benefit from Dee's agile bass playing. Sadly, Dee passed away from skin cancer in 1992. As for Nigel, other than contributing backing vocals with Dee on the *Reg Strikes Back* album, he did not work with Elton again until 2001.

RESTLESS

Elton John, Bernie Taupin / 5:16

Musicians: Elton John: lead and backing vocals, synthesizer / **Davey Johnstone:** electric guitar, backing vocals / **Dee Murray:** bass, backing vocals / **Nigel Olsson:** drums, backing vocals **Recorded:** AIR Studios, Montserrat (Caribbean): December 1983 **Technical Team: Producer:** Chris Thomas / **Sound Engineer:** Renate Blauel / **Tape Operator:** Steve Jackson / **Mastering:** Tim Young (UK), Greg Fulginiti (USA) **Single Release:** *Wrap Her Up / Restless* (live) **UK Release:** November 1985 on Rocket Record Company (ref. EJS 10) **Best UK Chart Ranking:** 12 • *Nikita / Restless* **US Release:** January 1986 on Geffen Records (ref. 7-28800) **Best US Chart Ranking:** 7

With a classic rock 'n' roll sound but written in blues-tinged language, "Restless" is based on an arrangement that could not be more organic, with guitar, bass, and drums as the natural backing. Only a few layers of discreet synthesizer are added to fill out the sound. Davey Johnstone's guitar riff is edgy and effective, as is his solo. Dee Murray constructs an evolving line, first following the guitar before linking in with the voice, and all while ornamenting his phrases with a few judiciously placed slaps. Behind the drums, Nigel Olsson aspires above all to create solidity via his unembellished playing style. The big success of the piece resides not only in the backing vocals but also in Elton's muscular vocal production. Bernie's lyrics capture the atmosphere of the period perfectly. Right in the middle of the Cold War, paranoia was reaching a fever pitch in the East and the West: "Everybody's restless / Everybody's scared / Everybody's looking for something that just ain't there," as Bernie puts it, condensing the general humor into a single phrase, clearly a reference to George Orwell's *1984*: "The walls have ears / Big Brother's watching." Elton later played "Restless" on stage many times, but always on the piano and in a faster version. In 1986, a live version of this song was chosen for Side B of the English and American singles derived from *Ice on Fire*.

SLOW DOWN GEORGIE (SHE'S POISON)

Elton John, Bernie Taupin / 4:10

Musicians: Elton John: vocals, synthesizer, backing vocals / **Davey Johnstone:** electric guitar, acoustic guitar, backing vocals / **Dee Murray:** bass, backing vocals / **Nigel Olsson:** drums, backing vocals **Recorded:** AIR Studios, Montserrat (Caribbean): December 1983 **Technical Team: Producer:** Chris Thomas / **Sound Engineer:** Renate Blauel / **Tape Operator:** Steve Jackson / **Mastering:** Tim Young (UK), Greg Fulginiti (USA)

By using the same formula, they employed on "Restless," the group channels a frantic brand of rock 'n' roll that skillfully prepares the way (via its enthusiastic verses) for a feverishly addictive refrain. Davey Johnstone adds a purposeful acoustic guitar, which is not unlike the playing, in certain flourishes, of the Who's Pete Townshend. Once again, the backing vocals consisted of Dee, Nigel, Davey, and Elton, and they helped create the ambiance surrounding the haunting performance by the singer. Elton's voice acts as a relay to express the friendship depicted by Bernie. The lyricist assigns the role of his protective friend to the narrator of his story, who warns a certain Georgie to be careful with his latest conquest, sometimes with a twist of humor: "The reputation of the woman you're dating's / About as nasty as the Berlin Wall / Slow down, Georgie, she's poison." He also acknowledges certain indisputable attractions that have affected Georgie's discernment, like "her big brown eyes and a body that could stop a clock." He expresses doubts concerning the virtue of the young woman, who he thinks collects prey and wants to fleece his friend, and encourages him to get away from her as quickly as possible: "You better cut her loose before she gets her hooks in you / If you give her the world, and it was covered in pearls / She'd only ask for the moon."

WHO WEARS THESE SHOES?

Elton John, Bernie Taupin / 4:03

Musicians: Elton John: vocals, piano, synthesizer, backing vocals / **Davey Johnstone:** electric guitar, backing vocals / **Dee Murray:** bass, backing vocals / **Nigel Olsson:** drums, backing vocals **Recorded:** AIR Studios, Montserrat (Caribbean): December 1983 **Technical Team:** Producer: Chris Thomas / **Sound Engineer:** Renate Blauel / **Tape Operator:** Steve Jackson / **Mastering:** Tim Young (UK), Greg Fulginiti (USA) **Single Release:** *Who Wears These Shoes? / Tortured* **UK Release:** October 15, 1984, with Rocket Record Company (ref. EJS 6/880 323-7) **Best UK Chart Ranking:** 50 • *Who Wears These Shoes? / Lonely Boy* **US Release:** October 23, 1984, with Geffen Records (ref. 7-29189) **Best US Chart Ranking:** 16 • *Who Wears These Shoes? / I Heard It Through the Grapevine / Tortured* **UK Release:** October 1984 with Rocket Record Company (ref. EJS 612) **Best UK Chart Ranking:** Did Not Chart

"Who Wears These Shoes?" is tinged with a deliciously retro color. An electric guitar marks the rhythm on the offbeat, while another lavishes very effectively harmonized strummed funk guitar rhythms. Both are linked into a tight bass/drums section with an elegant reverb, on a solid tempo at around 85 bpm. The clearest mark of this meticulous production is provided by the resplendent backing vocals around Elton's lead voice, which is perfectly assured, even when it descends unfalteringly into the lower register on some of the verses. The singer, restlessly animated, incarnates the insanely jealous character depicted in Bernie's lyrics. The man addresses his former sweetheart, explaining that he does not wish to cause her problems. However, he spies on her slightest movements, thinks about her constantly, and feels like the "old jukebox" always playing the same song. But, in addition to understanding the reason for their breakup, which obsesses him most, he wants to know who has replaced him in the heart of his former partner: "Who Wears These Shoes?" And too bad if his friends "all think" he must be crazy. Performing better in the charts in the United States than in the United Kingdom, "Who Wears These Shoes?" is one of the best of Elton's "soft rock" singles.

BREAKING HEARTS (AIN'T WHAT IT USED TO BE)

Elton John, Bernie Taupin / 3:34

Musicians: Elton John: vocals, piano, backing vocals / **Davey Johnstone:** backing vocals / **Dee Murray:** backing vocals / **Nigel**

Olsson: backing vocals **Recorded:** AIR Studios, Montserrat (Caribbean): December 1983 **Technical Team:** Producer: Chris Thomas / **Sound Engineer:** Renate Blauel / **Tape Operator:** Steve Jackson / **Mastering:** Tim Young (UK), Greg Fulginiti (US) **Single Release:** *Breaking Hearts (Ain't What It Used to Be) / In Neon* **UK Release:** February 1985 on Rocket Record Company (ref. EJS 7/880 486-7) **Best UK Chart Ranking:** 59

"Breaking Hearts (Ain't What It Used to Be)" is an abrupt departure from the rock atmosphere of the first three pieces on the album. This piano ballad, in which Elton's voice is overlaid with the celestial backing vocals of his fellow musicians, expresses profound emotion with a sometimes uncertain but always sincere vibrato, and in the process it gives the singer one of his most difficult vocal performances of the entire album. Oscillating between the low and high registers, "Breaking Hearts (Ain't What It Used to Be)" also offers some touching sequences, for example, when Elton's voice breaks slightly (at 3:20). It should be said that the theme of loneliness resonated particularly with Elton, who had had his share of emotional roller coasters during the course of the previous fifteen years. The narrator bitterly regrets having played with the feelings of his partners, even confessing: "And now I know what lonely means / I used to give so little and gain everything." He launches into devastating self-deprecation, albeit late in the day, which leads him to express his empathy toward his victims and his decision to live as a recluse in future: "Can't say I blame them all for being hurt / After all, I treated each and every one like dirt / Who wants a heart that's never home? / I face the facts and lock myself into a life alone." Its minimalist production was the diametric opposite of Elton's recent, more vigorous hits, but that did not prevent the single from hitting the British charts, seemingly in recognition of the singer's peerless talent for writing melodies.

LI'L 'FRIGERATOR

Elton John, Bernie Taupin / 3:37

Musicians: Elton John: vocals, piano, synthesizer, Hammond organ, backing vocals / **Davey Johnstone:** electric guitar / **Dee Murray:** bass / Nigel Olsson: drums / Andrew Thompson: saxophone **Recorded:** AIR Studios, Montserrat (Caribbean): December 1983 **Technical Team:** Producer: Chris Thomas / **Sound Engineer:** Renate Blauel / **Tape Operator:** Steve Jackson / **Mastering:** Tim Young (UK), Greg Fulginiti (USA)

Despite all the kick that characterizes this song, absolutely nothing original emerges from "Li'l 'Frigerator," in either form or substance. Bernie extends the theme previously set out in "Slow Down Georgie (She's Poison)," warning a friend of the dangers represented by a young woman he considers to be cold and calculating, having bewitched him with her "kiss of death." Uncompromisingly, he ends his narrative with a terse declaration: "She's an empty shell, you're a piece of meat / Just another statistic on her readout sheet." Regarding the form of the song, the arrangement is not inventive, but it is jubilant and catchy: Elton lets himself go on the piano like a wild thing, hammering out the high notes with a sadistic pleasure, and Andrew Thompson injects some fire at 2:15 with a short saxophone solo. During this time the underused rhythm section contents itself with run-of-the-mill output, simply gaining in tension what it lacks in variety, and Davey Johnstone compensates for what is missing in general creativity by adding some much-needed energy on the guitar.

PASSENGERS

Elton John, Bernie Taupin, Davey Johnstone, Phineas Mkhize / 3:23

Musicians: Elton John: vocals, synthesizer, harmonium / **Davey Johnstone:** acoustic guitar, backing vocals / **Dee Murray:** bass, backing vocals / **Nigel Olsson:** drums, backing vocals **Recorded:** AIR Studios, Montserrat (Caribbean): December 1983 **Technical Team:** Producer: Chris Thomas / **Sound Engineer:** Renate Blauel / **Tape Operator:** Steve Jackson / **Mastering:** Tim Young (UK), Greg Fulginiti (USA) **Single Release:** *Passengers / Lonely Boy* **UK Release:** August 6, 1984, with Rocket Record Company (ref. ESJ 5/880 167-7) **Best UK Chart Ranking:** 5

In October 1983, two months before the recording of "Passengers," Elton John performed at Sun City, a hotel complex in Bophuthatswana, a Bantustan created from scratch by the South African government to ameliorate the image and impact of its racist policies. In addition to Elton, other superstars of the rock and pop scene of the 1980s, including Rod Stewart and Queen, performed there. Technically, they were not playing in a country led by Frederik De Klerk and therefore circumventing the boycott set forth by the United Nations and supported by the African National Congress. Elton somewhat naïvely thought that he would be performing in a country spared from the horrific segregation that was happening in South Africa, seemingly not realizing that the cost of tickets was prohibitive for much of the Black South African population, and also seemingly unaware that the South African population suffering under apartheid wanted artists to join in the United Nations boycott. As Elton himself wrote later, "You couldn't achieve anything positive by going there. So there's no point trying to justify it. Sometimes you fuck up, and you have to hold your hand up and admit it. [...] When I got back I signed a public pledge put together by anti-apartheid campaigners, saying I would never go there again."[3]

With "Passengers," which was composed during the recording sessions at Monserrat, Elton, Bernie, and Davey sought to make amends for the controversy of the Sun City appearance by directly condemning apartheid in song. The lyrics do indeed castigate rich white people who made their fortunes on "a blood bank." They also reproach their selfishness for refusing to share trains that would enable poor Black people to get to work more easily. The passengers of the title have been refused access to the train, which forces the narrator to wonder: "who want[s] to get on," emphasizing that this train seems not to be the train of progressiveness. Musically, the song draws its inspiration from a version of a South African folk song ("Isonto Lezayone"), which was recorded by the artist Phineas Mkhize in 1963. "Passengers" also takes an unexpected dip into world music, a terrain explored and popularized by Paul Simon on his album *Graceland* in 1986, which is considered by many to be the first disc in this genre.

IN NEON

Elton John, Bernie Taupin / 4:19

Musicians: Elton John: vocals, synthesizers, piano, Fender Rhodes, harpsichord, backing vocals / **Davey Johnstone:** electric guitar, acoustic guitar, backing vocals / **Dee Murray:** bass, backing vocals / **Nigel Olsson:** drums, backing vocals **Recorded:** AIR Studios, Montserrat (Caribbean): December 1983 **Technical Team:** Producer: Chris Thomas / **Sound Engineer:** Renate Blauel / **Tape Operator:** Steve Jackson / **Mastering:** Tim Young (UK), Greg Fulginiti (USA) **Single Release:** *Breaking Hearts / In Neon* **UK Release:** February 1985 on Rocket Record Company (ref. EJS 7/880 486-7) **Best UK Chart Ranking:** 59 • *In Neon / Tactics* **US Release:** November 1984 on Geffen Records (ref. 7-29111) **Best US Chart Ranking:** 38

A ballad that is melancholic in the extreme and outrageously presented under a thick layer of reverb and seraphic backing vocals, "In Neon" details the pathetic existence of a young woman who is too immersed in the illusions of beauty, fame, and fashion. Dreaming of notoriety, she ends up living in sordid obscurity. Dreaming of the city lights, she ends up in the shadows, behind a counter, her eyes inert, "A hot cup of coffee held in her fingers." She continued to hope that "a stranger could walk in" and save her. Elton does not skimp on the pathos in the piece, which he adorns with subtle touches of synthesizers. There is nothing new here for the very disciplined rhythm section of Dee and Nigel or for Davey's guitar, which is surprisingly muzzled on this occasion and reduced to a perfunctory contribution. The backing vocals, on the other hand, once again contribute to a high-caliber performance and bring out a refrain that otherwise would have been fairly lackluster. Borderline soporific, "In Neon" was on the B side of "Breaking Hearts" in the United Kingdom, but it fared better in the United States, where it was promoted to Side A and flanked by "Tactics" on Side B.

Sporting a boater hat, Elton sits backstage and prepares to wow the public at Wembley on June 30, 1984. (left)

Following page: Elton never renounced his penchant for flamboyant costumes, as evidenced by this drag ensemble worn during a concert in 1984.

BURNING BUILDINGS

Elton John, Bernie Taupin / 4:02

Musicians: Elton John: vocals, piano, backing vocals / **Davey Johnstone:** electric guitar, acoustic guitar, backing vocals / **Dee Murray:** bass, backing vocals / **Nigel Olsson:** drums, tambourine, backing vocals **Recorded:** AIR Studios, Montserrat (Caribbean): December 1983 **Technical Team:** Producer: Chris Thomas / **Sound Engineer:** Renate Blauel / **Tape Operator:** Steve Jackson / **Mastering:** Tim Young (UK), Greg Fulginiti (USA)

"Burning Buildings" creates a strong image to describe an amorous relationship consumed by anger and bitterness. Long gone are the times when the narrator enthused about the "sweet sensation" of love, for which he felt "no price [was] too high." Coping badly with "Such hard knocks" inflicted upon his heart, he laments the fact that his once pleasant relationship has given way to "Cold stares and angry words." From the midst of these harsh words, the expression "Live our life on borrowed time" jumps out. One might imagine that this sentiment was "borrowed" from John Lennon and his song "Borrowed Time," which was unveiled a few weeks earlier, in January 1984, on the posthumous album *Milk and Honey*. Elton explained in his autobiography that Yoko Ono had asked him to help with the creation of this album, but that he had refused because he was overwhelmed by the responsibilities that such a task would entail. From a musical perspective, Elton remains in poignant ballad territory until 2:41, which is when the bridge opens up. Guided by a guitar with nylon strings, this moment prepares the listener for the final assault of the refrain by way of a conventional but appealing melody. The musicians shine in their contributions on backing vocals rather than via their instruments, which are closeted behind Elton's piano.

DID HE SHOOT HER?

Elton John, Bernie Taupin / 3:21

Musicians: Elton John: vocals, synthesizers, piano, backing vocals / Davey Johnstone: electric guitar, sitar, backing vocals / **Dee Murray:** bass, backing vocals / **Nigel Olsson:** drums, backing vocals **Recorded:** AIR Studios, Montserrat (Caribbean): December 1983 **Technical Team:** Producer: Chris Thomas / **Sound Engineer:** Renate Blauel / **Tape Operator:** Steve Jackson / **Mastering:** Tim Young (UK), Greg Fulginiti (USA)

Davey Johnstone's guitar often enhanced many of Elton John's songs, and it was rare that his contribution proved as controversial as it did on this track. It is not so much the guitar part itself—which is workmanlike without being flamboyant—that is at issue, as much as it is his irrepressible urge to play the sitar, an instrument popularized by George Harrison in the 1970s, which Davey had mastered somewhat less well. The horrible chords banged out by Elton doggedly double down on a sense of havoc that cannot be saved by Nigel Olsson's clumsy drums, which smother the song under rolls from the toms, or by the very bland bass of Dee Murray, which is oddly hard to hear. The lyrics, which concern a man who allegedly shot a woman, similarly fail to brighten the already somber tone of this otherwise forgettable piece.

SAD SONGS (SAY SO MUCH)

Elton John, Bernie Taupin / 4:56

Musicians: Elton John: vocals, piano, synthesizers, Clavinet, backing vocals / **Davey Johnstone:** acoustic guitar, backing vocals / **Dee Murray:** bass, backing vocals / **Nigel Olsson:** drums, backing vocals **Recorded:** AIR Studios, Montserrat (Caribbean): December 1983 **Technical Team: Producer:** Chris Thomas / **Sound Engineer:** Renate Blauel / **Tape Operator:** Steve Jackson / **Mastering:** Tim Young (UK), Greg Fulginiti (USA) **Single Release:** *Sad Songs (Say So Much)* / *A Simple Man* **UK Release:** May 22, 1984, on Rocket Record Company (ref. PH 7/822 087-7) **Best UK Chart Ranking:** 7 **US Release:** May 22, 1984, on Geffen Records (ref. 7-29292) **Best US Chart Ranking:** 5

If there is one thing that the years have not changed in Elton John, it is certainly his spontaneity. It is perhaps this quality above all others that has allowed him to remain so prolific. "Sometimes a song only takes as long to write as it does to listen to," as he explains in his autobiography. "'Sad Songs (Say So Much)' was like that—I sat down, read the lyric and played it, pretty much the same as you hear on the record."[3] It is true that the song's melody remains self-evidently implacable, almost childlike, and that it is easy to imagine Elton eagerly filling in the chords on his piano to enrich it. "I've never had writer's block, I've never sat down with one of Bernie's lyrics and nothing has come out. I don't know why. I can't explain it and I don't want to explain it. Actually, I love that I can't explain it. It's the spontaneity of it that's beautiful,"[3] as he put it. Everything in the song seems disarmingly straightforward, from Elton's clear and limpid voice to the gentle and deliciously doo-wop backing vocals of Nigel, Dee, and Davey, as well as the copious, varied keyboards. Bernie keeps his lyrics simple; they describe how someone who experienced sadness or lost someone dear to them can find comfort in listening to the old blues classics on the radio: "When all hope is gone / Sad songs say so much / If someone else is suffering enough oh to write it down / When every single word makes sense."

"Sad Songs (Say So Much)" didn't receive as much airplay as one might have hoped, but it managed to win over the public through its communicative good nature, and the song had no difficulty reaching the top ten on both sides of the Atlantic, hitting number seven in the United Kingdom and number five in the United States.

A SIMPLE MAN

Elton John, Gary Osborne / 3:48

Single: *Sad Songs (Say So Much)* / *A Simple Man* **UK Release:** May 22, 1984, on Rocket Record Company (ref. PH 7/822 087-7) **Best UK Chart Ranking:** 7 **US Release:** May 22, 1984, on Geffen Records (ref. 7-29292) **Best US Chart Ranking:** 5 **Musicians:** Elton John: vocals, piano / Davey Johnstone: guitar / Dee Murray: bass / Nigel Olsson: drums **Recorded:** AIR Studios, Montserrat (Caribbean): September 1982 **Technical Team:** Producer: Chris Thomas / Sound Engineer: Bill Price

In 1978, Gary Osborne was contacted by his friend Jack O'Halloran. The actor was working on an adaptation of *The Informer*, a 1935 John Ford film. Jack asked Gary if he could write the words for a potential song to be included in the film. Gary did as he was asked. The lyrics unfold the story of a "simple man" who, feeling that death is not far off, sums up his life as a long journey filled with difficulties and loneliness. Gary submitted his work to Elton, who lost no time wrapping the lyrics in a melody. The film never saw the light of day, and "A Simple Man" stayed untouched until Elton resurrected it for Side B of "Sad Songs (Say So Much)." Oscillating between blues and country, "A Simple Man" has the benefit of a fine arrangement, notably the guitars and keyboards. The guitars have an accompanying role, but the parts played discreetly with the bottleneck are very effective. The excellent solo flows perfectly between the warm keyboard sounds. The only point of occasional debate: Elton's vocal contribution; his wavering voice seems to lack emotion, except for the refrain, which is slow but engaging.

LONELY BOY

Elton John, Gary Osborne / 4:50

Singles: *Passengers* / *Lonely Boy* **UK Release:** August 6, 1984, on Rocket Record Company (ref. ESJ 5/880 167-7) **Best UK Chart Ranking:** 5 • *Who Wears These Shoes?* / *Lonely Boy* **US Release:** October 23, 1984, on Geffen Records (ref. 7-29189) **Best US Chart Ranking:** 16 **Musicians:** Elton John: vocals, keyboards / Steve Lukather ?: electric guitar / Reggie McBride: bass / Alvin Taylor: drums **Recorded:** Super Bear Studios, Berre-les-Alpes, France:

August 1979 / Sunset Sound Recorders, Los Angeles: January–March 1980 **Technical Team:** Producers: Clive Franks, Elton John / Sound Engineers: Clive Franks, Patrick Jauneaud / Assistant Sound Engineers: David Burgess, David Leonard, Peggy McCreary, Stephen McManus / Mastering: Bernie Grundman / Album Coordinator: Adrian Collee

For Side B of "Passengers," Elton brought out another song recorded during the sessions for *21 at 33* in 1979. Initially called "Lonely Man," the song appeared on the soundtrack for a television adaptation of the popular British comic book series *Dan Dare: Pilot of the Future*. Gary Osborne was chosen as the musical director of the series, and he turned to Elton for the composition of the music. He knew that Elton would be receptive to the proposal because he and Bernie had already written an homage to the character on *Rock of the Westies* in 1975. Eventually, the TV series was scrapped, but the song was not abandoned. With slightly reworked lyrics and a new name, "Lonely Boy" took the form of a bluesy ballad that's illuminated by an almost cosmically wonderful electric guitar solo.

I HEARD IT THROUGH THE GRAPEVINE (LIVE)

Norman Whitfield, Barrett Strong / 5:46

Single: *Who Wears These Shoes?* / *I Heard It Through the Grapevine* / *Tortured* **UK Release:** October 1984 on Rocket Record Company (ref. EJS 612) **Best UK Chart Ranking:** Did Not Chart **Musicians:** Elton John: vocals, piano / Davey Johnstone: electric guitar, backing vocals / Cooker Lo Presti: bass, backing vocals / James Newton Howard: keyboards / Roger Pope: drums / Other backing vocals: Uncredited / Live Recording: Wembley Empire Pool, London: November 3, 1977 **Technical Team:** Producer: Clive Franks

For its appearance as a maxi single, "Who Wears These Shoes?" was joined by "Tortured" and a live recording of "I Heard It Through the Grapevine" that was captured on November 3, 1977, from the stage of the Empire Pool in Wembley, London. Elton performed there with the group China, which consisted of three of the singer's fellow musicians: Davey Johnstone, Roger Pope, and James Newton Howard. Together they offered a lively version of "I Heard It Through the Grapevine," a popular soul anthem made famous by Marvin Gaye. Elton seems almost possessed in this rendition of the song, and the musicians more or less race to keep up with the frenzied rhythm set by his piano at the beginning of the piece.

ALBUM

ICE ON FIRE

This Town . Cry to Heaven . Soul Glove . Nikita . Too Young . Wrap Her Up .
Satellite . Tell Me What the Papers Say . Candy by the Pound . Shoot Down the Moon

RELEASE DATES
UK Release: November 4, 1985
Reference: Rocket Record Company—HISPD 26, 826 213-1
Best UK Chart Ranking: 3
US Release: November 4, 1985
Reference: Geffen Records—GHS 24077
Best US Chart Ranking: 48

With *Ice on Fire*, Elton mixed music and geopolitics in the midst of the Cold War.

THE COLD WAR IN SONG

In January 1985, Elton was back home in England and ready to compose *Ice on Fire*. Although not strictly a concept album in the style of *Captain Fantastic and the Brown Dirt Cowboy*, a single theme that is linked to the geopolitical context of the time runs through all the songs on this album: the Cold War. Even if, at this period, relations between East and West were thawing somewhat thanks to the arrival of Mikhail Gorbachev as leader of the Soviet Union, Elton had become aware of the ideological and cultural antagonism between the two blocs during the concerts he had given in the USSR in 1979, and again during his European tour in 1984, when he had given four concerts on the eastern side of the Iron Curtain. "Nikita" is the most striking example of Elton's willingness to explore the frosty relations between East and West, as it tells the story of a man who has fallen in love with a border guard at the Berlin Wall. "Cry to Heaven" speaks of what might happen if war broke out. "Tell Me What the Papers Say" dwells on the role of the media as a conveyor of propaganda, which is often a destructive force. "Shoot Down the Moon" was in the running for inclusion on the soundtrack of the James Bond film *A View to a Kill*, which features a Soviet villain. Given the context of the album, cheerfulness is hard to come by. The album's cover is even more restrained than that of *Breaking Hearts*, consisting only of a black-and-white photo by Terry O'Neill that shows Elton in a fedora with his face turned away and his eyes concealed behind dark glasses.

Searching for a New Rhythm

Musically, Elton was obsessed with the Tina Turner album *Private Dancer*, which was released in May 1984, and he decided to imitate the Queen of Rock 'n' Roll by choosing new bass and drum players. The rhythm sections he approached were Paul Westwood (who had worked with Peter Green and Cliff Richard) and Charlie Morgan (who had worked with Judie Tzuke, Roy Harper, and Nik Kershaw), Deon Estus (famous for his bass line in Wham!'s "Wake Me Up Before You Go-Go") and Mel Gaynor (Simple Minds), David Paton (Alan Parsons Project) and

Dave Mattacks (Fairport Convention), as well as John Deacon and Roger Taylor, the inimitable duo from Queen. To accommodate all of these new faces, Gus Dudgeon returned as producer, replacing Chris Thomas, who was not available because he was busy working with INXS.

In addition to these famous pairs, numerous guest musicians came into Sol Studios, chosen by Elton in preparation for his nineteenth album. Sol Studios was the new name for the old Mill Studios, which were now owned by Jimmy Page, who had purchased the structure from Gus Dudgeon in 1980, when Gus had been forced to sell in order to pay his debts. Elton brought in guest musicians whenever the opportunity arose, so when he heard that Sister Sledge and Millie Jackson were coming to England as part of their respective tours, he seized on his chance to take advantage of their warm, mellow voices for "This Town" and "Act of War." He was also able work with Nik Kershaw, who had been a fan of Elton's since he was a teenager. The twenty-seven-year-old guitarist shone with his silky playing on "Nikita," the song that would eventually become the album's biggest hit, going all the way to number three in the UK. "Nikita" also inspired the name of the album, with Elton choosing *Ice on Fire* from a lyric describing the eyes of the fabled Nikita.

But perhaps the guest who left the most important mark on the album was George Michael. In addition to contributing backing vocals for two songs ("Nikita" and "Wrap Her Up"), he also had an important influence on Elton with his more modern style of music. Ready to listen to advice, Elton adopted elements from George Michael's repertoire, which resulted in a cleverly measured mixture of sugary synth-pop, synthetic funk, and modern soul. Despite the large number of guest artists that appear on this album, Gus Dudgeon and Elton John succeeded in giving the project a unified sound and a firm sense of coherence.

Unfortunately, Americans gave *Ice on Fire* a chilly reception, sending it no higher than forty-eighth on the *Billboard* charts. The UK was much more welcoming to Elton's latest project; it went all the way to number three in the album rankings.

THIS TOWN

Elton John, Bernie Taupin / 3:57

Musicians: Elton John: lead vocals, piano / Davey Johnstone: electric guitar / Paul Westwood: bass / Charlie Morgan: drums / Fred Mandel: synthesizers / Rick Taylor: trombone / Raul D'Oliveira: trumpet / Paul Spong: trumpet / David Bitelli: direction, arrangements, baritone saxophone / Orchestra: Onward International Horns / Sister Sledge: vocals **Recorded:** Sol Studios, Cookham, UK: January 1985 **Technical Team:** Producer: Gus Dudgeon / Sound Engineer: Stuart Epps / Mixing and Editing: Graham Dickson, Gus Dudgeon / Additional Mixing and Editing: Tom Pearce / Mastering: Gordon Vicary

Ice on Fire opens with a song that is a slice of social commentary, introducing the listener to the blue-collar workers of a small, economically depressed town. Life has nothing to offer these workers, trapped in their moribund town, faced with unemployment, and stuck in the past. The musical setting provided for "This Town" has a few piano chords, but its insistent disco bass line and clinical brass sound overwhelm the track. Backing vocals by Sister Sledge come to the rescue of a tuneless melody, and a prominent trumpet solo at 1:46 offers some saving grace. Even Elton's vocal improvisations at 3:42 seem unoriginal and almost dated from the moment he utters them. Although perfectly produced by Gus Dudgeon, "This Town" was probably not the best choice for the album's opening track.

CRY TO HEAVEN

Elton John, Bernie Taupin / 4:17

Musicians: Elton John: lead vocals, piano / Davey Johnstone: classical guitar, synth guitar / Paul Westwood: bass / Charlie Morgan: drums / Fred Mandel: keyboards **Recorded:** Sol Studios, Cookham, UK: January 1985 **Technical Team:** Producer: Gus Dudgeon / Sound Engineer: Stuart Epps / Mixing and Editing: Graham Dickson, Gus Dudgeon / Additional Mixing and Editing: Tom Pearce / Mastering: Gordon Vicary **Single Release:** *Cry to Heaven* / *Candy by the Pound* **UK Release:** February 1986 on Rocket Record Company (ref. EJS 11/884 533-7) **Best UK Chart Ranking:** 47

Much more appealing than "This Town," "Cry to Heaven" has the advantage of a very evocative text. Bernie Taupin depicts a world standing still, paralyzed by war, holding its breath during a fragile truce symbolized by a white flag fluttering on a high building. The scenes of desolation pile up one after the other, illustrating the poverty and suffering of victims of collateral damage. The fighting isn't shown—there's no need, since the total destitution of the children, many of whose fathers will have died, is enough to illustrate the consequences of war: desolation, broken families, and pointless sacrifice. At the end, Bernie introduces the metaphor of a cat playing with a mouse until it gets bored and kills it. Humans are the same; they play their warlike games, and inevitably they turn to war itself. Initially sounding like a gentle piano ballad, "Cry to Heaven" is progressively enriched with synthetic sounds and an inspired rhythm section. Elton gives his best here; his voice is low and gripping at the beginning of the song and heartrending by the end.

SOUL GLOVE

Elton John, Bernie Taupin / 3:31

Musicians: Elton John: lead vocals, piano / Davey Johnstone: electric guitar, vocals / Deon Estus: bass / Mel Gaynor: drums / Fred Mandel: keyboards / Frank Ricotti: congas, tambourine, shaker / Bob Sydor: tenor saxophone / Rick Taylor: trombone / Raul D'Oliveira: trumpet / Paul Spong: trumpet / James Newton Howard: direction, string arrangements / Gus Dudgeon: direction, brass arrangements / David Bitelli: direction, brass arrangements, tenor saxophone / Orchestra (brass): Onward International Horns / Orchestra (strings): not credited / Alan Carvell, Kiki Dee, Katie Kissoon, Pete Wingfield: vocals / **Recorded:** Sol Studios, Cookham, UK: January 1985 **Technical Team:** Producer: Gus Dudgeon / Sound Engineer: Stuart Epps / Mixing and Editing: Graham Dickson, Gus Dudgeon / Additional Mixing and Editing: Tom Pearce / Mastering: Gordon Vicary

"Soul Glove" is characterized from the very outset by flashy brass, and Elton John takes a back seat vocally speaking, ceding ground to the backing singers. While the attractive melody (particularly in the refrain) benefits once again from skilled production, there are a number of elements that upset the whole. They include Deon Estus's disco-style bass, which is tiring and positively oppressive and fills all the available space—just try counting the number of notes played between 2:32 and 2:34! And although Bernie's text is a good deal less insistent, it's every bit as insipid. The clichés pile up in an attempt to describe a strained relationship: "Pressure tends to get the best of you / Well don't let them break your spirit / Keep the faith and you will come on through." If the text wasn't punctuated with terms of endearment such as *baby* and *honey*, it might have come straight out of a self-help manual.

"Soul Glove" was originally intended for Kiki Dee, but Elton decided to keep it for himself, using the displaced singer in the backing vocals instead.

Elton John and British actress, model, and athlete Anya Major in the music video for the single "Nikita."

FOR ELTON ADDICTS

The name Nikita was also used as the title of a popular Luc Besson film, which starred Anne Parillaud and premiered in 1990.

NIKITA

Elton John, Bernie Taupin / 5:43

Musicians: Elton John: lead vocals, Yamaha GS1 piano, synthesizer, vocals / **Nik Kershaw:** electric guitar, vocals / **David Paton:** fretless bass / **Dave Mattacks:** drums, percussion / **Fred Mandel:** synthesizers / Davey Johnstone, George Michael: vocals **Recorded:** Sol Studios, Cookham, UK: January 1985 **Technical Team: Producer:** Gus Dudgeon / **Sound Engineer:** Stuart Epps / **Mixing and Editing:** Graham Dickson, Gus Dudgeon / **Additional Mixing and Editing:** Tom Pearce / **Mastering:** Gordon Vicary **Single Release:** *Nikita / The Man Who Never Died* **UK Release:** September 1985 on Rocket Record Company (ref. EJS 9/884 173-7) **Best UK Chart Ranking:** 3 • *Nikita / Restless* **US Release:** January 1986 on Geffen Records (ref. 7-28800) **Best US Chart Ranking:** 7

Genesis and Lyrics

After forty years of the Cold War, the 1980s represented a détente of sorts between Ronald Reagan and Mikhail Gorbachev. The situation had changed since 1979, the year when Elton performed on the other side of the Iron Curtain as one of the few singers from the West who have managed to do so, alongside Cliff Richard and Boney M. This geopolitical breakthrough inspired Bernie to compose a story about a British man living in West Berlin who falls in love with Nikita, a Soviet frontier guard living in East Berlin. The music video that accompanied the song depicts Nikita as a woman—the model Anya Major—but it is no secret that Nikita is a man's name in Russia.

Bernie compares the eyes of this fatal beauty from a cold land to "ice on fire," words that provide the title for the album. Overcome with sadness, the narrator laments that politics prevent him from meeting his love openly. He wonders if the Russian, "a captive in the snow," ever counts "the stars at night," the sky being the only place the two of them can share.

Production

The clarity and production quality on this track give each instrument its due, most notably the fretless bass played by David Paton, which is less well used on the other tracks of this album. Dave Mattacks's solid drumming, including a muted snare drum, compensates for the rather harsh synthetic sounds and lends warmth to the piece. The same can be said for Nik Kershaw's discreet guitar, which provides a few cleverly placed funky phrases, especially in the intro. Elton is particularly good here, in a melody exactly suited to his voice, which is at its best in the lower register. He is supported by wonderful backing vocals from Nik Kershaw, Davey Johnstone, and especially George Michael. The synthesizers played by Elton fit well into the arrangement, a good example coming during the long solo at 3:40. Perfect both in content and in form, "Nikita" is an island of creativity among the other songs on this album. The public recognized it as something outstanding, and the song went to number one in Belgium, Germany, Ireland, the Netherlands, and Portugal.

TOO YOUNG

Elton John, Bernie Taupin / 5:13

Musicians: Elton John: lead vocals, piano / Davey Johnstone: electric guitar, vocals / John Deacon: bass / Roger Taylor: drums / Gus Dudgeon: electronic Simmons drums / Dave Mattacks: snare drum / Frank Ricotti: timbales, cymbals / Fred Mandel: synthesizers / Alan Carvell, Kiki Dee, Katie Kissoon, Pete Wingfield: vocals **Recorded:** Sol Studios, Cookham, UK: January 1985 **Technical Team:** Producer: Gus Dudgeon / **Sound Engineer:** Stuart Epps / **Mixing and Editing:** Graham Dickson, Gus Dudgeon / **Additional Mixing and Editing:** Tom Pearce / **Mastering:** Gordon Vicary

It was a strange decision to cede the rhythm section of this soporific ballad to John Deacon and Roger Taylor, respectively the bass player and the drummer of Queen and composers of some of the most up-tempo, relentless stadium anthems of the period. The two men are underexploited by Elton here, and they seem to be bored to death in "Too Young," which is a conventional slow number with banal words despite the promise of the theme. Bernie describes the complex relationship between two people of very different ages. The parents of the young woman strongly disapprove of her love, as do the many jealous men who would give anything to trade places with the object of her desire. Regretfully, the protagonist realizes that his relationship is impossible, and that the fault lies with critics who will "get us in the long run." Although it is not enough to rescue the song, Elton's voice is excellent, and the backing vocals are very successful. Davey Johnstone's little guitar solo also brings a bit of edge and a welcome change to an otherwise sleepy track.

WRAP HER UP

Elton John, Bernie Taupin, Davey Johnstone, Fred Mandel, Charlie Morgan, Paul Westwood / 6:21

Musicians: Elton John: lead vocals / George Michael: featured vocals / Davey Johnstone: electric guitar, vocals / Paul Westwood: bass / Charlie Morgan: drums / Fred Mandel: keyboards, sequencing / Phil Todd: alto saxophone / Rick Taylor: trombone / Raul D'Oliveira: trumpet / Paul Spong: trumpet / James Newton Howard: direction, string arrangements / Gus Dudgeon: direction, brass arrangements / David Bitelli: direction, brass arrangements, baritone saxophone, tenor saxophone / Orchestra (brass): Onward International Horns /

Orchestra (strings): not credited / Kiki Dee, Katie Kissoon, Pete Wingfield: vocals **Recorded:** Sol Studios, Cookham, UK: January 1985 **Technical Team:** Producer: Gus Dudgeon / **Sound Engineer:** Stuart Epps / **Mixing and Editing:** Graham Dickson, Gus Dudgeon / **Additional Mixing and Editing:** Tom Pearce / **Mastering:** Gordon Vicary **Single Release:** *Wrap Her Up / Restless (live)* **UK Release:** November 1985 on Rocket Record Company (ref. EJS 10) **Best UK Chart Ranking:** 12 • *Wrap Her Up / The Man Who Never Died* **US Release:** October 1985 on Geffen Records (ref. 7-28873) **Best US Chart Ranking:** 20

Determined to revisit "Dream Baby," a sensual rock 'n' roll number by Roy Orbison, Elton was persuaded against it by George Michael. The younger singer could see no point in rehashing Orbison's song, suggesting instead that Elton could draw on the mood and style of Orbison's original in order to compose an entirely new song. The cover version was abandoned, and "Wrap Her Up" appeared in its place. Caught between synth-pop and new wave, its very pronounced synthetic sounds are present even on the acoustic instruments, including the brass and drums. The intrinsic quality of the piece is not in doubt, as evidenced by its performance in the charts: it went to number twelve in the UK and to number twenty in the US. It is sung as a duet by Elton and George Michael, with the latter singing in an impressive falsetto. In the video they behave like two schoolboys, at one point even throwing a cream pie in poor Kiki Dee's face. Given how chummy they seemed, it's hard to imagine that the two men were estranged for several years in the 2000s because of comments Elton made in the press regarding George's dissolute lifestyle. "I loved George," Elton wrote in his autobiography. "He was ludicrously talented, and he went through a lot, but he was the sweetest, kindest, most generous man. I miss him so much."[3] The real attraction of this number is the dazzling sound of the brass, which helpfully fleshes out a rather dull and obsessive melody. The expertly directed strings take off in the intoxicating finale (5:51), after Elton and George indulge themselves by listing the names of iconic women, including Marlene Dietrich, Marilyn Monroe, Brigitte Bardot, Doris Day, and Billie Jean King.

English singer-songwriter Nik Kershaw, whose 1984 hit "I Won't Let the Sun Go Down on Me" peaked at number two in the UK, appeared as a guitarist on "Satellite."

SATELLITE

Elton John, Bernie Taupin / 4:38

Musicians: Elton John: lead vocals, synthesizer / Davey Johnstone: synth guitar, vocals / Nik Kershaw: electric guitar / Deon Estus: bass / Mel Gaynor: drums / Fred Mandel: keyboards, electric guitar, finger snaps / Alan Carvell, Pete Wingfield: vocals **Recorded:** Sol Studios, Cookham, UK: January 1985 **Technical Team:** Producer: Gus Dudgeon / **Sound Engineer:** Stuart Epps / **Mixing and Editing:** Graham Dickson, Gus Dudgeon / **Additional Mixing and Editing:** Tom Pearce / **Mastering:** Gordon Vicary

Benefiting from impeccable orchestration and production, "Satellite" has a very rough lead singer part, which, paradoxically, takes advantage of Elton's fluctuating vocal form. To spare his voice (his vocal cords had been overtaxed by the intense amount of touring he'd done in the previous years), Elton opted for the lower register and sang with a slightly husky timbre that is uniquely charming. Deon Estus on bass takes care of the overall groove, while Nik Kershaw gives us a minimalist but perfectly judged guitar line. Meanwhile, Bernie describes an attraction between two people, one of whom is "starving for affection, waiting to be fed." He uses the vocabulary of space ("come on like a comet," "surround me like a satellite") to illustrate his idea but overextends his metaphors in the process.

TELL ME WHAT THE PAPERS SAY

Elton John, Bernie Taupin / 3:40

Musicians: Elton John: lead vocals, piano / Davey Johnstone: electric guitar, vocals / David Paton: bass / Dave Mattacks: drums / Fred Mandel: keyboards / Alan Carvell, Kiki Dee, Katie Kissoon, Pete Wingfield: vocals **Recorded:** Sol Studios, Cookham, UK: January 1985 **Technical Team:** Producer: Gus Dudgeon / **Sound Engineer:** Stuart Epps / **Mixing and Editing:** Graham Dickson, Gus Dudgeon / **Additional Mixing and Editing:** Tom Pearce / **Mastering:** Gordon Vicary

A cheerful and jubilant atmosphere permeates the catchy "Tell Me What the Papers Say." David Paton's bass stands out immediately: played dryly with a pick, favoring the high frequencies, it leaves it to Fred Mandel's keyboards to flesh out the low register and give it warmth. Fred emulates a brass section throughout the song, particularly brilliantly from 2:15 onward. Elton's piano, unleashed in a wild rock 'n' roll style, really takes off at 2:34. Davey Johnstone's guitar is underexploited, just as it is on the rest of the album, and here it's confined to a role as accompaniment, something that seems to have been required in this creative period that was dominated by keyboards. Davey makes an important contribution to the successful backing vocals, where Kiki Dee's voice can also be clearly heard. Suffering from bad treatment by an often hostile press, Elton delighted in the bitterly ironic words of this song, which features lyrics that use stock phrases constantly reproduced by the press.

Dave Mattacks (shown here in 1971) contributed his subtle playing on "Nikita," "Candy by the Pound," and "Shoot Down the Moon."

CANDY BY THE POUND

Elton John, Bernie Taupin / 3:57

Musicians: Elton John: lead vocals, synthesizer / Davey Johnstone: electric guitar, vocals / David Paton: bass / Dave Mattacks: drums / Fred Mandel: keyboards / Frank Ricotti: vibraphone / Nick Pentelow: tenor saxophone / Pete Thomas: tenor saxophone / Chris Pyne: trombone / Raul D'Oliveira: trumpet / Paul Spong: trumpet / Rick Taylor: trombone, arrangements / David Bitelli: direction, arrangements, baritone saxophone / Orchestra: Onward International Horns / Alan Carvell, Kiki Dee, Katie Kissoon, Pete Wingfield: vocals **Recorded:** Sol Studios, Cookham, UK: January 1985 **Technical Team:** Producer: Gus Dudgeon / Sound Engineer: Stuart Epps / Mixing and Editing: Graham Dickson, Gus Dudgeon / Additional Mixing and Editing: Tom Pearce / Mastering: Gordon Vicary **Single Release:** *Cry to Heaven / Candy by the Pound* **UK Release:** February 1986 on Rocket Record Company (ref. EJS 11/884 533-7) **Best UK Chart Ranking:** 47

A very conventional blues-rock shuffle provides the basis for "Candy by the Pound," which was intended to imitate the sound of the Miracles. The only truly original thing about the piece is the brass section, particularly active on the refrains of an all-purpose melody that the brass's creativity does a lot to compensate for. The opposite is true for the bass, drums, and guitars, which are completely locked in, contributing no variety to the song. To give a couple of examples: the longest contribution on guitar from Davey Johnstone is barely a second long, while Frank Ricotti's vibraphone solo starts at 3:18 and continues for about ten seconds before fading away. The backing vocals get the job done without adding any value. The lyrics lack interest as well, and Bernie seems to have had to force himself to write this love song wherein the ecstasies of love are compared to the delicious pleasures of stuffing oneself with a pound of candy.

SHOOT DOWN THE MOON

Elton John, Bernie Taupin / 5:09

Musicians: Elton John: lead vocals, piano / Pino Palladino: fretless bass / Fred Mandel: synthesizers, arrangements / Gus Dudgeon: arrangements / **Recorded:** Sol Studios, Cookham, UK: January 1985 **Technical Team:** Producer: Gus Dudgeon / Sound Engineer: Stuart Epps / Mixing and Editing: Graham Dickson, Gus Dudgeon / Additional Mixing and Editing: Tom Pearce / Mastering: Gordon Vicary

Elton John hoped that "Shoot Down the Moon" would be chosen as the theme for the James Bond film *A View to Kill*. Unfortunately, he was beaten out by Duran Duran, who offered up a more clinical, synth-pop track that reflected the trends of the time. Nevertheless, "Shoot Down the Moon" bears many stylistic traces of the self-imposed exercise of writing for Britain's most famous spy. Even the words—*gun, bullet, shoot*—link the song to the world of covert intelligence. After the song was rejected for the movie's soundtrack, Elton put it away until George Michael insisted that he include it on the track list for *Ice on Fire*.

This heartrending ballad telling a story of betrayed love starts with a few grandiose and overwhelming bars from Elton on piano. His voice is uncertain, particularly as he reaches into the higher register at "Oh you robbed me blind." This is followed by "Of what little hope remained," where he ends up sounding out of breath. From this point on the arrangement gets a bit lost in a torrent of unpleasant-sounding keyboards, though not so much so that we forget Elton's elegant piano playing and the lightness of Pino Palladino's fretless bass.

ACT OF WAR

Elton John, Bernie Taupin / 4:41

Single Release: Act of War Part 1 / Act of War Part 2 **UK Release:** June 1985 on Rocket Record Company (ref. EJS8 880 882-7) **Best UK Chart Ranking:** 32 **US Release:** June 1985 on Geffen Records (ref. 7-28956) **Best US Chart Ranking:** Did Not Chart **Musicians:** Elton John: lead vocals, piano, Yamaha TX81C synthesizer / Millie Jackson: lead vocals, vocals / Davey Johnstone: electric guitar / Nik Kershaw: electric guitar / Deon Estus: bass / Mel Gaynor: drums / Gus Dudgeon: electronic Simmons drums / Fred Mandel: guitar, Yamaha DX7 synthesizer, Jupiter 8 synthesizer **Recorded:** Sol Studios, Cookham, UK: January 1985 **Technical Team:** Producer: Gus Dudgeon / **Sound Engineer:** Stuart Epps / **Mixing and Editing:** Graham Dickson, Gus Dudgeon / **Additional Mixing and Editing:** Tom Pearce / **Mastering:** Gordon Vicary

After covering love affairs thwarted by the geopolitics of the Cold War, here Bernie tackles the subject of war between couples. We see a relationship tearing itself apart against a backdrop of alcohol and domestic tedium. The metaphors come in straightaway, and sounds of submachine guns and shelling (created by Gus Dudgeon using an electronic drum) are added to the already aggressive musical arrangement to drive home Bernie's point about the tensions between the couple. Davey Johnstone and Nik Kershaw take center stage with their dazzling guitars, providing a highly addictive main riff and an incendiary final solo. The clarity of the guitars allows for a background of organized chaos created by an abundance of keyboards, with Elton playing on a Yamaha TX81C and Fred Mandel playing on a Yamaha DX7 as well as a Jupiter 8.

Above all it is the singing of Elton and Millie Jackson, who convincingly plays the role of the angry woman, that livens up this number. Elton and Bernie had hoped to get Tina Turner for this part, but she turned them down. Strangely, "Act of War" was not taken seriously when it came out, possibly because of the music video that showed the two singers standing in front of cheap-looking cardboard scenery. The song went to number thirty-two in the United Kingdom, but Geffen Records in the US did nothing to promote the track, and it quickly faded from public view, much to Elton's disappointment.

THE MAN WHO NEVER DIED

Elton John / 5:13

Single Release: *Nikita / The Man Who Never Died* **UK Release:** September 1985 by Rocket Record Company (ref. EJS 9/884 173-7) **Best UK Chart Ranking:** 3 • *Wrap Her Up / The Man Who Never Died* **US Release:** October 1985 by Geffen Records (ref. 7-28873) **Best US Chart Ranking:** 20 **Musicians:** Elton John: lead vocals, piano / Richie Zito: electric guitar? / Jeff Porcaro: rhythm box programming? / James Newton Howard: synthesizer **Recorded:** June 1981 **Technical Team:** Producers: Clive Franks, Elton John / **Sound Engineer:** Clive Franks

This emotional tribute to John Lennon has echoes of "Song for Guy" both in its subject matter and in its arrangement. It was composed shortly after the assassination of the former Beatle and then recorded in June 1981, between sessions for *The Fox* and *Jump Up!* It remained on the shelf for a long time after that because Bernie Taupin had written another, more successful tribute to Lennon, "Empty Garden," which was included on the *Jump Up!* album. Mainly instrumental, this touching song is composed around a beautiful piano, behind which there are discreet layers of synthesizer and programmed drums. The only voices heard sound like they're coming from a great distance, almost drowned in reverb as they repeat their mantra over and over again: "Imagine…the man who never died."

Elton John stands between
Roger Daltrey and Sting during
the finale of the Live Aid
concert on July 13, 1985.

ELTON'S AWAKENING TO CHARITABLE WORK

In 1985, the music world was vibrating with the rhythm of charitable operations on a hitherto unknown scale. Bob Geldof, leader of the Boomtown Rats, was the first to launch the movement, with the release of the charity single "Do They Know It's Christmas?" a spontaneous reaction to the distress of the famine-stricken Ethiopian population. He found out about his humanitarian catastrophe with horror, when he chanced upon a BBC documentary in which the special correspondent Michael Buerk revealed the scale of the disaster that was unfolding in this country in the Horn of Africa: images of starving families, prostrate in the dirt, on death's door, were striking in their unacceptable violence. All the more so because this was taking place in the face of the general indifference of the Western world. "Do They Know It's Christmas?" which brought together, among others, Sting, Bono, Boy George, Phil Collins, and George Michael under the name of Band Aid, sold 11.7 million copies worldwide and raised £8 million pounds sterling (almost $10.5 million). With this money, pallets of food were sent to Ethiopia, but Geldof quickly discovered that $10.5 million could not halt this famine for more than two weeks...More had to be done, even though other artists joined in with similar initiatives. In fact, his charity single was very quickly emulated: in the United States, Lionel Richie and Michael Jackson enrolled a multitude of American artists under the USA for Africa flag, to record "We Are the World," composed in the context of a momentum of generosity toward the Ethiopians.

Live Aid: July 13, 1985

In spring 1985, Geldof had the idea of uniting all these goodwill initiatives under the same momentum, by organizing the biggest charity concert in history. This came together on July 13, 1985, as a double festival organized on two stages thousands of miles apart: Wembley Stadium, in London, and the John F. Kennedy Stadium, in Philadelphia (other initiatives in Sydney and Moscow also joined the project). All the big names in music were present for this satellite broadcast show: among others, Status Quo, Elvis Costello, Black Sabbath, Sting, Phil Collins (the only artist to play in both cities on the same day!), Crosby, Stills & Nash, Judas Priest, the Beach Boys, Dire Straits, Queen, David Bowie, the Pretenders, Santana, Wham!,

Madonna, Paul McCartney, Tom Petty, Neil Young, Led Zeppelin, Mick Jagger, Tina Turner, Bob Dylan, and, of course, Elton John. Elton was one of the first to respond in the affirmative to Geldof's call when he set out his project, on March 13, 1985, during the Ivor Novello Awards ceremony. Elton assured Geldof of his involvement. John Reid also gave his total support and even offered his assistance with the organization. He used all his influence to encourage the artists from his wide network to take part in this major undertaking. He had no hesitation in citing Elton's participation to convince any that were reticent about it, that the show would be involving artists of the first order. Live Aid, which was followed by nearly 2 billion viewers, was successful beyond all expectations. At around 5:00 GMT, Bob Geldof—"Saint Bob," we should say—entered the press room at Wembley. In front of the camera he was barely able to disguise his terrible back pain, and also particularly his anger at the injustice and the urgency of the Ethiopian situation. He was even exaggeratedly direct toward the viewers when urging them to donate. Despite this intervention, considered by some to be rather cavalier, the operation raised nearly $196 million.

A Massive Success

Elton was one of the last acts to appear, at 8:50, just after the Who and before Freddie Mercury and Brian May, who brought the audience at Wembley to their knees. Paul McCartney closed the evening. It should also be said that Elton was given a key slot as a headliner. He also had the longest set, in which he included seven songs from his repertoire. Flamboyant in his suit embroidered with sequins and wearing a sort of wedge cap decorated with a long feather, Elton launched into a frenzied version of "I'm Still Standing." This did not last long. A series of terrible chording errors by Davey Johnstone and disappointing backing vocals made this an apocalyptic performance, despite all the energy deployed by Elton, who struggled mightily to make everything work. Fortunately, the remainder of the performance went much better, with the rhythm section formed by Charlie Morgan on bass and David Paton on drums, demonstrating their cohesion on "Bennie and the Jets." With the delicate "Rocket Man," it was Cooper who distinguished

himself, sprinkling the number with subtle carillons or cymbal crashes. But next came the pieces that aroused the greatest fervor: "Don't Go Breaking My Heart" with a radiant Kiki Dee, and "Don't Let the Sun Go Down on Me" with Wham!, who performed with a sense of investiture. George Michael took full charge of the song, while Elton opted to remain back behind his piano, leaving the lead vocals entirely to him. Thus were sown the seeds for what became a single with the duo in 1991—before appearing on the album *Duets*, and Elton's first double number one in the charts (United Kingdom and United States) since "Don't Go Breaking My Heart." The mini set concluded with a rhythm 'n' blues version with aspects of gospel, of "Can I Get a Witness," borrowed from Marvin Gaye. The nightmarish opening was forgotten, the public expressed their enthusiasm, and the evening was saved.

Elton's Major Campaign in the Fight Against AIDS

This same year, in 1985, Elton began another campaign, one that was particularly close to his heart: the fight against a devastating illness that was still relatively unknown: AIDS. Dionne Warwick asked the singer to record alongside Stevie Wonder, Gladys Knight, and renowned studio musicians such as Michael Landau (guitar), David Foster (synthesizer), and Paulinho da Costa (percussion). They were working on a new version of "That's What Friends Are For," written by Burt Bacharach and Carole Bayer Sager, and previously recorded by Rod Stewart in 1982. Elizabeth Taylor, who happened to be in the studio on the day of the recording in her capacity as an ambassador in the fight against AIDS, suggested that the revenues from the single could be donated to fund research on treatment of the disease. Released in October 1985, the song went to number one in the United States and very quickly became the most widely sold singles of the year in Great Britain. It was Elton's biggest hit of the period.

Elton extended his charitable momentum into the following year. On June 20, 1986, he acted as master of ceremonies for the Prince's Trust gala, a charitable organization founded by Prince Charles, which raised funds to help young people find work and education. On this occasion Elton was part of an ephemeral super group combining, among others, Sting, Eric Clapton, Mark Knopfler, Phil Collins, and Rod Stewart.

Elton did not confine himself to supporting the AIDS movement during these pivotal years (1985 and 1986) in which the music world began supporting the most disadvantaged; he continued his charitable commitments, most notably through a foundation he created himself in 1992, the EJAF (Elton John AIDS Foundation), as a way to support innovative programs for the prevention of AIDS, and to assist in the treatment of patients suffering from the disease.

ALBUM

LEATHER JACKETS

Leather Jackets . Hoop of Fire . Don't Trust That Woman .
Go It Alone . Gypsy Heart . Slow Rivers . Heartache All Over the World .
Angeline . Memory of Love . Paris . I Fall Apart

RELEASE DATES
UK Release: October 15, 1986
Reference: Rocket Record Company—EJLP 1
Best UK Chart Ranking: 24
US Release: November 3, 1986
Reference: Geffen Records—GHS 24114
Best US Chart Ranking: 91

Ever the showman, Elton often incorporated fantastical hair styling into his stage wardrobe.

On November 18, 1986, the musicians of the Melbourne Symphony Orchestra made Elton John an honorary member for life.

LIVE IN AUSTRALIA

Live in Australia with the Melbourne Symphony Orchestra was recorded in Sydney on December 14, 1986, and released on June 13, 1987. The album features a series of exceptional concerts given by Elton and the Melbourne Symphony during Elton's 1986 Tour De Force concert tour.

A RECORDING CATASTROPHE

"It was about as close to an unmitigated disaster as anything I've ever released," Elton John frankly acknowledged in his autobiography. "I had always tried to be strict about not using drugs in the studio, but this time, that rule went completely out of the window. The coke had precisely the impact on my creative judgement you might expect. I stuck any old crap on *Leather Jackets*."[3] There are few who would disagree with the artist's assessment, so unworthy of his talent is this album. The American public basically disregarded this album when it was released, and posterity was no more favorable. *Leather Jackets*, like *Victim of Love* before it, brought fans together only in shared disdain for the album.

A Train Wreck Waiting to Happen

Leather Jackets is a widely acknowledged low point in Elton's career, and it can be explained via one important fact: Elton was consuming a titanic amount of cocaine at the end of 1985 and into early 1986. Gus Dudgeon recalled: "He'd go out and do some coke and it'd be all over his mouth, his nose would be running and I'd go: 'Oh God, this is just awful.'"[129] The

producer, who could no longer endorse such a waste, eventually left the production team after this album was completed. Elton included some really subpar numbers on this album both in style ("Heartache All over the World," "Go It Alone") and in substance ("Memory of Love"). The songs were almost spectacular in their vacuousness and banality, not to mention very misogynistic in the case of "Don't Trust That Woman," which was co-written with Cher. Interestingly, Cher declined to record the song for her own repertoire, which tells us all we need to know.

The conditions for the recording process were also unfavorable to the overall cohesion of the album. Six of the eleven tracks actually come out of the *Ice on Fire* sessions in 1985. At that time, Elton had planned to record enough songs to fill two albums, but he changed his mind and only released one: *Ice on Fire*. Then, in the spring of 1986, Elton went back to work to finalize his twentieth opus, and he found that the new series of songs he had composed was mediocre at best. He decided to poach from the surplus of tracks created for *Ice on Fire*, including "Leather Jackets,"

The musicians were photographed as bikers for the album cover (left to right): Fred Mandel, Davey Johnstone, Elton John, Charlie Morgan, and David Paton. (above)

As always, Elton John gave himself free reign when it came to stagewear. (right)

"Hoop of Fire," "Go It Alone," "Gypsy Heart," "Slow Rivers" (which includes the voice of Cliff Richard), and "Angeline." The new pieces were put to bed in the Netherlands between May and August 1986, during a break that the exhausted singer granted himself between the European and North American parts of his *Ice on Fire* tour, which ran from March through October of that year.

In addition to problems with the writing, Elton was having problems with his voice. The singer struggled to control his voice and sometimes even lost his voice completely, especially when he ventured too low into the deep register. "Sometimes I would sound fine. Other times I would rasp and croak and wheezily fail to hit the notes."[3] A specialist diagnosed cysts on his vocal cords, possibly due to his excessive consumption of marijuana, and recommended that Elton end his tour as soon as possible—an inconceivable option for the singer. Despite his voice failing numerous times, Elton went right through to the

end of the tour. Under these conditions, Gus Dudgeon did his best to hide the misery of his singer by placing the lead vocals as far back as possible in the mix, which is especially apparent on "Leather Jackets" and "Go It Alone."

Finally, Elton and Gus made a series of questionable choices. A majority of the songs on the album employed electronic percussion (played by Gus himself and his sound engineer, Graham Dickson) and numerous synthesizers with metallic tones that deprived the pieces of any inherent warmth or heart. Occasional bursts of hard rock intensity from Davey Johnstone in directionless songs like "Go It Alone" were also unable to compensate for this coldness. Elton extended his lack of discernment all the way to the choice for the album title, and the photo selected for the back of the album sleeve, which shows the album's musicians wearing studded leather jackets and serious expressions, posing like members of a biker gang.

A Last Gasp of Extravagance

Luckily for Elton John, the public's disaffection only manifested itself in the charts. The world tour promoting *Ice on Fire*, which was divided into three parts and ran from November 1985 to October 1986, was a big success, and most of the concerts were played to sold-out venues. Elton responded to this enthusiasm with even more exuberance, returning to the extravagant touring wardrobe of the old days. The designer Bob Mackie, who also dressed Cher, designed the most conspicuous, glittery, and luminous costumes imaginable, and he had no hesitation in giving Elton increasingly voluminous wigs to wear along with them. The wigs were iridescent with fuchsia peaks or done in the colors of the American flag—nothing was too over-the-top for the star. Elton aptly settled for a baroque white wig with a pigtail on the last leg of his 1986 Australian tour, which ran from November 5 to December 14. The tour was titled "Tour De Force," and Elton was accompanied by the Melbourne Symphony Orchestra, which he considered a major achievement. Recordings from these dates led to the release, in June 1987, of one of Elton's best live albums: *Live in Australia*.

LEATHER JACKETS

Elton John, Bernie Taupin / 4:14

Musicians: Elton John: vocals, Yamaha GS1 synthesizer / **Davey Johnstone:** acoustic guitar, electric guitar / **Fred Mandel:** synthesizers, synthesizer sequencer programming / **Gus Dudgeon:** drum machine programming, electronic percussion / **Graham Dickson:** electronic percussion **Recorded:** Sol Studios, Cookham, UK: January 1985 **Technical Team: Producer:** Gus Dudgeon / **Sound Engineer:** Graham Dickson / **Assistant Sound Engineers:** Albert Boekholt, Ronald Prent / **Mixing:** Graham Dickson, Gus Dudgeon / **Mastering:** Greg Fulginiti / **Studio Coordinators:** Steve Brown, Adrian Collee

"Be a cool jerk / Don't work," is the proclamation in Bernie Taupin's lyrics. While this eulogy of laziness is mainly addressed to "them boys in leather jackets"—an evocation of rock icons such Elvis or Buddy Holly, the advice seems to have been taken at face value by a breathless Elton. Poor Gus Dudgeon had no choice but to drown Elton's tired voice in a magma flow of strident synthesizers, a technique that is particularly audible in the refrain, with its painful "Look at them boys." It is difficult to become attached to all those synthetic instruments or find any scrap of warmth in "Leather Jackets," an intrinsically cold piece: percussion and drums take the electronic highway, programming out any trace of nuance. The bass—also played on a synthesizer—and the pseudo-strings and brass were particularly indigestible for fans right from the outset; fans no longer saw in this music the symphonic and moving Elton of his beginnings, now substituted with a cocaine-ridden phantom taking all the most predictable turnings. Only Davey Johnstone attempts to infuse some organic content into the piece—a wasted effort. For an opening number, "Leather Jackets" leaves one fearing the worst for the rest of the album.

HOOP OF FIRE

Elton John, Bernie Taupin / 4:16

Musicians: Elton John: vocals, grand piano, Roland JX-8P synthesizer / **Davey Johnstone:** acoustic guitar, electric guitar, backing vocals / **David Paton:** bass / **Dave Mattacks:** drums / **Fred Mandel:** Yamaha DX7 synthesizer / **Frank Ricotti:** percussion / **Alan Carvell, Katie Kissoon, Pete Wingfield:** backing vocals **Recorded:** Sol Studios, Cookham, UK: January 1985 / **Wisseloord Studios,**

Hilversum, Netherlands: May–September 1986 **Technical Team: Producer:** Gus Dudgeon / **Sound Engineer:** Stuart Epps / **Assistant Sound Engineers:** Albert Boekholt, Ronald Prent / **Mixing:** Graham Dickson, Gus Dudgeon / **Mastering:** Greg Fulginiti / **Studio Coordinators:** Steve Brown, Adrian Collee

"It wasn't all bad: 'Hoop of Fire' was pretty classy, especially compared to the company it was keeping."[3] In his autobiography, Elton provides a lucid and uncompromising assessment of *Leather Jackets*. His desperate wish to save something from his most spectacular musical train wreck is touching, but while it is true that "Hoop of Fire" is at least listenable, it is still a terrible caricature of a ballad, artificially doped with a sixties spirit worthy of Phil Spector. Melodically, Elton provides the bare minimum with his voice, which at this point was still unaffected by his problems with capricious vocal cords. Bernie's lyrics are a heavy evocation of a couple's sexual tension, focusing on a man living constantly on the edge and a young woman whom the man considers to be too shy. Bernie describes their situation metaphorically, inviting her to flirt with a "hoop of fire." Davey Johnstone's guitar is drowned in reverb and syrupy to the max, and the rhythm section is very basic, with some truly unbearable castanets.

DON'T TRUST THAT WOMAN

Cher, Lady Choc Ice / 4:59

Musicians: Elton John: vocals, MIDI piano, Roland JX-8P synthesizer / **Davey Johnstone:** acoustic guitar, electric guitar / **David Paton:** bass / **Charlie Morgan:** drums / **Fred Mandel:** Korg DW-8000 synthesizer / **Graham Dickson:** electronic percussion / **Jody Linscott:** percussion **Recorded:** Wisseloord Studios, Hilversum, Netherlands: May–September 1986 **Technical Team: Producer:** Gus Dudgeon / **Sound Engineer:** Graham Dickson / **Assistant Sound Engineers:** Albert Boekholt, Ronald Prent / **Mixing:** Graham Dickson, Gus Dudgeon / **Mastering:** Greg Fulginiti / **Studio Coordinators:** Steve Brown, Adrian Collee

Elton John and Cher recorded "Don't Trust That Woman," with lyrics co-written by Cher.

Elton does not mince words when describing this track: "There was a terrible song I co-wrote with Cher called 'Don't Trust That Woman,' the lyrics of which were beyond belief: 'you can rear-end her, oooh, it'll send her.' You could tell what I thought of that by the fact that I declined to put my own name to it, crediting the song to Cher and my old made-up studio character Lady Choc Ice. Of course, if you hate a song so much that you won't actually admit you wrote it, it's generally speaking a good idea not to record and release it."[3] The appalling lyrics deal with the distrust that a woman instills in a man, incorporating every possible stereotype in the process: "Don't trust that woman [...] She's a man-eater [...] She's a liar [...] she'll bring you down to your knees." In his book *Sir Elton: The Definitive Biography of Elton John*, Philip Norman

floats the theory (contradicted by Elton himself in his own autobiography) that Renate Blauel was a co-author of the song: "a track written by Renate under the pseudonym Lady Choc Ice. There was also a credit line: 'Special thanks to Lady Choc Ice for being a continued source of inspiration.'"[17] This is not a completely unreasonable idea to explore, since Elton had also previously used the alias Lord Choc Ice for himself on Side B of *Jump Up!*

Although the piece gives David Paton the opportunity to play a fluid and bounding bass line, there are few musical aspects worth saving. The arrangement is weighed down considerably by the electronic steel drums that punctuate each section. So, with Sir Elton's permission, this one goes straight to the scrap heap.

GO IT ALONE

Elton John, Bernie Taupin / 4:29

Musicians: Elton John: vocals, grand piano / **Davey Johnstone:** acoustic guitar, electric guitar, backing vocals / **Charlie Morgan:** drums, electronic percussion / **Fred Mandel:** synthesizer programming, sequencing, Roland JX-8P synthesizer / **Gus Dudgeon:** electronic percussion / **Graham Dickson:** electronic percussion / **Alan Carvell, Shirley Lewis, Gordon Neville:** backing vocals **Recorded:** Sol Studios, Cookham, UK: January 1985 **Technical Team:** Producer: Gus Dudgeon / **Sound Engineer:** Graham Dickson / **Assistant Sound Engineers:** Albert Boekholt, Ronald Prent / **Mixing:** Graham Dickson, Gus Dudgeon / **Mastering:** Greg Fulginiti / **Studio Coordinators:** Steve Brown, Adrian Collee

With its electronic programming and synthesizers permanently in the forefront, the frenetic rhythm of "Go It Alone" is locked into the synthetic era of the mid-1980s, a style that had already gone out of fashion some five years earlier. Naturally, Davey Johnstone remains the source of organic salvation, providing some naturalistic riffs that are eventually nullified by his seeming lack of commitment. He never manages to make himself stand out among all the impassive machines. As for Elton's piano, it remains inaudible until an existential awakening from 3:44. Try as the singer might to inject some feeling of rage into his vocals, we do not for one moment believe in this sordid story of two individuals tearing each other apart with the narrator appearing to angrily disown their time spent together before consigning himself to building something new "brick by brick" with "a girl that fits."

GYPSY HEART

Elton John, Bernie Taupin / 4:45

Musicians: Elton John: vocals, grand piano / **Davey Johnstone:** acoustic guitar, electric guitar, backing vocals / **David Paton:** bass / **Dave Mattacks:** drums / **Fred Mandel:** Roland Jupiter 8 synthesizer / **Alan Carvell, Shirley Lewis, Gordon Neville:** backing vocals **Recorded:** Sol Studios, Cookham, UK: January 1985 / Wisseloord Studios, Hilversum, Netherlands: May–September 1986 **Technical Team:** Producer: Gus Dudgeon / **Sound Engineer:** Stuart Epps / **Assistant Sound Engineers:** Albert Boekholt, Ronald Prent / **Mixing:** Graham Dickson, Gus Dudgeon / **Mastering:** Greg Fulginiti / **Studio Coordinators:** Steve Brown, Adrian Collee

On this song, which was taken from the *Ice on Fire* sessions, Elton shows himself off to advantage both in his vocals and on the piano, and he's not afraid to take his ballad into the realms between waltz and gospel. He's helped along by a rhythm section in good form and by effective backing vocals from Shirley Lewis's penetrating voice. "Gypsy Heart" is one of the rare items on this disk to elicit some emotion, probably because it is one of the few songs that makes relatively little use of synthetic machinery. Even so, Bernie's lyrics are soon bogged down in a quagmire of clichés typical of the most banal kind of love song, as evidenced by the turgid content of certain passages such as "Your gypsy heart will never find / Any arms as warm as mine / And gypsy, when we meet again / I'll play my part and wrap you up inside my arms."

SLOW RIVERS

Elton John, Bernie Taupin / 3:08

Musicians: Elton John: vocals, grand piano / **Cliff Richard:** vocals / **Davey Johnstone:** electric guitar / **Paul Westwood:** bass / **Charlie Morgan:** drums / **Fred Mandel:** Yamaha DX7 synthesizer, Roland Jupiter 8 synthesizer / **James Newton Howard:** string arrangements, conductor / **Gavyn Wright:** orchestra leader / **Orchestra:** uncredited / **Kiki Dee:** backing vocals **Recorded:** Sol Studios, Cookham, UK: January 1985 **Technical Team:** Producer: Gus Dudgeon / **Sound Engineer:** Graham Dickson / **Sound Engineer (Sol Studios):** Stuart Epps / **Assistant Sound Engineers:** Albert Boekholt, Ronald Prent / **Mixing:** Graham Dickson, Gus Dudgeon / **Mastering:** Greg Fulginiti / **Studio Coordinators:** Steve Brown, Adrian Collee **Single Release:** *Slow Rivers / Billy and the Kids* (45 rpm) **UK Release:** November 24, 1986, on Rocket Record Company (ref. EJS 13) **Best UK Chart Ranking:** 44 • *Slow Rivers / Billy and the Kids / Lord of the Flies* (12") **UK Release:** November 1986 on Rocket Record Company (ref. EJS 1312) **Best UK Chart Ranking:** Did Not Chart

This harmless ballad is one of the rare successes of the Elton/ Bernie duo on this opus. In this piece Elton has composed one of his most mystical melodies, the diametric opposite of everything he had previously done. It is imbued with this kind of contained sorrow that only someone who has experienced the breakup of a failed relationship can sing. Bernie's lyrics elegantly and with finesse compare a dying romance to a

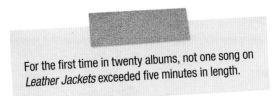

For the first time in twenty albums, not one song on *Leather Jackets* exceeded five minutes in length.

slow-flowing river that he watches with a heart cold as winter: "Slow rivers run cold, / Shallow waters never sank so low […] The bitter wind just bites through me like a wild dog. / I still see in your eyes tonight like headlights through the fog." As an unconditional fan of Cliff Richard, Elton wanted to record a duet with him, but in the end, Cliff did not contribute very much to this number. Their voices even seem quite unsynchronized, but this mixture of tenderness and robustness, although not transcendent, never handicaps the song. The discreet strings arrangement, the comfortable mattress provided by the rhythm section consisting of Charlie Morgan and Paul Westwood, and the vibrations of the metallic synthesizers of Fred Mandel suggest a river deprived of life and a romance empty of all passion. Despite its redeeming qualities, "Slow Rivers" did not survive the train wreck of *Leather Jackets*.

HEARTACHE ALL OVER THE WORLD

Elton John, Bernie Taupin / 4:16

Musicians: Elton John: vocals / Davey Johnstone: acoustic guitar, electric guitar, backing vocals / Charlie Morgan: drums / Fred Mandel: synthesizer sequencer programming, Roland P60 synthesizer, Prophet 2000 synthesizer / Gus Dudgeon: electronic percussion / Graham Dickson: electronic percussion / Vicki Brown, Alan Carvell, Gordon Neville: backing vocals **Recorded:** Wisseloord Studios, Hilversum, Netherlands: May–September 1986 **Technical Team:** Producer: Gus Dudgeon / **Sound Engineer:** Graham Dickson / **Assistant Sound Engineers:** Albert Boekholt, Ronald Prent / **Mixing:** Graham Dickson, Gus Dudgeon / **Mastering:** Greg Fulginiti / **Studio Coordinators:** Steve Brown, Adrian Collee **Single Release:** *Heartache All over the World / Highlander* **UK Release:** September 1986 on Rocket Record Company (ref. EJS 12) **Best UK Chart Ranking:** 45 **US Release:** September 1986 on Geffen Records (ref. 7-28578) **Best US Chart Ranking:** 55

In September 2001, Elton issued a categorical judgment of "Heartache All over the World" in an interview granted to the British magazine *Uncut*. Referring to it as "pretty insubstantial,"[129] he even stated that it was probably the worst song he had ever recorded. The reasons for this contempt are clear: an all-purpose melody, insipid lyrics about a man looking for girls

who would have "pity" on him, and an instrumentation dominated by keyboards that sound like extracts from animated cartoon credits. Nothing could save this piece, which nonetheless hit the charts on both sides of the Atlantic. Perhaps its catchy rhythm and the short bridge passage (from 3:31 to 3:43) helped it gain a modicum of traction with the public.

ANGELINE

Elton John, Bernie Taupin, Alan Carvell / 3:56

Musicians: Elton John: vocals, Yamaha GS1 synthesizer / Davey Johnstone: electric guitar, backing vocals / John Deacon: bass / Roger Taylor: drums / Jody Linscott: tambourine / Alan Carvell, Shirley Lewis, Gordon Neville: backing vocals **Recorded:** Sol Studios, Cookham, Berkshire: January 1985 / Wisseloord Studios, Hilversum, Netherlands: May–September 1986 **Technical Team:** Producer: Gus Dudgeon / **Sound Engineer:** Stuart Epps / **Assistant Sound Engineers:** Albert Boekholt, Ronald Prent / **Mixing:** Graham Dickson, Gus Dudgeon / **Mastering:** Greg Fulginiti / **Studio Coordinators:** Steve Brown, Adrian Collee

While recovering from an illness, Elton called to his sickbed the magic duo from Queen, consisting of John Deacon on bass and Roger Taylor on drums. Although this new input was not enough to make "Angeline" a great song, it did enable it to rise above the rest of *Leather Jackets*. Recorded during the joint sessions with *Ice on Fire*, "Angeline" also wins the prize for the most misogynistic piece on the album, and perhaps even reaches the level of "Don't Trust That Woman." Could there, in fact, be a more repugnant man than Angeline's boyfriend? She seems to be good only for feeding him, supplying him with drugs, and making love on command ("…bite me, Angeline, let me use / You like a sex machine"), and worse still, the narrator of the song is convinced that Angeline actually enjoys being subjugated to this extent. Elton adopts a tone that's hard as leather, while motorcycles rev their engines to support the testosterone-laden rhythm section. Alan Carvell features with a series of backing vocals that make the song slightly more palatable. Elton, who was impressed by the backing vocals, gave Carvell a credit as co-composer.

MEMORY OF LOVE

Elton John, Gary Osborne / 4:09

Musicians: Elton John: vocals / **Davey Johnstone:** acoustic guitar, electric guitar, backing vocals / **David Paton:** bass / **Charlie Morgan:** drums / **Fred Mandel:** Yamaha DX7 synthesizer, Roland P60 synthesizer / **Alan Carvell, Shirley Lewis, Gordon Neville:** backing vocals / **Albert Boekholt:** voice synthesizer, samples **Recorded:** Wisseloord Studios, Hilversum, Netherlands: May–September 1986 **Technical Team:** Producer: Gus Dudgeon / **Sound Engineer:** Graham Dickson / **Assistant Sound Engineer:** Albert Boekholt, Ronald Prent / **Mixing:** Graham Dickson, Gus Dudgeon / **Mastering:** Greg Fulginiti / **Studio Coordinators:** Steve Brown, Adrian Collee

"Memory of Love" is an unremittingly bland ballad that owes its clammily ordinary lyrics ("Emotions can deceive you," "never ever take love for granted," "Love will grow, it comes and goes," "My love will never, never, never leave you") to Gary Osborne, who seems to have been somewhat lacking in inspiration. Fred Mandel has as much fun as he can manage with his Yamaha DX7, which is the real attraction on this slow number. This ultra-multitasking synthesizer, capable of producing all kinds of interesting sounds, was very overused by artists in the 1980s. In subsequent years it was largely forgotten before coming back into fashion in the 2000s as a rare and prized collector's item. Nevertheless, the rhythm section on this track becomes so contemplative that it sometimes gives the impression of being behind the beat. Davey Johnstone contents himself with a few crumbs left over for the guitar.

PARIS

Elton John, Bernie Taupin / 4:00

Musicians: Elton John: vocals, grand piano / **Davey Johnstone:** electric guitar, backing vocals / **David Paton:** bass / **Charlie Morgan:** drums / **Fred Mandel:** Korg DW-8000 synthesizer, Roland Jupiter 8 synthesizer, Yamaha TX816 Rhodes synthesizer / **Alan Carvell, Shirley Lewis, Gordon Neville:** backing vocals **Recorded:** Wisseloord Studios, Hilversum, Netherlands: May–September 1986 **Technical Team:** Producer: Gus Dudgeon / **Sound Engineer:** Graham Dickson / **Assistant Sound Engineers:** Albert Boekholt, Ronald Prent / **Mixing:** Graham Dickson, Gus Dudgeon / **Mastering:** Greg Fulginiti / **Studio Coordinators:** Steve Brown, Adrian Collee

A declaration of love to the City of Light that was composed in London at the Mayfair Hotel, "Paris" commits the cardinal sin of sentimentality. Bernie's lyrics linger over Montmartre and the Rive Gauche in order to explain the narrator's feelings. Davey Johnstone adds some warmth to the piece with his electric arpeggios engorged with reverb, but the harmonic progression is clumsy and conventional. Here too, the synthesizers, with their undigestible sound layers and woeful strings emulations, dominate at the core of this song, composed in one go by Elton, who was as efficient as he was uninspired in this case. He never embodies the excited dream of the narrator, and he remains firmly on the outskirts of the City of Light.

I FALL APART

Elton John, Bernie Taupin / 4:01

Musicians: Elton John: vocals, Roland JX-8P synthesizer, Yamaha CP-80 synthesizer / **Davey Johnstone:** electric guitar / **David Paton:** bass / **Charlie Morgan:** drums / **Fred Mandel:** Roland JX-8P synthesizer, Roland Jupiter 8 synthesizer, grand piano **Recorded:** Wisseloord Studios, Hilversum, Netherlands: May–September 1986 **Technical Team:** Producer: Gus Dudgeon / **Sound Engineer:** Graham Dickson / **Assistant Sound Engineers:** Albert Boekholt, Ronald Prent / **Mixing:** Graham Dickson, Gus Dudgeon / **Mastering:** Greg Fulginiti / **Studio Coordinators:** Steve Brown, Adrian Collee

"A ballad called 'I Fall Apart' was another example of Bernie's uncanny ability to put words in my mouth that so perfectly expressed my personal situation I might have written them myself."[3] In his autobiography, Elton has nothing but praise for his colleague and for this piece, which sets out the anguish, loneliness, and fear of emptiness that regularly overwhelmed him. The narrator is confronted with the worst: he loves someone who loves someone else ("For every rose you give her, I'll give you three"). David Paton's fretless bass serves as the basis for this ballad, with its ordinary melody. At 3:09 a micro solo by Davey Johnstone makes things a little more poignant, but Elton wanders through the song rather zombielike, perhaps as a way of conveying just how much he has fallen apart.

HIGHLANDER

Elton John / 3:34

Single Release: *Heartache All over the World / Highlander* **UK Release:** September 29, 1986, with Rocket Record Company (ref. EJS 12) **Best UK Chart Ranking:** 45 **US Release:** September 1986 with Geffen Records (ref. 7-28578) **Best US Chart Ranking:** 55 **Musician:** Elton John: synthesizers **Recorded:** Woodside Studios, Berkshire, UK: summer 1985 **Technical Team:** Producer: Adrian Collee

Russell Mulcahy, the producer of many of Elton's music videos in the 1980s, was also prominent in the cinema. Following the notable horror film *Razorback*, released in 1984, he followed up with *Highlander*, which portrays a merciless battle between a group of immortal beings that plays out over several centuries until only one remains. Queen contributed a number of tracks to the film's soundtrack, but Elton also tried his hand at creating an atmospheric instrumental piece performed entirely on synthesizer. This experiment eventually ended up as Side B of "Heartache All over the World." The number enabled Elton to pile on synthetic sounds in an attempt to create a certain kind of mood before launching into an outlandish jazz digression at 2:48 into the song.

BILLY AND THE KIDS

Elton John, Bernie Taupin / 4:22

Single Release: *Slow Rivers / Billy and the Kids* (45 rpm) **UK Release:** November 1986 on Rocket Record Company (ref. EJS 13) **Best UK Chart Ranking:** 44 • *Slow Rivers / Billy and the Kids / Lord of the Flies* (12") **UK Release:** November 1986 on Rocket Record Company (ref. EJS 1312) **Best UK Chart Ranking:** Did Not Chart **Musicians:** Elton John: vocals, keyboards / Unidentified

musicians: ? **Recorded:** Sol Studios, Cookham, UK: May–June 1985 **Technical Team:** Producer: Gus Dudgeon / **Sound Engineers:** Graham Dickson, Stuart Epps

As the B-side selection for "Slow Rivers," "Billy and the Kids" seemed like an odd choice since it didn't actually have any relation to the famous Billy the Kid of the American West. In reality, the song is merely a banal story of a breakup. A jovial arrangement accompanies this narrative full of bitterness—synthesizers with perky sonorities, glitzy brass, groovy bass, gospel backing vocals—and the contrast between the music and the lyrics is somewhat disconcerting.

LORD OF THE FLIES

Elton John, Bernie Taupin / 4:30

Single Release: *Slow Rivers / Billy and the Kids / Lord of the Flies* (12") **UK Release:** November 1986 on Rocket Record Company (ref. EJS 1312) **Best UK Chart Ranking:** Did Not Chart **Musicians:** Elton John: vocals, keyboards / Unidentified musicians: ? **Recorded:** Sol Studios, Cookham, UK: May–June 1985 **Technical Team:** Producer: Gus Dudgeon

"Lord of the Flies" offers a jubilant piano-bar atmosphere that Elton could quite easily have recorded a decade earlier. Focusing on ambition and pride, Bernie's lyrics once again seem darker than the cheerful arrangement might suggest. This is based on sassy brass emulations, an unbearable piano in the honky-tonk manner, nice backing vocals, and a breathless rhythm section, notably the appealing bass, played mostly with a pick. Then there is a masterful bridge passage at 2:36, tackled with a light touch by a banjo.

ALBUM

REG STRIKES BACK

Town of Plenty . A Word in Spanish . Mona Lisas and Mad Hatters (Part Two) .
I Don't Wanna Go On with You Like That . Japanese Hands . Goodbye Marlon Brando .
The Camera Never Lies . Heavy Traffic . Poor Cow . Since God Invented Girls

RELEASE DATES
UK Release: June 24, 1988
Reference: Rocket Record Company—EJLP 3/834 701-1
Best UK Chart Ranking: 18
US Release: June 24, 1988
Reference: MCA Records—MCA-6240
Best US Chart Ranking: 16

In September 1988, Elton auctioned off many of his most famous stage costumes at Sotheby's, along with jewelry, furniture, and various works of art. The auction fetched around $8.2 million. Among the more unusual items up for sale was the pair of giant shoes that Elton wore in the movie *Tommy*, which were bought by a representative from Dr. Martens for $20,000.

BALANCING THE ACCOUNTS

At the end of the 122-concert *Ice on Fire* tour, which spanned from November 1985 through much of 1986, and the twenty-eight-date "Tour de Force" in Australia, Elton found himself in serious trouble. On January 6, 1987, a number of cysts were removed from his vocal cords. This was anything but trivial, since the cysts could have turned out to be cancerous and very well might have prevented Elton from singing ever again, or they could've drastically changed the sound of his voice. Fortunately, the first two possibilities never came to pass, and the change to Elton's voice—it became lower and more husky—delighted him. He had to accept that his famous falsetto was no more, but otherwise all was well. Now armed with a new vocal sound, Elton started work on a new album, *Reg Strikes Back*.

Resurrection

In October 1987, Elton began recording his twenty-first album at AIR Studios in London. After a painful year spent convalescing after his operation, dealing with the disintegration of his marriage to Renate, processing his split from Geffen Records (he eventually moved to MCA Records), and fending off the endless allegations about his sex life in the British tabloids, a time of relative creative productivity did him a world of good. With a cheerful and communicative Chris Thomas once more at his side, and with lyrics once again written by Bernie Taupin, Elton felt reinvigorated. *Reg Strikes Back* has a title that echoes "The Bitch Is Back," and it covers the gamut of Elton's melodic styles: long ballads ("Japanese Hands," "Since God Invented Girls"), Latin music ("A Word in Spanish"), urban funk ("Mona Lisas and Mad Hatters (Part Two)"), rock ("Goodbye Marlon Brando"), bubblegum pop ("Town of Plenty"), and

a smattering of world music ("Heavy Traffic"). Thomas invited Nigel Olsson and Dee Murray back to do the supporting vocals, and guests who had already worked in the studio with Elton began to gravitate back to the production process: Pete Townshend contributed an acoustic guitar to "Town of Plenty," while Bruce Johnston and Carl Wilson contributed vocals on "Since God Invented Girls." For the rest of the songs, Elton placed his trust in his touring group: Davey Johnstone, David Paton, Fred Mandel, Charlie Morgan, Jody Linscott, and the indispensable Ray Cooper.

The album cover was designed by Gered Mankowitz under the direction of David Costa, and it set out the intentions of a newly focused Elton: a photograph shows his imposing collection of stage costumes arranged to resemble the Beatles' famous cover from *Sgt. Pepper's Lonely Hearts Club Band*, as if to declare to the public that the wild extravagance of his last tour was a kind of last stand. He had now shed his exotic clothes like a snake sloughing off its skin. The new Elton appeared sober (at least in dress) and ready to take an accounting of his career so far. More alert and involved than he had been on some of his earlier albums, Elton seemed reinvigorated and full of new and original musical ideas. The public responded to this change of direction favorably, and the album hit the top 20 on both sides of the Atlantic. In the US, the album went to number sixteen thanks to the efforts of MCA, who stood fully behind Elton and organized an intense promotional campaign. The hard work bore fruit, and critics were also enthusiastic. Harold Goldberg of *Rolling Stone* commented on the singer's renewed energy, writing: "Throughout *Reg Strikes Back*, Elton grips gritty rock reality by the throat and never releases that hold."[30]

TOWN OF PLENTY

Elton John, Bernie Taupin / 3:41

Musicians: Elton John: vocals, Roland RD-1000 digital piano / **Davey Johnstone:** electric guitar, vocals / **Pete Townshend:** acoustic guitar / **David Paton:** bass / **Charlie Morgan:** drums / **Fred Mandel:** synthesizers / **Dee Murray, Nigel Olsson:** vocals **Recorded:** AIR Studios, London: October 1987 **Technical Team:** Producer: Chris Thomas / **Sound Engineers:** Bill Price, Michael Mason, Paul Wertheimer / **Assistant Sound Engineer:** Karl Lever / **Mastering:** Tim Young **Single Release:** *Town of Plenty* / *Whipping Boy* **UK Release:** August 1988 on Rocket Record Company/Phonogram (ref. EJS 17/870 618-7) **Best UK Chart Ranking:** 74

Bernie's lyrics for "Town of Plenty" represent an all-out attack on Ronald Reagan's America. In the mid-1980s, the politicians' greed seemed to prevail over the public good, jeopardizing American social programs to an extent not seen since the 1920s. The media, on the other hand, was flourishing and engaged in a dangerous race for ratings. Elton knew all about this, having been on the receiving end of the media's glare in 1987. Bernie, putting himself in the shoes of a man who has come to the city to take advantage of its wealth, uses the song to make a general denunciation of this kind of grasping behavior, just as he did in "Goodbye Yellow Brick Road," in which a young man grows tired of the excesses of the big city and returns home to the farm where he grew up. Elton seems to have recovered well from the operation on his vocal cords, and he sings with abandon. What he loses in subtlety he gains in power. The relaxed acoustic guitar from Pete Townshend is scarcely audible but fits well as background accompaniment to the rhythm section and the inevitable keyboards. Davey Johnstone punctuates the verses with well-placed chords on the electric guitar and joins in with the returning musicians Dee Murray and Nigel Olsson for the excellent backing vocals. "Town of Plenty" is a joyous celebration of the new Reginald!

A WORD IN SPANISH

Elton John, Bernie Taupin / 4:39

Musicians: Elton John: vocals, synthesizers, organ / **Davey Johnstone:** electric guitar, acoustic guitar, vocals / **David Paton:** bass / **Charlie Morgan:** drums / **Fred Mandel:** synthesizers / **Dee Murray, Nigel Olsson:** vocals / **Recorded:** AIR Studios, London: October 1987 **Technical Team:** Producer: Chris Thomas / **Sound Engineers:** Bill Price, Michael Mason, Paul Wertheimer / **Assistant Sound Engineer:** Karl Lever / **Mastering:** Tim Young

Davey Johnstone's guitar takes something of a back seat on much of this album because of the dominance of the keyboards in the orchestration, but in "A Word in Spanish" his playing comes into its own. Davey uses nylon strings on his instrument, and his playing excels in precision and clarity, providing a perfect link with the lyrics. Written by Bernie, the lyrics are so romantic that you might think they were by Gary Osborne, were it not for the tiny hint of satire lurking in the background. They evoke the trials and tribulations of a young man who, having failed to win over the woman of his heart, believes that he could succeed in winning her over, no longer being "a ghost" in her eyes, if he could just say that Spanish word— never revealed—heard in a movie. Naïvely, he thinks that this word has some almost magical effect: "And the words he spoke in Spanish brought the female lead to tears." But there's a problem: "If you only would listen."

Elton entrusted the choreography of the colorful video for "A Word in Spanish" to Kenny Ortega, the choreographer responsible for *Dirty Dancing* and the future director of *High School Musical* and Michael Jackson's *This Is It*.

MONA LISAS AND MAD HATTERS (PART TWO)

Elton John, Bernie Taupin / 4:13

Musicians: Elton John: vocals, Roland RD-1000 digital piano / **Davey Johnstone:** electric guitar, vocals / **David Paton:** bass / **Charlie Morgan:** drums / **Fred Mandel:** synthesizers / **Freddie Hubbard:** trumpet, flugelhorn / **Dee Murray, Nigel Olsson:** vocals **Recorded:** AIR Studios, London: October 1987 **Technical Team:** Producer: Chris Thomas / **Sound Engineers:** Bill Price, Michael Mason, Paul Wertheimer / **Assistant Sound Engineer:** Karl Lever / **Mastering:** Tim Young

As the title makes clear, "Mona Lisas and Mad Hatters (Part Two)" relates to the song "Mona Lisas and Mad Hatters," which appeared on *Honky Château* some fifteen years earlier. The first song was inspired by a shooting that occurred under the window of Bernie's New York hotel room, thereby destroying his romantic view of the city. In part 2, Bernie looks back to that event with greater maturity, now recognizing "the madness that makes this city hard" while conceding that it "took away the kid in [him]." This does not discourage the song's narrator from wandering around the streets of the Big Apple again, soaking up its atmosphere and culture, and evoking the names of Little Italy, Spanish Harlem, Lady Liberty, and Central Park in the process. Once Elton set the lyrics to music, the tight and exhilarating song magically brought the densely populated city, with its massive urban concentration, to life. The oppression is relieved by Freddie Hubbard's bright trumpet and flugelhorn solos, and by the crisp vocal backing from Nigel, Dee, and Davey. At 2:18 we also hear the famous "Beep-beep'm, beep-beep, yeah!" from the Beatles' "Drive My Car." Elton's powerful voice sails with ease through this bold blend of rock, jazz, and Latin music.

Davey Johnstone, Elton's loyal guitarist, was promoted to musical director on *Reg Strikes Back*.

I DON'T WANNA GO ON WITH YOU LIKE THAT

Elton John, Bernie Taupin / 4:35

Musicians: Elton John: vocals, Roland RD-1000 digital piano / **Davey Johnstone:** acoustic guitar, vocals / **David Paton:** bass / **Charlie Morgan:** drums / **Fred Mandel:** synthesizers / **Dee Murray, Nigel Olsson:** vocals **Recorded:** AIR Studios, London: October 1987 **Technical Team:** Producer: Chris Thomas / **Sound Engineers:** Bill Price, Michael Mason, Paul Wertheimer / **Assistant Sound Engineer:** Karl Lever / **Mastering:** Tim Young **Single Release:** *I Don't Wanna Go On with You Like That* / *Rope Around a Fool* **UK Release:** May 1988 on Rocket Record Company (ref. EJS 16) **Best UK Chart Ranking:** 30 **US Release:** May 31, 1988, on MCA Records (ref. MCA-53345) **Best US Chart Ranking:** 2

Definitely the biggest hit off this album, "I Don't Wanna Go On with You Like That" would, in time, become one of the most significant numbers in Elton's repertoire. At the moment of its release, however, it represented an important creative departure, and it showed what Elton could do with his "new" voice following the operation on his vocal cords. More powerful and lower in register, this song provides the ideal accompaniment to the singer's energetic playing on a Roland RD-1000 digital piano. While giving Elton a number where he could excel, Bernie's theme is not exactly original. The song is about a man who is demanding that his partner love no one else but him. He threatens to leave her if there is "One more set of boots on your welcome mat," and warns her that "I ain't no puzzle piece that needs to fit," and adding that he "Don't want to be a feather in your cap." With a linear but perfectly maintained tempo coming from the rhythm section, composed of David Paton on bass and Charlie Morgan on drums, Fred's synthesizers add substance to the sound while Davey's acoustic guitar stays almost inaudible. Together they provide a comfortable ambiance for Elton's voice and his unrestrained piano. He gives us a groove-filled solo beginning at 3:19, which is perhaps one of his most inspired from recent albums. The backing vocals provided by a quartet made up of Davey, Elton, Dee Murray, and Nigel Olsson are dazzling in their effectiveness, harkening back to the glory days of the fearless band they formed in the 1970s, when nothing seemed impossible.

JAPANESE HANDS

Elton John, Bernie Taupin / 4:41

Musicians: Elton John: vocals, synthesizers, acoustic piano / **Davey Johnstone:** acoustic guitar, electric guitar, vocals / **David Paton:** bass / **Charlie Morgan:** drums / **Fred Mandel:** synthesizers / **Dee Murray, Nigel Olsson:** vocals **Recorded:** AIR Studios, London: October 1987 **Technical Team:** Producer: Chris Thomas / Sound Engineers: Bill Price, Michael Mason, Paul Wertheimer / **Assistant Sound Engineer:** Karl Lever / **Mastering:** Tim Young

Bernie's lyrics describe a beautiful Japanese woman and a fascination with her country. The words play with a series of contrasts between the Land of the Rising Sun and the narrator's own country. Bernie uses periphrases that shroud his evocations in mystery; yin and yang, for example, are suggested by the words "symbols painted black and white." Many elements add to the uncomfortable feeling of exoticism that pervades this song: "paper walls" (shoji, the translucent interior walls of traditional Japanese houses), earthquakes, "bamboo," the "secrets of the east," "silk." In the middle of this list of stereotypes, Bernie opts to use "hands" as a stand-in for the body as a whole, and he also uses comparisons between heat and cold as a metaphor for sexual excitement: as in "the hot wind," "the moon grows cold."

Unlike Iggy Pop's and David Bowie's versions of "China Girl" (a song they wrote together, with Iggy bringing out a version in 1977 and David in 1983), Elton opted to use an excessively pared down arrangement with just a hazy layer of synthesizer supporting his voice. The backing vocals, provided by his one-time rhythm section of Dee Murray and Nigel Olsson, have the same lightness as the keyboards. In the middle of this floating arrangement, majestic entries from the electric guitar crown the moment of plenitude and perfectly match Bernie's blissful lyrics.

GOODBYE MARLON BRANDO

Elton John, Bernie Taupin / 3:31

Musicians: Elton John: vocals, synthesizers / **Davey Johnstone:** acoustic guitar, electric guitar, vocals / **David Paton:** bass / **Charlie Morgan:** drums / **Fred Mandel:** synthesizers / **Ray Cooper:** maracas, tambourine, timbales / **Dee Murray, Nigel Olsson:** vocals **Recorded:** AIR Studios, London: October 1987 **Technical Team:** Producer: Chris Thomas / Sound Engineers: Bill Price, Michael Mason, Paul Wertheimer / **Assistant Sound Engineer:** Karl Lever / **Mastering:** Tim Young

Often underemployed on the preceding recordings, Davey Johnstone's electric guitar makes a dramatic return in "Goodbye Marlon Brando." Starting with a power-chord riff, the guitarist's performance is the main attraction of this heavy metal rock track that is otherwise a bit conventional while being full of testosterone. Elton's macho "ooh" at the beginning of the track sets a less than subtle tone. The rhythm section hammers it out in the background. Only the backing vocals and a few interjections from a bouncy synthesizer on the verses beginning at 2:27 are able to provide a bit of relief to the otherwise heavy sound of the song. The music suits Bernie's words well: he lets rip, suggesting that the great actor Marlon Brando be forgotten, probably because he represents a bygone era. The number of targets in Bernie's sights is long: politicians ("the clowns in congress"), new age music, sentimental soaps, tabloids, and also real people, including the Beach Boys and Sylvester Stallone ("Say goodbye to Rocky Five, Six, Seven and Eight"), who were both well liked by Elton.

THE CAMERA NEVER LIES

Elton John, Bernie Taupin / 4:36

Musicians: Elton John: vocals, acoustic piano / **Davey Johnstone:** electric guitar, vocals / **David Paton:** bass / **Charlie Morgan:** drums / **Fred Mandel:** synthesizers / **Ray Cooper:** maracas, tambourine, timbales / **Dee Murray, Nigel Olsson:** vocals **Recorded:** AIR Studios, London: October 1987 **Technical Team:** Producer: Chris Thomas / **Sound Engineers:** Bill Price, Michael Mason, Paul Wertheimer / **Assistant Sound Engineer:** Karl Lever / **Mastering:** Tim Young

Always guarded when questioned about the true meanings of his songs, Elton was evasive when asked about "The Camera Never Lies" and Bernie was no more forthcoming on the song's true meaning; nevertheless, the metaphor of a husband discovering his wife's unfaithfulness and collecting proof of it in the form of photographs is a clear reference to Elton's overexposure in the media in much of the 1980s. Despite the subject matter, the melody is unexpectedly invigorating, with a rolling bass and Elton playing a particularly bouncy and natural-sounding acoustic piano. It is as if the seriousness of the husband's accusations needs to be compensated for by a light musical accompaniment. Anger and rage are present in abundance, especially in the singer's voice, which makes another strong showing on this convincing track, marred only by an indifferent bridge at 2:55.

As a symbol of the glam rock period, these 1974 monogrammed boots sold for $10,000 in an auction at Sotheby's in 1988.

HEAVY TRAFFIC

Elton John, Bernie Taupin, Davey Johnstone / 3:30

Musicians: Elton John: vocals, acoustic piano / Davey Johnstone: electric guitar, acoustic guitar, vocals / David Paton: bass / Charlie Morgan: drums / Fred Mandel: synthesizers / Ray Cooper: maracas, tambourine, timbales / Dee Murray, Nigel Olsson: vocals **Recorded:** AIR Studios, London: October 1987 **Technical Team:** Producer: Chris Thomas / **Sound Engineers:** Bill Price, Michael Mason, Paul Wertheimer / **Assistant Sound Engineer:** Karl Lever / **Mastering:** Tim Young

The intricate melody of "Heavy Traffic" owes as much to Elton John's effectiveness as it does to Davey Johnstone's creativity. Both names are credited on this festive number—dating from the recording sessions for *Leather Jackets*—where piano and guitars interweave and complement one another throughout. Meanwhile, Davey shines both on the acoustic guitar, with skilled fingerpicking, and on the electric guitar that is able to offer a wider range of sound in the second part of the song. Sounding rather distant in the final mix, the backing vocals add a touch of wackiness. Notable contributions also come from the elastic sound of the bass and from the silky-smooth sound of the snare drum. In his lyrics Bernie gives us a gallery of caricatures (Billy, Mack, Judy, Cindy, Jackie...) who are marginalized Californians living close to the Mexican border. These rejects from the American Dream live by their wits, involved in drug trafficking, pimping, and prostitution. In this modern America, where success is denied to them, they are inevitably sucked into a destructive spiral filled with drug addiction, murder, and suicide.

POOR COW

Elton John, Bernie Taupin / 3:51

Musicians: Elton John: vocals, synthesizers / Davey Johnstone: electric guitar, vocals / David Paton: bass / Charlie Morgan: drums / Fred Mandel: synthesizers / Ray Cooper: maracas, tambourine, timbales / Dee Murray, Nigel Olsson: vocals **Recorded:** AIR Studios, London: October 1987 **Technical Team:** Producer: Chris Thomas / **Sound Engineers:** Bill Price, Michael Mason, Paul Wertheimer / **Assistant Sound Engineer:** Karl Lever / **Mastering:** Tim Young

Perhaps created in response to criticism of his very masculine approach to "Since God Invented Girls," here Bernie has written words that are full of empathy for a young woman. He paints a tragic picture: the girl has married out of necessity and in imitation of the women she sees all around her. Her husband pays little attention to her and prefers "factory girls." He is not only adulterous but also violent, which we deduce from the words "the back of his hand." Bernie's character works all hours to keep things afloat, and she is hugely brave but also slightly naïve.

On this synth-pop track, the slamming drums, the bouncing bass, and the haunting motif played by Elton on the keyboard with the left hand set the song on track. Elton can then have a field day vocally. He offers an admirable variety of moods and range, energizing the text by fiercely accentuating certain words that seem to fall like metaphorical blows from the woman's husband.

Elton John's short-lived marriage to Renate Blauel ended in divorce in 1988.

SINCE GOD INVENTED GIRLS

Elton John, Bernie Taupin / 4:54

Musicians: Elton John: vocals, Roland RD-1000 digital piano / **Davey Johnstone:** electric guitar, vocals / **David Paton:** bass / **Charlie Morgan:** drums / **Fred Mandel:** synthesizers / **Adrian Baker, Bruce Johnston, Dee Murray, Nigel Olsson, Carl Wilson:** vocals
Recorded: AIR Studios, London: March 1988 **Technical Team:** Producer: Chris Thomas / **Sound Engineers:** Bill Price, Michael Mason, Paul Wertheimer / **Assistant Sound Engineer:** Karl Lever / **Mastering:** Tim Young

Deeply depressed and limited by his convalescence post-surgery, Elton had never gone for such a long time without playing his piano. This may be why a certain feverishness can be detected in his first attempts to compose for the *Reg Strikes Back* album. "Since God Invented Girls," the first song he managed to complete—in a single shot, to boot—was to provide the catalyst he needed. He composed it at home, in the presence of his personal sound engineer, who had the inspired idea of bringing out the recording the moment the melody emerged from Elton's improvisational playing.

Ironically, while he was going through a difficult period in his relationship with Renate and realizing that the feelings of love that had brought them together were at odds with his homosexuality, Elton was able to work on Bernie's somewhat macho text that praised women and thanked God for them as if they were a gift from on high.

Bernie may have been expecting something more rocking and upbeat than the music that was eventually composed by Elton. Instead, inspired by the lyricist's mention of Brian Wilson, Elton aimed for a gentle anthem à la the Beach Boys. To underline this tribute, Elton once more invited Beach Boy Bruce Johnston to record the vocals with his partner in the group, tenor Carl Wilson. Echoes of the Beach Boys are everywhere: from the swinging rhythm to the sequence of minor and major chords (*E* minor–*E* flat major–*B* flat major–*F*), in the expansive drumming, inspired by Dennis Wilson's style, and of course in the angelic vocals. Elton's voice passes its first test with flying colors. His vocal signature is still present but has settled into a slightly lower register with greater projection.

Elton John at a 1988 concert in Paris.

ROPE AROUND A FOOL

Elton John, Bernie Taupin / 3:48

Single Release: *I Don't Wanna Go On with You Like That / Rope Around a Fool* **UK Release:** May 1988 on Rocket Record Company (ref. EJS 16) **Best UK Chart Ranking:** 30 **US Release:** May 31, 1988, on MCA Records (ref. MCA-53345) **Best US Chart Ranking:** 2 **Musicians:** Elton John: lead singer, Roland RD-1000 digital piano / Davey Johnstone: electric guitar / David Paton: bass / Charlie Morgan: drums / Synthesizers: ? **Recorded:** AIR Studios, London: October 1987 **Technical Team:** Producer: Chris Thomas / Sound Engineers: Bill Price, Michael Mason, Paul Wertheimer / Assistant Sound Engineer: Karl Lever / Mastering: Tim Young

With its bluesy feel, providing Elton with the opportunity to compose a beautiful piano score and a rousing solo, "Rope Around a Fool" scores with the intensity of its arrangement. The rhythm section flexes its muscles, Elton's voice shines with confidence, and Davey Johnstone's guitar, though slightly far back, is very sharp. Bernie's text is cryptic. It is not clear if the song is criticizing a society where no one is prepared to acknowledge their responsibilities, preferring to find a scapegoat and string him up ("And it's easier sometimes to throw a rope around a fool"), or whether, more prosaically, it is a protest against capital punishment ("We got mass determination making up the rules"). Either way, the subject is serious, and the music is not well adapted to it. Even if it is not entirely clear, there are some memorable phrases, including "We got Miss Communication kicking out the stool," punning with "miscommunication." Despite its qualities, "Rope Around a Fool" was not selected for the *Reg Strikes Back* album, but it did make an appearance on Side B of "I Don't Wanna Go On with You Like That."

ALBUM

SLEEPING WITH THE PAST

Durban Deep . Healing Hands . Whispers . Club at the End of the Street .
Sleeping with the Past . Stone's Throw from Hurtin' . Sacrifice .
I Never Knew Her Name . Amazes Me . Blue Avenue

RELEASE DATES
UK Release: August 29, 1989
Reference: Rocket Record Company—838 839-1
Best UK Chart Ranking: 1
US Release: August 29, 1989
Reference: MCA Records—MCA-6321
Best US Chart Ranking: 23

For their next album, Elton and Bernie created songs inspired by Motown Records, Chess Records, and Stax Records.

SOUL BROTHERS

Did the Puk studios have an unexpectedly soothing effect? Three albums created there contain the word *sleep*: *Sleeping with the Past* by Elton John, *Sleeping Beauty Waltz and Other Great Dances from Europe*, and 2016's *The Violent Sleep of Reason* by Meshuggah.

During the second half of 1988, the clouds darkening Elton's skies started to disperse. The results from *Reg Strikes Back* quickly redressed his situation in the sales charts, following the slide that began with *Leather Jackets*. The *Sun* newspaper made honorable amends with their "Sorry Elton" headline to apologize for printing almost a year's worth of articles containing false accusations about the singer. Finally, an auction of his collection of personal objects in September 1988 helped him amass nearly $8.2 million. This was a substantial return that enabled him to cover the cost of his divorce from Renate Blauel (among other things), which was a separation negotiated without acrimony.

In November 1988, it was with a newly freed spirit that Elton John approached the recording sessions for *Sleeping with the Past* at the Puk Recording Studios, which had been created in a converted farmhouse in Demark by John "Puk" Quist and his wife in 1978. George Michael recorded his *Faith* album there in May 1987 and recommended the recording complex to Elton. The premises, which were modern and spacious—notably including a paneled mixing cabin, open at the rear with a vast picture window—also came equipped with cutting-edge recording equipment and a wide range of leisure facilities (spa, jacuzzi, pool, etc.) that very quickly won over an international clientele (Depeche Mode, the Kinks, Judas Priest, etc.). Like Hérouville or Caribou, this was a location that was conducive to creativity. It provided Elton with a total change of scenery and beneficial seclusion, far from all the temptations liable to distract him or plunge him back into his addictions (which did not, on the other hand, prevent him from copious consumption of the alcohol on the premises). This was a vital prerequisite, since Elton did not have any new songs up his sleeve and planned to compose everything on the spot as soon as he arrived at the studios.

Soul Inspiration

Following the stylistic panoply offered in his previous opus, the singer felt it was necessary to set guidelines for this next album. He and Bernie agreed to create an album inspired by the soul music of the 1960s that had so richly nurtured their youthful compositions. Obviously, it was not the first time the duo had drawn on this musical genre. "Take Me to the Pilot," "Bennie and the Jets," and the *Thom Bell Sessions* also owe their existence to this early source of inspiration. But never before had their intentions been so clearly defined. The two men even put in place an original working method: Bernie Taupin's mission was to immerse himself in this musical ambiance by listening to as many songs as possible from this period during his writing, including standards by Chess, Stax, and from all of Motown. Once the lyrics had been written, he would write the sources of his inspiration at the bottom of each song so that Elton could be inspired during his musical composition. Naturally, Elton sometimes strayed from these stylistic indications, but they were useful nonetheless.

Inevitably, a certain nostalgia infiltrated the album as the two men delved back into a musical heritage that was so intimately linked with their teenage selves, thereby also reinforcing their bond of friendship and artistic collaboration. Elton included the following touching dedication on the back of the album cover: "This album's for you, Bernie...."

Davey Earns His Stripes

True to form, Elton lined up the songs one after the other, starting with "Whispers," "Amazes Me," and "Sleeping with the Past." The mechanism was a well-oiled machine: In the morning, Elton picked up Bernie's lyrics and started composing in the presence of Chris Thomas, who recorded everything, and with Davey Johnstone now enthroned as musical director. Once the fundamentals had been laid down, the other musicians arrived at around eleven in the morning. All the alumni from the *Reg Strikes Back* tour were present: keyboard players Guy Babylon, and Fred Mandel, bassist Romeo Williams, drummer Jonathan Moffett, and backing vocalists Natalie Jackson (now Kudisan Kai), Mortonette Jenkins, and Marlena Jeter. They went into the studio, and at that point Davey Johnstone came onstage while Elton disappeared. Having been briefed by Elton, the guitarist had a clear vision of the expected results. Very often it was Davey who dictated the parts to each of the musicians. Once the instrumental parts had been finalized, Elton came back to add first the vocal line for the ensemble, and then his definitive vocals. Each piece was completely processed this way throughout the course of the working day.

From one kingdom to another, on his return from Denmark Elton was given a princely welcome in his home country. The album went to number one in the UK as soon as it was released in August 1989, and it was certified triple platinum. The situation was less flattering in the United States, where the opus achieved an otherwise honorable twenty-third place and stayed there for fifty-three weeks.

1989

DURBAN DEEP

Elton John, Bernie Taupin / 5:29

Musicians: Elton John: lead and backing vocals, Roland RD-1000 digital piano / **Davey Johnstone:** guitars, backing vocals / **Fred Mandel:** guitars, keyboards / **Romeo Williams:** bass / **Jonathan Moffett:** drums / **Guy Babylon:** keyboards / **Peter Iversen:** Fairlight CMI digital synthesizer and programming **Recorded:** Puk Recording Studios, Randers, Denmark: November 1988 **Technical Team:** Producer: Chris Thomas / **Sound Engineers:** David Nicholas, John Quist / **Assistant Sound Engineer:** Karl Lever / **Mastering:** Greg Fulginiti / **Album Coordinator:** Steve Brown / **Studio Coordinators:** Adrian Collee, Dee Whelan

"Durban Deep" was inspired by "Working in the Coal Mine," Lee Dorsey's hit released in 1966 and written by one of Elton's idols, Allen Toussaint—with this one big difference, that the song in this case is not about a coal mine but rather the famous Durban Deep, nicknamed the "Grand Old Lady," a gigantic South African gold mine located about twenty kilometers from Johannesburg, which stopped operating in 2001. Bernie gives the narrative to one of the miners. He suffers from "the killin' heat" that dominates in the depths of the mine, the coal dust he breathes all the time, and the blisters inflicted on his flesh by the heavy work. He bows to the invectives of his boss, who calls him "lazy," because he has to feed his "family, they go hungry." When he returns to the surface, he is blinded by a "big red sun" which "Look a lot like fire" or by this "old blue heaven / [which] Look a lot like your eyes."

Elton opts for an arrangement that is borderline reggae in style, seeking to convey through the nonchalance of the music the repetitive and oppressive nature of the work at the bottom of the mine. Davey Johnstone's guitar produces a very inspired solo from 3:03, even though he takes some liberties with the melody developed by Elton's piano (at 3:17 and 3:21).

HEALING HANDS

Elton John, Bernie Taupin / 4:30

Musicians: Elton John: lead and backing vocals, keyboards / **Davey Johnstone:** guitars, backing vocals / **Romeo Williams:** bass / **Jonathan Moffett:** drums / **Guy Babylon:** keyboards / **Fred Mandel:** keyboards / **Peter Iversen:** Fairlight CMI digital synthesizer, programming / **Natalie Jackson, Mortonette Jenkins, Marlena Jeter:** backing vocals **Recorded:** Puk Recording Studios, Randers, Denmark: November 1988 **Technical Team:** Producer: Chris Thomas / **Sound Engineers:** David Nicholas, John Quist / **Assistant Sound Engineer:** Karl Lever / **Mastering:** Greg Fulginiti / **Album Coordinator:** Steve Brown / **Studio Coordinators:** Adrian Collee, Dee Whelan **Single Release:** *Healing Hands / Dancing in the End Zone* **UK Release:** August 14, 1989, on Rocket Record Company (ref. EJS 19) **Best UK Chart Ranking:** 45 **US Release:** July 5, 1989, on MCA Records (ref. MCA-53692) **Best US Chart Ranking:** 13 • *Sacrifice / Healing Hands* **UK Release:** May 25, 1990, on Rocket Record Company (ref. EJS 22/875 808-7) **Best UK Chart Ranking:** 1

A soul and even gospel ambiance is asserted in "Healing Hands," with its rousing refrain, which illustrates all of Elton's melodic facility—as much vocally as on his keyboards. He even provides a small piano solo in the middle of the piece. This heartfelt tribute to the famous Four Tops hit "Reach Out I'll Be There," both in its soul color and in the text, describes the care lavished on a loved one to heal their wounds. We also encounter the famous "reach out," repeated several times in the refrains. "I never knew it could hurt so bad / When the power of love is dead," the narrator explains at the beginning, even conceding that there "Ain't no cure for the pain / You gotta wade into the water / You gotta learn to live again." But in the end, he hopes that "healing hands" will enable him to see the light again, "where the darkness ends." In order to convey this message of hope, Elton uses a fairly conventional rhythm section with keyboards very much in evidence and, above all, the finely honed backing vocals. Davey Johnstone very ably weaves an electrical bed of sound in the background to fill out the song's harmonic musculature.

WHISPERS

Elton John, Bernie Taupin / 5:26

Musicians: Elton John: vocals, Roland RD-1000 digital piano / **Davey Johnstone:** guitars / **Romeo Williams:** bass / **Jonathan Moffett:** drums / **Guy Babylon:** keyboards / **Fred Mandel:** keyboards / **Peter Iversen:** Fairlight CMI digital synthesizer, programming **Recorded:** Puk Recording Studios, Randers, Denmark: November 1988 **Technical Team:** Producer: Chris Thomas / **Sound Engineers:** David Nicholas, John Quist / **Assistant Sound Engineer:** Karl Lever / **Mastering:** Greg Fulginiti / **Album Coordinator:** Steve Brown / **Studio Coordinators:** Adrian Collee, Dee Whelan **Single Release:** *Club at the End of the Street / Whispers* **UK Release:** August 1990 on Rocket Record Company (ref. EJS 23) **Best UK Chart Ranking:** 47

The hit "Whispers" is another opportunity for paying homage to soul, this time to the sunny Jackie Wilson and his hit "Whispers Gettin' Louder," released in 1966. Elton's ballad, constructed on a slow tempo, is principally based on a delicate electronic piano score, some light percussion, a fluid bass, and electric guitar with a carefully dosed reverb. Elton's voice is impressive here, as it seems always to be on the edge, oscillating between power and gentleness. The song concludes with a magnificent piano movement, which brings out the gentleness of the melody. Bernie's lyrics, provided upstream, were already impregnated with sensuality at the turn of each verse: "Look at me twice with wildcat eyes / Promise me everything / Except a blue night," but also "Melt in embraces / Of crazy eyed past" or "A distant smile framed / Her lips are soft and moist." Despite its status as a B-side and the modest forty-seventh place achieved in the United Kingdom by the single "Club at the End of the Street," "Whispers" established itself as one of Elton's emblematic numbers, confirming his intuition: From the demo stage, he had felt "the old spine-tingling feeling"[132] that confirmed this was going to be a hit.

CLUB AT THE END OF THE STREET

Elton John, Bernie Taupin / 4:52

Musicians: Elton John: vocals, Roland RD-1000 digital piano / **Davey Johnstone:** guitars, backing vocals / **Fred Mandel:** guitars, organ / **Romeo Williams:** bass / **Jonathan Moffett:** drums / **Guy Babylon:** keyboards / **Vince Denham:** saxophone / **Peter Iversen:** Fairlight CMI digital synthesizer, programming **Recorded:** Puk Recording Studios, Randers, Denmark: November 1988 **Technical Team:** Producer: Chris Thomas / **Sound Engineers:** David Nicholas, John Quist / **Assistant Sound Engineer:** Karl Lever / **Mastering:** Greg Fulginiti / **Album Coordinator:** Steve Brown / **Studio Coordinator:** Adrian Collee, Dee Whelan / **Single Release:** *Club at the End of the Street / Whispers* **UK Release:** August 1990 on Rocket Record Company (ref. EJS 23) **Best UK Chart Ranking:** 47 • *Club at the End of the Street / Give Peace a Chance* **UK Release:** April 1990 on Rocket Record Company (ref. EJS 21) • *Club at the End of the Street / Sacrifice* **US Release:** April 1990 on MCA Records (ref. MCA-79026) **Best US Chart Ranking:** 28

"I love 'Club at the End of the Street,'" Elton has often explained. "We wanted to write a song like the Drifters would record, one of those Goffin-King, Brill Building songs. It's the closest we ever got to one."[35] In fact, the warm and rounded backing vocals on this piece are laced with doo-wop references, while the text narrates the adventure of two lovers who enjoy meeting in a fashionable club where "the sound of Otis" and the "voice of Marvin Gaye" resound. Bernie depicts the location in a very cinematographic way, sketching a New York firmly implanted in the collective imagination: "In this smoky room / There's a jukebox plays all night / And we can dance real close / Beneath the pulse of a neon light" or "There's a downtown smell of cooking / From the flame on an open grill." The moderate tempo sits particularly well with the catchy melody of the refrain, which is brought out well by Elton, who is full of haunting presence, and whose French accent is irresistible on the "rendezvous" which is made to rhyme with the physical "Me and you." Most of the keyboards fill out the arrangement skillfully and generously (with the exception of one of these, a crude strings emulation on the bridge passages between the verses and refrains) and are brilliantly supplemented by Vince Denham's torrid saxophone.

SLEEPING WITH THE PAST

Elton John, Bernie Taupin / 4:52

Musicians: Elton John: vocals, Roland RD-1000 digital piano / **Davey Johnstone:** guitars, backing vocals / **Romeo Williams:** bass / **Jonathan Moffett:** drums / **Guy Babylon:** keyboards / **Fred Mandel:** keyboards / **Peter Iversen:** Fairlight CMI digital synthesizer, programming / **Natalie Jackson, Mortonette Jenkins, Marlena Jeter:** backing vocals

Recorded: Puk Recording Studios, Randers, Denmark: November 1988 **Technical Team:** Producer: Chris Thomas / **Sound Engineer:** David Nicholas, John Quist / **Assistant Sound Engineer:** Karl Lever / **Mastering:** Greg Fulginiti / **Album Coordinator:** Steve Brown / **Studio Coordinators:** Adrian Collee, Dee Whelan

Among the first numbers on the album to be recorded, "Sleeping with the Past" gave the album its name, and has some elements that are reminiscent of the Temptations, who were one of the most emblematic American soul and rhythm 'n' blues groups of the 1960s. The arrangement is very rich, with very good and very enveloping keyboards; a nice, raucous electric guitar launching straight into a punchy riff, and a rhythm section with an impeccable groove, underpins the abrasive brass. It is in this context that the story of a woman whose heart has been broken by a man unfolds. The narrator urges her to extricate herself from his influence: "Like a thief he's come, like a thief he's gone / He's stolen your tears one by one / You're proud to love him, it's a foolish sign / You're a broken heart at the scene of the crime." He even implores her not to "go sleepin' with the past" and not to "go prayin' he'll come back," concluding, bluntly: "You're an empty doll in the power of a fool."

STONE'S THROW FROM HURTIN'

Elton John, Bernie Taupin / 4:44

Musicians: Elton John: vocals, Roland RD-1000 digital piano / **Davey Johnstone:** guitars, backing vocals / **Fred Mandel:** guitars / **Romeo Williams:** bass / **Jonathan Moffett:** drums / **Guy Babylon:** keyboards / **Peter Iversen:** Fairlight CMI digital synthesizer and programming / **Natalie Jackson, Mortonette Jenkins, Marlena Jeter:** backing vocals: Puk Recording Studios, Randers, Denmark: November 1988 **Technical Team:** Producer: Chris Thomas / **Sound Engineers:** David Nicholas, John Quist / **Assistant Sound Engineer:** Karl Lever / **Mastering:** Greg Fulginiti / **Album Coordinator:** Steve Brown / **Studio Coordinators:** Adrian Collee, Dee Whelan

More blues than soul, "Stone's Throw from Hurtin'" was written by Bernie with the American duo Sam & Dave in mind, while Elton John initially evoked the musical influence of Marvin Gaye. Finally, the searing, venomous guitars of Davey Johnstone are above all reminiscent of Canned Heat or JJ Cale and deliver a trenchant solo, obscuring the anecdotal presence of the keyboards. In contrast, Elton's voice, which is of exceptional gentleness, also carries along the blues entailed in a faded sentimental relationship: "We're just a couple of kids with a broken toy," as Bernie subtly describes it. This was in reality the demo vocal take, the one artists generally record as a guide for subsequent attempts. The voice of Natalie Jackson (Kudisan Kai) can be heard on the fade-out of the piece, discreetly singing "stone's throw from hurtin'," a phrase that had him pulling his hair out. In fact, Elton thought that her "hurtinnnn'" was either too long or too short and had her redo the take a dozen times.

SACRIFICE

Elton John, Bernie Taupin / 5:04

Musicians

Elton John: vocals, Roland RD-1000 digital piano
Davey Johnstone: guitars
Romeo Williams: bass
Jonathan Moffett: drums
Guy Babylon: keyboards
Fred Mandel: keyboards
Peter Iversen: Fairlight CMI digital synthesizer, programming

Recorded

Puk Recording Studios, Randers, Denmark: November 1988

Technical Team

Producer: Chris Thomas
Sound Engineers: David Nicholas, John Quist
Assistant Sound Engineer: Karl Lever
Mastering: Greg Fulginiti
Album Coordinator: Steve Brown
Studio Coordinators: Adrian Collee, Dee Whelan

Single Release

Sacrifice / Love Is a Cannibal
  UK Release: October 1989 on Rocket Record Company (ref. EJS 20/876 330-7)
  Best UK Chart Ranking: 55
  US Release: January 1990 on MCA Records (ref. MCA-53750)
  Best US Chart Ranking: 18
• *Sacrifice / Healing Hands*
  UK Release: May 25, 1990, on Rocket Record Company (ref. EJS 22/875 808-7)
  Best UK Chart Ranking: 1
• *Club at the End of the Street / Sacrifice*
  US Release: April 1990 on MCA Records (ref. MCA-79026)
  Best US Chart Ranking: 28

Genesis and Lyrics

While Elton John entered the studio very confident of the potential of the album he was about to record, he did have major doubts about one of the songs on the track list: "Sacrifice." Not without some irony, he returned to this episode in his autobiography: "Demonstrating again the infallible commercial instincts that led me to announce I was going to strangle Gus Dudgeon if 'Don't Let the Sun Go Down on Me' was ever released, I said I didn't want it ['Sacrifice'] on the album. I was talked round, but then the record company wanted to release it as a single, which just seemed stupid—it was a five-minute-long ballad, no one was going to play it."[3] In October 1989 the song was released in the United Kingdom, in the wake of album, as a single with "Love Is a Cannibal" on the B-side. But it plateaued at fifty-fifth place, unworthy of Elton's status, until spring 1990. It was at this time that Steve Wright, a DJ on BBC Radio 1 who was enchanted by "Sacrifice," decided to promote it by scheduling it to be played regularly. Given the renewed popularity that this initiative conferred on the number, in May 1990 Rocket Record launched a new offensive, and rereleased it as a double A-side together with "Healing Hands," which Elton considered "much more commercial."[3] Three weeks later, the singer achieved his first solo number one in the United Kingdom. The plaintive ballad gradually established itself as one of the most powerful in his career, causing Gus Dudgeon to comment sardonically, with ironic humor, in 1993: "[Producer Chris Thomas] had the first solo number one in England with Elton and I didn't!,"[133] not forgetting to add as a reminder that he had actually been behind a very large number of his emblematic hits: "That really did me in, because I was determined that I was going to be the guy to do that...."[133]

Often compared to one of the other great Elton ballads, "Your Song," "Sacrifice" also begins with the words "It's a...." But this is the only similarity, as Bernie explains: "It's a simple lyric, but it's an intelligent, adult lyric. It's basically about the rigors of adult love, and it's a million miles away from 'Your Song.' Elton came up with a brilliant melody, and his performance on it gives it a lot of integrity and meaning."[133] The lyricist, who admitted having been influenced by the 1967 Aretha Franklin hit "Do Right Woman, Do Right Man" when writing the lyrics for "Sacrifice," holds this song in very high esteem—even considering it to be his finest collaboration with Elton.

Production

Naturally, the keyboards contribute significantly to the success of "Sacrifice"—and not only the famous Roland RD-100 digital piano played by Elton. According to producer Chris Thomas, it was Guy Babylon who provided the most mythical contribution to the song: "Certainly, I remember Guy's work on 'Sacrifice.' That sort of tinkling response-line to the vocal...the riff? That was one of Guy's things."[133] While the percussion, which is light, as in "Whispers," is included in the background, Elton provides the song with one of his finest vocal performances on the disk: deep and powerfully melancholic. Then there is Davey Johnstone's guitar, which produces an ethereal gimmick bathed in twang in homage to one of his idols, guitarist Hank Marvin of the Shadows, the 1960s group whose famous "Apache" resonates in the distance in "Sacrifice" when one hears this warm, respectful nod in its direction.

All the profits from this single were given to charitable organizations linked to AIDS: the Terrence Higgins Trust, which seeks to raise awareness of the disease; the London Lighthouse, a treatment center; the Jefferiss Research Trust, a treatment unit at St. Mary's Hospital, Paddington, that conducts research into treatment; and Body Positive, a center supporting recently diagnosed patients.

I NEVER KNEW HER NAME

Elton John, Bernie Taupin / 3:28

Musicians: Elton John: vocals, Roland RD-1000 digital piano / **Davey Johnstone:** guitars, backing vocals / **Fred Mandel:** guitars / **Romeo Williams:** bass / **Jonathan Moffett:** drums / **Guy Babylon:** keyboards / **Peter Iversen:** Fairlight CMI digital synthesizer, programming / **Natalie Jackson, Mortonette Jenkins, Marlena Jeter:** backing vocals **Recorded:** Puk Recording Studios, Randers, Denmark: November 1988 **Technical Team:** Producer: Chris Thomas / **Sound Engineers:** David Nicholas, John Quist / **Assistant Sound Engineer:** Karl Lever / Mastering: Greg Fulginiti / **Album Coordinator:** Steve Brown / **Studio Coordinators:** Adrian Collee, Dee Whelan

It is irrepressible love at first sight for the narrator, who, as an unwitting wedding guest, is smitten by the bride. Far from wanting to disrupt the union of the couple on this special day, he contents himself with closely observing the newly married woman and allowing his heart to "Whisper words that never reached her." Once the vows have been pronounced and the blessing given, he resigns himself to having to remain "In love with the bride of a handsome man" and to letting her pass through his life "like summer rain," fleetingly, without even having known her name. In order to set to music this impossible story of love imagined by Bernie, Elton uses Romeo Williams's percussive slap bass and the clear drumming of Jonathan Moffett, who assert themselves as the two real pillars of the piece. Davey Johnstone remains discreet on guitar except for the inverted effect that is very noticeable at 1:58. The keyboards have the main role in filling out the arrangement, particularly in the well-emulated brass sonorities—albeit not as warm as the real brass would be. The backing vocals are directly inspired by gospel music, while Elton's piano is anchored in soul, recalling the spirit of "Don't Play That Song" by Aretha Franklin.

AMAZES ME

Elton John, Bernie Taupin / 4:36

Musicians: Elton John: vocals, Roland RD-1000 digital piano / **Davey Johnstone:** guitars, backing vocals / **Romeo Williams:** bass / **Jonathan Moffett:** drums / **Guy Babylon:** keyboards / **Fred Mandel:** keyboards / **Peter Iversen:** Fairlight CMI digital synthesizer, programming / **Natalie Jackson, Mortonette Jenkins, Marlena Jeter:** backing vocals **Recorded:** Puk Recording Studios, Randers, Denmark: November 1988 **Technical Team:** Producer: Chris Thomas / **Sound Engineers:** David Nicholas, John Quist / **Assistant Sound Engineer:** Karl Lever / Mastering: Greg Fulginiti / **Album Coordinator:** Steve Brown / **Studio Coordinators:** Adrian Collee, Dee Whelan

Ray Charles, who would have been proud of the fact, was the main inspiration for this number with its unique vibration from the states of the American South. Davey Johnstone's guitar is very present here, first in the precise arpeggios with a clean sound before lavishing some ostinato hooks with a saturated sound between two verses, then a trenchant solo at 3:17, animated by some passing notes using tapping. This well-written solo evolves into a slow and very heavy rhythmic section, while Elton's voice, which is in fine shape, marries ideally with the fantastic backing vocals provided by Natalie Jackson (Kudisan Kai), Mortonette Jenkins, and Marlena Jeter. Jackson (Kai) was even invited back into the studio after these sessions to add some ad libs, which reinforce the powerfully gospel character of this melancholic, expressive song. It is a pity, in a song of such warmth, that the pizzicato violin is not played on a real instrument rather than produced by a synthesizer emulation.

BLUE AVENUE

Elton John, Bernie Taupin / 4:19

Musicians: Elton John: vocals, Roland RD-1000 digital piano / **Davey Johnstone:** guitars, backing vocals / **Romeo Williams:** bass / **Jonathan Moffett:** drums / **Guy Babylon:** keyboards / **Fred Mandel:** keyboards / **Peter Iversen:** Fairlight CMI digital synthesizer, programming **Recorded:** Puk Recording Studios, Randers, Denmark: November 1988 **Technical Team:** Producer: Chris Thomas / **Sound Engineers:** David Nicholas, John Quist / **Assistant Sound Engineer:** Karl Lever / Mastering: Greg Fulginiti / **Album Coordinator:** Steve Brown / **Studio Coordinators:** Adrian Collee, Dee Whelan

"Blue Avenue" feels like the most anecdotal number on *Sleeping with the Past*. There is an accumulation of keyboard layers over a somber digital piano motif, but these make no sense: notably, the (fake) brass, such as the pseudo muted trumpet, sounds very synthetic, as do the syrupy layers of strings programmed in the background. The arrival of Davey Johnstone's acoustic guitar, perfectly recorded, at least provides some space to breathe in this hitherto stifled arrangement, as does the rhythm section, which comes in quite late, at 2:57. Although the gentleness of the backing vocals and of Elton's voice are among the positive points in "Blue Avenue," its melody seems convoluted and not particularly catchy. Incomprehensibly, a sitar (also a synthesizer emulation) comes in on the final bar, accentuating the strange color of this piece, which is the diametric opposite of the world of rhythm 'n' blues, soul, or gospel that is developed on the rest of the album.

BONUS TRACK

Used as B-sides for "Healing Hands" and "Sacrifice," the numbers "Dancing in the End Zone" and "Love Is a Cannibal" finally joined the track list of *Sleeping with the Past* in 1998, with the joint reissue of the album by Mercury (314 558 479-2), Rocket Record Company (314 558 479-2), and Island Records (314 558-479-2).

DANCING IN THE END ZONE

Elton John, Bernie Taupin, Davey Johnstone / 3:53

Single Release: *Healing Hands / Dancing in the End Zone* **UK Release:** August 14, 1989, on Rocket Record Company (ref. EJS 19) **Best UK Chart Ranking:** 45 **US Release:** July 5, 1989, on MCA Records (ref. MCA-53692) **Best US Chart Ranking:** 13 **Musicians:** Elton John: vocals, Roland RD-1000 digital piano / Davey Johnstone: electric guitar, backing vocals / David Paton: bass / Charlie Morgan: drums / Fred Mandel: synthesizers / Fred McFarlane: programming / Ray Cooper: percussion / Dee Murray, Nigel Olsson: backing vocals **Recorded:** Puk Recording Studios, Randers, Denmark: November 1988 **Technical Team:** Producer: Chris Thomas / Sound Engineers: David Nicholas, John Quist / Assistant Sound Engineer: Karl Lever / Mastering: Greg Fulginiti / Album Coordinator: Steve Brown / Studio Coordinators: Adrian Collee, Dee Whelan

An unbearable sound mush overdosed with brass emulation synthesizers, "Dancing in the End Zone" appears on the reissue of *Sleeping with the Past* in 1998 and on Side B of "Healing Hands" in 1989. Recorded during the *Reg Strikes Back* sessions, the piece was unsurprisingly banished from the album track list …before being once again left out of the next one, too. The woefully banal lyrics simply set out an invitation to dance over interminable verses and a refrain that quickly becomes irritating. There is unfortunately nothing to be saved on "Dancing in the End Zone." Elton and Bernie are both in autopilot mode. Even poor Davey Johnstone, who co-wrote the piece with them, is overwhelmed by the weight of the ensemble and only manages to appear on a meager riff, which is also very run-of-the-mill.

LOVE IS A CANNIBAL

Elton John, Bernie Taupin, Davey Johnstone / 3:53

Single Release: *Sacrifice / Love Is a Cannibal* **UK Release:** October 1989 on Rocket Record Company (ref. EJS 20/876 330-7) **Best UK Chart Ranking:** 55 **US Release:** January 1990 on MCA Records (ref. MCA-53750) **Best US Chart Ranking:** 18 **Musicians:** Elton John: vocals, piano / Davey Johnstone: electric guitar, backing vocals / David Paton: bass / Charlie Morgan: drums / Fred Mandel: synthesizers / Fred McFarlane: programming / Dee Murray, Nigel Olsson: backing vocals **Recorded:** Puk Recording Studios, Randers, Denmark: November 1988 **Technical Team:** Producer: Chris Thomas / Sound Engineers: David Nicholas, John Quist / Assistant Sound Engineer: Karl Lever / Mastering: Greg Fulginiti / Album Coordinator: Steve Brown / Studio Coordinator: Adrian Collee, Dee Whelan

Barely more presentable than "Dancing in the End Zone," another title from the *Reg Strikes Back* sessions, "Love Is a Cannibal" at least has the merit of winding up the discussions at a breakneck speed. The song has huge problems, however: The melody is forgettable and nearly nonexistent; and Elton's voice, which is down-mixed, is imperceptible in an arrangement that is confused by the appearance at 1:56 of a keyboard that could been derived from the circuits of R2-D2. As for Bernie's cryptic and very brief lyrics, one never really knows what they are arguing against, unless it is that "Love is a cannibal," "Woman is a criminal," or, alternatively, that "man is the animal." Despite its obvious defects, the number has the honor of appearing on the B-side of "Sacrifice," and it also showed up on the soundtrack of *Ghostbusters II.*

A LIFE-SAVING BREAK: TREATMENT FOR ADDICTION IN SUMMER 1990

Elton John owed his recovery from addiction to two people: Ryan White and Hugh Williams. The singer read about Ryan's case in an article in *Newsweek*. Ryan was a teenager from Kokomo, Indiana, who suffered from hemophilia after becoming infected with the HIV virus through a blood transfusion. As if that wasn't enough for him to handle, Ryan found himself becoming increasingly ostracized by the inhabitants of his hometown: The family car was vandalized, insulting graffiti appeared around town, and there were petitions to have him removed from school. Hearing that the young man loved his music, Elton got in contact with the family and established strong links with them over the following months. He regularly called Ryan or would go and visit him. When he heard that Ryan had to be sedated and put on a ventilator on March 29, 1990, Elton went straight to his bedside in Indianapolis.

Growing Awareness

To Ryan's family and friends, Elton was no longer an inaccessible pop star, but rather a kind man doing everything he could to make their daily life more bearable. He did this through a host of small gestures. Everything that his assistants would normally do for him, he did for these people, including tidying Ryan's room, fetching sandwiches for everyone, having flowers delivered to the entire hospital department, and answering hundreds of phone calls from people offering good wishes and support until the tragic day, April 8, 1990, when Ryan succumbed to his illness.

Ryan's funeral was attended by Elton and numerous other well-known people, including Michael Jackson and Barbara Bush, and he became symbolic of the fight against AIDS. Elton was one of the pallbearers and he played "Skyline Pigeon" in memory of the young man. Seeing how Ryan's mother had dealt with all these events with the greatest dignity and no bitterness, Elton began to reflect on his own way of dealing with life's difficulties: "I spent half my life feeling angry and resentful about things that didn't matter. I was the kind of person who got on the phone and shouted at people because the weather outside my Park Lane hotel didn't suit me. Whatever else had been wrong with my childhood, I hadn't been brought up to behave that way."[3] This new awareness came with feelings of shame when he looked at the images of the funeral that aired on television: "I was bloated and gray. My hair was white. I looked worn out, exhausted, ill. I was forty-three years old, and I looked about seventy. God, the state of me. Something had to change."[3]

The Second Wake-Up Call

A few months after this event, another sobering incident took place. At the time, Elton was in a relationship with a young twentysomething from Atlanta named Hugh Williams. Hugh accompanied him on continuous bouts of drug and alcohol abuse. Seemingly out of nowhere, Hugh announced that he was finished with all that, and he was going to rehab. Stunned by the news, Elton flew into a violent rage, insulting and reproaching Hugh and accusing him of being weak. The unacceptable truth was that it brought Elton face-to-face with his own demons and his inability to control them. He found himself alone with his addictions, and now he no longer had a partner to help justify them. Rather than follow his partner's lead, Elton decided to cut himself off even more, shutting himself up in his rented house in London for two weeks. He spent his days in a bathrobe stained with vomit—the result of his bulimia—drinking whiskey, sniffing coke, watching endless porno movies, and making all kinds of lists: the songs he had written, the artists he'd like to work with, and so on. Cutting himself off in a state of paranoia, he no longer answered the phone. Filled with self-disgust, he finally agreed to Hugh's suggestion that they go see his psychologist for a kind of couple's therapy. At one of these sessions, the specialist asked them to draw up a list of things they held against each other. Hugh's list described in minute detail Elton's erratic behavior; his addiction to drugs, sex, and food; and his needy dependence on others. Elton, on the other hand, listed nothing but unimportant details: Hugh put discs back in the wrong sleeves, left his stuff lying about. Elton realized he needed help, and on July 29, 1990, he entered Chicago's Parkside Lutheran Hospital under an assumed name, George King, and began detox treatment. The regime at the hospital was strict, and the staff did not give him special treatment just because he was a star; quite the opposite in fact: He had to wash his own clothes and manage his purchases on $10 pocket money, and he was not allowed to communicate with the outside world. When he reemerged from the center in September, Elton was a new man. He had finally freed himself from his addictions, but it was too soon to start working again. He visited Rocket Records to tell the team that he was taking a break. It was to last almost two years.

ALBUM

THE ONE

Simple Life . The One . Sweat It Out . Runaway Train . Whitewash County .
The North . When a Woman Doesn't Want You . Emily . On Dark Street .
Understanding Women . The Last Song

RELEASE DATES
UK Release: June 22, 1992
Reference: Rocket Record Company—512 360-1
Best UK Chart Ranking: 2
US Release: June 22, 1992
Reference: MCA Records—MCAD-10614
Best US Chart Ranking: 8

A NEW START

Although he took an artistic break that lasted nearly three years to deal with treating his addictions, Elton John did manage to make some new additions to his discography during this time. *The Very Best of Elton John* is one such addition, and it included two new compositions: "You Gotta Love Someone" and "Easier to Walk Away." The compilation did not come out until October 1, 1990, but when it finally released it hit the top of the sales charts in many countries—though not in the United States, where it was never released. In North America, Elton opted to put out a four-CD box set called *To Be Continued…*, which came out on November 8, 1990, and included two additional new pieces: "Made for Me" and "I Swear I Heard the Night Talkin'." Finally, on October 22, 1991, *Two Rooms: Celebrating the Songs of Elton John & Bernie Taupin* was released and featured covers from major talents including Kate Bush, Sting, the Who, and George Michael. George Michael was also included in the November 25 release of a live version of "Don't Let the Sun Go Down on Me," which became number one in multiple countries.

Somehow, in spite of the fact that he was "taking a break," Elton still managed to be prolific as ever. Nevertheless, when he went back into the studio to record his twenty-third album, he was gripped with fear. Recording sessions for *The One* were set to take place at Studio Guillaume Tell in Paris in November 1991, but Elton worried whether inspiration would still be there after such a long period of inactivity. During the first moments of recording, the singer became overwhelmed by what was at stake, but he quickly recovered himself and the process moved forward smoothly. Unfortunately, recording sessions for *The One* served as a backdrop for a rare clash between Elton John and Bernie Taupin, in which, unsurprisingly, the singer came out on top. The lyricist felt that the drum machines were omnipresent on the album, to the point of distraction. Controlled by drummer Olle Romö, they dominated each song. Once he had the lyrics in hand, Elton asked Romö to create a rhythm at a given tempo before composing the rest of the music to match the drums, which meant they were the driving force of each composition. Thankfully, the melodies here are more addictive than they were on *Leather Jackets* and they do not get strangled by overbearing synth-pop arrangements. Chris Thomas worked hard to place Elton's acoustic piano (a Yamaha Disklavier) in the foreground when the demos were recorded. As usual, Davey Johnstone, Guy Babylon, Kiki Dee, and Nigel Olsson were all back to work on the new album, but the rest of the recording crew was made up of newcomers: Adam Seymour supported Davey Johnstone on guitar, while Mark Taylor doubled up on keyboards with Guy Babylon. Pino Palladino completed the team on bass. A few big names were also brought in to add some extra flare, including Eric Clapton on "Runaway Train" and Pink Floyd guitarist David Gilmour on "Understanding Women."

Death and Rebirth

The One offers a more human, and more melodic, approach to songwriting than some of its predecessors. This is owed in significant part to Elton John's restored mental state, as well as to Bernie Taupin's agile pen. The writer always knew how to translate Elton's torments into hit songs. He even managed to link together the dramas experienced by Elton John and Eric Clapton in "Runaway Train," while at the same time retaining an admirable deference to both men. Never afraid to take on delicate subjects, he penned a violent takedown of racism in "Whitewash County" and a polemic against sexism in "When a Woman Doesn't Want You," before touching on old age and death in "Emily," the homeless in "On Dark Street," and AIDS and the acceptance of homosexuality in "The Last Song." The seriousness and sadness contained in these songs reverberated in the recording studio on January 15, 1992, when the musicians learned of the sudden death of Dee Murray, who had been battling skin cancer when he had a stroke. He had not appeared alongside Elton for eight years, but Elton's grief was still intense. Six months later, on July 6, another close friend of Elton's died prematurely: Vance Buck, who had been Elton's onetime lover and remained one of his closest friends, died of complications from AIDS at age thirty-two. Ten years after the release of "Blue Eyes," which he had inspired, *The One* was dedicated Vance. While Elton was reborn artistically, a part of his past also died.

Following a brief contribution on *Ice on Fire*, Pino Palladino (shown here in 2000) served as the official bassist on *The One*.

SIMPLE LIFE

Elton John, Bernie Taupin / 6:26

Musicians: Elton John: vocals, piano / Adam Seymour: guitar / Pino Palladino: bass / Olle Romö: drums, percussion, drum machine programming / Mark Taylor: keyboards **Recorded:** Studio Guillaume Tell, Paris: November 1991 **Technical Team:** Producer: Chris Thomas / **Sound Engineer:** David Nicholas / **Assistant Sound Engineers:** Alex Firla, Andy Strange / **Album Coordinator:** Steve Brown / **Studio Coordinators:** Adrian Collee, Sam Stell **Single Release:** *Simple Life* / *The Last Song* **UK Release:** May 1993 on Rocket Record Company (ref. EJS 31) **Best UK Chart Ranking:** 44 • *Simple Life* / *The North* **US Release:** March 1993 on MCA Records (ref. MCAS7 54581) **Best US Chart Ranking:** 30

Genesis and Lyrics

While getting one's life back on the right track is never a simple mater, the lyrics deployed by Bernie on "Simple Life" are intentionally straightforward, and they serve as the perfect opening for Elton's redemption album. *The One* became the first album in a very long time that Elton recorded while sober. Galvanized by his regained faculties, the singer sets himself a clear objective: "We're gonna get back to the simple life again." The parallels are clear: Elton is setting himself on a new path and the listener is invited to take the journey with him.

Production

Although entirely synthetic, the bass/drums section sustains the ensemble solidly and creates the regular, continuous rhythm of a locomotive that's running at full speed. Similarly, Mark Taylor manages to emulate a harmonica with his keyboards, which evokes the sound of a train entering the station. Beyond this musically re-created railway setting, Elton delivers a fine performance on piano and vocals, which are slightly metallic in timbre—as though the singer, with his steely voice, is seeking to merge himself with the roaring wheels of the train that have been created by the musicians in his band. When "Simple Life" was released as a single, the refrain was cut after the second verse and extra harmonica was added in its place; this shortened the single's running time by just over a minute and a half in comparison with the full-length version that appeared on the album.

THE ONE

Elton John, Bernie Taupin / 5:53

Musicians: Elton John: vocals, piano / Adam Seymour: guitar / Davey Johnstone: guitar / Pino Palladino: bass / Olle Romö: drums, percussion, drum machine programming / Mark Taylor: keyboards / Guy Babylon: keyboards, programming **Recorded:** Studio Guillaume Tell, Paris: November 1991 **Technical Team:** Producer: Chris Thomas / **Sound Engineer:** David Nicholas / **Assistant Sound Engineers:** Alex Firla, Andy Strange / **Album Coordinator:** Steve Brown / **Studio Coordinators:** Adrian Collee, Sam Stell / **Single Release 45 rpm:** *The One* / *Suit of Wolves* **UK Release:** May 25, 1992, on Rocket Record Company (ref. EJS 28) **Best UK Chart Ranking:** 10 **US Release:** May 1992 on MCA Records (ref. MCAS7-54423) **Best US Chart Ranking:** 9

Genesis and Lyrics

Bernie's lyrics on "The One" describe the feeling of elation you have when you finally discover your perfect partner after years spent searching. The images invoked seemed to give Elton a powerful connection with the text, and they inspired one of his most heartrending ballads. As described, the meeting of this soulmate is staged in an almost cinematographic way within the lyrics. Various romantic settings are offered up, including "freedom fields where wild horses run," alongside other stock romantic imagery: "I saw you dancin' out the ocean / Running fast along the sand"; "When stars collide like you and I / No shadows block the sun / You're all I've ever needed." At this point in his life, Elton had no difficulty placing himself in this intimate and passionate text.

Production

Pino Palladino's fretless bass and the layers of Guy Babylon's and Mark Taylor's benevolent keyboards constitute the twin pillars of "The One," leaving the limelight to Davey Johnstone, who executes elegant flights of guitar fancy on his EBow. His instrument confers an epic dimension to this number that is perfectly supported by Elton's loquacious piano. Between 3:22 and 3:47, Elton uses his technique to splash out the climax of the piece, preparing with bravura for the redescent toward the

"Sweat It Out" and its final keyboard section symbolize Elton's return as a musician.

final sequence, which is admirably constructed. Above all, Elton sings with an undeniable sincerity and communicative emotion one of the catchiest melodies of the second part of his career. Upon its release in May 1992, "The One" asserted itself by appearing in the top 10 in both the US and the UK charts, and the following year it was nominated for Best Vocal Pop Performance at the Grammy Awards. Unfortunately, the song lost out to "Tears in Heaven" by Eric Clapton.

FOR ELTON ADDICTS

Famed designer Gianni Versace was entrusted with the cover design for *The One*. Versace designed a Baroque floral motif, which he used as a border surrounding a black-and-white photo of Elton taken by French fashion photographer Patrick Demarchelier.

SWEAT IT OUT

Elton John, Bernie Taupin / 6:39

Musicians: Elton John: vocals, piano / **Davey Johnstone:** guitar / **Pino Palladino:** bass / **Olle Romö:** drums, percussion, drum machine programming / **Mark Taylor:** keyboards / **Guy Babylon:** keyboards, programming **Recorded: Studio Guillaume Tell, Paris:** November 1991 **Technical Team: Producer:** Chris Thomas / **Sound Engineer:** David Nicholas / **Assistant Sound Engineers:** Alex Firla, Andy Strange / **Album Coordinator:** Steve Brown / **Studio Coordinators:** Adrian Collee, Sam Stell

Genesis and Lyrics

With "Sweat It Out," Bernie steps out of his usual role and gives us a protest song in the spirit of "Subterranean Homesick Blues" by Bob Dylan. In other words, a montage of fairly disparate images are used to draw focus to some of the worst political and social transgressions of the era. He is addressing subjects here that are more pressing than on the rest of the album, and above all chastising the galloping materialism of the 1980s and the indifference of humanity to the state of the world. Among other things, he accuses UN forces ("Peace keepers") of throwing fuel on the fire in certain parts of the globe and triggering new conflicts, and he also deplores environmental tragedies including the *Exxon Valdez* spill that had happened three years earlier, in 1989 ("Oil slicks put us on the ropes"), and the inability of American banks to support the population ("Man it's hard to handle / When the bank's broke"). Surprisingly, Bernie does not spare his own family or his fellow musicians and artists, and he deplores the futility of their songs and charity concerts ("Band aids on dead doorways").

Production

With his rigorous drum machine programming, Olle Romö provides Elton with an "industrial" environment that works well given the direction of the song's lyrics. Pino Palladino plays his warm bass in unison, and once the rhythm section is installed, Mark Taylor's and Guy Babylon's keyboards adeptly prepare the terrain for Elton, who has no hesitation venturing into the verses. Davey Johnstone's guitar, which is more discreet here, is nonetheless indispensable as it provides one of the only organic touches in this almost completely synthetic arrangement; the guitarist even provides some very effective acoustic arpeggios. Elton, whose voice is slightly modulated to convey more of a raw sound, never departs from the effective melody devised in the refrain. Elton often commented in interviews that *The One* marked his return to form as a proper musician, and in fact he recorded his very impressive piano part on this track in a single take.

RUNAWAY TRAIN

Elton John, Bernie Taupin, Olle Romö / 5:23

Musicians

Elton John: vocals, organ
Eric Clapton: guitar, vocals
Davey Johnstone: guitar
Pino Palladino: bass
Olle Romö: drums, percussion, drum machine programming
Guy Babylon: keyboards, programming
Beckie Bell, Carol Fredericks, Joniece Jamison: backing vocals

Recorded

Studio Guillaume Tell, Paris: November 1991 / Townhouse Studios, London: ?

Technical Team

Producer: Chris Thomas
Sound Engineer: David Nicholas
Assistant Sound Engineers: Andy Bradfield, Alex Firla, Andy Strange
Album Coordinator: Steve Brown
Studio Coordinators: Adrian Collee, Sam Stell

Single Release

Runaway Train / Understanding Women (extended mix)
UK Release: July 1992 on Rocket Record Company (ref. EJS 29)
Best UK Chart Ranking: 31
US Release: August 1992 on MCA Records (ref. MCAS7-54452)
Best US Chart Ranking: Did Not Chart

1992

FOR ELTON ADDICTS

"Runaway Train" also appears on the soundtrack of the film *Lethal Weapon 3*.

Genesis and Lyrics

Even before Elton John and Eric Clapton worked together on "Runaway Train," negotiations were underway to set up a series of concerts that would see them both at the top of the bill. Elton asked Bernie to write the lyrics for a duet that reflected both of their eventful lives, particularly reflecting the tragedy that had struck Eric Clapton the previous year (the loss of his four-year-old son in a fall from the fifty-third floor of an apartment building in New York) and also touching on Elton's recovery process after finally confronting his addictions. Given this directive, Bernie wrote lyrics that focused on sorrow and loss. While he does not shy away from dark times—"I've lost and seen the world shut down / It's a darkness no one knows"—the lyricist prefers to emphasize the theme of rebirth: "Found a way home written on this map," the narrator sings, "I'm starting to feel a little muscle again" and "Trying to get a grip on my life again." At this point, the singer (and therefore Bernie) is a little older and a little wiser, and he knows that shadow and darkness can reappear at any time, so a note of caution concludes the optimistic lyrics: "Nothing hits harder than a runaway train."

Production

The trenchant guitar of Eric Clapton pretty much immediately declares itself as the star of this song. Clapton, nicknamed "Slowhand," has the opportunity to demonstrate his talent in a number of incandescent solos. Although the two men sing together on this demanding quest for redemption, they are able to share the instrumental spotlight as well, and Elton also shines on his Roland RD-1000 digital piano. Still, the voices of Elton John and Eric Clapton marry perfectly, particularly on the refrain to the catchy melody, which incorporates gentle backing vocals from Beckie Bell, Carol Fredericks, and Joniece Jamison. Beginning at 3:52, Elton's vocals give way to the best moment on the track, when Elton John's and Eric Clapton's solos entwine in a striking moment of communion. While bassist Pino Palladino's presence is rather discreet, as is the presence of Davey Johnstone's rhythm guitar, Swedish drummer and percussionist Olle Romö produces highly colored drum sounds that earned him a joint credit for the composition of the number.

Eric Clapton and Elton John finally managed to perform together a few times between June and August of 1992. They appeared at Dodger Stadium in LA and in various other locations around the world, but the highlight of their joint appearances was a series of three evenings at Wembley Stadium in the UK, which took place on June 26, 27, and 28, 1992.

WHITEWASH COUNTY

Elton John, Bernie Taupin / 5:30

Musicians: Elton John: vocals, piano, organ / **Davey Johnstone:** guitar / **Pino Palladino:** bass / **Olle Romö:** drums, percussion, drum machine programming / **Guy Babylon:** keyboards, programming **Recorded:** Studio Guillaume Tell, Paris: November 1991 **Technical Team: Producer:** Chris Thomas / **Sound Engineer:** David Nicholas / **Assistant Sound Engineers:** Alex Firla, Andy Strange / **Album Coordinator:** Steve Brown / **Studio Coordinators:** Adrian Collee, Sam Stell

In "Whitewash County," Bernie violently attacks the subject of racism. The county depicted in the song is in the midst of an election, and minds are focused on one candidate in particular. The narrator is not taken in by this racist, hateful character, even though he "Talks sweet as sugar cane," as Bernie puts it. Reading between the lines, it seems clear that this sweet-talking character is meant to evoke David Duke, the white supremacist militant and former Grand Wizard of the Ku Klux Klan, who ran for president in 1988. "He's got a shiny new wax face" is surely a reference to the excessive amount of cosmetic surgery Duke had undertaken, which changed his face but not his repulsive views.

A skillful mix of rock and country, the song opens with violins (created mechanically in this case) typical of the square dance, cleverly linking tradition with modernity. Halfway through, Davey's catchy guitar and Elton's impossible piano consolidate the song's infernal pace, particularly in the finale, where Elton's chords are thunderous.

THE NORTH

Elton John, Bernie Taupin / 5:16

Musicians: Elton John: vocals, piano / **Adam Seymour:** guitar / **Pino Palladino:** bass / **Olle Romö:** drums, percussion, drum machine programming / **Mark Taylor:** keyboards **Recorded:** Studio Guillaume Tell, Paris: November 1991 **Technical Team: Producer:** Chris Thomas / **Sound Engineer:** David Nicholas / **Assistant Sound Engineers:** Alex Firla, Andy Strange / **Album Coordinator:** Steve Brown / **Studio Coordination:** Adrian Collee, Sam Stell **Single Release:** *Simple Life* / *The North* **US Release:** March 1993 on MCA Records (ref. MCAS7 54581) **Best US Chart Ranking:** 30

"'The North' I love a lot; that's my favorite song without question [on *The One*],"[35] Elton said in an interview in 2013. This is certainly because it celebrates his renewal as a man and as an artist. Bernie uses the metaphor of the North to express the aspect of darkness that slumbers in each of us and that Elton had explored so much, before managing to come out of it: "Have you seen the North / That cold grey place / Don't want

A shadow was cast over the sessions for *The One* when Dee Murray (shown here in 1983) passed away.

its shadow anymore / On my face." In parallel, this enables the lyricist to question his own past, having left the grayness of northern England for the sun of California: "The North was my mother / But I no longer need her," he writes. For his part, Elton applies himself to making "The North" a magnificent ballad, illuminated by his assured voice and a fine arrangement dominated by his piano, which is both gentle and benevolent, with precise arpeggios. Mark Taylor's keyboards pleasingly enrich the refrain, while Pino Palladino's sliding bass is very creative in the background. As Davey Johnstone is absent, it is Adam Seymour, normally consigned to a more utilitarian role, who assumes responsibility for weaving the deep and subtle guitar lines in the finale, using an EBow.

WHEN A WOMAN DOESN'T WANT YOU

Elton John, Bernie Taupin / 4:56

Musicians: Elton John: vocals, piano / **Adam Seymour:** guitar / **Davey Johnstone:** guitar, backing vocals / **Pino Palladino:** bass / **Olle Romö:** drums, percussion, drum machine programming / **Mark Taylor:** keyboards / **Guy Babylon:** keyboards, programming / **Kiki Dee, Nigel Olsson:** backing vocals **Recorded:** Studio Guillaume Tell, Paris: November 1991 **Technical Team: Producer:** Chris Thomas / **Sound Engineer:** David Nicholas / **Assistant Sound Engineers:** Alex Firla, Andy Strange / **Album Coordinator:** Steve Brown / **Studio Coordinators:** Adrian Collee, Sam Stell

Bernie had seemingly had enough of the depiction of women as systematically debased and objectified by men, which he himself had done in previous songs like "Since God Invented Girls," "Angeline," and "Li'l 'Frigerator." So he gives men a blunt warning with this track: "'Cause you can't take a woman / When she doesn't want you / And you can't be a man / If you're blind to reason." Elton slightly dilutes the strength of the lyrics by lacing this smooth ballad with country and soul sounds, which seem like a response to the famous "When a Man Loves a Woman" by Percy Sledge. Elton's typically gospel piano, the layers of discreet keyboards, the crystalline acoustic guitar arpeggios, and a slightly laid-back rhythm section all contribute to making "When a Woman Doesn't Want You" the ultimate ballad on this album. Adam Seymour and Davey Johnstone weave a comfortable guitar sound into the background, ably constituted from twang arpeggios, offbeat chords, and distortion notes that confer a healthy touch of rhythm 'n' blues to the proceedings, while Elton's voice has a harsher overall timbre that makes sense given the song's tone of warning.

Elton performed "The North" for the first time onstage during two concerts given at the Grand Ole Opry in Nashville on March 15, 1992, as part of a fundraiser for the family of Dee Murray, his bassist, who had died a month earlier.

Freddie Mercury also passed away during the recording session for *The One*. Elton paid homage to Freddie alongside Axl Rose at Wembley Stadium on April 20, 1992.

EMILY

Elton John, Bernie Taupin / 4:58

Musicians: Elton John: vocals, piano / **Davey Johnstone:** guitar, backing vocals / **Pino Palladino:** bass / **Olle Romö:** drums, percussion, rhythm box programming / **Guy Babylon:** keyboards, programming **Recorded:** Studio Guillaume Tell, Paris: November 1991 **Technical Team: Producer:** Chris Thomas / **Sound Engineer:** David Nicholas / **Assistant Sound Engineers:** Alex Firla, Andy Strange / **Album Coordinator:** Steve Brown / **Studio Coordinators:** Adrian Collee, Sam Stell

It is unusual for Bernie's lyrics to contain characters who have names, and even more so for those names to be used as the title of the song. The lyricist breaks this rule with "Emily," a song in which he presents an elderly woman who is preparing to meet her maker: "The old girl hobbles, nylons sagging [...] But Emily don't be afraid / When the weight of angels weighs you down." He depicts the changing seasons, a skillful metaphor for the description of time passing inexorably and leading to an ineluctable destiny: "When summer bends to the winter's rage / Emily walks through the cemetery." Seeking the "faded hero" to whom she prays, she draws near to him in a painful solitude. However, as in "Song for Guy," Elton chooses to address death with some lighter mood music. With a moderate tempo he creates a cheerful melody, and reserves a short, ethereal piano solo to illustrate the moment when the main character passes from this world to the next.

ON DARK STREET

Elton John, Bernie Taupin / 4:43

Musicians: Elton John: vocals, electronic piano / Davey Johnstone: guitar, backing vocals / Olle Romö: drums, percussion, drum machine programming / Guy Babylon: keyboards, programming / Kiki Dee, Nigel Olsson: backing vocals **Recorded:** Studio Guillaume Tell, Paris: November 1991 **Technical Team:** Producer: Chris Thomas / Sound Engineer: David Nicholas / Assistant Sound Engineers: Alex Firla, Andy Strange / Album Coordinator: Steve Brown / Studio Coordination: Adrian Collee, Sam Stell

When Bernie presented his musical partner with the first draft of "On Dark Street," which then had the temporary title "All I Ever Wanted Was You," the text was rejected. Elton considered the title to be corny and thought some of the verses were weak. Bernie had to revise his copy, notably the refrain. He returned with the story of a homeless family forced to live on the streets and having a difficult time: "Oh and we must have got lost / Living on Dark Street / Looking for an exit / Sleeping on the concrete." However, Elton almost incongruously instills the spirit of luxuriant Philly Soul into this story… The melody skillfully accentuates the most important words in Bernie's text, and the song feels like the most commercial one on the album, with its keyboard layers, its catchy riff emulating a sitar, and impressive backing vocals by Kiki Dee and Nigel Olsson.

UNDERSTANDING WOMEN

Elton John, Bernie Taupin / 5:03

Musicians: Elton John: vocals, electronic piano / David Gilmour: guitar / Pino Palladino: bass / Olle Romö: drums, percussions, drum machine programming / Guy Babylon: keyboards, programming Kiki Dee: backing vocals **Recorded:** AIR Studios, London: ? **Technical Team:** Producer: Chris Thomas / Sound Engineer: David Nicholas / Assistant Sound Engineers: Alex Firla, Andy Strange / Album Coordinator: Steve Brown / Studio Coordinators: Adrian Collee, Sam Stell **Single Release:** *Runaway Train (featuring Eric Clapton) / Understanding Women* (extended mix) **UK Release:** July 1992 on Rocket Record Company (ref. EJS 29) **Best UK Chart Ranking:** 31 **US Release:** August 1992 on MCA Records (ref. MCAS7-54452) **Best US Chart Ranking:** Did Not Chart

"Understanding Women" is what the narrator of this song aspires to do as a man whose pride has been injured following a separation: "And I'm not any man you've ever known before," he insists, while he would like to be "the final word / In the book we haven't written." To set to music the torments of this man who finally seems to renounce the idea of achieving his objective, Elton conceived a typically new wave arrangement. The song shimmers with keyboards as complex as the narrator's problem, while the verses, where his piano expresses itself with more delicacy, are much more melodic, especially with the contribution of Kiki Dee's soaring vocals. In this industrial musical environment, the trenchant guitar of legendary Pink Floyd guitarist David Gilmour surges in like a flash of lightning at 3:08, adding tension to the last sequence of the piece.

THE LAST SONG

Elton John, Bernie Taupin / 3:33

Musicians: Elton John: vocals, piano / Guy Babylon: keyboards, programming **Recorded:** Studio Guillaume Tell, Paris: November 1991 **Technical Team:** Producer: Chris Thomas / Sound Engineer: David Nicholas / Assistant Sound Engineers: Alex Firla, Andy Strange / Album Coordinator: Steve Brown / Studio Coordination: Adrian Collee, Sam Stell **Single Release:** *The Last Song / The Man Who Never Died / Song for Guy* **UK Release:** November 1992 on Rocket Record Company (ref. CD: EJSCD 30/864 477-2)) **Best UK Chart Ranking:** 21 • *The Last Song* **US Release:** October 6, 1992, on MCA Records (ref. MCA5P-2425) **Best US Chart Ranking:** 23 • *Simple Life / The Last Song* **UK Release:** May 10, 1993, on Rocket Record Company (ref. EJS 31) **Best UK Chart Ranking:** 44

"The Last Song" was one of the first songs written for *The One*. In it, Bernie Taupin depicts a rapprochement between a father and his homosexual son, who is dying of AIDS. The lyricist, who had lost friends to this illness, does not in any way skirt around the painful death of the protagonist and the progressive deterioration of his physical condition: "As light as straw and brittle as a bird / Today I weigh less than a shadow on the wall." In a way he regrets the juvenile recklessness that exposed him to the illness: "I only thought I'd win / I never dreamed I'd feel this fire beneath my skin." Certain that his father would not have been at his side, he is overwhelmed by his support: "I can't believe you love me / I never thought you'd come / I guess I misjudged love between a father and his son." To illustrate the fear of stigmatization musically, Elton, with his infallible melodic instinct, creates an air that is clear, pure, and heartrending. Constructed like a funeral dirge, he supports his astonishing voice just with an expressive piano, and benevolent keyboards. Bernie, who had initially called the song "Song for '92," changed the title because Elton was convinced that it would never achieve posterity if a specific date was attached to anchor the song in a specific time period. In Elton's view, AIDS, like homophobia, was unfortunately here to stay.

The One proved to be a great
success for Elton, and his
return to form was confirmed.

SIDE B

SUIT OF WOLVES

Elton John, Bernie Taupin / 5:48

Single Release 45 rpm: *The One* / *Suit of Wolves* **UK Release:**
May 25, 1992, on Rocket Record Company (ref. EJS 28)) **Best UK
Chart Ranking:** 10 **US Release:** May 1992 on MCA Records (ref.
MCAS7-54423) **Best US Chart Ranking:** 9 • **Maxi CD:** *The One* /
Suit of Wolves / *Fat Boys and Ugly Girls* **UK Release:** May 1992 on
Rocket Record Company (ref. EJ CDJ 28/866 937-2) **Musicians:**
Elton John: vocals, keyboards / Davey Johnstone: guitar / Pino
Palladino: bass / Olle Romö: drums, percussion, drum machine
programming / Guy Babylon: keyboards, programming **Recorded:**
AIR Studios, London: July 1991 **Technical Team: Producer:** Chris
Thomas / **Sound Engineer:** David Nicholas / **Assistant Sound
Engineers:** Alex Firla, Andy Strange / **Album Coordinator:** Steve
Brown / **Studio Coordinators:** Adrian Collee, Sam Stell

A conventional ballad, "Suit of Wolves" was recorded during
the same session as "Understanding Women," which was organized at AIR Studios in July 1991 for inclusion of these two
numbers in the British edition of the *To Be Continued…* box set,
to appear in November of the same year. Bernie provided an
abstruse text with multiple possible interpretations. The character, who could be a man or a woman, wears a metaphorical wolf's clothing and rushes into the arms of a "hungry man."
"And when you can't get what you want / You take anything
you can," proclaims the narrator before confusing the issue
between vulnerability and domination when referring to their
"prayers between two hungry arms." The most obvious route
seems to be adultery, symbolized by "dangerous flowers / All
around my bed," and "some want rings and some just want /
And those who'd like to see me dead." These last elements,
associated with the evocation of the "wolf," the "beast," and
the resentment of "this dirty little town," by which the narrator seems to have been rejected, might also suggest a witch
hunt. Either way, neither Bernie nor Elton divulged the key to
this song that went relatively unnoticed, despite its presence on
Side B of *The One* single and in the remastered version of the
album released in 1998 by Rocket Record Company and Mercury (ref. 558 480-2).

Accompanying "The One" in its release on maxi
CD format, "Fat Boys and Ugly Girls" is also
included in the 1998 remastered version of *The
One* sold by Rocket Record Company and Mercury (ref. 558 480-2).

SIDE B

FAT BOYS AND UGLY GIRLS

Elton John, Bernie Taupin / 4:14

Maxi CD: *The One* / *Suit of Wolves* / *Fat Boys and Ugly Girls* **UK
Release:** May 1992 on Rocket Record Company (ref. EJ CDJ 28/866
937-2) **Musicians:** Elton John: vocals, piano ? / **Other instruments:**
unidentified **Recorded:** Studio Guillaume Tell, Paris: November 1991
Technical Team: Producer: Chris Thomas / **Sound Engineer:** David
Nicholas / **Assistant Sound Engineers:** Alex Firla, Andy Strange /
Album Coordinator: Steve Brown / **Studio Coordinators:** Adrian
Collee, Sam Stell

In "Fat Boys and Ugly Girls" Bernie provides a long and (extra)
large look at the concerns of "fat boys" and "ugly girls"—the former being continually rejected by the latter, who, in turn, suffer their own indignities when handsome boys reject them. But
what happens when the "fat boys" and the "ugly girls" fall in
love with each other? They spurn the superficiality of the people
around them and realize they are actually happier together. Elton
counters this slightly far-fetched and simplistic story with some
deliciously retro rock 'n' roll styling. Synthetic but sassy brass,
raucous guitars, cheeky keyboards, and a sustained rhythm section frame Elton's exhilarating voice. He holds back when, at
2:32, a guitar solo comes in with a certain swing to it.

DUETS

Teardrops (with k.d. lang) . When I Think About Love (I Think About You) (with P. M. Dawn) . The Power (with Little Richard) . Shaky Ground (with Don Henley) . True Love (with Kiki Dee) . If You Were Me (with Chris Rea) . A Woman's Needs (with Tammy Wynette) . Old Friend (with Nik Kershaw) . Go On and On (with Gladys Knight) . Don't Go Breaking My Heart (with RuPaul) . Ain't Nothing Like the Real Thing (with Marcella Detroit) . I'm Your Puppet (with Paul Young) . Love Letters (with Bonnie Raitt) . Born to Lose (with Leonard Cohen) . Don't Let the Sun Go Down on Me (with George Michael) . Duets for One

RELEASE DATES
UK Release: November 23, 1993
Reference: Rocket Record Company—518 478-1 (2x LP) / 518 478-2 (CD)
Best UK Chart Ranking: 5
US Release: November 30, 1993
Reference: MCA Records—MCAD-10926 (CD)
Best US Chart Ranking: 25

CREATIVE RECREATION

The idea of an album of duets came up in 1993 via a suggestion from the Phonogram record company. They wanted to put together a compilation of Elton John's earlier collaborations with other artists in time to go on sale for the holidays. Elton was firmly against any opportunistic attempts to exploit his catalog, and he preferred the idea of creating an album of all-new duets. This presented the perfect opportunity for him to act on musical dreams he'd been harboring for a long time, including singing a duet with Bonnie Raitt.

An Ambitious Undertaking

The project began to take shape in early summer 1993. The first recording laid down was a duet with Bonnie Raitt called "*Love Letters.*" The song was originally an instrumental number that appeared in a 1945 film with the same name and was revived in 1961 when Ketty Lester released a new version with lyrics added. Elvis also covered it in 1966, and it was this version that Elton particularly liked. Bonnie and Elton's duet is uplifting in its spontaneity and shared joy, and it marked the beginning of a rapid recording campaign. At a rate of one song per day, Elton John toured studios all across the United States and England on a tight schedule devised by John Reid. The goal was to record all the tracks on the album in the space of just eight weeks during July and August of 1993. Obviously, the main constraint was matching the guest singers' calendars with Elton's, and, not surprisingly, some of the names on his list had to be left out due to scheduling conflicts. Many prospective duet partners—including Bono, Neil Young, Axl Rose (of Guns N' Roses), James Taylor, and Steve Winwood—were unavailable because they were on tour or working on other projects. Nevertheless, Elton managed to link up with many of his idols, including Gladys Knight, Marcella Detroit, and Leonard Cohen.

Elton valued spontaneity, which he believed had become too rare in the music of the 1990s. This spontaneity is evident in the speed with which this album was recorded, and the relatively simple instrumentation that was used in order to increase the rate of production. "Love Letters" is a good example of this working practice. A single piano and a lone guitar played with a bottleneck were all that was required to create a tender relationship between Elton and Bonnie Raitt. Similarly, "When I Think About Love" was composed in a slower tempo to focus on the velvety backing vocals of P. M. Dawn, which meant that the song could be recorded in a very short time.

Choosing the Backing Vocalists

The song selection process was hugely critical since speed was the name of the game on this album. *Duets* is built around a number of cover versions, including Womack & Womack's "Teardrops" (with k.d. lang) and the Temptations' hit "Shakey Ground" (with Don Henley). Marcella Detroit opted for a cover version of "Ain't Nothing Like the Real Thing," which had originally been popularized by Marvin Gaye and Tammi Terrell. Detroit personally organized the main elements of the orchestration, including the memorable harmonica. Soul and R & B numbers make up the majority of the songs chosen for the album. Only Leonard Cohen injects a note of jazz, with a cover version of country singer Ted Daffan's "Born to Lose."

Interspersed among these cover tracks are some of Elton John's own songs, including "Don't Let the Sun Go Down on Me," with George Michael, and "Don't Go Breaking My Heart," with drag icon RuPaul taking over for Kiki Dee. The king of disco and electro, Giorgio Moroder, came on board for the production and turned "Don't Go Breaking My Heart" into an audacious dance track. Kiki Dee does also get a chance to sing on Cole Porter's "True Love," a song that Elton had loved since childhood. Chris Rea and Nik Kershaw, whose particular singing styles provided a nice contrast with Elton's own voice, were given the privilege of reinterpreting their own songs, "If You Were Me" and "Old Friend," respectively. Gladys Knight brings her powerful voice to "Go On and On," which was composed, written, supervised, and, for the most part, played on the album by Stevie Wonder.

Only three new numbers were written for the album: "A Woman's Needs," "The Power," and "Duets for One." Elton John composed "A Woman's Needs" with Tammy Wynette's voice in mind, even before asking her to join him in the project.

Designed expressly for her strong and expressive voice, this ballad is set in waltz time and driven by Elton's piano arpeggios as well as delicate country ornamentation on the guitar. It is an excellent example of the dynamic between the two singers. The dialogue between the two relates to the end of a love affair, fitting perfectly with the music with its fluctuating disillusion and optimism between each couplet and each bridge.

Little Richard, a major influence on Elton's love of rock 'n' roll, deserved a song specially tailored to him. Elton and Bernie put together "The Power" specifically for this album, and for Little Richard. With a melody that is contemplative but propelled by a snappy drumbeat, this song, as well judged in its music as in its lyrics, offers a much softer side of the rock 'n' roll pioneer than we might expect, and seems to take account of Little Richard's decision in 1958 to become a Seventh Day Adventist. The fervent backing vocals give the feel of a gospel choir, perhaps as a tribute to Little Richard, whose music education started with church music.

An anomaly at the end of this collaborative album is a song called "Duets for One" that has Elton singing on his own, his old happiness recovered as he embarks on a new stage of his life. Chris Difford of Squeeze wrote the lyrics to the song, and Elton liked Squeeze so much that he is said to have bought every copy of their album *Some Fantastic Place* (1993) that was on sale in a record shop near his home. Dean Parks and Chris Rea share guitar-playing duties on the track, so perhaps this is where the duet angle gets worked into the single?

Covering the decades from the 1940s to the 1970s and embracing soul, country, pop, and R & B, *Duets* takes Elton on an exciting journey of creativity and shows yet again (after previous hit duets with Kiki Dee, John Lennon, and Dionne Warwick) how comfortable he is working with other major artists.

A Stream of Singles

Six singles were taken from this album: *Don't Let the Sun Go Down on Me / I Believe (When I Fall in Love It Will Be Forever)* was released in the UK in November 1991 on Epic (ref. 657646 7) and in the US by Columbia (ref. 38-74086). The single went to number one on both sides of the Atlantic. On November 8, 1993, Rocket Records brought out *True Love / The Show Must Go On* (ref. EJS 32/858060-7), which went to number two in the charts. That same month, MCA Records released *True Love / Runaway Train* (ref. MCAS7 54762), a disk that did not do especially well and only hit number fifty-six in the rankings. In February 1994, Rocket Records released *Don't Go Breaking My Heart / Donner Pour Donner* (ref. EJS 33/858404-1) in the UK and it went to number seven, while MCA Records put together *Don't Go Breaking My Heart* alongside a collection of remixes (ref. MCA8P 2981). This collection only hit number ninety-two in the charts. Last, London Records brought out *Ain't Nothing Like the Real Thing / Break the Chain* (ref. LON 350/857 528-7) on May 2, and the single went all the way to number twenty-four.

THE LION KING:
AN ACCLAIMED SOUNDTRACK

Elton John and Tim Rice previously collaborated on "Legal Boys" before reuniting on a much larger scale to create the soundtrack to the 1994 mega-hit, *The Lion King*.

Circle of Life (Carmen Twillie, Lebo M.)
I Just Can't Wait to Be King (Jason Weaver, Rowan Atkinson, Laura Williams)
Be Prepared (Jeremy Irons, Whoopi Goldberg, Cheech Marin, Jim Cummings)
Hakuna Matata (Nathan Lane, Ernie Sabella, Jason Weaver, Joseph Williams)
Can You Feel the Love Tonight (Joseph Williams, Sally Dworsky, Nathan Lane, Ernie Sabella, Kristle Edwards)
This Land (Hans Zimmer)
. . . To Die For (Hans Zimmer)
Under the Stars (Hans Zimmer)
King of Pride Rock (Hans Zimmer)
Circle of Life (Elton John)
I Just Can't Wait to Be King (Elton John)
Can You Feel the Love Tonight (Elton John)

ALBUM

Release Dates
UK Release: May 31, 1994
Reference: Mercury—522 690-2 / Walt Disney Records—0126902DNY
Best UK Chart Ranking: Did Not Chart
US Release: May 31, 1994
Reference: Walt Disney Records—60858-2
Best US Chart Ranking: 1

Musicians
Elton John: composition (songs), lead vocals, keyboard
Tim Rice: words
Hans Zimmer: composition (instrumental numbers), arrangements
Davey Johnstone: guitar
Phil Spalding: bass
Chuck Sabo: drums
Guy Babylon: programming
Olle Romö: programming
Bob Daspit: programming
Bruce Fowler: direction, arrangements
Nick Glennie-Smith: direction, arrangements
Bobbi Page: arrangements
Mark Mancina: arrangements
Lebo M.: choir leader
Mbongeni Ngema: choir leader
Andraé Crouch: choir leader
London Community Gospel Choir: backing vocals

Recorded
Media Ventures, Los Angeles / Ocean Way Recording, Los Angeles / Snake Ranch, London / Angel Recording Studios, London / BOP Studios, Mmabatho (South Africa): 1993–1994

Technical Team
Producers: Hans Zimmer, Mark Mancina, Jay Rifkin, Chris Thomas

Sound Engineers: Steven Stern, David Appelt, Michael Farrow, Steve Price, Jay Rifkin, Brett Newman, Alister Glyn, Tanja Somers
Mixing: Bruce Botnick

Single Releases
Can You Feel the Love Tonight / Can You Feel the Love Tonight (Instrumental)
   Single 45 rpm
   UK Release: June 27, 1994, on Mercury (ref. EJS 34)
   Best UK Chart Ranking: 14
Can You Feel the Love Tonight
   CD single
   US Release: May 12, 1994, on Hollywood Records (ref. HR-64543-2)
   Best US Chart Ranking: 4
Circle of Life / Circle of Life (Cast Version) */ I Just Can't Wait to Be King / This Land* (Instrumental)
   CD Single
   UK Release: 1994 on Mercury (ref. 856 219-2; EJSCD 35)
   Best UK Chart Ranking: 11
Circle of Life
   CD Single
   US Release: August 9, 1994, on Hollywood Records (ref. HR-64516-2)
   Best US Chart Ranking: 18

Before establishing itself on Disney's long list of classic movies, *The Lion King* was a long time in the making. Development began in 1988 and production started in earnest in 1991. While location scouting was being carried out in Kenya, George Scribner, the director, opposed to the idea of making a musical film and walked off the project. He was replaced by Rob Minkoff, who had the story and the script revised. In the meantime, *Aladdin*, which was conceived at the same time, was proceeding more rapidly and soon became the top priority inside the Disney studios. The music for *Aladdin* was composed by the duo also working on *The Little Mermaid*: Alan Menken and Howard Ashman. Suffering from AIDS, Howard Ashman died prematurely on March 14, 1991. Tim Rice, the lyricist for *Jesus Christ Superstar*, was brought in to complete Ashman's unfinished projects, including *Aladdin* and *Beauty and the Beast*. It seemed obvious that the thing to do was to hire Tim Rice to work on *The Lion King*. Menken, the composer, was unavailable, so Tim Rice took advantage of the situation to put forward a novel idea: Why not bring in a pop star to replace Menken?

A Good Bet

Tim Rice first approached the Swedish group ABBA, but their composer, Benny Andersson, was already involved in writing another musical in his home country, *Kristina från Duvemåla*. Next, Rice put forward Elton John's name, having worked with him in 1981 on the *Jump Up!* album. To Rice's surprise, Elton said

he would be interested. Walt Disney's nephew, Roy E. Disney, was not keen on the idea. Nevertheless, the Disney company agreed, seemingly convinced that the singer-composer's fame could be of help to the project.

Elton and Tim began their long-distance collaboration in 1993. Tim would fax his lyrics to Elton in Los Angeles, then Elton would mail back his demo tapes to London. From the very outset, Tim Rice was hoping that Elton might be involved in more than just the songs (the instrumentals were being composed by Hans Zimmer) and asked him to sing some of the songs himself, even though it was standard for the actors playing the characters to handle the vocals. Among these "independent" songs from the movie, the first one the duo took on was "Can You Feel the Love Tonight." Two versions of the song were used in the movie: the one sung by the voice actors (Joseph Williams, Sally Dworsky, Nathan Lane, Ernie Sabella, and Kristle Edwards) and the one sung by Elton. The words of the latter version differ slightly from the version sung by the characters in the movie itself, and they're more overtly romantic.

The next song to emerge was "Circle of Life," one that also appears in two versions on the album. One version is sung by Carmen Twillie and Lebo M., the other by Elton. The song draws on the main themes of the movie. As Tim Rice put it: "Generations passing on the flame, one generation dying out and a new one taking over, and animals eating each other. All of these things are part of the 'Circle of Life.'"[134] Unlike the others, this song took shape in front of Rice, who was in London and had dropped into the AIR Studios on Oxford Street. Elton insisted that he bring the words with him to the studio. Rice

was reluctant, saying they were not ready, but Elton was having none of that. Snatching the unfinished lyrics from Rice's hand, he added the main melody. He played it several times to check the lyrics fit, and then suddenly everything fell into place.

A Popular Success

Elton threw himself wholeheartedly into the project, even when he found himself faced with words that seemed strange when taken out of context, such as "When I was a young warthog" in "Hakuna Matata." Tim Rice had found the song's famous catch-phrase "Hakuna matata" in a book written in Swahili. Its literal meaning is "No worries." He immediately imagined it as a kind of mantra for Timon and Pumbaa, two beloved comical characters from the movie. Tim, speaking in an interview, said of them: "The main thing is they're comic relief. They represent a different aspect of life. It's not all about lions and prides."[134] Initial feedback from Disney was unenthusiastic. However, their doubts were dispelled when they heard the orchestral versions of the songs. As for the public, they were instantly won over. The album went to the top of the *Billboard* ranking chart, and in 1994 it sold almost 5 million copies in the United States alone. Elton John told *Rolling Stone* magazine: "The Lion King changed my life. It gave me the opportunity to write for the stage. It gave me more strings to my bow. After The Lion King, I wrote *Aida*, I wrote *Billy Elliot*, and I wrote *The Vampire Lestat*—four stage musicals. Up until that point, I was just doing records, videos, and touring. Of course, nobody knew it was going to be this big. I'm so proud to be involved in it, and I have Tim Rice to thank for it."[35]

ALBUM

MADE IN ENGLAND

Believe . Made in England . House . Cold . Pain . Belfast .
Latitude . Please . Man . Lies . Blessed

RELEASE DATES
UK Release: March 20, 1995
Reference: Rocket Record Company/Mercury—526 185-2
Best UK Chart Ranking: 3
US Release: March 21, 1995
Reference: Rocket Record Company—314-526 915-2
Best US Chart Ranking: 13

A heightened feeling of patriotism took hold of the local boy made good when Elton went to the new AIR Studios in London to record *Made in England*.

FOR ELTON ADDICTS

With the exception of "Made in England," every track on this album was given a single-word title. This was done as a tip of the hat to the *John Lennon/Plastic Ono Band* album, which included similarly short titles, like "Mother," "Love," and "God."

A BRITISH SYMPHONY

Nineteen ninety-four was the year of Elton John's consecration as a rock legend. On January 19, the singer joined the Rock and Roll Hall of Fame and became officially recognized as one of popular music's most immortal musicians. During this year he also achieved an unprecedented success with the soundtrack for the film *The Lion King*, which earned him an Oscar for "Can You Feel the Love Tonight." Before this tidal wave of acclaim began, the composer first set out to record *Made in England*, which, as the name indicates, was to be an entirely home-based production.

British AIR Ways

Elton decides once again to place his confidence in George Martin's AIR Studios. This time, however, the recording sessions would not take place in the Caribbean paradise of Montserrat, nor at the studios in Oxford Street. The Montserrat location had been devastated during Hurricane Hugo in 1989, and Oxford Street closed its doors in 1991. The former producer of the Beatles had relocated his operation to a Victorian church in Hampstead, a district to the north of London. The new studios set up in this grandiose and unusual space were inaugurated in December 1992. They contain a hexagonal space with a vast suspended acoustic canopy, which meant that the studio not only had exceptional acoustics, but it could also accommodate a larger symphony orchestra and a choir. This was an ideal location for Elton, who planned to renew his focus on the rich orchestrations of his early days. He also met up again with Paul Buckmaster, with whom he had not worked since *A Single Man* in 1978, and who would provide the direction for the prestigious London Session Orchestra on "Believe," "House," "Cold," and "Belfast," leaving only "Latitude" to George Martin, and "Man" to Gavyn Wright. The singer and his group set themselves up at the AIR Studios for thirteen weeks, from February to April 1994. This time, Elton did not content himself with recording his parts and then taking his leave; he took a full-time role in the recording and served as a co-producer. Also on board as a producer was Greg Penny, who came in to replace Chris Thomas.

The Ideal Bassist

Another contributor who made his first appearance on *Made in England* was Bob Birch, who was called on to work as Elton's new bassist. Bob had been a friend of Guy Babylon's since 1985, and he was introduced to Davey Johnstone four years later. The three men eventually formed the band Warpipes alongside Nigel Olsson. When Pino Palladino declined an invitation to take part in the *The One* tour in 1992 due to the imminent birth of his child, Johnstone suggested Birch take his spot. He had everything that Elton liked: classical musical training, a pronounced taste for jazz, and he also played several instruments (bass, saxophone, and bassoon) in addition to having an extreme passion for the Motown sound. To make things even more perfect, he was a formidably efficient studio musician, which earned him the nickname "first-take Bob."

Elton had three keyboards at his disposal during recording: a Yamaha grand piano, a Bösendorfer grand piano, and a Roland electronic piano. As productive as ever, he composed numerous songs but only used eleven of them, which meant

The newly formed Elton John Band. Standing, left to right: Bob Birch, Guy Babylon, Ray Cooper. Seated: Davey Johnstone, Elton John, Charlie Morgan.

that "Building a Bird," "Leaves," "Hell," "Skin," "Tick-Tock," "Undone," "Red," and "Horses" were all set aside. Most of these tracks were forgotten, with the exception of "Horses," which was later reworked on *The Big Picture* and given the name "Live Like Horses"; and "Building a Bird," which Nigel Olsson included on his 2001 album, *Move the Universe*. In spite of the fact that it wasn't used on the album, "Building a Bird" was the first to be laid down on tape. Elton followed it with "Belfast" and "Believe," and the alliterative nature of the song titles caused some amusement among the musicians, who began to wonder if Bernie was only capable of writing songs that started with the same letter as his name. Curiously, the original title of this album was *Believe*, until Elton and Bernie agreed to go with *Made in England* as a way to emphasize the fact that it had been recorded in Elton's home country.

The release of *Made in England* was initially scheduled for autumn 1994 but was pushed back to March 1995 due to the success of *The Lion King* soundtrack, which was released on May 31, 1994. The motion picture soundtrack album was certified gold in the United Kingdom, and it sold a million copies in the United States, where it also hit the thirteenth spot on the *Billboard* album charts.

BELIEVE

Elton John, Bernie Taupin / 4:55

Musicians

Elton John: vocals, piano, backing vocals
Davey Johnstone: guitars
Bob Birch: bass
Charlie Morgan: drums
Guy Babylon: keyboards, programming
Ray Cooper: percussion
Paul Buckmaster: direction, arrangements
Orchestra: London Session Orchestra

Recorded

AIR Lyndhurst Hall, London: February 24, 1994

Technical Team

Producers: Elton John, Greg Penny
Sound Engineer: Jon Ingoldsby
Assistant Sound Engineer: Andy Strange
Mixing: Greg Penny, Jon Ingoldsby
Mastering: Chris Bellman
Album Coordinator: Steve Brown
Studio Coordinator: Adrian Collee

Single Release

Believe / The One (live) / The Last Song (live)
UK Release: February 20, 1995, on Rocket Record Company (ref. EJSCD 36) and Mercury (ref. 856 015-2)
Best UK Chart Ranking: 15

• *Believe / The One (live)*
US Release: February 1995 on Rocket Record Company/Island (ref. 422-856 014-7)
Best US Chart Ranking: 13

Maxi CD

• *Believe / The One (live) / The Last Song (live) / Sorry Seems to Be the Hardest Word (live) / Believe (live)*
US Release: February 1995 on Rocket Record Company/Island (ref. 422-856 713-2)
Best US Chart Ranking: Did Not Chart

Genesis and Lyrics

"Nothing seemed to be taking shape until I wrote the music for *Believe*…. With *Believe*, I thought, 'That's the benchmark for this album,'[32] explained Elton. In this song, the subject—love—turns from the individual and takes on a universal dimension. At the time the song was written, Bernie himself had found love once more and was spending happy days with his third wife, Stephanie Haymes. They lived in California's Santa Ynez Valley, where Bernie bred horses and helped Stephanie with the management of her Italian restaurant. But his father, whom he arranged to have join him in America, was dying, and Bernie was powerless to do anything about it; all he could do was put words to paper to express his gratitude. He did so quite freely, laying bare his sadness in "Believe": "War makes money, cancer sleeps, / Curled up in my father and that means something to me." Without love, nothing makes sense, and only this feeling can transcend political movements and institutions: "Churches and dictators, politics and papers / Everything crumbles sooner or later / But love, I believe in love." Satisfied with this homage, Bernie asked the impossible of Elton: to write a song as definitive as John Lennon's "Imagine."

Production

With this monumental reference in mind, Elton set to work. Paul Buckmaster was called on to create a bed of searing strings while Davey Johnstone's acoustic guitar accompanied Elton's somber piano. A rhythmic motif played on the tabla was to open the piece, but this was cut during the final stages; it reappeared, however, when the song was performed onstage. Elton's voice, cradled by a desperate optimism, is particularly poignant, evoking the dichotomy of life, which offers the best things and the worst. The refrain of "Believe" asserts itself as the most memorable on the album: It is based on the depth of Elton's voice as much as the melody—which is strangely comforting—shaping the image of Bernie's text, in which pain is always overtaken by love. At 2:19, Davey Johnstone's electric guitar, which hitherto had been confined to finely executed distortion arpeggios, launches into a huge solo written with great precision, with a sound close to that of a sitar. Then, at 4:08, the light strings directed by Paul Buckmaster take over the orchestral coda very effectively. The piece is finally overlaid by metallic noise announcing the next piece, "Made in England."

MADE IN ENGLAND

Elton John, Bernie Taupin / 5:08

Musicians: Elton John: lead and backing vocals, piano / **Davey Johnstone:** guitars / **Bob Birch:** bass / **Charlie Morgan:** drums / **Ray Cooper:** percussion / **Guy Babylon:** keyboards, programming
Recorded: AIR Lyndhurst Hall, London: March 18, 1994 **Technical Team:** Producers: Elton John, Greg Penny / **Sound Engineer:** Jon Ingoldsby / **Assistant Sound Engineer:** Andy Strange / **Mixing:** Greg Penny, Jon Ingoldsby / **Mastering:** Chris Bellman / **Album Coordinator:** Steve Brown / **Studio Coordinator:** Adrian Collee **Single Release:** *Made in England / Whatever Gets You Through The Night* (live) / *Lucy in the Sky with Diamonds* (live) / *I Saw Her Standing There* (live) **UK Release:** May 8, 1995, on Rocket Record Company (ref. EJSDD 37) and Mercury (ref. 856 893-2) **Best UK Chart Ranking:** 18 • *Made in England / Lucy in the Sky with Diamonds* (live) **US Release:** June 1995 on Rocket Record Company (ref. 422-852 172-7) **Best US Chart Ranking:** 52

Genesis and Lyrics

Like a veritable compendium of Elton's life, "Made in England" called on all of Bernie's songwriting powers and made good use of his privileged position as a spectator during Elton's meteoric rise to the status of global celebrity. "We've known each other for over twenty-seven years," declared the lyricist. "In that time, I've learned everything there is to know about him, about his childhood and whatever loneliness he may have existed in, and also that it's the music that's always kept him alive and kept him going…. It's always been the music that's kept him afloat."[32] Bernie now returned to those who had forged Elton's destiny: an absent father and an attention-seeking mother ("I had a quit-me father / I had a love-me mother"), and of course, his earliest idols, Little Richard and Elvis Presley. Bernie recalled that Stanley Dwight's indifference to his son's love of music caused Elton many torments, but also indirectly led to Bernie and Elton's meeting ("Face down on a playground / Crying, 'God, send me a brother'"). This brother, who understands him so well, is clearly Bernie—who, in a moment of patriotic fervor, also emphasizes Elton's capacity to overcome all the outrages in which he found himself embroiled, because he was "made in England" and therefore "built to last."

Made in England evokes the fraternal link that binds Bernie and Elton, who are shown here in a photograph taken by Mike Ross at the very beginning of their careers.

Production

It is impossible not to think of the opening chord of the Beatles' "A Hard Day's Night" when listening to the opening of "Made in England," a reference that is clearly acknowledged by Elton John. Clear and trenchant, Davey Johnstone's guitar then takes up one of the most important roles at the heart of the arrangement; meanwhile, the rhythm section is launched like a locomotive without any brakes. Despite its introspective and nostalgic lyrics, Elton opted to make "Made in England" into an exhilarating anthem, with a refrain that a group like Coldplay might feel proud of today, and which was designed to appeal to crowds singing in stadiums. As the song enters its final phase, it becomes even more dynamic as a loop of programmed, swirling strings combine with Elton's rambling piano and the ethereal, enchanting backing vocals.

HOUSE

Elton John, Bernie Taupin / 4:27

Musicians: Elton John: vocals, piano, backing vocals / **Davey Johnstone:** guitars / **Bob Birch:** bass / **Charlie Morgan:** drums / **Ray Cooper:** percussion / **Guy Babylon:** keyboards, programming / **Paul Buckmaster:** direction, arrangements / **Orchestra:** London Session Orchestra **Recorded:** AIR Lyndhurst Hall, London: March 1, 1994 **Technical Team: Producers:** Elton John, Greg Penny / **Sound Engineer:** Jon Ingoldsby / **Assistant Sound Engineer:** Andy Strange / **Mixing:** Greg Penny, Jon Ingoldsby / **Mastering:** Chris Bellman / **Album Coordinator:** Steve Brown / **Studio Coordinator:** Adrian Collee

"House" refers back, very powerfully, to the darkest days of Elton's pop star life, when he was plagued by loneliness and dependence on cocaine. Bernie observes his friend—the narrator—on a downward path and imagines him in the process of sinking. Prostrate in his bedroom, he talks to himself, as though to conjure up the madness that haunts him, listing all that he sees: "This is my house / This is where I live [...] Those are the trees / I can hear them breathe / This is my bed / This is where I sleep." But this inventory inevitably begs other, more painful questions: "What is my soul / Where is my tired heart / That is the question / Where is the answer?" "As soon as I read the lyrics, I thought of when I used to do cocaine and wouldn't come out of my room for two weeks at a time," Elton told journalist Robert Hilburn in 1995. "I would creep around my own house so slowly that it would take me fifteen minutes to walk across my bedroom floor."[135] This waltz, depressing but also imbued with hope—with the narrator continuing to evoke his dreams—is based on Elton's delicate piano lines, whose vocals sound worn down, but also a subtle harp sound emulated by a keyboard. On the second level, the slow percussion of Charlie Morgan, the elegant guitar of Davey Johnstone, the poignant strings directed by Paul Buckmaster, and Bob Birch's sliding guitar complete an effective arrangement.

COLD

Elton John, Bernie Taupin / 5:37

Musicians: Elton John: vocals, piano, backing vocals / **Davey Johnstone:** guitars / **Bob Birch:** bass / **Charlie Morgan:** drums / **Ray Cooper:** percussion / **Guy Babylon:** keyboards, programming / **Paul Buckmaster:** direction, arrangements / **Orchestra:** London Session Orchestra **Recorded:** AIR Lyndhurst Hall, London: February 23, 1994 **Technical Team: Producers:** Elton John, Greg Penny / **Sound Engineer:** Jon Ingoldsby / **Assistant Sound Engineer:** Andy Strange / **Mixing:** Greg Penny, Jon Ingoldsby / **Mastering:** Chris Bellman / **Album Coordinator:** Steve Brown / **Studio Coordinator:** Adrian Collee

While the first three tracks on the album are interlinked by orchestral bridges imagined by Paul Buckmaster, Elton reboots the tone of the album with "Cold," which starts in an autumnal way, almost abruptly. There is nothing autobiographical in this melancholic, searing ballad, unlike "House": We do not know exactly if the love story depicted by Bernie involves a homosexual or heterosexual couple. There is no "he" or "she"; perhaps this is a way in which the lyricist evokes gay love, because hitherto, during his break with Bernie, Elton had always depended on Tom Robinson and Gary Osborne to address this subject. Elton shows his talent in the way he anchors the complex melody of "Cold" in rhythm 'n' blues while his powerful voice oscillates between blues and gospel with an impressive measure of feeling, particularly when he switches into an intoxicating falsetto at 4:28. As for the surgical guitars of Davey Johnstone, they exchange brilliantly with Paul Buckmaster's light but solemn strings. At the very least a tormented number, "Cold" is certainly one of the most successful songs on *Made in England*.

George Martin's new AIR
Studios were constructed in an
old Victorian church that
featured exceptional acoustics.

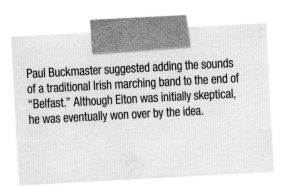

Paul Buckmaster suggested adding the sounds of a traditional Irish marching band to the end of "Belfast." Although Elton was initially skeptical, he was eventually won over by the idea.

PAIN

Elton John, Bernie Taupin / 3:51

Musicians: Elton John: vocals, piano, backing vocals / **Davey Johnstone:** guitars / **Bob Birch:** bass / **Charlie Morgan:** drums / **Ray Cooper:** percussion / **Guy Babylon:** keyboards, programming **Recorded:** AIR Lyndhurst Hall, London: March 2, 1994 **Technical Team:** Producers: Elton John, Greg Penny / **Sound Engineer:** Jon Ingoldsby / **Assistant Sound Engineer:** Andy Strange / **Mixing:** Greg Penny, Jon Ingoldsby / **Mastering:** Chris Bellman / **Album Coordinator:** Steve Brown / **Studio Coordinator:** Adrian Collee

"Pain" draws closely on Bernie and Elton's shared past. The pain described by the lyricist is felt on several levels and actually becomes the song's main character. Bernie clearly alludes to the physical pain of his sick father but also to his own pain, which is emotional in nature, because he cannot bear to see his father suffer. There is also the psychological pain of his favorite subject, Elton, who tried for years to mask his fragilities beneath outlandish costumes, and who took refuge in drugs and alcohol. Bernie interrogates the song's enigmatic protagonist on the subject of suffering. And this suffering, which lurks in every corner of our existence, takes the time to explain the ways that it intends to exert itself on humanity: "My name is Pain, you belong to me / You're all I wanted, I'm all you'll ever be / From the beginning in a world without end / I am the air, I am Pain." In singing this anthem, Elton does not sink into pathos but instead takes the orchestration in a style reminiscent of the Rolling Stones. Davey Johnstone's guitar riff and solo compare very favorably with those of Keith Richards's classic work on songs like "Can't You Hear Me Knocking" and "Brown Sugar."

BELFAST

Elton John, Bernie Taupin / 6:31

Musicians: Elton John: lead and backing vocals, piano / **Davey Johnstone:** guitars / **Bob Birch:** bass / **Charlie Morgan:** drums / **Ray Cooper:** percussion / **Guy Babylon:** keyboards, programming / Teddy Borowiecki: accordion / Paul Brennan: bagpipes, flute / **Paul Buckmaster:** orchestral arrangements / **Gavyn Wright:** conductor / **Orchestra:** London Session Orchestra **Recorded:** AIR Lyndhurst Hall, London: March 4, 1994 **Technical Team:** Producers: Elton John, Greg Penny / **Sound Engineer:** Jon Ingoldsby / **Assistant Sound Engineer:** Andy Strange / **Mixing:** Greg Penny, Jon Ingoldsby / **Mastering:** Chris Bellman / **Album Coordinator:** Steve Brown / **Studio Coordinator:** Adrian Collee **Single Release:** *Please / Belfast / Lies* **UK Release:** 1995 on Rocket Record Company (ref. 852 729-2) and Mercury (ref. INT 852 729-2) **Best UK Chart Ranking:** 33

Even though the name of the song is taken from the capital of Northern Ireland, according to Elton it has no direct link to it, and he attributes a more universal meaning to the track: "You can substitute Belfast for Chechnya," said Elton. "It could be any place where human beings are being subject to intolerable pressure and pain. It's about the human spirit...and being able to battle through those conditions...and being stronger than all of that."[32] Even so, Bernie's lyrics do explicitly evoke Belfast, and the ravages inflicted by an endless war on its inhabitants: "All I see are dirty faces [...] / No more enchanted evenings / The pubs are closed / And all the ghosts are leaving [...] But I never saw a braver place, / Belfast." Elton's music itself is filled with Irish themes—way beyond Paul Buckmaster's cinematic introduction, which is interpreted by the London Session Orchestra, conducted by Gavyn Wright. Elton's voice merges with his piano, particularly during the prologue, before he allows himself to be carried by the elegant strings and is joined by a discreet flute and bagpipes. These almost switch the end of some verses in the direction of traditional Irish music. "Belfast" was nearly left off the disk at the last minute due to a ceasefire that occurred shortly after its recording, but after further consideration Elton opted to keep it in.

1995

LATITUDE

Elton John, Bernie Taupin / 3:36

Musicians: Elton John: lead and backing vocals, piano, harmonium / **Davey Johnstone:** guitars, mandolin, banjo / **Bob Birch:** bass / **Charlie Morgan:** drums / **Ray Cooper:** percussion / **Guy Babylon:** keyboards, programming / **George Martin:** direction, arrangements / **Orchestra:** London Session Orchestra **Recorded:** AIR Lyndhurst Hall, London: March 30, 1994 **Technical Team: Producers:** Elton John, Greg Penny / **Sound Engineer:** Jon Ingoldsby / **Assistant Sound Engineer:** Andy Strange / **Mixing:** Greg Penny, Jon Ingoldsby / **Mastering:** Chris Bellman / **Album Coordinator:** Steve Brown / **Studio Coordinator:** Adrian Collee **Single Release:** *Blessed* / *Latitude* **US Release:** October 1995 on Rocket Record Company (ref. 422-852 394-7) **Best US Chart Ranking:** 34

Bernie is second to none in his capacity for recycling good ideas: Here he evokes the distance that separates him from his beloved, as he has previously done on "I Guess That's Why They Call It the Blues." This time it is his wife, Stephanie Haymes, that he longs for. The lyricist set to work on his text following a transatlantic telephone conversation with her. When Bernie gave his text to Elton, Elton set to work on the first instrument at hand, a harmonium. He composed the song straightaway and ten minutes later recorded a voice demo for it, which was finally retained as it was without further modification. For this melody, which is incredibly reminiscent of the Beatles, Elton dreamed of having the input of George Martin's expertise—Martin being the legendary producer who had fashioned most of the successes of the Fab Four and was also the owner of the AIR studios, where the album was being recorded. Greg Penny and Elton therefore tried their luck during a meal break and approached Martin as he was quietly eating a sandwich in the common room. Without departing one iota from his characteristic elegance and composure, the producer assured them that he would call in to listen to the song when he had finished his sandwich. He was charmed by the piece and engaged fully with the process. His brilliant work on the strings arrangement, which is light and ethereal, and on the solemn brass makes this folk waltz a precious moment on the album. This piece is also attractively reinforced by Davey Johnstone on banjo.

FOR ELTON ADDICTS

The harmonium played on "Latitude" was a gift from Davey Johnstone to Elton. It can be seen in the 1973 documentary *Elton John and Bernie Taupin Say Goodbye Norma Jean and Other Things.*

Elton John was honored for his "exceptional contribution to music" during the 1995 Brit Awards.

PLEASE

Elton John, Bernie Taupin / 3:53

Musicians: Elton John: lead and backing vocals, keyboards / **Davey Johnstone**: guitars, mandolin, backing vocals / **Bob Birch**: bass, backing vocals / **Charlie Morgan**: drums / **Ray Cooper**: percussion / **Guy Babylon**: keyboards, programming, backing vocals **Recorded:** AIR Lyndhurst Hall, London: March 9, 1994 **Technical Team:** Producers: Elton John, Greg Penny / **Sound Engineer:** Jon Ingoldsby / **Assistant Sound Engineer:** Andy Strange / **Mixing:** Greg Penny, Jon Ingoldsby / **Mastering:** Chris Bellman / **Album Coordinator:** Steve Brown / **Studio Coordinator:** Adrian Collee Maxi CD Release: *Please / Honky Cat* (live) / *Take Me to the Pilot* (live) / *The Bitch Is Back* (live) **UK Release:** 1995 on Rocket Record Company (ref. EJSDD40) and Mercury (ref. 852687) **Best UK Chart Ranking:** 33

Following years of turbulence in his private life, Elton was finally at peace. His relatively new relationship with David Furnish brought him a sense of stability that had been sorely lacking. He felt happy and had no difficulty celebrating fidelity and love in these lyrics by Bernie, which are full of hope and promise: "After everything we've been through, what's left to prove / So please, [...] let me grow old with you." Bernie, too, had discovered more serenity in his life, and so "Please" refers as much to their sentimental lives as to their shared adventure, having been able to cope with the lean times and their redeeming break, to give their partnership a second youth: "We've been crippled in love, [...] / We've chalked on the walls a slogan or two about life / [...] We've been flipped like a coin, both of us landing facedown." With its rousing melody and Davey's mandolin, which accentuates the crystalline effect already obtained by the contribution of a twelve-string guitar, "Please" is the only example on the album of an incursion into country music territory. This is a positive-minded, relaxed, and sincere song, enabling Bob Birch and Guy Babylon to perform in a backing vocals trio with Davey Johnstone, a moving reference to the matchless trio formed a few years earlier with Dee Murray and Nigel Olsson. Another acknowledged reference was addressed to the Beatles, with a refrain strongly reminiscent of "Please Please Me." It took just one attempt by Elton to finalize the vocals part for the piece, Greg Penny having retained the demo track in the final mix.

MAN

Elton John, Bernie Taupin / 5:16

Musicians: Elton John: lead and backing vocals, piano, arrangements / **Davey Johnstone:** guitars / **Bob Birch:** bass / **Charlie Morgan:** drums / **Ray Cooper:** percussion / **Guy Babylon:** keyboards, programming, arrangements / **Paul Carrack:** Hammond organ / **Gavyn Wright:** direction / **Orchestra:** London Session Orchestra **Recorded:** AIR Lyndhurst Hall, London: March 28, 1994 **Technical Team: Producers:** Elton John, Greg Penny / **Sound Engineer:** Jon Ingoldsby / **Assistant Sound Engineer:** Andy Strange / **Mixing:** Greg Penny, Jon Ingoldsby / **Mastering:** Chris Bellman / **Album Coordinator:** Steve Brown / **Studio Coordinator:** Adrian Collee

A superficial reading of the lyrics of this song might lead fans to imagine that Elton had suddenly taken up a traditional view of masculinity like those commonly espoused by groups like the Promise Keepers, an Evangelical organization for men that originated in the United States in the early 1990s and taught that men should take on more of a leadership role within the family unit. However, it is unimaginable that Bernie would have had Elton singing the praises of an organization that was opposed to gay marriage. In fact, the lyricist was unconcerned by any decline in so-called masculine values; on the contrary, he merely intended to celebrate modern manhood, with all its associated failings and imperfections. While Elton first sings "Man stands in all his glory," he then leads into a more nuanced perspective: "Man breathes his own deceit / Man worships his own defeat [...] Man stumbles on his own belief." "It's very important for me, being gay, to say I'm a man, too," he said. "It's just affirming I'm proud to be a gay male."[32] To underline his message, Elton devised an epic gospel sound for the piece, in which Paul Carrack's Hammond organ shines through. The string arrangement, this time written by Guy Babylon, is once again performed by the versatile London Session Orchestra under the direction of Gavyn Wright, and Elton's voice has rarely sounded so strong and accomplished.

LIES

Elton John, Bernie Taupin / 4:28

Musicians: Elton John: lead and backing vocals, piano / **Davey Johnstone:** guitars / **Bob Birch:** bass / **Charlie Morgan:** drums / **Ray Cooper:** percussions / **Guy Babylon:** keyboards, programming **Recorded:** AIR Lyndhurst Hall, London: March 29, 1994 **Technical Team: Producers:** Elton John, Greg Penny / **Sound Engineer:** Jon Ingoldsby / **Assistant Sound Engineer:** Andy Strange / **Mixing:** Greg Penny, Jon Ingoldsby / **Mastering:** Chris Bellman / **Album Coordination:** Steve Brown / **Studio Coordination:** Adrian Collee

In "Lies," Bernie reminds Elton of the lies he told before entering rehab to treat his dependency on drugs and alcohol: "I've lied to lie with danger / I've lied for a drug or two / I've lied about most everything / But I never lied to you." Bernie also addresses Elton's sexuality, making reference to his failed marriage to Renate Blauel and to the subconscious denial of his homosexuality: "Some lie about who they love," sings Elton. While melodically not as strong as most of the other pieces on *Made in England*, "Lies" does have a directness to it that strikes the listener square in the heart. Bernie knows that Elton's wounds have scarred over, and he's not afraid to engage with them. Elton brings out the best in the lyrics by fashioning a swaggering and exhilarating arrangement, including some spectacular flights of virtuosic piano playing.

BLESSED

Elton John, Bernie Taupin / 5:01

Musicians: Elton John: lead and backing vocals, piano / **Davey Johnstone:** guitars / **Bob Birch:** bass / **Charlie Morgan:** drums / **Ray Cooper:** percussion / **Guy Babylon:** keyboards, programming **Recorded:** AIR Lyndhurst Hall, London: March 14, 1994 **Technical Team: Producers:** Elton John, Greg Penny / **Sound Engineer:** Jon Ingoldsby / **Assistant Sound Engineer:** Andy Strange / **Mixing:** Greg Penny, Jon Ingoldsby / **Mastering:** Chris Bellman / **Album Coordinator:** Steve Brown / **Studio Coordinator:** Adrian Collee **Single Release:** *Blessed* / *Latitude* **US Release:** October 1995 on Rocket Record Company (ref. 422-852 394-7) **Best US Chart Ranking:** 34

In "Blessed," Bernie expresses his desire to have children. As someone who had always put his career first, Bernie was apparently surprised to discover how much he enjoyed being around Stephanie Haymes's children from a previous marriage. He was impatient to welcome his own flesh and blood into the world: "Hey you, you're a child in my head / You haven't walked yet / Your first words have yet to be said / But I swear you'll be blessed." He imposes no conditions on the fulfillment of his dream: The child's eyes can be blue or green, but they will have "the best, I promise you that." The lyrics are of course reminiscent of the first joint Elton/Bernie hit, "Your Song," and particularly the verse: "So excuse me forgetting but these things I do / You see I've forgotten if they're green or they're blue / Anyway the thing is what I really mean / Yours are the sweetest eyes I've ever seen." The resemblance is limited to the lyrics, however, since from a musical point of view "Blessed" has more similarities with a track on *Sleeping with the Past* called "Blue Avenue," which is also constructed around wrenching piano chords.

LOVE SONGS (AMERICAN VERSION)

Can You Feel the Love Tonight (*The Lion King*, 1994)

The One (*The One*, 1992)

Sacrifice (*Sleeping with the Past*, 1989)

Daniel (*Don't Shoot Me I'm Only the Piano Player*, 1973)

Someone Saved My Life Tonight (*Captain Fantastic and the Brown Dirt Cowboy*, 1975)

Your Song (*Elton John*, 1970)

Don't Let the Sun Go Down on Me (Live, Wembley Arena) (*Duets*, 1993)

Believe (*Made in England*, 1995)

Blue Eyes (*Jump Up!*, 1982)

Sorry Seems to Be the Hardest Word (*Blue Moves*, 1976)

Blessed (*Made in England*, 1995)

Candle in the Wind (Live, Sydney Entertainment Centre) (*Live in Australia with the Melbourne Symphony Orchestra*, 1997)

You Can Make History (*Young Again*) (previously unreleased)

No Valentines (previously unreleased)

Circle of Life (*The Lion King*, 1994)

ALBUM

US Release Date: September 24, 1996
Reference: MCA Records—MCAD-11481
Best US Chart Ranking: 24

Love Forever

In May 1996, a few months before recording began on *The Big Picture*, a short session was organized at the Townhouse Studios to prepare two new songs intended for inclusion in the American edition of the compilation *Love Songs*, which was schedule to go on sale on September 24, 1996, just under a year after the UK edition had been released on November 6, 1995, on the Rocket Record and Mercury labels. The two new numbers were intended to give some consistency and originality to this compilation of love songs, Bernie and Elton's absolute favorite theme. To record them, Elton turned to the five musicians who were to join with him a few months later for the *Big Picture* sessions: Davey Johnstone (guitars), John Jorgenson (guitars), Bob Birch (bass), Charlie Morgan (drums, percussion), and Guy Babylon (keyboards).

Of the fifteen titles on the track list, eleven come from previous albums, two were live versions of old songs ("Candle in the Wind" and "Don't Let the Sun Go Down on Me") and two were original songs specially composed for the album: "You Can Make History (Young Again)" and "No Valentines." In addition to these two extra songs, there are other small differences between the UK and US releases: "I Guess That's Why They Call It the Blues," "Nikita," "True Love," "Please," and "Song for Guy" are no longer present on the US version, but "Believe" does make an appearance.

The album was very successful when it was released, going to the top of the charts in Chile, Norway, and New Zealand. It was a platinum disc in nine countries and multiplatinum in nine others. A compilation of videos came out at the same time on LaserDisc, VHS, and CD Video.

Love was celebrated on the compilation of romantic ballads that Elton released in 1996, and it remains one of his favorite topics (shown here during a concert in Las Vegas in 2004).

YOU CAN MAKE HISTORY (YOUNG AGAIN)

Elton John, Bernie Taupin / 3:50

Musicians: Elton John: vocals, piano / **Davey Johnstone:** guitars / **Bob Birch:** bass / **Charlie Morgan:** drums, percussion / **Guy Babylon:** keyboards **Recorded:** Townhouse Studios, London: May 1996 **Technical Team:** Producer: Chris Thomas

This gentle ballad is about a lover who makes the narrator feel young again. Bernie is almost certainly alluding to the one-time advertising executive, Canadian David Furnish. Fifteen years younger than Elton, David and he had begun a relationship two years earlier. But alongside the words of love are cruel reminders that time is beginning to take its toll: "I can feel the years crawling through my skin." Of the members of the group that were to return again and again to work with Elton, the only missing one here is guitarist John Jorgenson. The arrangement includes a guitar strung with nylon, some beautiful and vibrant (albeit synthetic) chords, and a credible emulation of a sitar.

NO VALENTINES

Elton John, Bernie Taupin / 4:08

Musicians: Elton John: vocals, piano / **Davey Johnstone:** guitars / **John Jorgenson:** guitars / **Bob Birch:** bass / **Charlie Morgan:** drums, percussion / **Guy Babylon:** keyboards **Recorded:** Townhouse Studios, London: May 1996 **Technical Team:** Producer: Chris Thomas

Backed up this time by John Jorgenson, Davey Johnstone's inspired melodies are impressive, providing some delightful arpeggios, but perhaps a little too close—both in construction and sonority—to those of "My Iron Lung," Radiohead's hit from *The Bends*, released in the spring of 1995. A few notes from the nylon-string guitar and some syrupy keyboards complete this bland ballad despite the efforts of the six-string guitar. Elton never bothered to promote it in live performances. Bernie's words create a picture of love gone sour: "No more Valentine's Day / No more Christmas cards / I've thrown them all away [. . .] / I gave you earth and sky [. . .] / I'll keep my bleeding heart / Just let me out of here."

THE BIG PICTURE

Long Way from Happiness . Live Like Horses . The End Will Come .
If the River Can Bend . Love's Got a Lot to Answer For . Something About the Way
You Look Tonight . The Big Picture . Recover Your Soul . January .
I Can't Steer My Heart Clear of You . Wicked Dreams

RELEASE DATES
UK Release: September 22, 1997
Reference: Rocket Record Company/Mercury—536 266-2
Best UK Chart Ranking: 3
US Release: September 22, 1997
Reference: Rocket Record Company—31453 6266 2
Best US Chart Ranking: 9

FOR ELTON ADDICTS

The Big Picture album cover featured a portrait of Elton made by the celebrated artist and film director Julian Schnabel. In addition to his artwork, Schnabel has directed popular films, including *Basquiat, Before Night Falls*, and *The Diving Bell and the Butterfly*.

LOVE IS IN THE AIR

The year 1996 offered Elton John some respite since he was not on tour, but that did not get in the way of him composing actively. During this time, he worked on music for the stage adaptation of *The Lion King*, as well as for *Aida*, which was inspired by the opera by Giuseppe Verdi and took the form of a conceptual album that released in 1999. Elton also worked on music for a new animated cartoon called *The Road to El Dorado*, which was later released by DreamWorks Pictures in 2000. On June 20, 1996, Elton took part in a Pavarotti & Friends charity concert organized by Luciano Pavarotti to raise money to benefit the War Child organization and support child victims of war. The concert also included other major musical artists like Eric Clapton, Sheryl Crow, Liza Minnelli, and Joan Osborne. During this event, the Italian tenor and the English singer unveiled "Live Like Horses," a song they also recorded together and included on Elton John's album *The Big Picture*.

Assembling a Team

Recording sessions for Elton's twenty-fifth studio album began in January 1997 at the London Townhouse Studios, and they ran through May of that year. Located in Shepherd's Bush, these studios were owned by Richard Branson, the founder of Virgin Records, and they were housed inside three homes that were numbered 1, 2,...and 4. While they did not have the benefit of the same prestigious aura as EMI Recording Studios, the Townhouse Studios could boast having recorded some of the greatest British rock anthems of the period, such as "In the Air Tonight" by Phil Collins in 1980, and it became one of Queen's favorite recording haunts between 1980 and 1989.

The whole tour team was present with Elton for recording: Davey Johnstone and John Jorgenson on guitars, Guy Babylon on keyboards, Bob Birch on bass, and Charlie Morgan on drums. Only Ray Cooper did not take part in the festivities. The various percussions were therefore provided by Charlie Morgan, with additional contributions from Matthew Vaughan on "I Can't Steer My Heart Clear of You." Paul Carrack, of Mike and the Mechanics and Squeeze, also came back into the fold after working on "Man" (*Made in England*) in 1994 and laid down the gentle sounds of his organ on "Something About the Way You Look Tonight."

Davey Johnstone and John Jorgenson both played guitar on *The Big Picture*.

The successful experience of working on *Made in England* encouraged Elton to pursue the same artistic tack by enveloping his new pieces with luxurious string arrangements, which were recorded at the AIR Studios because they were more suitable for that level of recording work. Paul Buckmaster was absent from this album, so the arrangements were entrusted to Guy Babylon and Anne Dudley, the latter assuming responsibility for the orchestral direction as well. As a composer, Anne was more used to film music (she won an Oscar in 1998 for *The Full Monty*), and she provided a cinematic vision to this album that helped play up the storytelling narratives of Bernie Taupin's lyrics.

This time Elton John stepped back from production duties, which had proved to be too onerous and time-consuming, and instead he called in the loyal Chris Thomas to handle the controls. The singer held his producer in high esteem, and for good reason; Thomas had been trained at the school of George Martin and he had many great qualities, including a background as a keyboard player (he played keyboards on "Piggies" by the Beatles, the Mellotron on "The Continuing Story of Bungalow Bill," and also piano on "Savoy Truffle"), an astonishing capacity for adaptation (he produced for

groups as diverse as Procol Harum, the Sex Pistols, INXS, and Pulp), an excellent ear, and above all else a modern touch in his production, which emphasized legibility of instrumentation and purity of the sound. Some of his best production work can be heard on Pink Floyd's 1973 masterpiece, *Dark Side of the Moon*.

Bernie's Frustration

The only issue that Elton and Bernie ran into during work on *The Big Picture* was a debate over the order in which their songs would appear on the final album. Bernie wanted to open *The Big Picture* with "Long Way from Happiness," followed by "Live Like Horses" and then "The End Will Come," but this sequence of tracks was too slow and contemplative for Elton's taste. Apparently, Bernie wanted this to be a "torch song" album, in the spirit of crooners like Frank Sinatra or Tony Bennett. In fact, a romantic mood pervades most of the songs on the album, which evoke all manner of amorous relationships. At the time, both Bernie and Elton had found love with their partners: David Furnish for Elton, and Stephanie Haymes for Bernie. Despite the subject matter inherent in the lyrics, Elton was keen to illustrate these sometimes intimate, melancholic,

Elton John and Luciano Pavarotti performed together during the War Child charity event on June 20, 1996.

and sensual texts with a more upbeat musical composition. Unfortunately, Bernie's lyrics did not lend themselves to this approach, and they seemed to cry out for a slower, more contemplative attitude. In spite of this friction over their dueling approaches to the album, Elton and Bernie were celebrating thirty years of collaboration in 1997. At this point, the two men knew each other so well that they could dispense with some of their long-held ways of working. Elton no longer hesitated in breaking away from the creative process that they had adopted almost as ritual since their earliest days. He had no qualms asking Bernie to shorten his extensive lyrics and even to rewrite the occasional refrain, as happened on "Long Way from Happiness." This proved to be a painful experience for Bernie, who could only watch helplessly as the album quickly diverged from the original concept that he had in mind. In the end, Bernie eventually ranked this as the worst album in Elton's discography, placing it even lower than *Leather Jackets* in his estimation, which is really saying something.

A Success Overshadowed by Mourning

The public did not share Bernie's opinion, and they greeted this new offering with enthusiasm when it was released in September 1997. The album hit number three on the charts in Great Britain, and it went to number nine in the United States. The album's solid performance should've been a cause for celebration, but Elton had been hit by two pieces of shocking and heartbreaking news in the months leading up to the album's release. Fashion designer Gianni Versace was one of Elton's close friends, and shortly after the two men had gone on holiday together, Versace was gunned down in front of his Miami Beach home on July 15, 1997. A month and a half later, Diana, Princess of Wales, died in a tragic car accident in Paris. Brutally overwhelmed by the drama in his personal life, Elton found himself at the center of a major historical event when he performed a revised version of "Candle in the Wind," rewritten to honor the memory of the "Princess of Hearts." Accompanied by "Something About the Way You Look Tonight," "Candle in the Wind 1997" appeared on September 13, nine days before *The Big Picture*, and it became the second most widely sold single of all time, after the perennial holiday classic "White Christmas" sung by Bing Crosby. Profits from the single were given to charitable foundations supported by the Diana, Princess of Wales Memorial Fund.

LONG WAY FROM HAPPINESS

Elton John, Bernie Taupin / 4:46

Musicians: Elton John: vocals, piano, organ / **Davey Johnstone:** guitars / **John Jorgenson:** guitars / **Bob Birch:** bass / **Charlie Morgan:** drums, percussion / **Anne Dudley:** direction, arrangements / **Guy Babylon:** keyboards, arrangements / **Carol Kenyon:** backing vocals / **Orchestra:** uncredited **Recorded:** Townhouse Studios, London / AIR Lyndhurst Hall, London: November 1996–May 1997 **Technical Team:** Producer: Chris Thomas / **Sound Engineer:** Pete Lewis / **Assistant Sound Engineers:** Ben Georgiades, Andy Green, Jay Reynolds / **Sessions Coordinators:** Maureen Hillier, Ranni Lewis, Derek MacKillop / **Studio Coordinators:** Adrian Collee, Pete Mills

As the opening track on *The Big Picture*, "Long Way from Happiness" leaves something to be desired. In fact, Elton and Bernie had difficulty getting their act together when it came to finding the right marriage of lyrics and music on this song. Elton took issue with the melody of the refrain, which he considered to be overly long and uneven. He called Bernie and asked him to simplify his text, which Bernie did without veering away from the main subject of the song: a kindly soul who takes on some of the stress and anxiety that a friend is struggling with following a failed relationship. The result of Elton and Bernie's tinkering is a sanitized composition that evokes previous songs from Elton's catalog, like "Blessed" and "Blue Avenue." A slow drum loop, a gliding synthesizer, and a guitar played with a staccato rhythm all coalesce around the stratospheric talent of backing vocalist Carol Kenyon and help to elevate "Long Way from Happiness" in the process.

LIVE LIKE HORSES

Elton John, Bernie Taupin / 5:02

Musicians: Elton John: vocals, piano / **Luciano Pavarotti:** vocals (single version) / **Davey Johnstone:** guitars / **John Jorgenson:** guitars / **Bob Birch:** bass / **Charlie Morgan:** drums, percussion / **Anne Dudley:** direction, arrangements / **Guy Babylon:** keyboards, arrangements / **Angel Voices Choir:** backing vocals / **Orchestra:** uncredited **Recorded:** Townhouse Studios, London / AIR Lyndhurst Hall, London: May 1996 **Technical Team:** Producer: Chris Thomas Maxi CD **Single Release:** *Live Like Horses* (Studio Version) / *Live Like Horses* (Live Finale Version) / *Step into Christmas* / *Blessed* **UK Release:** 1996 on Rocket Record Company (ref. LLHDD 1) / Mercury (ref. 578 877-2) **Best UK Chart Ranking:** 9

Recorded during the first week of May 1996 at Townhouse Studios and AIR Lyndhurst Hall (for the orchestral arrangements), "Live Like Horses" appeared as a single after it was performed at a Pavarotti & Friends charity concert given in support of the War Child organization. The song was not intended to be included on the track list for *The Big Picture*, but Elton gave in to pressure from fans, who called vociferously for it to be included on the album. The track is characterized by its theme of liberty and stands out from the other pieces on the album, which are centered around the theme of human relationships.

In addition to its effective and rousing melody, the song benefits from a very open sound and Elton's powerful voice, which both contribute to the expression of liberty generated in the song's lyrics and metaphorically represented by the image of a galloping horse. Some piano notes are played in suspension to open the song, while the melody is enriched by very precise guitar chords, but the soaring strings and discreet but magnetic backing vocals elevate "Live Like Horses" into something truly captivating. While Elton sang this song solo on his album, he performed it alongside Luciano Pavarotti for the single release, which includes a live version of the song, the studio version, and two other songs: "Step into Christmas" and "Blessed."

THE END WILL COME

Elton John, Bernie Taupin / 4:53

Musicians: Elton John: vocals, piano / **Davey Johnstone:** guitars / **John Jorgenson:** guitars / **Bob Birch:** bass / **Charlie Morgan:** drums, percussion / **Anne Dudley:** direction, arrangements / **Guy Babylon:** keyboards, arrangements / **Orchestra:** uncredited **Recorded:** Townhouse Studios, London / AIR Lyndhurst Hall, London: November 1996–May 1997 **Technical Team:** Producer: Chris Thomas / **Sound Engineer:** Pete Lewis / **Assistant Sound Engineers:** Ben Georgiades, Andy Green, Jay Reynolds / **Sessions Coordinators:** Maureen Hillier, Ranni Lewis, Derek MacKillop / **Studio Coordinators:** Adrian Collee, Pete Mills

"The End Will Come" evokes the strange sentiment of alienation felt by a couple facing predictions of the end of their relationship despite that they've only just found each other.

The two lovers want to prove their naysayers wrong, but the seeds of doubt have been sown despite their best efforts. So, they adopt an approach of self-persuasion: "And so they say, the end will come for us [...] But I don't believe, I don't believe / That the end will come for us." The song is distinctive for its slow rhythm, which is sometimes countered by Elton's nervy chords on piano, such as during the unexpected interlude that begins at 2:50 and is quickly followed by string instruments that come in during the refrain. Davey Johnstone's and John Jorgenson's guitars paint a delicate canvas in the background. While the first two verses have Elton's voice drowned in echo, which recalls some of the Beatles' pop sound, "The End Will Come," marked by its surprising marriage of folk and jazz, is a complete break from the music Elton had played during the past three decades.

IF THE RIVER CAN BEND

Elton John, Bernie Taupin / 5:22

Musicians: Elton John: chant, piano, organ / **Davey Johnstone:** guitars / **John Jorgenson:** guitars / **Bob Birch:** bass / **Charlie Morgan:** drums, percussion / **Anne Dudley:** direction, arrangements / **Guy Babylon:** keyboards, arrangements / **Orchestra:** uncredited / **East London Gospel Choir:** backing vocals **Recorded:** Townhouse Studios, London / AIR Lyndhurst Hall, London: November 1996–May 1997 **Technical Team:** Producer: Chris Thomas / **Sound Engineer:** Pete Lewis / **Assistant Sound Engineers:** Ben Georgiades, Andy Green, Jay Reynolds / **Sessions Coordinators:** Maureen Hillier, Ranni Lewis, Derek MacKillop / **Studio Coordinators:** Adrian Collee, Pete Mills Maxi CD Release: *If the River Can Bend* (Edit) / *Don't Let the Sun Go Down on Me* (Recorded Live in Paris) / *Guess That's Why They Call It the Blues* (Recorded Live in Paris) / *Sorry Seems to Be the Hardest Word* (Recorded Live In Paris) **UK Release:** June 1998 on Rocket Record Company (ref. EJS DD43) / Mercury (ref. 568 961-2) **Best UK Chart Ranking:** 32

At first glance, staying true to one's convictions, against all odds and regardless of where the winding paths of destiny may take you, seems to be the theme of "If the River Can Bend." However, another reading is also possible. In the same way that "Please" (off the *Made in England* album) served as a postscript for "Two Rooms at the End of the World" (off *21 At 33*), "If the River Can Bend" presents itself as a sequel to "Harmony," which

originally appeared on *Goodbye Yellow Brick Road*. In fact, in this song's lyrics Bernie makes a very clear reference to the partnership he and Elton have maintained for so many years, and he makes direct reference to "Harmony." As he wrote: "All the twists and turns / We've made together / All the boats you rocked / With your harmony." The parallel with the verse in "Harmony" is clear: "Harmony and me / We're pretty good company / Looking for an island / In our boat upon the sea." With its powerful pop refrain that's tinged with hints of gospel, "If the River Can Bend" is the first piece on the album with pace; Elton's staccato voice explodes on the tense refrain, while Bob Birch's bass prepares the way for the massive strings and raw rock guitar that come in at 4:12.

LOVE'S GOT A LOT TO ANSWER FOR

Elton John, Bernie Taupin / 5:00

Musicians: Elton John: vocals, piano, organ / **Davey Johnstone:** guitars / **John Jorgenson:** guitars / **Bob Birch:** bass / **Charlie Morgan:** drums, percussion / **Anne Dudley:** direction, arrangements / **Guy Babylon:** keyboards, arrangements / **Orchestra:** uncredited **Recorded:** Townhouse Studios, London / AIR Lyndhurst Hall, London: November 1996–May 1997 **Technical Team:** Producer: Chris Thomas / **Sound Engineer:** Pete Lewis / **Assistant Sound Engineers:** Ben Georgiades, Andy Green, Jay Reynolds / **Sessions Coordinators:** Maureen Hillier, Ranni Lewis, Derek MacKillop / **Studio Coordinators:** Adrian Collee, Pete Mills

As a mannered ballad, "Love's Got a Lot to Answer For" distills its run-of-the-mill melody over a slow rhythm, while layers of cocooning synthesizers envelop the lyrics in harmonic compassion. In the lyrics, Bernie assumes the persona of a thwarted lover who is heartbroken by the end of a romance. The protagonist wanders along the streets on a cold night and drowns himself in dark thoughts on love: "Is loneliness the same as being free?" he asks, before continuing: "Freedom's like the stars in the sky / Alone and cold and burning / Each one keeps its distance / If only we were stars, you and I." Desperate and lugubrious, Elton's voice has difficulty extracting itself from a song that's weighed down with self-pity.

SOMETHING ABOUT THE WAY YOU LOOK TONIGHT

Elton John, Bernie Taupin / 5:09

Musicians: Elton John: vocals, piano / **Davey Johnstone:** guitars / **John Jorgenson:** guitars / **Bob Birch:** bass / **Charlie Morgan:** drums, percussion / **Paul Carrack:** organ / **Anne Dudley:** direction, arrangements / **Guy Babylon:** keyboards, arrangements / **Orchestra:** uncredited / **Carol Kenyon, Jackie Rawe:** backing vocals **Recorded:** Townhouse Studios, London / AIR Lyndhurst Hall, London: January 13, 1997 **Technical Team:** Producer: Chris Thomas / **Sound Engineer:** Pete Lewis / **Assistant Sound Engineers:** Ben Georgiades, Andy Green, Jay Reynolds / **Sessions Coordinators:** Maureen Hillier, Ranni Lewis, Derek MacKillop / **Studio Coordinators:** Adrian Collee, Pete Mills / Maxi CD Release: *Something About the Way You Look Tonight / Candle in the Wind 1997 / You Can Make History (Young Again)* **UK Release:** September 13, 1997, on Rocket Record Company (ref. PTCD 1) / Mercury (ref. 568 109-2) **Best UK Chart Ranking: 1 Single Release:** *Something About the Way You Look Tonight / Candle in the Wind 1997* **US Release:** September 13, 1997, on Rocket Record Company (ref. 31456 8108 7) **Best US Chart Ranking:** 1

Bernie Taupin's writing was becoming increasingly concise, if not necessarily pushing in new directions. The few verses that make up "Something About the Way You Look Tonight" tell the story of a lover who is besotted with their partner. Bernie's lyrics dive headfirst into clichés: "I need to tell you / How you light up every second of the day / But in the moonlight / You just shine like a beacon on the bay," writes Bernie, in his most "easy listening" song yet. He continues with astonishingly gauche compliments: "And I can't explain / But it's something about the way you look tonight / Takes my breath away" / [...] "I don't know where to start," he concludes. The song is helped immensely by Elton, who sublimes Bernie's insipid lyrics inside an epic song that lasts for more than five minutes and which is imbued with pop, rhythm 'n' blues, and gospel. To achieve this, Elton transforms the narrator's clumsiness into musical gentleness, which is all the better for its ability to express desire that is in danger of boiling over. Elton's arrangement is a model of construction. The impressive brass and intense strings, magnificently directed by Anne Dudley, support Elton's very effective vocal performance, which is occasionally distinguished by an irresistibly breaking voice. Davey Johnstone delivers a very nice electric guitar solo, and at 4:22 the seductive play resumes in an unexpected finale that intelligently illustrates the growing excitement of the protagonist. Elton, the master of melody, strikes again and transforms fairly mawkish lyrics into a convincing declaration of amorous affection.

THE BIG PICTURE

Elton John, Bernie Taupin / 3:45

Musicians: Elton John: vocals, piano, organ / **Davey Johnstone:** guitars / **John Jorgenson:** guitars / **Bob Birch:** bass / **Charlie Morgan:** drums, percussion / **Anne Dudley:** direction, arrangements / **Guy Babylon:** keyboards, arrangements / **Orchestra:** uncredited **Recorded:** Townhouse Studios, London / AIR Lyndhurst Hall, London: November 1996–May 1997 **Technical Team:** Producer: Chris Thomas / **Sound Engineer:** Pete Lewis / **Assistant Sound Engineers:** Ben Georgiades, Andy Green, Jay Reynolds / **Sessions Coordinators:** Maureen Hillier, Ranni Lewis, Derek MacKillop / **Studio Coordinators:** Adrian Collee, Pete Mills

The narrator imagined by Bernie wants to be the poster child in the movie of his life: "tell me do I fit in the big picture / Do I have a shot at the big part." With varying degrees of skill, he runs the film metaphor through to its eventual happy ending. For his part, Elton has no equal in musically dressing Bernie's most intimate thoughts: He starts softly on the piano, with a velvety voice, and he establishes an ambiance that seems to suggest confidence. But soon the musical environment becomes more theatrical with the intervention of tumultuous strings, a slightly distorted guitar, and a solid rhythm section that signifies the narrator is proudly asserting their right to appear in the "big picture." As a musical roller coaster, "The Big Picture" successfully links together its disparate movements, but it gives no answer to its central question: Does the narrator get to kiss the "big star" in the end?

RECOVER YOUR SOUL

Elton John, Bernie Taupin / 5:18

Musicians: Elton John: vocals, piano, organ / **Davey Johnstone:** guitars / **John Jorgenson:** guitars **Bob Birch:** bass / **Charlie Morgan:** drums, percussion / **Guy Babylon:** keyboards / **Paul Clarvis:** tabla / **Carol Kenyon, Jackie Rawe:** backing vocals **Recorded:** Townhouse Studios, London / AIR Lyndhurst Hall, London: November 1996–May 1997 **Technical Team:** Producer: Chris Thomas / **Sound Engineer:** Pete Lewis / **Assistant Sound Engineers:** Ben Georgiades, Andy Green, Jay Reynolds / **Sessions Coordinators:** Maureen Hillier,

Ranni Lewis, Derek MacKillop / **Studio Coordinators:** Adrian Collee, Pete Mills / Maxi CD Releases: *Recover Your Soul* (Single Remix) */ Big Man in a Little Suit / I Know Why I'm in Love / Recover Your Soul* (Album Version) **UK Release:** February 1998 on Rocket Record Company (ref. EJSCD 42) / Mercury (ref. 568 219-2) **Best UK Chart Ranking:** 16 *Recover Your Soul* (Single Remix) */ I Know Why I'm in Love / Big Man in a Little Suit* **US Release:** April 1, 1998, on Island Records (ref. 314-568-762-8) **Best US Chart Ranking:** 55

The melody of "Recover Your Soul" shows signs of an assured arrangement, starting with its fine percussion, which is surrounded by the benevolent backing vocals of Carol Kenyon and Jackie Rawe. Elton and his mellow organ sound sit comfortably alongside a warm acoustic guitar, a rounded bass, and slightly nonchalant drums all coming to the rescue of Bernie, whose inspiration has left him high and dry, narrating yet another story of lost love. "Love was a fire but it stopped burning," he writes. But Elton and his group construe it all in a different way and transform the song into an anthem full of hope, around which Elton's artfully modulated voice pulsates, undulating between gentleness and virility. No fatalities here: With "Release, relax, let go," Elton finds an anchor point and turns it into the song's positive mantra.

JANUARY

Elton John, Bernie Taupin / 4:00

Musicians: Elton John: vocals, piano / **Davey Johnstone:** guitars / **John Jorgenson:** guitars **Bob Birch:** bass / **Charlie Morgan:** drums, percussion / **Anne Dudley:** direction, arrangements / **Guy Babylon:** keyboards, arrangements / **Orchestra:** uncredited **Recorded:** Townhouse Studios, London / AIR Lyndhurst Hall, London: November 1996–May 1997 **Technical Team:** Producer: Chris Thomas / **Sound Engineer:** Pete Lewis / **Assistant Sound Engineers:** Ben Georgiades, Andy Green, Jay Reynolds / **Sessions Coordinators:** Maureen Hillier, Ranni Lewis, Derek MacKillop / **Studio Coordinators:** Adrian Collee, Pete Mills

Seasons come and go, and sometimes they're accompanied by the birth of a passionate love. But the month of January remains engraved in the memory of the narrator, for a night of passion spent together with a lover under the stars by the warmth of a camp fire: "Must have kissed you till I hurt you / Must have been a wild night / Must have rolled in the ashes at the break of day." The music does not in any way express this romanticism, with a harmonic and instrumental development that is difficult to follow. The keyboards dominate initially, until Davey's and John's guitars in turn make timid entries. Bob Birch's bass seems to have been amputated from its fundamental frequencies, supplanted by superfluous strings. As for Elton's voice, it is the worst feature, sounding like an extra in his own song.

I CAN'T STEER MY HEART CLEAR OF YOU

Elton John, Bernie Taupin / 4:08

Musicians: Elton John: vocals, piano / **Davey Johnstone:** guitars / **John Jorgenson:** guitars / **Bob Birch:** bass / **Charlie Morgan:** drums, percussion / **Matthew Vaughan:** keyboards, percussion / **Anne Dudley:** direction, arrangements / **Guy Babylon:** arrangements **Recorded:** Townhouse Studios, London / AIR Lyndhurst Hall, London: November 1996–May 1997 **Technical Team:** Producer: Chris Thomas / **Sound Engineer:** Pete Lewis / **Assistant Sound Engineers:** Ben Georgiades, Andy Green, Jay Reynolds / **Sessions Coordinators:** Maureen Hillier, Ranni Lewis, Derek MacKillop / **Studio Coordinators:** Adrian Collee and Pete Mills

As influential as he was in Elton's career, Bernie Taupin was unsuccessful in imposing his idea of creating an album in the same vein as Frank Sinatra or Tony Bennett. Only the penultimate number in the track list, "I Can't Steer My Heart Clear of You," comes fairly close to the sounds of classic crooners, with its full melody and orchestral dimension. The swirling and stormy strings sequence owes much to the orchestral direction of Anne Dudley, enabling the melody to be lifted higher before eventually cresting and falling like an immense wave. This song is one of the most complex arrangements on the album, and it has careful keyboards provided by guest player Matthew Vaughan. Davey Johnstone's and John Jorgenson's guitars also shine out alongside the keyboards. The ensemble serves the lyrics perfectly, which compare life to a ship that is difficult to maneuver in the face of the squalls of desire that often send a boat off its course.

WICKED DREAMS

Elton John, Bernie Taupin / 4:40

Musicians: Elton John: vocals, piano, organ / **Davey Johnstone:** guitars / **John Jorgenson:** guitars / **Bob Birch:** bass / **Charlie Morgan:** drums, percussion / **Anne Dudley:** direction, arrangements / **Guy Babylon:** keyboards, arrangements **Orchestra:** uncredited **Recorded:** Townhouse Studios, London / AIR Lyndhurst Hall, London: November 1996–May 1997 **Technical Team:** Producer: Chris Thomas / **Sound Engineer:** Pete Lewis / **Assistant Sound Engineers:** Ben Georgiades, Andy Green, Jay Reynolds / **Sessions Coordinators:** Maureen Hillier, Ranni Lewis, Derek MacKillop / **Studio Coordinators:** Adrian Collee, Pete Mills

The melody of "Wicked Dreams" is fairly straightforward and it has very little variation between the verses and the refrains, but this never undermines its effectiveness. This piece is one of the few on the album, along with "If the River Can Bend," that manages to take on a fairly sustained tempo. The group of musicians had an opportunity with this number to interact in a more natural way than on the more elaborate songs. Above all, Elton wanted to conclude *The Big Picture* on a positive note, with a cheerful melody—even if this was in contrast with the lyrics, which consist of an invitation from the narrator to join in his most indecent dreams. While Davey Johnstone's and John Jorgenson's guitars are present at the start, "Wicked Dreams" is mainly built on a foundation of vibrant strings directed by Anne Dudley, while Elton adds a nice, dynamic piano in the background.

Elton John was filled with energy during a concert at Madison Square Garden on October 21, 2000.

Elton John One Night Only—The Greatest Hits was released on November 13, 2000, less than one month after it was recorded at Madison Square Garden. Contrary to what the title suggests, the live album was recorded over two evenings on October 20 and 21, 2000.

I KNOW WHY I'M IN LOVE

Elton John, Bernie Taupin / 4:27

Maxi CD: *Recover Your Soul* (Single Remix) / *Big Man in a Little Suit* / *I Know Why I'm in Love* / *Recover Your Soul* (Album Version) **UK Release:** February 1998 on Rocket Record Company (ref. EJSCD 42) / Mercury (ref. 568 219-2) **Best UK Chart Ranking:** 16 **Maxi CD:** *Recover Your Soul* (Single Remix) / *I Know Why I'm in Love* / *Big Man in a Little Suit* **US Release:** April 1, 1998, on Island Records (ref. 314-568-762-8) **Best US Chart Ranking:** 55 **Musicians:** Elton John: vocals, piano / **Davey Johnstone:** guitars / **John Jorgenson:** guitars / **Bob Birch:** bass / **Charlie Morgan:** drums, percussion / **Anne Dudley:** direction, arrangements / **Guy Babylon:** keyboards, arrangements / **Orchestra:** uncredited **Recorded:** Townhouse Studios, London / AIR Lyndhurst Hall, London: January 16, 1997 **Technical Team: Producer:** Chris Thomas / **Sound Engineer:** Pete Lewis / **Assistant Sound Engineers:** Ben Georgiades, Andy Green, Jay Reynolds / **Sessions Coordinators:** Maureen Hillier, Ranni Lewis, Derek MacKillop / **Studio Coordinators:** Adrian Collee, Pete Mills

Elton's melodic approach to "I Know Why I'm in Love" was constructed around a moderate tempo, with elegant backing vocals and a swaying arrangement that owes much to the Beach Boys. The strings—arranged by Guy Babylon and Anne Dudley, and directed by Anne Dudley—add warmth, in the same way as the guitar, with a fine distortion provided by Davey Johnstone, and the deliberately exaggerated voice of Elton. Playful keyboards adorn the string playing in the finale, while the guitars discreetly accompany the movement. Still short of inspiration, Bernie lists the reasons why the narrator is in love with his other half. The words often seem naïve, although rather tender, as in the first verse: "I wake up and I look at the clock / In the middle of the night my heart stops / When I see you in the moonlight / I know why I'm in love." Recorded during the sessions for *The Big Picture*, the song was held in reserve and used as a B-side of "Something About the Way You Look Tonight" in 1997 and "Recover Your Soul" (Single Remix) in 1998.

BIG MAN IN A LITTLE SUIT

Elton John, Bernie Taupin / 4:25

Maxi CD: *Recover Your Soul* (Single Remix) / *Big Man in a Little Suit* / *I Know Why I'm in Love* / *Recover Your Soul* (Album Version) **UK Release:** February 1998 on Rocket Record Company (ref. EJSCD 42) / Mercury (ref. 568 219-2) **Best UK Chart Ranking:** 16 *Recover Your Soul* (Single Remix) / *I Know Why I'm in Love* / *Big Man in a Little Suit* **US Release:** April 1, 1998, on Island Records (ref. 314-568-762-8) **Best US Chart Ranking:** 55 **Musicians:** Elton John: chant, piano / **Davey Johnstone:** guitars / **John Jorgenson:** guitars / **Bob Birch:** bass / **Charlie Morgan:** drums, percussion / **Guy Babylon:** keyboards **Recorded:** Townhouse Studios, London / AIR Lyndhurst Hall, London: April 27, 1997 **Technical Team: Producer:** Chris Thomas / **Sound Engineer:** Pete Lewis / **Assistant Sound Engineers:** Ben Georgiades, Andy Green, Jay Reynolds / **Sessions Coordinators:** Maureen Hillier, Ranni Lewis, Derek MacKillop / **Studio Coordinators:** Adrian Collee, Pete Mills

"Big Man in a Little Suit" was unjustly left off the final track listing of *The Big Picture*, which is too bad because it could've added a little energy to the track list. Approached in a youthful, even regressive way by Elton, who gave Davey Johnstone's raw slide guitar the keys to the bus on this occasion, the B-side of "Recover Your Soul" temporarily plunges the singer back into the crazy years of the 1970s. It's too bad that Bernie's lyrics fail to stand out in their originality. This song is about a man trying to reconquer a love abandoned for the sake of his career after he realizes that work isn't the only thing that matters: "I want to get back to loving you / Give me one more chance / Won't you warm the hands of this cold headed fool?"

ALBUM

SONGS FROM THE WEST COAST

The Emperor's New Clothes . Dark Diamond . Look Ma, No Hands . American Triangle .
Original Sin . Birds . I Want Love . The Wasteland . Ballad of the Boy in the Red Shoes .
Love Her Like Me . Mansfield . This Train Don't Stop There Anymore

RELEASE DATES
UK Release: October 1, 2001
Reference: Rocket Record Company/Mercury—586 330-2
Best UK Chart Ranking: 2
US Release: October 1, 2001
Reference: Mercury—314 586 330-2
Best US Chart Ranking: 15

I'm still standing.

Want strong bones? Drinking enough lowfat milk now can help prevent osteoporosis later.

got milk?

Elton appeared in a "Got milk?" campaign in 2001.

Songs from the West Coast (2001) displayed Elton's renewed sense of vitality and enthusiasm for his work.

A CAREER TURNING POINT

He was now to be addressed as "Sir Elton John." On February 24, 1998, the artist was received by Queen Elizabeth II at Buckingham Palace to become a knight and a Commander of the Most Excellent Order of the British Empire, under the very proud gaze of his mother, his stepfather, and David Furnish, his partner. Elton's father, Stanley Dwight, had unfortunately passed away in December 1991 and was not able to witness this major achievement in his son's career.

A few days after the ceremony, a cold dose of reality was delivered. Elton learned that some of his employees had not been paid for several months and that he was on the brink of financial ruin. How could the star be debt-ridden when he had had so many commercial successes? All questions led to John Reid. Elton's manager and right-hand man since the beginning of the 1970s—and also his lover for many years—Reid, it seems, had been at the very least negligent in the management of the singer's assets, of which he'd had total control. In 2000, Elton instigated legal proceedings against Reid, and the case was eventually settled out of court with John Reid agreeing to pay nearly $5 million in compensation to the artist.

The Ryan Adams Moment

The second millennium seemed to begin rather favorably for Elton, who had seen two years of continuous musical success: The stage adaptation of *The Lion King* won him a Tony Award in 1998, as did *Aida* in 1999, which also earned him a Grammy in 2001. In 2000, his discography was augmented by a new film score for the animated film *The Road to El Dorado*, co-written with Tim Rice. Finally, a live album also saw the light of day: *One Night Only: The Greatest Hits* was derived from a performance recorded by Phil Ramone at Madison Square Garden on October 20 and 21, 2000, and it was released very shortly afterward, on November 13.

Despite this flurry of activity, Elton's fans were languishing. It had been nearly four years since the artist had conceived a studio album. But 2001 gave the fans what they were waiting for, thanks to Ryan Adams. The young songwriter, who reenergized the country-folk genre with his anarchic mix of nonchalance and sensitivity, released his first album, *Heartbreaker*, on September 5, 2000, and it was a real revelation for Elton—to the extent that the fifty-three-year-old star thanked Adams,

Producer Pat Leonard (here with Elton John in 2001) took the controls for the new opus and applied some drastic changes to the singer's working patterns.

in the credits of his twenty-seventh opus, *Songs from the West Coast*, for having "inspired me to do better." Elton John shared this musical revelation with Bernie while they were staying in the South of France in 2000, and at the same time announced his desire to get back to work. What Elton took from Ryan Adams's album was the simplicity of his intent: "I think Elton realized that for a long time he might have been chasing trends in music, not necessarily setting them like he once did," Bernie Taupin later said. "After writing all those songs for Broadway and movies, I think he wanted to get his hands dirty again and do something without thinking about the marketplace or whether it is going to get on the radio or what is most likely to sell."[137]

The star wanted to establish different working methods and to rediscover the freshness of his earliest days. Elton asked Bernie to write as many lyrics as possible. When they met again in Los Angeles in September 2000 to finalize the compositions, the two men set out a new working protocol. For the first time in their careers, they would be working together in the same room. While this may seem like a natural way to operate for most writer/composer teams, Bernie and Elton had never worked in this manner.

The Pat Leonard Effect

Evoking the past, even as a way of trying to move on from it, inevitably caused a wave of nostalgia for Bernie. This focus on this past served as his inspiration for all the songs on the album, particularly with "This Train Don't Stop There Anymore," one of the standout pieces on the disk that was chosen as a single and ranked twenty-fourth in the United Kingdom

when it was released. But the first number composed for the album was something rare for Bernie: "American Triangle" was written as an homage to Matthew Shepard, a young student who was tortured and killed in Laramie, Wyoming, because of his homosexuality.

Once the new batch of songs was put together, Elton John turned to Patrick Ray Leonard, known as Pat Leonard, the producer who had assisted him on *The Road to El Dorado*. He had previously worked with Bryan Ferry (*Bête Noire*, 1987), Roger Waters (*Amused to Death*, 1992), and Madonna. Pat was not a man given to compromise. He had heard about Elton John's need for change, and he took this need literally, first checking to make sure that this was not just posturing on the part of the artist. Once this need for change was confirmed, Pat pushed Elton completely outside of his comfort zone by bringing in a new group of musicians. Guy Babylon, Bob Birch, and John Mahon, who had accompanied him on tour for some time, were all suddenly out. Instead, Elton was joined by percussionist Jay Bellerose, guitarist Rusty Anderson, drummer Matt Chamberlain, and bassist Paul Bushnell. Patrick Leonard gave himself a major role as well by playing various keyboards on the album. "I have to say that one of the biggest regrets of my life is that I've not fallen out, but I've drifted away from Pat," confessed Elton. "I feel very ungrateful to Pat that I didn't make another record with him. We were so close on that record, he shifted me so much in the direction that I wanted to go."[35] This infusion of new blood did not, per se, mean a complete departure from the past; in fact, some of the dream team were brought back: Paul Buckmaster, Davey Johnstone, and Nigel Olsson were all once

Elton John showed an interest in a rising star from a new generation: Rufus Wainwright.

In the panoramic photo used for the cover of the album, Elton's partner David Furnish can be seen dressed as a cowboy.

again on the recording docket. Some guest stars also made appearances on some songs, including Rufus Wainwright on "American Triangle," Stevie Wonder on harmonica on "Dark Diamond," and Billy Preston, who makes his Hammond B3 organ sing on "I Want Love," "The Wasteland," and "Love Her Like Me."

Life at the Château

Patrick Leonard was a memorable character in his own right, and he liked working in the traditional way. At a time when many studios were moving entirely to digital, the producer liked the use of analog tapes to preserve the warmth of the instruments. He and Elton were on the same page on this point. This time Elton would not be composing on top of a drum loop. The singer wanted to return to the feelings of the old days, recording with a reduced team and creating a musical roar via guitar, bass, drums, and, of course, piano. "I'm there at the piano, singing these songs as we were putting down the rough tracks and thinking, 'God, this sounds really good.' It was how we used to do it years ago at the Château with the old

band."[138] If this leaves one imagining ideal recording sessions filled with direct takes, well, the reality was less idyllic. Recording sessions were split between several studios, which detracted slightly from the team's spontaneity. In fact, Elton's vocals were immortalized at the Townhouse Studios in London, while Rufus Wainwright recorded his vocals at Ocean Way Recording in Los Angeles, the Stevie Wonder takes took place at Wonderland Studios (LA), and the strings and brass arrangements were done at Cello Studios (LA). The rest of the recording sessions took place at Johnny Yuma Recording and at Sony Music Studios, also located in Los Angeles.

The press unanimously praised this lively new direction that Elton's career was taking. Carried by the singles "I Want Love," "This Train Don't Stop There Anymore," and "Original Sin," whose music videos featured appearances from celebrities like Robert Downey Jr., Justin Timberlake, and Elizabeth Taylor, Elton's first opus of the twenty-first century went to second place in the charts in the United Kingdom, and to fifteenth place in the United States. The public had not forgotten Elton, just as he had not forgotten where he came from.

THE EMPEROR'S NEW CLOTHES

Elton John, Bernie Taupin / 4:29

Musicians: Elton John: vocals, piano / Davey Johnstone: guitars, backing vocals / Paul Bushnell: bass, backing vocals / Nigel Olsson: drums, backing vocals / Jay Bellerose: percussion / Paul Buckmaster: direction, arrangements / Orchestra: uncredited **Recorded:** Townhouse Studios, London / Cello Studios, Sony Music Studios, Johnny Yuma Recording, Los Angeles: September 18, 2000–April 30, 2001 **Technical Team:** Producer: Patrick Leonard / **Sound Engineers:** Joe Chiccarelli, Brian Scheuble / **Assistant Sound Engineers:** Andy Green, Jennifer Hilliard, Katrina Leigh, Jonathan Merritt, Alan Sanderson, Todd Shoemaker, Tom Stanley / **Artistic Direction Coordinators:** Todd Interland, Derek MacKillop / **Production Coordinators:** Adrian Collee, Suzanne Ybarra / **Mixing:** Bill Bottrell / **Mixing Assistant:** Alan Sanderson / **Mastering:** Stewart Whitmore

"The Emperor's New Clothes" takes its title from a tale written by Hans Christian Andersen in 1837, in which a vain emperor demands new clothes be made for him. Two passing swindlers pretend to be tailors and play on his credulousness: They manage to persuade him that they have made clothes that only stupid people cannot see. The emperor thus walks around unclothed until he realizes the deception. With this literary projection, Bernie recalls his partnership with Elton at the beginning of the 1970s, when they were completely broke but had fun pretending that the world was their oyster. In this piece, Elton gives in to fans who wanted him to put the piano back at the center of his arrangements, and he leaves out his sound experimentations, playing only piano/voice during the composition phase. This is how he laid down this song that Billy Joel might have been proud of. With discreet backing vocals, the instrumental parts create a very American groove, which takes us back to the golden days of *Tumbleweed Connection* or *Madman Across the Water*. Elton's voice, as fresh as it was in the 1970s, is given perfect prominence: It delicately accentuates the word "clothes" and gives us a very fine vibrato in the finale, at 3:53, followed by a "Yeah" of heartfelt satisfaction at 3:56.

DARK DIAMOND

Elton John, Bernie Taupin / 4:27

Musicians: Elton John: vocals, piano / Davey Johnstone: guitars, backing vocals / Paul Bushnell: bass, backing vocals / Matt Chamberlain: drums / Patrick Leonard: Hammond B3 organ / Stevie Wonder: Clavinet, harmonica / Nigel Olsson: backing vocals **Recorded:** Townhouse Studios, London / Sony Music Studios, Johnny Yuma Recording, Wonderland Studios, Los Angeles: September 18, 2000–April 30, 2001 **Technical Team:** Producer: Patrick Leonard / **Sound Engineers:** Joe Chiccarelli, Brian Scheuble, Ralph Sutton / **Assistant Sound Engineers:** Andy Green, Jennifer Hilliard, Steve Jones, Katrina Leigh, Jonathan Merritt, Alan Sanderson, Todd Shoemaker, Tom Stanley / **Artistic Direction Coordinators:** Todd Interland, Derek MacKillop / **Production Coordinators:** Adrian Collee, Suzanne Ybarra / **Mixing:** Bill Bottrell / **Mixing Assistant:** Alan Sanderson / **Mastering:** Stewart Whitmore

Elton surprises us with this swaying reggae piece, which is at times reminiscent of "Durban Deep" on *Sleeping with the Past*. With a funky bass and a refrain with an irresistible swing, it includes, above all, the contribution of Stevie Wonder on his rhythmic Clavinet and generating positive waves with his highly distinctive harmonica. Wonder adds a great deal to this haunting piece, alongside Patrick Leonard's Hammond organ. Nigel Olsson boosts the backing vocals alongside Davey Johnstone, with his discreet guitar, and bassist Paul Bushnell. Bernie's lyrics are polished like a diamond and they constitute an anthem to perseverance and the need to steel oneself in the face of a broken heart. Unfortunately, Elton has not performed "Dark Diamond" onstage with any kind of frequency, which is a shame since this piece would lend itself very well to live performance.

LOOK MA, NO HANDS

Elton John, Bernie Taupin / 4:22

Musicians: Elton John: vocals, piano / Davey Johnstone: electric guitar, backing vocals / David Channing: acoustic guitar / Paul Bushnell: bass, backing vocals / Nigel Olsson: drums, backing vocals / Patrick Leonard: organ / Jay Bellerose: percussion **Recorded:** Townhouse Studios, London / Sony Music Studios, Johnny Yuma Recording, Los Angeles: September 18, 2000–April 30, 2001 **Technical Team:** Producer: Patrick Leonard / **Sound Engineers:** David Channing, Joe Chiccarelli, Brian Scheuble / **Assistant Sound Engineers:** Andy Green, Jennifer Hilliard, Katrina Leigh, Jonathan Merritt, Alan Sanderson, Todd Shoemaker, Tom Stanley / **Artistic Direction Coordinators:** Todd Interland, Derek MacKillop / **Production Coordinators:** Adrian Collee, Suzanne Ybarra / **Mixing:** Bill Bottrell / **Mixing Assistant:** Alan Sanderson / **Mastering:** Stewart Whitmore

This song starts with an authentic seventies feeling, once again sounding similar to *Tumbleweed Connection* even though the tempo is slightly faster. This seventies vibe eventually subsides with the very prominent appearance of the drums, which anchor the piece more in the 1990s. Bernie's lyrics refer to one of his adolescent passions shared with Elton—science fiction: "Been down in Roswell when the Martians came / [...] I'm a super power, I'm a handy man." But it is also a question of making his mother proud, a desire of Elton's for a large part of his life: "Didn't I turn out, didn't I turn out to be / Everything you wanted Ma, ain't you proud of me?" the narrator asks her. In this piece, with its very pronounced country spirit, Elton's soothing piano and comforting voice particularly stand out, with the precision of the backing vocals magnificently enveloping him until the ecstasy of the last bars, and also Davey Johnstone's effective solo at 3:51.

AMERICAN TRIANGLE

Elton John, Bernie Taupin / 4:49

Musicians: Elton John: vocals, piano / **Rufus Wainwright:** vocals / **Rusty Anderson:** electric guitar / **Bruce Gaitsch:** acoustic guitar / **Paul Bushnell:** bass / **Matt Chamberlain:** drums / **Patrick Leonard:** Hammond B3 organ, keyboards **Recorded:** Townhouse Studios, London / Sony Music Studios, Johnny Yuma Recording, Ocean Way Studios, Los Angeles: September 18, 2000–April 30, 2001 **Technical Team: Producer:** Patrick Leonard / **Sound Engineers:** Joe Chiccarelli, Brian Scheuble / **Assistant Sound Engineers:** Andy Green, Jennifer Hilliard, Katrina Leigh, Jonathan Merritt, Alan Sanderson, Todd Shoemaker, Tom Stanley / **Artistic Direction Coordinators:** Todd Interland, Derek MacKillop / **Production Coordinators:** Adrian Collee, Suzanne Ybarra / **Mixing:** Bill Bottrell / **Mixing Assistant:** Alan Sanderson / **Mastering:** Stewart Whitmore

Elton has a particular affection for "American Triangle," a poignant piano ballad that he refers to with great emotion in his autobiography, calling it "a very harrowing, angry song about the homophobic murder of Matthew Shephard [sic] in Wyoming in 1998."[3] Bernie's lyrics are indeed powerful and uncompromising: "God hates fags where we come from [...] It's a cold wind blowing, Wyoming / See two coyotes run down a deer / Hate what we don't understand / You pioneers give us your children / But it's your blood that stains their hands." Elton's vocal performance, which is unusually somber, is striking, and Rufus Wainwright's backing vocals are brilliantly executed. While there is absolutely nothing to reproach in the arrangement, which is understated and perfect, an alternative version limited only to piano and vocals would certainly have won over many fans. Played onstage beginning in April 2000, a few months before the song was actually recorded, "American Triangle" was then constructed around a more sustained tempo before being laid down on the album.

ORIGINAL SIN

Elton John, Bernie Taupin / 4:49

Musicians: Elton John: vocals, piano / **Rusty Anderson:** guitars / **Paul Bushnell:** bass / **Matt Chamberlain:** drums / **Patrick Leonard:** keyboards / **Jay Bellerose:** percussion / **Paul Buckmaster:** direction, arrangements / **Orchestra:** uncredited **Recorded:** Townhouse Studios, London / Cello Studios, Sony Music Studios, Johnny Yuma Recording, Los Angeles: September 18, 2000–April 30, 2001 **Technical Team: Producer:** Patrick Leonard / **Sound Engineers:** Joe Chiccarelli, Brian Scheuble / **Assistant Sound Engineers:** Andy Green, Jennifer Hilliard, Katrina Leigh, Jonathan Merritt, Alan Sanderson, Todd Shoemaker, Tom Stanley / **Artistic Direction Coordinators:** Todd Interland, Derek MacKillop / **Production Coordinators:** Adrian Collee, Suzanne Ybarra / **Mixing:** Bill Bottrell / **Mixing Assistant:** Alan Sanderson / **Mastering:** Stewart Whitmore **Single Release:** CD1: *Original Sin / I'm Still Standing* (Live) / *This Train Don't Stop There*

Anymore (Live) **UK Release:** April 1, 2002, on Rocket Record Company/Mercury (ref. 588 999-2) **Best UK Chart Ranking:** 39 **Maxi CD:** *Original Sin / Original Sin* (Live) / *All The Girls Love Alice* (Live) **UK Release:** April 1, 2002, on Rocket Record Company/Mercury (ref. 582 850-2) **Best UK Chart Ranking:** Did Not Chart

At the first hearing of the album in front of a panel of fans, "Original Sin" clearly stood out as one of the favorite pieces. This is quite an amusing outcome when one realizes that this song includes the least amount of Elton's piano. Elton uses his instrument in particular in the finale to insert a subtle reference to "Did He Shoot Her," a song from *Breaking Hearts*. He never concealed that he had a particular affection for "Original Sin," considering it "one of the best songs [he had] ever written."[35] In this atmospheric track with its catchy refrain and full melody, the country guitar arpeggios played by Rusty Anderson are slightly reminiscent of "Conquer the Sun," while the restrained arrangements by Paul Buckmaster work very effectively. Bernie's heartbreaking lyrics linger on a one-sided love, perhaps for a celebrity as the music video may suggest via a plot that features Mandy Moore worshipping Elton, who in turn only has eyes for Elizabeth Taylor—but there could be many other possible interpretations.

BIRDS

Elton John, Bernie Taupin / 3:52

Musicians: Elton John: vocals, piano, harmonium / **Rusty Anderson:** guitars / **David Channing:** Dobro / **Paul Bushnell:** bass / **Matt Chamberlain:** drums, percussion **Recorded:** Townhouse Studios, London / Sony Music Studios, Johnny Yuma Recording, Los Angeles: September 18, 2000–April 30, 2001 **Technical Team: Producer:** Patrick Leonard / **Sound Engineers:** Joe Chiccarelli, Brian Scheuble / **Assistant Sound Engineers:** Andy Green, Jennifer Hilliard, Katrina Leigh, Jonathan Merritt, Alan Sanderson, Todd Shoemaker, Tom Stanley / **Artistic Direction Coordinators:** Todd Interland, Derek MacKillop / **Production Coordinators:** Adrian Collee, Suzanne Ybarra / **Mixing:** Bill Bottrell / **Mixing Assistant:** Alan Sanderson / **Mastering:** Stewart Whitmore

Although the West Coast is specifically referenced in the album title, "Birds" sounds like it comes straight out of the Deep South. This song is also clearly reminiscent of the cheerful "Jack Rabbit," an outtake from *Goodbye Yellow Brick Road* in 1973. Elton's very lively piano is well-supported by a harmonium, while David Channing's rough Dobro pairs with Rusty Anderson's fiery guitar. Bernie's lyrics are sometimes rather choice, as with this typically childlike phrase: "How come birds / Don't fall from the sky when they die?" which elicits a response that is both poetic and touching: because they always look for a quiet place to hide. As the watermark of the song, Bernie is referring to parts of ourselves that we hide from the outside world.

An exploration of American music would not be complete without paying homage to the great Robert Johnson.

The music video for "I Want Love" was filmed in one continuous take. It featured actor Robert Downey Jr. walking through a giant California mansion while singing the song in playback. The sixteenth take was eventually used for the video.

I WANT LOVE

Elton John, Bernie Taupin / 4:35

Musicians: Elton John: vocals, piano / **Davey Johnstone:** electric guitar, backing vocals / **Bruce Gaitsch:** acoustic guitar / **Paul Bushnell:** bass, backing vocals / **Nigel Olsson:** drums, backing vocals / **Billy Preston:** Hammond B3 organ / **Jay Bellerose:** percussion / **Kudisan Kai:** backing vocals **Recorded:** Townhouse Studios, London / Sony Music Studios, Johnny Yuma Recording, Los Angeles: September 18, 2000–April 30, 2001 **Technical Team:** Producer: Patrick Leonard / **Sound Engineers:** Joe Chiccarelli, Brian Scheuble / **Assistant Sound Engineers:** Andy Green, Jennifer Hilliard, Katrina Leigh, Jonathan Merritt, Alan Sanderson, Todd Shoemaker, Tom Stanley / **Artistic Direction Coordinators:** Todd Interland, Derek MacKillop / **Production Coordinators:** Adrian Collee, Suzanne Ybarra / **Mixing:** Bill Bottrell / **Mixing Assistant:** Alan Sanderson / **Mastering:** Stewart Whitmore **Single Release:** CD1: *I Want Love / The North Star / Tiny Dancer* **UK Release:** September 24, 2001, on Rocket Record Company/Mercury (ref. 588 706-2) **Best UK Chart Ranking:** 9 CD2: *I Want Love / God Never Came There / The One* **UK Release:** September 24, 2001, on Rocket Record Company/Mercury (ref. 588 707-2) **Best UK Chart Ranking:** 9

Bernie submits himself to an exercise in contrition on "I Want Love," which was an indisputable hit and the first single from the album. In the song he describes himself as "irresponsible," "dead in places," as someone who feels "nothing, just old scars," as though with a hard heart, but nonetheless aspiring to a love he considers to be "impossible." The lyricist also does not shy away from addressing the autobiographical aspect of his text: "It's very close [to the truth], but you have to remember that most of the songs you write are only moments of time. You might feel the emotion of the song just for a few hours or a few days, then feel totally different by the time the song is finished or recorded. When you listen to it then, you might go, 'My God, I don't feel like that anymore. It's so bitter.' But if everyone edited themselves like that, we would have lost some of the greatest songs ever written."[137]

"I Want Love" very clearly evokes "Free as a Bird," which was published by the three remaining Beatles, Paul McCartney, Ringo Starr, and George Harrison, on the first volume of their *Anthology* in 1995. "I Want Love" features the same heavy drums that come in after an intimate introduction, the same moderate tempo, the same guitar tinged with tremolo in the accompaniment, and the same wailing guitar on the solo. Everything here is reminiscent of the Liverpool Fab Four, and even the harmonic framework seems not too far from that of "Free as a Bird."

Three pillars provided Elton with marvelous support on "I Want Love": Nigel Olsson's drums contribute a solid line over which Paul Bushnell simply has to fit his bass, while Davey Johnstone shines brightly on electric guitar. In addition, the three men blend in impressive vocal harmonies, which helpfully envelope Elton's powerful voice. More discreet, but no less indispensable to the bedrock of the song, Bruce Gaitsch shows great discipline on acoustic guitar and contributes an extra layer of brilliance to the ensemble. Like a final musical reference to the Beatles, Billy Preston, who was a prospective recruit for the Beatles before they split up, here delivers a warm Hammond organ line. One of Elton's favorite pieces, "I Want Love" rose to ninth place in the British charts and was played over two hundred times onstage by the singer, who was nominated for the 44th Annual Grammy Awards in 2002 in the Best Male Pop Vocal Performance category, although the award was taken home by James Taylor for "Don't Let Me Be Lonely Tonight."

THE WASTELAND

Elton John, Bernie Taupin / 4:21

Musicians: Elton John: vocals, piano / Davey Johnstone: guitars / Paul Bushnell: bass / Nigel Olsson: drums / Billy Preston: Hammond B3 organ / Kudisan Kai, Táta Vega: backing vocals **Recorded:** Townhouse Studios, London / Sony Music Studios, Johnny Yuma Recording, Los Angeles: September 18, 2000–April 30, 2001 **Technical Team:** Producer: Patrick Leonard / Sound Engineers: Joe Chiccarelli, Brian Scheuble / Assistant Sound Engineers: Andy Green, Jennifer Hilliard, Katrina Leigh, Jonathan Merritt, Alan Sanderson, Todd Shoemaker, Tom Stanley / Artistic Direction Coordinators: Todd Interland, Derek MacKillop / Production Coordinators: Adrian Collee, Suzanne Ybarra / Mixing: Bill Bottrell / Mixing Assistant: Alan Sanderson / Mastering: Stewart Whitmore

As the first piece on the album with a sustained tempo, "The Wasteland" anchors itself solidly in blues-rock territory and forcefully illustrates Elton's musical roots, which were very much influenced by the music of the United States' West Coast. The piece begins with a classic blues riff before evolving in the direction of a hybrid melodic rock whose secret is well-known to Elton. Bernie emphasizes the piece's blues pedigree with a marked reference to Robert Johnson, the famous guitarist around whom a myth grew up wherein he sold his soul to the devil in exchange for his virtuosity: "Come on Robert Johnson / Though we're worlds apart / You and I know what it's like / With the devil in our heart." The legendary Billy Preston, just as much at ease at the front of the stage as in the role of session musician, seasons the line played on his Hammond organ with a warm, retro sound. His precise musical placement enables him to slot in some short, snappy punctuation on the track.

BALLAD OF THE BOY IN THE RED SHOES

Elton John, Bernie Taupin / 4:52

Musicians: Elton John: vocals, piano / Davey Johnstone: acoustic guitar, mandolin, backing vocals / Paul Bushnell: bass, backing vocals / Nigel Olsson: drums, backing vocals / Jay Bellerose: percussion / Paul Buckmaster: direction, arrangements / Orchestra: uncredited **Recorded:** Townhouse Studios, London / Cello Studios, Sony Music Studios, Johnny Yuma Recording, Los Angeles: September 18, 2000–April 30, 2001 **Technical Team:** Producer: Patrick Leonard / Sound Engineers: Joe Chiccarelli, Brian Scheuble / Assistant Sound Engineers: Andy Green, Jennifer Hilliard, Katrina Leigh, Jonathan Merritt, Alan Sanderson, Todd Shoemaker, Tom Stanley / Artistic Direction Coordinators: Todd Interland, Derek MacKillop / Production Coordinators: Adrian Collee, Suzanne Ybarra / Mixing: Bill Bottrell / Mixing Assistant: Alan Sanderson / Mastering: Stewart Whitmore

An elegant ritornello worthy of *Madman Across the Water*, "Ballad of the Boy in the Red Shoes" has a luxuriant arrangement masterfully directed by Paul Buckmaster. The presence of Davey Johnstone, who irrigates the piece with magnificent mandolin ornaments, is decisive. Elton has played this number very often onstage and always presents it in the same way, explaining that its narrator is a dancer suffering from AIDS who cannot be resigned to losing everything that makes his life worth living. Bernie's lyrics are strikingly emotional: "Screaming on the inside / Give me your water, help me survive / Gonna miss the sunlight / When I lose my eyesight / Give me my red shoes, I want to dance." At the finale, Bernie's heartrending lyrics "Take my red shoes, I can't wear them anymore" are a direct allusion to "Knockin' on Heaven's Door" by Bob Dylan, echoing the lyrics of the folk troubadour: "put my guns in the ground / I can't shoot them anymore."

LOVE HER LIKE ME

Elton John, Bernie Taupin / 3:58

Musicians: Elton John: vocals, piano / **Rusty Anderson:** guitars / **Paul Bushnell:** bass, backing vocals / **Matt Chamberlain:** drums / **Patrick Leonard:** Mellotron / **Billy Preston:** Hammond B3 organ / **Davey Johnstone, Nigel Olsson:** backing vocals **Recorded:** Townhouse Studios, London / Sony Music Studios, Johnny Yuma Recording, Los Angeles: September 18, 2000–April 30, 2001 **Technical Team:** Producer: Patrick Leonard / **Sound Engineers:** Joe Chiccarelli, Brian Scheuble / **Assistant Sound Engineers:** Andy Green, Jennifer Hilliard, Katrina Leigh, Jonathan Merritt, Alan Sanderson, Todd Shoemaker, Tom Stanley: **Artistic Direction Coordinators:** Todd Interland, Derek MacKillop / **Production Coordinators:** Adrian Collee, Suzanne Ybarra / **Mixing:** Bill Bottrell / **Mixing Assistant:** Alan Sanderson / **Mastering:** Stewart Whitmore

2001

With its production anchored in the 1990s and its effective although run-of-the-mill refrain, "Love Her Like Me" could quite easily have been part of *Made in England*. The contribution of Billy Preston, the keyboard player in whom Ray Charles saw his successor, is almost inaudible because his Hammond organ is drowned in the sound spectrum. Davey Johnstone puts down his guitar to provide some syrupy backing vocals, leaving Rusty Anderson in charge of interpreting a motif that is catchy, but that remains pegged to the rhythm and whose qualities are above all loud, with his very California *twang*. Elton's piano remains in the background, giving greater scope to the group. Once again Bernie's lyrics tell a story of lost love. In this case a rich man has married the narrator's ex, which sends her a clear message: He may make this new woman change her name and let her live on top of a mountain of money, but he will never be able to love her in the same way.

MANSFIELD

Elton John, Bernie Taupin / 4:53

Musicians: Elton John: vocals, piano / **Davey Johnstone:** acoustic guitar, backing vocals / **Rusty Anderson:** electric guitar, bouzouki / **Paul Bushnell:** bass, backing vocals / **Matt Chamberlain:** drums / **Patrick Leonard:** keyboards / **Paul Buckmaster:** direction, arrangements / **Orchestra:** uncredited / **Nigel Olsson:** backing vocals **Recorded:** Townhouse Studios, London / Cello Studios, Sony Music Studios, Johnny Yuma Recording, Los Angeles: September 18, 2000–April 30, 2001 **Technical Team:** Producer: Patrick Leonard / **Sound Engineers:** Joe Chiccarelli, Brian Scheuble / **Assistant Sound Engineers:** Andy Green, Jennifer Hilliard, Katrina Leigh, Jonathan Merritt, Alan Sanderson, Todd Shoemaker, Tom Stanley / **Artistic Direction Coordinators:** Todd Interland, Derek MacKillop / **Production Coordinators:** Adrian Collee, Suzanne Ybarra / **Mixing:** Bill Bottrell / **Mixing Assistant:** Alan Sanderson / **Mastering:** Stewart Whitmore

Elton's singing sounds as though it is coming from far away at the beginning of "Mansfield," and this is not helped by the overloaded production, which weakens the overall ensemble.

The convoluted melody, which is very unintuitive, prevents the song from asserting itself as one of the strong points on *Songs from the West Coast*. The finale is much more successful, with a nice movement that starts at 3:33 when it's launched by slamming drums and then sublimated by impeccable backing vocals. Bernie confirms his talent for re-creating moments from life in his lyrics. "Sometimes the magic of the past is all we've got," he says in "Mansfield," which is about two friends who have found themselves setting out on a love story.

THIS TRAIN DON'T STOP THERE ANYMORE

Elton John, Bernie Taupin / 4:38

Musicians: Elton John: vocals, piano / **Paul Bushnell:** bass, backing vocals / **Matt Chamberlain:** drums / **Paul Buckmaster:** direction, arrangements / **Orchestra:** uncredited / Gary Barlow, Kudisan Kai, **Davey Johnstone, Nigel Olsson:** backing vocals **Recorded:** Townhouse Studios, London / Cello Studios, Sony Music Studios, Johnny Yuma Recording, Los Angeles: September 18, 2000–April 30, 2001 **Technical Team:** Producer: Patrick Leonard / **Sound Engineers:** Joe Chiccarelli, Brian Scheuble / **Assistant Sound Engineers:** Andy Green, Jennifer Hilliard, Katrina Leigh, Jonathan Merritt, Alan Sanderson, Todd Shoemaker, Tom Stanley / **Artistic Direction Coordinators:** Todd Interland, Derek MacKillop / **Production Coordinators:** Adrian Collee, Suzanne Ybarra / **Mixing:** Bill Bottrell / **Mixing Assistant:** Alan Sanderson / **Mastering:** Stewart Whitmore **Single Release:** CD1: *This Train Don't Stop There Anymore / Did Anybody Sleep with Joan of Arc? / I Want Love* (Live) **UK Release:** December 2001 on Rocket Record Company / Mercury (ref. 588 896-2) **Best UK Chart Ranking:** 24 **Maxi CD:** *This Train Don't Stop There Anymore / American Triangle* (Live) / *Philadelphia Freedom* (Live) **UK Release:** 2001 on Rocket Record Company / Mercury (ref. 588 897-2)

"This Train Don't Stop There Anymore" really shows the quality of *Songs from the West Coast* and rounds it off in the best possible way. In the song, Elton delivers one of his finest vocal performances. The backing vocals by Gary Barlow, Kudisan Kai, Davey Johnstone, and Nigel Olsson provide a compassionate accompaniment to Elton's melancholy. After a magnificent overture on the piano that's worthy of "Goodbye Yellow Brick Road," Elton brings Bernie's lyrics to life. The narrator is a thinly disguised Bernie, once again dealing with affairs of the heart and affirming that "The sentimental things [he'd] write / Never meant that much to [him]," and Elton, conscious that the end is now closer than the beginning: "I used to be the main express [...] / But [...] / This train don't stop there anymore." The moving music video, created by David LaChapelle presents a youthful Elton John in the form of Justin Timberlake, who wears the emblematic attire of the artist from the 1970s. The young singer was so convincing in his portrayal that for a time he was considered for the role of Elton in the 2019 biopic *Rocketman*.

ELTON JOHN   SONGS FROM THE WEST COAST

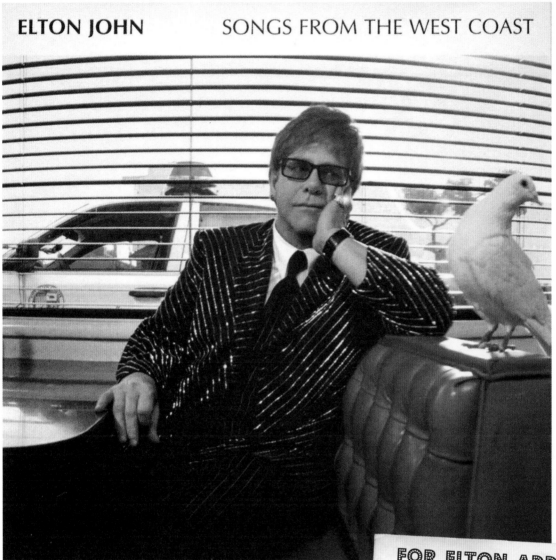

After exploring different musical genres, *Songs from the West Coast* marked a return to the intimacy of Elton's earlier albums.

FOR ELTON ADDICTS

The diner featured in the photo on the album cover is Rae's Restaurant in Santa Monica. This famous spot can also be seen in *True Romance* (1993) and in *Lords of Dogtown* (2005).

THE NORTH STAR

Elton John, Bernie Taupin / 5:31

Musicians: Elton John: vocals, piano? **Recorded:** Townhouse Studios, London / Sony Music Studios, Johnny Yuma Recording, Los Angeles: September 18, 2000–April 30, 2001 **Technical Team: Producer:** Patrick Leonard / **Sound Engineers:** Joe Chiccarelli, Brian Scheuble / **Assistant Sound Engineers:** Andy Green, Jennifer Hilliard, Katrina Leigh, Jonathan Merritt, Alan Sanderson, Todd Shoemaker, Tom Stanley / **Artistic Direction Coordinators:** Todd Interland, Derek MacKillop / **Production Coordinators:** Adrian Collee, Suzanne Ybarra / **Mixing:** Bill Bottrell / **Mixing Assistant:** Alan Sanderson / **Mastering:** Stewart Whitmore

Electric guitar arpeggios bathed in tremolo and an intense piano imprint their delicacy on the introduction of this blues ballad, which soon extends to include a deep bass, discreet percussion, backing vocals anchored in gospel, and some velvet keyboard sounds. Elton's voice is particularly animated on the refrain, which is the main point of interest in the song even as it's also marked by a mysterious guitar line that's present right at the beginning of the number. Although cryptic, Bernie's lyrics seem to stress the metaphor of the North Star to define the fundamental point of reference that certain individuals represent in other people's lives. Initially left out of the album, "The North Star" ended up appearing as a bonus track on the rerelease of *Songs from the West Coast*, which was released simultaneously on Rocket Record Company and Mercury (ref. 063 087-0) in 2002.

ALBUM

PEACHTREE
ROAD

Weight of the World . Porch Swing in Tupelo . Answer in the Sky .
Turn the Lights Out When You Leave . My Elusive Drug . They Call Her the Cat .
Freaks in Love . All That I'm Allowed (I'm Thankful) . I Stop and I Breathe . Too Many Tears .
It's Getting Dark in Here . I Can't Keep This from You

RELEASE DATES
UK Release: November 9, 2004
Reference: Rocket Record Company/Mercury—9867611
Best UK Chart Ranking: 21
US Release: November 9, 2004
Reference: Rocket Record Company/Universal Records—
B0003647-02
Best US Chart Ranking: 17

Peachtree Road is dedicated to the memory of Elton's former record producer Gus Dudgeon and his wife, Sheila, who both tragically died in a car accident on July 21, 2002.

HEADING SOUTH

Galvanized by his success with the stage adaptations of *The Lion King* (1997) and *Aida* (1998), in 2003 Elton embarked on creating the music for *Billy Elliot: The Musical*, based on the 2000 movie directed by Stephen Daldry and a story by Lee Hall. The show, with Elton's music, came out in 2005 at the Victoria Palace Theatre in London's West End. It proved to be yet another hit for a composer still basking in the success of his *Greatest Hits 1970–2002*, a platinum disk that was issued in the UK in 2002.

So, it was with the confidence of an artist at the height of his power that Elton began recording sessions for a new studio album, *Peachtree Road*, in January 2004. He had already recorded some numbers in April 2003, but not all of these were used for the new album, and some eventually ended up being used as B-sides for later releases. For this twenty-eighth album, Elton John took control of the artistic direction himself. His plan was to build on the success of his 2001 album, *Songs from the West Coast*, by once again drawing on American music for inspiration. His choice was also governed by the desire to create a more intimate style that couldn't have been more different from the demonstrative nature of the musicals he'd been working on. Opting to record at Atlanta's Tree Sound Studios, Elton soaked up the atmosphere of the American South as he worked on the album.

A Meeting Point of Different Genres

Influenced as always by his surroundings while recording, Elton John's aim was to bring the spirit of the American South to life through his new ballads. For someone from Britain, the sometimes harsh and arid landscapes found in Texas, Alabama, Tennessee, and Mississippi were both foreign and fascinating. These same landscapes, frozen in time and empty of all human life, were captured by London photographer Sam Taylor-Wood and used for the album's booklet. The image on the cover shows a railroad crossing in Douglasville, a town on the outskirts of Atlanta. This image summed up in a single photograph

the feeling of melancholy and sobriety that Elton aspired to for this album, even though almost all the numbers have a string orchestra and several of them have excellent backing vocals performed by various invited singers. The backing vocalists add harmonies that embellish the melodies so beautifully crafted by Elton to go with Bernie Taupin's romantic lyrics, and they are responsible for injecting a dose of gospel on songs like "Porch Swing in Tupelo" and "Answer in the Sky."

Apart from these added elements, recording sessions took place with a dedicated core of musicians who operated in isolation. For this album, Davey Johnstone rediscovered the plain folk-country style he had adopted originally before being "contaminated" by rock, bringing out some of his favorite instruments (dobro, baritone guitar, sitar, mandolin, Leslie speaker, etc.). Now without Patrick Leonard, Elton's touring team was back together: Guy Babylon on keyboards, Bob Birch on bass, Nigel Olsson on drums, and John Mahon on percussion. Guy Babylon ably directs the orchestra, as he had done for *The Big Picture* in 1997. Adapting to Elton's pared-down choices and relying on nothing more than his acoustic piano and a Fender Rhodes (for "Too Many Tears"), Guy confines himself to a Hammond organ and a Rhodes, giving the songs a retro feel that evokes the 1970s.

But more than anything else, this album is redolent of America and various subgenres of American music, including jazz ("My Elusive Drug"), soul ("Freaks in Love"), gospel ("Porch Swing in Tupelo"), and country ("Turn the Lights Out When You Leave"). With both the modesty of a Brit arriving in the musical holy land of America and a thorough knowledge of this heritage, Elton places himself at the center of all these genres that have nourished his creativity. Perhaps unsurprisingly, his intentions were more readily accepted by the American public, where the album went to number seventeen on the *Billboard* charts. The British public was slightly less enthusiastic, but the album still hit a very respectable number twenty-one in the rankings.

WEIGHT OF THE WORLD

Elton John, Bernie Taupin / 3:58

Musicians: Elton John: lead and backing vocals, piano / **Davey Johnstone:** electric guitar, acoustic guitar, dobro, backing vocals / **Bob Birch:** bass, backing vocals / **Nigel Olsson:** drums, backing vocals / **John Mahon:** percussion, backing vocals / **Guy Babylon:** programming, arrangements, direction **Orchestra:** Steve Erdody, Martin Tillman: cellos / Brian Dembrow, Victoria Miskolczy, Simon Oswell, James V. Ross: violas / Charlie Bisharat, Joel Derouin, Bruce Dukow, Endre Granat, Eric J. Hosler, Dimitrie Leivichi, Phillip Levy, Robin Olson, Sid Page, Mark Robertson, Anatoly Rosinsky, Lisa M. Sutton: violins **Recorded:** Tree Sound Studios, Atlanta / The Record Plant, Los Angeles / Silent Sound, Atlanta: January 2004 **Technical Team: Producer:** Elton John / **Sound Engineer:** Matt Still / **Assistant Sound Engineers:** Jason Carson, John Holmes, Josh McDonnell, Josh "Frodo" Monroy, Rob Skipworth, Tom Tapley / **Mixing:** Matt Still / **Mastering:** Bob Ludwig

An attractive and contemplative melody in *G* major, "Weight of the World" starts with a simplicity similar to that of the Beatles' "Let It Be." After a solo piano begins the track, Elton is joined progressively by spare drum beats, elegant strings, warm backing vocals, and the constant presence of Davey Johnstone. The guitarist first adds some magnificent chords on the acoustic guitar with some restrained touches of electric guitar here and there and, most importantly, a surprising dobro solo at 2:31. Bernie's theme is expressed in brilliant lyrics: in them, the narrator, partly melancholy, partly pleased, admits that he has moved on to a new stage of his life, and that he's no longer shouldering the weight of the world. "Fortune and fame is so fleeting / These days I'm happy to say / I'm amazed that I'm still around / And the weight of the world is off my back." Inevitably, we see a parallel with the lives of Bernie and Elton, with both men conscious of the road they have traveled and the responsibilities they have acquired along the way.

PORCH SWING IN TUPELO

Elton John, Bernie Taupin / 4:39

Musicians: Elton John: vocals, piano / **Guy Babylon:** programming, orchestral arrangements, Hammond organ / **Davey Johnstone:** electric guitar, acoustic guitar, dobro / **Bob Birch:** bass / **Nigel Olsson:** drums / **John Mahon:** percussion / Charles Bullock, Terrence Davis, Todd Honeycutt, Adam McKnight, Rosalind McKnight, L'Tanya Shields, M. Denise Sims, Alecia Terry: backing vocals **Orchestra:** Steve Erdody, Martin Tillman: cellos / Brian Dembrow, Victoria Miskolczy, Simon Oswell, James V. Ross: violas / Charlie Bisharat, Joel Derouin, Bruce Dukow, Endre Granat, Eric J. Hosler, Dimitrie Leivichi, Phillip Levy, Robin Olson, Sid Page, Mark Robertson, Anatoly Rosinsky, Lisa M. Sutton: violins **Recorded:** Tree Sound Studios, Atlanta / The Record Plant, Los Angeles / Silent Sound, Atlanta: January 2004 / **Technical Team: Producer:** Elton John / **Sound Engineer:** Matt Still / **Assistant Sound Engineers:** Jason Carson, John Holmes, Josh McDonnell, Josh "Frodo" Monroy, Rob Skipworth, Tom Tapley / **Mixing:** Matt Still / **Mastering:** Bob Ludwig

A wonderful ballad with a gospel sound, "Porch Swing in Tupelo" has a huge number of singers for the backing vocals. Davey Johnstone contributes a few well-placed notes on the dobro and, above all, provides the song's groove with the clarity of his electric guitar. Guy Babylon's Hammond organ is also brought to the fore, given as much prominence as Elton's intense piano. Elton gives us a vocal performance full of character and nuance in this tribute to one of the idols of his youth: Elvis Presley. Because this song is all about Elvis, even if the narrator initially lingers on images of the old days in the American South, it eventually focuses on the porch swing of a house in Tupelo, the town where Elvis was born. The "truck drivin' boy / With the grease monkey look and the rock 'n' roll voice" is, of course, Elvis. The narrator imagines that the singer might have sat on this porch in Tupelo, "Singing all praise to God through poverty's tears," the words referring to the humble beginnings of the boy who would become the so-called King of Rock 'n' Roll.

2004

ANSWER IN THE SKY

Elton John, Bernie Taupin / 4:04

Musicians: Elton John: lead and backing vocals, piano / **Davey Johnstone:** electric guitar, acoustic guitar, baritone guitar, slide guitar / **Bob Birch:** bass / **Nigel Olsson:** drums / **Guy Babylon:** programming, Hammond organ, arrangements, direction / **John Mahon:** percussion / Rosalind McKnight, L'Tanya Shields, M. Denise Sims, Alecia Terry: backing vocals Orchestra: Steve Erdody, Martin Tillman: cellos / Brian Dembrow, Victoria Miskolczy, Simon Oswell, James V. Ross: violas / Charlie Bisharat, Joel Derouin, Bruce Dukow, Endre Granat, Eric J. Hosler, Dimitrie Leivichi, Phillip Levy, Robin Olson, Sid Page, Mark Robertson, Anatoly Rosinsky, Lisa M. Sutton: violins **Recorded:** Tree Sound Studios, Atlanta / The Record Plant, Los Angeles / Silent Sound, Atlanta: January 2004 **Technical Team:** Producer: Elton John / **Sound Engineer:** Matt Still / **Assistant Sound Engineers:** Jason Carson, John Holmes, Josh McDonnell, Josh "Frodo" Monroy, Rob Skipworth, Tom Tapley / **Mixing:** Matt Still / **Mastering:** Bob Ludwig

The need to look for something greater than ourselves is a common human characteristic, and it lies at the heart of Bernie Taupin's message in "Answer in the Sky." He invites us to look at the night sky to see "celestial light," faith, and hope. Bernie uses the metaphor of the sky to look into the depths of his soul, searching for answers to life's most unanswerable questions. "And if your heart is empty / And there's no hope inside / There's a chance you'll find an answer in the sky." Rock and gospel (and an important role for the strings) collide here, giving the piece its energy. Elton's voice comes through strongly, as do the gravelly repetitions of "sometimes" in the refrains, which are admirably supported by the impressive backing vocals. The musical arrangement is effective, both conventional and elegant, as is Elton's intense piano playing, supported by the dry drumming of Nigel Olsson and inventive guitar playing by Davey Johnstone.

TURN THE LIGHTS OUT WHEN YOU LEAVE

Elton John, Bernie Taupin / 5:02

Musicians: Elton John: lead and backing vocals, piano / **Davey Johnstone:** electric guitar, acoustic guitar / **John Jorgenson:** pedal steel guitar / **Bob Birch:** bass / **Nigel Olsson:** drums / **Guy Babylon:** programming, Hammond organ, arrangements, direction / **John Mahon:** percussion Orchestra: Steve Erdody, Martin Tillman: cellos / Brian Dembrow, Victoria Miskolczy, Simon Oswell, James V. Ross: violas / Charlie Bisharat, Joel Derouin, Bruce Dukow, Endre Granat, Eric J. Hosler, Dimitrie Leivichi, Phillip Levy, Robin Olson, Sid Page, Mark Robertson, Anatoly Rosinsky, Lisa M. Sutton: violins **Recorded:** Tree Sound Studios, Atlanta / The Record Plant, Los Angeles / Silent Sound, Atlanta: January 2004 **Technical Team:** Producer: Elton John / **Sound Engineer:** Matt Still / **Assistant Sound Engineers:** Jason Carson, John Holmes, Josh McDonnell, Josh "Frodo" Monroy, Rob Skipworth, Tom Tapley / **Mixing:** Matt Still / **Mastering:** Bob Ludwig Release as **Maxi CD:** *Turn the Lights Out When You Leave / How's Tomorrow / Peter's Song* **UK Release:** April 2005 by Mercury (ref.: 9870663) **Best UK Chart Ranking:** 32 • *Turn the Lights Out When You Leave (Radio Edit)/ Things Only Get Better with Love* **UK Release:** April 2005 by Mercury (ref.: 9870664) **Best UK Chart Ranking:** Did Not Chart

A country ballad with a wonderful refrain, "Turn the Lights Out When You Leave" owes much of its retro feel to both the gentle weeping sound of the pedal steel guitar, played by a returning John Jorgenson, and the nicely judged reverb effect applied to Elton's voice. At 3:08 Elton delivers an attractive and delicate solo on piano. Once again, the theme of the song is the breakup of a relationship. The narrator is determined to assure the woman leaving him—her "bags out on the bed" and the "closet's all cleared out"—that he'll survive without her. "I ain't gonna die, I ain't gonna cry [...] I ain't gonna shake, I ain't gonna break," he sings, even if he sounds not completely convinced of himself. Though she may still look pretty "In that lacy little dress," he accepts that their love "is all worn out" and, bitterly, asks her to turn the lights out when she leaves.

MY ELUSIVE DRUG

Elton John, Bernie Taupin / 4:12

Musicians: Elton John: vocals, piano / **Davey Johnstone:** electric guitar, backing vocals, slide guitar, Leslie speaker / **Bob Birch:** bass, backing vocals / **Nigel Olsson:** drums, backing vocals / **Guy Babylon:** programming, Hammond organ, arrangements, direction / **John Mahon:** percussion, backing vocals Orchestra: Steve Erdody, Martin Tillman: cellos / Brian Dembrow, Victoria Miskolczy, Simon Oswell, James V. Ross: violas / Charlie Bisharat, Joel Derouin, Bruce Dukow, Endre Granat, Eric J. Hosler, Dimitrie Leivichi, Phillip Levy, Robin Olson, Sid Page, Mark Robertson, Anatoly Rosinsky, Lisa M. Sutton: violins **Recorded:** Tree Sound Studios, Atlanta / The Record Plant, Los Angeles / Silent Sound, Atlanta: January 2004 **Technical Team:** Producer: Elton John / Sound Engineer: Matt Still / Assistant Sound Engineers: Jason Carson, John Holmes, Josh McDonnell, Josh "Frodo" Monroy, Rob Skipworth, Tom Tapley / **Mixing:** Matt Still / **Mastering:** Bob Ludwig

As soon as he saw the words for "My Elusive Drug," Elton knew immediately that he would turn it into a heart-rending ballad rather than a colorful rock number. And no wonder, because the song is clearly about his drug addiction. Now he can say "I'm not the same as I used to be" but admits throughout the song that "Sure I've made mistakes, haven't we all / I've been loose as a cannon and dumb as a wall." All his life, he says, he has been searching for his "elusive drug"—in other words, the true and unconditional love of the person he calls "the sweetest addiction." Undeservedly neglected, "My Elusive Drug" is an impeccably performed and produced piece that features vibrant strings, gentle backing vocals, a minimalist solo from Davey Johnstone at 3:04, and, most importantly, an Elton in marvelous vocal form, as evidenced by the well-controlled vibrato and the intensity of the ending.

THEY CALL HER THE CAT

Elton John, Bernie Taupin / 4:27

Musicians: Elton John: lead and backing vocals, piano / **Davey Johnstone:** electric guitar, dobro, baritone guitar / **Bob Birch:** bass / **Nigel Olsson:** drums / **Guy Babylon:** programming, Hammond organ, Rhodes piano / **John Mahon:** percussion / **Larry Klimas:** baritone saxophone / **Walter Parazaider:** tenor saxophone / **James Pankow:** trombone, brass arrangements / **Lee Loughnane:** trumpet / **Terrence Davis, Todd Honeycutt, Adam McKnight, Rosalind McKnight, L'Tanya Shields, M. Denise Sims, Alecia Terry, Mark Ford:** backing vocals **Recorded:** Tree Sound Studios, Atlanta / The Record Plant, Los Angeles / Silent Sound, Atlanta: January 2004 **Technical Team:** Producer: Elton John / Sound Engineer: Matt Still / Assistant Sound Engineers: Jason Carson, John Holmes, Josh McDonnell, Josh "Frodo" Monroy, Rob Skipworth, Tom Tapley / **Mixing:** Matt Still / **Mastering:** Bob Ludwig

"Just a little boy lost in the land of the free" is how Bernie's narrator describes Billy, "the wildest thing I've ever seen." Billy has transitioned from male to female—"was just plain mister once" and now has "hips like Mick, she's a Rolling Stone." Now "Billy got a kitty," as the narrator crudely puts it, "they call her the cat." Elton wanted the song to be an uninhibited rock number with wild piano, prominent backing vocals, and punchy brass. Davey Johnstone, who gives the song a Rolling Stones–like feel with his electric guitar, also performs a dobro riff that represents a high point in the recording. Guy Babylon's warm keyboards and Nigel Olsson's robust drums are also excellent.

FREAKS IN LOVE

Elton John, Bernie Taupin / 4:31

Musicians: Elton John: lead and backing vocals, piano / **Davey Johnstone:** electric guitar, acoustic guitar / **Bob Birch:** bass / **Nigel Olsson:** drums / **Guy Babylon:** programming, Hammond organ, Rhodes piano, arrangements, direction / **John Mahon:** percussion / **Charles Bullock, Terrence Davis, Adam McKnight, Mark Ford:** backing vocals Orchestra: Steve Erdody, Martin Tillman: cellos / Brian Dembrow, Victoria Miskolczy, Simon Oswell, James V. Ross: violas / Charlie Bisharat, Joel Derouin, Bruce Dukow, Endre Granat, Eric J. Hosler, Dimitrie Leivichi, Phillip Levy, Robin Olson, Sid Page, Mark Robertson, Anatoly Rosinsky, Lisa M. Sutton: violins **Recorded:** Tree Sound Studios, Atlanta / The Record Plant, Los Angeles / Silent Sound, Atlanta: January 2004 **Technical Team:** Producer: Elton John / Sound Engineer: Matt Still / Assistant Sound Engineers: Jason Carson, John Holmes, Josh McDonnell, Josh "Frodo" Monroy, Rob Skipworth, Tom Tapley / **Mixing:** Matt Still / **Mastering:** Bob Ludwig

With "Freaks in Love," Elton temporarily moves away from blues and rock and returns to soul music. While it's easy to imagine bands like the Temptations, the Four Tops, or even Earth, Wind & Fire singing this ballad, from the intro on it bears a striking resemblance to Simply Red's 1989 version of Harold Melvin & the Blue Notes' 1972 hit "If You Don't Know Me by Now." Featuring mellow Hammond organ, slightly laid-back electric guitar and drums, and doo-wop-inspired backing vocals accompanying Davey Johnstone's lovely solo: all the ingredients of a vibrant ballad are present and accounted for. Elton delivers an assured vocal performance of this rather unusual melody. Bernie's lyrics tell of two fools who are madly in love and heedless of the rest of the world, which sees them as outsiders, as "idiots among the hawks and doves." But "Happy is the union / Of fools and freaks alike."

2004

ALL THAT I'M ALLOWED (I'M THANKFUL)

Elton John, Bernie Taupin / 4:52

Musicians: Elton John: lead and backing vocals, piano / **Davey Johnstone:** electric guitar, acoustic guitar, sitar / **Bob Birch:** bass / **Nigel Olsson:** drums / **Guy Babylon:** programming, Hammond organ, Rhodes piano, direction, arrangements / **John Mahon:** percussion / **Charles Bullock, Terrence Davis, Adam McKnight, Mark Ford:** backing vocals **Orchestra:** Steve Erdody, Martin Tillman: cellos / Brian Dembrow, Victoria Miskolczy, Simon Oswell, James V. Ross: violas / Charlie Bisharat, Joel Derouin, Bruce Dukow, Endre Granat, Eric J. Hosler, Dimitrie Leivichi, Phillip Levy, Robin Olson, Sid Page, Mark Robertson, Anatoly Rosinsky, Lisa M. Sutton: violins **Recorded:** Tree Sound Studios, Atlanta / The Record Plant, Los Angeles / Silent Sound, Atlanta: January 2004 **Technical Team:** Producer: Elton John / Sound Engineer: Matt Still / Assistant Sound Engineers: Jason Carson, John Holmes, Josh McDonnell, Josh "Frodo"

Monroy, Rob Skipworth, Tom Tapley / **Mixing:** Matt Still / **Mastering:** Bob Ludwig **Single Release:** *All That I'm Allowed (I'm Thankful) / Keep It a Mystery* **UK Release:** November 1, 2004, on Rocket Record Company/Mercury (ref.: 9868258) **Best UK Chart Ranking:** Did Not Chart • **Maxi CD:** *All That I'm Allowed (I'm Thankful) / So Sad the Renegade / A Little Peace* **UK Release:** 2004 on Rocket Record Company/Mercury (ref.: 9868257) **Best UK Chart Ranking:** Did Not Chart

Full of good vibes and gratitude, "All That I'm Allowed (I'm Thankful)" is a hymn to happiness and the good fortune to have gotten "All that I'm allowed" from life. "It'll do for me, I'm thankful now," sings the narrator/Elton. With hindsight, Bernie tells him that their ambitions may not have been as far-fetched as they seemed when they were younger. Now is the time to thank life for all the blessings they've received: "I see hope in every cloud." With its all-male backing vocals and melodic clarity, the refrain of "All That I'm Allowed (I'm Thankful)" is perhaps the album's most memorable and enduring track. Shining at the heart of this stellar ballad is Davey Johnstone's beautiful sitar playing.

I STOP AND I BREATHE

Elton John, Bernie Taupin / 3:39

Musicians: Elton John: vocals, piano / **Davey Johnstone:** electric guitar, acoustic guitar / **Bob Birch:** bass / **Nigel Olsson:** drums / **Guy Babylon:** programming, Hammond organ, Rhodes piano, direction, arrangements / **John Mahon:** percussion, programming / **Charles Bullock, Terrence Davis, Adam McKnight, Mark Ford:** backing vocals **Orchestra: Steve Erdody, Martin Tillman:** cellos / **Brian Dembrow, Victoria Miskolczy, Simon Oswell, James V. Ross:** violas / **Charlie Bisharat, Joel Derouin, Bruce Dukow, Endre Granat, Eric J. Hosler, Dimitrie Leivichi, Phillip Levy, Robin Olson, Sid Page, Mark Robertson, Anatoly Rosinsky, Lisa M. Sutton:** violins **Recorded:** Tree Sound Studios, Atlanta / The Record Plant, Los Angeles / Silent Sound, Atlanta: January 2004 **Technical Team: Producer:** Elton John / **Sound Engineer:** Matt Still / **Assistant Sound Engineers:** Jason Carson, John Holmes, Josh McDonnell, Josh "Frodo" Monroy, Rob Skipworth, Tom Tapley / **Mixing:** Matt Still / **Mastering:** Bob Ludwig

The sophisticated melody of "I Stop and I Breathe" demonstrates that Elton is not just a singer of interchangeable ballads. The unusually complex harmonic progression of the song is matched by an impressively elegant arrangement, with Elton's piano playing the leading role. Bernie's lyrics describe a couple who have overcome their differences. In the words of the narrator: "We are still all right [...] No one ever wins / But we're strong enough." Elton's voice is powerful and sincere, mirrored by his piano, which sounds deep and intense. Guy Babylon's poignant arrangement for strings is just what is needed, and the same goes for Davey Johnstone, who tactfully accompanies the narrator's intimate confessions with his delicate arpeggios using the distortion pedal.

John Jorgenson with his Selmer DG-300 guitar.

TOO MANY TEARS

Elton John, Bernie Taupin / 4:15

Musicians: Elton John: lead and backing vocals, piano, Rhodes piano / **Davey Johnstone:** electric guitar, dobro, backing vocals, slide guitar, mandolin / **Bob Birch:** bass, backing vocals / **Nigel Olsson:** drums, backing vocals / **Guy Babylon:** programming, direction, arrangements / **John Mahon:** percussion, backing vocals **Orchestra: Steve Erdody, Martin Tillman:** cellos / **Brian Dembrow, Victoria Miskolczy, Simon Oswell, James V. Ross:** violas / **Charlie Bisharat, Joel Derouin, Bruce Dukow, Endre Granat, Eric J. Hosler, Dimitrie Leivichi, Phillip Levy, Robin Olson, Sid Page, Mark Robertson, Anatoly Rosinsky, Lisa M. Sutton:** violins **Recorded:** Tree Sound Studios, Atlanta / The Record Plant, Los Angeles / Silent Sound, Atlanta: January 2004 **Technical Team: Producer:** Elton John / **Sound Engineer:** Matt Still / **Assistant Sound Engineers:** Jason Carson, John Holmes, Josh McDonnell, Josh "Frodo" Monroy, Rob Skipworth, Tom Tapley / **Mixing:** Matt Still / **Mastering:** Bob Ludwig

Like "Answer in the Sky," "Too Many Tears" has a spiritual element to it. It mourns the tragedies that have plagued human history and questions our collective role in them. The lyricist suggests that peace and brotherhood are our individual responsibilities, and that it is up to each of us to draw inspiration from models who have shown us the way: "Just look into that beautiful blue / That beautiful blue, blue sky / And know too many tears, too many tears / Have been cried." Bernie refers to the assassinations of John F. Kennedy ("Did you go to Dallas on that day? / Have you been to where they broke a dream?"), Martin Luther King Jr. ("Why a balcony in Memphis, Tennessee / Seems trapped in time"), and perhaps also to Gandhi ("The barefoot man lived a simple life"), albeit indirectly. Despite a beautiful piano score and the inspired playing of Davey Johnstone on dobro and mandolin, "Too Many Tears" is probably one of the most melodically conventional tracks on the album, and this may explain why Elton never performed it in a concert.

IT'S GETTING DARK IN HERE

Elton John, Bernie Taupin / 3:50

Musicians: Elton John: vocals, piano / Davey Johnstone: electric guitar, acoustic guitar / Bob Birch: bass / Nigel Olsson: drums, backing vocals / Guy Babylon: programming, Hammond organ, Rhodes piano, direction, arrangements / John Mahon: percussion, programming / Charles Bullock, Terrence Davis, Adam McKnight, Mark Ford: backing vocals Orchestra: Steve Erdody, Martin Tillman: cellos / Brian Dembrow, Victoria Miskolczy, Simon Oswell, James V. Ross: violas / Charlie Bisharat, Joel Derouin, Bruce Dukow, Endre Granat, Eric J. Hosler, Dimitrie Leivichi, Phillip Levy, Robin Olson, Sid Page, Mark Robertson, Anatoly Rosinsky, Lisa M. Sutton: violins **Recorded:** Tree Sound Studios, Atlanta / The Record Plant, Los Angeles / Silent Sound, Atlanta: January 2004 **Technical Team:** Producer: Elton John / Sound Engineer: Matt Still / Assistant Sound Engineers: Jason Carson, John Holmes, Josh McDonnell, Josh "Frodo" Monroy, Rob Skipworth, Tom Tapley / **Mixing:** Matt Still / **Mastering:** Bob Ludwig

"It's Getting Dark in Here" is a typical Elton ballad, drawing in the listener at the beginning with its slow tempo, dark chords on the piano, and strong backing vocals with a gospel-style Hammond organ and a memorable refrain. Elton is in fine voice, and his projection in the lower register is exemplary, with just the right amount of precise vibrato. "It's Getting Dark in Here" describes the narrator's depression—and his paranoia. A suffocating feeling of oppression assails him in every verse ("I'm afraid of my shadow […] I'm scared of strangers […] World's so ugly / I can't breathe." Considering the darkness of the text, the choice of such a luminous arrangement seems daring.

I CAN'T KEEP THIS FROM YOU

Elton John, Bernie Taupin / 4:35

Musicians: Elton John: lead and backing vocals, piano / Davey Johnstone: electric guitar, acoustic guitar / Bob Birch: bass / Nigel Olsson: drums / Guy Babylon: programming, Hammond organ, direction, arrangements / John Mahon: percussion / Charles Bullock, Terrence Davis, Adam McKnight, Mark Ford: backing vocals Orchestra: Steve Erdody, Martin Tillman: cellos / Brian Dembrow, Victoria Miskolczy, Simon Oswell, James V. Ross: violas / Charlie Bisharat, Joel Derouin, Bruce Dukow, Endre Granat, Eric J. Hosler, Dimitrie Leivichi, Phillip Levy, Robin Olson, Sid Page, Mark Robertson, Anatoly Rosinsky, Lisa M. Sutton: violins **Recorded:** Tree Sound Studios, Atlanta / The Record Plant, Los Angeles / Silent Sound, Atlanta: January 2004 **Technical Team:** Producer: Elton John / Sound Engineer: Matt Still / Assistant Sound Engineers: Jason Carson, John Holmes, Josh McDonnell, Josh "Frodo" Monroy, Rob Skipworth, Tom Tapley / **Mixing:** Matt Still / **Mastering:** Bob Ludwig

Fans have given *Peachtree Road* the unofficial title of "ballad album," and it is entirely justified; the only number not to fall into this demanding category is "They Call Her the Cat." "I Can't Keep This from You" is an intense ballad that, from its first notes, is not unlike "Don't Let the Sun Go Down on Me," especially at the ends of the refrains. Chosen to end the album, this piece relies heavily on Elton's assured (if somewhat forced) singing, Guy Babylon's dreamy keyboards, and above all the gospel backing vocals from Charles Bullock, Terrence Davis, Adam McKnight, and Mark Ford. A dramatic solo from Davey Johnstone comes in at the emotional climax of the song, and Bernie's lyrics concern a man who has decided to reveal his love, saying "It's the time to tell the truth / Keeping it from you is wrong." Another love song for Elton and Bernie, but a good one!

KEEP IT A MYSTERY

Elton John, Bernie Taupin / 4:13

Single Release: *All That I'm Allowed (I'm Thankful) / Keep It a Mystery* **UK Release:** November 1, 2004, on Rocket Record Company/Mercury (ref. 9868258) **Best UK Chart Ranking:** Did Not Chart **Musicians:** Elton John: vocals, piano / Davey Johnstone: guitars, mandolin / Bob Birch: bass / Nigel Olsson: drums / Guy Babylon: keyboards / John Mahon: percussion / Harmonica: not credited **Recorded:** Tree Sound Studios, Atlanta / The Record Plant, Los Angeles / Silent Sound, Atlanta: April 2003 **Technical Team:** Producer: Elton John / Sound Engineer: Matt Still / Assistant Sound Engineers: Jason Carson, John Holmes, Josh McDonnell, Josh "Frodo" Monroy, Rob Skipworth, Tom Tapley / **Mixing:** Matt Still / **Mastering:** Bob Ludwig

"Keep It a Mystery" was recorded a few months before the *Peachtree Road* sessions, and it has a good theme on the piano as well as a pleasing melody. It is backed by a playful mandolin, a groovy electric guitar, precise backing vocals, and a warm harmonica sound. While the musicians' instrumentation succeeds in capturing some of the mystery referred to in the song's title, it fails to convey the sensuality and desire that underlies the lyrics. Deemed to be too different from the other compositions on the album, which were mainly ballads, "Keep It a Mystery" was set aside when the final track list was drawn up. It came out a year and a half later as the B side on the "All That I'm Allowed (I'm Thankful)" single.

SO SAD THE RENEGADE

Elton John, Bernie Taupin / 5:05

Maxi CD: *All That I'm Allowed (I'm Thankful) / So Sad the Renegade / A Little Peace* **UK Release:** 2004 on Rocket Record Company/Mercury (ref. 9868257) **Best UK Chart Ranking:** Did Not Chart **Musicians:** Elton John: vocals, piano / Davey Johnstone: guitars / John Jorgenson: pedal steel guitar / Bob Birch: bass / Nigel Olsson: drums / John Mahon: percussion / Guy Babylon: keyboards, arrangements, direction / Orchestra: not credited **Recorded:** Tree Sound Studios, Atlanta / The Record Plant, Los Angeles /

Silent Sound, Atlanta: April 2003 **Technical Team:** Producer: Elton John / Sound Engineer: Matt Still / **Assistant Sound Engineers:** Jason Carson, John Holmes, Josh McDonnell, Josh "Frodo" Monroy, Rob Skipworth, Tom Tapley / **Mixing:** Matt Still / **Mastering:** Bob Ludwig

Even though it was recorded some months before the sessions for *Peachtree Road* took place, "So Sad the Renegade" fulfilled all the requirements for the new album. Nevertheless, it was not included, and was instead set aside until it was included on the 2004 maxi CD promoting "All That I'm Allowed (I'm Thankful)." This is an excellent ballad that benefits from Davey Johnstone's admirable acoustic guitar playing, which is restrained and precise, as well as from John Jorgenson playing on pedal steel guitar. John Mahon's percussion is also great here, while Elton's piano playing blends perfectly with the overall arrangement.

A LITTLE PEACE

Elton John, Bernie Taupin / 4:00

Maxi CD: *All That I'm Allowed (I'm Thankful) / So Sad the Renegade / A Little Peace* **UK Release:** 2004 on Rocket Record Company/Mercury (ref. 9868257) **Best UK Chart Ranking:** Did Not Chart **Musicians:** Elton John: vocals, piano / Davey Johnstone: guitars, banjo / Bob Birch: bass / Nigel Olsson: drums / Guy Babylon: keyboards **Recorded:** Tree Sound Studios, Atlanta / The Record Plant, Los Angeles / Silent Sound, Atlanta: April 2003 **Technical Team:** Producer: Elton John / Sound Engineer: Matt Still / **Assistant Sound Engineers:** Jason Carson, John Holmes, Josh McDonnell, Josh "Frodo" Monroy, Rob Skipworth, Tom Tapley / **Mixing:** Matt Still / **Mastering:** Bob Ludwig

Elton John plays up his vigorous vibrato on this track, which features a catchy groove that helps it stand out from the rest of the album. Elton's piano playing is remarkable here, especially on the solo that radiates "good vibes" beginning at 2:00. Between the mischevous banjo and the electric guitar, Davey Johnstone stands out as the other central anchor on "A Little Peace."

HOW'S TOMORROW

Elton John, Bernie Taupin / 5:22

Maxi CD: *Turn on the Lights When You Leave / How's Tomorrow / Peter's Song* **UK Release:** April 2005 on Mercury (ref. 9870663) **Best UK Chart Ranking:** 32 **Musicians:** Elton John: vocals, piano / Davey Johnstone: guitar / Guy Babylon: keyboards / John Jorgenson: lap steel guitar / Bob Birch: bass / Nigel Olsson: drums **Recorded:** Tree Sound Studios, Atlanta / The Record Plant, Los Angeles / Silent Sound, Atlanta: April 2003 **Technical Team:** Producer: Elton John / Sound Engineer: Matt Still / Assistant Sound Engineers: Jason Carson, John Holmes, Josh McDonnell, Josh "Frodo" Monroy, Rob Skipworth, Tom Tapley / Mixing: Matt Still / Mastering: Bob Ludwig

Recorded several months before the rest of the *Peachtree Road* album, "How's Tomorrow" was eventually shelved before finally being released in 2005. Despite its placement on the back burner, this country-soul ballad acquits itself nicely. The guitars of Davey Johnstone and John Jorgensen meld beautifuly with Elton's powerful vocals, and his lovely piano playing, which is most notable beginning at 4:30.

PETER'S SONG

Elton John, Bernie Taupin / 3:41

Maxi CD: *Turn on the Lights When You Leave / How's Tomorrow / Peter's Song* **UK Release:** April 2005 on Mercury (ref. 9870663) **Best UK Chart Ranking:** 32 **Musicians:** Elton John: vocals, piano / Davey Johnstone: guitar, mandolin / Guy Babylon: keyboards / Bob Birch: bass / Nigel Olsson: drums **Recorded:** Tree Sound Studios, Atlanta / The Record Plant, Los Angeles / Silent Sound, Atlanta: April 2003 **Technical Team:** Producer: Elton John / Sound Engineer: Matt Still / Assistant Sound Engineers: Jason Carson, John Holmes, Josh McDonnell, Josh "Frodo" Monroy, Rob Skipworth, Tom Tapley / Mixing: Matt Still / Mastering: Bob Ludwig

"Peter's Song" is written in the style of a folk ballad and it's given great lift by Davey Johnstone's guitar and mandolin. There was hope for a time that the song would be featured on the soundtrack for the 2004 feature film *Neverland*, about the life of *Peter Pan* author, J.M. Barrie, but the partnership never materialized and "Peter's Song" was eventually released in 2005.

THINGS ONLY GET BETTER WITH LOVE

Elton John, Bernie Taupin / 5:18

Single: *Turn on the Lights When You Leave / Things Only Get Better with Love* **UK Release:** April 2005 on Mercury (ref. 9870664) **Best UK Chart Ranking:** Did Not Chart **Musicians:** Elton John: vocals, piano / Davey Johnstone: guitar / Guy Babylon: keyboards, orchestration and arrangements / Bob Birch: bass / Nigel Olsson: drums / Orchestra: uncredited **Recorded:** Tree Sound Studios, Atlanta / The Record Plant, Los Angeles / Silent Sound, Atlanta: April 2003 **Technical Team:** Producer: Elton John / Sound Engineer: Matt Still / Assistant Sound Engineers: Jason Carson, John Holmes, Josh McDonnell, Josh "Frodo" Monroy, Rob Skipworth, Tom Tapley / Mixing: Matt Still / Mastering: Bob Ludwig

Guy Babylon shines on "Things Only Get Better with Love," which benefits from his finely crafted orchestral arrangements, most notably in the finale. Babylon also directed the massive backing vocals that envelop Elton's relaxed voice. Bernie's lyrics here aren't the most original, but they serve as a perfect springboard for the song's slow crescendo toward musical ecstasy. The song was originally recorded before the main *Peachtree Road* sessions, in April 2003, but it wasn't released until two years later on the B-side of "Turn the Lights Out When You Leave."

BILLY ELLIOT:
A SEMI-AUTOBIOGRAPHICAL MUSICAL COMEDY

Tracklist

The Stars Look Down (7:31)
Shine (6:07)
Grandma's Song (4:40)
Solidarity (8:55)
Expressing Yourself (5:13)
The Letter (3:48)
Born to Boogie (4:25)
Angry Dance (3:50)
Merry Christmas Maggie Thatcher (3:26)
Deep into the Ground (3:36)
He Could Be a Star (4:51)
Electricity (5:54)
Once We Were Kings (4:14)
The Letter (Reprise) (2:53)
Finale (5:35)
The Letter (Bonus track) (Elton John) (2:33)
Merry Christmas Maggie Thatcher (Bonus track) (Elton John) (3:38)
Electricity (Bonus track) (3:31)

ALBUM
Release Dates

UK Release: 2005 Reference: Polydor 987 537-2
US Release: 2005 Reference: DECCA Broadway B000613072
Recorded: Angel Recording Studios, London
Single Release: "Electricity" / "Indian Sunset" (Edit) UK Release: July 11, 2005 Rocket Record Company/Mercury (ref.: 98721842)
Best UK Chart Ranking: 4

Margaret Thatcher died on April 8, 2013, and Billy Elliot audience members were asked to decide whether "Merry Christmas Maggie Thatcher," which contains lyrics like "We all celebrate today, 'cause it's one day closer to your death" would remain in the show. The audience voted overwhelmingly to keep the song in, and the performance took place as usual.

At the 2000 Cannes Film Festival, Elton John emerged from a movie screening for an upcoming feature called *Dancer*. Based on a script by Lee Hall, and directed by Stephen Daldry, the film told the story of an eleven-year-old boy from a small mining town in England who dreamed of becoming a ballet dancer. Over the course of the story, the young Billy Elliot comes up against the prejudices of an unforgiving society as well as his own father. Though he is encouraged to pursue boxing as a more appropriate interest, Billy is fascinated by the poise and grace of ballet. The boy's stubborn insistence on pursuing his interest in dance against all odds inspired Elton to look back on his own life, to the point where he felt compelled to ask Stephen Daldry and Lee Hall if they'd be interested in making a musical of their film, which was eventually released under the name of *Billy Elliot*.

Four years later, Elton John completed the soundtrack for *Billy Elliot: The Musical*. Performed for the first time in London in 2005, the musical won numerous awards and eventually ran on Broadway. Elton John himself performed three of the thirteen songs composed for the show: "The Letter," "Electricity," and "Merry Christmas Maggie Thatcher." These songs were included on the reissue of *Peachtree Road* when it was released as a CD by Rocket Record Company/Mercury (ref. 9871101) in 2005.

"The Letter" is a splendid and heartbreaking ballad written in the form of a letter sent to Billy from his recently deceased mother, who says that she will love and support him no matter what. Meanwhile, the perky and highly addictive "Merry Christmas Maggie Thatcher" refers to the British prime minister who ran the country from 1979 to 1990. Margaret Thatcher was known for setting up a series of radical economic reforms, which Billy Elliot and his family suffer from mightily. Finally, "Electricity" also appeared on the reissue of *Peachtree Road*, and it was also selected as a single alongside "Indian Sunset," which was an excerpt from *Madman Across the Water*. In the musical, "Electricity" is performed by Billy Elliot during his audition for the Royal Ballet School, and it represents the young boy's ability to overcome all obstacles to achieve his dreams. The song eventually became the sixty-third Elton John track to rank in the British Top 40 when it went to number four on the charts.

Shown here in 2008, Elton John posed with three different Billies cast in *Billy Elliot*: Trent Kowalik, David Alvarez, and Kiril Kulish.

ALBUM

THE CAPTAIN & THE KID

Postcards from Richard Nixon . Just Like Noah's Ark . Wouldn't Have You Any Other Way (NYC) . Tinderbox . And the House Fell Down . Blues Never Fade Away . The Bridge . I Must Have Lost It on the Wind . Old '67 . The Captain and the Kid

RELEASE DATES
UK Release: November 18, 2006
Reference: Rocket Record Company/Mercury—1706491
Best UK Chart Ranking: 6
US Release: September 18, 2006
Reference: Interscope Records—B0007673-02
Best US Chart Ranking: 18

Bernie at his ranch in Santa Ynez, California. The lyricist found peace in the rural life, and he delved back into his memories to find inspriation for the sequel to *Captain Fantastic*.

An official photograph of the civil partnership of David Furnish and Elton John, which occurred on December 21, 2005.

LOOKING BACK

A kind of mature acceptance mixed with a hint of melancholy starts to be discernable in Elton and Bernie Taupin's later creations. With the passing of time, the two men began to find comfort in an idealized memory of their early years. At the same time, they were now enjoying fulfilling personal lives. Elton and David Furnish formed a civil partnership on December 21, 2005, the first day that civil partnerships for same-sex couples were allowed in Britain. Elton's career was still flourishing. Bernie had taken American citizenship and was living with Heather Kidd, his fourth partner. Now, at last, he was able to enjoy the delights of fatherhood; his daughter, Charley Indiana, was born on May 18, 2005. But perhaps it was precisely because Elton and Bernie had finally found long-wished-for fulfillment that they were able to cast a more objective look at their past. Merck Mercuriadis, Elton's manager since the dismissal of John Reid in 1998, put forward the idea that the two of them do an album that, by tracing the story of their careers, would be a continuation of *Captain Fantastic and the Brown Dirt Cowboy* (1975). Elton and Bernie greeted the proposal with enthusiasm. But while they willingly looked back on their younger years with varying degrees of nostalgia, this brief glance in the rearview mirror did not divert them from the road ahead, which they intended to continue to travel together.

No Muss, No Fuss

With the subject already decided on, there was no need for Bernie to produce a lot of disparate lyrics for the new album. Instead, he wrote eleven beautifully crafted songs that, rather than trying to chronologically trace their career, are like representative snapshots of those years: the conquest of the United States ("Postcards from Richard Nixon"), showbiz life ("Just Like Noah's Ark"), the discovery of New York ("Wouldn't Have You Any Other Way [NYC])," their volatile relationship ("Tinderbox"), cocaine addiction ("And the House Fell Down"), friends who had died ("Blues Never Fade Away"), their career choices ("The Bridge," "The Captain and the Kid"), their love affairs ("I Must Have Lost It on the Wind"), the earliest years ("Old '67"), and Elton's flamboyant costumes ("Across the River Thames").

The problem was trying to find time to record, given Elton's many live concert bookings. In February 2004, he began a residency at Caesars Palace in Las Vegas with the title "The Red Piano," which he was to perform until March 2009—concerts that took up much of his time. In 2006, the only slots he had available were the end of February, the beginning of March, and May. Just as with recording for *Peachtree Road*, he needed to find studios easily reached from his residence in Atlanta. This time he opted for Center Stage, a complex including

In 2006, (from left to right) Elton John, Guy Babylon, Bob Birch, and Nigel Olsson performed under the spotlights at Caesar's Palace as part of Elton's The Red Piano concert residency.

several concert halls that he was to turn into a provisional recording studio. Recording eventually began in the spring of 2006. The unusual acoustics of these spaces proved to be ideal for this album and its very raw sound. Elton John personally directed in collaboration with Matt Still, a local producer who also did the recording and mixing. The singer's voice is deliberately to the fore, presented with very few effects to create a sense of intimacy. The musicians and instruments are modest in number: Elton records on his Yamaha DC7 Disklavier grand piano. Guy Babylon uses Yamaha Motif synthesizers. Bob Birch alternates between his Fender Jazz Bass and his Music Man Silhouette. Nigel Olsson plays on a drum kit with a DW double bass drum pedal and Paiste cymbals. John Mahon uses a drum kit with Yamaha Latin percussion and Zildjian cymbals. Davey Johnstone is greedier, using not only his custom-made "Captain Fantastic" Gibson CS Les Paul, but also his Les Paul Black Beauty, a Fender Stratocaster, a Takamine EN15, an Ovation MM68AX mandolin, and Hughes & Kettner amps. Despite being so intermittent, the sessions worked out wonderfully well, and they were completed in a relatively short amount of time: "It was the quickest album we'd done since the '70s. Twenty days, writing and recording. The pressure was off."[139]

A thousand miles from the surrealist album cover (which was peppered with symbols designed by the pop artist Alan Aldridge) on *Captain Fantastic and the Brown Dirt Cowboy*, the cover of *The Captain & the Kid* is, like the musical mood of the songs, much more restrained. Photo sessions were organized with the photographer Ryan McGinley under the direction of David Costa, the latter having also overseen the design of many of Elton's other album art from *Goodbye Yellow Brick Road* in 1973 to *To Be Continued...* in 1991. Here we see Elton and Bernie brought together virtually in a sepia-colored landscape, Elton at the piano at his English home, Woodside, and Bernie on horseback on his ranch in California—certainly as a nod to his nickname, Brown Dirt Cowboy.

Such a personal album by rights ought to have been successful, but the absence of a single ("The Bridge" was used only as a promotional single on the radio) meant that sales were flat. Outside the UK, where it went to number six in the charts (a triumph in itself, given the below-average performance of *Peachtree Road*), the album languished in the international charts, peaking at number eighteen in the United States, where it sold just over 150,000 copies.

Davey Johnstone plays a Gibson guitar emblazoned with *Captain Fantastic* artwork.

Arthur, Elton's dog, died in 2018 at the age of fourteen. In Arthur's memory, Elton played a deeply felt version of *"Don't Let the Sun Go Down on Me"* onstage in Las Vegas, where he was in residence. The cocker spaniel, Elton's faithful companion, was given to him for his fifty-sixth birthday and was a witness at the civil partnership ceremony between Elton and David Furnish in 2005.

POSTCARDS FROM RICHARD NIXON

Elton John, Bernie Taupin / 5:15

Musicians: Elton John: vocals, piano / Davey Johnstone: electric guitar, acoustic guitar, banjo, mandolin, harmonica, backing vocals / Bob Birch: bass, backing vocals / Nigel Olsson: drums, backing vocals / Guy Babylon: keyboards, arrangements / John Mahon: percussion, backing vocals / Matt Still: backing vocals **Recorded:** Center Stage, Atlanta: Spring 2006 **Technical Team:** Producers: Elton John, Matt Still / **Sound Engineer:** Matt Still / **Assistant Sound Engineer:** Tom Rickert / **Mixing:** Matt Still / Assistant **Mixing:** Dan Porter / **Mastering:** Bob Ludwig / **Studio Coordinator:** Adrian Collee

The Captain & the Kid journeys back through time with *"Postcards from Richard Nixon,"* a song that picks up the story of Elton and Bernie's career together from where *Captain Fantastic and the Brown Dirt Cowboy* had left off, which is to say on the brink of their conquest of the United States, their ultimate fantasy. The song starts with the former president Richard Nixon greeting these two unsophisticated young Englishmen with open arms. Bernie affectionately describes Elton and himself as "Twin spirits soaking up a dream." He also refers to the "big red bus," the double-decker bus chartered by Elton's American record company for his first tour of North America in order to make sure the young singer made a big impact. Unsurprisingly, the song has a dig at Nixon, saying that "he's sent so many [soldiers] overseas" and suggesting that the American president was hoping that Elton and Bernie might distract people from the negative remarks being made about him in the press about his management of the Vietnam War: "A small diversion caused by two / Pale kids come to play," as Bernie put it. By way of a diversion, Elton was to stage an artistic takeover, with "Someone Saved My Life Tonight" rising to fourth place on the *Billboard* charts. His memories of that glorious period are summed up in an invigorating piano rock motif, well supported by Davey Johnstone's acoustic guitar. This followed by Nigel Olsson's drums, adding a little more muscle to the proceedings, while airy backing vocals effectively underline the refrain.

JUST LIKE NOAH'S ARK

Elton John, Bernie Taupin / 5:33

Musicians: Elton John: vocals, piano / Davey Johnstone: electric guitar, acoustic guitar, banjo, mandolin, harmonica, backing vocals / Bob Birch: bass, backing vocals / Nigel Olsson: drums, backing vocals / Guy Babylon: keyboards, arrangements / John Mahon: percussion, backing vocals / Matt Still: backing vocals / Arthur: barking **Recorded:** Center Stage, Atlanta: Spring 2006 **Technical Team:** Producers: Elton John, Matt Still / **Sound Engineer:** Matt Still / **Assistant Sound Engineer:** Tom Rickert / **Mixing:** Matt Still / **Mixing Assistant:** Dan Porter / **Mastering:** Bob Ludwig / **Studio Coordinator:** Adrian Collee

"Just Like Noah's Ark" oozes rock 'n' roll from every pore, and it is so strongly influenced by the Rolling Stones that it might seem like a pastiche. Elton's song has, however, a greater musical complexity than many of the more instinctive numbers by Keith Richards and Mick Jagger: unexpected changes of rhythm and breaks in the harmonic progressions make this a joyful piece where each musician is allowed to shine. Guy Babylon, for example, embarks on a wild keyboard solo at 3:29, brilliantly picked up by Davey Johnstone at 3:51. Nigel Olsson and Bob Birch provide an uncompromising and slightly laidback rhythm section. In the words, Bernie paints a caustic picture of the music business, depicting it as a decadent Noah's Ark: "Pretty girls and boys in drag […] Italiano promotion men / Chomping a big cigar […] Radio boss dipping his nose in a little white packet." But Elton and Bernie assure us that they will not fall for all this: "We're not as dumb as we might look." At the end of the song, Arthur, Elton's dog, barks to the rhythm of the music: frightened by the bell John Mahon was trying to play, he couldn't be silenced. Matt Still, in charge of mixing, was delighted by the effect of this extraordinarily rhythmic barking and so decided to keep it in—and to credit Arthur for his artistic contribution!

Bob Birch and Elton John at Wembley Stadium during a performance on December 11, 2002.

WOULDN'T HAVE YOU ANY OTHER WAY (NYC)

Elton John, Bernie Taupin / 4:39

Musicians: Elton John: vocals, piano / Davey Johnstone: electric guitar, acoustic guitar, banjo, mandolin, harmonica, backing vocals / Bob Birch: bass, backing vocals / Nigel Olsson: drums, backing vocals / Guy Babylon: keyboards, arrangements / John Mahon: percussion, backing vocals / Matt Still: backing vocals **Recorded:** Center Stage, Atlanta: Spring 2006 **Technical Team:** Producers: Elton John, Matt Still / **Sound Engineer:** Matt Still / **Assistant Sound Engineer:** Tom Rickert / **Mixing:** Matt Still / Assistant **Mixing:** Dan Porter / **Mastering:** Bob Ludwig / **Studio Coordinator:** Adrian Collee

This nostalgic ballad dedicated to New York is built around vivid and almost cinematographic evocations of the metropolis: the long black limousines, Central Park in the snow, the famous yellow cabs, the subway rumbling below ground night and day, the ghost of the famous mafioso Joe Gallo haunting the streets, the famous disco Studio 54 on Broadway. New York has lost none of its attraction for Bernie. He uses the city as the background for several of his songs—not always in such a positive way—summing up his view in a simple phrase: "This city's got a thing about it, don't try to understand it." Although successful, the song is musically disappointing, given the potential of its subject and Bernie's treatment of it. The arrangement and melody are unimaginative despite some nice guitar touches from Davey Johnstone and backing vocals that are effective but sound too distant. Expressive piano playing helps the piece as a whole.

TINDERBOX

Elton John, Bernie Taupin / 4:26

Musicians: Elton John: vocals, piano / Davey Johnstone: electric guitar, acoustic guitar, banjo, mandolin, harmonica, backing vocals / Bob Birch: bass, backing vocals / Nigel Olsson: drums, backing vocals / Guy Babylon: keyboards, arrangements / John Mahon: percussion, backing vocals / Matt Still: backing vocals **Recorded:** Center Stage, Atlanta: Spring 2006 **Technical Team:** Producers: Elton John, Matt Still / **Sound Engineer:** Matt Still / **Assistant Sound Engineer:** Tom Rickert / **Mixing:** Matt Still / Assistant **Mixing:** Dan Porter / **Mastering:** Bob Ludwig / **Studio Coordinator:** Adrian Collee

It would have been tempting for Bernie to smooth over any rough edges in his relationship with Elton when writing his musical memoirs, but he doesn't shy away from it. In "Tinderbox," the lyricist does not attempt to conceal the tensions that could have upset their musical partnership: "We've been living in a tinderbox / And two sparks can set the whole thing off"; "Pressure's gonna cook us if we don't unlock it." Bernie even refers to the time the two men stopped working together, only to come back again better than ever—although there was no guarantee of that at the time: "We've gotta climb out of the other one's pocket / Or we're gonna burn out on this beautiful rocket." The "beautiful rocket" is, of course, a reference to the song "Rocket Man" as well as the Rocket Record Company, the name of their label. "Tinderbox" depends largely on Elton's charismatic voice, which seems at times to mimic a furious Paul McCartney, along with his expressive piano playing. The piano is joined by Davey Johnstone's delicately saturated guitars, the dry sound of Nigel's drums is reinforced by the brightness of a tambourine, and Bob Birch on bass provides reliable support. An impressive vocal backing contributes to the overall sound of "Tinderbox," which is one of the most successful numbers on *The Captain & the Kid*.

AND THE HOUSE FELL DOWN

Elton John, Bernie Taupin / 4:49

Musicians: Elton John: vocals, piano / **Davey Johnstone:** electric guitar, acoustic guitar, banjo, mandolin, harmonica, backing vocals / **Bob Birch:** bass, backing vocals / **Nigel Olsson:** drums, backing vocals / **Guy Babylon:** keyboards, arrangements / **John Mahon:** percussion, backing vocals / **Matt Still:** backing vocals **Recorded: Center Stage, Atlanta:** Spring 2006 **Technical Team: Producers:** Elton John, Matt Still / **Sound Engineer:** Matt Still / **Assistant Sound Engineer:** Tom Rickert / **Mixing:** Matt Still / **Assistant Mixing:** Dan Porter / **Mastering:** Bob Ludwig / **Studio Coordinator:** Adrian Collee

The Captain & the Kid is anything but a hagiography. Here the most depraved aspects of Elton's and Bernie's careers are exposed to public view. Bernie does not spare himself in the process and particularly not in "And the House Fell Down," a song that sheds an unflinching light on his addictions and growing paranoia when in a downward spiral. The story of the Three Little Pigs referred to in this number is used to describe his dependency: the image of the Big Bad Wolf threatening to blow his house down, ready to eat him, is his way of expressing his vulnerability and the collapse of his social life in moments of crisis. He invites the listener to see into his troubled psyche: "The sun is up and the shades are all pulled down / I'm more paranoid with every little sound […] Oh the TV's on and the colors really hurt my head / If I could think straight I'd wish that I was dead." He doesn't shy away from the sordid details: "With a rolled up note I'm hovering on that line / Three days on a diet of cocaine and wine / And a little weed just to level me sometime." Constructed on a rhythm section with a driving groove, with particularly prominent bass playing, the song features one of the most beautiful piano sequences on the album. Having already produced an irresistible motif at the beginning of the song, Elton throws himself into an amazing swing solo at 3:06. His great vocal performance, enhanced by the backing vocals, makes "And the House Fell Down" one of the most brilliant successes of the record.

BLUES NEVER FADE AWAY

Elton John, Bernie Taupin / 4:45

Musicians: Elton John: vocals, piano / **Davey Johnstone:** electric guitar, acoustic guitar, banjo, mandolin, harmonica, backing vocals / **Bob Birch:** bass, backing vocals / **Nigel Olsson:** drums, backing vocals / **Guy Babylon:** keyboards, arrangements / **John Mahon:** percussion, backing vocals / **Matt Still:** backing vocals **Recorded: Center Stage,** **Atlanta:** Spring 2006 **Technical Team: Producers:** Elton John, Matt Still / **Sound Engineer:** Matt Still / **Assistant Sound Engineer:** Tom Rickert / **Mixing:** Matt Still / **Mixing Assistant:** Dan Porter / **Mastering:** Bob Ludwig / **Studio Coordinator:** Adrian Collee

Blues and gospel are woven together in "Blues Never Fade Away," a moving ballad with words by Bernie remembering Ryan White, John Lennon, and Gianni Versace. And not just them; so many other dead friends are recalled by implication in this song (Marc Bolan, Freddie Mercury, Lady Di, Dee Murray, and Gus and Sheila Dudgeon). It laments the cruelty of fate and the unspeakable pain caused by these losses. Elton's words for the former Beatle are simple but eloquent: "I miss John Lennon's laugh." Gianni Versace is alluded to by the sentence: "His passions hung upon his walls and were printed onto cloth." He is more direct speaking of the death of Ryan White: "He wasn't famous but I sure did love him / I've got his picture in a little frame / He lost his life to a big disease before it even had a name." "Who makes the call and who gets to choose? / Who gets to win and who gets to lose?" "And how did we get so lucky?" the narrator asks guiltily, aware that he has lived life dangerously but has survived nevertheless. The arrangement of "Blues Never Fade Away" is a model of crescendo construction. Starting out with just the piano, it is gradually enriched with, first, a stunning mandolin, and then angelic backing vocals, warm keyboards in the background, and a lively rhythm section. The whole is driven by Elton's singing, which encourages uninhibited electric guitar playing by Davey Johnstone. The last section, from 3:33, begins gently; as it grows in intensity, Elton's voice at 3:48 gives you goose bumps. The emotional effect of the song's conclusion is sublime.

THE BRIDGE

Elton John, Bernie Taupin / 3:38

Musicians: Elton John: vocals, piano; backing vocals: uncredited **Recorded: Center Stage, Atlanta:** Spring 2006 **Technical Team: Producers:** Elton John, Matt Still / **Sound Engineer:** Matt Still / **Assistant Sound Engineer:** Tom Rickert / **Mixing:** Matt Still / **Mixing Assistant:** Dan Porter / **Mastering:** Bob Ludwig / **Studio Coordinator:** Adrian Collee

The opening piano chords of this moving minimalist ballad bring "Your Song" to mind, the song that was Elton's stepping stone to success. But Bernie does not forget that to get there, hard and demanding decisions had to be made and that one should never shy away from an essential choice, here imagined as a bridge: "And every one of us has to face that day / Do you cross the bridge or do you fade away?" In Bernie's lyrics, the bridge becomes a metaphor for life, "Strong enough to hold the weight of time / Long enough to leave some of us behind." As the song goes on, the lyrics calls on the narrator to risk all and overcome his fears: "And the bridge—it shines / Oh, cold, hard iron / Saying come and risk it all / Or die trying." Elton's deeper voice asserts itself, confidently tackling the harmonic gymnastics of a melody that is more complex than it might seem. The Elton/Bernie duo makes a strong impact with "The Bridge," in a perfect illustration of the complementary way they work together. This piece has something of the flavor of the classics of their 1970s heyday.

I MUST HAVE LOST IT ON THE WIND

Elton John, Bernie Taupin / 3:53

Musicians: Elton John: vocals, piano / **Davey Johnstone:** electric guitar, acoustic guitar, banjo, mandolin, harmonica, backing vocals / **Bob Birch:** bass, backing vocals / **Nigel Olsson:** drums, backing vocals / **Guy Babylon:** keyboards, arrangements / **John Mahon:** percussion, backing vocals / **Matt Still:** backing vocals **Recorded: Center Stage, Atlanta:** Spring 2006 **Technical Team: Producers:** Elton John, Matt Still / **Sound Engineer:** Matt Still / **Assistant Sound Engineer:** Tom Rickert / **Mixing:** Matt Still / **Mixing Assistant:** Dan Porter / **Mastering:** Bob Ludwig / **Studio Coordinator:** Adrian Collee

Indispensable musician Davey Johnstone is firing on all cylinders in "I Must Have Lost It on the Wind"; whether it's his incisive acoustic guitar, warm harmonica, or understated mandolin, he single-handedly provides the song's country sound. Over this, Elton provides his signature piano playing. Guy Babylon on keyboards adds in some light and cheerful notes, which are one of the important elements of this song. The rhythm section, relegated to the background in the mix, does a reliable job, its swinging groove supporting Davey's harmonica, the key feature of this arrangement. Bernie's words deal with past loves and other failed relationships, putting himself in the shoes of a philosophical narrator: "I could say my list of lovers doesn't matter anymore / But some are always in my heart / And some I'm not so sure

/ Either way they all left their mark / And for some I found a cure." Vocally, Elton is at ease but doesn't pull out all the stops. He can, however, count on the fine backing vocals on the refrains to make this essentially cheerful piece more emotionally telling.

> Each episode of the television series *Grey's Anatomy* takes its title from a famous song. "I Must Have Lost It on the Wind" was the title of the first episode of its eleventh season.

OLD 67

Elton John, Bernie Taupin / 4:01

Musicians: Elton John: vocals, piano / **Davey Johnstone:** electric guitar (slide), acoustic guitar, banjo, mandolin, backing vocals / **Bob Birch:** bass, backing vocals / **Nigel Olsson:** drums, backing vocals / **Guy Babylon:** keyboards, arrangements / **John Mahon:** percussion, backing vocals / **Matt Still:** backing vocals **Recorded: Center Stage, Atlanta:** Spring 2006 **Technical Team: Producers:** Elton John, Matt Still / **Sound Engineer:** Matt Still / **Assistant Sound Engineer:** Tom Rickert / **Mixing:** Matt Still / **Mixing Assistant:** Dan Porter / **Mastering:** Bob Ludwig / **Studio Coordinator:** Adrian Collee

Without worrying about chronological coherence, in the aptly named "Old '67" Bernie Taupin takes us back to the year 1967, the dawn of his career with Elton. The two men remember how they "nearly froze to death on Oxford Street." Now they are "sitting in the South of France," looking back at their past career while listening to the "cicadas singing." "Old '67 what a time it was / What a time of innocence, / what a time we've lost / Raise a glass and have a laugh." "Old '67" has all the hallmarks of Elton's style, with a wonderful harmonic progression, beautiful interjections from Davey Johnstone on slide guitar, and the silky keyboard playing of Guy Babylon. These elements, coupled with faraway backing vocals, convey and reinforce the song's nostalgia. Elton's voice, clear and powerful, blends perfectly with his honkytonk piano, particularly where it starts to sound slightly more rasping toward the end. "Old '67" would not have been out of place on albums such as *Tumbleweed Connection* or *Honky Château*.

"The Captain and the Kid" stands out as the song that most directly evokes the artist's musical past.

THE CAPTAIN AND THE KID

Elton John, Bernie Taupin / 5:02

Musicians: Elton John: vocals, piano / **Davey Johnstone:** electric guitar, acoustic guitar, banjo, mandolin, backing vocals / **Bob Birch:** bass, backing vocals / **Nigel Olsson:** drums, backing vocals / **Guy Babylon:** keyboards, arrangements / **John Mahon:** percussion, backing vocals / **Matt Still:** backing vocals **Recorded: Center Stage, Atlanta:** Spring 2006 **Technical Team: Producers:** Elton John, Matt Still / **Sound Engineer:** Matt Still / **Assistant Sound Engineer:** Tom Rickert / **Mixing:** Matt Still / **Mixing Assistant:** Dan Porter / **Mastering:** Bob Ludwig / **Studio Coordinator:** Adrian Collee

Given the brief to make a direct connection with the 1975 album *Captain Fantastic and the Brown Dirt Cowboy*, "The Captain and the Kid" treads on dangerous ground. Written by Bernie, "the Kid," the text is written from the point of view of "Captain" Elton. It dwells on the differences between the two men, differences that make them complement one another. There are many allusions to the pair's classic works, while *Goodbye Yellow Brick Road*, *Tumbleweed Connection*, "Rocket Man," and *Captain Fantastic and the Brown Dirt Cowboy* are specifically mentioned. Elton and Bernie are forced to acknowledge one thing, something that justifies their constant artistic progress: "And you can't go back / And if you try it fails." So, despite this look back to the past, the road has not yet come to an end for these two friends who are still looking ahead to the future. Imbued with a country music sound, "The Captain and the Kid" is more proof of Davey Johnstone's contribution to Elton John's world: the occasional interventions of his electric guitar are beautifully judged, his banjo playing is delightful, and his driving acoustic guitar encourages the rhythm section to follow him in a gentle shuffle rhythm. Elton's piano slips mischievously into the gaps. As for the backing vocals, they complete a heartwarming arrangement for long winter evenings. The mixing of the whole is a model of clarity.

None of Elton's penchants for eccentric clothing are spared in "Across the River Thames."

ACROSS THE RIVER THAMES

Elton John, Bernie Taupin / 4:32

Musicians: Elton John: vocals, piano / Davey Johnstone: electric guitar, acoustic guitar, banjo, mandolin, backing vocals, musical direction / Bob Birch: bass, backing vocals / Nigel Olsson: drums, backing vocals / Guy Babylon: keyboards, arrangements / John Mahon: percussion, backing vocals / Matt Still: backing vocals
Recorded: Center Stage, Atlanta: Spring 2006 **Technical Team:** Producers: Elton John, Matt Still / Sound Engineer: Matt Still / Assistant Sound Engineer: Tom Rickert / Mixing: Matt Still / Mixing Assistant: Dan Porter / Mastering: Bob Ludwig / Studio Coordinator: Adrian Collee

Bernie knew he could count on Elton's sense of humor and self-deprecation when he handed over the delectable words of the joyful rock number "Across the River Thames." In the very first lines of the song, Elton admits: "Good taste at times I've sometimes lacked / I won't deny the truth / I got dressed up as Donald Duck / Making up for my repressed youth." He then refers to "Disco balls and spandex pants / On questionable friends," as if to recall the disastrous showing of his only disco album, *Victim of Love*, in 1979. He does not hide that he had been called a "dinosaur" by the punk movement, whose members tried to tell him "that the times was changing / And all good things must end." No matter, an amused Elton responds, "I'm still here and the fog still rolls across the River Thames." Changing fashions have not affected his lasting popularity. Without sacrificing the rock aspect (as can be heard from Davey Johnstone's very credible solo at 3:14), the arrangement of "Across the River Thames" is easy listening. Elton's piano is less audible than Guy Babylon's keyboards, but the backing vocals, ideal for a football stadium, and the rhythm section, energetic if slightly uncoordinated, give solid support to this number recorded during the *Peachtree Road* sessions.

ALBUM

THE UNION

If It Wasn't for Bad . Eight Hundred Dollar Shoes . Hey Ahab . Gone to Shiloh .
Jimmie Rodgers' Dream . There's No Tomorrow . Monkey Suit . The Best Part of the Day .
A Dream Come True . When Love Is Dying . I Should Have Sent Roses . Hearts Have
Turned to Stone . Never Too Old (To Hold Somebody) . In the Hands of Angels

RELEASE DATES
UK Release: October 20, 2010
Reference: Mercury—2748480
Best UK Chart Ranking: 12
US Release: October 19, 2010
Reference: Decca—B0014840-02
Best US Chart Ranking: 3

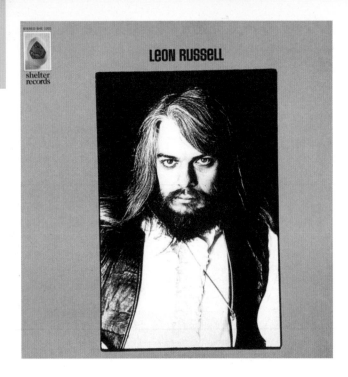

Leon Russell was released in 1970, and the album inspired Elton John's long-term admiration for the American songwriter.

A MOVING REUNION

The story of *The Union* and the link between Elton John and Leon Russell says more about the British star than all his accolades, distinctions, and millions of albums sold. It speaks to the importance Elton attached to music as art, of course, as well as to the human qualities he placed above all other artistic considerations. The years might well have gone by, but Elton never forgot his idol, any more than the *Leon Russell* LP that he wore out on his turntable, or the haunting melody of "Song for You" (note the proximity with "Your Song," released the same year, in 1970) and the particularly unique voice of its performer. It was from Leon Russell that Elton learned rock could also be the realm of the pianist, and that one could marry different musical styles with elegance (folk, country, gospel, bluegrass, blues) and without losing direction. He also learned that a session musician could be proud of their profession (Russell had played with George Harrison, Doris Day, Barbra Streisand, B.B. King, Willie Nelson, Frank Sinatra, the Rolling Stones, Ray Charles, Eric Clapton, Bob Dylan...). Elton had also not forgotten the attendance of Russell at his concert at the Troubadour, on August 26, 1970. He had almost fallen off his chair when he noticed Russell in the audience—and not only that, but when the American songwriter actually invited Elton to visit him, Elton thought, "He's going to invite me up there and tie me to a chair and whip me and say 'This is how to play the piano!'...and

ohhh...I was really scared...and I've never been scared of meeting anyone..."[40]

Out of Touch

The years went by, and the two men gradually lost touch with each other until January 2009. At the time, Elton was on safari in South Africa with David Furnish. David had prepared a playlist on his iPod according to Elton's suggestions. One evening, when they were getting ready to eat, Elton started the playlist, which began with "Back to the Island" by Leon Russell. The effect of this nostalgic song on Elton was immediate: overwhelmed by the memories it unearthed, he burst into tears. Once he was back in London, Elton picked up his telephone and asked his manager for Leon Russell's number. "I asked how he was. He said he was in bed, watching *Days of Our Lives* on TV: 'I'm all right. Just about making ends meet.' That was one way of putting it. Leon had made some bad business decisions, he had a lot of ex-wives, and times had changed. Now he was touring anywhere that would have him. One of the finest musicians and songwriters in the world, and he was playing sports bars and pubs, beer festivals and motorbike conventions, towns I'd never heard of in Missouri and Connecticut."[3] It is true that since *One for the Road*, an album recorded with Willie Nelson in 1979 that received two Grammy nominations, Leon Russell had totally disappeared off the charts. When he

Elton John and Leon Russell in concert on October 19, 2010, at the Beacon Theatre in New York.

put down the phone, Elton realized that what had driven him to contact Leon after such a long time was the desire to record something together. The singer straightaway contacted T-Bone Burnett, whom he did not know personally, but whose work as a musician and producer he admired. T-Bone had the ideal profile for this kind of project. A former member of Bob Dylan's Rolling Thunder Revue, Burnett was a fan of jazz just as much as he was of country and had worked with a number of artists that Elton held in high esteem, including Elvis Costello, Roy Orbison, k.d. lang, and B.B. King. Luckily, the project stirred T-Bone's interest. So Elton redialed Leon's number to ask if he would agree to make an album with him "My God, forty-five years I don't hear from you [actually thirty-five] and now twice in ten minutes?"[3] Leon burst out laughing. The musician was tempted, but he did raise some provisos due to his failing physical health: He walked with a cane and had accumulated a raft of other issues. However, Elton did not have to press Leon for too long before he gave in and they agreed to work together.

A Dream Come True

The Union was written by four people. An exceptional lyricist in his own right, Leon did, however, leave most of the texts to Bernie. Certain themes common to several pieces emerged: mutual gratitude for this moment of artistic communion ("A Dream Come True," "In the Hands of Angels"), lost love ("Hearts Have Turned to Stone," "I Should Have Sent Roses," "When Love Is Dying," "Mandalay Again"), death and the passing of time ("Never Too Old," "There's No Tomorrow"), and—something more unusual for Bernie—humor ("Eight Hundred Dollar Shoes," "The Best Part of the Day"). "Gone to Shiloh," in which Taupin evokes the American Civil War with admirable precision, stands out from the rest of the tracks and inspired the title of the album, *The Union*, with a double meaning, as it evokes both the Union army and also the association between Leon and Elton.

The album's recording sessions started at the Village Recorder in Los Angeles, on November 20, 2009, or thirty-nine years to the day after the concert given by Leon Russell at Fillmore East in New York, where Elton played. The creation of

the songs was not compartmentalized. Writing, composition, and recording all intertwined together over a period of four months, until March 2010. For the first time since *Victim of Love* in 1979, Elton John did not call upon his tour musicians. The turnover of personnel was significant for all the tracks on this album, although a core group did emerge with drummers and percussionists Jay Bellerose and Jim Keltner, bassist Dennis Crouch, keyboard player Booker T. Jones, guitarist Marc Ribot, and trumpet player Darrell Leonard. Among the artists invited to these reunions, was, of course, Neil Young, who poured out emotion into the number "Gone to Shiloh," as well as Brian Wilson, who took charge of the backing vocals direction on "When Love Is Dying." After working with Bruce Johnston and Carl Wilson, Elton now had the benefit of collaborating with another member of the legendary Beach Boys. The recording sessions flowed along with disconcerting efficiency. The sessions barely lasted longer than two hours a day, since it was

difficult for Leon Russell to work prolonged hours. In fact, the team was interrupted in the middle of one of the sessions due to a sudden medical issue when Leon suffered from a loss of cerebrospinal fluid. "There were moments when I wondered if his contributions to the album were going to be released post-humously. One day, his nose started running: it was fluid leak-ing from his brain. He was rushed into hospital for surgery and treated for heart failure and pneumonia while he was there."[3] A week later, the indefatigable Russell, with his long hair and white beard, was back in the studio to wrap up the album.

The Resurrection of King Leon

The Union was released in October 2010, and Leon Russell and Elton John promoted it together with thirty or so con-certs scheduled to run until April 2 of the following year. The two artists made the promotional rounds together, which went against the grain for Leon, since he had hitherto shunned all

forms of publicity. Leon made appearances with good grace as a way to thank his partner, who had enabled him to expe-rience an unexpected worldwide success. With some glow-ing reviews, the album was ranked in most of the international charts and even reached third place on the *Billboard* charts. On December 1, 2010, "If It Wasn't for Bad" was nominated for a Grammy Award in the category of Best Pop Collaboration with Vocals. On March 14, Leon was also recognized by his peers when he was inducted into the Rock and Roll Hall of Fame. And naturally, it was Elton who gave the induction speech. Unfortunately, five years later, on November 13, 2016, Leon Russell passed away at the age of seventy-four. "My darling Leon Russell passed away last night," Elton wrote on his Ins-tagram account. "He was a mentor, inspiration and so kind to me. Thank God we caught up with each other and made 'The Union.' He got his reputation back and felt fulfilled. I loved him and always will."[141]

IF IT WASN'T FOR BAD

Leon Russell / 5:15

Musicians: Elton John: vocals / Leon Russell: vocals, piano, backing vocals arrangement / Marc Ribot: electric guitar / Dennis Crouch: acoustic bass / Jim Keltner: drums, percussion / Jay Bellerose: drums, percussion / Booker T. Jones: Hammond B3 organ / Keefus Ciancia: keyboards / Darrell Leonard: trumpet, bass trumpet, brass direction and arrangement / Ira Nepus: trombone / Maurice Spears: trombone / George Bohanon: trombone, baritone horn / William Roper: tuba / Bill Maxwell: backing vocals direction / Rose Stone, Judith Hill, Alfie Silas-Durio, Tata Vega, Jean Witherspoon: backing vocals **Recorded:** Quad Studios, Nashville, Tennessee / The Village Recorder, Los Angeles: November 20, 2009–March 2010 **Technical Team:** Producer: T-Bone Burnett / Executive Producers: Johnny Barbis, Elton John / Sound Engineers: Mike Piersante, Jason Wormer / Assistant Sound Engineers: Kory Aaron, Kyle Ford, Mark Lambert, Brett Lind, Ben McAmis, Chris Owens, Vanessa Parr / Mixing: Mike Piersante / Editing: Jason Wormer / Mastering: Gavin Lurssen / Production Coordinators: Adrian Collee, Jon Howard, Ivy Skoff

"If you didn't see him, I'm sorry: you missed out. Leon Russell was the greatest."[3] Of all the artists with whom Elton had been able to rub shoulders during his career, Leon Russell is the one who has received the most enthusiastic praise. More than just words, it is the music itself that speaks such volumes for the talent of this unjustly neglected artist: the collaborative album created by the two men begins with a grandiose composition, 100 percent the work of this genius from Oklahoma. "If It Wasn't for Bad" exudes pure class over more than five minutes, and one hardly lingers over Elton's vocal performance, which is difficult to make out. Leon Russell inhabits the piece totally due to his powerful piano playing and his mesmerizing, bluesy voice. The discreet appearance of the brass always adds enhanced majesty to the ensemble, especially from 1:53, while Booker T. Jones's Hammond organ offers a soft bed for Marc Ribot's electric guitar, who was already acknowledged for his exceptional work with Tom Waits since his *Rain Dogs* album. The American musician delivers a solo that is both short and incisive at the end of this intense piece, sublimated by stunning backing vocals. The dark lyrics dwell on the unhappy experience of a man who is the victim of a toxic relationship, punctuated by lies and cheap shots. As the music supports them, the words cut like razor blades: "I knew from the first night I met you / Something just wasn't quite right / [...] I only saw what I wanted to see / You were a dream in my mind." With this highly successful introductory piece, *The Union* sets the bar very high.

EIGHT HUNDRED DOLLAR SHOES

Elton John, Bernie Taupin / 3:23

Musicians: Elton John: vocals, piano / Leon Russell: vocals, piano / Marc Ribot: electric guitar / Dennis Crouch: acoustic bass / Jim Keltner: drums, percussion / Jay Bellerose: drums, percussion / Keefus Ciancia: keyboards / Bill Maxwell: backing vocals direction and arrangement / Bill Cantos, Lou Pardini, Jason Scheff, Tata Vega: backing vocals **Recorded:** Quad Studios, Nashville, Tennessee / The Village Recorder, Los Angeles: November 20, 2009–March 2010 **Technical Team:** Producer: T-Bone Burnett / Executive Producers: Johnny Barbis, Elton John / Sound Engineers: Mike Piersante, Jason Wormer / Assistant Sound Engineers: Kory Aaron, Kyle Ford, Mark Lambert, Brett Lind, Ben McAmis, Chris Owens, Vanessa Parr / Mixing: Mike Piersante / Editing: Jason Wormer / Mastering: Gavin Lurssen / Production Coordinators: Adrian Collee, Jon Howard, Ivy Skoff

While Elton John and Leon Russell were bound by a profound admiration and mutual respect, everything would lead one to believe that the characters portrayed in "Eight Hundred Dollar Shoes" represented the two artists. Life had distanced them from each other, one a victim of his own success, and seeming to have forgotten where he came from, and the other remaining in obscurity. "I saw you cross the landing descending marble stairs / Like Caesar crossed the Rubicon you seemed to walk on air," wrote the lyricist to emphasize the gap between the two protagonists. And to illustrate it further, he takes the example of overpriced shoes: "Oh you came to town in headlines / And eight hundred dollar shoes." To set this story to music, Elton opted for a melancholic ballad, in which the piano has the star role. Marc Ribot's guitar colors the arrangement discreetly, always judiciously, without superfluous playing effects. Some elements of rhythm and play on cymbals come in, also to provide density to the song. A cello sound, subtly emulated on Keefus Ciancia's keyboards, imparts a certain solemnity, while the distant backing vocals benevolently envelop Leon Russell's voice, which appears very sporadically.

HEY AHAB

Elton John, Bernie Taupin / 5:39

Musicians: Elton John: vocals, piano / Leon Russell: vocals, piano / Marc Ribot: electric guitar / T-Bone Burnett: electric guitar / Dennis Crouch: acoustic bass / Jim Keltner: drums, percussion / Jay Bellerose: drums, percussion / Keefus Ciancia: keyboards / Mike Piersante: tambourine / Bill Maxwell: backing vocals direction and arrangement / Tanya Balam, Bill Cantos, Judith Hill, Kellye Huff, Perry Morgan, Alfie Silas-Durio, Tiffany Smith, Rose Stone, Tata Vega, Jean Witherspoon: backing vocals **Recorded:** Quad Studios, Nashville, Tennessee / The Village Recorder, Los Angeles: November 20–March 2010 **Technical Team:** Producer: T-Bone Burnett / Executive Producers: Johnny Barbis, Elton John / Sound Engineers: Mike Piersante, Jason Wormer / Assistant Sound Engineers: Kory Aaron, Kyle Ford, Mark Lambert, Brett Lind, Ben McAmis, Chris Owens, Vanessa Parr / Mixing: Mike Piersante / Editing: Jason Wormer / Mastering: Gavin Lurssen / Production Coordinators: Adrian Collee, Jon Howard, Ivy Skoff

"It's a constant struggle getting up that hill," writes Bernie at the beginning of "Hey Ahab," but he leaves solid ground behind during the subsequent verses, sailing on a boat of fortune and searching for a "great white whale." The use of the name Ahab is a reference to the novel *Moby Dick* by Herman Melville, published in 1851, in which a whaling captain called Ahab relentlessly pursues vengeance against a white whale that bit off his leg. In one reading, the whale in the book can be seen to symbolize the ideals a person might wish to attain, but only at the cost of major self-harm and sacrifice. By citing Jonah in the second verse, Bernie also ventures an allusion to the Biblical prophet, who, according to the famous story, was swallowed by a whale and then regurgitated after three days and three nights.

This rhythm 'n' blues piece is based on a fine piano duet between Elton and Leon. Elton's voice in this track is massive, and he's joined by Leon's on the refrains along with the company of backing vocalists who once again perform with great precision.

GONE TO SHILOH

Elton John, Bernie Taupin / 4:50

Musicians: Elton John: vocals, piano / Leon Russell: vocals, piano / Neil Young: vocals / Marc Ribot: electric guitar / Dennis Crouch: acoustic bass / Jim Keltner: drums, percussion / Jay Bellerose: drums, percussion / Keefus Ciancia: keyboards / Jason Wormer: dulcimer / Darrell Leonard: trumpet, brass direction and arrangement / Ira Nepus: trombone / Maurice Spears: trombone / George Bohanon: trombone, baritone horn / William Roper: tuba **Recorded:** Quad Studios, Nashville, Tennessee / The Village Recorder, Los Angeles: January 2010 **Technical Team:** Producer: T-Bone Burnett / Executive Producers: Johnny Barbis, Elton John / Sound Engineers: Mike Piersante, Jason Wormer / Assistant Sound Engineers: Kory Aaron, Kyle Ford, Mark Lambert, Brett Lind, Ben McAmis, Chris Owens, Vanessa Parr / Mixing: Mike Piersante / Editing: Jason Wormer / Mastering: Gavin Lurssen / Production Coordinators: Adrian Collee, Jon Howard, Ivy Skoff

For the heartrending "Gone to Shiloh," a song that's evocative of the repertoire of the Band, Bernie takes his inspiration from a dark episode in the history of the United States: the battle of Shiloh, a bloody confrontation between the Union and the Confederate armies that took place on April 6 and 7, 1862, in Hardin County, Tennessee. The Confederate troops of generals Albert Sidney Johnston and Pierre Gustave Toutant de Beauregard attacked the Union troops, which were under the command of Major General Ulysses S. Grant, taking them by surprise when they had just set up their camp. The victory of the Union soldiers came at a cost of terrible losses on both sides: Out of 110,000 soldiers present, nearly 3,500 died and 16,000 were wounded. At the time, it was the bloodiest battle in the country's history.

At the heart of the wider history, Bernie, good storyteller that he is, opted for a smaller scale narrative. That of Luther, who sets off to join the Union army, leaving behind his two children who are "gonna have to share the weight together." He does not dwell on his departure but becomes more verbose when depicting the horror of the field of battle. He does this with surgical precision: "When flags and bullets start to fly [...] / the stunned surprise in the eyes of dying men [...] / The old black rooster sang him down that dirt road." The musical arrangement is also very striking. The voices of three heroes from the 1970s—Elton John, Leon Russell, and Neil Young—marry together with overwhelming, spine-tingling clarity. The piano is serious, and the brass solemn, almost funereal. "'Gone to Shiloh' is a song that feels like a movie," explained Elton. "It was a pivotal moment for the record I did with Leon, *The Union*, and a pivotal moment for us as writers."[35]

Jimmie Rodgers, the legend of American country and yodeling, circa 1931.

JIMMIE RODGERS' DREAM

Elton John, Bernie Taupin, T-Bone Burnett / 3:43

Musicians: Elton John: vocals, piano / Leon Russell: vocals, piano / Marc Ribot: electric guitar / T-Bone Burnett: electric guitar / Russ Pahl: pedal steel / Dennis Crouch: acoustic bass / Jim Keltner: drums, percussion / Jay Bellerose: drums, percussion / *Keefus Ciancia:* keyboards / Debra Dobkin: calabash / Bill Maxwell: backing vocals direction and arrangement / Bill Cantos, Lou Pardini, Jason Scheff, Tata Vega: backing vocals **Recorded:** Quad Studios, Nashville, Tennessee / The Village Recorder, Los Angeles: November 20, 2009–March 2010 **Technical Team:** Producer: T-Bone Burnett / **Executive Producers:** Johnny Barbis, Elton John / **Sound Engineers:** Mike Piersante, Jason Wormer / **Assistant Sound Engineers:** Kory Aaron, Kyle Ford, Mark Lambert, Brett Lind, Ben McAmis, Chris Owens, Vanessa Parr / **Mixing:** Mike Piersante / **Editing:** Jason Wormer / **Mastering:** Gavin Lurssen / **Production Coordinators:** Adrian Collee, Jon Howard, Ivy Skoff

As a pioneer of country music, the American singer Jimmie Rodgers was barely able to enjoy any of his fame before he died prematurely in 1933, aged thirty-five. He became famous because of the original timbre of his voice, his ability to yodel, and his guitar-playing skills. He suffered from terrible anxiety, which had a fatal impact on his health. Legend has it that when he was close to death, he wanted to record his final song, "Years Ago," with just his guitar as accompaniment, once more rediscovering the simplicity of his happier days. Elton sings the story of this musical hero that Leon Russell reveres in "Jimmie Rodgers' Dream." Bernie Taupin takes the liberty of giving voice to Jimmie: "I'm looking at a funeral wagon rolling down." In fact, when he died, the body of Jimmie Rodgers was taken by train to Meridian, his place of birth, which Bernie also mentions. Later, the narrator demonstrates a chilling lucidity when he feels that death is close: "In that mirror maybe that's what's left of me." When he lays down his arms, Jimmie Rodgers clearly sees his famous dream, that is referred to in the song's title: "Now I'm just looking for some cleaner air to breathe / In this room all alone / I dream of you." Elton and Leon complement each other marvelously well in this swaying country piece with its communicative serenity. For this homage to a guitarist, the pianos are deliberately kept in the background, leaving open the field for Marc Ribot's and T-Bone Burnett's guitars to express themselves and paint a remarkable picture, in the midst of which Russ Pahl's pedal steel takes all the limelight.

THERE'S NO TOMORROW

Elton John, Leon Russell, T-Bone Burnett, James Timothy Shaw / 3:45

Musicians: Elton John: vocals, piano / Leon Russell: vocals, piano, backing vocals arrangement / **Marc Ribot:** electric guitar / Robert Randolph: pedal steel / Dennis Crouch: acoustic bass / Jim Keltner: drums, percussion / Jay Bellerose: drums, percussion / Keefus Ciancia: keyboards / Marty Grebb: keyboards / Bill Maxwell: backing vocals direction / Judith Hill, Alfie Silas-Durio, Tata Vega, Jean Witherspoon: backing vocals **Recorded:** Quad Studios, Nashville, Tennessee / The Village Recorder, Los Angeles: November 20, 2009–March 2010 **Technical Team:** Producer: T-Bone Burnett / **Executive Producers:** Johnny Barbis, Elton John / **Sound Engineers:** Mike Piersante, Jason Wormer / **Assistant Sound Engineers:** Kory Aaron, Kyle Ford, Mark Lambert, Brett Lind, Ben McAmis, Chris Owens, Vanessa Parr / **Mixing:** Mike Piersante / **Editing:** Jason Wormer / **Mastering:** Gavin Lurssen / **Production Coordinators:** Adrian Collee, Jon Howard, Ivy Skoff

"There's No Tomorrow" is an extremely dark song that addresses the theme of death, as does "Jimmie Rodgers' Dream." But it does so with a fatalism that leaves no room for poetry. In the text, an individual presents himself at the door of death. Nothing characterizes him because he represents the human being in his universality: "We all know the story / We've heard it before / We end up no question / Outside of death's door." The outcome is inevitable, "There's no place to hide," and whether or not one accepts one's destiny changes nothing: "There's no tomorrow / There's only today." This slow, fat blues would not have been out of place on an album by Tom Waits. Elton's chilling vibrato has within its wake the compassionate voice of Leon Russell and an army of backing vocals sounding like so many lost souls. The funereal piano occasionally comes to life among the blistering guitar spasms of Marc Ribot or the luminous steel pedal of Robert Randolph.

MONKEY SUIT

Elton John, Bernie Taupin / 4:46

Musicians: Elton John: vocals, piano / Leon Russell: vocals, piano / Mike Piersante: tambourine / Marc Ribot: acoustic guitar / Dennis Crouch: acoustic bass / Jim Keltner: drums, percussion / Jay Bellerose: drums, percussion / Keefus Ciancia: keyboards / Darrell Leonard: trumpet, brass direction and arrangement / Thomas Peterson: saxophone / Joseph Sublett: saxophone / Jim Thompson: saxophone / Bill Maxwell: backing vocals direction and arrangement / Tanya Balam, Bill Cantos, Judith Hill, Kellye Huff, Perry Morgan, Alfie Silas-Durio, Tiffany Smith, Rose Stone, Tata Vega, Jean Witherspoon: backing vocals **Recorded:** Quad Studios, Nashville, Tennessee / The Village Recorder, Los Angeles: November 20, 2009–March 2010 **Technical Team:** Producer: T-Bone Burnett / Executive **Producers:** Johnny Barbis, Elton John / Sound Engineers: Mike Piersante, Jason Wormer / **Assistant Sound Engineers:** Kory Aaron, Kyle Ford, Mark Lambert, Brett Lind, Ben McAmis, Chris Owens, Vanessa Parr / **Mixing:** Mike Piersante / **Editing:** Jason Wormer / **Mastering:** Gavin Lurssen / **Production Coordinators:** Adrian Collee, Jon Howard, Ivy Skoff

At the intersection between basic rock 'n' roll and rhythm and blues, "Monkey Suit" enabled Elton to fulfill one of his musical dreams: to offer his idol, Leon Russell, a piece liable to revive his verve of the 1970s: "With 'Monkey Suit,' I wanted to write the kind of song that Leon and Joe Cocker and Leon's band The Shelter People might have performed on the Mad Dogs and Englishmen Tour in 1970—lots of brass, big backing vocals,"[142] explained Elton. (*Mad Dogs* was a double live album by Joe Cocker. It was considered to be his best stage performance,

with Leon Russell accompanying him, particularly on guitars, piano, vocals, and backing vocals.) The arrangement is dense, with powerful female backing vocals, torrid brass, a breathless rhythm section, and an unbridled piano in the background. Together with all this, Elton tells the story of a man "dressed to kill in [his] monkey suit." Clearly bad news, the man is driving south "in a bullet-riddled stolen car" with "nothing left to prove." Although he intervenes very little in this piece, Leon would certainly have appreciated Elton's gesture.

THE BEST PART OF THE DAY

Elton John, Bernie Taupin / 4:45

Musicians: Elton John: vocals, piano / Leon Russell: vocals, piano / Marc Ribot: electric guitar / Dennis Crouch: acoustic bass / Jim Keltner: drums, percussion / Jay Bellerose: drums, percussion / Booker T. Jones: Hammond B3 organ / Keefus Ciancia: keyboards / Bill Maxwell: backing vocals direction and arrangement / Bill Cantos, Lou Pardini, Jason Scheff, Tata Vega: backing vocals **Recorded:** Quad Studios, Nashville, Tennessee / The Village Recorder, Los Angeles: November 20, 2009–March 2010 **Technical Team:** Producer: T-Bone Burnett / **Executive Producers:** Johnny Barbis, Elton John / **Sound Engineers:** Mike Piersante, Jason Wormer / **Assistant Sound Engineers:** Kory Aaron, Kyle Ford, Mark Lambert, Brett Lind, Ben McAmis, Chris Owens, Vanessa Parr / **Mixing:** Mike Piersante / **Editing:** Jason Wormer / **Mastering:** Gavin Lurssen / **Production Coordinators:** Adrian Collee, Jon Howard, Ivy Skoff

While the story of the friendship developed in "The Best Part of the Day" is touching, and even sometimes funny—as in the intro, where Bernie writes: "I hear you singing, 'I Shall Be Released' / Like a chainsaw running through a masterpiece / But that's all right, that's okay"—the melody lacks depth. Despite the moments of "panache" present on the recording, no one particularly stands out, except perhaps Booker T. Jones on the Hammond organ, but he only delivers a few lines. Marc Ribot's guitar is desperately transparent, and the rhythm section is clumsy. The value of the song lies elsewhere, in Elton's and Leon's evident enjoyment sharing verses and piano sequences.

A DREAM COME TRUE

Elton John, Leon Russell / 5:07

Musicians: Elton John: vocals, piano / Leon Russell: vocals, piano, backing vocals arrangement / **Marc Ribot:** electric guitar / **Dennis Crouch:** acoustic bass / **Jay Bellerose:** drums, percussion / **Keefus Ciancia:** keyboards / **Bill Maxwell:** backing vocals direction / **Rose Stone:** backing vocals, tambourine / **Judith Hill, Alfie Silas-Durio, Tata Vega, Jean Witherspoon:** backing vocals **Recorded:** Quad Studios, Nashville, Tennessee / The Village Recorder, Los Angeles: November 20, 2009–March 2010 **Technical Team:** Producer: T-Bone Burnett / **Executive Producers:** Johnny Barbis, Elton John / **Sound Engineers:** Mike Piersante, Jason Wormer / **Assistant Sound Engineers:** Kory Aaron, Kyle Ford, Mark Lambert, Brett Lind, Ben McAmis, Chris Owens, Vanessa Parr / **Mixing:** Mike Piersante / **Editing:** Jason Wormer / **Mastering:** Gavin Lurssen / **Production Coordinators:** Adrian Collee, Jon Howard, Ivy Skoff

This number by the John-Russell duo is probably the most emblematic in the backstory of *The Union*: It is manifestly a matter of Elton, an accomplished star at the height of his celebrity, coming to look for his forgotten master, to place him back in the limelight with this collaborative album. The old man expresses to him all his gratitude, but also his pleasure at the idea of tackling this project that offers him a second lease of youth. The lyrics are touching and acknowledge this—almost in real time—via the progress of the album, a veritable "dream come true" for Russell: "Somehow I know / That you're a dream come true / It takes my breath / When it sounds that way / Seems like you / Chase the clouds away / And I feel so good." The arrangement of the piece translates the mixture of excitement and solace that Leon Russell feels, with a breathless "leadership struggle" on piano (a very fine sequence at 2:35!), a question-and-answer exchange on the verses, rousing rhythm parts, and the mischievous guitar of Marc Ribot, who knits a nervy background sound. Some slight negatives: The impressive backing vocals are mixed in the background of the arrangement, and the kick drum seems slightly too overbearing at times.

WHEN LOVE IS DYING

Elton John, Bernie Taupin / 4:51

Musicians: Elton John: vocals, piano / Leon Russell: vocals, piano / T-Bone Burnett: electric guitar / Dennis Crouch: acoustic bass / Jim Keltner: drums, percussion / Jay Bellerose: drums, percussion / Keefus Ciancia: keyboards / Bill Maxwell: backing vocals direction and arrangement / Brian Wilson: backing vocals, backing vocals arrangement / Bill Cantos, Rose Stone, Lou Pardini, Jason Scheff, Alfie Silas-Durio, Tata Vega, Jean Witherspoon: backing vocals **Recorded:** Quad Studios, Nashville, Tennessee / The Village Recorder, Los Angeles: January 2010 **Technical Team:** Producer: T-Bone Burnett / **Executive Producers:** Johnny Barbis, Elton John / **Sound Engineers:** Mike Piersante, Jason Wormer / **Assistant Sound Engineers:** Kory Aaron, Kyle Ford, Mark Lambert, Brett Lind, Ben McAmis, Chris Owens, Vanessa Parr / **Mixing:** Mike Piersante / **Editing:** Jason Wormer / **Mastering:** Gavin Lurssen / **Production Coordinators:** Adrian Collee, Jon Howard, Ivy Skoff

Bernie finds the right words (and surely the simplest ones, too) to describe the feeling of impotence that overwhelms the narrator when he understands that love is dying: "Nobody ever tells you / When love is dying, when love is dying / It just gets a little colder / And we stop trying." For this tearful ballad, which seems at first sight to be located beyond the album's waterline, the vocal gentleness of Leon Russell is called upon in some of the verses, leaving the power of Elton to express himself on his own in the refrains. The melody of the refrain, which ostensibly recycles elements from "Circle of Life," is catchy, with the contribution of massive backing vocals. T-Bone Burnett's guitar delivers an economic performance while the often discreet piano part becomes more dominant at the end of the refrains. "When Love Is Dying" is not one of the best pieces on *The Union*, but one must acknowledge the diabolical capacity of the John-Taupin duo to create cleverly put-together ballads that can be hard to get out of one's head.

I SHOULD HAVE SENT ROSES

Leon Russell, Bernie Taupin / 5:21

Musicians: Elton John: vocals, piano / **Leon Russell:** vocals, piano / **Doyle Bramhall II:** electric guitar / **Don Was:** bass / **Jim Keltner:** drums, percussion / **Jay Bellerose:** drums, percussion / **Booker T. Jones:** Hammond B3 organ / **Keefus Ciancia:** keyboards / **Mike Piersante:** percussion / **Mike Ford:** percussion / **Jason Wormer:** percussion / **Darrell Leonard:** trumpet, bass trumpet, brass direction and arrangement / **Ira Nepus:** trombone / **Maurice Spears:** trombone / **George Bohanon:** trombone, baritone horn / **William Roper:** tuba / **Thomas Peterson:** saxophone / **Joseph Sublett:** saxophone / **Jim Thompson:** saxophone **Recorded:** Quad Studios, Nashville, Tennessee / The Village Recorder, Los Angeles: November 20, 2009–March 2010 **Technical Team:** Producer: T-Bone Burnett / **Executive Producers:** Johnny Barbis, Elton John / **Sound Engineers:** Mike Piersante, Jason Wormer. **Assistant Sound Engineers:** Kory Aaron, Kyle Ford, Mark Lambert, Brett Lind, Ben McAmis, Chris Owens, Vanessa Parr / **Mixing:** Mike Piersante / **Editing:** Jason Wormer / **Mastering:** Gavin Lurssen / **Production Coordinators:** Adrian Collee, Jon Howard, Ivy Skoff

Marc Ribot served as the guitarist on *The Union*.

Leon Russell's moving voice calls up an intense wave of emotions on the deliciously retro "I Should Have Sent Roses," which invokes the musical territory typically trod by the likes of Neil Young and Van Morrison. Elton, as a true vocal chameleon, provides an impeccable repartee on bewitching refrains, where Russell seems to abandon himself to his sadness. Exuding a blues feel even in the slightest silence, this song is one of the most beautiful on the disk. The narrator's angst is caused by the avoidable loss of his great love. He regrets his clumsiness and lack of consideration: "I didn't know how to love you / Though I loved you so much / And I should have sent roses." Burdened by regrets, he simply considers himself as "half the man I should be." To do justice to this touching repentance, solemn brass, both serious and elegant, are convened to the sickbed of this suffering soul. The work of Doyle Bramhall II, punctuating each phrase with lightning guitar pyrotechnics, commands admiration. The brass finale is held slightly back to allow breathing space for some piano notes. The brass, together with the united vibrato of Elton and Leon, provides a princely exit, and the ensemble matches this high standard overall.

HEARTS HAVE TURNED TO STONE

Leon Russell / 3:47

Musicians: Elton John: vocals / Leon Russell: vocals, piano, backing vocals arrangement / Doyle Bramhall II: electric guitar / Don Was: bass / Davey Faragher: bass / Jim Keltner: drums, percussion / Jay Bellerose: drums, percussion / Booker T. Jones: Hammond B3 organ / Keefus Ciancia: keyboards / Darrell Leonard: trumpet, brass direction and arrangement / Thomas Peterson: saxophone / Joseph Sublett: saxophone / Jim Thompson: saxophone / Bill Maxwell: backing vocals direction / Judith Hill, Alfie Silas-Durio, Tata Vega, Jean Witherspoon: backing vocals **Recorded:** Quad Studios, Nashville, Tennessee / The Village Recorder, Los Angeles: November 20, 2009–March 2010 **Technical Team:** Producer: T-Bone Burnett / **Executive Producers:** Johnny Barbis, Elton John / **Sound Engineers:** Mike Piersante, Jason Wormer / **Assistant Sound Engineers:** Kory Aaron, Kyle Ford, Mark Lambert, Brett Lind, Ben McAmis, Chris Owens, Vanessa Parr / **Mixing:** Mike Piersante / **Editing:** Jason Wormer / **Mastering:** Gavin Lurssen / **Production Coordinators:** Adrian Collee, Jon Howard, Ivy Skoff

On "Hearts Have Turned to Stone," the voice of Leon Russell is clear and redolent, with an engaging blues feel that is supported by dynamic backing vocals, a discreet but effective Elton, and a brilliant brass section. With less influence on this number than on the rest of the album, the piano gives way a little to Booker T. Jones's Hammond B3 organ and to the keyboards of Keefus Ciancia. Doyle Bramhall II, the distinguished guitarist also known for having crossed swords with Eric Clapton, distills some very well-judged interventions.

The lyrics are not up the standard of the instrumentation and are forgettable in their lack of depth. The words deal with a love that has waned ("Hearts have finally turned to stone.") Everything is just pain and solitude, as attested by the lugubrious lexical field: "rain," "sadness," "sorrow," "pain" …The narrator feels "lost and all alone"; "sadness deep inside me"; "I'm out here in the darkness / I hear the howling wind." Will he find a new love? The answer eludes him, "Not an easy thing to find / Out here in the wilderness."

T-Bone Burnett represents the intersection of country and bluegrass.

NEVER TOO OLD (TO HOLD SOMEBODY)

Elton John, Bernie Taupin / 4:58

Musicians: Elton John: vocals, piano / Leon Russell: vocals, piano / Marc Ribot: electric guitar / Dennis Crouch: acoustic bass / Jim Keltner: drums, percussion / Jay Bellerose: drums, percussion / Keefus Ciancia: keyboards / Bill Maxwell: backing vocals direction and arrangement / Lou Pardini, Jason Scheff, Bill Cantos, Alfie Silas-Durio, Judith Hill, Tata Vega: backing vocals **Recorded:** Quad Studios, Nashville, Tennessee / The Village Recorder, Los Angeles: November 20, 2009–March 2010 **Technical Team:** Producer: T-Bone Burnett / **Executive Producers:** Johnny Barbis, Elton John / **Sound Engineers:** Mike Piersante, Jason Wormer / **Assistant Sound Engineers:** Kory Aaron, Kyle Ford, Mark Lambert, Brett Lind, Ben McAmis, Chris Owens, Vanessa Parr / **Mixing:** Mike Piersante / **Editing:** Jason Wormer / **Mastering:** Gavin Lurssen / **Production Coordinators:** Adrian Collee, Jon Howard, Ivy Skoff

"Never Too Old (To Hold Somebody)" evokes the passing of time that eventually breaks bodies, but it does not have to be synonymous with solitude or prevent the exchange of tokens of friendship to those who love us. As the narrator emphasizes: "Don't you know, you're never too old / You're never too old to hold somebody." The piano parts, which are meticulous and delicate, lead the dance into this ballad where Elton's and Leon's voices rival each other in technique, particularly in the vibrato. The ingenious keyboards of Keefus Ciancia play cat and mouse: sometimes cocooning and blending into the arrangement, and sometimes standing in the light, such as where they emulate some welcome sitar notes. Marc Ribot's guitar is very discreet (perhaps too discreet?), contenting himself with punctuating the Elton-Leon duo interventions, without much display of imagination. At 3:39, a moving finale appears, with the two men taking up the refrain with one voice, like a mantra, supported by gospel choirs to great effect.

IN THE HANDS OF ANGELS

Leon Russell / 4:43

Musicians: Leon Russell: vocals, piano, backing vocals arrangement / Drew Lambert: electric bass / Marty Grebb: keyboards / Bill Maxwell: backing vocals direction / Rose Stone, Tanya Balam, Kellye Huff, Tiffany Smith, Perry Morgan, Bill Cantos, Judith Hill, Alfie Silas-Durio, Tata Vega, Jean Witherspoon: backing vocals **Recorded:** Quad Studios, Nashville (Tennessee) / The Village Recorder, Los Angeles: November 20, 2009–March 2010 **Technical Team:** Producer: T-Bone Burnett / **Executive Producers:** Johnny Barbis, Elton John / **Sound Engineers:** Mike Piersante, Jason Wormer / **Assistant Sound Engineers:** Kory Aaron, Kyle Ford, Mark Lambert, Brett Lind, Ben McAmis, Chris Owens, Vanessa Parr / **Mixing:** Mike Piersante. **Editing:** Jason Wormer / **Mastering:** Gavin Lurssen / **Production Coordinators:** Adrian Collee, Jon Howard, Ivy Skoff

The Union opened with a piece written entirely by Leon Russell and it closes in the same way, with "In the Hands of Angels." This song is touched by the grace of its gospel backing vocals, and the veteran artist seeks to thank Elton for bringing him back from obscurity. As he did not know what to give him, presuming that an artist of his standing should have everything he wanted in life, Leon gave Elton the thing he knew best: a song. At the time when it was recorded, he went into the studio and performed it in a single take, which stunned those listening, and above all Elton John. "It breaks my heart. I love that,"[142] Elton confided to T-Bone Burnett, in the control booth, before letting out an "oh fuck" and retreating into the little adjoining kitchen because he was overwhelmed with emotion. Unfortunately, this first take was not good enough for Leon's taste because he felt he had sung it two tones too high. So he did a second take, which is the one used on the album. Johnny Barbis, executive producer, was also an intended recipient of this homage by Leon, since he had also done everything to make the recording possible at a time when Russell had almost resigned himself to giving up music. "I could have been sick / I could have died / I could have given up," Leon sings with gravity, and then that "Johnny and the governor" had in a way brought him back to life. He added: "They made me feel just like a king [...] / They knew who I needed and who needed me [...] / I was in the hands of angels." "The angels are never gonna let you go, you know that?"[143] Elton answered him, when Leon came back into the common room. The musical arrangement is based on intense piano chords, keyboards humming with pleasure, and, above all, Leon's true, steady voice, launching an unerring arrow into the hearts of his hosts…and the fans.

MY KIND OF HELL

Elton John, Bernie Taupin / 3:16

Musicians: Elton John: vocals, piano / **Leon Russell:** vocals, piano / **Marc Ribot:** electric guitar / **Dennis Crouch:** acoustic bass / **Jim Keltner:** drums, percussion / **Jay Bellerose:** drums, percussion / **Keefus Ciancia:** keyboards / **Darrell Leonard:** trumpet, bass trumpet, brass direction and arrangement / **Thomas Peterson:** saxophone / **Joseph Sublett:** saxophone / **Jim Thompson:** saxophone / **Bill Maxwell:** backing vocals direction and arrangement / **Bill Cantos, Judith Hill, Alfie Silas-Durio, Tata Vega:** backing vocals **Recorded:** Quad Studios, Nashville, Tennessee / The Village Recorder, Los Angeles: November 20, 2009–March 2010 **Technical Team:** Producer: T-Bone Burnett / **Executive Producers:** Johnny Barbis, Elton John / **Sound Engineers:** Mike Piersante, Jason Wormer / **Assistant Sound Engineers:** Kory Aaron, Kyle Ford, Mark Lambert, Brett Lind, Ben McAmis, Chris Owens, Vanessa Parr / **Mixing:** Mike Piersante / **Editing:** Jason Wormer / **Mastering:** Gavin Lurssen / **Production Coordinators:** Adrian Collee, Jon Howard, Ivy Skoff

With its disconcerting rhythmic fluctuations, "My Kind of Hell" almost seems alien to the rest of *The Union*. At 1:45, a conflict of sound even seems to place piano and brass in opposition, giving the song an air of recreation for the musicians, who are able to release their excess energy without worrying about the harmony. The drums, although technical, feel slapdash where the tempo accelerates, Marc Ribot's guitar is undermixed, and the brass and backing vocals never really find their place in the sound magma of the finale. "My Kind of Hell" was also not originally present on the track list, which shows that it was not among the choice numbers for *The Union*, but it was subsequently added as a bonus on the deluxe CD, vinyl, and digital editions. As for the lyrics, Bernie picks up his subject of choice: separation. His convoluted lyrics depict a long-term couple who end up thoroughly detesting each other. The two partners are at odds even down to the smallest details: "Your hot coffee and my black tea." "I can't say I ever liked you much," concludes the narrator, "but you're my kind of hell."

MANDALAY AGAIN

Elton John, Bernie Taupin / 4:54

Musicians: Elton John: vocals, piano / **Leon Russell:** vocals, piano / **Marc Ribot:** electric guitar / **Dennis Crouch:** acoustic bass / **Jim Keltner:** drums, percussion / **Jay Bellerose:** drums, percussion / **Keefus Ciancia:** keyboards / **Bill Maxwell:** backing vocals direction and arrangement / **Bill Cantos, Judith Hill, Alfie Silas-Durio, Tata Vega:** backing vocals **Recorded:** Quad Studios, Nashville, Tennessee / The Village Recorder, Los Angeles: November 20, 2009–March 2010 **Technical Team:** Producer: T-Bone Burnett / **Executive Producers:** Johnny Barbis, Elton John / **Sound Engineers:** Mike Piersante, Jason Wormer / **Assistant Sound Engineers:** Kory Aaron, Kyle Ford, Mark Lambert, Brett Lind, Ben McAmis, Chris Owens, Vanessa Parr / **Mixing:** Mike Piersante / **Editing:** Jason Wormer / **Mastering:** Gavin Lurssen / **Production Coordinators:** Adrian Collee, Jon Howard, Ivy Skoff

Mandalay is a city in Myanmar (formerly the British colony known as Burma) that's known to the British via a poem of the same name written by Rudyard Kipling, which appeared in 1892 in the collection *Barrack-Room Ballads, and Other Verses*. In it, an English soldier back in his own country nostalgically recalls his love abandoned in Burma. The famous Kipling poem extends into Bernie's lyrics, which are also imbued with melancholy when recalling happy times in Mandalay. The wall of sound concocted by the musicians forms a soft bubble from which some notes escape on the guitar by Marc Ribot, expanded by a sad tremolo, as well as some discreet backing vocals. Calm and rousing drums seem to beat out the rhythm of the narrator's heartbeat, while the piano contributes a solid framework to the song. A fine instrumental sequence joins in with the two pianists together from 3:22. Their two voices unite in an astonishing symbiosis in this hidden treasure, which appeared only on the deluxe CD and vinyl editions of *The Union*.

ALBUM

THE DIVING BOARD

Oceans Away . Oscar Wilde Gets Out . A Town Called Jubilee . The Ballad of Blind Tom . Dream #1 . My Quicksand . Can't Stay Alone Tonight . Voyeur . Home Again . Take This Dirty Water . Dream #2 . The New Fever Waltz . Mexican Vacation (Kids in the Candlelight) . Dream #3 . The Diving Board

RELEASE DATES
UK Release: September 13, 2013
Reference: Mercury—3742534
Best UK Chart Ranking: 3
US Release: September 24, 2013
Reference: Capitol Records / Mercury—B001866802
Best US Chart Ranking: 4

DIVING INTO DEEP WATER

The creative enrichment that he derived from his collaborative project with Leon Russell on *The Union*, in 2010, led Elton John seek out collaborations with other artists over the following years. This need also doubled as a pursuit for legitimacy with a new generation of fans and singers. One singer, in particular, presented similarities with Elton himself: Lady Gaga. As well as his taste for exuberant and cumbersome costumes, she shared the same profile as a singer-pianist, with a keen feeling for a catchy melody, which, in her case, came packaged in a highly effective dance pop formula. The two musicians met on the stage at the Grammy Awards on January 31, 2010, and performed on their pianos facing each other: "Poker Face," "Speechless," and "Your Song," were offered as a medley that, when released as a single, reached ninety-fourth place on the Canadian charts. The following year, the original soundtrack of the new animated film *Gnomeo & Juliet* appeared. It contained some of Elton's greatest hits, and two new titles, "Hello Hello" (also with Lady Gaga) and "Love Builds a Garden." Subsequently, Elton continued to indulge his thirst for collaboration. He contributed to "Hard Times" by the rapper Plan B, alongside the singer Paloma Faith, which was released on May 19, 2011. Beginning on September 28, 2011, he began a new residency at Las Vegas, which ran until 2018, and which was called "The Million Dollar Piano." The show took its name from the massive Yamaha piano that dominated the stage. This technological jewel was adorned with LED screens that displayed videos and lighting effects. In 2012, Elton took on a collaborative project with Pnau, the Australian electro duo that had signed on with the Rocket Record Company. Elton suggested doing an album with them, and he entrusted them with some of his original recordings from the 1970s. The two members of Pnau, Peter Mayes and Nick Littlemore, made numerous samples from the original tracks, which they then assembled into new compositions. The result, *Good Morning to the Night*, was released on July 13, 2012. The following year, Elton also released "Save Rock and Roll" with the band Fall Out Boy, "Oh, Well" with 2Cellos, and "Face to Face" with Gary Barlow.

T-Bone Burnett's Magic Formula

In parallel with this operation to win over a new generation of listeners, the question of a new solo album also emerged. Elton's record company was pushing him to record at the end of 2011, and they specifically wanted either a Christmas album or an album of covers of Motown standards. This met with no response from Elton. Only a new album of original work could get him back in the studios, even though he still had some doubts when he eventually arrived in January 2012. *The Union* had been released a year earlier, and its promotional schedule had left him feeling worn out and tired.

But when Elton got to the Village Recorder studio in Los Angeles, which had previously hosted the sessions for *The Union*, his reticence evaporated. Not only did he appreciate the studio's vintage equipment, he had also been seduced by the spacious premises—located in a former Masonic temple built in 1922 that had also been used in the 1960s by Maharishi Mahesh Yogi for his transcendental meditation courses. This equipment included Neve consoles, and a collection of antique microphones that captured an incomparable, warm sound; these brought out to an ideal degree all the nuances of the singer's voice, whose timbre was becoming more serious and deeper with age.

T-Bone Burnett returned as Elton's producer on *The Diving Board* after previously working on *The Union*.

FOR ELTON ADDICTS

The initial working title, *The Diving Board*, had been used for months before Bernie and Elton suggested calling the album *Voyeur*. Bernie even went so far as to officially announce *Voyeur* as the title on his website before the two men eventually changed their minds.

T-Bone Burnett was brought back following his work on *The Union*, which had been unanimously praised, and he planned to take advantage of the maturation of Elton's voice by giving it prominence and combining it with pure piano sound, which he wanted to be very organic. As an old-style producer, he had a precise artistic vision for this album, which he envisaged as running counter to other contemporary productions, and in total opposition to the recent series of Elton collaborations. In T-Bone Burnett's mind, this kind of emphasis was accompanied by a necessary return to the core of Elton's music. For him, this also meant returning to the antediluvian format constructed onstage by Elton John, Dee Murray, and Nigel Olsson: piano, bass, and drums. However, Bernie later stated, "A lot of people are referring to this record by saying it's going back to the style of *Tumbleweed Connection* and the earlier albums. In essence, it's really not. We never really did studio recordings with the original trio. It was always much more a band situation. On things like *Madman Across the Water*, *Tumbleweed*, and especially *Elton John*, which had a full-on orchestra on it, those records were more band-oriented records."[67]

Either way, this marked the moment when the previously immovable Davey Johnstone was replaced. Upon Elton's suggestion, the renowned bassist and neosoul vocalist Raphael Saadiq was recruited for the album. Then the drummer-percussionist Jay Bellerose was called upon to complete this pivotal core group. A few other contributors gravitated around the team: keyboard player Keefus Ciancia, a preferred colleague of T-Bone Burnett's and a regular contributor with Mike Patton, Iggy Pop, and Father John Misty, who specialized in film soundtracks (*Ali*, *Spider-Man 2*, *The Hunger Games*). Guitarist Doyle Bramhall II was also engaged to distill some blues atmosphere on "A Town Called Jubilee" and "Take That Dirty Water." And finally, Jack Ashford, a Motown veteran, who had sprinkled his tambourine sounds over hundreds of numbers in the course of his career. To this extended musical company Burnett then added lots of brass, which was responsible for amplifying the soul dimension of the album, and backing vocalists were brought in to round out the sound.

Extended Sessions

While he had appeared initially hesitant to return to the studio so soon after *The Union* was released, Elton committed to the project with characteristic efficiency. Inspired by the diversity of Bernie Taupin's lyrics, who had honed his storytelling and submitted particularly poignant texts on the subject of his father ("Oceans Away"), Oscar Wilde ("Oscar Wilde Gets Out"), the exceptional life of Tom Wiggins ("The Ballad of Blind Tom"), and the subject of deviant love ("Voyeur"), in January 2012 Elton John composed no fewer than twelve new songs in two days. The songs were then recorded in the four days following that. Elton was delighted with the result, and it was announced that the album would go on sale in October 2012. "Then we basically sat on it for almost eight months, and then Elton called me in again and said he wanted to go back in and record some more songs,"[67] Bernie recalled. A new release date was then set for February 2013, but this deadline was too short, since it was not possible to arrange recording sessions until January 2013. The release was then delayed until May 2013, and then again to September. Bernie said, "The thing is, there was no scheduled release date from the day we started recording.

Nigel Olsson and Davey Johnstone onstage in October 2015.

[…] Nobody was in a hurry for a new Elton John and Bernie Taupin album. We could really wait and see when it was the best time to put it out. We went back in and recorded another five or six songs, and put everything together and re-listened to the whole thing. It was a great idea to go back. It really revitalized us and gave us a greater appreciation of things we did before."[67] A total of seventeen songs formed the copious tracklist of *The Diving Board*, before "5th Avenue," a slow tearjerker, was cut and "Candlelit Bedroom" shunted to the deluxe version of the album.

For the album cover, Elton contacted a contemporary photographer whose works he collected, Ryan McGinley, and asked him if he might have an image he could use. McGinley immediately thought of the photograph of one of his friends, Tim Barber, which showed the back of the young man, fully clothed and standing at the end of a diving board. Below him, an oil-smooth sea merges with a cloudy sky and makes the subject stand out, reinforcing the dramatic nature of the image. This visual, which is evocative of the work of Storm Thorgerson, the photographer who designed most of the Pink Floyd album covers, was not the result of a montage or staging. In fact, the image was taken about ten years earlier, somewhere between Vancouver and Squamish, in British Colombia. The rural locale, popular with teenagers, was located at the top of a cliff that is difficult to reach. McGinley framed the picture well, and the image, which perfectly illustrates the title, was chosen for the album.

Did the repeated delays generate excitement on the part of the public? Or was it perhaps the unusually sober-minded approach to the production process? Maybe it was the seriousness of Bernie's lyrics, and the deep melancholy of the album that is dominated by piano and vocals? Whatever the cause, fans on both sides of the Atlantic accepted the album with open arms, lifting it to third place on the charts in the United Kingdom and to fourth place on the charts in the United States.

On the advice of T-Bone Burnett, Elton's piano became the focal point on *The Diving Board*.

OCEANS AWAY

Elton John, Bernie Taupin / 3:58

Musicians: Elton John: vocals, piano **Recorded:** The Village Recorder, Los Angeles: January 2012 or January 2013 **Technical Team:** Producer: T-Bone Burnett / **Sound Engineer:** Jason Wormer / **Assistant Sound Engineers:** Jeff Gartenbaum, Chris Owens, Vanessa Parr / **Mixing:** Jason Wormer / **Mastering:** Gavin Lurssen

The Diving Board opens with a cautionary note: On this album, priority is given to the piano-vocal combination. In fact, Elton performs alone in this configuration, delivering one of his sorrowful ballads in the way he particularly knows how to do. But the emotional range of the number also owes a great deal to Bernie's lyrics, since the writer, who hides more often than not behind some obscure wording, this time penned material for a very intimate score. He pays homage to his father, Captain Robert Taupin, who served in the British army during the

Second World War. The lyricist also wrote a dedication to him in the booklet accompanying the disk. But Bernie, through this paternal figure, emphasizes the general applicability of his words to all soldiers, and not only those who fell in combat, buried "beneath a little wooden cross oceans away," but also the veterans, who deserve care and attention. "Call 'em up, n' dust 'em off, let 'em shine / The ones who hold on to the the ones / They had to leave behind," Bernie writes, calling for the old soldiers to be cherished together with the historic memory that they represent, before they disappear for good. This mark of respect and gratitude is not new in the work of Elton and Bernie, since they wrote about this subject very early on, in the song "Talking Old Soldiers" in *Tumbleweed Connection*. "Oceans Away" is a touching number, and it has become one of the most significant works in Bernie and Elton's catalog.

OSCAR WILDE GETS OUT

Elton John, Bernie Taupin / 4:35

Musicians: Elton John: vocals, piano / Raphael Saadiq: bass / Jay Bellerose: drums / Keefus Ciancia: keyboards / Stjepan Hauser: cello / Luka Šulić: cello **Recorded:** The Village Recorder, Los Angeles: January 2012 **Technical Team:** Producer: T-Bone Burnett / Sound Engineer: Jason Wormer / Assistant Sound Engineers: Jeff Gartenbaum, Chris Owens, Vanessa Parr / Mixing: Jason Wormer / Mastering: Gavin Lurssen

"I can be anywhere or anyplace and an idea will strike me. I could walk past a bookcase and there's a book about Oscar Wilde on it. I'll think, 'Here's a good idea. Put yourself in Oscar Wilde's mind after he's spent time in Reading Gaol. How did that change his perception of his life?'"[67]

The name Reading Gaol refers to an episode in the life of Oscar Wilde. In 1895, the Irish novelist and dramatist was sentenced to two years of hard labor for "gross indecency," due to his homosexual relationship with Lord Alfred Douglas, known as "Bosie." Homosexuality was a criminal offense at the time. During his transfer to Reading Gaol, the prison in which he was to serve his term, Wilde suffered a severe humiliation when he was forced to stand in public for half an hour while wearing convict's attire. He was quickly recognized, and suffered jeering, spitting, and abuse from the crowd that gathered around him. Bernie cites this event in the song, comparing Wilde's fate to that of Christ on his road to the cross, berating the eyes that "pierced his heart like crucifixion nails." Bernie addresses himself directly to Wilde with empathy: "You never stood a chance." Then Bernie remembers that Oscar Wilde sought refuge in France upon his release in 1897: "You turned your eyes to France." Paris was also where Wilde died, three years later, impoverished and using an assumed name, but not without having recorded his traumatizing experience in prison in his final work, *The Ballad of Reading Gaol*. When Elton discovered the words of "Oscar Wilde Gets Out," he was immediately inspired, and in a very short time he devised what would be the first song recorded for *The Diving Board*.

Production

Elton had perfectly grasped the seriousness of the events described by Bernie, and launched into the composition of an intense melody, developed by an impressive piano movement, in minor key. The cellos, magnificent in their subtlety, soon join Elton's powerful, deep voice, while the sober rhythm section seems to beat at the rhythm of a heart in distress. At 2:57, however, the sequence becomes even more engaging: the snare drum, hitherto excluded, finally enters. Elton's piano and the intelligent keyboards of Keefus Ciancia are the major contributors to the finale of this breathless piece, which recalls the spirit of an album such as *Madman Across the Water*, but inexplicably has been very little performed onstage.

A TOWN CALLED JUBILEE

Elton John, Bernie Taupin / 4:30

Musicians: Elton John: vocals, piano / Doyle Bramhall II: electric guitar / Raphael Saadiq: bass / Jay Bellerose: drums / Keefus Ciancia: keyboards / Jack Ashford: tambourine / Bill Maxwell: backing vocals arrangement / Bill Cantos, Alvin Chea, Carmel Echols, Judith Hill, Perry Morgan, Louis Price: backing vocals **Recorded:** The Village Recorder, Los Angeles: January 2012 or January 2013 **Technical Team:** Producer: T-Bone Burnett / Sound Engineer: Jason Wormer / Assistant Sound Engineers: Jeff Gartenbaum, Chris Owens, Vanessa Parr / Mixing: Jason Wormer / Mastering: Gavin Lurssen

Based on the image of an American farm put up for sale, Bernie unfolds the story of those who are forced to abandon the place. The lyrics, imbued with sadness and nostalgia for happier times, describe a desolate environment. However, the narrator does not lose hope and wants to start over somewhere new: "Gonna set things right and set up house / In a town called Jubilee." Little Lily, who "pulled a horseshoe from a pile of junk" and keeps it for good luck, and brother Jake and his old black dog accompany the narrator on the journey to Jubilee, and all their baggage is "A pinewood box, a rocking horse." The melody is pleasant, and the arrangement in particular is sophisticated, with elegant backing vocals and Doyle Bramhall II's electric guitar, just velvety enough to enable one to imagine oneself under the blazing Californian sun. A very nice piano movement by Elton begins at 3:14 and completes the persuasive charm of "A Town Called Jubilee."

THE BALLAD OF BLIND TOM

Elton John, Bernie Taupin / 4:12

Musicians: Elton John: vocals, piano / Raphael Saadiq: bass / Jay Bellerose: drums / Keefus Ciancia: keyboards / Jack Ashford: tambourine / Stjepan Hauser: cello / Luka Šulić: cello / Bill Maxwell: backing vocals arrangement / Bill Cantos, Perry Morgan, Louis Price, Alvin Chea: backing vocals **Recorded:** The Village Recorder, Los Angeles: January 2012 or January 2013 **Technical Team:** Producer: T-Bone Burnett / Sound Engineer: Jason Wormer / Assistant Sound Engineers: Jeff Gartenbaum, Chris Owens, Vanessa Parr / **Mixing:** Jason Wormer / **Mastering:** Gavin Lurssen

Genesis and Lyrics

The trumpeter Dizzy Gillespie had played for several heads of state over the course of his career, but for Tom Wiggins, alias Blind Tom, Gillespie made a special detour and visited his tomb, breaking the silence of the cemetery as he played "When the Saints Go Marching In." When Bernie Taupin found his 2009 biography, *The Ballad of Blind Tom*, by Deirdre O'Connell, he was transported by the story of a slave born on a cotton plantation in 1849 and sold with his family when he was not yet one year old. Blind and autistic, young Tom Wiggins could barely communicate as a child, but when he was set in front of a piano—an instrument that he mastered by the age of four— he was transformed. He was capable of reproducing complex compositions after hearing them only once, and he could play a different melody with each hand while singing at the same time. "When I read that book, I thought to myself, 'If this isn't a song, nothing is,'" testified Bernie. "It appealed to my method of writing. I had to literally make the *Reader's Digest* version of the book, condense it into a song. I think it worked."[67] Each verse accurately depicts the phenomenon that was Tom Wiggins and the appalling exploitation to which he was subjected. While some praise him as "a wonderment" others mock this "freak" and shamelessly exploit his handicap ("'Boy wouldn't know from money' / Just throw old Blind Tom a bone").

Production

Bernie Taupin establishes an implicit link between Blind Tom and Elton John, who, as a child, had a similar capacity to reproduce entire songs by ear, though to a lesser degree than Blind Tom. The singer, who was shaken by this story, created a melody that was both rich and well-defined, based on four chords (G minor, A7/G, C minor/G, and G minor). The sequence, emphatically melancholic with its minor keys, is a perfect match for the simplicity of the arrangement. In fact, the piano—the instrument that reigns on this album—allows some space for the others, set back in the mix by T-Bone Burnett. As such, their importance is key for the ambiance and dynamic of the piece, as with Jack Ashford's hypnotic tambourine from 0:15,

which is suffused with a slight reverb, or Raphael Saadiq's deep bass, whose entry into the track gives it new momentum at 1:02. The intangible, sepulchral voices in the background rise up (at 1:26 and at 2:00) in haunting elegy to the life and talent of Blind Tom.

DREAM #1

Elton John / 0:40

Musicians: Elton John: piano **Recorded:** The Village Recorder, Los Angeles: January 2012 or January 2013 **Technical Team:** Producer: T-Bone Burnett / **Sound Engineer:** Jason Wormer / **Assistant Sound Engineers:** Jeff Gartenbaum, Chris Owens, Vanessa Parr / **Mixing:** Jason Wormer / **Mastering:** Gavin Lurssen

A classically inspired instrumental interlude of just forty seconds, "Dream #1" serves as a melancholy introduction to one of the great pieces on the album: "My Quicksand."

MY QUICKSAND

Elton John, Bernie Taupin / 4:47

Musicians: Elton John: vocals, piano / Raphael Saadiq: bass / Jay Bellerose: drums / Keefus Ciancia: keyboards **Recorded:** The Village Recorder, Los Angeles: January 2012 or January 2013 **Technical Team:** Producer: T-Bone Burnett / **Sound Engineer:** Jason Wormer / **Assistant Sound Engineers:** Jeff Gartenbaum, Chris Owens, Vanessa Parr / **Mixing:** Jason Wormer / **Mastering:** Gavin Lurssen

Genesis and Lyrics

"I can never say what inspires things [...] But there are certain songs that you just get a first couple of lines and the songs form themselves,"[67] Bernie once said regarding "My Quicksand." By his own admission, he only had the title at the outset, but straightaway he understood that he would be able to do something with the "quicksand": "This is a good metaphor for sinking in a relationship."[67] In theory, the song refers to a man who goes to Paris and becomes bogged down in a relationship. In practice, the real meaning of the song is much more cryptic, and Bernie operates by means of impressionistic touches that seem to jump from one idea to the next on each new verse. "The thing is, some of my songs could be three songs in one. You can get a triple metaphor in a song where it's relatable on different levels to different people. I always like to have a little mystery in the songs."[67]

Production

Elton has often said that he was particularly proud of "My Quicksand" and that it is one of his greatest songs. "I thought, 'That's the best track I've ever recorded, right there.' Pianowise, vocalwise, everything about it. I've never played the piano like that on a record before—the solo was improvised."[35] With this absolutely heart-rending ballad, Elton could see how much progress he'd made since starting out as a young musician in the 1970s, when his story had yet to be written: "It's just a very musical moment that I was very proud of on this record. [...] This is the kind of song that I never thought I'd be singing when I started out. My days of making pop records like *Goodbye Yellow Brick Road* and *Don't Shoot Me I'm Only the Piano Player*, they were when I was younger. I'm not that guy anymore. I'm this guy. It's the most honest record I've ever made."[35] In fact, Elton's voice has a rare depth to it on this track, and it is accompanied by a particularly moving vibrato. Even though other musicians are present in the arrangement, Elton gives the impression of being alone in the world, and of wanting to give people the love that they have given him over the years: "I'm at a stage where I want to give back as much as I can. It's all kind of unexplainable, you know. There was this little boy, not the normal prototype; there was no one else like me in rock. [...] And I think people realize that I genuinely appreciate their love and affection and their loyalty. It's so fucking joyous after all this time. I wasn't always comfortable in my own skin. They were with me when I didn't know who I was."[35] Combining his love for soul, blues, and pop, and in some aspects recalling earlier numbers like "Come Down in Time" from *Tumbleweed Connection* and "Idol" from *Blue Moves*, "My Quicksand" has proved to be one of the most emblematic numbers of the second half of Elton John's career. It is therefore all the more surprising that he has almost never played it onstage.

CAN'T STAY ALONE TONIGHT

Elton John, Bernie Taupin / 4:49

Musicians: Elton John: vocals, piano / Raphael Saadiq: bass / Jay Bellerose: drums / Keefus Ciancia: keyboards / Jack Ashford: tambourine / Bill Maxwell: backing vocals arrangement / Bill Cantos, Alvin Chea, Perry Morgan, Louis Price: backing vocals **Recorded:** The Village Recorder, Los Angeles: January 2012 or January 2013 **Technical Team: Producer:** T-Bone Burnett / **Sound Engineer:** Jason Wormer / **Assistant Sound Engineers:** Jeff Gartenbaum, Chris Owens, Vanessa Parr / **Mixing:** Jason Wormer / **Mastering:** Gavin Lurssen **Single Release:** *Can't Stay Alone Tonight* **UK Release:** March 1994 on Virgin EMI Records (digital version only) **Best UK Chart Ranking:** Did Not Chart

In automatic-pilot mode, Bernie once again considers the subject of a thwarted relationship, this time with a rather insipid result that has a much too homely feel to it. No metaphors here, and the lyricist really goes to town: "Should have called you up this morning / But I'm such a fool at times." He describes a man who is too proud to admit his mistakes. He engaged in a "cold war of words," he recognizes that he "can't stay alone tonight" but does nothing to change things. For his part, Elton is no more successful in salvaging the situation. Naturally, this country-folk ballad is pleasing to the ear, but the melody is very ordinary. Even the bridge of the song, which comes in at 3:12, leaves a disagreeable sensation of having been heard somewhere before. On the plus side, this track features a nice piano score, attractive backing vocals, and Raphael Saadiq's rounded bass playing.

VOYEUR

Elton John, Bernie Taupin / 4:16

Musicians: Elton John: vocals, piano / Raphael Saadiq: bass / Keefus Ciancia: keyboards / Jay Bellerose: drums / Jack Ashford: tambourine **Recorded:** The Village Recorder, Los Angeles: January 2012 or January 2013 **Technical Team: Producer:** T-Bone Burnett / **Sound Engineer:** Jason Wormer / **Assistant Sound Engineers:** Jeff Gartenbaum, Chris Owens, Vanessa Parr / **Mixing:** Jason Wormer / **Mastering:** Gavin Lurssen

The more astute fans of Cat Stevens will notice a clear resemblance between the intro riff on "Voyeur" and "Matthew and Son," one of the British folk troubadour's hits. But although the motif returns frequently in "Voyeur," the resemblance between the two songs stops there. In his song, Bernie tells the story of a man who nurtures an unhealthy fascination for a woman, who he spends time watching while sitting in a tree, or on the roof of a hotel. This is a situation reminiscent of the one in "Every Breath You Take" by the Police. "Voyeur" does contain some powerful images, including "A whisper in the darkness / Holds more truth than a shout." Above all, it subtly depicts the psychological mechanisms that drive the voyeur to violate the privacy of his prey, and the intimacy he believes he is sharing with her when spying on her: "I see things [...] Through a hawk's eyes gliding silent on the wind / And in every secret rendezvous where illicit lovers park / I'll come away with something to keep you in my heart." Elton designs a nice musical framework around Bernie's lyrics: the gentleness and roundness of Raphael Saadiq's bass has one of the most important roles in this, as does Elton's relaxed and aerial piano. There is a good drums entry at 1:35, which is enriched by Jack Ashford's discreet tambourine. But the best moment in the piece is still the bridge starting at 3:01, with Elton's rending and disembodied distant voice, which gives way to a magnificent musical sequence between 3:15 and 3:36.

Elton sings "Home Again" during the 2013 Emmy Awards. The song was also chosen as the single from *The Diving Board*.

FOR ELTON ADDICTS

Elton John performed this song at the Emmy Awards on September 22, 2013, as part of an homage to Liberace, who was the subject of a nominated biopic, *Behind the Candelabra*. Elton explained that "Home Again" reminded him of Liberace, the piano genius, who had once told Elton that what he loved most in life was coming back home.

HOME AGAIN

Elton John, Bernie Taupin / 5:01

Musicians: Elton John: vocals, piano / **David Plitch:** bass / **Jay Bellerose:** drums / **Keefus Ciancia:** keyboards / **George Bohanon:** baritone saxophone / **Bruce Fowler:** trombone / **Chuck Findley:** bugle / **Darrell Leonard:** bugle, arrangement / **William Roper:** tuba **Recorded: The Village Recorder, Los Angeles:** January 2012 or January 2013 **Technical Team: Producer:** T-Bone Burnett / **Sound Engineer:** Jason Wormer / **Assistant Sound Engineers:** Jeff Gartenbaum, Chris Owens, Vanessa Parr / **Mixing:** Jason Wormer / **Mastering:** Gavin Lurssen **Single:** *Home Again* **UK Release:** 2013 on Mercury (digital version only) **Best UK Chart Ranking:** Did Not Chart • *Home Again* (Radio Edit) / *Home Again* **US Release:** 2013 on Capitol Records (digital version only) **Best US Chart Ranking:** Did Not Chart

With its wistful piano and poignant lyrics, "Home Again" has the true stature of an Elton John classic. Beyond the lament from a narrator who is desperate to get back home, Bernie is above all evoking life's circuitous routes of destiny, and the need to return to one's roots. "Even 'Home Again,' the single, although it seems like a straight-ahead song, it's really not," he commented. [...] "To me, home again isn't [as] obvious as it seems to certain people. To me, it can be a metaphor for a lot of things. It's a state of mind. It certainly doesn't mean that I want to go back to where I came from. In fact, that's the last place I want to go. [Laughs] So it's slightly contradictory on my part, but at the same time it means a lot more than what it means to the average person."[67] Bernie, who grew up in the small village of Owmby-by-Spital, in Lincolnshire, had to give this same explanation when his brother, having heard the song, asked him if he had written it nostalgically. "If I'd never left I'd never have known / We all dream of leaving," Bernie explains in the song's lyrics. But he is also emphasizing our paradoxical human inconsistency, which drives us to want to fly the nest, only to want to return once we are far away. In order to do justice to the melancholic lyrics, Elton provides an intense melody as well as a moving vocal performance. Discreet brass provide additional solemnity, and the drums are confined to some light cymbal effects. Elton's extremely expressive piano concludes alone, after a particularly fine movement between 3:27 and 3:55. As beautiful as "Home Again" is, its selection as the first single from *The Diving Board* was quite a gamble, since it was a classical ballad releasing in an era when the top 40 was basically devoid of such music. The gamble did not pay off, and the song failed to hit the charts on both sides of the Atlantic.

Bassist Raphael Saadiq (shown here in 2009) joined the musical team during production on *The Diving Board*.

TAKE THIS DIRTY WATER

Elton John, Bernie Taupin / 4:25

Musicians: Elton John: vocals, piano / Doyle Bramhall II: electric guitar / Raphael Saadiq: bass / Jay Bellerose: drums / Keefus Ciancia: keyboards / Jack Ashford: tambourine / Bill Maxwell: backing vocals arrangement / Bill Cantos, Carmel Echols, Judith Hill, Rose Stone: backing vocals **Recorded:** The Village Recorder, Los Angeles: January 2012 or January 2013 **Technical Team Producer:** T-Bone Burnett / **Sound Engineer:** Jason Wormer / **Assistant Sound Engineers:** Jeff Gartenbaum, Chris Owens, Vanessa Parr **Mixing:** Jason Wormer / **Mastering:** Gavin Lurssen

With "Take This Dirty Water," one might imagine that Bernie is seeking to contribute to the wider discourse on self-respect and perseverance given the extent to which he seems to be emphasizing these imperative clichés: "You get to make the rules," "Fight the tide and find the shore," "If the heart becomes a prisoner / Your soul will turn you loose," "Get back to the wellspring / Purify the stream," "Running like a river." But beneath this number lies a deeper meaning: the "dirty water" is above all a metaphor that describes all the problems and all the harmful things that pollute a person's life. For the narrator, the way to purify this "water," is to rediscover the innocence of childhood. "Search out days that never end [...] / feel just like a child again." Appropriately enough, as a hymn to resilience, "Take This Dirty Water" takes the gospel route, with the backing vocals nicely reinforcing that little internal voice that urges us all to follow our

own pathway in life. From the intro, Elton provides a typically blues piano sound, which returns several times throughout the course of the song before reappearing in the final moments. The benevolent sound that is generated throughout "Take This Dirty Water" owes a great deal to Doyle Bramhall II's plaintive guitar. Despite its rousing refrain and resolutely positive message, this number has hardly ever been performed by Elton onstage.

DREAM #2

Elton John / 0:43

Musicians: Elton John: piano **Recorded:** The Village Recorder, Los Angeles: January 2012 or January 2013 **Technical Team: Producer:** T-Bone Burnett / **Sound Engineer:** Jason Wormer / **Assistant Sound Engineers:** Jeff Gartenbaum, Chris Owens, Vanessa Parr / **Mixing:** Jason Wormer / **Mastering:** Gavin Lurssen

The pop structures and artifices that accompany many of Elton John's compositions have often eclipsed—or at least muted—the classical influences that have forged his musical education. The presence of this very short instrumental piece is a reminder of those influences.

THE NEW FEVER WALTZ

Elton John, Bernie Taupin / 4:39

Musicians: Elton John: lead and backing vocals, piano / Keefus Ciancia: keyboards / Raphael Saadiq: bass / Jay Bellerose: drums / George Bohanon: trombone, euphonium / Ira Nepus: trombone / Darrell Leonard: bugle, brass arrangement, trumpet / William Roper: tuba / Stjepan Hauser: cello / Luka Šulić: cello **Recorded:** The Village Recorder, Los Angeles: January 2012 or January 2013 **Technical Team:** Producer: T-Bone Burnett / Sound Engineer: Jason Wormer / Assistant Sound Engineers: Jeff Gartenbaum, Chris Owens, Vanessa Parr / Mixing: Jason Wormer / Mastering: Gavin Lurssen

Bernie Taupin most commonly ensures that his lyrics resist interpretation and takes care to cover his tracks as soon as any kind of Ariadne's thread seems too obvious. This also applies in "The New Fever Waltz," whose martial vocabulary ("war," "white flag," "muddy boots") and references to desolation ("ruins," "dirt and damp," "burned out broken walls") initially set out a battlefield décor. But, in a to-and-fro movement this is alternated with the décor of a ballroom and dancers who seem undisturbed by anything. This switch between the battlefield and ballroom is performed through the verse "I was shaking with a fever," which suggests the fevered mind of the narrator, probably a wounded soldier, imagining that he's dancing with his partner.

There is another possible reading: It could be the dance marathons of the United States' Great Depression, during which couples danced as long as they could until they collapsed with exhaustion. These competitions could last several days, with the key being a prize of several hundred dollars for the winners. In addition to the bruised feet and muscle pain, these marathons sometimes caused severe neurological problems for the participants, due to the lack of sleep. If we follow this interpretation, the reference to the "last good horse [that] went down" could be an allusion to Sydney Pollack's film *They Shoot Horses, Don't They?* (1969).

Whatever Bernie's intention, "it's just about pain and agony and, you know, desperation,"[145] explained Elton in an interview in 2013. "I love miserable songs. […]It's so easy to write songs about misery and hard times and sadness. It's much more difficult to write songs about happy and chirpy stuff."[145] As one of the most successful numbers on the disk, "The New Fever Waltz" is quite logically referred to by Elton as his favorite song: "This is probably my favorite song on the album. It's just so beautiful, and yet so harsh. The melody is so beautiful and the piano interlude and the orchestral interlude with the horns is so—it's moving."[145] The arrangement—especially the brass and cellos—is in fact very solemn, while Elton's piano, which sounds almost desperate, shows great delicacy right through to the last, deliberately low note.

MEXICAN VACATION (KIDS IN THE CANDLELIGHT)

Elton John, Bernie Taupin / 3:34

Musicians: Elton John: vocals, piano / Raphael Saadiq: bass / Jay Bellerose: drums / Jack Ashford: tambourine / Bill Maxwell: backing vocals arrangement / Bill Cantos, Alvin Chea, Carmel Echols, Judith Hill, Perry Morgan, Louis Price: backing vocals **Recorded:** The Village Recorder, Los Angeles: January 2012 or January 2013 **Technical Team:** Producer: T-Bone Burnett / Sound Engineer: Jason Wormer / Assistant Sound Engineers: Jeff Gartenbaum, Chris Owens, Vanessa Parr / Mixing: Jason Wormer / Mastering: Gavin Lurssen **Single Releases:** *Mexican Vacation (Kids in the Candlelight)* **UK Release:** 2013 on Mercury (on YouTube only) **Best UK Chart Ranking:** Did Not Chart • *Mexican Vacation (Kids in the Candlelight)* **US Release:** 2013 on Capitol Records (on YouTube only) **Best US Chart Ranking:** Did Not Chart

Having been chosen as the album's second single, "Mexican Vacation (Kids in the Candlelight)" is a perfect illustration of Bernie's facility with writing lyrics inside of lyrics. These holidays in Mexico clearly begin in the most romantic way possible: "I carried you in my arms / Through the hotel to our room / The night was filled with music." But the words become much more cryptic when he introduces the vision of "kids in the candlelight." The atmosphere suddenly takes a dive with these verses: "You said their stories should be told / Did they suffer when they died?" The identity of these children and their sad fate remain a mystery. With this emphasis on extreme contrast between his cocoon of love and the violence going on outside, the couple wakes up in the small hours of the morning to the sound of the television, and the narrator's partner throws the "pillow that [she] dream[ed] on" at the screen, on which a drug lord appears, before she bursts into tears. It is therefore possible that the two parallel stories—the one with the children, and the other with the drug baron—are linked? As for the music of "Mexican Vacation (Kids in the Candlelight)," it indulges Elton's passion for the blues, soul, and gospel, and his piano playing is alert and precise. At 1:47, the solo is inspired, and Elton's verve is contagious. The song's steady and appealing rhythm also demonstrates the complementary styles of Jay Bellerose on drums and Raphael Saadiq on bass.

DREAM #3

Elton John / 1:37

Musicians: Elton John: piano / Raphael Saadiq: bass / **Jay Bellerose:** drums **Recorded:** The Village Recorder, Los Angeles: January 2012 or January 2013 **Technical Team:** Producer: T-Bone Burnett / **Sound Engineer:** Jason Wormer / **Assistant Sound Engineers:** Jeff Gartenbaum, Chris Owens, Vanessa Parr / **Mixing:** Jason Wormer / **Mastering:** Gavin Lurssen

"Dream #3" stands out as the most convincing of the three instrumental tracks that punctuate *The Diving Board*: first, because it is longer and more elaborate than the others; and second, because its structure is more complex and involves a rhythm section consisting of Raphael Saadiq on bass and Jay Bellerose on drums. The two musicians, guided by Elton's edgy piano playing, contribute supportive and subtle touches to this minimalist, short jazz-rock piece, which is evocative of the worlds of Aaron Copland and Dave Brubeck. The finale, from 1:22, has a delicious lightness.

THE DIVING BOARD

Elton John, Bernie Taupin / 5:59

Musicians: Elton John: vocals, piano / **Larry Goldings:** Hammond B3 organ / **Raphael Saadiq:** bass / **Jay Bellerose:** drums / **George Bohanon:** trombone, euphonium / **Ira Nepus:** trombone / **Darrell Leonard:** bugle, brass arrangement / **William Roper:** tuba **Recorded:** The Village Recorder, Los Angeles: January 2012 or January 2013 **Technical Team:** Producer: T-Bone Burnett / **Sound Engineer:** Jason Wormer / **Assistant Sound Engineers:** Jeff Gartenbaum, Chris Owens, Vanessa Parr / **Mixing:** Jason Wormer / **Mastering:** Gavin Lurssen

Bernie's propensity for cultivating his work around subjects that are germane to Elton's life might lead one to believe that the title song on *The Diving Board* relates to some of the singer's personal experiences, or to their shared struggles with drugs. In fact, while its subject is indeed the question of the high price of celebrity, Bernie was more inspired by two former child stars who are often depicted as living on the edge (or, in this case the diving board). Sir Elton did tell the British magazine *Event*: "[You might think it's about] the drugs, the excesses, the millions on flowers, the tantrums, the outfits and the glasses... But it isn't. It's about Lindsay Lohan, Justin [Bieber], all these kids who are out there now not knowing what the hell is going on."[146] He continued: "I hate to think of Lindsay because she had a talent, she was a great actress, and then it became all about the madness, the parties and everyone forgets about what put them there in the first place: they get lost in the idea that they are famous for who they are, not what they are. I feel sorry for these kids... I worry that these kids will just get swallowed up. [...] I couldn't help Amy [Winehouse], Whitney [Houston] or Michael [Jackson]... but I did save myself."[146]

Ornamented with a slight reverb that's gently retro, Elton's magnetic voice alone holds the entire arrangement, and keeps the accompanying instruments attentively following. First in line is, of course, his piano, which has a docile, bluesy sound that allows space for the singer to indulge his vibrato. The jazzy drums are played with brushes and prolong Elton's angst-laden sound, while the discreet brass provides a touch of solace. This song is clearly a classic.

Doyle Bramhall II appears on two tracks from *The Diving Board* and he has a very particular style of playing. Bramhall II is known for playing a left-handed guitar with the stringing reversed.

CANDLELIT BEDROOM

Elton John, Bernie Taupin / 4:14

Musicians: Elton John: vocals, piano / Doyle Bramhall II: electric guitar / Raphael Saadiq: bass / Jay Bellerose: drums / Jack Ashford: tambourine **Recorded:** The Village Recorder, Los Angeles: January 2012 or January 2013 **Technical Team:** Producer: T-Bone Burnett / **Sound Engineer:** Jason Wormer / **Assistant Sound Engineers:** Jeff Gartenbaum, Chris Owens, Vanessa Parr / **Mixing:** Jason Wormer / **Mastering:** Gavin Lurssen

On this slow, retro number Elton shows himself off to some advantage, offering a pleasing melody without pianistic artifice while taking some risks with the vocals. This is the case mostly on the ends of phrases, where Elton's vibrato is called upon to reach down to the lowest register (impressive at 0:37 or at 1:03, for example). The rhythm section, which is austerely academic, remains supportive throughout the song, and is enriched by the presence of Jack Ashford's tambourine.

While Raphael Saadiq allows himself the liberty of some intricacy on the bass, Jay Bellerose's drums remain on the straight and narrow. This enables Elton to show what he can do with some very fine vocal placement, alternatively matching the kick drum and the snare drum and thereby creating the effect of generously hammering out the words. Doyle Bramhall's II's guitar, which is not very present on the album, delivers discreet arpeggios in the background, and he has his moment of glory from 2:27 on an old-fashioned style solo that is very well judged. Although well-written, the lyrics ("The sound of one heart breaking, the sound of someone waking / To the cold hard truth before the sun goes down / If I could ever catch you a little bit of that / I'd wrap it up and bury it in the deep dark ground"), suffer because they once again revolve around a subject that has been very well trod by the lyricist: heartbreak.

ALBUM

WONDERFUL CRAZY NIGHT

Wonderful Crazy Night . In the Name of You . Claw Hammer . Blue Wonderful .
I've Got 2 Wings . A Good Heart . Looking Up . Guilty Pleasure . Tambourine . The Open Chord

RELEASE DATES
UK Release: February 5, 2016
Reference: Mercury—4765866
Best UK Chart Ranking: 6
US Release: February 5, 2016
Reference: Island Records—B0024335-02
Best US Chart Ranking: 8

Deviating from his usual approach to their collaboration, Elton asked Bernie to write happy lyrics for his 32nd album.

Two years after the release of *Wonderful Crazy Night*, his last noncollaborative studio album, Elton began his farewell tour, rightly titled: Farewell Yellow Brick Road Tour.

A CELEBRATORY SALVO

The visual contrasts between the album covers for *The Diving Board* and *Wonderful Crazy Night* are striking. With his previous album, Elton showed the back of an individual literally standing on the edge of the precipice. With *Wonderful Crazy Night*, Elton John's humor and spontaneity are ecstatically captured by photographers Juergen Teller and Joseph Guay. "This is a happy album. Because I've never been happier,"[149] Elton reflected with disarming simplicity. However, not everything was so rosy. At this point in 2016, Elton had no more contact with his mother, Sheila Farebrother. He found it unacceptable that she continued to be in contact with John Reid, his former manager, and Bob Hayley, his assistant and chauffeur. He also believed she had spread gossip in the press about David Furnish. With his typically British sense of sangfroid, Elton let none of this personal strife show through to the public. He had deliberately chosen to create a much more positive album for principally artistic reasons, and he had no desire to tread water.

The Lyricist's Forced Smile

Wonderful Crazy Night is a complete one-eighty from its predecessor. This was the direction he gave to Bernie Taupin a few months before the start of recording, in January 2015. To get into the proper headspace, Taupin, who was going through a Van Morrison period, grouped together various numbers that he considered to be the happiest from the Irish songwriter's repertoire, particularly "Wild Night" and "(Straight to Your Heart) Like a Cannonball." He struggled somewhat with this happier directive, as he had a natural penchant for writing moving, dramatic stories and for focusing on relationships that unfolded under difficult circumstances. There was no denying that this new creative approach left the lyricist well outside of his comfort zone. "I've always maintained that the underbelly of life and heartbreak is much more satisfying to write about; the hardest thing for me is to write an upbeat, uplifting song."[150] Having become a father quite late in life, Bernie Taupin felt that as far as he was concerned, the quickest route to happiness, and the purest and most inexhaustible source of pure joy, was children. He knew that the same was true for Elton, who was now father to two boys: Zachary Jackson Levon, born in 2010, and Elijah Joseph Daniel, born in 2013. Thus, a feeling of paternal love permeates "A Good Heart" and the bonus track "Children's Song." Another kind of inspirational, happy-inducing love is the love of one's partner: "Blue Wonderful" and "In the Name of You" express this in a conventional way and without much success, since they aren't written in the kind of language that Bernie typically uses. With a preference for more nebulous or surrealist text, Bernie found himself slightly closer to his instincts on "Tambourine" and "The Open Chord," which use musical metaphors in an amorous context. Finally, there was still Bernie's original muse: Elton himself. Sir Elton's presence is felt in its more sociable and festive aspects ("Wonderful Crazy Night"), and in its occasional tendency to veer toward combativeness and pride ("Looking Up").

A Guitar Album

Although Elton imposed a paradigm shift with an insistence on upbeat lyrics, he once again booked the Village Recorder studios (U2 was rehearsing on the floor above during the recording sessions for this album). Elton once again put his trust in T-Bone Burnett, who proved his expertise through a warm and authentic production. This time the singer served as joint producer, and he was counting on the return of his most loyal musicians, those who had accompanied him onstage: John

Jazz bassist Matt Bissonette replaced Bob Birch and Davey Johnstone onstage (shown here in 2014) and on the album.

Mahon, who was supplemented on some numbers by Ray Cooper, as well as the most recent recruit, Matt Bissonette, along with Nigel Olsson, and Davey Johnstone, who recorded hours and hours of riffs and ornamentations for the album. The fact that he worked on his lines so much was because T-Bone expected spontaneity from the musicians during the takes, which, paradoxically required a complete mastery of each person's individual parts well in advance of recording. Most of the tracks were recorded live, as a group, with the piano, guitar, bass, and drums. Some other tracks were recorded with piano, bass, and percussion. In both cases, no more than one or two takes proved to be necessary. The overdub phase of the production process was used mainly by Davey, who added a number of acoustic guitar and solo inflections, doubling his tracks, and adding effects to create varied textures that gave the disk its heavy guitar inflection.

Fourteen songs (four of which were included only on the Deluxe and Super Deluxe versions) were wrapped up in just seventeen days, between January and April 2015, at a rate of one song a day, more or less. The routine had not changed since Elton's early beginnings: "Elton shows up in the morning and goes directly to the piano," John Mahon said. "With the tape running he picks a Bernie lyric to start creating a song with. He will pretty much stay at the piano until he has written a song in its basic form. Sometimes we will join him in the room by the piano and let him bounce suggestions off of us—melody, harmony, tempo, groove, song form, etc....From there we decide which instrumentation will be the best way to record the song. This all happens in the first hour or two. Once the basic song is recorded he will record the lead vocal. After that is done, it's time to add the other instruments that were not recorded in the first go-around. Then it's overdubbing more parts where needed, and usually last is vocal harmonies. By the end of the day we have a song in the bag. Pretty much a twelve to eight p.m. day."[151]

Once the album was completed, it was sent to Capitol Records, who rejected it. This decision sealed the end of their collaboration with Elton. The album was then offered to Island Records, who were delighted to welcome the superstar into their fold. *Wonderful Crazy Night* was finally released on February 5, 2016, more than a year after the start of its recording. At nearly sixty-nine years old, Elton dazzled the world with this stirring album that's full of good vibes. The album went to sixth place on the UK charts, and to number eight in the United States. Even though the sales on this album seem slim when compared to those of Elton's heyday (*Wonderful Crazy Night* sold fifty-eight thousand copies in America), the numbers must be viewed in the context of the musical industry of the twenty-first century, which saw a drop in the sale of physical discs in favor of streaming and downloads.

2016

John Mahon, Davey Johnstone, and Elton John at the BBC Radio 2 Festival on September 11, 2016.

WONDERFUL CRAZY NIGHT

Elton John, Bernie Taupin / 3:14

Musicians: Elton John: vocals, piano / **Davey Johnstone:** guitars / **Matt Bissonette:** bass / **Nigel Olsson:** drums / **Kim Bullard:** keyboards / **John Mahon:** percussion **Recorded:** The Village Recorder, Los Angeles: January–April 2015 **Technical Team:** **Producers:** Elton John, T-Bone Burnett **Associate Producer:** Kylie Kempster / **Sound Engineer:** Jason Wormer / **Assistant Sound Engineers:** Gabriel Burch, Jeff Gartenbaum, Vanessa Parr, Alex Williams / **Mixing:** Jason Wormer / **Editing:** Mike Piersante / **Mastering:** Gavin Lurssen **Single Release:** *Wonderful Crazy Night* **UK Release:** 2016 on Mercury Records **Best UK Chart Ranking:** Did Not Chart

"Some things you don't forget [...] / What a wonderful crazy night that was": a privileged testimony to the many antics of Elton John. Bernie does not specify which "crazy night" in particular he chose to evoke, and was careful not to reveal any details, referring only to a "Calypso moon," a "Warm wind," a "cool, cool drink," "loose clothes," and "ice cubes on the back of your neck." The rest is left to the imagination of the listeners. And "didn't it feel like the clocks had stopped," he says, underpinning the gentle nostalgia of the hedonism of this

piece. The second single of the album, this title song takes the form of an up-tempo rock number, in which the rhythm section distills an irresistible rock groove, with Matt Bissonette's swaying bass, and Nigel Olsson rock solid behind his drums. On piano, Elton is cheerful and effusive, particularly in a devastating solo in the middle of the piece. His refreshing playing style, reminiscent of Allen Toussaint in a New Orleans ambiance, perfectly integrates with the silky keyboards of Kim Bullard and Davey Johnstone's acoustic rhythm guitar. Clearly, the singer's aim is to place "Wonderful Crazy Night" in a continuous line with glorious numbers such as "Honky Cat" or "Bennie and the Jets," and the harmony binding the group in the number is, in any case, palpable. "When I got the lyric to 'Wonderful Crazy Night,' which is the second song I wrote for the album, I thought, 'Wow, this is a) a great title for the record, and b) it's got to be up-tempo with that lyric,'"[147] explained Elton. "So this was the template, really, for the album. After we finished that track I had no problem writing up-tempo tracks. The floodgates opened after that."[147]

IN THE NAME OF YOU

Elton John, Bernie Taupin / 4:34

Musicians: Elton John: vocals, piano / Davey Johnstone: guitars / Matt Bissonette: bass / **Nigel Olsson:** drums / **Kim Bullard:** keyboards / John Mahon: percussion **Recorded:** The Village Recorder, Los Angeles: January–April 2015 **Technical Team:** Producers: Elton John, T-Bone Burnett / **Associate Producer:** Kylie Kempster / **Sound Engineer:** Jason Wormer / **Assistant Sound Engineers:** Gabriel Burch, Jeff Gartenbaum, Vanessa Parr, Alex Williams / **Mixing:** Jason Wormer / **Editing:** Mike Piersante / **Mastering:** Gavin Lurssen **Single Release:** *In the Name of You* **UK Release:** 2016 on Virgin EMI Records **Best UK Chart Ranking:** Did Not Chart

An astonishing cross of multiples influences, right from its intro "In the Name of You" evokes "Tusk" by Fleetwood Mac and "That's All" by Genesis. Bernie Taupin's concise lyrics show less boldness. They unenthusiastically list everything that the narrator would be willing to do for another person: "To the bottom of the ocean / I would surely dive / To find the oldest oyster / With the biggest pearl inside" is probably the best strophe of the piece—and that is saying something. . . . Elton and his group, on the other hand, are at work refining a solid rock ballad, with a very elaborate structure, albeit without a very original melody. The rounded bass of Matt Bissonette fills even the smallest spaces left by Nigel Olsson, who is more robust than ever on drums. Davey Johnstone is omnipresent with his guitars, whether simply as an accompaniment, as biting as one could wish for, or in a cutting and inspired solo from 2:37. This is also the first Elton song for a long time to put the guitar back at the center of the action: "'In the Name of You' is one of my favorite tracks," explained the singer. "I just love the way the song builds. The chorus to me is so hook-y. Every song on the album has two or three hooks in it, whether it's a riff or a chorus or a verse. But 'In the Name of You' is full of hooks. That's the first real guitar-based track that we recorded. It has a funky intro, and then in the chorus the twelve-strings come rattling in. A lot of it is kind of a throwback to the '70s in a way, but it sounds modern, too. And it sounds a bit Little Feat–ish, that track, to me."[147]

CLAW HAMMER

Elton John, Bernie Taupin / 4:23

Musicians: Elton John: vocals, piano / Davey Johnstone: guitars, backing vocals / **Matt Bissonette:** bass, backing vocals / **Nigel Olsson:** drums, backing vocals / **Kim Bullard:** keyboards / **John Mahon:** percussion, backing vocals / **Gabe Witcher:** direction, arrangements / **Ken Stacey:** backing vocals **Ray Cooper:** tambourine **Recorded:** The Village Recorder, Los Angeles: January–April 2015 **Technical Team:** Producers: Elton John, T-Bone Burnett / **Associate Producer:** Kylie Kempster / **Sound Engineer:** Jason Wormer / **Assistant Sound Engineers:** Gabriel Burch, Jeff Gartenbaum, Vanessa Parr, Alex Williams / **Mixing:** Jason Wormer / **Editing:** Mike Piersante / **Mastering:** Gavin Lurssen

With an effective refrain in a major key, "Claw Hammer" features the work of Davey Johnstone with his intricate introductory riff on guitar and his dazzling interventions on a twelve-string electric guitar. Elton does, however, stress the fact that the song was initially written based on a piano motif: "All the riffs are piano riffs that are then adapted to the guitar or whatever. But the riff is so great. I just love that riff!"[147] The most impressive aspect of "Claw Hammer" is certainly its incredible versatility. The song explores various musical horizons, to the great enjoyment of its performer: "It starts off one way and goes another way, and at the end it goes berserk and very funky," explains Elton, "with Kim Bullard playing incredible brass parts on the synthesizer—which you think are real brass—because the samples are so good."[147] It's impossible not to cite Peter Gabriel when assessing this piece that combines prog rock, pop, and jazz, which Elton fully acknowledges: "Peter Gabriel's records were always influential on me because he used so many different instruments. You wouldn't think at the end of 'Claw Hammer' that you'd get a brass section coming in. Then the brass comes in and it really lifts the whole ending of the track. It starts off one way—a bit Steely Dan–ish—and then it goes another way and ends up Peter Gabriel–ish. And Elton John–ish! What can I tell you? It's certainly a track that by the end of it you wouldn't have thought it would go there when you listened to the first eight bars. That's what I love about that track."[147] This same craziness embraces Bernie Taupin's lyrics, which are a series of short and incisive phrases without any specific meaning. The one thing that is certain is that it is one of the very few songs in the entire history of modern pop whose words include the term "ontological." This warrants some explanation: Ontology is a philosophical concept that relates to the nature of being. Why do Bernie Taupin's lyrics contain such profound reflection? Who's to say, since ultimately the main value of "Claw Hammer" resides in its meticulous musical construction.

Elton John works the crowd at a free *Wonderful Crazy Night* concert in Los Angeles on February 27, 2016.

BLUE WONDERFUL

Elton John, Bernie Taupin / 3:38

Musicians: Elton John: vocals, piano / Davey Johnstone: guitars, backing vocals / Matt Bissonette: bass, backing vocals / Nigel Olsson: drums, backing vocals / Kim Bullard: keyboards / John Mahon: percussions, backing vocals **Recorded:** The Village Recorder, Los Angeles: January-April 2015 **Technical Team:** Producers: Elton John, T-Bone Burnett / Associate Producer: Kylie Kempster / Sound Engineer: Jason Wormer / Assistant Sound Engineers: Gabriel Burch, Jeff Gartenbaum, Vanessa Parr, Alex Williams / Mixing: Jason Wormer / Editing: Mike Piersante / Mastering: Gavin Lurssen

In fourth position in the track list, "Blue Wonderful" is the song that sets the tone for the album, which makes sense since it was the first number recorded during the sessions at the Village Recorder studios in LA. "I looked at the lyric and thought, 'Oh God, this is such a great title,'" explained Elton John. "But it was just so simple to write. It came together quickly. We were off to a good start."[147] Bernie's lyrics are based on the stock image of a blue-eyed lover, whose gaze is compared to the blue of the ocean ("I dive in, I dive deep, I just swim"). He also plays on the homophony of the word "blues," the musical genre, and it is implied that he's attached to the musical

blues as much as he's attached to the blue eyes of the one he loves. Elton is sensitive to these words and not lacking in inspiration in the composition of the music. "It reminded me a little bit of 'Tiny Dancer,'" he admits. "It's very Californian. That kind of vibe. It's full of electric guitars; very West Coast–y. Again, it was very quick to write, and it turned out exactly the way I wanted it."[147] It is true that Davey Johnstone's guitars, whether the arpeggios played on twelve-string electric guitar or lap steel that are present in the background, are reminiscent of the Eagles. Even so, more than "Tiny Dancer," "Blue Wonderful" directly evokes many other Elton songs, such as "Skyline Pigeon," "Harmony," "Chameleon," "The North," "Goodbye Yellow Brick Road," and "Man." Their common feature? All of them use Elton John's favorite chord progression: a descending diatonic scale sequence or "canon," as in Pachelbel's Canon. This sequence is also present in songs such as "Let It Be" and "A Day in the Life" by the Beatles, "All the Young Dudes," written by David Bowie for Mott the Hoople before he took it back, and "Mind Games" by John Lennon. With this proven effective harmonization, Elton and his group just have to run the sequence and provide a very fine climax on the double solo for piano and guitar beginning at 1:48.

Elton John released *Wonderful Crazy Night* on February 5, 2016, with a concert at the Olympia Hall in Paris.

I'VE GOT 2 WINGS

Elton John, Bernie Taupin / 4:35

Musicians: Elton John: vocals, piano / Davey Johnstone: guitars / Matt Bissonette: bass / Nigel Olsson: drums / Kim Bullard: keyboards / John Mahon: percussion / Ray Cooper: tambourine **Recorded:** The Village Recorder, Los Angeles: January–April 2015 **Technical Team:** Producers: Elton John, T-Bone Burnett / **Associate Producer:** Kylie Kempster / **Sound Engineer:** Jason Wormer / **Assistant Sound Engineers:** Gabriel Burch, Jeff Gartenbaum, Vanessa Parr, Alex Williams / **Mixing:** Jason Wormer / **Editing:** Mike Piersante / **Mastering:** Gavin Lurssen

Just as he had paid homage to Tom Wiggins on *The Diving Board*, in "I've Got 2 Wings" Bernie Taupin revives the memory of the Reverend Utah Smith, a preacher from Louisiana who preached in music, in the 1940s, in the Southern United States. One of his particularities was that he wore two large white paper wings on his back, which are transformed in the song into real wings when he rises up into paradise: "I was a light for the living / And I spoke of peace and love / With two wings and my old Gibson / I bought blessings from above [...] / But I went from paper wings / To the real thing at last." "I have this terrible tendency in my work to resurrect the neglected," explained a laughing Bernie concerning "I've Got 2 Wings." "It's great ammunition for songs. I mean, a Louisiana guitar-playing evangelist who wears a pair of wings? What's not to love about

that?"[148] To illustrate the story of this little-known hero, Elton strays into country terrain, rather than the blues. But he admits that he had never heard of the preacher before: "When Bernie gave me the lyric to 'I've Got 2 Wings,' I had no idea that this person existed, Elder Utah Smith," he confesses. "Then T-Bone said this guy really existed, and Bernie showed me the You-Tube footage of him with the wings. It made the song even better to write, because this guy was something else. [He was] this beautiful, wonderful black preacher who went into the church with a little amplifier, an electric guitar, and played with these wings on. Wow, that's something."[147] The song's soothing backing vocals seem to celebrate the celestial reward granted to the protagonist after so many years of hard labor and such unshakable faith. Davey's warm electric guitar, loaded with an effective acoustic accompaniment, backs them with gentleness through to the finale. "I've Got 2 Wings" gave Elton a great deal of satisfaction: "Music brings people together. When you hear music in a church, no matter whether it's sacred music, gospel music, blues music, or anything, it has a certain resonance that brings people together. It's very moving. Writing this song, 'I've Got 2 Wings,' it was very important that I knew [the story] beforehand."[147]

A GOOD HEART

Elton John, Bernie Taupin / 4:51

Musicians: Elton John: piano, vocals / Kim Bullard: keyboards / Davey Johnstone: guitars, backing vocals / Matt Bissonette: bass, backing vocals Nigel Olsson: drums, backing vocals / John Mahon: percussion, backing vocals / Tom Peterson: baritone saxophone / Joe Sublett: tenor saxophone / Jim Thomson: tenor saxophone / John Grab: trombone / Nick Lane: trombone / William Roper: tuba / Allen Fogle: French horn / Dylan Hart: French horn / Gabe Witcher: brass direction, arrangements **Recorded:** The Village Recorder, Los Angeles: January–April 2015 **Technical Team:** Producers: Elton John, T-Bone Burnett / **Associate Producer:** Kylie Kempster / **Sound Engineer:** Jason Wormer / **Assistant Sound Engineers:** Gabriel Burch, Jeff Gartenbaum, Vanessa Parr, Alex Williams / **Mixing:** Jason Wormer / **Editing:** Mike Piersante / **Mastering:** Gavin Lurssen **Single Release:** *A Good Heart* **UK Release:** July 29, 2016, on Virgin EMI Records **Best UK Chart Ranking:** Did Not Chart

The fifth single from *Wonderful Crazy Night*, "A Good Heart" is one of those powerful ballads for which the John-Taupin duo has been so celebrated. The narrator's identity is not initially clear: it could be Bernie addressing his daughters; Elton and his husband, David Furnish; or quite simply the close relationship between Elton and Bernie, after five decades spent together. Certain phrases have a paternal dimension ("Don't slip, don't trip on life / I'll be the moon inside your eyes / Don't be afraid of all my years / What you see or what you hear / It's all yours and yours alone"); others evoke the years that make one afraid, probably referring to the years separating Bernie and Heather Kidd and Elton and David Furnish; others refer to former loves ("Oh, sure [my heart has] cracked a time or two"). Elton at one time thought Bernie had been inspired by him and David Furnish as a couple, but the lyricist refuted this theory, and confirmed that it was about the transmission of the message from a father to his children: "Well, I think we have a mirror image on that because we both have young kids. Mine are a little older than his, but it's interesting. That ties us together because we're such radically different characters, but the one thing that ties us together is the kids. We can both understand the perils, pitfalls and joys of raising kids. He's got two boys and I have two girls that are seven and ten. But you draw so much energy from them, and I drew from that in a couple of songs. They're about the feeling you get from raising kids and the things you want to instill in them."[148] "A Good Heart" is definitely one of those pieces. Elton did not immediately like this song, which did, however, subsequently become one of his favorites on the album as the recording sessions progressed. It should be said that it does in a way combine the pop effectiveness of the Beatles that he had always loved and the power of sixties soul that he had always tried to emulate: "I wasn't so keen on it at first. Then we put the brass on it and it all came together. And the guitar playing is phenomenal. It's like a Steve Cropper kind of guitar sound; something you would hear on an old Stax record. I love the way I sing it and the way it builds."[147] Davey Johnstone, with his Midas touch on the six-string, splashes his class all over the song, while Elton uses his baritone voice to marvelous effect.

LOOKING UP

Elton John, Bernie Taupin / 4:07

Musicians: Elton John: vocals, piano / Davey Johnstone: guitars / Matt Bissonette: bass / Nigel Olsson: drums / Kim Bullard: keyboards / John Mahon: percussion **Recorded:** The Village Recorder, Los Angeles: January–April 2015 **Technical Team:** Producers: Elton John, T-Bone Burnett / **Associate Producer:** Kylie Kempster / **Sound Engineer:** Jason Wormer / **Assistant Sound Engineers:** Gabriel Burch, Jeff Gartenbaum, Vanessa Parr, Alex Williams / **Mixing:** Jason Wormer / **Editing:** Mike Piersante / **Mastering:** Gavin Lurssen **Single Release:** *Looking Up* **UK Release:** December 22, 2015, on Mercury and Virgin EMI **Best UK Chart Ranking:** Did Not Chart

A solid rock piece written in A major, "Looking Up" is the first single from *Wonderful Crazy Night*, and it re-creates the atmosphere of some of Elton's classic standards, like "Saturday Night's Alright (For Fighting)" and "Crocodile Rock." "It's the 2016 version of 'I'm Still Standing,' in a way," says Elton. "It's about my life. It's a really joyous song about being happy. [...] It reminds me a bit of Canned Heat and southern rock and roll. This, for me, was the standout, no-brainer single."[147] The subject of the song, which is resolutely positive, is condensed into the first line of the refrain: "Now I'm looking up more than I look down." This is a celebration of life in its fullest sense, albeit with some platitudes in the lyrics, such as "Time is wasted looking back," or "It's my life, do things my way." But, as is often the case in *Wonderful Crazy Night*, the main thing is the music. Elton's virile piano, Davey Johnstone's assured acoustic guitar, his fairly unoriginal but well executed electric guitar blues-rock solo, the full-powered drums of Nigel Olsson, and Bissonette's bass, which ricochets in all corners, are above all the expression of shared enjoyment by the musicians. It was nonetheless very far from enough to enable it to feature in any of the international charts.

GUILTY PLEASURE

Elton John, Bernie Taupin / 3:39

Musicians: Elton John: vocals, piano / Davey Johnstone: guitars / Matt Bissonette: bass / Nigel Olsson: drums / Kim Bullard: keyboards / John Mahon: percussion / Ken Stacey: backing vocals / **Recorded:** The Village Recorder, Los Angeles: January–April 2015 **Technical Team:** Producers: Elton John, T-Bone Burnett / **Associate Producer:** Kylie Kempster / **Sound Engineer:** Jason Wormer / **Assistant Sound Engineers:** Gabriel Burch, Jeff Gartenbaum, Vanessa Parr, Alex Williams / **Mixing:** Jason Wormer / **Editing:** Mike Piersante / **Mastering:** Gavin Lurssen

Lively and rousing, with its introductory clapping, "Guilty Pleasure" plays on its ambivalence between the bouncing character of its up-tempo pop, driven by the acoustic guitar, and pessimistic lyrics depicting a lover assailed by doubts. The narrator wonders about the sincerity and depth of feelings of their partner: "Am I the love of your life my love / Or just some guilty pleasure?" goes the lament, and these questions are never answered. The energy of the song, which counterbalances the pathos of the words and the relative melodic weakness, lies mainly in Davey Johnstone's acoustic rhythm guitar. Further into the song he provides a very well-constructed solo, this time on electric guitar. The rhythm section, which is very academic, plays its role in supporting Elton's powerful voice, whose piano only appears upstage, except in the finale. It is then alone in what seems to be more like an instrumental transition into the following piece, than a completely separate section of "Guilty Pleasure." This is without doubt the piece on the album that sounds the most "live." Even so, Elton has only rarely performed it onstage.

TAMBOURINE

Elton John, Bernie Taupin / 4:17

Musicians: Elton John: vocals, piano / Davey Johnstone: guitars / Matt Bissonette: bass / Nigel Olsson: drums / Kim Bullard: keyboards / John Mahon: percussion / Ray Cooper: tambourine **Recorded:** The Village Recorder, Los Angeles: January–April 2015 **Technical Team:** Producers: Elton John, T-Bone Burnett / **Associate Producer:** Kylie Kempster / **Sound Engineer:** Jason Wormer / **Assistant Sound Engineers:** Gabriel Burch, Jeff Gartenbaum, Vanessa Parr, Alex Williams / **Mixing:** Jason Wormer / **Editing:** Mike Piersante / **Mastering:** Gavin Lurssen

The arrangement in "Tambourine" is a model of complementarity between the instruments it employs. Once again Davey Johnstone irradiates the piece with good vibes, first in his rhythmic playing, mainly on acoustic guitar, and subsequently with little touches on electric guitar, with a clear sound setting and a slight, additional warm reverb. At 2:42, for example, the guitarist demonstrates his own writing talent on a short solo with its memorable ornamentations. Elton's piano is relegated to an upstage mix location, but this is not the most important aspect, since Kim Bullard's keyboards offer a comfortable bed for the rousing rhythm section and, in particular, Matt Bissonette's elastic bass. Finally, legendary percussionist Ray Cooper makes his return to Elton as literally the embodiment of the song's protagonist: the tambourine itself. In fact, the narrator, sighing, imagines himself as a tambourine in the hands of the loved one: "Smack in the middle / Toss it in the air / I don't care / You can play me anywhere." Rather than confining it to a simple accompanying role, Ray Cooper turns the instrument into a key component in the song, crossing all conventions and disseminating his flickering rhythmic sounds wherever he sees fit, but always with an implacable sense of rhythm. Vocally, Elton exudes a clear assurance without making too much of it and serves the vivacious melody to very good effect.

THE OPEN CHORD

Elton John, Bernie Taupin / 4:04

Musicians: Elton John: vocals, piano / **Davey Johnstone:** guitars, backing vocals / **Matt Bissonette:** bass, backing vocals / **Nigel Olsson:** drums, backing vocals / **Kim Bullard:** keyboards / **John Mahon:** percussion, backing vocals **Recorded:** The Village Recorder, Los Angeles: January–April 2015 **Technical Team:** Producers: Elton John, T-Bone Burnett / **Associate Producer:** Kylie Kempster / **Sound Engineer:** Jason Wormer / **Assistant Sound Engineers:** Gabriel Burch, Jeff Gartenbaum, Vanessa Parr, Alex Williams / **Mixing:** Jason Wormer / **Editing:** Mike Piersante / **Mastering:** Gavin Lurssen

A fervent music lover, and occasional singer—he wrote a spoken word album in 1971 called *Taupin*, and two other sung albums, *He Who Rides the Tiger* (1980) and *Tribe* (1987)—Bernie Taupin had never evinced particular leanings as an instrumentalist. However, over the years, he familiarized himself with the guitar in order to perfect the musicality of his texts. "I sort of need it in order to write. It's very hard for me to sit on a plane with a notepad. I can write lines and title ideas, but to construct a song I need to be in my office at home with a guitar on my knee and a pad and a piece of paper and a computer. I'll write things down and then transfer them to my computer, so that I can actually see it better. I look at it on the computer and then just chord stuff on the guitar to give myself an idea. It has nothing to do with the ultimate melody. It just gives me a better sense of the rhythm of the lyric."[67]

As a guitarist, Bernie familiarized himself with certain aspects of playing, such as the open chords. This consists of using a scordatura, providing a simplified fingering in order to make the chords easier to play. With his writer's mind he saw in this simplicity a source of happiness that was transposable for amorous relationships. He therefore constructs his words from this phrase with its sensual underlying meaning: "You're an open chord I wanna play all day." The gentleness induced by such a declaration is translated into music by a soft and silky arrangement that once again focuses on Elton's piano after a number of pieces left to the good offices of Davey Johnstone's guitars. The guitars are still present but clearly further back in the mix, to the benefit of Kim Bullard's keyboards in particular, emulating strings, and accompanying Elton with layers of sound on the refrain or rising up here and there in pizzicato mode. The melody of the refrain is catchy and rounds off *Wonderful Crazy Night* with great delicacy.

FREE AND EASY

Elton John, Bernie Taupin / 3:56

Musicians: Elton John: vocals, piano / **Davey Johnstone:** guitars, backing vocals / **Matt Bissonette:** bass, backing vocals / **Nigel Olsson:** drums, backing vocals / **Kim Bullard:** keyboards / **John Mahon:** percussion, backing vocals **Recorded:** The Village Recorder, Los Angeles: January–April 2015 **Technical Team:** Producers: Elton John, T-Bone Burnett / **Associate Producer:** Kylie Kempster / **Sound Engineer:** Jason Wormer / **Assistant Sound Engineers:** Gabriel Burch, Jeff Gartenbaum, Vanessa Parr, Alex Williams / **Mixing:** Jason Wormer / **Editing:** Mike Piersante / **Mastering:** Gavin Lurssen

Curiously left out since this would have been one of the best candidates for inclusion in *Wonderful Crazy Night*, the folk ballad "Free and Easy" boasts some impressive arrangements (the harpsichord from 2:20, the finely honed guitars, the warm bass, the incredibly varied backing vocals…). Elton is vocally impeccable, providing a marvelous illustration of the narrator's insouciance, full of calm, love, and liberty, after a life lived at full speed. In default of a better fate, the piece finally found refuge as a bonus track on the Deluxe version of the album (released in the UK on Mercury / Virgin EMI Records and in the United States on Island Records).

ENGLAND AND AMERICA

Elton John, Bernie Taupin / 3:56

Musicians: Elton John: vocals, piano / **Davey Johnstone:** guitars, backing vocals / **Matt Bissonette:** bass, backing vocals / **Nigel Olsson:** drums, backing vocals / **Kim Bullard:** keyboards / **John Mahon:** percussion, backing vocals **Recorded:** The Village Recorder, Los Angeles: January–April 2015 **Technical Team:** Producers: Elton John, T-Bone Burnett / **Associate Producer:** Kylie Kempster / **Sound Engineer:** Jason Wormer / **Assistant**

Sound Engineers: Gabriel Burch, Jeff Gartenbaum, Vanessa Parr, Alex Williams / **Mixing:** Jason Wormer / **Editing:** Mike Piersante / **Mastering:** Gavin Lurssen

Although it's probably exhilarating for the musicians, who are playing at lightning speed, "England and America" suffers from its conventional structure and inopportune grandiloquence. It was therefore logical that it missed out on being included in the main album and was relegated to the deluxe version of *Wonderful Crazy Night* (released in the UK on Mercury / Virgin EMI Records and in the United States on Island Records). As an American citizen since 1990, in this song Bernie pays homage to his country of birth, and also to the country of his heart: England and America. As the lyricist reminds us through the powerful voice of his singer and colleague: "And if I fall it's good to know / There's England and America."

NO MONSTERS

Elton John, Bernie Taupin / 4:58

Musicians: Elton John: vocals, piano / **Davey Johnstone:** guitars, backing vocals / **Matt Bissonette:** bass, backing vocals / **Nigel Olsson:** drums, backing vocals / **Kim Bullard:** keyboards / **John Mahon:** percussion, backing vocals / **Tom Peterson:** baritone saxophone / **Joe Sublett:** tenor saxophone / **Jim Thomson:** tenor saxophone / **John Grab:** trombone / **Nick Lane:** trombone / **William Roper:** tuba / **Allen Fogle:** French horn / **Dylan Hart:** French horn / **Gabe Witcher:** brass direction, arrangements / **Ken Stacey:** backing vocals **Recorded:** The Village Recorder, Los Angeles: January–April 2015 **Technical Team:** Producers: Elton John, T-Bone Burnett / **Associate Producer:** Kylie Kempster / **Sound Engineer:** Jason Wormer / **Assistant Sound Engineers:** Gabriel Burch, Jeff Gartenbaum, Vanessa Parr, Alex Williams / **Mixing:** Jason Wormer / **Editing:** Mike Piersante / **Mastering:** Gavin Lurssen

In "No Monsters," Bernie evokes a relationship between two lovers that has turned sour due to a difficult past: "But I was damaged and adrift then / Afraid I'd break your pure and perfect heart." The couple meet again when the narrator finally feels ready to move forward.

Following pages: Elton John and his men in black during the Farewell Yellow Brick Road Tour in September 2018: (left to right) Ray Cooper, Matt Bissonette, Kim Bullard, Nigel Olsson, Elton John, Davey Johnstone, and John Mahon.

CHILDREN'S SONG

Elton John, Bernie Taupin / 3:49

Musicians: Elton John: vocals, piano / Davey Johnstone: guitars, backing vocals / Matt Bissonette: bass, backing vocals / Nigel Olsson: drums, backing vocals / Kim Bullard: keyboards / John Mahon: percussion, backing vocals / Tom Peterson: baritone saxophone / Joe Sublett: tenor saxophone / Jim Thomson: tenor saxophone / John Grab: trombone / Nick Lane: trombone / William Roper: tuba / Allen Fogle: French horn / Dylan Hart: French horn / Gabe Witcher: brass direction, arrangements / Ken Stacey: backing vocals
Recorded: The Village Recorder, Los Angeles: January–April 2015

Technical Team: Producers: Elton John, T-Bone Burnett / **Associate Producer:** Kylie Kempster / **Sound Engineer:** Jason Wormer / **Assistant Sound Engineers:** Gabriel Burch, Jeff Gartenbaum, Vanessa Parr, Alex Williams / **Mixing:** Jason Wormer / **Editing:** Mike Piersante / **Mastering:** Gavin Lurssen

As was the case on "A Good Heart," Bernie wrote the lyrics to "Children's Song" in reference to his own children, as well as to Sir Elton's two sons. Humbly, and with great tenderness, the lyricist, having been battered by a tumultuous life spent in the spotlight, passes on to his descendants what wisdom he has gleaned over the years: "Paint in colors bold and bright / Don't fade into the gray / Live every second like it counts / Go ahead and seize the day." Touching, but probably considered too naïve, "Children's Song" appeared only on the limited-edition box set version of *Wonderful Crazy Night* (released in the UK on Mercury / Virgin EMI Records / Island Records).

ELTON: JEWEL BOX—AN 8 CD BOX SET

Release Dates

UK Release: November 13, 2020

Reference: UMC / EMI / Rocket Entertainment—071 590-8

Best UK Chart Ranking: 68

US Release: November 13, 2020

Reference: UMC / EMI / Rocket Entertainment—071 590-8

Best US Chart Ranking: Did Not Chart

Diamonds are Forever

After demonstrating that he was still artistically relevant with 2016's *Wonderful Crazy Night*, Elton John was once again led to cast an eye over his past due to the approaching fiftieth anniversary of his collaboration with Bernie Taupin. The celebration took the form of a compilation album called *Diamonds*, whose deluxe edition combined fifty-one of Elton John's greatest successes. Sir Elton also used this moment to make a bittersweet announcement to his fans. He began to publicize his farewell tour, "Farewell Yellow Brick Road," which would be a marathon of three hundred dates played around the world. The tour began on September 8, 2018, in Allentown, Pennsylvania. The following year, Elton's biopic, *Rocketman*, was released after gestating in development since the early 2000s. The much-celebrated film was made under the close supervision of Elton and via the direction of Dexter Fletcher, and it was carried by the very convincing performance of actor Taron Egerton. The cherry on the cake of all these glittering achievements was the fall 2019 publication of Elton's frank autobiography, *Me*, which was praised by the critics and fans alike.

A Fantasy Fulfilled

True musical completists remained unsatisfied. Just as Prince fans knew that their idol had hours of unreleased material tucked away inside Paisley Park, Elton's fans also knew that before becoming a musician of genius, he was above all a music lover…and a compulsive collector. It was therefore impossible to imagine that Elton did not have in his possession priceless archives of his own productions, unreleased material, rare recordings, or other nuggets dating from his Reginald period, and well before hurricane Elton hit the world.

This is the gap that *Elton: Jewel Box* filled when it was released in 2020. The massive box set consisted of eight CDs that were divided into four categories: two disks of *Deep Cuts*, three dics of *Rarities*, two more disks of *B-Sides 1976–2005*, and one disk simply called *And This Is Me…* The collection, which also exists in vinyl editions, is accompanied by a lavishly illustrated sixty-page booklet containing copious information on songs, photos, advertising material, and extracts from the lyrics. In it, Elton also makes some fascinating revelations: "But I never thought of myself as a singles artist. […] I wanted to make albums. […] They had hits on them, but they became hits almost by accident."[152] This is how Elton justifies highlighting this hitherto unknown legacy, even adding: "I've made a lot of records over the last fifty-two years: there

The cover design for *Elton: Jewel Box* was inspired by this Terry O'Neill photo taken in 1973.

could easily have been another thirty or forty songs on here. Think of it as an alternative history of Elton John."[152] Elton's initiative, whose placement is clearly aimed at the fans, is effectively that of an artist wishing to provide a different perspective of his rich career. More than a third of the pieces are new, and the compilation work is no mean feat: "I knew I was busy back then, but when did we sleep? But that said, I have a great archivist and a wonderful team behind me who have an extensive and systematized approach to collating and storing my work."[153]

On the two *Deep Cuts* CDs there are pieces that Elton felt that he had somewhat neglected, like "Monkey Suit," recorded with Leon Russell, "Mellow" from *Honky Château* (which Elton felt included what is probably the best piano solo he had ever recorded), and "The Ballad of Danny Bailey (1909–34)," from *Goodbye Yellow Brick Road*, which Elton also considered to be one of his group's finest performances.

Elton's Treasure

Most of the pieces on the *B-Sides 1976–2005* discs and on *And This Is Me* had already been released but remained relatively unheard. Some of them (seventeen, to be precise) had never even been made available on CD, such as the wild instrumental "Choc Ice Goes Mental" (B-side of "Kiss the Bride" in the United States) or even "Snow Queen," a duet with Kiki Dee that many fans would not necessarily remember was featured

on side B of their legendary collaboration, "Don't Go Breaking My Heart." "However, rediscovering tracks like 'The Angel Tree,' 'Tartan Coloured Lady' or 'The Tide Will Turn for Rebecca' are such special songs and mean a lot to me," Elton confessed. "I really believe that if Bernie and I had not written those songs together early on, we would never have progressed as songwriters. They remind me of the beautiful musical journey we have both been through."[153]

But the real highlight for fans is certainly the *Rarities 1965–1971* trio of discs, which notably features "Come Back Baby," the first song that Reg Dwight wrote as part of Bluesology: "'Come Back Baby' is a track I will never forget. I distinctly remember recording it at Philips [studio] in Stanhope Place, Marble Arch [in London]."[153] There is also a demo version of "Scarecrow," Elton's first musical setting of Bernie Taupin's lyrics, and the exuberant "Dick Barton Theme (Devil's Gallop)," credited to the Bread and Beer Band, a collective of session musicians with whom Elton played. "The 'Rarities' tracks, which go all the way back to the mid-to-late '60s," explained Elton, "were primarily archived at my record company, Universal, in the UK. They had been digitized piecemeal over the years. It's an art in itself, really!"[153]

While *Diamonds* offers a fine vision of Elton's official creative journey, *Jewel Box* is a complement to this, providing a different reading that makes it a must-have for fans who want to enjoy the entire panorama of Elton's rich recording catalog.

REGIMENTAL SGT. ZIPPO

When I Was Tealby Abbey . And the Clock Goes Around . Sitting Doing Nothing .
Turn to Me . Angel Tree . Regimental Sgt. Zippo . A Dandelion Dies in the Wind .
You'll Be Sorry to See Me Go . Nina . Tartan Coloured Lady .
Hourglass . Watching the Planes Go By

RELEASE DATES
Worldwide Release: June 12, 2021, on Record Store Day
References: Rocket Entertainment / EMI / UMC / DJM Records—0602435557878;
Rocket Entertainment / EMI / UMC—RSDRSZ2021
Best UK Chart Ranking: Did Not Chart
Best US Chart Ranking: 197
On vinyl only
Limited series of 7,000 copies

Elton and Bernie circa 1970.

PSY'COVER

Assembled for release on Record Store Day in 2021, this album cover is adorned with a period psychedelic visual: a pen and ink drawing by David Larkham, the historical designer of Elton's first album covers.

SMOKE WITHOUT FIRE

2021

While the world was in lockdown in 2020 and reeling from the full force of the COVID-19 pandemic, Elton John used the downtime to delve back into his discography to exhume *Regimental Sgt. Zippo*. The idea had come to him while he was carrying out research for the gargantuan *Elton: Jewel Box*, a box set of treasures from the singer's archives that had appeared the previous year. It was on this occasion that the ill-fated *Regimental Sgt. Zippo* resurfaced. Between November 1967 and May 1968, Elton—then known as Reginald Dwight—had recorded twelve songs with the secret hope of releasing them one day on an album with DJM Records, for which he had even chosen the title: *Regimental Sgt. Zippo*. In the end, they were left on one side at the advice of Steve Brown, who was convinced that the Elton-Bernie duo had not yet given the best it could offer.

He wanted them to record some new, more promising numbers. *Regimental Sgt. Zippo* was thus nipped in the bud by *Empty Sky*, which started the ball rolling for Elton's discography in June 1969. Half a century later, the singer decided to do justice to this original opus, and he released it as part of Record Store Day in June 2021. Among the twelve numbers on his track list, only "You'll Be Sorry to See Me Go" was genuinely new; the others had already been included in 2020's *Jewel Box* release—some of them in their definitive form ("Turn to Me," "Tartan Coloured Lady," "Hourglass"), and others in their demo form ("When I Was Tealby Abbey," "And the Clock Goes Round," "A Dandelion Dies in the Wind"), and still others were released in alternative versions ("Sitting Doing Nothing," "Angel Tree," "Regimental Sgt. Zippo," "Nina," "Watching the Planes Go By").

WHEN I WAS TEALBY ABBEY
Elton John, Bernie Taupin / 2:35

Musicians: Elton John: vocals, piano, organ / **Caleb Quaye:** guitar, flute, timbales, cymbals, backing vocals / **Dee Murray:** bass, backing vocals / **David Hynes:** drums, backing vocals / **Paul Fenoulhet Orchestra:** orchestra / **Zack Laurence:** arrangements **Recorded:** Dick James Music Studios, London: April 5, 1968 **Technical Team:** Producer: Caleb Quaye / **Sound Engineer:** Frank Owen / **Remix (2021):** John Barrett

"When I Was Tealby Abbey" was worked on in the studio on April 5, 1968. In the end it was the seventh take of this song, with its sophisticated arrangements, that landed on the *Regimental Sgt. Zippo* disc. The track evokes the church in the village of Tealby, not far from Market Rasen, in Lincolnshire, where Bernie grew up.

AND THE CLOCK GOES AROUND
Elton John, Bernie Taupin / 3:06

Musicians: Elton John: vocals, piano, electric piano / **Caleb Quaye:** guitar, percussion, backing vocals / **Dee Murray:** bass, backing vocals / **David Hynes:** drums, backing vocals **Recorded:** Dick James Studios, London: April 4, 1968 **Technical Team:** Producer: Caleb Quaye / **Sound Engineer:** Frank Owen / Remix (2021): John Barrett

Evincing a Dylan-esque gravitas with its deliberate guitar playing, "And the Clock Goes Round" presents more of a folkish side to the type of artist that Elton was at the time—even though the unexpectedly dreamlike bridge passage in the middle of the piece also says a great deal about the song's psychedelic leanings.

SITTING DOING NOTHING
Caleb Quaye, Elton John / 2:30

Musicians: Elton John: vocals, piano / **Caleb Quaye:** guitar, backing vocals / **Dee Murray:** bass, backing vocals / **David Hynes:** drums, backing vocals **Recorded:** Dick James Studios, London: March 7, 1968 **Technical Team:** Producer: Caleb Quaye / **Sound Engineer:** Frank Owen / **Remix (2021):** John Barrett

"Sitting Doing Nothing" cannot disguise the musical influence of the Beatles, any more than its lyrics, which owe a great deal to "I'm Only Sleeping." Elton (lyrics) and Caleb (music) used the fourth take for the definitive version.

TURN TO ME
Elton John, Bernie Taupin / 3:16

Musicians: Elton John: vocals, piano, organ / **Caleb Quaye:** guitar, backing vocals / **Dee Murray:** bass, backing vocals / **David Hynes:** drums, backing vocals / **Paul Fenoulhet Orchestra:** brass / **Zack Laurence:** arrangements **Recorded:** Dick James Studios, London: March 10, 1968 **Technical Team:** Producer: Caleb Quaye / **Sound Engineer:** Frank Owen / **Remix (2021):** John Barrett

March 10 was a prolific day for the team, who recorded three pieces, including "Turn to Me." This number echoes the legendary riff by the Troggs on "Wild Thing," and also includes some nice brass. "Turn to Me" was covered by Plastic Penny in 1969. The members of this group included a certain Nigel Olsson, future drummer for Elton.

ANGEL TREE
Elton John, Bernie Taupin / 2:04

Musicians: Elton John: vocals, piano / **Caleb Quaye:** guitar, tambourine, backing vocals / **Dee Murray:** bass, backing vocals / **Roger Pope:** drums, backing vocals / **Paul Fenoulhet Orchestra:** brass / **Zack Laurence:** arrangements **Recorded:** Dick James Studios, London: December 13, 1967 **Technical Team:** Producer: Caleb Quaye / **Sound Engineer:** Frank Owen / **Remix (2021):** John Barrett

Recorded during the demo stage according to the Dick James studio archives, "Angel Tree" saw the light of day on December 13, 1967. Elton was unable to record the definitive version the following week, as he was mobilized to provide backing vocals on the Tom Jones hit "Delilah." The version used for *Regimental Sgt. Zippo* was the third take, which was recorded on January 11, 1968, with some glitzy brass. The backing vocals were recorded eight days later. An amusing detail: in the lyrics there is reference to a tree in Lincolnshire...the same one referred to later in "Burn Down the Mission."

REGIMENTAL SGT. ZIPPO
Elton John, Bernie Taupin / 4:44

Musicians: Elton John: vocals, piano, organ / **Caleb Quaye:** guitar, flute, backing vocals / **Dee Murray:** bass, backing vocals / **David Hynes:** drums, backing vocals **Recorded:** Dick James Studios, London: May 20, 1968 **Technical Team:** Producer: Caleb Quaye / **Sound Engineer:** Frank Owen / **Remix (2021):** John Barrett

As Elton's schedule allowed him very few slots for recording "Regimental Sgt. Zippo," he had to attend a session on May 20, 1968, and by the second take he and his fellow musicians were satisfied with this psychedelic homage, explicitly dedicated to *Sgt. Pepper's Lonely Hearts Club Band* by the Beatles.

2021

A DANDELION DIES IN THE WIND

Elton John, Bernie Taupin / 3:14

Musicians: Elton John: vocals, piano, organ / **Caleb Quaye:** guitar, backing vocals / **Dee Murray:** bass, backing vocals / **David Hynes:** drums, backing vocals **Recorded:** Dick James Studios, London: March 10, 1968 **Technical Team:** Producer: Caleb Quaye / Sound Engineer: Frank Owen / **Remix (2021):** John Barrett

The second song recorded on March 10, 1968, "A Dandelion Dies in the Wind" was completed after its second take. The song is evocative of Procol Harum, who had a big influence on Reginald in his early days.

YOU'LL BE SORRY TO SEE ME GO

Caleb Quaye, Elton John / 2:34

Musicians: Elton John: vocals, piano / **Caleb Quaye:** guitar, tambourine, claps, backing vocals / **Dee Murray:** bass, claps, backing vocals / **Roger Pope:** drums, claps, backing vocals **Recorded:** Dick James Studios, London: April 4, 1968 **Technical Team:** Producer: Caleb Quaye / Sound Engineer: Frank Owen / **Remix (2021):** John Barrett

Gently naïve, with its intentionally innocent-sounding backing vocals, "You'll Be Sorry to See Me Go" has the benefit of some effusive playing by Caleb Quaye, who also co-wrote the lyrics.

NINA

Elton John, Bernie Taupin / 3:50

Musicians: Elton John: vocals, piano, organ / **Caleb Quaye:** guitar / **Dee Murray:** bass / **David Hynes:** drums / **Paul Fenoulhet Orchestra:** orchestra / **Zack Laurence:** arrangements **Recorded:** Dick James Studios, London: November 15, 1967 **Technical Team:** Producer: Caleb Quaye / Sound Engineer: Frank Owen / **Remix (2021):** John Barrett

"Nina" is the oldest number on this opus: its demo was recorded on November 3, 1967, just after the release of the third and final Bluesology single, "Since I Found You Baby," and just before the Elton-Bernie duo signed their contract with Dick James. The version that appears on *Regimental Sgt. Zippo* is the seventh take, which was recorded on November 15 with the entire group. Baroque and wild, above all it has quite a slap-dash feel to it, although its energy is infectious.

TARTAN COLOURED LADY

Elton John, Bernie Taupin / 4:09

Musicians: Elton John: vocals, harpsichord / **Caleb Quaye:** guitar, flute / **Dee Murray:** bass / **David Hynes:** drums / **Paul Fenoulhet Orchestra:** orchestra / **Zack Laurence:** arrangements **Recorded:** Dick James Studios, London: February 16, 1968 **Technical Team:** Producer: Caleb Quaye / Sound Engineer: Frank Owen / **Remix (2021):** John Barrett

"Tartan Coloured Lady" was wrapped up on February 16 in a single take. It clearly stands out because of Elton's harpsichord playing, a warm-up for the legendary "Skyline Pigeon."

HOURGLASS

Elton John, Bernie Taupin / 2:44

Musicians: Elton John: vocals, piano, electric piano / **Caleb Quaye:** guitar, backing vocals / **Dee Murray:** bass, backing vocals / **David Hynes:** drums, backing vocals **Recorded:** Dick James Studios, London: March 10, 1968 **Technical Team:** Producer: Caleb Quaye / Sound Engineer: Frank Owen / **Remix (2021):** John Barrett

The bucolic "Hourglass," with its charming backing vocals, was the third piece to be wrapped up on March 10, 1968, marking the closure of this pivotal day for the album.

WATCHING THE PLANES GO BY

Elton John, Bernie Taupin / 4:07

Musicians: Elton John: vocals, piano, organ / **Caleb Quaye:** guitar, backing vocals / **Dee Murray:** bass, backing vocals / **David Hynes:** drums, backing vocals / **Paul Fenoulhet Orchestra:** brass / **Zack Laurence:** arrangements **Recorded:** Dick James Studios, London: February 6, 1968 **Technical Team:** Producer: Caleb Quaye / Sound Engineer: Frank Owen / **Remix (2021):** John Barrett

In February 1968, Elton and his musicians wrapped up two numbers intended for the album: "Tartan Coloured Lady" and "Watching the Planes Go By." Recorded in a single take on the sixth, this track was one of Caleb Quaye's favorite pieces. Inspired by the Beatles, it boasts a psychedelic orchestration and luxuriant brass.

ALBUM

THE LOCKDOWN SESSIONS

Cold Heart (Pnau Remix) (with Dua Lipa) . Always Love You (with Young Thug and Nicki Minaj) . Learn to Fly (with Surfaces) . After All (with Charlie Puth) . Chosen Family (with Rina Sawayama) . The Pink Phantom (with Gorillaz and 6lack) . It's a Sin (with Years & Years) . Nothing Else Matters (with Miley Cyrus, Watt, Yo-Yo Ma, Robert Trujillo, and Chad Smith) . Orbit (with SG Lewis) . Simple Things (with Brandi Carlile) . Beauty in the Bones (with Jimmie Allen) . One of Me (with Lil Nas X) . E-Ticket (with Eddie Vedder) . Finish Line (with Stevie Wonder) . Stolen Car (with Stevie Nicks) . I'm Not Gonna Miss You (with Glen Campbell)

RELEASE DATES
UK Release: October 22, 2021
Reference: EMI—EMICD 2051 /
Rocket Entertainment—00602438711673
Best UK Chart Ranking: 1
US Release: October 22, 2021
Reference: EMI / Interscope Records /
Rocket Entertainment—B0034529-02
Best US Chart Ranking: 10

A JOYOUS CACOPHONY

His Farewell Yellow Brick Road Tour, which had started on September 8, 2018, was going well, but Elton was obliged to suspend it following his performance in Sydney on March 7, 2020.

As countries around the world began going into lockdown in order to contain the spread of the COVID-19 virus, Elton John found himself in a state of forced inactivity. This was an intolerable situation for him, as he had only rarely taken a break since his earliest days. But in a world that was now ultra-connected, lockdown didn't necessarily mean a total break from work and creativity. Sir Elton decided to work remotely with other artists, and to put all their collaborations together on one album, aptly named *The Lockdown Sessions*.

The singer organized these collaborations according to artists he admired, opportunities that presented themselves, and to musical discoveries that he made along the way. This gave him scope for a surprising mixture of styles and generations, which confirmed his status as a sponsor of modern pop (earned through duets with emerging artists) while maintaining his aura of glory from the 1970s. Who else, in fact, could boast combining so much diversity on the same disk? Here we encounter all in one place the calibrated pop of Dua Lipa, Charlie Puth, Rina Sawayama, Years & Years, and Ed Sheeran; the rap of Nicki Minaj, Young Thug, and Lil Nas X; the mixture of neo-soul pop from Surfaces; the melancholic trip-hop of Gorillaz; the rock conversion of Miley Cyrus; the funky house music of SG Lewis; the pop rock of Brandi Carlile; the country pop of Jimmie Allen; the rock of Eddie Vedder; the soul of Stevie Wonder; the soft rock of Stevie Nicks; and the country folk of the late Glen Campbell. As for the age of the participants, from Lil Nas X (twenty-two) the youngest, to Stevie Nicks (seventy-three), here too the range was very large.

Just Like the Good Old Days

However disparate the participants may have been, *The Lockdown Sessions* was a heterogeneous album in terms of its construction. Of the seventeen songs that make up the final track list, seven are compositions in which Elton was involved ("Always Love You," "After All," "Orbit," "Simple Things," "E-Ticket," "Finish Line," and "Stolen Car"), five were conceived by his colleagues ("Learn to Fly," "Chosen Family," "The Pink Phantom," "Beauty in the Bones" and "One of Me") three are covers, which are challenging in their audacity ("Nothing Else Matters," "It's a Sin," and "I'm Not Gonna Miss You"), and one is a mash-up ("Cold Heart"). Sometimes Elton John appears almost an extra on his own disc, like a deluxe session musician sublimating his piano part to the work of others. This is the case on "One of Me" with Lil Nas X, for which Elton John created a short, dreamy piano motif. A supporting role might seem incompatible with his superstar status, but Elton approached the song with an almost teenage degree of avidity and curiosity. He even affirmed this role as a musician in the shadows with a certain pride, which brought back nice memories for him: "All the tracks I worked on were really interesting and diverse, stuff that was completely different to anything I'm known for, stuff that took me out of my comfort zone into completely new territory. And I realized there was something weirdly familiar about working like this. At the start of my career, in the late '60s, I worked as a session musician. Working with different artists during lockdown reminded me of that. I'd come full circle: I was a session musician again. And it was still a blast."[154] But it is when he expresses himself in his preferred territory of rock and soul, and when he is more involved in the song's artistic direction, that Elton John seems more at ease.

Elton used time spent in lockdown to create a series of duets with a who's-who of the new pop generation.

Some of the songs on the album were revealed to the public even before the album's official release, such as "Chosen Family," which was included on the eponymous album by Sawayama and released in April 2020. "It's a Sin" came out in May 2021, "Learn to Fly" and "Nothing Else Matters" were broadcast in June, and "One of Me" was included on the album *Montero* by Lil Nas X and released in September. "The Pink Phantom" was an integral part of *Song Machine, Season One: Strange Timez,* the seventh album by Gorillaz, released on October 23, 2020.

The recordings were subdivided and carried out (wherever possible) with the artists physically present; either from a little home studio equipped with Pro Tools or at the largest London studios. A whole host of precautions were required to prevent any contamination. Plexiglas windows separated the artists when they were singing together. When distance prevented the artists from meeting, recordings were carried out using Zoom videoconference software.

The Lockdown Sessions was unveiled to the public on October 22, 2021, and received good press, with critics recognizing the value of the initiative taken by everyone involved. The public was also enthusiastic, but at the time of the release, there was stiff competition at the top of the British charts, with new deliveries from Lana Del Rey, Biffy Clyro, and Duran Duran. In the end, this did not prevent Elton from winning first place, a position he regained some nine years after *Good Morning to the Night* was released with Pnau. The United States was not left behind either, and Elton went to tenth place on *Billboard*. A new edition of the album also appeared with the number "Merry Christmas" included. This is a good-natured, catchy song written with Ed Sheeran, and which also earned a place at the top of the British charts.

After the release of *The Lockdown Sessions*, plans were put in place to resume the Farewell Yellow Brick Road Tour in 2022 and 2023, which should be met with resounding success.

On *The Lockdown Sessions*, Elton offers a fireworks display of colors and styles ranging from rap and R&B to electropop, soul, and rock.

Together with Pnau, Elton John and Dua Lipa recorded "Cold Heart," a clever mash-up of some of Elton's most emblematic numbers.

COLD HEART (PNAU REMIX)

Elton John, Bernie Taupin, Peter Mayes, Nicholas Littlemore, Sam Littlemore / 3:22 /

Digital Single Release: *Cold Heart* (Pnau Remix) **Worldwide Release:** August 13, 2021, on EMI Records (digital version only) **Best UK Chart Ranking:** 1 **Best US Chart Ranking:** 1

The fruit of a mutual admiration between Elton John, Dua Lipa, and Pnau, "Cold Heart" might leave one feeling apprehensive about the outcome of a mash-up created by the collision of influences ranging from "Rocket Man," "Sacrifice," "Kiss the Bride," and "Where's the Shoorah?" all set in a new-disco context that might be considered sacrilege by some fans. But this is an exercise in deconstruction and reconstruction from the Australian producers of Pnau, and it is not lacking in interest from a harmonic point of view. Pnau manages to construct a cohesive, solid melody from the various samples used. This piece, with its infectious groove, is surmounted by Dua Lipa's clear, suave voice. "Cold Heart" was a global success, reaching the top 10 in more than forty countries, and taking the top spot in Great Britain. When "Cold Heart" hit number one in the UK, Sir Elton John became the only artist to have songs in the UK top 10 for six consecutive decades. Selected as a single, "Cold Heart" does prove anomalous from the rest of the album in one specific way: It is the only track that revisits the pianist's own repertoire.

ALWAYS LOVE YOU

(WITH YOUNG THUG AND NICKI MINAJ)

Elton John, Andrew Wotman, Ali Tamposi, Louis Bell, Jeffrey Lamar Williams, Billy Walsh, Onika Maraj / 4:17

The first song to be worked on in the studio, "Always Love You" is still a solitary work. "It began its life as very much an Elton John song," Elton commented, "and I didn't really like it, it needed something. And that's what Andrew [Watt, producer of the album] did, he chopped up the song and moved the chorus to the beginning."[155] Then the two men called upon rappers Young Thug and Nicki Minaj, but unfortunately after their contributions were incorporated, the worlds of pop and rap still never seemed to fully coexist on the track.

LEARN TO FLY

(WITH SURFACES)

Forrest Frank, Colin Padalecki / 3:31

"Learn to Fly" was the first song created via Zoom. This time, Forrest Frank and Colin Padalecki (the singers and guitarists of Surfaces and the authors of the hit "Sunday Best") submitted a feel-good neosoul composition that immediately seduced Elton, who was always on the lookout for new things. The

musician added a piano part and vocal harmonies after a series of rehearsals via videoconference. "Learn to Fly" was issued as a single in June 2020 by the TenThousand Projects label.

neighbor added a vocal track before producing it. It was used as the second single for the album, after "Cold Heart."

AFTER ALL
(WITH CHARLIE PUTH)

Elton John, Charlie Puth,
Jacob Kasher Hindlin / 3:28

Digital Single Release: *After All* **Worldwide Release:**
September 22, 2021, on EMI Records (digital version only) **Best UK Chart Ranking:** Did Not Chart **Best US Chart Ranking:** Did Not Chart

Elton John admired Charlie Puth, and the two eventually formed a real friendship. Following a chance meeting in a restaurant, the two artists realized that they lived on the same street. Charlie Puth became a regular visitor to the John-Furnish household, often dropping round for pizza on Sundays. It was therefore quite natural for Elton and Charlie to start recording together. Elton presented "After All" to Charlie, and his young

CHOSEN FAMILY
(WITH RINA SAWAYAMA)

Rina Sawayama, Jonny Lattimer,
Danny L. Harle / 4:40

The Japanese artist Rina Sawayama had set herself up in London and was able to record directly with Elton, after isolating for two weeks beforehand. Elton discovered this artist with her magnetic charisma while preparing an episode of his Apple radio program *Rocket Hour*. Their involvement, which arose from regular email exchanges, was thus extended through the song "Chosen Family," a pop number with an epic life force to it, on which Elton laid a piano part and which he performed with his stentorian voice, contrasting with Rina Sawayama's agile and high-pitched voice.

THE PINK PHANTOM

(WITH GORILLAZ AND 6LACK)

*Damon Albarn, Remi Kabaka,
Ricardo Valdez Valentine Jr. / 4:13*

This slow number, combining Gorillaz and Elton John, mixing trip-hop, pop, and rap, was assembled remotely: Damon Albarn was in Devon, the rapper 6lack was in Atlanta, and Elton was in London. Elton had to rein in his instinct, which drove him to create a whole melodic dynamic on piano, as Damon Albarn had opted to pare down as far as possible the instrumental part and to concentrate on the vocal harmonies between the tracks, which were very different between Elton, 6lack, and his own. The result is ethereal and melancholic, and has an accomplished gentleness. It delighted Elton, a big fan of the Blur singer's musical eclecticism.

IT'S A SIN

(WITH YEARS & YEARS)

Neil Tennant, Chris Lowe / 4:44

"It's a Sin" is another adventurous cover. Elton John was literally shaken by Olly Alexander's true and nuanced performance in the television series produced by Russell T. Davies, which took its name from the Pet Shop Boys hit. To illustrate this series, which portrays two young gay men confronted by the apparition of AIDS, in the 1980s, Olly Alexander, who is also the singer with Years & Years, delivers an intense acoustic version of the piece. Elton then suggested to the young man the idea of performing it together at the Brit Awards ceremony in 2021, and then recorded it in the studio for inclusion in the album. All the profits from this number will be paid to Elton John's foundation supporting the fight against AIDS. While the song retains the same emphasis, with piano-voice on the intro, it diverges along the way and goes completely astray in a "fireman's ball" type of arrangement that, in one fell swoop, loses all the emotional charge that it had managed to establish.

NOTHING ELSE MATTERS

(WITH MILEY CYRUS, WATT, YO-YO MA, ROBERT TRUJILLO, AND CHAD SMITH)

James Hetfield, Lars Ulrich / 6:35

We knew that Elton was capable of working with hard rockers like Alice in Chains ("Black Gives Way to Blue," on their eponymous album in 2009), Queens of the Stone Age ("Fairweather Friends," on the album...*Like Clockwork* in 2013), Ozzy

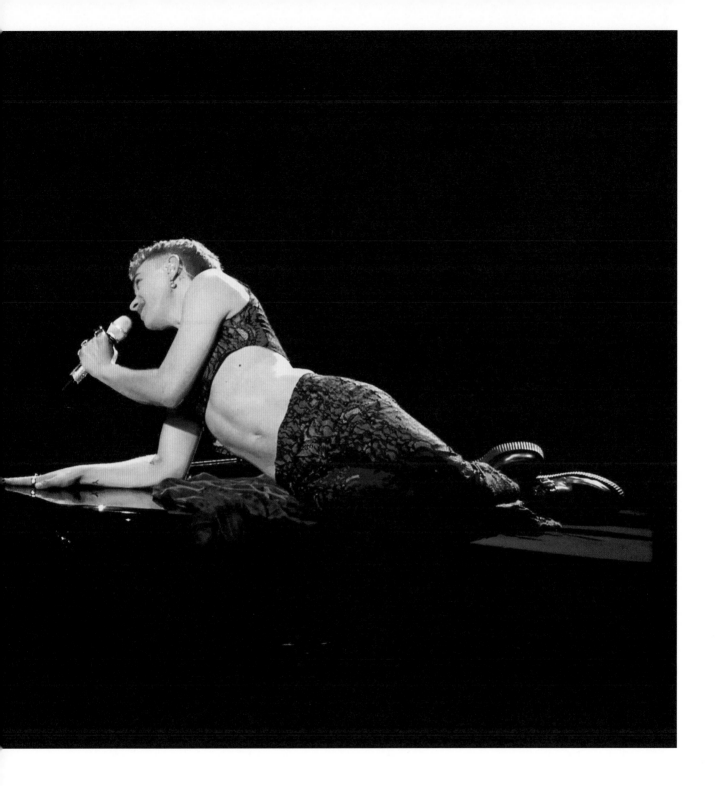

Osbourne ("Ordinary Man" on his eponymous album in 2020), but to tackle Metallica's classic? Even so, Elton had nothing but praise for this piece: "This is one of the best songs ever written, to me. I mean, it's a song that never gets old,"[156] as he said on the *Howard Stern Show*, in the presence of James Hetfield, the band's singer, who shed a tear while receiving the compliment. This idea, suggested by producer Andrew Watt, seemed about as sensible as pouring absinthe into a milkshake. But Watt would play guitar on Elton's cover, which would even be given

a blessing by the group itself, who included it on the tribute album *Metallica Blacklist* (released September 10, 2021). However, from an instrumental point of view, it withstood the test completely, due to the contributions of cellist Yo-Yo Ma; Robert Trujillo, bassist with Metallica; and Chad Smith, drummer with the Red Hot Chili Peppers. This was quite a feat, achieved via Zoom. The voice of Miley Cyrus does leave one with some apprehensions, despite the wide tessitura she uses and an entirely irreproachable technical performance.

ORBIT

(WITH SG LEWIS)

*Elton John, Samuel George Lewis,
Sophie Frances Cooke / 3:28*

"Orbit" suffers from "studio musician syndrome." Recorded in the studio alongside producer SG Lewis, this number in its initial version was considered too close to Elton's usual style. Lewis had then taken it away and created a completely new, very electro rhythm, to the extent that only the star's voice still reminds us that this song is actually on an Elton album.

SIMPLE THINGS

(WITH BRANDI CARLILE)

*Elton John, Andrew Wotman,
Roman Campolo / 4:11*

Elton felt it was important to include Brandi Carlile, his friend of nearly eighteen years, on the new album. He suggested that she should take part in "Simple Things," a piece he had composed with Andrew Wotman (alias Watt) and that exudes a sense of authentic friendship with its harmonized voices and radiant backing vocals.

BEAUTY IN THE BONES

(WITH JIMMIE ALLEN)

Jimmie Allen, Taylor Bird, Phil Bentley, Bruce Roberts / 3:50

One might have expected more from the association between Elton and country singer and musician Jimmie Allen on "Beauty in the Bones." Instead of this, the two of them get bogged down in an unpalatable dance number.

ONE OF ME

(WITH LIL NAS X)

Montero Hill, John Cunningham, Jasper Sheff, Ilsey Juber / 2:41

Admiring the commitment to the LGBTQIA+ community espoused by the performer of the surprise hit "Old Town Road," Elton quickly became great friends with Lil Nas X.

He also showed great trust in him, giving him free range to edit his piano parts as he saw fit. This was something the young artist, with all his twenty-two years, did not hesitate to do, significantly pruning Elton's track, removing some of the funk elements, and retaining only the main melodic line. He also left out the star's vocal line. This had the effect of reducing Elton's contribution to a ravishing melodic motif but rendered the song's place on the album almost illegitimate.

E-TICKET

(WITH EDDIE VEDDER)

Elton John, Eddie Vedder, Andrew Wotman / 3:18

Alongside Eddie Vedder on "E-Ticket," Elton delivers a rock 'n' roll song in which his impossible piano playing completely meshes with a rhythm section that never steals the limelight. Andrew Watt's bounding bass forms an explosive duo with the hammering drums of Taylor Hawkins, the drummer with Foo Fighters, while Elton John and Eddie Vedder rant and rave with an obvious enjoyment. Although one may consider that the timbre of such an exceptional singer as the Pearl Jam vocalist has been underused here, the energy is so infectious that it is sufficient to make this an enjoyable listening experience. With this number, Elton was responding to a request by Eddie Vedder, who had one day passed him a little note backstage indicating that he would like to do a duo with him.

FINISH LINE

(WITH STEVIE WONDER)

Elton John, Andrew Wotman, Ali Tamposi, Roman Campolo / 4:24

The duo combining Stevie Wonder and Elton John was a completely natural one. The two men had an association going back fifty years and had worked together but had never recorded a duo in the strict sense of the word. "Finish Line" puts this right, in the most brilliant way, with a sugary and groovy number. Even so, it was not originally planned that Stevie Wonder would be contributing with his voice; he was only intended to provide a piano and harmonica part. But on hearing the Kanye West choir, which inundates the piece with its gospel song, he could not resist taking part in what turned out to be the best song on the album.

STOLEN CAR

(WITH STEVIE NICKS)

Elton John, Andrew Wotman, Ali Tamposi / 5:37

The shared artistic sensibilities of Elton and Stevie Nicks are on full display in "Stolen Car." An elegant introduction, distantly reminiscent of the harmonic progression in "Your Song," opens on a refrain in which the two voices are combined with great commitment and technique. Even though the voice of the ex–Fleetwood Mac singer may seem tired at certain moments, she finds a new youthfulness in the refrains.

I'M NOT GONNA MISS YOU

(WITH GLEN CAMPBELL)

Glen Campbell, Julian Raymond / 2:56

In this virtual duo, Elton reinterpreted "I'm Not Gonna Miss You" at the request of the family of Glen Campbell, the country artist, who had died in 2017. Elton takes up this poignant song with emotion, which deals with the subject of Alzheimer's disease, from which Glen suffered. Glen released his original version of the song three years before he died, and Elton added his vocals in the Abbey Road studios for the *Lockdown Sessions* version.

MERRY CHRISTMAS

(WITH ED SHEERAN)

Elton John, Ed Sheeran, Steve Mac / 3:28

"This is my first track with Ed and I'm so happy it's a Christmas song!" Elton said. "It has been so much fun to make this song with such a close friend and the music video was an absolute blast to film: Pastiches of some of the best Christmas songs out there and Ed dressed up as Mariah Carey—what more could you want!?"[155]

In December 1973, Elton gave a series of six concerts in London alongside Davey Johnstone, Nigel Olsson, and Dee Murray. The concert on December 22, 1973, was broadcast on BBC Radio 1.

LIVE ALBUMS

17-11-70
(11-17-70 IN THE UNITED STATES)

Recorded 17/11/1970 (New York)

Release Date: April 9, 1971 (United Kingdom) May 10, 1971 (United States) / **Reference:** DJM Records – DJLPS 414 (United Kingdom) / Uni Records – UNI 98105 (United States) / **UK Best Ranking:** 20 – **US Best Ranking:** 11 / **Track Listing:** Take Me to the Pilot • Honky Tonk Women • Sixty Years on • Can I Put You on • Bad Side of the Moon • Burn Down the Mission/My Baby Left Me/Get Back

HERE AND THERE

Recorded 18/05/1974 and 28/11/1974 (London)

Release Date: April 30, 1976 (United Kingdom) May 3, 1976 (United States) / **Reference:** DJM Records – DJLPH 473 (United Kingdom) / MCA Records – MCA-2197 (United States) / **UK Best Ranking:** 6 – **US Best Ranking:** 4 / **Track Listing:** Skyline Pigeon • Border Song • Honky Cat • Love Song • Crocodile Rock • Funeral for a Friend/Love Lies Bleeding • Rocket Man (I Think It's Going to Be a Long, Long Time) • Bennie and the Jets • Take Me to the Pilot

LIVE IN AUSTRALIA
(WITH THE MELBOURNE SYMPHONY ORCHESTRA)

Recorded 1/12/1986 (Sydney)

Release Date: June 1987 (United Kingdom) July 6, 1987 (United States) / **Reference:** Rocket Record Company – EJLP 2 (United Kingdom) / MCA Records – MCA2-8022 (United States) / **UK Best Ranking:** 43 – **US Best Ranking:** 24 / **Track Listing:** Sixty Years On • I Need You to Turn To • The Greatest Discovery • Tonight • Sorry Seems to Be the Hardest Word • The King Must Die • Take Me to the Pilot • Tiny Dancer • Have Mercy on the Criminal • Madman Across the Water • Candle in the Wind • Burn Down the Mission • Your Song • Don't Let the Sun Go Down on Me

ONE NIGHT ONLY – THE GREATEST HITS

Recorded 20 and 21/10/2000 (New York)

Release Date: November 13, 2000 / **Reference:** Mercury – 548 334-2 (United Kingdom) / Universal Records – 440 013 050-2 (United States) / **UK Best Ranking:** 7 – **US Best Ranking:** 65 / **Track Listing:** Goodbye Yellow Brick Road • Philadelphia Freedom • Don't Go Breaking My Heart • Rocket Man (I Think It's Going to Be a Long, Long Time) • Crocodile Rock • Sacrifice • Can You Feel the Love Tonight? • Bennie and the Jets • Your Song • Sad Songs (Say So Much) • Candle in the Wind • Saturday Night's Alright (for Fighting) • I'm Still Standing • Don't Let the Sun Go Down on Me • I Guess That's Why They Call It the Blues

LIVE FROM MOSCOW 1979
(WITH RAY COOPER)

Recorded 28/05/1979 (Moscow)

Release Date: April 13, 2019 / **Reference:** Rocket Entertainment – 7713590/Virgin EMI Records – 00602577135903/UMC/BBC – 602577135903 (United Kingdom) / Virgin EMI Records - 7713590, BBC - 7713590, Rocket Entertainment – 7713590, UMC - 7713590 (United States) / **UK Best Ranking:** Did Not Chart – **US Best Ranking:** Did Not Chart / **Track Listing:** Daniel Skyline • Pigeon • Take Me to the Pilot • Rocket Man (I Think It's Going to Be a Long, Long Time) • Don't Let the Sun Go Down on Me • Goodbye Yellow Brick Road • Candle in the Wind • I Heard It Through the Grapevine • Funeral for a Friend • Tonight • Better Off Dead • Bennie and the Jets • Sorry Seems to Be the Hardest Word • Crazy Water • Saturday Night's Alright (for Fighting)/Pinball Wizard • Crocodile Rock • Get Back/Back in the USSR

ORIGINAL SOUNDTRACKS

FRIENDS

Release Date: April 1971 (United Kingdom) March 5, 1971 (United States) / Reference: Paramount Records – SPFL269 (United Kingdom) / Paramount Records – PAS6004 (United States) / **UK Best Ranking:** Did Not Chart – **US Best Ranking:** 36 / **Track Listing:** Friends • Honey Roll • Variations on Friends • Theme (The First Kiss)/Seasons • Variations on Michelle's Song (A Day in the Country) • Can I Put You On • Michelle's Song • I Meant to Do My Work Today (A Day in the Country) • Four Moods • Seasons Reprise

THE LION KING (ORIGINAL MOTION PICTURE SOUNDTRACK)

Release Date: May 31, 1994 / Reference: Mercury – 522 690-2/Walt Disney Records – 0126902DNY (Europe) / Walt Disney Records – 60858-2 (United States) / **UK Best Ranking:** Did Not Chart – **US Best Ranking:** 1 / **Track Listing:** Carmen Twillie – Circle of Life • Jason Weaver – I Just Can't Wait to Be King • Jeremy Irons – Be Prepared • Nathan Lane, Ernie Sabella – Hakuna Matata • Joseph Williams, Sally Dworsky – Can You Feel the Love Tonight? • This Land (instrumental) • To Die For (instrumental) • Under the Stars (instrumental) • King of Pride Rock (instrumental) • Elton John – Circle of Life • Elton John – I Just Can't Wait to Be King • Elton John – Can You Feel the Love Tonight

THE LION KING (ORIGINAL BROADWAY CAST RECORDING)

Release Date: 1997 / Reference: Walt Disney Records – 0104552DNY (Europe) / Walt Disney Records – 60802-7 (United States) / **UK Best Ranking:** Did Not Chart – **US Best Ranking:** Did Not Chart / **Track Listing:** Circle of Life • Grasslands • The Morning Report • The Lioness Hunt • I Just Can't Wait to Be King • Chow Down • They Live in You • Be Prepared • The Stampede • Rafiki Mourns • Hakuna Matata • One By one • The Madness of King Scar • Shadowland • The Lion Sleeps Tonight • Endless Night • Can You Feel the Love Tonight? • He Lives in You (Reprise) • Simba Confronts Scar • King of Pride Rock (Circle of Life Reprise)

ELTON JOHN AND TIM RICE'S AIDA

Release Date: March 22, 1999 / Reference: Rocket Record Company – 524 651-2 (United Kingdom) / Rocket Record Company/Island Records – 314-524 628-2 (United States) / **UK Best Ranking:** 29 – **US Best Ranking:** 41 / **Track Listing:** Sting – Another Pyramid • Elton John, LeAnn Rimes – Written in the Stars • Tina Turner, Angelique Kidjo – Easy As Life • Spice Girls – My Strongest Suit • Elton John, Janet Jackson – I Know the Truth • Boyz II Men – Not Me • Shania Twain – Amneris' Letter • Elton John, Heather Headley, Sherie Rene Scott – A Step Too Far • Lenny Kravitz – Like Father, Like Son • Heather Headley – Elaborates Lives • James Taylor – How I Know You • Elton John, Lulu – The Messenger • Kelly Price – The Gods Love Nubia • Dru Hill – Enchantment Passing Through • Orchestral Finale

THE MUSE

Release Date: August 24, 1999 / Reference: Rocket Record Company/Island Records – 546 517-2 (Europe) / Rocket Record Company – 314 546 517-2 (United States) / **UK Best Ranking:** Did Not Chart – **US Best Ranking:** Did Not Chart / **Track Listing:** Driving Home • Driving to Universal • Driving to Jack's • Walk of Shame • Better Have a Gift • The Wrong Gift • The Aquarium • Are We Laughing? • Take a Walk with Me • What Should I Do? • Back to the Aquarium • Steven Redecorates • To the Guesthouse • The Cookie Factory • Multiple Personality • Sarah Escapes • Back to Paramount • Meet Christine • The Muse • The Muse (Remix by Jermaine Dupri)

THE ROAD TO EL DORADO

Release Date: March 14, 2000 / Reference: DreamWorks Records – 450 219-2 (Europe) / DreamWorks Records – 0044-50219-2 (United States) / **UK Best Ranking:** Did Not Chart – **US Best Ranking:** 63 / **Track Listing:** El Dorado • Someday out of the Blue (Theme from El Dorado) • Without Question • Friends Never Say Goodbye • The Trail We Blaze • 16th Century Man • The Panic in Me • It's Tough to Be a God (with Randy Newman) • Trust Me • My Heart Dances • Queen of Cities • Cheldorado (instrumental) • The Brig (instrumental) • Wonders of the New World (instrumental)

BILLY ELLIOT THE MUSICAL

Release Date: 2005 / Reference: Polydor 987 537-2 (United Kingdom) / Decca Broadway B000613072 (United States) / **UK Best Ranking:** Did Not Chart – **US Best Ranking:** Did Not Chart / **Track Listing:** The Stars Look Down • Shine • Grandma's Song • Solidarity • Expressing Yourself • The Letter • Born to Boogie • Angry Dance • Merry Christmas Maggie Thatcher • Deep into the Ground • He Could Be a Star • Electricity • Once We Were Kings • The Letter – Reprise • Finale • The Letter (Elton John) • Merry Christmas Maggie Thatcher (Elton John) • Electricity (Elton John)

GNOMEO & JULIET

Release Date: February 8, 2011 / Reference: Buena Vista Records – 50999 026752 2 0 (Europe) / Buena Vista Records – D001341292 (United States) / **UK Best Ranking:** Did Not Chart – **US Best Ranking:** Did Not Chart / **Track Listing:** Hello Hello (Album Version) • Crocodile Rock (with Nelly Furtado) • Saturday's Night Alright (for Fighting) • Don't Go Breaking My Heart (with Kiki Dee) • Love Builds a Garden • Your Song • Rocket Man (I Think It's Going to Be a Long, Long Time) • Tiny Dancer • Bennie and the Jets • Gnomeo & Juliet (instrumental) • Dandelions (instrumental) • Bennie and the Bunnies (instrumental) • Terrafirminator (instrumental) • The Tiki, Tiki, Tiki Room (instrumental)

ROCKETMAN

Release Date: May 24, 2019 / Reference: Virgin EMI Records – CD V3231 (Europe) / Universal – 7790358 (United States) / **UK Best Ranking:** 5 – **US Best Ranking:** 4 / **Track Listing:** (numbers performed by Taron Egerton unless indicated otherwise) Taron Egerton, Sebastian Rich – The Bitch Is Back (Introduction) • Kit Connor, Gemma Jones, Bryce Dallas Howard, Steven MacKintosh – I Want Love • Taron Egerton, Kit Connor – Saturday Night's Alright (for Fighting) • Thank You for All Loving • Border Song • Rock and Roll Madonna (Interlude) • Your Song • Amoreena • Crocodile Rock • Tiny Dancer • Take Me to the Pilot • Hercules • Taron Egerton, Rachel Muldoon – Don't Go Breaking My Heart (Interlude) • Taron Egerton, Richard Madden – Honky Cat • Pinball Wizard (Interlude) • Rocket Man (It's Going to Be a Long, Long Time) • Bennie and the Jets (Interlude) • Taron Egerton, Colinde Schoenmaker – Don't Let the Sun Go Down on Me • Sorry Seems to Be the Hardest Word • Taron Egerton, Jamie Bell – Goodbye Yellow Brick Road • I'm Still Standing • Taron Egerton, Elton John – (I'm Gonna) Love Me Again

THE LION KING
(2019 SOUNDTRACK)

Release Date: July 11, 2019 / Reference: Walt Disney Records – 8742300 (Europe) / Walt Disney Records – D003166302 (United States) / **UK Best Ranking:** Did Not Chart – **US Best Ranking:** 13 / **Track Listing:** Brown Lindiwe Mkhize, Lebo M. – Circle of Life/Nants' Ingonyama (2019 Version) • Hans Zimmer – Life's Fair • Hans Zimmer – Rafiki's Fireflies • JD McCrary, Shahadi Wright Joseph, John Oliver – I Just Can't Wait to Be King • Hans Zimmer – Elephant Graveyard • Chiwetel Ejiofor – Be Prepared (2019 Version) • Hans Zimmer – Stampede • Hans Zimmer – Scar Takes the Throne • Billy Eichner, Seth Rogen, JD McCrary, Donald Glover – Hakuna Matata • Hans Zimmer – Simba Is Alive! • Billy Eichner, Seth Rogen – The Lion Sleeps Tonight • Beyoncé, Donald Glover, Billy Eichner, Seth Rogen – Can You Feel the Love Tonight • Hans Zimmer – Reflections of Mufasa • Beyoncé – Spirit • Hans Zimmer – Battle for Pride Rock • Hans Zimmer, Ensemble, Lebo M. – Remember/King of Pride Rock/Circle of Life (Finale) • Elton John – Never Too Late • Lebo M. – He Lives in You • Lebo M. – Mbube

COMPILATIONS

GREATEST HITS

Release Date: November 8, 1974 / Reference: DJM Records – DJLPH 442 (United Kingdom)/MCA – MCA-2128 (United States) / **UK Best Ranking:** 1 – **US Best Ranking:** 1 / **Track Listing:** Your Song • Daniel • Honky Cat • Goodbye Yellow Brick Road • Saturday Night's Alright for Fighting • Rocket Man (I Think It's Going to Be a Long, Long Time) • Bennie and the Jets • Don't Let the Sun Go Down on Me • Border Song • Crocodile Rock

GREATEST HITS VOLUME II

Release Date: September 30, 1977 / Reference: DJM Records – DJH 20520 (United Kingdom) / MCA Records – MCA-3027 (United States) / **UK Best Ranking:** 6 – **US Best Ranking:** 21 / **Track Listing:** The Bitch Is Back • Lucy in the Sky with Diamonds • Sorry Seems to Be the Hardest Word • Don't Go Breaking My Heart • Someone Saved My Life Tonight • Philadelphia Freedom • Island Girl • Grow Some Funk of Your Own • Bennie and the Jets (replaced by Levon on the North American version) • Pinball Wizard

THE COMPLETE PICTURE – MILESTONES

Release Date: 1980 / Reference: K-Tel – TU 2640 (United States) / **US Best Ranking:** Did Not Chart / **Track Listing:** Don't Go Breaking My Heart • Island Girl • The Bitch Is Back • Don't Let the Sun Go Down on Me • Bennie and the Jets • Someone Saved My Life Tonight • Don't Let the Sun Go Down on Me • Sorry Seems to Be the Hardest Word • Mama Can't Buy You Love • Philadelphia Freedom • Crocodile Rock • Rocket Man (I Think It's Going to Be a Long, Long Time) • Daniel • Lucy in the Sky with Diamonds • Your Song • Goodbye Yellow Brick Road

LADY SAMANTHA

Release Date: February 1980 (cassette and 8-track cartridge release in 1974) / Reference: DJM Records – DJM 22085 (United Kingdom) / UK **Best Ranking:** 56 / **Track Listing:** Rock and Roll Madonna • Whenever You're Ready (We'll Go Steady Again) • Bad Side of the Moon • Jack Rabbit • Into the Old Man's Shoes • It's Me That You Needed • Ho, Ho, Ho (Who'd Be a Turkey At Christmas) • Skyline Pigeon • Screw You • Just Like Strange Rain • Grey Seal • The Honey Roll • Lady Samantha • Friends

THE VERY BEST OF ELTON JOHN

Release Date: October 1980 / Reference: K-Tel – NE 1094 (United Kingdom) / UK **Best Ranking:** 24 / **Track Listing:** Your Song • Goodbye Yellow Brick Road • Daniel • Song for Guy • Candle in the Wind • Friends • Tiny Dancer • Rocket Man (I Think It's Going to Be a Long, Long Time) • Don't Go Breaking My Heart • Sorry Seems to Be the Hardest Word • Border Song • Someone Saved My Life Tonight • Mona Lisas and Mad Hatters • Harmony • High Flying Bird • Don't Let the Sun Go Down on Me

THE BEST OF ELTON JOHN, VOLUME I

Release Date: 1981 / Reference: Columbia Special Products – P 16196 (United States) / US **Best Ranking:** Did Not Chart / **Track Listing:** Border Song • Philadelphia Freedom • Lucy in the Sky with Diamonds • Honky Cat • Daniel • Pinball Wizard • Saturday Night's Alright for Fighting • The Bitch Is Back • Don't Let the Sun Go Down on Me • Bennie and the Jets

THE BEST OF ELTON JOHN, VOLUME II

Release Date: 1981 / Reference: Columbia Special Products – P 16197 (United States) / US **Best Ranking:** Did Not Chart / **Track Listing:** Your Song • Goodbye Yellow Brick Road • Rocket Man (I Think It's Going to Be a Long, Long Time) • Candle in the Wind • Crocodile Rock • Someone Saved My Life Tonight • Island Girl • Grow Some Funk of Your Own • Harmony • Tiny Dancer

LOVE SONGS

Release Date: 1981 / Reference: Columbia Special Products – T.V.A. 3 (United Kingdom) / UK **Best Ranking:** Did Not Chart / **Track Listing:** Blue Eyes • Little Jeannie • Sartorial Eloquence • Shine on Through • Chloe • Elton's Song • Tonight • Song for Guy • Sorry Seems to Be the Hardest Word • Princess • Chameleon • Return to Paradise • Never Gonna Fall in Love Again • Strangers • Someone's Final Song • All Quiet on the Western Front

THE NEW COLLECTION

Release Date: 1983 / Reference: Everest Collection – CBR 1027 (United Kingdom) / UK **Best Ranking:** Did Not Chart / **Track Listing:** Crocodile Rock • Don't Let the Sun Go Down on Me • Saturday Night's Alright (for Fighting) • It's Me That You Need • Someone Saved My Life Tonight • Whatever Gets You Through the Night/Lucy in the Sky with Diamonds • The Bitch Is Back • High Flying Bird • Elderberry Wine • Candle in the Wind • Your Sister Can't Twist (But She Can Rock 'n' Roll) • Daniel

THE NEW COLLECTION, VOLUME I

Release Date: 1983 / Reference: Everest Collection – CBR 1036 (United Kingdom) / UK **Best Ranking:** Did Not Chart / **Track Listing:** Your Song • Benny and the Jets • Harmony • Take Me to the Pilot • Island Girl • Rocket Man (I Think It's Going to Be a Long, Long Time) • Goodbye Yellow Brick Road • Honky Cat • Philadelphia Freedom • Skyline Pigeon • Roy Rogers • I Think I'm Going to Kill Myself

THE SUPERIOR SOUND OF ELTON JOHN (1970–1975)

Release Date: 1983 / Reference: DJM Records – 810 062-2 (Europe) / UK **Best Ranking:** Did Not Chart / **Track Listing:** Your Song • Crocodile Rock • Rocket Man (I Think It's Going to Be a Long, Long Time) • Daniel • Saturday Night's Alright (for Fighting) • Goodbye Yellow Brick Road • Funeral for a Friend/Love Lies Bleeding • Don't Let the Sun Go Down on Me • Philadelphia Freedom • Someone Saved My Life Tonight • We All Fall in Love Sometimes/Curtains

YOUR SONGS

Release Date: 1985 / Reference: MCA Records – MCA-37266 (United States) / US **Best Ranking:** Did Not Chart / **Track Listing:** Your Song • Country Comfort • Tiny Dancer • Burn Down the Mission • Friends • Take Me to the Pilot • Candle in the Wind • Elderberry Wine • Razor Face • Harmony

GREATEST HITS VOLUME III

Release Date: November 12, 1987 / Reference: Geffen Records – 9 24153-2 (United States) / **US Best Ranking:** 84 / **Track Listing:** I Guess That's Why They Call It the Blues • Mama Can't Buy You Love • Little Jeannie • Sad Songs (Say So Much) • I'm Still Standing • Empty Garden (Hey Hey Johnny) • Heartache All over the World • Too Low for Zero • Kiss the Bride • Blue Eyes • Nikita • Wrap Her Up

THE COLLECTION

Release Date: 1989 / Reference: Pickwick Music - PWKS 551 (United Kingdom) / **UK Best Ranking:** Did Not Chart / **Track Listing:** Funeral for a Friend/Love Lies Bleeding • Sweet Painted Lady • Elderberry Wine • Come Down in Time • I Need You to Turn To • Border Song • Crocodile Rock • Mona Lisas and Mad Hatters • The Greatest Discovery • Country Comfort • Blues for My Baby and Me • Harmony • Teacher I Need You • Ballad of a Well-Known Gun

THE VERY BEST OF ELTON JOHN

Release Date: October 26, 1990 / Reference: Phonogram – 846 947-2 (United Kingdom) / **UK Best Ranking:** 1 / **Track Listing:** Your Song • Rocket Man (I Think It's Going to Be a Long, Long Time) • Honky Cat • Crocodile Rock • Daniel • Goodbye Yellow Brick Road • Saturday Night's Alright for Fighting • Candle in the Wind • Don't Let the Sun Go Down on Me • Lucy in the Sky with Diamonds • Philadelphia Freedom • Someone Saved My Life Tonight • Pinball Wizard • Don't Go Breaking My Heart • Bennie and the Jets • Sorry Seems to Be the Hardest Word • Song for Guy • Part Time Love • Blue Eyes • I Guess That's Why They Call It the Blues • I'm Still Standing • Kiss the Bride • Sad Songs • Passengers • Nikita • I Don't Wanna Go on with You Like That • Sacrifice • Easier to Walk Away • You Gotta Love Someone

TO BE CONTINUED...

Release Date: November 8, 1990 / Reference: Rocket Record Company – 848 236-2 (United Kingdom) / Reference: MCA Records – MCAD4-10110 (United States) / **UK Best Ranking:** Did Not Chart - **US Best Ranking:** 82 / **Track Listing:** Come Back Baby • Lady Samantha • It's Me That You Need • Your Song (demo) • Rock and Roll Madonna • Bad Side of the Moon • Your Song • Take Me to the Pilot • Border Song • Sixty Years On • Country Comfort • Grey Seal • Friends • Levon • Tiny Dancer • Madman Across the Water • Honky Cat • Mona Lisas and Mad Hatters • Rocket Man (I Think It's Going to Be a Long, Long Time) • Daniel • Crocodile Rock • Bennie and the Jets • Goodbye Yellow Brick Road • All the Girls Love Alice • Funeral for a Friend/Love Lies Bleeding • Whenever You're Ready (We'll Go Steady Again) • Saturday Night's Alright for Fighting • Jack Rabbit • Harmony • Screw You (Young Man's Blues in the American version) • Step into Christmas • The Bitch Is Back • Pinball Wizard • Someone Saved My Life Tonight • Philadelphia Freedom • One Day at a Time • Lucy in the Sky with Diamonds • I Saw Her Standing There • Island Girl • Sorry Seems to Be the Hardest Word • Don't Go Breaking My Heart • I Feel Like a Bullet (in the Gun of Robert Ford) (Live) • Ego • Song for Guy • Mama Can't Buy You Love • Cartier • Little Jeannie • Donner Pour Donner • Fanfare • Chloe • The Retreat • Blue Eyes • Empty Garden (Hey Hey Johnny) • I Guess That's Why They Call It the Blues • I'm Still Standing • Sad Songs (Say So Much) • Act of War • Nikita • Candle in the Wind (Live) • Carla/Etude (Live) • Don't Let the Sun Go Down on Me (Live) • I Don't Wanna Go on with You Like That (12" Mix) • Give Peace a Chance • Sacrifice • Made for Me • Easier to Walk Away • Suit of Wolves • Understanding Women

SONG BOOK

Release Date: 1992 / Reference: Pickwick Music – PWKS 4126P (United Kingdom) / **UK Best Ranking:** Did Not Chart / **Track Listing:** All Quiet on the Western Front • Tiny Dancer • Where to Now St. Peter? • Ego • Shooting Star • Wrap Her Up • Texan Love Song • Nobody Wins • Empty Garden • Lady What's Tomorrow • Who Wears These Shoes? • Just Like Belgium • Empty Sky • Crazy Water • Island Girl • Friends

RARE MASTERS

Release Date: 1992 / Reference: DJM Records/Chronicles – 514 305-2 (United Kingdom) / Reference: Polydor – 514 305-2 (United States) / **UK Best Ranking:** Did Not Chart - **US Best Ranking:** Did Not Chart / **Track Listing:** I've Been Loving You • Here's to the Next Time • Lady Samantha • All Across the Havens • It's Me That You Need • Just Like Strange Rain • Bad Side of the Moon • Rock and Roll Madonna • Grey Seal • Friends • Michelle's Song • Seasons • Variation on Michelle's Song (A Day in the Country) • Can I Put You On • Honey Roll • Variation on Friends • I Meant to Do My Work Today (A Day in the Country) • Four Moods • Seasons Reprise • Madman Across the Water • Into the Old Man's Shoes • Rock Me When He's Gone • Slave • Skyline Pigeon • Jack Rabbit • Whenever You're Ready (We'll Go Steady Again) • Let Me Be Your Car • Screw You (Young Man's Blues) • Step into Christmas • Ho! Ho! Ho! Who'd Be a Turkey at Christmas • Sick City • Cold Highway • one Day at a Time • I Saw Her Standing There • House of Cards • Planes • Sugar on the Floor

GREATEST HITS 1976–1986

Release Date: November 3, 1992 / **Reference:** MCA Records – MCAD-10693 (United States) / **US Best Ranking:** Did Not Chart / **Track Listing:** I'm Still Standing • Mama Can't Buy You Love • Sorry Seems to Be the Hardest Word • Little Jeannie • Blue Eyes • Don't Go Breaking My Heart • Empty Garden (Hey, Hey Johnny) • Kiss the Bride • I Guess That's Why They Call It the Blues • Who Wears These Shoes? • Sad Songs (Say So Much) • Wrap Her Up • Nikita

CHARTBUSTERS GO POP

Release Date: 1994 (United Kingdom) 1998 (United States) / **Reference:** RPM Records – RPM 142 (United Kingdom) / **Reference:** Purple Pyramid – CLP 0237-2 (United States) / **UK Best Ranking:** Did Not Chart - **US Best Ranking:** Did Not Chart / **Track Listing:** My Baby Loves Lovin' • Cottonfields • Lady D'Arbanville • Natural Sinner • United We Stand • Spirit in the Sky • Travelin' Band • I Can't Tell the Bottom from the Top • Good Morning Freedom • Young Gifted and Black • In the Summertime • Up Around the Bend • Snake in the Grass • Neanderthal Man • She Sold Me Magic • Come and Get It • Love of the Common People • Signed Sealed Delivered • It's All in the Game • Yellow River

LOVE SONGS

Release Date: November 6, 1995 (Europe) September 24, 1996 (United States) / **Reference:** Rocket Record/Mercury – 528 788-2 (United Kingdom) / **Reference:** MCA Records – MCAD-11481 (United States) / **UK Best Ranking:** 4 - **US Best Ranking:** 24 / **Track Listing:** Sacrifice • Candle in the Wind • I Guess That's Why They Call It the Blues • Don't Let the Sun Go Down on Me • Sorry Seems to Be the Hardest Word • Blue Eyes • Daniel • Nikita • Your Song • The One • Someone Saved My Life Tonight • True Love • Can You Feel the Love Tonight • Circle of Life • Blessed • Please • Song for Guy

GREATEST HITS 1970–2002

Release Date: November 11, 2002 / **Reference:** Mercury – 063 449-2 (United Kingdom) / **Reference:** Mercury – 440 063 478-2 (United States) / **UK Best Ranking:** 3 - **US Best Ranking:** 12 / **Track Listing:** Your Song • Levon • Tiny Dancer • Rocket Man (I Think It's Going to Be a Long, Long Time) • Honky Cat • Crocodile Rock • Daniel • Saturday Night's Alright for Fighting • Goodbye Yellow Brick Road • Candle in the Wind • Bennie and the Jets • Don't Let the Sun Go Down on Me • The Bitch Is Back • Philadelphia Freedom • Someone Saved My Life Tonight • Island Girl • Sorry Seems to Be the Hardest Word • Don't Go Breaking My Heart • Little Jeannie • I'm Still Standing • I Guess That's Why They Call It the Blues • Sad Songs (Say So Much) • I Don't Wanna Go on with You Like That • Nikita • Sacrifice • The One • Can You Feel the Love Tonight? • Circle of Life • Believe • Blessed • Something About the Way You Look Tonight • Written in the Stars • I Want Love • This Train Don't Stop There Anymore

ROCKET MAN: THE DEFINITIVE HITS

Release Date: March 26, 2007 / **Reference:** Rocket Record Company/Mercury – 172 6047 (Europe) / **Reference:** Mercury/Rocket Record Company/Island Records/Chronicles/Ume – B0008661-02 (United States) / **UK Best Ranking:** 2 - **US Best Ranking:** 9 / **Track Listing:** Crocodile Rock • Daniel • Rocket Man (I Think It's Going to Be a Long, Long Time) • I Guess That's Why They Call It the Blues • Blue Eyes • Don't Let the Sun Go Down on Me • Sacrifice • Candle in the Wind • Sad Songs (Say So Much) • I'm Still Standing • Saturday Night's Alright (for Fighting) • Your Song • Sorry Seems to Be the Hardest Word • Can You Feel the Love Tonight • Nikita • Don't Go Breaking My Heart • Goodbye Yellow Brick Road • Tinderbox

DIAMONDS

Release Date: November 10, 2007 / **Reference:** Rocket Record Company/Virgin EMI Records/UMC – 6700657 (United Kingdom) / **UK Best Ranking:** 5 / **Reference:** Rocket Record Company/Island Records – B0027369-02 (United States) / **US Best Ranking:** 7 / **Track Listing:** Your Song • Tiny Dancer • Rocket Man (I Think It's Going to Be a Long, Long Time) • Honky Cat • Crocodile Rock • Daniel • Saturday Night's Alright (for Fighting) • Goodbye Yellow Brick Road • Candle in the Wind • Bennie and the Jets • The Bitch Is Back • Philadelphia Freedom • Island Girl • Someone Saved My Life Tonight • Don't Go Breaking My Heart • Sorry Seems to Be the Hardest Word • Little Jeannie • Song for Guy • Blue Eyes • I'm Still Standing • I Guess That's Why They Call It the Blues • Sad Songs (Say So Much) • Nikita • I Don't Wanna Go on with You Like That • Sacrifice • Don't Let the Sun Go Down on Me • Something About the Way You Look Tonight (Single Edit) • I Want Love • Can You Feel the Love Tonight • Are You Ready for Love? • Electricity • Home Again • Looking Up • Circle of Life • Skyline Pigeon (Piano Version) • Lucy in the Sky with Diamonds • Pinball Wizard • Mama Can't Buy You Love • Part Time Love • Victim of Love • Empty Garden (Hey Hey Johnny) • Kiss the Bride • That's What Friends Are For • The One • True Love • Believe • Live Like Horses • Written in the Stars • This Train Don't Stop there Anymore • Good Morning to the Night • Step into Christmas

ELTON: JEWEL BOX

Release Date: November 13, 2020 / Reference: UMC/EMI/Rocket Entertainment – 071 590-8 (United Kingdom) / **UK Best Ranking:** 68 / Reference: UMC/EMI/Rocket Entertainment – 071 590-8 (United States) / **US Best Ranking:** Did Not Chart / **Track Listing:**

CD1 – Deep Cuts: 1

Monkey Suit • Where to Now St. Peter? • Mellow • The Ballad of Danny Bailey (1909–34) • Chameleon • Gone to Shiloh • We All Fall in Love Sometimes • Too Low for Zero • The Power • All That I'm Allowed • The Bridge • The New Fever Waltz • Stone's Throw from Hurtin' • The North • Hoop of Fire • Boogie Pilgrim

CD2 – Deep Cuts: 2

Ticking • Crystal • All Quiet on the Western Front • Tell Me When the Whistle Blows • Freaks in Love • Never Too Old (to Hold Somebody) • The Emperor's New Clothes • House • (Gotta Get a) Meal Ticket • Understanding Women • Shoot Down the Moon • Have Mercy on the Criminal • Blues for My Baby and Me • My Quicksand • Street Kids

CD3 – Rarities Part One: 1965–1968

Come Back Baby • Mr. Frantic • Scarecrow (Piano/Tambourine Demo) • A Dandelion Dies in the Wind (Piano Demo) • Velvet Fountain (Piano Demo) • A Little Love Goes a Long Way (Piano Demo) • If You Could See Me Now (Piano Demo) • Mr. Lightning Strikerman (Piano Demo) • Countryside Love Affair (Piano Demo) • I Could Never Fall in Love with Anybody Else (Piano Demo) • I Get a Little Bit Lonely (Piano Demo) • The Witch's House (Piano Demo) • Get Out of This Town (Piano/Tambourine Demo) • Year of the Teddy Bear (Piano Demo) • Where It's At (Piano/Percussion Demo) • Who's Gonna Love You (Piano/Percussion Demo) • Nina (Band Version) • Angel Tree (Piano/Guitar/Tambourine Demo) • Here's to the Next Time (Piano/Tambourine Demo) • Thank You for All Your Loving (Band Version) • Watching the Planes Go By (Band Version) • When the First Tear Shows (Arranged Band Version) • Tartan Colored Lady (Arranged Band Version)

CD4 – Rarities Part Two: 1968

Hourglass (Band Version) • 71-75 New Oxford Street (Band Demo) • Turn to Me (Arranged Band Version) • Reminds Me of You (Piano Demo) • I Can't Go on Living Without You (Arranged Band Version) • And the Clock Goes Round (Piano Demo) • When I Was Tealby Abbey (Piano Demo) • I'll Stop Living When You Stop Loving Me (Piano Demo) • Trying to Hold on to a Love That's Dying (Piano Demo) • Sitting Doing Nothing (Band Version) • Regimental Sergeant Zippo (Band Version) • Cry Willow Cry (Band Demo) • There Is Still a Little Love (Band Demo) • If I Asked You (Band Demo) • Skyline Pigeon (Piano Demo) • Two of a Kind (Arranged Band Version) • The Girl on Angel Pavement (Arranged Band Version) • Smokestack Children (Arranged Band Version) • Baby I Miss You (Band Demo) • All Across the Havens (Piano/Guitar Demo) • Bonnie's Gone Away (Piano/Guitar Demo) • Just an Ordinary Man (Piano Demo) • There Is Still Time for Me (Piano/Guitar/Tambourine Demo)

CD5 – Rarities Part Three: 1968–1971

The Tide Will Turn for Rebecca (Piano Demo) • Dick Barton Theme (Devil's Gallop) • Breakdown Blues • Taking the Sun from My Eyes (Arranged Band Version) • It's Me That You Need (Band Demo) • Sing Me No Sad Songs (Band Demo) • The Flowers Will Never Die (Piano Demo) • In the Morning (Band Demo) • Open Your Eyes to the Sun (Piano/Tambourine Demo) • One Time, Sometime or Never (Band Demo) • Slow Fade to Blue (Piano/Guitar Demo) • Rolling Western Union (Piano Demo) • My Father's Gun (Piano Demo) • Amoreena (Piano Demo) • Burn Down the Mission (Piano Demo) • Razor Face (Piano Demo) • Madman Across the Water (Piano Demo) • Holiday Inn (Piano Demo) • All the Nasties (Piano Demo)

CD6 – B-Sides Part One: 1976–1984

Snow Queen • Conquer the Sun • Cartier • White Man Danger • Tactics • Steal Away Child • Love So Cold • Les Aveux • Donner Pour Donner • J'veux D'la Tendresse • Fools in Fashion • Can't Get Over Getting Over Losing You • Tortured • Hey Papa Legba • Take Me Down to the Ocean • Where Have All the Good Times Gone? (Alternate Mix) • The Retreat • Choc Ice Goes Mental • A Simple Man

CD7 – B-Sides Part Two: 1984–2005

Lonely Boy • Highlander • Billy and the Kids • Lord of the Flies • Rope Around a Fool • Medicine Man • I Know Why I'm in Love • Big Man in a Little Suit • God Never Came Here • The North Star • Did Anybody Sleep with Joan of Arc? • So Sad the Renegade • A Little Peace • Keep It a Mystery • How's Tomorrow • Peter's Song • Things Only Get Better with Love

CD8 – And This Is Me…

Empty Sky • Lady Samantha • Border Song • My Father's Gun • All the Nasties • I Think I'm Going to Kill Myself • Philadelphia Freedom • Song for Guy (Single Edit) • Sartorial Eloquence • Elton's Song • Cold As Christmas (in the Middle of the Year) • I Fall Apart • Amazes Me • The Last Song • American Triangle • (I'm Gonna) Love Me Again

TRIBUTE ALBUMS

TWO ROOMS: CELEBRATING THE SONGS OF ELTON JOHN & BERNIE TAUPIN

Release Date: October 14, 1991 (United Kingdom) / Reference: Mercury – 845 749-2 (United Kingdom) / Reference: Polydor – 845 750-2 / **UK Best Ranking:** Did Not Chart / **US Best Ranking:** 18 / **Track Listing:** Eric Clapton – Border Song • Kate Bush – Rocket (I Think It's Going to Be a Long, Long Time) • Sting – Come Down in Time • The Who – Saturday Night's Alright (for Fighting) • The Beach Boys – Crocodile Rock • Wilson Phillips – Daniel • Joe Cocker – Sorry Seems to Be the Hardest Word • Jon Bon Jovi – Levon • Tina Turner – The Bitch Is Back • Daryl Hall & John Oates – Philadelphia Freedom • Rod Stewart – Your Song • Oleta Adams – Don't Let the Sun Go Down on Me • Bruce Hornsby – Madman Across the Water • Sinead O'Connor – Sacrifice • Phil Collins & the Serious Band – Burn Down the Mission • George Michael – Tonight

REVAMP: REIMAGINING THE SONGS OF ELTON JOHN & BERNIE TAUPIN

Release Date: April 6, 2018 / Reference: Virgin EMI Records – CDV 3205 (Europe) / Reference: Virgin EMI Records/Rocket Record Company/Island Records – B0028164-02 / **UK Best Ranking:** Did Not Chart / **US Best Ranking:** 13 / **Track Listing:** Elton John, Pink, Logic – Bennie and the Jets (2018 Version) • Coldplay – We All Fall in Love Sometimes • Alessia Cara – I Guess That's Why They Call It the Blues • Ed Sheeran – Candle in the Wind (2018 Version) • Florence + the Machine – Tiny Dancer • Mumford & Sons – Someone Saved My Life Tonight • Mary J. Blige – Sorry Seems to Be the Hardest Word • Q-Top, Demi Lovato – Don't Go Breaking My Heart • The Killers – Mona Lisas and Mad Hatters • Sam Smith – Daniel • Miley Cyrus – Don't Let the Sun Go Down on Me • Lady Gaga – Your Song • Queens of the Stone Age – Goodbye Yellow Brick Road

RESTORATION: REIMAGINING THE SONGS OF ELTON JOHN & BERNIE TAUPIN

Release Date: April 6, 2018 / Reference: MCA Nashville – 00602567409199 (Europe) / Reference: MCA Nashville – B0028066-2 / **US Best Ranking:** 36 / **Track Listing:** Little Big Town – Rocket Man • Maren Morris – Mona Lisas and Mad Hatters • Don Henley, Vince Gill – Sacrifice • Brothers Osborne – Take Me to the Pilot • Miranda Lambert – My Father's Gun • Chris Stapleton – I Want Love • Lee Ann Womack – Honky Cat • Kacey Musgraves – Roy Rogers • Rhonda Vincent, Dolly Parton – Please • Miley Cyrus – The Bitch Is Back • Dierks Bentley – Sad Songs (Say So Much) • Rosanne Cash, Emmylou Harris – This Train Don't Stop There Anymore • Willie Nelson – Border Song

EP

THE THOM BELL SESSIONS '77

Release Date: June 1979 / Reference: Rocket Record Company – XPRES 1312 (United Kingdom) / Reference: MCA Records – MCA 13921 / **US Best Ranking:** 51 / **Track Listing:** Are You Ready for Love • Three Way Love Affair • Mama Can't Buy You Love

THE COMPLETE THOM BELL SESSIONS

Release Date: February 1989 / Reference: MCA Records – MCA-39115 (United States) / **US Best Ranking:** Did Not Chart / **Track Listing:** Nice and Slow • Country Love Song • Shine on Through • Mama Can't Buy You Love • Are You Ready for Love • Three Way Love Affair

REMIXED

Release Date: December 30, 2003 / Reference: Rocket Record Company/Mercury/Chronicles – B0002071-22 (United States) / **US Best Ranking:** Did Not Chart / **Track Listing:** Are You Ready for Love ('79 Radio Edit) • Are You Ready for Love (Ashley Beddle's Love And Protection Mono Edit) • Candle in the Wind (Acoustic Mix) • Rocket Man '03 • Song for Guy (Remix)

GLOSSARY

Backing track: an instrumental or vocal track, sometime only rhythmic, recorded to accompany a singer or group.

Bend: a guitar technique consisting of pulling or pushing one or more strings parallel to the neck. This has the effect of raising the sound of the note(s) played by approximately half a tone or more.

Bottleneck: glass or metal tube that the guitarist places on a finger and slides over the strings to obtain a metallic sound. Blues players developed this way of playing by using (literally) a bottleneck.

Bridge: a transition between passages of a song. Most commonly designating the sequence located between the verse and the refrain.

Brill Building Pop: a musical movement current at the end of the 1950s and early 1960s, characterized by a sophisticated form of pop intended for a young audience. It takes its name from the Brill Building, a building in New York, in which teams of professional composers worked.

Chop: whether of the "open" [without palm-muting], "closed" [with palm-muting] or "skank" [especially, off-beat Reggae] type, a guitar technique involving note by note play, used above all in funk music.

Coda: word of Italian origin meaning the concluding passage of a piece of music.

Cowbell: small bell used as a percussion instrument. Its name comes from bells worn by herds of cows.

Crunchy: describes a slight distortion of sound, or of an instrument intended to intentionally reduce its clarity and at the same time to give it a momentarily warm and powerful sound.

Delay: audio effect reproducing the acoustic phenomenon of an echo. Incorporated in a pedal activated effect or on a mixing console, it can be applied to a voice or instrument, to repeat a sound regularly by delaying its signal over time.

Detuning: modification of the pitch of a note or series of notes, obtained by deliberately putting an instrument or recorded signal out of tune.

Distortion: sound effect created by degrading the quality of an audio signal with the saturation of the channel of an amplifier, using the distortion effect incorporated in the equipment, or by using a distortion pedal.

Dobro: make of guitar whose sound is amplified using a metallic resonator. The word "Dobro" comes from the contraction of the name of its creators, Americans of Slovak origin: the Dopyera Brothers.

Doo-wop: popular musical style from the 1950s. Inspired by gospel, it is based on precise close vocal harmony.

Easy listening: style of music close to a kind of music referred to as "ambient," in which the sonorities, often devoid of any roughness, are pleasant and liable to please a large number of listeners.

EBow: enclosed unit containing an electromagnet, which, when placed near guitar strings, causes them to vibrate continuously.

Emulation: imitation of the sound of an instrument implemented using a keyboard, or software.

Fader: a vertical control button located on the mixing table, which is used to adjust the volume of each recording track.

Falsetto: word of Italian origin designating a singing technique that enables male singers to reach the highest notes in their register.

Feedback: a physical phenomenon that is produced when the amplified output (speaker, for example) and receiver (singer's microphone, or instruments, for example) are placed too close together. The sound produced is like a strident whistling noise or hum. Some rock electric guitarists, such as Jimi Hendrix in the 1960s, have used it creatively as a sound effect in some pieces.

Finger-picking: guitar playing technique, particularly on acoustic guitar, specific to American folk music, blues, and bluegrass, where the melody and rhythm are played at the same time.

Fretless: type of musical instrument that has no frets on the neck, unlike the standard model (guitar, bass, banjo).

Fundamental: bass note on which a chord is constructed.

Fuzz: sound effect that consists of producing a sound, that is saturate, thick and heavy. Popularized by artists like the Rolling Stones or Jimi Hendrix, fuzz is applied mainly to electric guitars.

Gimmick: a short series of notes whose easily recognizable melody retains one's attention and remains in the listener's memory. With jazz origins, this technique progressively spread to use in other musical genres.

Groove: abstract term that applies mainly to the rhythm of a song created by the bass and drums. The word emerged in the wake of Black American music from the beginning of the twentieth century.

Harmonization: technique of the multiplication of vocal or instrumental line, by adding to it a note in unison or at the octave. If the line added that is complementary to the original line is played or sung on another note (at an interval of a third, or a fifth, for example), this is referred to as polyphonic harmonization.

High hat: diminutive of "Charleston"; a drum kit component consisting of two cymbals actioned by a foot pedal.

Honky-tonk: style of country music, popularized by musicians such as Jimmie Rodgers and Hank Williams, and played in bars of the same name, principally in the Southern United States.

Jam session: improvisation session involving several musicians gathered together informally simply for the enjoyment of playing music together.

Laid back: literally "relaxed." Style of playing slightly behind the rhythm to create a "relaxed" effect.

Lap steel: Hawaiian type of guitar, played when laid flat, on the knees.

Leslie cabinet: named after its inventor, Donald Leslie, an amplification cabinet equipped with a rotary baffle chamber in front of the speaker, which creates a vibrato effect.

Mash-up: song constructed from several preexisting numbers.

Midtempo: term defining a song played at a moderate tempo.

Outtake: piece of studio or live recorded music that is not selected for use in the official version of an album. This may be an unpublished piece, or an alternative version to an existing number, which may be revived, in the event of a compilation issue, or reissue of the album.

Overdubs: a set of new sounds recorded (voices and/or instruments) and added to pre-existing recorded material.

Pattern: a rhythmic or melodic sequence which repeats in a piece.

Phasing: sound effect obtained by filtering a signal and creating a series of highs and lows in the frequency spectrum. Available as a pedal mechanism or rack-mounted, the effect often creates a sensation of a wave sound or swirling wind.

Pizzicato: playing technique used on bowed string instruments where the strings are plucked rather than using a bow.

Reverb: natural or artificial echo effect applied to an instrument or voice during the recording or mixing of a piece.

Reverse: deliberate playing of a sound backward on an audio track.

Riff: short fragment of a few notes that regularly return during a piece, and which accompanies the melody. The origin of the word "riff" comes from an abbreviation of the English expression "rhythmic figure."

Scat: vocal style specific to jazz, where the use of syllables prevails over the singing of comprehensible texts.

Setlist: list of songs played by an artist or group during a concert.

Skiffle: in the United Kingdom, a folk music style in the 1950s, inspired by jazz and blues, and where the use of homemade instruments was a characteristic distinctive feature.

Slap: electronic bass technique used mainly in funk and disco music, where the strings are struck by the thumb and pulled by the other fingers of the right hand.

Slide: technique used on a guitar that designates a continuous and rapid sliding of a chord or single note to another, with intermediate notes continuing to sound.

Songwriter: English term designating a writer-composer of a song.

Staccato: musical passage played with [short] detached notes.

Storytelling: art of narration in writing [song] lyrics.

Synth pop: musical style that appeared in the 1980s, in which the use of a synthesizer is dominant.

Talk box: effect enabling a musician to modulate the sound using a plastic tube connecting between a speaker and the mouth and creating synthetic sounds similar to the human voice.

Track list: list of songs presented on an album.

Twang: sharp sound, like the onomatopoeia of its name, produced particularly by certain electric guitars, especially the Fender Telecaster model.

Wah-wah: audio effect, mainly used on electric guitars, using the pedal of the same name, produced by the oscillation of the sound frequency between the low and high sounds; the sound created is reminiscent of that of a human voice repeating the onomatopoeia "wah."

BIBLIOGRAPHY

1 – Paul Gambaccini, "Elton John: The Rolling Stone Interview," *Rolling Stone*, August 16, 1973.

2 – Elton John, "Elton John: Billy Elliot's Dad Does What Mine Never Could," Sunday Times Magazine, May 12, 2015, https://www.thetimes.co.uk/article/elton-john-billy-elliots-dad-does-what-mine-never-could-dhrk8639bqt.

3 – Elton John, Me, New York, Henry Holt, 2019.

4 – Chris Roberts, L'Histoire illustrée de Rocket Man, Paris, Éditions Place des Victoires, October 2019.

5 – Timothy White, "Elton John: The Billboard Interview," Billboard, October 4, 1997.

6 – Craig Rosen, "Bernie Taupin: The Billboard Interview," Billboard, October 4, 1997.

7 – Paul Sexton, "Bernie and the Hits: Elton's Backroom Boy," Times (London), September 14, 2006.

8 – Bernie Taupin, A Cradle of Haloes: Sketches of a Childhood, London, Aurum Press, October 1988, https://archive.org/details/cradleofhaloessk00taup/page/n199/mode/2up?q=distinguished.

9 – John F. Higgins, Interview with Ray Williams, 1992, eltonjohn.com, https://www.eltonjohn.com/stories/ad_that_rocketed_two_careers_50.

10 – Rob Tannenbaum, "Bernie Taupin on His 53-Year Musical Marriage to Elton John: It's 'God's Right Hand,'" Los Angeles Times, January 29, 2020.

11 – Tom Doyle, Captain Fantastic: Elton John's Stellar Trip Through the '70s, New York, Ballantine Books, 2017.

12 – Pete Paphides, "Record Collecting Saved Me," Record Collector, Christmas 2020.

13 – John F. Higgins, "Empty Sky—Elton's First Album Turns 50 Today," Elton John (website), June 6, 2019, https://www.eltonjohn.com/stories/empty-sky-50.

14 – Peter Kearns, Elton John in the 1970s: Every Album, Every Song (1969–1979), Tewkesbury, UK: Sonicbond Publishing, 2019.

15 – Ian Ravendale, interviews and testimonies with Bernie Taupin and Elton John, Classic Pop Presents Elton John—Special Edition, March 2017.

16 – Claude Bernardin and Tom Stanton, Rocket Man: Elton John from A–Z, Westport, CT, Greenwood Publishing Group, 1996.

17 – Philip Norman, Sir Elton: The Definitive Biography of Elton John, London, Sidgwick & Jackson, 1991.

18 – Andy Greene, "Bernie Taupin on His 53-Year Saga with Elton John and Hopes for the Future," Rolling Stone, November 2, 2020.

19 – John Woolcombe, Interview with Ray Williams, Elton John's first manager, https://www.youtube.com/watch?v=hTnctUODmJI.

20 – Keith Hayward, Tin Pan Alley: The Rise of Elton John, London, Soundcheck Books, 2013.

21 – John F. Higgins, "50 Years On: Remembering the Elton John Album—Part 1," Elton John (website), April 10, 2020, https://www.eltonjohn.com/stories/ej50-part-1.

22 – John F. Higgins, "Paul Buckmaster: In His Own Words," Elton John (website), January 19, 2018, https://www.eltonjohn.com/stories/paul-buckmaster:-in-his-own-words.

23 – John Peel, interview with Elton John, John Peel's Night Ride, BBC Radio, December 25, 1973.

24 – Paul Gambaccini, The Elton John Story: Keyboard Wizard, BBC Radio 1, July 3, 1976.

25 – John F. Higgins, "50 Years On: Remembering the Elton John Album—Part 2," Elton John (website), August 7, 2020, https://www.eltonjohn.com/stories/50-years-on-remembering-the-elton-john-album-part-2.

26 – Terry Towne, interview with Elton John, Jazz and Pop, 1971.

27 – John Mendelsohn, "Elton John," album review, Rolling Stone, November 12, 1970.

28 – Interview with Bernie Taupin given to Radio Times, August 2002, quoted in "Talking Taupin," Hercules, September 2002.

29 – Paul Zollo, More Songwriters on Songwriting, Boston, Da Capo Press, 2016.

30 – Penny Valentine and Jerry Gilbert, "Fotheringay, Royal Albert Hall, London," Sounds, October 1970.

31 – David John DeCouto, Captain Fantastic: The Definitive Biography of Elton John in the '70s, Chandler, AZ, Triple Wood Press, 2018.

32 – Elizabeth J. Rosenthal, His Song: The Musical Journey of Elton John, New York, Billboard Books, 2001.

33 – Scott Robinson, Harmony: Analyzing the Music of Elton John, 1968–1977, self-published, 2021.

34 – Life, Special Issue, vol. 19, no. 13, May 17, 2019.

35 – Cameron Crowe, "Elton John: My Life in 20 Songs," Rolling Stone, October 10, 2013, https://www.rollingstone.com/music/music-lists/elton-john-my-life-in-20-songs-10473/.

36 – Paul Gambaccini, A Conversation with Elton John and Bernie Taupin, London, Flash Books, 1975.

37 – David Wright, Interview with Gus Dudgeon, Hercules, June 2002.

38 – Franck Ernould, "Gus Dudgeon: A Production Ace!" Interview published in Home Studio, 1998, and on Franck Ernould (website), http://www.ernould.com/Ingeson/dudgeon.html. Translated from the French.

39 – Jérôme Soligny, Interview with Gus Dudgeon, David Bowie: Rainbow Man, 1967–1980, Paris, Gallimard, 2019, p. 99. Translated from the French.

40 – Quoted in "The Funeral of Gus and Sheila Dudgeon," Angelfire, https://www.angelfire.com/in2/Elton/DudgeonFuneral.html.

41 – Elton John, "Farewell Paul Buckmaster," Facebook, November 8, 2017, https://www.facebook.com/EltonJohn/photos/farewell-paul-buckmaster-so-heartbroken-he-helped-make-me-the-artist-i-am-today-/1840198779342554/.

42 – Interview with Elton John, New Potato Caboose, June 28, 1971.

43 – Jon Tiven, "Gus Dudgeon," International Musician, October 1975.

44 – Testimony of Caleb Quaye, March 2020, www.eltonjohn.com.

45 – Michelle Lanz, "Inside the Rock Star's Studio with Music Arranger Paul Buckmaster," The Frame, May 16, 2016, https://www.scpr.org/programs/the-frame/2016/05/16/48900/inside-the-rock-star-s-studio-with-music-arranger/.

46 – Andy Greene, "Flashback: Elton John Performs a Stunning 'Sixty Years On' at the Troubadour in 1970," Rolling Stone, August 25, 2020, https://www.rollingstone.com/music/music-news/elton-john-troubadour-sixty-years-on-1049548/.

47 – John F. Higgins, "The Troubadour—50 Years On," Elton John (website), August 25, 2020, https://www.eltonjohn.com/stories/troubadour-50.

48 – Roy Carr, "The Man Behind Elton John," New Musical Express, February 13, 1971.

49 – Ronnie Friend, "Elton John LIVE at the Troubadour, LA 1970—'Sixty Years On,'" August 6, 2019, YouTube, video, https://www.youtube.com/watch?v=QWhg0-39wQU.

50 – Quoted in "From the Archives: Robert Hilburn's 1970 Review of Elton John at the Troubadour—'New Rock Talent,'" Los Angeles Times, May 23, 2019, https://www.latimes.com/entertainment/music/la-et-ms-elton-john-1970-at-the-troubadour-hilburn-20190523-story.html.

51 – Michel Magne, L'Amour de vivre [Love of Life], Nice, Ed. Alain Lefeuvre, 1980. Translated from the French.

52 – John Katsilometes, "As an Intuitive Drummer, Elton John's Nigel Olsson Can't Be Beat," Las Vegas Sun, October 17, 2012.

53 – Andy Greene, "Nigel Olsson Reflects on 50 Years of Playing Drums for Elton John," Rolling Stone, August 22, 2018, https://www.rollingstone.com/music/music-news/nigel-olsson-reflects-on-50-years-of-playing-drums-for-elton-john-713606/.

54 – Joe Bosso, "Exclusive Interview: Nigel Olsson—My Career with Elton John," MusicRadar, April 11, 2011, https://www.musicradar.com/news/drums/exclusive-interview-nigel-olsson-my-career-with-elton-john-419704.

55 – George Matlock, "Honey Roll: Nigel Olsson Talks Exclusively to George Matlock from California," Part 2, Elton John World, November 15, 1999, http://www.eltonjohnworld.com/index.php/archives/old-news-special/3700-honeyroll.

56 – Quoted in John F. Higgins, "Tumbleweed Connection at 50," Elton John (website), October 30, 2020, https://www.eltonjohn.com/stories/tumbleweed50.

57 – Front page of Melody Maker, November 28, 1970.

58 – Two Rooms: Celebrating the Songs of Elton John & Bernie Taupin, Universal Music Group, 2005, DVD.

59 – Jon Landau, "Tumbleweed Connection," Rolling Stone, February 18, 1971.

60 – Rock History Music, "Ray Williams Talks Elton's 'Amoreena,'" Producer Gus Dudgeon & Marc Bolan," February 26, 2020, YouTube, video, https://www.youtube.com/watch?v=ghz9GqElu8U.

61 – Elvis Costello, Interview with Elton John, Spectacle, Channel 4 (UK), CTV (Canada), 2008.

62 – Michael Kaplan, "'I Knew It Was About Me': Maxine Taupin Talks 'Tiny Dancer,' Other Elton John Hits," New York Post, December 7, 2019, https://nypost.com/2019/12/07/i-knew-it-was-about-me-maxine-taupin-talks-tiny-dancer-other-elton-john-hits/.

63 – Alexis Petridis, "'This Is a Very Good Question, Bob Dylan': Elton John, Interviewed by Famous Fans," Guardian, October 12, 2019, https://www.theguardian.com/music/2019/oct/12/this-is-a-very-good-question-bob-dylan-elton-john-interviewed-by-famous-fans.

64 – Susan Black, Elton John: In His Own Words, London, Omnibus Press, 1995.

65 – George Matlock, "Backstage: Two Rooms at the End of the World: Clive Frank's Interview Part 3," Elton John World, July 31, 2000, http://www.eltonjohnworld.com/index.php/archives/old-news-special/3690-backstagetwooomsattheendo.

66 – Live recording in the BBC studios for the television series Sounds for Saturday, November 11, 1971, Philip Anness, "Elton John—Levon (1971) Live at BBC Studios," October 18, 2011, YouTube, video, https://www.youtube.com/watch?v=mire1WJKdR8.

67 – Andy Greene, "Bernie Taupin on Elton John's New LP: 'It's Kudos All Around,'" Rolling Stone, September 26, 2013, https://www.rollingstone.com/music/music-news/bernie-taupin-on-elton-johns-new-lp-its-kudos-all-around-102572/.

68 – Rick Clark, "Rick Clark's Music I Love Blog: Gus Dudgeon on Elton, Part 2," Rick Clark Productions, September 2, 2020, https://rickclarkproductions.com/music-i-love-blog/tag/Gus+Dudgeon.

69 – Austin Scaggs, "The Rolling Stone Interview: Elton John," Rolling Stone, February 17, 2011, https://www.rollingstone.com/music/music-news/the-rolling-stone-interview-elton-john-100053/.

70 – Keith Hayward, Elton John: From Tin Pan Alley to the Yellow Brick Road, Bedford, UK, Wymer Publishing, 2015.

71 – Robert Sandall, "Bernie Taupin: Him Indoors," Q, July 1992.

72 – Claude Bernardin, "'If I Was an Artist, Who Paints with His Eyes': Claude Bernardin's Top 30 Elton John List. Celebrating the 30th Anniversary of AllSongsList," eltonjohnallsongslist, April 10, 2014, http://eltonjohnallsongslist.blogspot.com/2014/04/if-i-was-artist-who-paints-with-his.html.

73 – Quoted in Paul Sexton, "'Don't Shoot Me I'm Only the Piano Player': How Elton John Fired a Classic," uDiscoverMusic, February 10, 2021, https://www.udiscovermusic.com/stories/elton-john-dont-shoot-me-im-only-the-piano-player/.

74 – Jon Landau, "Honky Château," album review, Rolling Stone, August 17, 1972, https://www.rollingstone.com/music/music-album-reviews/honky-chateau-93596/.

75 – "Davey Johnstone Celebrates His 3,000th Show—Interview," Elton John (website), October 2, 2019, https://www.eltonjohn.com/stories/davey-3000.

76 – Andy Greene, "Guitarist Davey Johnstone Looks Back on His Five-Decade Odyssey with Elton John," Rolling Stone, September 7, 2018, https://www.rollingstone.com/music/music-news/elton-john-guitarist-davey-johnstone-on-their-history-and-final-tour-720041/.

77 – Olivier Roubin, "Young American in London," Rock First, 2011. Interview with Tony Visconti, translated from the French.

78 – Eileen Shapiro, "Caleb Quaye: Louder than Rock—Interview," Louder than War November 14, 2018, https://louderthanwar.com/caleb-quaye-louder-rock/.

79 – George Matlock, "Backstage: Make Strange Sounds, Strange Sounds It Seems: Clive Frank's Interview Part 2," Elton John World, July 30, 2000, http://www.eltonjohnworld.com/index.php/archives/old-news-special/3665-backstagemakestrangesounds.

80 – David Buckley, Elton: The Biography, 3rd ed., Chicago Review Press, 2007; London, André Deutsch, 2019.

81 – "The Story Behind 'Daniel'," eltonjohnallsongslist, December 17, 2007, http://eltonjohnallsongslist. blogspot.com/2007/12/story-behind-daniel.html.

82 – Alexis Petridis, "Why Marc Bolan Was 'the Perfect Pop Star,' by Elton John, U2 and More," Guardian, September 4, 2020, https://www.theguardian. com/music/2020/sep/04/marc-bolan-perfect-pop-star-t-rex-singer-tribute-album-elton-john-u2.

83 – "Unforgettable People (VII): Caleb Quaye," January 31, 2008, eltonjohnallsongslist, http:// eltonjohnallsongslist.blogspot.com/2008/01/ unforgettable-people-v-caleb-quaye_4058.html.

84 – Interview with Elton John, Beat Instrumental, December 1975.

85 – Cal Fussman, "Bernie Taupin: What I've Learned," Esquire, January 2, 2012, https://www.esquire.com/ entertainment/interviews/a11922/bernie-taupin-quotes-0112/.

86 – Interview with Davey Johnstone, Guitar Player, January 1, 1972.

87 – "One Night on the Yellow Brick Road, as Experienced by Leroy Gomez," Elton John World, February 23, 2014, http://www.eltonjohnworld.com/ index.php/cheryl-s-specials/4072-one-night-on-the-yellow-brick-road-as-experienced-by-leroy-gomez.

88 – Elton John: "Goodbye Yellow Brick Road," Classic Albums documentary, directed by Bob Smeaton, Eagle Rock Entertainment, 2001, DVD. Some quotes were taken from the commentary on the DVD; these quotes were translated from the French.

89 – "Engineer David Hentschel Talks About Goodbye Yellow Brick Road," Elton John (website), October 4, 2013, https://www.eltonjohn.com/stories/ engineerdavidhentscheltalksaboutgoodbyeyellowbrickroad.

90 – Andy Greene, "Elton John and Bernie Taupin Look Back at Goodbye Yellow Brick Road," Rolling Stone, March 14, 2014, https://www.rollingstone.com/ music/music-news/elton-john-and-bernie-taupin-look-back-at-goodbye-yellow-brick-road-205112/.

92 – Legs McNeil and Gillian McCain, Please Kill Me: The Uncensored Oral History of Punk, Australian ed., Abacus, 1997.

93 – Interview with John Carsello, video "Inside Caribou Ranch," Rocky Mountain News, 2008.

94 – Roger Catlin, "The Top 5 Tower of Power Horn Riffs," Songfacts, March 25, 2021, https://www.songfacts. com/blog/writing/top-5-tower-of-power-horn-riffs.

95 – Quoted in rokritr, "Elton John Album by Album Thread," Steve Hoffman Music Forums, June 11, 2010, https://forums.stevehoffman.tv/threads/ elton-john-album-by-album-thread.214152/ page-14#post-5530453.

96 – Romuald Ollivier, "Profession: Producer," Guitar Part, June 2003. Interview with Jimmy Page, translated from the French.

97 – Andy McKaie, interview with Elton John and Bernie Taupin, from the booklet accompanying the box set To Be Continued…, November 8, 1990.

98 – Elton John, "Champagne, Bingo, and the 'Gucci-Pucci' crowd: A Day in the Life of Elton John circa 1974," Vogue (UK), September 1974.

99 – Radio interview with Elton John and Bernie Taupin, Classic Albums, February 24, 1990.

100 – Gus Dudgeon quoted in Paul Gambaccini, "Captain Fantastic and the Brown Dirt Cowboy," from the booklet accompanying the Captain Fantastic and the Brown Dirt Cowboy Deluxe Edition, 2005.

101 – Caroline Coon, "I Want to Chug, Not Race," Melody Maker, June 21, 1975.

102 – Jon Landau, "Captain Fantastic and the Brown Dirt Cowboy," album review, Rolling Stone, July 17, 1975.

103 – Paul Roland, Elton John, London, Proteus Books, 1984.

104 – clevelandlivemusic, "Elton John + Billie Jean King—Interview—Tonight Show 9/20/93," YouTube, video, https://www.youtube.com/watch?v=YgtXvamVuck.

105 – Interview with Elton John, Rocket Hour, Beats 1, Apple, audio, September 8, 2018.

107 – Elton John, "Elton John: They Wanted to Tone Down the Sex and Drugs. But I Haven't Led a PG-13 Life," Guardian, May 26, 2019, https://www.theguardian. com/global/2019/may/26/elton-john-in-my-own-words-exclusive-my-life-and-making-rocketman.

109 – John F. Higgins, "Billie Jean King Talks About 'Philadelphia Freedom,'" Elton John (website), September 10, 2018, https://www.eltonjohn.com/stories/ billie-jean-king-talks-about-philadelphia-freedom.

110 – Rock History Music, "Caleb Quaye Looks Back At Elton John's Rock of the Westies / Blue Moves Band," September 19, 2018, YouTube, video, https:// www.youtube.com/watch?v=5ozNCsb6g28.

111 – Robert Hilburn, "John and Taupin's Playback Session: Songwriting Duo Strolls Through Its Song Catalogue," Los Angeles Times, August 13, 1989, https://www.latimes. com/archives/la-xpm-1989-08-13-ca-797-story.html.

112 – George Cole, "Elton John, the Beach Boys and the Fine Art of Pop Alchemy," Guardian, September 30, 2010, https://www.theguardian.com/music/2010/ sep/30/arranging-brian-wilson-paul-buckmaster.

113 – Cliff Jahr, "Elton John: It's Lonely at the Top," Rolling Stone, October 7, 1976, https:// www.rollingstone.com/artists/davidbowie/articles/ story/8718858/elton_john_its_lonely_at_the_top.

114 – Jon Kutner and Spencer Leigh, 1000 UK Number One Hits, London, Omnibus Press, 2005.

115 – "Davey Johnstone Guitar Collection: The Sitar," October 25, 2016, Facebook, video, 2:48, https://www. facebook.com/johnstonedavey/videos/991662700960326/.

116 – Stephen Spignesi and Michael Lewis, Elton John: Fifty Years On: The Complete Guide to the Musical Genius of Elton John and Bernie Taupin, New York and Nashville, Post Hill Press, 2019.

117 – "'Blue Moves' Celebrates an Anniversary," Elton John (website), October 2016, https://www.eltonjohn. com/stories/blue-moves-celebrates-an-anniversary.

118 – Stephen Holden, "A Single Man," album review, Rolling Stone, January 25, 1979, https://www.rollingstone. com/music/music-album-reviews/a-single-man-86074/.

119 – Stephen Holden, "Victim of Love," album review, Rolling Stone, December 13, 1979, https://www.rollingstone.com/ music/music-album-reviews/victim-of-love-2-189621/.

120 – Martha Hume, "Elton's Comeback Ignites On-Stage but Not on Record," a review of Victim of Love, US magazine, November 27, 1979.

121 – Romuald Ollivier, "Steve Lukather, côté Son," Guitar Part, October 2003. Translated from the French.

122 – Toni Tennille, "Daryl's Music Dream Come True: Rumbo Recorders Studio," Toni Tennille (website), January 16, 2016, https://www.tonitennille.net/blog/2016/1/16/ daryls-music-dream-come-true-rumbo-recorders-studio.

123 – From the booklet accompanying the box set Jewel Box, 2020.

124 – Andy Peebles, radio interview with Elton John, BBC, London, December 28, 1980.

125 – "Diamond Moments: 'I'm Still Standing,'" Elton John (website), October 26, 2017, https://www.eltonjohn. com/stories/diamond-moments-im-still-standing.

126 – Spencer Leigh, Bob Dylan: Outlaw Blues (Carmarthen, UK: McNidder & Grace, 2020).

127 – Sam Inglis, "Gus Dudgeon: Producer," Sound on Sound, July 2001, https://www.soundonsound. com/people/gus-dudgeon-producer.

128 – Joe Bosso, "Exclusive Interview: Davey Johnstone—My Career with Elton John," MusicRadar, April 4, 2011, https:// www.musicradar.com/news/guitars/exclusive-interview-davey-johnstone-my-career-with-elton-john-413589.

129 – Jon Wilde, "Elton: The Magnificent Showman," Uncut, September 2001.

130 – Harold Goldberg, "Reg Strikes Back," album review, Rolling Stone, October 6, 1988, https://www.rollingstone. com/music/music-album-reviews/reg-strikes-back-193237/.

131 – Radio interview with Elton John, NRJ, Spring 1988.

132 – John F. Higgins, Testimony by Elton John, ""Sleeping with the Past" Turns 30," eltonjohn.com, September 2, 2019, https://www.eltonjohn.com/stories/sleeping-with-the-past-30.

133 – "Diamond Moments: 'Sacrifice,'" Elton John (website), December 7, 2017, https://www.eltonjohn. com/stories/diamond-moments-:-sacrifice.

134 – Matt Patches, "The Lion King Turns 20: Lyricist Tim Rice Talks About Writing 5 Iconic Songs," Vulture, June 23, 2014, https://www.vulture.com/2014/06/lion-king-lyricist-tim-rice-songs-20th-anniversary.html.

135 – Robert Hilburn, "Get Back, Honky Cats," Los Angeles Times, April 2, 1995.

136 – Johnnie Walker, The Radio 2 Breakfast Show, BBC Radio 2, March 25, 1995.

137 – Robert Hilburn, "The Man with the Words," Los Angeles Times, September 30, 2001, https://www.latimes. com/archives/la-xpm-2001-sep-30-ca-51510-story.html.

138 – Bruce Britt, "With 'Songs from the West Coast,' Elton John Returns to His Roots," MusicWorld, October 31, 2001, https://www.bmi.com/news/entry/20011101elton_john_with_songs_from_the_west_coast_elton_john_returns_to.

139 – Tom Doyle, "Fantastic Voyage," Mojo, October 2006.

140 – Mike Quigley, Tracy Lee Hearst, and Rick McGrath, "This Is Your Song: The Elton John Interview," April 22, 1971, Mike Quigley (website), http://www. mjq.net/interviews/EltonJohnInterview1971.htm.

141 – Elton John (eltonjohn), "My darling Leon Russell passed away last night," Instagram, November 13, 2016, https://www.instagram.com/p/BMwSXfvl_BM/.

142 – Elton John, "Monkey Suit," from the booklet accompanying the Jewel Box set, 2020.

143 – The Union, directed by Cameron Crowe, documentary, Vinyl Films, 2011.

145 – Terry Gross, "A More Reflective Leap on Elton John's 'Diving Board,'" WHYY-FM, originally broadcast September 19, 2013, NPR, January 1, 2014, audio and transcript, https:// www.npr.org/transcripts/256607935?t=1644845572878.

146 – Louise Gannon, "'I Was Just Minutes from Death': Elton John Reveals How Appendicitis Nearly Killed Him on Tour—and His Desperate Bid to Save Whitney and Amy," Mail Online, September 7, 2013, https://www.dailymail.co.uk/ home/event/article-2412455/Elton-John-exclusive-interview-I-help-Amy-Whitney-Michael-I-did-save-myself.html.

147 – Jeff Slate, "The Bitch Is Back: Elton John's 'Wonderful Crazy Night' Soars," Tidal, February 5, 2016, https:// tidal.com/magazine/article/the-bitch-is-back-elton-johns-wonderful-crazy-night-soars-share/1-22137.

148 – Andy Greene, "Bernie Taupin on 48 Years Writing with Elton John and Their New LP," Rolling Stone, November 24, 2015, https://www.rollingstone. com/music/music-news/bernie-taupin-on-48-years-writing-with-elton-john-and-their-new-lp-59194/.

149 – Stephen Rodrick, "Elton: The Bitch at Peace," Rolling Stone, February 25, 2016, https://rollingstone.com/music/ music-news/elton-john-the-bitch-at-peace-1140/.

150 – Cameron Crowe, "Elton John and Bernie Taupin: 'The Hardest Thing Is to Write an Uplifting Song,'" inews.co.uk, November 9, 2017, https://inews.co.uk/culture/music/elton-john-bernie-taupin-hardest-thing-write-uplifting-song-102954.

151 – "John Mahon Talks to East End Lights," eltonfan. net, February 13, 2016, https://www.heimbecker. net/ef/news/archive/news-archive-2-2016.html.

152 – Elton John, from the booklet accompanying Jewel Box, 2020.

153 – Gillian G. Gaar, "Elton John's Collection of Jewels," Goldmine, January 28, 2021, https://www.goldminemag. com/interviews/elton-john-collection-of-jewels.

154 – Ben Beaumont-Thomas, "Elton John Announces New Album Made with A-List Guests in Lockdown," Guardian, September 1, 2021, https://www.theguardian. com/music/2021/sep/01/elton-john-announces-new-album-made-with-a-list-guests-in-lockdown.

155 – Elton John, "The Lockdown Sessions," Elton John (website), 2021, https://thelockdownsessions. eltonjohn.com/#tracklisting.

156 – "Elton John Calls This Metallica Track 'One of the Best Songs Ever Written,'" Howard Stern Show, September 10, 2021, YouTube, video, 0:58, https:// www.youtube.com/watch?v=wofWGD5TUxo.

INDEX

The songs, albums, and singles analyzed in this book are emphasized in bold, along with portraits of specific performers.

Cooper, Ray 119–131, 146, 180, 195, 207, 212, 214–226, 236–449, 254–275, 278–297, 302–316, 320, 322, **325**, 366–369, 375, 380, 390, 399, 414, 418, 419, 431, 459–465, 472, 556, 558, 560, 562

Cordell, Denny 60

Corvettes, The 10

Costa, David 414, 512

Costa, Paulinho da 322, 326–329, 340, 399

Country Comfort 78, 81, 82, **89**, 106, 112

Country Love Song 307

Cox, Terry 51, 70, 71, 119–121

Crazy Water 283, **286**

Crocodile Rock 42, 139, 156, 160–162, 168, **168–169**, 170, 176, 191, 195, 211, 252, 254, 296, 561

Croker, David 364–373

Crosby, David 285, 292

Crosby, Stills & Nash 398

Crouch, Andraé 452–453

Crouch, Dennis 524–534

Crowe, Cameron 113, 148, 527

Crudup, Arthur 81, 107

Cry to Heaven 390, **392**, 396

Crystal 369, **373**

Curtains 234, **244**

Cyril Davies R&B All Stars 12

D'Oliveira, Raul 392–396

Daldry, Stephen 506

Dan Dare (Pilot of the Future) 259, 386

Dancing in the End Zone 426, **431**

Dancing in the Street 266

Dangereusement vôtre [film] 390, 396

Daniel 40, 42, 156, **158–160**, 176, 211, 241, 252, 259, 466, 554

Dark Diamond 487, **488**

Daspit, Bob 452–453

David Hynes 574–575

Davies, Roy 322, 326–329

Davis, Terrence 498, 500–503

Dawn, P.M. 450

Deacon, John 390, 394, 409

Dear God 334, **338**, 341, 342

Dear John 358

Dee, Brian 67, 68, 96, 116

Delaney & Bonnie 48, 68, 76

Denham, Vince 427

Denny, Sandy 81

Derek and the Dominos 165, 263

Desper, Steve 334, 338

Detroit, Marcella 450

Diamond, Neil 82, 83

Diamonds [Compilation] 42, 568, 569

Dick James Demos 24

Dick James Music Studios 20, 21, 23, 30, 34–45, 574–575

Dick James Records 43

Dickson, Graham 392–397

Did He Shoot Her? **385**

Diddley, Bo 265

Dirty Little Girl 193, **194**, 195

Dixie Lily 215

DJM Records 24, 28, 31, 32, 48, 52, 180

Do They Know It's Christmas? 398

Dodger Stadium 34, 252, 266, 269, 274, 441

Don't Go Breaking My Heart 108, 264, 276, 277, **278–279**, 304, 336, 399, 450, 451, 569

Don't Let the Sun Go Down on Me 200, 207, 208, 219, **222–223**, 224, 225, 252, 291, 399, 428, 436, 450, 451, 456, 475, 503, 514

Don't Shoot Me I'm Only the Piano Player [album] 42, 60, 66, **150–173**, 276, 380, 456, 545

Don't Trust That Woman 402, **406–407**, 409

Donne, John 348

Donner Pour Donner 340

Downey Jr., Robert 487, 490

Doyle, Tom 182

Dragon, Daryl 222, 283, 286, 335, 363

Drake, Nick 122

Dread, Judge 192

Dream #1 544

Dream #2 548

Dream #3 550

Dreamboat 373, **375**

Dua Lipa 578, 582

Duck, Ian 44, 89–91, 108, 109

Dudgeon, Angus Boyd (Gus) 42, 43,50, 51–56, **60**, 61–72, 78–97, 102–122, 126–149, 155–173, 176–201, 208–226, 234–249, 254–269, 274–297, 302, 304, 366, 390–397, 402–411, 428, 496, 510, 516

Dudley, Anne 472–480

Duets [album] **450–451**

Duke, David 442

Duncan, Kirk 13

Duncan, Lesley 62–72, 86–93, 95, 104, 113, 120, 121

Dunne, Phil 364–373

Durban Deep 426, 488

Dwight, Geoff 10

Dwight, Reggae 192

Dwight, Reginald Kenneth (Reg) 6, 8, 10, 11, 15, 18, 32, 44, 58, 108, 126, 240, 560, 572

Dwight, Stanley 6, 460, 484

Dyer, Rod 368

Dylan Hart 557–565

Dylan, Bob 16, 17, 39, 439, 491

Dynamic Sounds Studio 176, 178

Dyson, Geoff 10

E-Ticket 587

Eagles, The 83, 254, 257, 338

Earn While You Learn 375

Eastern Sound Studio 274, 282–296

Egan, Mike 96

Ego 314

Eight Hundred Dollar Shoes 526

Elderberry Wine 162

Eli, Bobby 306

Elton: Jewel Box [compilation] 568–569

Elton 60 – Live At Madison Square Garden (2007) [Compil] 87, 135

Elton John [album] **46–73**

Elton John AIDS Foundation 399

Elton John Greatest Hits [album] 252

Elton's Song 346, **352**

Emblow, Jack 118

Emerson, Keith 109

Emily 444

Empty Garden (Hey Hey Johnny) 361

Empty Sky [album] 20–25, **26–45**, 48, 51, 52, 78, 79, 82, 85, 92, 108, 165, 207, 232

Empty Sky 14, 24, 28, 30, **34**, 55

England and America 564

Epps, Stuart 22, 28, 56, 146, 308–316, 375, 392–397, 406, 408, 409, 411,

Epstein, Brian 24

Estus, Deon 390, 392, 395, 397

Every Day I Have the Blues 11

Evette Benton, 306

Fairport Convention 167

Family Dogg, The 32

Farebrother, Fred (Derf) 9

Farebrother, Sheila 554

Farewell Yellow Brick Road Tour 565, 568, 578, 581

Fascist Faces 346, **349**

Fat Boys and Ugly Girls 438, **446**

Fay, Don 31, 34, 37, 45

Feed Me 255, 256, **265**

Feibelman, Maxine 58, 102, 110,129, 137, 140, 188, 212, 235, 255, 262, 263, 274, 278, 282, 291, 296, 316

Feldman, Victor 336, 339

Feliciano, José 63

Fillmore East 100, 524

Findley, Chuck 336, 337

Finish Line 587

First Episode At Hienton 65, 70

Fletcher, Dexter 568

Flinstone Boy 305, **315**

Flowers, Herbie 54, 56, 81, 88, 89, 96, 119–121, 136, 312

Fontana Records 10, 11

Fools in Fashion 349, **353**

Forbes, Bryan 152, 157

Ford, Mark 500–503

Forsey, Keith 322, 326–329

Fortin, Carl 288

Foster, Alex 364–373

Fowler, Bruce : 452–453

Franklin, Aretha 239, 249, 285, 428, 430

Franks, Clive 21–23, 31,34–40, 45, 154, 176, 212–225, 265, 269, 304–316, 334–342, 346, 348, 350, 352, 353, 363, 375, 386, 397

Franz, Johnny 14

Freaks in Love 500

Fredericks, Carol 440

Free and Easy 564

Friends [album BO] **104–105**

Friends [film] 66, 100, 102, 126, 144, 335, 399

Frome Court 10, 14, 34, 41, 48, 50, 58, 68

Funeral for a Friend [Love Lies Bleeding] **182–183**

Furnish, David 464, 467, 473, 484, 487, 510, 514, 522, 554, 561

Gabriel, Peter 122, 558

Gaitsch, Bruce 489–491

Gall, France 340, 341

Garner, Kay 62–72, 86, 90 91

Gate, The 10

Gaynor, Mel 390, 392, 395, 397

Geffen Records 342, 346–411

Geldof, Bob 398–399

Gene Page Strings, The 296, 297

Georgia 311

Gets You Thru the Night 451

Gilbert, John 104

Gillette, Mic 219

Gilliam, Terry 66, 325

Gilmour, David 245, 436, 445

Give Me the Love 339

Glennie-Smith, Nick 452–453

Gloud, Venette 336, 337, 339

Glover, David 21, 44, 72, 86, 87, 90–92, 97, 108, **109**, 110–113, 120

Glover, Sue 90, 110

Gnomeo & Juliet 538

Go It Alone 402, 404, **408**

Gomez, Leroy 173, 189, 198

Gone to Shiloh 527

Goodbye 122

Goodbye Marlon Brando 418

Goodbye Yellow Brick Road [album] 174–201

Goodbye Yellow Brick Road 188–189

Gorbachev, Mikhail 390, 393

Gorillaz & 6lack 584

Grabham, Mick 129

Gralto Publishing 13

Grasse 320, 332, 346

Green, Andy 116, 474–480, 488–493

Green, Colin 54, 56, 67, 68

Greenaway, Roger 82

Grey Seal 52, 72, **191**

Grimsby 214

Grow Some Funk of Your Own 256, **261**, **262**

Guercio, Jeff 236–249, 255–269, 278

Guercio, Jim 206, 257

Guercio, Mark 236–249, 255–269, 278

Guilty Pleasure 562

Gulliver / Hay Chewed / Reprise 45

Guns N' Roses 66, 182, 193, 450

Guthrie, Woody 17

Gypsy Heart 408

Halcox, Pat

Hall, Larry 339

Hall, Lee 506

Hall, Tony 66

Hammersmith Odeon 66, 368, 589

Hampson, Frank 269

Hard Luck Story 264

Harmony 200–201

Harris, Sheila 6

Harrison, George 163, 191, 325, 385, 491, 522

Hatot, Alain 129, 134, 162, 164, 166

Hauser, Stjepan 543, 544, 549

Have Mercy on the Criminal 66, 164, **165**, 2240, 264

Haymes, Stephanie 459, 463, 473

Hazzard, Tony 62, 64, 68, 70, 72, 86, 91, 144, 149

Healing Hands 426

Heart in the Right Place 348

Heartache All over the World 409

Hearts Have Turned to Stone 530

Heavy Traffic 419

Heels of the Wind 351

Heep, Uriah 38, 80, 132

Hendrix, Jimi 45, 187, 212

Hentschel, David 52, 54, 61–72, 129, 140, 143, 172, 179–201, 214–226, 234, 244

Hercules 149

Here and There [compilation] 135

PHOTO CREDITS

© **ALAMY:** AF archive/Alamy Banque D'Images 347 • Allstar Picture Library Ltd./Alamy Banque D'Images 86, 453 • Fabio Dien/Alamy Banque D'Images 485 • Fine Art Images/Heritage Images 490 • INTERFOTO/Alamy Banque D'Images 322 • Lebrecht Music & Arts/Alamy Banque D'Images 22 • Martyn Goddard/Alamy Banque D'Images 367 • Neil Munns PA Images/Alamy Banque D'Images 471 • PA Images/Alamy Banque D'Images 149 • Pictorial Press Ltd/Alamy Banque D'Images 233, 395 • Records/Alamy Banque D'Images 306 • Sayre Berman/Alamy Banque D'Images 501 • Sheri Determan/Alamy Live News 565 • Vinyls/Alamy Banque D'Images 314 • © **BRIDGEMAN IMAGES:** Bridgeman Images 321 • Claude Schwartz/Bridgeman Images 128, 129, 130, 178 • SSPL/UIG/Bridgeman Images 361 • © **GETTY IMAGES:** Al Seib/Los Angeles Times via Getty Images 511 • Albert Foster/Daily Mirror/Mirrorpix/Getty Images 334–335 • Anthony Barboza/Getty Images 407 • Anwar Hussein/Getty Images 185, 277 • Arthur Grimm/United Archives via Getty Images 41 • Baron/Hulton Archive/Getty Images 184 • Bernard Weil/Toronto Star via Getty Images 429 • Bettmann/Getty Images 285 • Bill Tompkins/Getty Images 443 • Bob King/Redferns/Getty Images 405 • Brendan Monks/Daily Mirror/Mirrorpix/Getty Images 369 • Brian Cooke/Redferns via Getty Images 351 • Brian Rasic/Getty Images 463, 473, 486 • Brian Shuel/Redferns/Getty Images 71 • Carl Bruin/Mirrorpix via Getty Images 370 • Case/Mirrorpix via Getty Image 384 • Chip HIRES/Gamma-Rapho via Getty Images 201 • Chris Farina/Corbis via Getty Images 497 • Dave Benett/Getty Images 19 • Dave Hogan/Hulton Archive/Getty Images 223, 357, 451, 481 • Dave J. Hogan/Getty Images 583 • David Gahr/The Estate of David Gahr/Getty Images 572 • David Lefranc/Kipa/Sygma via Getty Images 433 • David M. Benett/Dave Benett/Getty Images 584–585 • David M. Benett/Getty Images for the Elton John AIDS Foundation 582 • David Redfern/Redferns/Getty Images 69, 81, 117, 142–143, 177, 588–589 • David Warner Ellis/Redferns/Getty Images 159 • David Wolff–Patrick/Redferns/Getty Images 560 • Dimitrios Kambouris/WireImage/Getty Images 548 • Don Preston/The Boston Globe via Getty Images 205 • Donaldson Collection/Getty Images 528 • Ebet Roberts/Redferns/Getty Images 439 • Erich Auerbach/Getty Images 65 • Estate Of Keith Morris/Redferns/Getty Images 166 • Evening Standard/Hulton Archive/Getty Images 156, 264 • Fairfax Media via Getty Images 402 • FG/Bauer-Griffin/Getty Images 399 • Fin Costello/Redferns/Getty Images 44, 64, 79, 89, 308 • GAB Archive/Redferns/Getty Images 30, 291 • Gabe Palacio/ImageDirect/Getty Images 472 • Gary Miller/Getty Images 541 • Gems/Redferns/Getty Images 25 • Geoff Garrett/Mirrorpix via Getty Images 240 • George Rose/Getty Images 288 • George Wilkes/Hulton Archive/Getty Images 92, 111 • Georges De Keerle/Getty Images 415 • Georges MERILLON/Gamma-Rapho via Getty Images 421 • Gijsbert Hanekroot/Redferns/Getty Images 294 • Gilles Petard/Redferns/Getty Images 239 • GONZALO/Bauer-Griffin/GC Images 559 • Hart/Daily Mirror/Mirrorpix/Getty Images 310 • Hayley Madden/Redferns/Getty Images 515 • Henry Diltz/Corbis via Getty Images 292 • Hiroyuki Ito/Getty Images 216 • Hulton Archive/Getty Images 179, 484, 498 • Ian Dickson/Redferns/Getty Images 173 • Ian Tyas/Keystone Features/Getty Images 241 • Images Press/IMAGES/Getty Images 280, 332 • Jack Robinson/Hulton Archive/Getty Images 49, 59, 63 • Jacques Haillot/Sygma/Sygma via Getty Images 340 • Jeff Hochberg/Icon and Image/Getty Images 12 • Jesse Wild/Guitarist Magazine/Future via Getty Images 502 • Jim McCrary/Redferns/Getty Images 396 • JMEnternational/JMEnternational for BRIT Awards/Getty Images 579 • Joe Kohen/WireImage/Getty Images 507 • John Mead/Evening Standard/Hulton Archive/Getty Images 290 • Jordi Vidal/Redferns via Getty Images 556 • Jorgen Angel/Redferns/Getty Images 114 (upper left, center and bottom), 114, 115 • Karjean Levine/Getty Images 438 • Kevin Mazur/Getty Images for Rocket Entertainment 566–567 • Kevin Mazur/WireImage for New York Post/Getty Images 523, 524–525 • Kevin Mazur/WireImage/Getty Images 487, 535, 540, 551, 555 • Keystone/Hulton Archive/Getty Images 363 • Koh Hasebe/Shinko Music/Getty Images 232 • Kyle Gustafson/For The Washington Post via Getty Images 580–581 • L. Cohen/WireImage/Getty Images 42 • L. Pemoni/Getty Images 563 • Larry Hulst/Michael Ochs Archives/Getty Images 326 • Len Trievnor/Express/Hulton Archive/Getty Images 35 • Lester Cohen/Getty Images 425 • LGI Stock/Corbis/VCG via Getty Images 380 • M. Stroud/Daily Express/Hulton Archive/Getty Images 199 • Marco Piraccini/Archivio Marco Piraccini/Mondadori via Getty Images 542 • Mark Sullivan/Contour by Getty Images 236 • McKeown/Popperfoto via Getty Images 10 • Michael Caulfield/WireImage for Twenty First Artists/Getty Images 467 • Michael Childers/Corbis via Getty Images 101 • Michael Kovac/Getty Images for EJAF 586 • Michael Ochs Archives/Getty Images 8 (left), 8 (right), 29, 33, 37, 39, 77, 78, 91, 95, 97, 119, 135, 144, 146, 165, 187, 206, 213, 235, 245, 255, 258, 263, 265, 276, 283, 284, 329, 333, 417, 522 • Michael Putland/Getty Images 18, 45, 50, 73, 84, 85, 103, 107, 118, 123, 137, 138, 139, 152, 183, 189, 191, 192, 215, 237, 279, 311, 325 • Michael Tran/FilmMagic/Getty Images 547 • Michael Webb/Keystone/Getty Images 157 • Mick Hutson/Redferns/Getty Images 444, 512 • Mike Maloney/Daily Mirror/Mirrorpix/Getty Images 387 • Mike Maloney/Mirrorpix/Getty Images 112 • Mike Prior/Redferns/Getty Images 339 • Movie Poster Image Art/Getty Images 140 • NASA/ullstein bild via Getty Images 141 • National Jazz Archive/Heritage Images/Getty Images 96 • Chopard &The Elton John Aids Foundation–Nick Harvey/ WireImage via Getty images 539 • Patrick Riviere/Getty Images 420 • Paul Bergen/Redferns/Getty Images 323 • Paul Natkin/Getty Images 287 • Paul Popper/Popperfoto via Getty Images 381 • Pete Still/Redferns/Getty Images 557 • Peter Stone/Mirrorpix/Getty Images 317 • PL Gould/IMAGES/Getty Images 249 • RB/Redferns/Getty Images 9 (left), 221, 269 • Richard Blanshard/Getty Images 324 • Richard E. Aaron/Redferns/Getty Images 244 • Rick Diamond/Getty Images 477 • Rino Petrosino/Mondadori Portfolio by Getty Images 153 • Robert Altman/Michael Ochs Archives/Getty Images 113 • Robert Knight Archive/Redferns/Getty Images 197, 217, 218, 307 • Robin Platzer/Twin Images/Getty Images 312 • Ron Galella/Ron Galella Collection via Getty Images 293 • Ron Howard/Redferns/Getty Images 56, 131, 167 • Ron Pownall/Corbis via Getty Images 242, 275, 298–299 • Ross Marino/Getty Images 403 • Sam Taylor-Wood/Handout/PA/EMPICS 510 • Samuel Dietz/Redferns/Getty Images 531 • Silver Screen Collection/Getty Images 360 • Spencer Weiner/Los Angeles Times via Getty Images 260 • SSPL/Getty Images 219 • Stephenson/Mirrorpix/Getty Images 21 • Steve Morley/Redferns/Getty Images 234, 246 • Steve Rapport/Getty Images 338 • Steve Schapiro/Corbis via Getty Images 87 • Terry Disney/Daily Express/Hulton Archive/Getty Images 93 • Tim Mosenfelder/Corbis via Getty Images 513, 532 • Tim Mosenfelder/Getty Images 554 • Tom Hill/WireImage/Getty Images 136, 170 • Tony Russell/Redferns/Getty Images 88 • Tristan Fewings/Getty Images /AFP 57 • TV Times via Getty Images 169 • Universal History Archive/Universal Images Group via Getty Images 259 • University of Westminster/Heritage Images/Getty Images 67 • Val Wilmer/Redferns/Getty Images 7, 15 • Watal Asanuma/Shinko Music/Getty Images 155 • Zangl/ullstein bild via Getty Images 230 • © **HEMIS:** Ben Molyneux/Alamy/Hemis 493 • Historic Collection/Alamy/Hemis 31 • kpa/United Archives GmbH/Alamy/Hemis 349 • MARKA/Alamy/Hemis 105, 190 • Nancy Kaszerman/ZUMA Wire/Alamy Live News/Hemis 419 • Paul Smith/Alamy Live News/Hemis 573 • Pictorial Press Ltd/Alamy/Hemis 13, 23, 231 • sjvinyl/Alamy/Hemis 104 • Stock Connection Blue/Alamy/Hemis 160 • © **ICONIC IMAGES:** Ed Caraeff/Iconic Images 43, 80, 83, 171, 208, 266, 268, 281 • Terry O'Neill/Iconic Images 17, 53, 127, 147, 209, 211, 253, 256, 257, 267, 270–271, 289, 297,303, 337, 343, 391, 437, 441, 457, 458, 519, 569 • Gered Mankowitz/Iconic Images 404 • Mike Ross/Iconic Images 36, 61, 102, 121, 181, 224, 460, 518 • James Fortune/Iconic Images 207 • © **MIRRORPIX:** Carl Bruin/Mirrorpix 359, 371 • Mirrorpix 379 • Peter Stone/Daily Mirror/Mirrorpix 304 • © **ROGER-VIOLLET:** Patrick Ullmann/Roger-Viollet 132, 133 • © **SHUTTERSTOCK:** Alan Messer/Shutterstock 9 (right) • Dezo Hoffman/Shutterstock 55 • George Harris/Evening News/Shutterstock 11 • Johnny Boylan/Shutterstock 447 • Northcliffe Collection/ANL/Shutterstock 6 • Philip Ollerenshaw/Shutterstock 393 • Shutterstock 464 • © **AUTRES:** Tout droits réservés : 76

ACKNOWLEDGMENTS

Olivier Roubin would like to thank Isabelle, Maxime, Benjamin, Michel and Catherine, Gilles and Anne.

Romuald Ollivier would like to thank Anne, Hugo, Alex, Fabrice and Patricia, Manuela, François, family and friends.

The authors would jointly like to thank Isabelle, Claire, Karine, Louise and Laurence.

The editor would like to thank Ellie for her invaluable help throughout the development of this book.